RELIGION AND THE INDIVIDUAL

RELIGION AND THE INDIVIDUAL

A Social-Psychological Perspective

C. Daniel Batson
Patricia Schoenrade
W. Larry Ventis

New York Oxford
OXFORD UNIVERSITY PRESS
1993

Oxford University Press

Oxford New York Toronto
Delhi Bombay Calcutta Madras Karachi
Kuala Lumpur Singapore Hong Kong Tokyo
Nairobi Dar es Salaam Cape Town
Melbourne Auckland

and associated companies in
Berlin Ibadan

Published by Oxford University Press, Inc.,
200 Madison Avenue, New York, New York 10016

The previous edition was entitled
The Religious Experience: A Social-Psychological Perspective

Library of Congress Cataloging-in-Publication Data
Batson, C. Daniel (Charles Daniel), 1943–
Religion and the individual : a social-psychological perspective /
C. Daniel Batson, Patricia Schoenrade, W. Larry Ventis.
p. cm. Rev. ed. of: The religious experience.
Includes bibliographical references and index.
ISBN 0-19-506208-6. ISBN 0-19-506209-4 (pbk.)
1. Experience (Religion) 2. Religion and sociology.
3. Psychology, Religious.
I. Schoenrade, Patricia. II. Ventis, W. Larry, 1943– .
III. Batson, C. Daniel (Charles Daniel), 1943–Religious experience.
IV. Title. BL53.B35
1993 200'.1'9—dc20

We would like to acknowledge the permission to quote material
from the following sources:
G. W. Allport and J. M. Ross. *Religious Orientation Scale.*
C. Castaneda. *The Teachings of Don Juan: A Yaqui Way of Knowledge.*
The University of California Press. Copyright 1968 by
The Regents of the University of California.
T. Leary. *High Priest.* Copyright 1968 by Peace Press.
Malcolm X, with the assistance of Alex Haley. *The Autobiography of Malcolm X.* Copyright 1964 by Random House, Inc.
J. Harding and H. Schuman. *Social Problems Questionnaire.*
R. Masters and J. Houston. *The Varieties of Psychedelic Experience.* Copyright 1966.
H. Smith. Do Drugs Have Religious Import?
Journal of Philosophy. Copyright 1964.
Time, Inc. "Hurry, My Children, Hurry." March 26, 1979.
A. Watts. "Psychedelics and Religious Experience." Copyright 1968,
California Law Review, Inc. Reprinted by permission.

1 3 5 7 9 8 6 4 2

Printed in the United States of America
on acid-free paper

Preface

Never discuss politics or religion. Far from indicating a lack of interest in these topics, this familiar maxim suggests much interest but much difference of opinion. Given the interest and controversy, one might think that religion would have received considerable attention from social psychologists. It has not. With a few notable exceptions, they have carefully adhered to the maxim of never discussing religion. We think this is unfortunate and offer this book as a step toward the development of a social psychology of religion.

More than a body of information, social psychology is the application of a particular method, the scientific method, to study the behavior of individuals in society. The scientific method includes two key elements: (1) development of explanatory theories based on empirical observation; and (2) testing these theories through subsequent empirical observation. This book reports our attempt to apply this method to the study of religion. Our concern is with the role of religion in the life of the individual—its origins, development, dynamics, functions, and consequences—rather than with religion as a social institution. It is for this reason that we speak of *individual* or *personal* religion. Our goal is to provide a clear and coherent social-psychological picture of individual religion, a picture that does not do violence to its diversity and mystery yet is still scientifically sound.

Pursuit of this goal has led us to consider the classic treatments by William James, Sigmund Freud, and Gordon Allport, as well as much of the more recent empirical literature. But we have drawn on the past selectively. We have not tried to provide a comprehensive, textbook review of the literature in psychology and sociology of religion. Instead, we have used whatever ideas and research contributed most directly to our analysis. Especially for theoretical insights, this has meant relying heavily on literature in social psychology that has not traditionally been classified as psychology or sociology of religion. It has also meant leaving out a sizeable portion of the traditional literature.

Such selectivity seems not only natural but necessary in the development of a coherent theoretical perspective. But it carries with it a danger. A reader could get the distorted view that our perspective is *the* social-psychological perspective on religion. The reader who is a professional in the field will know that this is not the case. We would like to assure other readers as well that it is not. The perspective presented is one that we have found quite helpful in understanding the nature and consequences of religion in individuals' lives. Further, it has stood up surprisingly well in initial empirical tests. But it is only one perspective among many possibilities.

Individual religion is extremely complex, and it is with some apprehension that we claim to offer even a selective social-psychological analysis of it. As will become apparent, our analysis has limitations. Most obviously, it was developed in the context of Western religion, specifically American Christianity. All three authors were raised within the religious traditions of American Protestantism, and no doubt this early experience shaped our conception of religion and its effects in ways of which we are not even aware. In addition, the existing empirical research on individual religion is almost exclusively Western. The vast majority of studies we shall discuss were conducted over the past four decades within the context of American Christianity. We hope that our conceptual analysis and the related empirical research are of sufficient generality to shed some light on the role of religion in the lives of people from other cultures. But that is a question that they, not we, must answer.

In writing, we tried to keep three different sets of readers in mind: (1) anyone with an interest in religion; (2) students—including students of social psychology, psychology of religion, and sociology of religion; and (3) our professional colleagues. These may seem to be very different audiences, so different that it would be impossible to write for all three at once. But we found that they blended rather quickly into one. This was no doubt because social psychology of religion is a very young science. A precise, specialized vocabulary of the sort that develops as a science matures, and tends to leave the uninitiated baffled, does not yet exist. Moreover, we wanted our perspective to be as clear as possible, and so decided that it should be painted with broad, bold strokes and without a great deal of attention to fine detail. The resulting picture is, we believe, accessible to any reader with an interest in religion, not only the student or professional scholar.

Although statistics are a valuable and necessary tool of the social psychologist, it may be reassuring to the reader without detailed knowledge of statistics that we tried to keep the presentation of statistical analyses to a minimum. The major exception occurs in Chapter 6, where it was necessary to include some discussion of a rather complex statistical technique, factor analysis. This was necessary because the three-dimensional model of ways of being religious introduced in that chapter and employed extensively in later chapters is based on factor analysis. But in Chapter 6 and throughout the book, the implications of statistical analyses are explicitly stated. So, although a reader with no statistical background may have to take our word for the implications of the statistics at a number of points, he or she should have no difficulty understanding the argument being made.

Readers familiar with the earlier book by Batson and Ventis, *The Religious Experience* (Oxford University Press, 1982), may want to know how the present book relates to it. The answer is simple; the present book is a revision, clarification, update, and expansion of the earlier one. The general character and style, and the perspective offered, are essentially the same as in the earlier book. But there are also some important changes.

First and most obviously, we have changed the title. We liked the old title, but apparently it was not clear. Some people read *The* as a claim on our part to know the single, true form of religious experience. Nothing could have been further from our intent. Others read *Religious Experience* to mean that we were limiting our analysis to the psychology of dramatic religious experience*s*, such as conversion experiences. Although we were certainly interested in dramatic religious experiences, our intent was—and is—to study *religion as experienced by the individual,* including the way a person's religion is influenced by and influences other aspects of life. We have no intention of limiting our analysis to the psychology of dramatic religious experiences, nor did we. The new title may seem a bit bland, but perhaps it will be less subject to misunderstanding.

Second, we have gained the additional perspective of a third author, Pat Schoenrade. In addition to helping make revisions throughout the book, Pat has been instrumental in several important additions. She contributed substantially to the new chapter on Individual Development and Religion (Chapter 3) and to the new section in Chapter 5 on music as a facilitator of religious experience.

Other major changes include the following: (1) Presentation of the latest version of our three-dimensional model for assessing personal religion as a means, end, and quest, including clarification and evaluation of that model in light of criticisms of earlier versions (Chapter 6). (2) Addition of evidence from almost a hundred more studies, most done during the last decade, to our analysis of the relation between personal religion and mental health (Chapter 8). (3) Addition of evidence from a number of recent studies to our analysis of the social consequences of personal religion, leading to the creation of two chapters in place of the previous one on this topic. Chapter 9 examines the relationship between personal religion and intolerance, prejudice, and bigotry; Chapter 10 examines the relationship between personal religion and a concern for (and helping of) others in need.

One feature of the earlier book that we have not changed is that, instead of creating an author index, we indexed the References. In brackets after each reference you will find listed the pages in this book where that reference is discussed. This should make it much easier to locate our discussion of a particular book, article, or research report.

We received much help with the preparation of this book and its predecessor. First and foremost, our students helped. Sometimes, their excitement and enthusiasm encouraged us; more often, their questions and criticism made us aware of the shortcomings of our thinking and the need for more and better empirical evidence. Friends and colleagues also helped by reading portions of the manuscript and providing comments and suggestions; among these were Michael Argyle, Cherie Baetz, Marc Boggs, Nell Brewer, Chris Burris, Clark Chinn, Richard Clark, Hob Crockett, Jean-Pierre Deconchy, Malcolm Diamond, James Dittes, Rick Gibbons, Bill Graziano, Bruce Hunsberger, Jack Keating, Satoru Kaneko, Kevin McCaul, Richard Machalek, Virginia Pych, Kelly Shaver, Peter Sherrard, Paweł Socha, Bernard Spilka, Mary Vanderplas, Ray Varey, and Lawrence Wrightsman. Both the University of Kansas and the College of William and Mary helped by providing study leaves, and Wolfson College at Oxford and the University Center for Human Values at Princeton both provided settings for portions of the writing. Katia Silva helped with manuscript preparation, and Joan Bossert of Oxford University Press provided much appreciated editorial support and understanding. Finally, Judy, Karl, Jonathan, Debbie, and Summer were patient, at least most of the time.

Fort Loudoun Lake, Tenn.
November 1992

C.D.B.
P.S.
W.L.V.

Contents

RELIGION AND THE INDIVIDUAL

1

Toward a Social Psychology of Religion

Social commentators, viewing modern society from the ivory towers of academia and the arts, have long predicted the demise of religion. Yet religion persists. Public opinion polls reveal that Americans of today, like their parents and grandparents, assign much importance to religion. In 1987, 94 percent reported that they believed in God; 90 percent reported that they pray; 85 percent reported that religion was either very important or fairly important to them; 71 percent expressed belief in life after death (Gallup & Castelli, 1989). Even in countries where church attendance has dropped dramatically in recent decades, reports of personal belief in God remain relatively high: 70 percent in the United Kingdom; 62 percent in France; and 79 percent in Australia (Gallup Poll International, 1984; see Brown, 1987). Although percentages in such polls are probably inflated by respondents' desire to give socially "right" responses (Demerath & Levinson, 1971), it is clear that when one ventures out of the ivory towers into the mainstream of modern life, religion still occupies a central role. Reviewing U.S. survey data over the last fifty years, Gallup and Castelli (1989) concluded that "perhaps the most appropriate word to use to describe the religious character of the nation as a whole over the last half century is 'stable.' Basic religious beliefs, and even religious practice, today differ relatively little from the levels recorded fifty years ago" (p. 4).

And even within the academic and artistic communities, religious concerns persist. A recent Gallup Poll of U.S. college students, who are often described as the most skeptical and least religious cohort in the society, reveals a strong interest in religion: 80 percent report that religion is important in their lives, and 55 percent had attended religious services once or more in the month preceding the survey (Associated Press, September 9, 1989). Although the answers given to religious questions may not be those of traditional institutions and doctrines, the questions are being asked: Is there any meaning and purpose to my life? How shall I deal with my death? How shall I relate to others? In fact, it is often to confront such questions more directly that the scholar, student, writer, and artist lay aside traditional religious answers. They strip themselves of the cloak of tradition to feel the chilling bite of the questions more sharply.

Religion not only persists; it has long had a dramatic impact on human life. It has given us some of our most memorable literature, lines that have provided comfort and challenge for centuries: "Yea, though I walk through the valley of the shadow of death . . ." "Blessed are the meek . . ." "But I say unto you, love your enemies. . . ." It has also given rise to celebrated acts of selfless concern for others. Albert Schweitzer's deep religious conviction led him to sacrifice prestige and comfort to go to Africa and provide medical care for thousands. Martin Luther King's dream of a society in which all people, black and white, would be free was essentially a religious vision. Religious conviction lay behind Mahatma Gandhi's life of asceticism and nonviolent protest. Mother Teresa, even as her own health deteriorated, did not cease to express her religious faith by caring for the needs of the poorest of the poor. And for literally millions of less celebrated people, the most significant, the most joyful, the most meaningful moments of their lives have been religious.

But if many of humanity's highest moments have been religious, so have many of its lowest. The mass suicide and murder of 913 members of the People's Temple in Jonestown, Guyana, in 1979 was a chilling reminder of the potential destructiveness of religious fervor. Wars and crusades have been waged in the name of religion, as have persecution and torture. Corrupt religious leaders—assisted by electronic media—continue to take advantage of their flock, fleecing rather than shepherding them. Throughout known history, religion has motivated callousness, elitism, and hypocrisy. "O Lord, I thank Thee that I am not as this poor beggar . . ." is an all too familiar prayer. It often seems, as Jonathan Swift put it, that "we have just enough religion to make us hate, but not enough to make us love one another."

When we contemplate the powerful effects of religion on human life, both for good and for ill, it is easy to become confused. We may yearn for understanding, including any understanding that social psychology can provide. But even to propose a social-psychological analysis of religion raises several difficult questions: What do we mean by religion? Is a social-psychological analysis of religion really possible? If it is, what should it involve? We shall address these three questions in this introductory chapter; our answers will provide the foundation on which the understanding of religion presented in subsequent chapters will be built.

WHAT DO WE MEAN BY RELIGION?

Our interest is in individual religion, that is, in religion as experienced by individuals, not in religion as a self-contained set of beliefs or an institution in society. But what is individual religion? In thinking about this question, it may help if we have some examples before us. Consider the following:

1. A middle-aged woman hurries during her lunch hour to the nearby Catholic Church to light a candle and pray for her son, a soldier serving overseas.

2. After preparing carefully, a young Jewish boy reads from the Torah at his Bar Mitzvah. The experience makes a deep impression on him; he senses for the first time that he is an active member of God's chosen nation, Israel. Although he does not attend synagogue regularly during his adult life, this impression stays with him.

3. A prostitute responds to an altar call in a storefront church. Convinced of her sin and deeply repentant, she goes forward and accepts Jesus as her personal Lord and Savior.

4. Five times a day an Islamic businessman faces Mecca, kneels, and prays. He tries to live all of his life according to the teachings of the Koran.

5. Put off by the hypocrisy of institutional religion and skeptical of traditional religious answers, a young woman comes to the conclusion that there is no God and no life after death. The only meaning in life is to be found in caring for others and living every day to the fullest.

6. A prosperous businessman and his wife attend church each Sunday because "it's the thing to do" and "good for business." Neither takes the spiritual side of the service seriously.

7. A young man decides to spend two weeks alone hiking and camping in the Canadian Rockies "just to have a chance to think about things and try to sort out what's important in my life."

Which of these are expressions of religion? Most of us would probably agree that the first four qualify; but what about the last three? Whether we consider any of them to be religious will depend on our definition of religion.

As early at 1912, James Leuba was able to catalog forty-eight different definitions of religion; doubtless one could list many more today. Given this range of possibilities, what definition should we adopt? In trying to decide, we are both chastened and comforted by the words of sociologist Milton Yinger: "Any definition of religion is likely to be satisfactory only to its author" (1967, p. 18). We can only add that the definition we shall propose is not fully satisfactory even to us. It has the status of a working definition, nothing more.

Still, if a working definition is going to work, it must be chosen carefully. Specifically, we believe that ours should be responsive to two pressures: First, it should reflect the uniqueness, complexity, and diversity of religion. Second, it should have heuristic value; that is, it should invite and encourage a social-psychological analysis by emphasizing the way that religion fits into, rather than stands apart from the ongoing life of the individual.

Uniqueness, Complexity, and Diversity of Religion

Uniqueness. It has frequently been noted that religious experience is unique, that it is somehow different from everyday experience. Rudolph Otto (1923) described religious experience as "wholly other." William James (1902) spoke of religion in terms of a unique emotion, "solemn joy." Paul Pruyser (1968) suggested that religion involves "serious" belief, behavior, feeling, and attitude. Yinger (1970) and, following him, Machalek and Martin (1976) considered religious concerns to be those that emerge when one is "thinking beyond the immediate problems of the day—however important—beyond headlines, beyond the temporary . . . to the most important concern or concerns of life" (Machalek & Martin, 1976, pp. 314–315).

Let us try to be more explicit about how religious experience is unique. Religious concerns seem to differ from everyday concerns both in the *comprehensiveness* of their scope and in their personal *centrality.* Everyday concerns might include what you will have for dinner, what the right answer was to the third question on today's history exam, or whether you will get the job you applied for yesterday. Although any of these concerns may seem all-consuming, at least for the moment, each deals with only a limited aspect of your life and does not touch the core. How you answer is not likely to change the way you look at yourself in relation to life itself. You may discover a new dish you like; you may learn that you do not know as much about the reign of Louis XIV as you thought you did; you may find yourself embarking on a new career. But you are not likely to change your fundamental notions of who you are as a person or whether your life has any ultimate meaning and purpose. Religious concerns and experiences are unique in that they *do* affect central perceptions about oneself and life itself; they *are* likely to change your notions of who you are and whether your life has any ultimate meaning and purpose.

Complexity. Because of its comprehensiveness and centrality, religion is psychologically complex. It involves a complex array of psychological categories—emotions, beliefs, attitudes, values, behaviors, and social environments. It is complex in another way as well. Even if we were to catalogue religious individuals' beliefs and attitudes about God, an afterlife, and the Church, few people would feel that such a catalogue adequately described their religion. Nor would it be sufficient simply to extend the catalogue to include various emotions, such as a sense of awe and mystery, or various behaviors, such as attending church and praying.

Religion often has a coherence that goes beyond a collection of beliefs, attitudes, emotions, and behaviors. It seems to combine and transcend these psychological categories, providing a sense of *integrity*. It not only expresses but also transforms the individual's life. To provide but one classic example, Saul was so changed that he adopted a new name, Paul, after his religious experience on the Damascus road. As he wrote later, "Everything old has passed away; see, everything has become new!" (II Cor. 5:17 NRSV).

Diversity. It need hardly be said that the religion of different individuals can be very different. If we consider only recognized world religions, the range of experiences is immense. Indeed, it seems impossible to identify any one characteristic that they all have in common. For example, one might think that at least all recognized world religions would include some notion of divinity, some God or gods. But not all do. There are well-established traditions within Buddhism and Confucianism that explicitly exclude such notions.

To compound the problem of diversity, it seems inappropriate to limit religion to recognized religious traditions. Sociological research suggests that many people now pursue religious concerns outside the structure of the recognized traditions (Luckmann, 1967; Machalek & Martin, 1976; Yinger, 1970). Personal growth groups, crisis-support networks, new-age workshops, encounter groups, political movements, meditation, and even parapsychology have come to serve religious functions. In the poignant words of Gary, a 13-year-old actively involved in both the Catholic and Protestant religious traditions of his divorced parents when interviewed by child psychiatrist Robert Coles (1990):

> You take the kids whose folks aren't into any religion; we have lots of them in our school, and they're no different than anyone, and some of them—I talk with them about what they believe—are really great, because they ask a lot of questions about life, and they want to stop and talk about things, about what's right and wrong, and what you should believe, and after I talk with them, I'll say to myself, hey, maybe if you have no religion, you end up being more religious. You know what I mean? (p. 279)

Given this diversity, it would seem impossible to provide a definition that includes a description of all the forms that religion takes.

A Functional Definition of Religion

Fortunately, it is possible to define religion by describing its *function* rather than all of its forms. We shall opt for a definition of this kind, one that we believe allows for the uniqueness, complexity, and diversity of religion. We shall define religion as *whatever we as individuals do to come to grips personally with the questions that confront us because we are aware that we and others like us are alive and that we will die.* Such questions we shall call *existential questions.*

No other species has the same degree of awareness that we human beings have of personal existence, of the personal existence of others, of the possibility of other worlds, and of personal finitude. As social psychologist M. Brewster Smith pointed out in his presidential address to the American Psychological Association, this existential awareness provokes profound questions.

> Self-consciousness with forethought and afterthought gives rise to the human existential predicament. At least for the last 50,000 years, we and our forebears have faced the puzzle (which we have had the words to pose to ourselves) of whence we came into the world, why we are here, and what happens when we die. But as we know, this is no matter of mere curiosity. Since reflective language made us persons, we have cared about ourselves and each other *as* persons. So the inevitability of the eventual death of self and loved ones and the arbitrary unpredictability of death from famine, disease, accident, predation, or human assault become the occasion not only for momentary animal terror, but also for a potentially unremitting human anguish. And the quest for meaning, for meanings compatible with a human life of self-conscious mortality, becomes a matter of life-and-death urgency. (Smith, 1978, p. 1055; also see Solomon, Greenberg, & Pyszczynski, 1991)

Existential questions may be articulated in the language of philosophy, as has been done by existentialists Martin Heidegger and Jean-Paul Sartre, or the language of theology, as has been done by Paul Tillich. But they can also be stated in less sophisticated, more direct language. It is in such language that most of us confront them:

> What is the meaning and purpose of my life?
> How should I relate to others?
> How do I deal with the fact that I am going to die?
> What should I do about my shortcomings?

We believe that religion arises from our attempt to deal with such questions. As M. Brewster Smith says, "Thus emerged the many worlds of myth, ritual, and religion that provide the traditional answers to the question of what it means to be human" (1978, p. 1055). Or, in the words of Tolstoy (1893/1987):

> What is the purpose of such momentary, uncertain and vacillating existence in this eternal, well-defined and never-ending world? . . . This question invariably faces each individual, and everyone answers it in one way or another. It is the answer to this question that comprises the essence of all religions. (p. 134)[1]

Having stated our definition of religion, we hasten to add four points of elaboration.

1. The existential questions listed above are illustrative only. The questions that arise as a result of existential awareness, the relative importance of these questions, and the form the questions take will vary from individual to individual.

2. The way different individuals deal with the questions will also vary. Our definition is intended to include all those ways of coming to grips with existential concerns that are traditionally associated with the term *religion*—belief in God and an afterlife, dramatic mystical or conversion experiences, worship and other forms of religious ritual, devout adherence to a prescribed code of conduct, prayer, meditation, ascetic self-denial, and so on. But the definition also allows for nontraditional forms of religion—belief in some impersonal cosmic force, focus on self-actualization in this life, participation in self-help or social-action rituals, even the experience of being converted away from one's religious heritage into the sense of personal freedom and responsibility that can accompany living without any gods.

The definition also allows for variation along another dimension, the degree of closure or finality in one's response. Many religious individuals sincerely believe that they have found the answer to one or more existential questions; they know the Truth. Others, like Hesse's *Siddhartha* (1951), may be intensely religious without ever reaching any clearly defined answers. For

1. There is some, admittedly sketchy, evidence that questions of this type are not simply a reflection of Western values. First, archaeologists have uncovered flower-lined burial graves dating from 50,000 years ago, attesting to concern about death and afterlife among our ancient ancestors (Marshak, 1976). Second, Yinger (1977) asked 751 individuals from five different countries (Japan, Korea, Thailand, New Zealand, and Australia) to indicate in response to an open-ended question what they considered to be the basic and permanent question(s) for mankind. Responses from each country were quite similar. Across the entire sample, meaning and purpose in life was mentioned by 60 percent of the respondents, suffering was mentioned by 54 percent, and injustice was mentioned by 38 percent. Finally, in 1980 a young Chinese worker wrote in a letter to *China Youth* magazine: "Life, is this the mystery you try to reveal? Is the ultimate end nothing more than a dead body?" Apparently, these questions struck a very resonant chord among other Chinese youth, for they prompted 60,000 letters in response.

There is also some evidence that people identify questions of this type with religion. In a survey of 2,509 American college students and adults, Braden (1947) found that the reason most frequently given for being religious was that "religion gives meaning to life." And in a large nationwide survey in Britain (ITA, 1970), it was found that *death* was the word that evoked religious associations (e.g., "God") for the largest percentage of respondents (64 percent). Similarly, Newman and Pargament (1990) found that in their undergraduate sample the problems most frequently linked to religion involved the death, illness, or injury of a family member.

them, seeking but never finding is a way of coming to grips with existential concerns.

3. Our definition of religion is not without precedent. Similar functional definitions have been proposed by other social scientists, although usually by sociologists rather than by psychologists. For example, Yinger defined religion as "a system of beliefs and practices by means of which a group of people struggle with the ultimate problems of human life" (1970, p. 7; see also Frank, 1977; Machalek & Martin, 1976). Although clearly similar, our definition differs from Yinger's in two ways. First, we do not wish to limit religion to beliefs and practices. To respect the complexity of religion, we have tried to allow for many ways of coming to grips with issues of existence, not only through beliefs and practices, but also through attitudes, values, emotions, and the dynamic integration of all these religious experiences. Second, to respect the diversity of religion, we have tried to allow for individual as well as group responses.

In addition to respecting the complexity and diversity of religion, we have tried to reflect its uniqueness. We have done this by identifying religion with a specific set of questions or concerns, those arising from existential awareness. Many profound personal questions are not religious: Should I ask Sally to marry or should I wait? Should I go into law or medicine? Such questions may be extremely important, and the answers one gives may have lasting effects on one's life. But coming to grips with such questions is not religious, for they do not concern matters of existence. By our definition, only when a person is responding to those issues that transcend problems in one's life and concern the nature of life itself is that individual dealing with religious questions.

This means that not everyone is religious, at least not all the time. One can easily imagine an individual who, at a given period in life, has no interest in confronting any existential questions. By our definition, at that point in his or her life, such an individual is not religious.

4. Although existential questions are often the basis for philosophical discussions, there is a difference between dealing with these questions in a philosophical and in a religious manner. As philosophical questions the issues tend to be dealt with in the abstract. Answers are universal, not personal, and are not necessarily assumed to affect one's own subsequent life. As religious questions, the same issues are confronted on an intensely personal level; answers are expected to have dramatic effects on one's life. Of course, the line between religion and philosophy, especially moral philosophy and metaphysics, is far from clear-cut. One can discuss religion philosophically, and one's response to philosophical questions can be deeply religious.

Who Is and Is Not Religious?

Equipped with this functional definition of religion, let us return to the seven examples presented on page 5. Which ones are examples of religion?

According to our definition, all are except example 6, in which a businessman and his wife attend church regularly for purely social reasons. In each of the other examples the individual involved appears to be dealing at some level with one or more existential concerns. The middle-aged woman finds meaning and comfort in knowing that her son is in God's hands; the young woman who opts for atheism finds meaning and purpose, bittersweet perhaps but nonetheless real, in trying to care for others and live every day to the fullest; the young hiker may come up with no answers, but he is addressing existential questions, and so on. In contrast, the businessman is not dealing with any issues of existence, even though he is frequenting a religious setting. Therefore, by our definition he is not religious.[2]

Of course, there are those who would disagree with our definition. Some would consider it too narrow. Gordon Allport (1950), for one, resists any attempt to specify the nature or function of religion at a general level. Rather, he says, "the subjective religious attitude of every individual is, in both its essential and non-essential features, unlike that of any other individual. The roots of religion are so numerous, the weight of their influence in individual lives so varied, and the forms of rational interpretation so endless, that uniformity of product is impossible" (1950, p. 26). Instead of attempting to develop a comprehensive definition as we have, Allport recommends that we "refer the task of characterizing the religious consciousness to the only authorities capable of knowing what it is—namely individuals who experience it" (Allport, 1950, p. 6). Clearly, if we did this, the businessman and his wife would be considered religious.

We find much merit in Allport's idea of listening with care to the way religious individuals characterize their own experience; indeed, we have tried to do this in our research. But we reject Allport's highly individualistic approach to defining religion because we fear that it would fail to give any clear direction or focus to our analysis. It would amount to having no definition at all.

At the other end of the spectrum, there are those who would consider our definition too broad. They would argue that some apprehension of or belief in a transcendent, divine reality is a necessary part of religion. For example, William James defines religion as "the feelings, acts, and experiences of individual men in their solitude, so far as they apprehend themselves to stand in relation to whatever they may consider the divine" (1902, p. 42). Similarly, sociologist Peter Berger favors what he calls substantive

2. This is not to say that the businessman and his wife will never consider existential questions. They may even be prompted by their attendance at church to do so, at least on occasion. And to the degree that they are, their experience becomes religious. Being religious by our definition is not an all-or-none phenomenon; it is more appropriately viewed as a matter of degree. Indeed, in Chapter 6 we shall suggest that it is a matter of degree along at least three distinct dimensions, and one of these dimensions explicitly takes account of the type of religious involvement shown by the businessman and his wife.

definitions over functional definitions: "Substantive definitions of religion generally include only such meanings and meaning-complexes as refer to transcendent entities in the conventional sense—God, gods, supernatural beings and worlds, or such metaempirical entities as, say, the *ma'at* of the ancient Egyptians or the Hindu law of *karma*" (Berger, 1974, pp. 127–128). According to either of these definitions, the young atheist in example 5 would not be religious.

Although we would readily accept that a divine or transcendent reality can be and often is a part of a person's religion, we have explicitly rejected the idea that it must be. We would agree that there is always a transcendent dimension to religion, but we have defined it in functional rather than metaphysical terms; the individual transcends everyday matters to deal with existential concerns. This functional rather than metaphysical approach to transcendence allows our definition to include greater diversity, including the young atheist. In addition, we believe that it has more heuristic value for a social-psychological analysis.

Heuristic Value of Our Functional Definition

While recognizing the uniqueness of religious experiences relative to everday experiences, our functional definition still emphasizes that religion is an integral and dynamic part of human life. It suggests that, by providing a new sense of reality and of one's own place within reality, religion is both a response to and a contributor to the individual's personality and social life.

This suggestion invites a number of important psychological questions: What leads an individual to become religious, to come to grips with one or more existential questions? What happens in a religious experience? What, psychologically, are the different dimensions of being religious? Is religion a source of personal freedom, of enslaving ideology, or both? In some people's lives religion seems constructive, in others it seems destructive; what accounts for this? We believe that questions like these are precisely the kind that a social psychology of religion should address. They are the questions, among others, that we shall attempt to address in subsequent chapters. But first, another preliminary question must be considered, for it casts doubt on our entire enterprise.

IS A SOCIAL PSYCHOLOGY OF RELIGION POSSIBLE?

The social psychologist interested in studying religion faces a problem. If the study is to provide insight into individuals' religion, then the subtlety, richness, and profundity of the religious experience must not be lost. If religion is deformed or distorted through oversimplification, the understanding achieved will suffer accordingly. At the same time, the psychologist must proceed scientifically because psychology is a science. He or she must be ready to subject individuals' religious experience to careful, critical scrutiny and systematic investigation, including detailed analysis of the nature and function of its components. To provide even tentative scientific answers to questions like the ones just listed, it is necessary to go beyond common sense to develop theories concerning the role of religion in human life and to test these theories by making careful empirical observations. Such testing is necessary if one is to find out whether religion actually functions in human life as one's theories say it does. Now the problem is this: Is there not a fundamental incompatibility between the requirements of respecting the integrity and complexity of the religious experience and of proceeding scientifically? If there is, then a social psychology of religion seems impossible.

To provide some perspective, it is important to remember that this kind of problem is not unique to the social psychologist studying religion. It is quite common in science. Consider, for example, a botanist studying a delicate, beautiful rose. While still respecting the integrity and complexity of the rose, the botanist may find it necessary to dissect it, to measure its different parts carefully and dispassionately, to analyze their chemical makeup, to examine their cell structure under a microscope, to compare them with similar parts of other flowers, and to consider how they interact with their environment both inside and outside the bush from which the rose was taken. A rose thus scrutinized may lose its beauty; indeed, it may not be recognizable as a rose at all. But few would question the value of the botanist's work. Not only does it seem worthwhile to try to understand the nature and function of the rose blossom, but success in doing so has contributed much to our having more and prettier roses to enjoy. And if those of us who are not botanists find roses no more beautiful as a result of the increased understanding, we do not find them less so.

In some ways the task of the social psychologist studying religion is analogous to that of the botanist studying roses, but in some important ways it is not. The goal of both is to understand the nature and function of a complex phenomenon. In pursuing this goal, both must go beyond the everyday reaction of awe, wonder, and reverence at the phenomenon to look more critically at its structure and function. The scientist's more critical look often involves subjecting the phenomenon to analysis, measurement, and experimental manipulation. At the same time, both the botanist and the psychologist must take care not to create a distorted picture of the phenomenon in the process of trying to understand it.

The clear success that botanists and other life scientists have had in conducting scientific analysis of complex, living systems underscores the fact that this basic scientific problem is not inherently insoluble. Analysis and measurement—even dissection and chemical decomposition—are not inconsistent with treating a rose as a complex, integrated living system. Far from inhibiting understanding, these techniques allow the botanist to go beyond simple awareness and appreciation to an understanding of why a rose is the way it is.

But, in spite of these similarities in their tasks, the social psychologist studying religion confronts three potential stumbling blocks that the botanist studying roses does not. First, some people object to the scientific study of religion. Second, the psychologist's preconceptions may lead him or her to approach religion with motives other than an honest desire to understand. Third, because an individual's religion is not observable in the same sense as a rose, some consider it impossible to apply the scientific method to its study. If we are to develop a social psychology of religion, we need to surmount each of these potential obstacles.

Concerns about a Scientific Study of Religion

Religion is a part of people; roses are not. It is hardly surprising, then, that people become more concerned when a psychologist scrutinizes religion than when a botanist does the same to roses. Seeing a rose dissected, we may regret the loss of some beauty, but there is no personal threat. One can imagine that the rosebush might take a very different view of the botanist's work; the bush has lost something potentially vital to survival. In a parallel manner, many people view religion as something vital to their survival, and they are naturally uneasy about having it subjected to analysis by a psychologist. They do not want their own or others' religion dissected, manipulated, or mutilated for any reason. Respecting this wish places severe constraints on social psychologists studying religion. They must avoid using research techniques that involve a risk of damaging individuals' religion.

But even if psychologists eschew research techniques that could do damage, a person whose religious beliefs are a matter of life and death still has reason to be concerned. This is because the person's beliefs are likely to include some ideas about the nature and function of his or her own religion, answers to questions such as: Why am I religious? What actually happened during this or that religious experience? What difference has my religion made in the way I act? As we noted earlier, the psychologist's task is to address these same questions, although in more general terms. The problem is that the psychologist's answers may provide plausible alternatives to the answers of the religious individual, thereby challenging the individual's beliefs.

It is important for the social psychologist to be honest at this point. Often, social psychologists bend over backward to emphasize the limited relevance and impact of their research. In stark contrast, our experience observing the reactions of religious individuals suggests that social-psychological research on religion has so much potential for relevance and impact that the consumer should be warned. It is frequently said that science cannot prove the existence or nonexistence of God, and we would agree. But it is frequently also said that a scientific study of religion carries no implications for a person's religious beliefs; here we would disagree.

Consider, for example, a reader of this book whose religious faith includes a belief that Jesus came to live in his heart when, as a teenager, he was on a religious retreat with a group of friends, all of whom were saying that Jesus had come to live in their hearts. He is likely to have some doubts about this belief when in Chapter 2 he encounters a social influence explanation for such experiences. He may, of course, reject this alternative explanation; he may decide that he is an exception to the general rule of social influence; or he may reconcile social influence with his religious conviction by concluding that "the Lord works in mysterious ways," one way being through peer pressure. Still, it seems both naive and misleading to suggest that the scientific study of religion has no relevance for and so cannot challenge personal beliefs. Exposure to research on religion may make it difficult ever again to look at one's own religion in the same way. Whether the religious individual is willing to face the questions that a social-psychological analysis of religion may raise about cherished experiences and beliefs—or, ideally, is eager to face them—is something that he or she must decide personally.

Because of the potential impact of a social-psychological analysis of religion on individuals' beliefs, we need to be very careful about jumping to conclusions. As Donald Campbell (1975) observed in his presidential address to the American Psychological Association, probably one reason that religious beliefs and practices have survived for centuries is that they serve important functions for individuals and for society. Before we even consider challenging them, we need to count the cost carefully. If we proceed with a psychological study of religion, as we have, it is important that we proceed responsibly. This rather obvious requirement brings us to the second potential stumbling block.

Motives of Psychologists Studying Religion

Although only a few social psychologists have studied religion, a number of other psychologists have. Indeed, there is a rather large literature in the psychology of religion. But even a cursory look at this literature underscores the fact that one can pursue a psychological study of religion for motives other than an honest attempt to understand. To be blunt, some psychologists have tried to conduct smear campaigns against religion in the guise of science; others have used the trappings of science to clothe the equally unscientific purpose of extolling the virtues of religion.

If a psychologist is to conduct a scientific analysis of religion, it seems essential that he or she remain open to a wide range of hypotheses, whether or not these hypotheses are flattering to religion. We believe that William James (1902) provided an ideal model in this regard, and we shall try to walk in his footsteps. He approached the varieties of religious experience carefully and critically, always looking for both potentially constructive and destructive aspects.

In part because ulterior motives have undermined concern for honest inquiry, the psychology of religion seems to have drifted into a rather stagnant backwater, far from the mainstream of modern psychology. As Bernard Spilka has noted, "Connections between the psychology of religion and psychology in general are not well established. The former utilizes methods and techniques from the mainstream of psychology, but rarely the ideas" (1978, p. 97).

At an earlier point in the history of psychology, this lack of contact with mainstream psychology might have been justified. After all, there may have been little of relevance to religion in the myriad studies of rats and pigeons used in the 1930s and 1940s to develop the learning theories of Skinner and Hull. But psychology has come a long way since then. Theory and research into complex information processing and creativity, into the formation and change of perceptions of one's reality and one's place in that reality, into the behavioral consequences of one's attitudes, beliefs, and values, even into possible neurophysiological substrates for the way we make sense of our world—all of these seem potentially relevant to understanding religion.

In offering these criticisms, we do not mean to suggest that the literature on psychology of religion contains nothing of value. There is much of value, both theoretical ideas and empirical research. Our points are simply that psychologists studying religion often appear to have ulterior motives, and they have not taken as much advantage of the developments in mainstream psychology as they should. We believe that psychology of religion should cast off these ulterior motives and return to the mainstream.

The Scientific Study of Religion: Phenomenological or Empirical?

The first two stumbling blocks may be overcome, at least in part, if the psychologist sticks to his or her business as a scientist, conducting a careful, sensitive, honest, and scholarly inquiry. But when attention is turned to conducting such an inquiry, a further problem arises. As individuals come to grips with existential questions, they often claim contact with an otherworldly realm—with God, Allah, the One, and so on. Does this otherworldliness not make it impossible to study religion scientifically? This is obviously a crucial and difficult question, one we must consider in some detail. It has proved to be the greatest hindrance to the development of a viable social psychology of religion.

Many people, including many psychologists of religion, believe that there is an irreconcilable incompatibility between the intensely personal, mysterious, otherworldly character of religion and the scientific demand for objective, empirical observations. Faced with this incompatibility, these people give us a choice: either insist on the irreducible character of religious experience and deny that it is amenable to scientific analysis, or insist on objective, empirical observations and deny that religious experience (as opposed to religious behavior) can be included in a scientific study of religion.

Those who choose the first option are often called *phenomenologists* or *humanists*. They believe that religious experience must occupy a central role in any study of religion and that the only way to study religious experience is to use wholistic techniques such as in-depth clinical interviews with religious individuals. Those who choose the second option are often called *empiricists* or *positivists.* They contend that the research techniques proposed by the phenomenologists do not produce the objective, empirical observations essential for scientific analysis. They further contend that if religious experience in its complexity and integrity does not yield such observations, then the psychologist cannot study religious experience. Instead, the psychological study of religion must be limited to observable behavior, such as going to church, praying, or marking agreement or disagreement with questionnaire items concerning religious attitudes and beliefs. According to this empiricist view, one can have a science of religious *behavior* but not of religious *experience.* (See Hanford, 1975; King, 1991; and Spilka, 1977, for further elaboration of the phenomenology-empiricism controversy in the study of religion.)

Which option should we choose? We believe we should choose neither. For, as is true in so many debates about underlying assumptions, both sides in this debate seem right in what they affirm, but wrong in what they deny. The phenomenologist affirms that we must respect the integrity and complexity of religious experience; it cannot be reduced to observable, quantifiable behavior. The empiricist affirms that any social-psychological study of religion must be scientifically respectable; it must be based on objective, empirical observations. Both sides deny the same thing, that one can use traditional scientific methods to study religious experience.

We believe that both sides are wrong in this denial, and we believe that their error stems from an inaccurate and outmoded view of science. This view, derived from logical positivism, has long been rejected by leading philosophers of science (e.g., Hanson, 1958; Kuhn, 1962; Popper, 1959) and was never an accurate description of more than a very small percentage of scientific research. We further believe that a more contemporary and realistic view of science enables one to transcend the phenomenology-empiricism controversy. This more contemporary view rests on understanding the relationship between personal experience and publicly verifiable observations.

The relationship between experience and empirically observable behavior in a contemporary view of science. According to the contemporary view, religious experience, like other experience, leaves publicly observable "tracks" in the life of the individual. The scientist can make much use of these tracks, as long as he or she is careful not to confuse the tracks with the experience that produced them. Just as children learn to recognize the presence of wind from observable facts—a snapping flag, a displaced hat, or chill on the skin—the observable fact that someone describes an experience that he has had as an encounter with God is part of a set of tracks that makes the experience, but not the experienced (i.e., God), amenable to scientific research.

To use another metaphor, one suggested by the philosopher Ludwig Wittgenstein, the behavioral consequences of religious experience function much like the symptoms of a disease. The symptoms are not the disease; instead, says Wittgenstein (1958), the symptoms serve as observable *criteria* for the disease. They are the observable tracks that allow a doctor to know when the disease is present. Similarly for a religious experience, the person's description of the experience, nonverbal cues, and changes in belief and behavior are all tracks or symptoms that serve as observable criteria. They provide clues both to the existence and to the character of the experience. The scientist can use these tracks or symptoms as publicly verifiable observations, making it possible to test explanatory theories concerning the nature and function of an individual's religious experience.

Of course, the scientist must be careful at this point. He or she cannot assume that a description is face-valid any more than the doctor can assume that a report of symptoms means that a particular disease is present. As a patient may be malingering, reporting symptoms that he is not really experiencing, a person can claim to have had a religious experience when he knows he has not. Or, as a hysterical patient can feel and honestly describe symptoms without having the underling disease, a person may describe a religious experience, honestly believing that she has accurately described what she experienced, when what she actually experienced was quite different. The doctor must be sensitive to these possibilities when diagnosing illness; similarly, the scientist studying religious experience must approach the available observable criteria carefully and critically in order to determine what experience actually lies behind them.

Two strategies have been developed to help scientists decide what experience lies behind the observable criteria. One is *convergence.* This strategy involves observing a range of relevant criteria—verbal statements, nonverbal cues, and subsequent behavior—and using them as checks on one another. To illustrate, if someone says, "I met God yesterday" in a matter-of-fact tone as he might say, "I met Fred yesterday," and then goes on talking about the weather, it would be very different from the person who haltingly and with deep emotion whispers, "I met God yesterday."

But even if all of the relevant criteria agree, what should we conclude actually occurred? Should we accept at face value the claim to have met God yesterday? Or should we assume that what the person actually experienced was quite different? At this point a second strategy provides some guidance: *the rule of parsimony.* Simply put, this rule states that if different explanations can account equally well for some phenomenon, we should prefer the simplest one. To illustrate, it is possible that all inanimate objects are imbued with invisible little engines that propel them about in a manner that conforms perfectly to the patterns predicted by the laws of physics. But, as long as the behavior of objects can be accounted for equally well in terms of an explanation that does not include the invisible-engine hypothesis, that simpler explanation is preferable.

The rule of parsimony suggests that as a matter of strategy (not as a statement of reality), the social-psychological analysis of experience should proceed at the simplest level that provides an adequate account of the observed criteria. If the claim to have met God yesterday can be as adequately accounted for in terms of simpler, more commonplace processes, such as socialized expectations, guilt, fatigue, and peer pressure, then this simpler explanation should be preferred.

But having said this, we hasten to add that even though the rule of parsimony is rather straightforward in principle, it is less clear-cut in practice. Which of two explanations is simplest is not always apparent. One may, for example, account for complex problem solving in terms of a complex array of relatively simple processes, such as trial-and-error consideration of all possible solutions. Alternatively, one may account for the same behavior in terms of a simple array of relatively complex processes, such as implementation of a heuristic strategy like reasoning by analogy. Which explanation is most parsimonious? The former assumes simpler processes; the latter, a simpler, more elegant array. There is no ready answer. Insofar as possible, the scientist tries to preserve parsimony of both types. But often, especially when explaining religious experience, simplicity in terms of simple processes and simplicity in terms of elegance are in conflict. Was it an encounter with God, or was it a combination of more commonplace processes such as peer pressure, guilt, and fatigue? Often, the most parsimonious explanation is not apparent, so we cannot say which explanation is better.

If the scientist can only approach religious experience indirectly through its tracks or symptoms, and if these cannot be taken at face value but must be interpreted using strategies like convergence and parsimony, strategies that often involve ambiguities, have we not lost the certainty and factual precision frequently claimed to be the hallmark of science? Yes, we have. In doing so, however, we have lost something that was never really there. This point lies at the heart of the contemporary view of science. As Polanyi (1958), Kuhn (1962), and others have pointed out, the scientist's facts and laws always involve subjective inference and interpretation. Scientists have long studied unobservable phenomena indirectly through reliance on publicly verifiable, but potentially distortable, criteria.

To provide some examples, the physicist only observes symptoms such as curved tracks in a cloud chamber or the wiggling of tiny molecules, yet infers the presence or absence of protons, electrons, and the ever-thickening fog of subatomic particles. This has by no means prohibited the development of scientific theories concerning these particles nor subjection of these theories to empirical test. In astrophysics, black holes can by definition never be seen; their immense gravitational force prevents any light from escaping them to reach other parts of the universe. Still, theories about their nature and function have been developed and are being tested through observation of their effects on other celestial bodies. Similarly, phychologists and physiologists never capture depression or stress in a test tube; they must rely on tracks or symptoms that serve as criteria for the presence of these states. Yet much valuable scientific work has been done on each.

Transcending the phenomenology-empiricism debate. Once we recognize the distinction between an unobservable event or experience and the observable tracks or symptoms that can serve as empirical criteria for that experience, we can see that the phenomenology versus empiricism debate rests on a failure to recognize this distinction. Both sides in the debate implicitly assume that because scientists insist on using publicly verifiable observations to test their theories, scientists can study only observable events. But as we have seen, explanatory theories concerning the nature and function of unobservable phenomena can be developed and, by using the observable criteria, tested empirically. It is not claimed that the criteria serve as an empirical equivalent of the phenomena, as is required by positivism (see Carnap, 1938); instead, it is claimed that the criteria serve as tracks or symptoms that permit us to make inferences about the unobservable event. As long as an event leaves observable tracks or symptoms (and it is not clear that we would ever know about it if it did not), it is amenable to empirical analysis. As long as religious experience in all its individuality, transcendence, and mystery leaves observable tracks or symptoms, it is amenable to empirical analysis.

When the distinction between unobservable experiential phenomena and the observable criteria for these phenomena is recognized and employed, the incompatibility between a phenomenological and an empirical approach to the study of religion disappears. It is possible to develop a social psychology of religion that is at once phenomenological *and* empirical: phenomenological in its focus on deeply felt and life-transforming religious experience as a central aspect of religious life, empirical in its reliance on empirical observations to test one's theories. It is our goal to develop just such a social psychology of religion, one that is both phenomenological and empirical. (For similar but more detailed discussions of the phenomenology versus empiricism debate in psychology in general, see Child, 1973; Mandler and Mandler, 1974; and Rychlak, 1977.)

WHAT SHOULD A SOCIAL-PSYCHOLOGICAL ANALYSIS OF RELIGION INVOLVE?

So what should a phenomenological and empirical social psychology of religion involve? We believe that it should involve application of the scientific method to the study of religion from the unique orientation of social psychology. Even though there is considerable overlap, each area of the social and behavioral sciences has its unique orientation. The unique orientation of social psychology is the study of psychological processes within the individual while at the same time recognizing that the individual is always subject to direct and indirect influence from his or her social environment. Consistent with this orientation, the theories making up our social-psychological perspective on religion attempt to explain the nature and consequences of religion in the individual's life, while at the same time keeping in mind the impact on the individual of his or her social environment.

As already suggested, the relevant theories will need to address questions such as: What leads an individual to choose one religious stance over another? Psychologically, what happens during a religious experience? What are the consequences of various ways of dealing with religious questions? Does being religious make a person more content, more open, more caring? In developing theories to answer such questions, the social psychologist studying religion needs to take advantage of theories developed in other areas of mainstream psychology, both inside and outside social psychology. Specifically, recent attempts to understand complex psychological processes such as social influence, attachment, creativity, the development and change of one's view of reality, managing death anxiety, belief intensification, and commitment would seem to hold much promise.

Theory development is an essential first step in a social psychology of religion, but it is only that. If our analysis is to be scientific, we must take a second step as well: Our theories must be subjected to empirical test. In the following chapters we shall present much empirical research relevant to the different theories proposed. To provide some basis for evaluating this research, the basic logic of the scientific method and the relative merits of three major research designs—experimental, correlational, and quasi-experimental—are discussed in the Appendix. The reader is invited to consult the Appendix now or whenever questions arise either about the role of research in social psychology of religion or about the strengths and weaknesses of the different research designs.

SUMMARY AND CONCLUSION

We have adopted a functional definition of religion: Religion is whatever we do to come to grips with existential questions—the questions that confront us because we are aware that we and others like us are alive and that we will die. Such questions include: What is the meaning or purpose of my life? How should I relate to others? How do I deal with the fact that I am going to die? What should I do about my shortcomings? This definition underscores the uniqueness, complexity, and diversity of religion. It suggests that religion is both a response and a contributor to the individual's total personality and social life, and so it invites psychological questions about the sources, nature, and consequences of religion. Such questions are, we believe, precisely the sort that a social psychology of religion should address.

But can social psychologists address such questions scientifically without at the same time doing violence to what is being studied, individuals' religion? We believe they can. The basic problem of respecting the integrity of complex phenomena while subjecting them to careful analysis is a common one in science, and the history of science provides ample evidence that it can be solved. Further, although several specific stumbling blocks stand in the way of the development of a social psychology of religion, none seem inherently insurmountable.

Considering three specific stumbling blocks in turn, the social psychologist can deal with the concern of religious individuals about the implications of a scientific study of religion by warning them that there may be challenges to their beliefs, by leaving it to them to find personal relevance in a social-psychological analysis as they see fit, and by resisting quick pronouncements about the practical implications of a social-psychological analysis, whether such pronouncements are favorable or unfavorable to religion. The problem of ulterior motives on the part of psychologists studying religion can, we hope, be overcome by adopting an attitude of open inquriy and by better integration of the psychological study of religion into mainstream psychology.

What is usually considered to be the most serious stumbling block standing in the way of the development of a social psychology of religion is, we believe, actually the easiest to overcome. The phenomenology versus empiricism debate—the debate over whether one will focus on the inner religious life of the person at the sacrifice of empirical observation (the phenomenological view) or will insist on empirical observation and so limit one's analysis to religious behavior rather than the inner religious life (the empiricist view)—seems to us to be based on a misunderstanding of what science is. In science, the phenomena being studied need not be observable as long as they leave observable tracks or symptoms. These tracks, rightly interpreted, can provide empirical criteria for the presence of inherently mysterious, unobservable, deeply personal experiences. Capitalizing on this approach, a social psychology of religion can, and we believe should, be both phenomenological and empirical: phenomenological, in that it focuses not only on religious behavior but also on religious experience; empirical, in that it employs the scientific method, including reliance on publicly verifiable observation.

With the way cleared of obstacles, it is time to take the humbling trip from possibility to reality, to consider what insights and information a social-psychological analysis of religion can provide. As we do, it is important that we not forget our goal, a scientifically sound perspective that does not do violence to the diversity and mystery of religion. Though at present far off, this is the Celestial City toward which we hope, like Bunyan's pilgrim, to make some progress.

I

Sources of the Individual's Religion

2

Social Sources of Personal Religion

If you are like most people, you consider your religion to be a very personal matter. You may listen to a lot of other people's ideas, but in the end you reserve the right to make up your own mind about whether you believe in God, in an afterlife, and so on. Others cannot dictate to you on religious matters; your faith, or lack of it, is between you and your God.

But is it really? Much social-psychological research suggests a very different possibility, that what may seem to be a freely chosen and highly personal religious stance is in large measure a product of social influence. To state this view strongly: You are free to choose only the religious stance that your particular social background dictates.

The idea that religious beliefs and even life-transforming religious experiences are a product of social influence can be unsettling. It calls into question the religious individual's conviction that his or her beliefs and experiences are a natural and necessary response to some spiritual reality. It also calls into question the skepticism of the atheist or agnostic, for if belief is a product of social influence, disbelief may also be. But, although it may be unsettling, this idea deserves careful consideration because there is a great deal of empirical evidence consistent with it.

PREDICTING RELIGION FROM SOCIAL BACKGROUND: THREE HYPOTHETICAL CASES

Perhaps the easiest way to appreciate the impact of social influence on religion is to consider predictions that we can make about a person's religion when we know a little about his or her social background. Imagine three children, each born today.

> Sally Morrison is born in an upper-middle-class suburb of New York City. She is white. Her father is a middle-level executive in a large manufacturing firm; her mother is a lawyer. Sally's parents belong to the local Episcopal Church but do not attend regularly; they consider religion to be primarily a collection of superstitions and myths, though they find the church useful in providing family rituals, such as christenings and weddings.
>
> Gloria Johnson is born in a small town in North Carolina. She is black. Her father works on a road construction crew, her mother in the local knitting mills. She is the first of five children. Gloria's mother regularly attends a small Pentecostal church; her father does not go to church.
>
> Tony Bassillio is born in Detroit. His parents are third-generation Italian. His father works at one of the automobile plants; his mother is a housewife. Tony has three older brothers and two older sisters. His parents are Catholic and attend Mass each Sunday.

Given only this limited information about social background, can we make any predictions about the religious experiences of these three children as they grow up? Indeed we can. For the purpose of demonstration, we shall make our predictions quite specific. They will not be totally accurate, of course, but they will be far better than chance.

Sally is the least likely of the three to be involved in institutional religion. Her approach to religion will include a somewhat angry, cynical questioning of traditional religious answers. In her college philosophy and literature courses she will encounter the writings of several existentialists. She will resonate with these authors and will, when pressed, call herself an existentialist. During her adult life Sally will only occasionally attend church; she will, however, participate in a number of group experiences (weekend workshops, encounter groups, etc.), will do some reading about Zen and Yoga, and will undergo psychotherapy for a short period in an attempt to "find more meaning in life."

Things will be very different for Gloria. She will have the first of a number of intensely emotional encounters with Jesus when she is 11. Most of these experiences will occur at tent revivals held every few months in or near her hometown. She will attend the same Pentecostal church her mother did, and she will talk to God regularly in prayer. Gloria will believe fervently that Jesus has saved her from her sins and that because she has accepted Him as Lord and Savior she will go to heaven when she dies. Sometimes she will read the Bible, but she will not read other literature about her faith. Much of Gloria's adult life will revolve around church functions and her personal religion.

Tony will attend a Catholic school. He will learn religious doctrines in much the same way he learns history and geography. When he is 13 Tony will have the first of several rather mysterious experiences. While saying his prayers at church he will feel the presence of the Blessed Virgin. The last of these experiences will occur when he is 16. For most of his adult life Tony will attend Mass in a rather mechanical way, but he will feel uncomfortable when he does not attend. Although he will seldom think about religion when not in church, Tony will have a positive feeling toward his religion, and will get very angry when someone makes fun of the Catholic Church or its teachings.

Where did we get our predictions? It may seem that we simply plucked them out of thin air, but we did not. Each has, as you will see, some basis in empirical research, and all are based on the general assumption that a person's social situation influences his or her religion. The plausibility of the predictions is underscored by the simple exercise of trying to mix the backgrounds and experiences. The chance that Gloria Johnson will become interested in existentialism is slim indeed, as is the chance that Sally Morrison will have an intensely emotional encounter with Jesus when she is 11. Had we broadened the spectrum of social backgrounds to include, for example, a boy born in Calcutta or a girl in Tokyo, we could have predicted with confidence even more dramatic differences in religious experience.

It is important to recognize that each of the three children we have described will feel that he or she is making very personal decisions about religious questions. Sally will feel a surge of independence as she renounces the stuffy, Establishment religion of the white middle class. Gloria will feel a deeply personal sense of warmth, release, and comfort each time she gives her life to Jesus. God's presence will be very real to her; He will live in her heart. Tony will not make as active a decision about religion, but he will still have a strong feeling that his religious views are his own, are right, and were in no way dictated to him by society.

But our ability to predict their personal religious experience in advance from minimal information about social background suggests that each of these children is actually living out a script written by society; each is free to choose only the religious stance that his or her place in society dictates. And is not each of us in the same position, believing that we have freely chosen a religious stance that is actually dictated to us by our social situation? It is time to take a step back and consider how social influence works.

HOW SOCIAL INFLUENCE WORKS

Social influence is a theoretical concept, but one that is too broad to allow us to speak of a single, unified theory of social influence. There are many theories. At their base they all share a common proposition: What we as individuals think, feel, and experience is strongly influenced by other people. This proposition has become so central to social psychology that the discipline has sometimes been defined as the study of social influence (e.g., Allport, 1968; Jones, 1987).

Social influence is obvious when those influencing us are physically present. For example, it is obvious when a person says that two lines of different lengths are the same just because everyone else in a group has said so (see Asch, 1956). It is also obvious when a person reluctantly complies with insistent instructions to administer what he believes to be extremely painful, perhaps lethal, electric shocks to another individual (see Milgram, 1963).

But social influence is by no means limited to face-to-face interactions. Our predictions for Sally, Gloria, and Tony suggest that each of us is subject to subtle forms of social influence simply as a result of being born into a particular niche in society. We are caught up in an ongoing social drama, and, as any actor who drops a line knows, there is strong pressure to stick to the script. Shakespeare put it clearly in *As You Like It* (Act II, Scene vii):

> All the world's a stage.
> And all the men and women merely players:
> They have their exits and their entrances;
> And one man in his time plays many parts. . . .

Many social psychologists and sociologists, most notably Erving Goffman (1959), have used this dramaturgical analogy between social life and a stage play to talk about subtle, indirect forms of social influence. In doing so, these psychologists and sociologists typically emphasize three concepts: social roles, social norms, and reference groups. Within the dramaturgical analogy, social roles are the parts to be played, social norms the script of the play, and reference groups the audience.

Social roles may be formally defined as behavior patterns that are characteristic, and expected, of a person or persons who occupy some position in a social structure. Less formally, they are the parts to be played in the social drama. Of course, playing roles in society is considerably more complex than playing a part in a play. Each of us is called on to play a number of different social roles at once. Some are very specific and well defined; others are general and ambiguous. For example, as a young man, Tony Bassillio might be called on to play simultaneously the roles of premedical student, son, brother, apartment-mate, Catholic, Democrat, part-time mechanic, fiancé, aware 20-year-old, and man. Each of these roles has its own more or less explicit script.

The scripts that tell the person playing a given social role what to do define *social norms*. More formally, social norms are a group's written or unwritten rules of appropriate behavior for those occupying particular roles. Although it is common to think of norms at a broad, societal level, such as the norms of the American middle class or of Japanese culture, each social role carries with it a set of social norms. Even as social roles can be general or specific, so the related social norms can be general or specific. General norms might include such cultural wisdom as "Children should be seen and not heard" or "The man should do the asking." Building on the example of Tony Bassillio as a premedical student, a specific norm might prescribe that he take courses in chemistry and biology and do well in them.

Sometimes the scripts for a person's different social roles conflict. For example, Tony might experience role conflict over the issue of abortion—his premed training, political liberalism, and desire to be an aware 20-year-old may argue in favor, but the scripts for his roles as a Catholic and the son of Catholic parents may argue against. The severe tension that can result from such role conflict provides a clue to the power of social roles and norms.

When our roles are in harmony with one another their power is less apparent because everything goes smoothly. But the power is still there. It produces what Daryl Bem (1970) has called a "nonconscious ideology," an absolute and unquestioned assurance that the script is right; indeed, that there could not be any other script. When this happens, our awareness of the script and of our roles disappears; like water for a fish, they become invisible. As in the case of the religious beliefs of Sally, Gloria, and Tony, they no longer define one approach to reality; they define reality itself.

Much of the pressure to conform to the prescriptions of social roles and norms comes from the fact that the social drama is not played in private; there is an audience. The audience includes the actor's *reference groups.* Reference groups are not the entire audience that witnesses the social drama; they are those members of the audience to whom the actor plays—his or her public, critics, and fellow actors. More formally, a reference group is any group whose judgment an individual values. As an actor looks to audience response to judge his or her performance, so we look to our reference groups to give us direction in social behavior. Any group typically specifies, either explicitly or implicitly, the appropriate social roles and norms for certain situations; it has expectations about the parts to be played and the scripts to be followed. Knowing this, the individual who values some group will look to the group's standards in deciding how to act. This is because the individual wants the reference group's approval; as actors on the social stage, we want applause.

A child's immediate family usually forms the first, primary reference group. The child plays to his or her parents, seeking their approval. As the child gets older and makes social contacts outside the home, he or she begins to play to other reference groups as well, especially groups formed by peers. One has only to think of the agonies of the adolescent who is struggling to be accepted by the "right" crowd to appreciate the power of reference-group approval. Whether the issue is not wanting to be seen with this or that person (including one's parents), not wearing this or that sweater, not endorsing this or that view on some social or political issue, the response is often, "Oh, I'd rather *die* than do that!" It is a terrible thing to be caught playing the wrong part or following the wrong script before an esteemed audience.

Just as we have a number of social roles and norms, each of us has an overlapping network of reference groups. In addition to people we know personally, our reference groups can include people we do not know, and even groups of which we are not members. All that is required for a group to serve as a reference group is that we look to it for guidance and approval. To illustrate, imagine Sally Morrison's overlapping network of reference groups while in college: her immediate family, other family members, her friends at college, existentialists, students at the college, current college students in general, liberated women, New Yorkers, the white middle class (though she might deny it), Republicans, Americans, etc. These groups will exert different degrees of influence on Sally depending on how much she values them. In addition, some will be particularly relevant for some decisions (e.g., "Should I go into law or nursing?") and not at all for others (e.g., "Does my life have any meaning?").

A CASE FOR SOCIAL INFLUENCE AS THE SOURCE OF PERSONAL RELIGION

Having introduced the concepts of social roles, norms, and reference groups, let us consider how they might affect the way one comes to grips with religious questions. The dramaturgical analogy suggests that religious questions, like all personally important questions, arise in the context of an ongoing social drama. Moreover, it suggests that a given actor's response to these questions is determined by his or her scripts. As a "mere player" he or she will feel pressure to respond to the call of God or not, to pursue the spiritual or not, according to what the scripts say is acceptable and appropriate for a person in his or her social position. Each of us has been assigned our part, the script is in the hand, and the audience awaits. Our religious beliefs and experiences—or lack of them—are simply one aspect of the part in the social drama we have been assigned to play.

Power of Social Influence on Religion

In fact, because religious questions transcend everyday objective reality, there is reason to expect the impact of social influence on religion to be particularly strong. For, as Leon Festinger pointed out in his theory of social comparison processes, nonobjective beliefs and attitudes are especially subject to social influence. According to Festinger (1954), "There exists a drive to evaluate one's opinions and abilities." When evaluating our abilities, we can usually rely on objective standards, but when evaluating opinions, beliefs, and attitudes, we cannot. And when we cannot use objective standards, says Festinger, the drive to evaluate leads to a greater reliance on social comparison.

To illustrate, a person can evaluate his ability at running the hundred-meter dash with a stopwatch, but he cannot use an objective measure to evaluate his belief in the dignity and worth of all human life. Instead, he evaluates this belief by comparison with the standards set by relevant reference groups. As a result, his beliefs about such issues are very likely to be influenced by these groups.

Although neither Festinger nor more recent interpreters of social comparison theory (e.g., Goethals & Darley, 1977) have explicitly applied this theory to religious beliefs and experiences, it seems quite relevant. Religion often involves dramatic, unexpected but deeply moving experiences that cannot be evaluated objectively. How is the individual to make sense of such "wholly other" experiences? Social comparison theory suggests that because of the absence of clear objective standards, the individual will rely all the more heavily on interpretations supplied by his or her reference groups.

Consider a rather simple example. Most of us have at one time or another had a sense that we were not alone when, in fact, it was clear that no one else was physically present. Was this experience a visitation by God, an experience of the oneness of all existence, or just a case of our mind playing tricks on us? A person who knew the views of our reference groups about such matters could probably predict with confidence the interpretation that we adopted.

The effect of social influence on religious beliefs is further illustrated in an experiment by Brown and Pallant (1962). For many people, one of their social roles is as a member of some religious denomination, and this membership carries normative pressure to adhere to the beliefs of the denomination (even though the individual may not understand exactly what these beliefs are). To demonstrate the impact of social influence on religion, Brown and Pallant (1962) had a group of Methodist teenagers complete a questionnaire measuring their religious beliefs. One week later these same teenagers were asked to complete the questionnaire again. But this time, some of them found that their copies of the questionnaire already contained someone else's responses. These responses, which were carefully prepared to differ moderately from the ones the teenager had expressed a week earlier, were marked in red. For some of the Methodist teenagers these marks were attributed to "Rev. A. S. Whitehead, a prominent Methodist minister," and for others, to "Rev. Father Sullivan, a prominent Roman Catholic priest."

Beliefs expressed by the teenagers on the second administration were clearly affected by this information. Those teenagers who thought that the red-marked responses were made by the Methodist Rev. Whitehead moved their own responses significantly more toward agreement with the red marks than did either those who thought the red-marked responses were made by the Catholic Rev. Father Sullivan or those whose questionnaires had no red-marked responses. Why were Rev. Whitehead's responses influential when Rev. Father Sullivan's were not? Presumably, it was because the former served as an expert representative of the denominational reference group, whereas the latter did not.[1]

The power of social influence to affect religious beliefs may seem rather benign in this experiment, but it is often far from benign. Consider, for example, the social influence that can operate in groups like the Hare Krishnas or the Unification Church (Moonies). New converts are encouraged to live with the group, to spend all their time on group activities, and to surrender all money and personal possessions. In this way, ties to old roles, norms, and reference groups are broken. Sometimes, the wedge between the convert and his or her old system of social influence is driven deeper by the suggestion that the Devil can work through parents and friends to lure the new convert from the path of Light. Then any attempt by family or friends to reestablish contact is viewed with suspicion; any attempt to question what is prescribed by the group is seen as the work of the Devil.

In place of the old social support system, the group provides the convert with a new set of clearly defined roles, norms, and reference groups. Right thoughts and right actions are specified. Often the leader of the group comes to embody the group as a whole, becoming the key reference group, all-seeing and all-knowing. If the transfer of social support systems is successful, the convert may soon become unable to resist the group's view of reality or the leader's commands.

Because of its powerful effects, this conversion process has attracted much attention; it has been labeled "mind control" or "brainwashing." But at its heart it often appears to involve nothing more than a powerful use of social influence to undermine the convert's old roles, norms, and reference groups, and to replace them with new ones (Jacobs, 1987; Long & Hadden, 1983). Just how powerful this process can be was dramatically illustrated in 1979 when hundreds of members of the People's Temple, after having given up homes and country to move to the jungles of Guyana, obeyed their leader Jim Jones's commands to commit suicide and even to murder their children and reluctant comrades. In the area of religion, social influence can be powerful indeed!

Empirical Evidence That Social Background Influences Religion

Most of us do not come under the intense, dramatic social pressure of religious groups requiring total commitment. Still, a social influence analysis

1. We must add a note of caution to our interpretation of the results of this experiment. As discussed in the Appendix, responses on a self-report questionnaire may not be an accurate index of true religious belief. We do not know whether the teenagers who saw Rev. Whitehead's responses changed their beliefs as well as their responses. All we know is that they changed what they *said* they believed. We shall have to await the evidence reported in the next section of this chapter before concluding that social influence can affect religious beliefs themselves.

suggests that the same social pressures, operating more subtly, can and do shape our religious stance. It suggests that differences in rather impersonal characteristics of our social background, which create different social roles, norms, and reference groups, lead to differences in personal religion. If this is true, then it should be possible to predict with some confidence a person's religion from a police-style description: male, Caucasion, 23 years old, and so on. Indeed, this does appear possible.

The list of social background characteristics that have been found to predict religion is long. It includes sex, race, age, socioeconomic status, educational level, town size, geographical region, family ethnic origin, parents' religion, political affiliation, and marital status. To give a flavor of the consistency and scope of the evidence, we shall look at the relationship between religion and six of these social background variables. Readers who would like a more comprehensive review may want to consult the one provided several years ago by Michael Argyle and Benjamin Beit-Hallahmi (1975).

We must add a caution before presenting the evidence. Although the empirical relationships between religion and these six social background variables are all well established, theoretical explanations for these relationships are not. This is primarily because the evidence for the relationships is correlational. As discussed in the Appendix, inferring causation from correlations is often difficult. Consistent with the case we are making, we shall focus on social influence explanations of these relationships. But, when appropriate, we shall consider other explanations as well.

Sex. There is considerable evidence that women are more likely to be interested and involved in religion than men. Women rate their religious beliefs as important more than do men, and they are more likely to report having had a religious or mystical experience (Sasaki, 1979). More women than men report having attended religious services in the past week (46 percent compared with 33 percent); more women hold membership in a church or synagogue (74 percent compared with 63 percent); and more women report watching religious programs (53 percent compared with 44 percent). Women are more likely than men to read the Bible at least monthly (56 percent compared with 41 percent) and to report having "a great deal of confidence" in organized religion (62 percent compared with 52 percent) (Gallup Report, 1987). Among Christian denominations, as one moves away from the established, traditional churches (e.g., Catholic, Eastern Orthodox, Episcopal) toward newer, less traditional ones (e.g., Assembly of God, Pentecostal) the proportion of women members relative to men increases (Argyle & Beit-Hallahmi, 1975). In sum, although the differences are not always large, they are remarkably consistent: Women appear to be more religious than men.

For a long time this sex difference was explained in terms of biological differences between men and women rather than in terms of social influence. In fact, two biological explanations remain popular among psychologists of religion, so we need to consider them before we consider a social influence explanation. The first, suggested by Freud, is that religious fervor is a result of displaced infantile sexual attachment to one's father.

Noting that most deities and most religious leaders are men, Freud claimed that "God is in every case modeled after the father, and that our personal relation to God is dependent upon our relation to our physical father, fluctuating and changing with him, and that God at bottom is nothing but an exalted father" (1913, p. 244). When the idea of God as a projected father figure is considered in the context of Freud's analysis of infantile sexuality, it is easy to predict sex differences in interest in religion. Boys are supposed to emerge from the Oedipus complex with ambivalent feelings toward their father; the father is feared because he is a more powerful competitor for the affections of the mother, but he is also emulated. Accordingly, men should feel ambivalence toward God, the projected Father. In contrast, girls should have a less ambivalent, more positive attachment to their father; he is the love object of their infantile sexuality. Projecting these feelings onto God, women should be more attracted to God.

Consistent with Freud's view, Stark (1965) noted that there were consecration ceremonies for nuns during the Middle Ages, some of which continue today, that included giving the young candidate a gold wedding ring and calling her a bride of Christ. One ceremonial response was, "I love Christ whose bed I have entered." Candidates were urged to "forget there [in Christ's bed] all the world, and there be entirely out of the body; there in glowing love embrace your beloved who is come down from heaven into your breast's bower, and hold Him fast until He shall have granted whatsoever you wish for." Some nuns believed that they had conceived by Christ, and some even sustained false pregnancies as a result of this belief. In a very different context, La Barre (1962) reported that women members of Appalachian snakehandling cults exhibit decidedly sexual responses while handling the snakes.

It has also been noted that clear sexual imagery can be found in women's descriptions of their religious experiences. Mechthild of Magdeburg (ca. 1212–ca. 1282), recounting her love affair with Christ, advised "all virgins to follow the most charming of all, the 18-year-old Jesus, so He might embrace them." Elsewhere she quoted the Song of Solomon, "Tell my Beloved that His chamber is prepared, and that I am sick with love for Him." And she described one experience in which "He took the soul into His divine arms, and placing His fatherly hand on her bosom, He looked into her face and kissed her well" (Stark, 1965). Saint Teresa of Avila (1515–1582) in her autobiography described her early experiences as "an intimate, friendly intercourse with God, in which the soul expresses her love freely to Him who loves her." Later, she depicted a dramatic scene in which she experienced God's love through an angel:

> In his hands I saw a great golden spear, and at the iron tip there appeared to be a point of fire. This he plunged into my heart several times so that it penetrated to my entrails. When he pulled it out, I felt that he took them with it, and left me utterly consumed by the great love of God. The pain was so severe

> that it made me utter several moans. The sweetness caused by this intense pain is so extreme that one cannot possibly wish it to cease, nor is one's soul then content with anything but God. This is not a physical, but a spiritual pain, though the body has some share in it—even a considerable share. So gentle is this wooing which takes place between God and the soul. . . . (1957, p. 210)

In addition to this anecdotal evidence, there is some empirical research that has been interpreted as supporting Freud's view. Researchers have found that God is described in terms quite similar to those used to describe one's father (Vergote, Tamayo, Pasquali, Bonami, Pattyn, & Custers, 1969) and that, in general, women's attitudes toward God correlate more positively with attitudes toward their father than do men's (Godin & Hallez, 1964). Moreover, attitudes toward God and their own father have been found to be most similar for nuns, followed by young unmarried women, followed by older women (Godin & Hallez, 1964). Finally, statistics indicate that there are proportionally more men involved in Catholicism than in the Protestant denominations (Argyle & Beit-Hallahmi, 1975). Could this be because Catholicism offers a mother figure to whom men can form an infantile sexual attachment, the Virgin Mary, as well as a father figure for women?

In spite of the cited evidence, Freud's theory that religion arises from displaced infantile sexual attachment to a projected father figure must be regarded with considerable skepticism. For, when examined more closely, none of the evidence clearly supports it. First, romantic and sexual imagery, such as nuns speaking of being in love with or married to Christ, may be used metaphorically in a religious context to indicate the intensity of feeling, not underlying sexual motivation. Second, the dramatic examples from the writings of Mechthild and Saint Teresa were by no means randomly selected; they were chosen precisely because they involved explicit sexual imagery. Many examples exist in which women, including these women, talk about their religious experiences in a way that does not suggest sexual connotations.

Third, researchers who interpret the positive relationship between women's attitudes toward God and their father as evidence for Freud's theory have typically failed to take account of a very likely confound. Most women in these studies view both God and their fathers very positively. Given this fact, it is neither surprising nor particularly noteworthy to find that their attitudes toward their father correspond closely to their attitudes toward God; their attitudes toward *any* especially well-liked and esteemed person would correspond closely to their attitudes toward God. Consistent with this reasoning, it has been found that among those women and men who view both parents positively, the attitudes toward mother as well as father correlate highly with attitudes toward God, and among those women and men who view their mothers more positively than their fathers, attitudes toward the mother correlate more positively than do attitudes toward the father (Godin & Hallez, 1964). These results suggest that the previously noted relationship between attitudes toward God and father among women is simply an artifact of both God and father being viewed positively. It provides no clear evidence that a causal link exists between attitudes toward the two, and so it provides no clear evidence for Freud's view that God is a projected father figure.

Finally, as to the proportion of men involved in Catholicism and Protestantism, these two branches of Christianity differ on many dimensions other than provision of a mother figure for religious devotion; for example, they differ in their ability to meet instrumental-masculine and expressive-feminine needs (Schoenfeld & Mestrovic, 1991). One or more of these other differences could easily account for the observed differences in the proportion of men participating in each.

The second biological explanation still popular among psychologists of religion is based on the belief that inborn personality differences exist between the sexes and that these differences lead women to have a greater need for religion. As evidence for this view, one can point to empirical research indicating that women express greater feelings of guilt than do men (Wright, 1971) and that they also score higher on measures of submissiveness, passivity, dependence, anxiety, worry, and distress (Garai, 1970; Garai & Scheinfeld, 1968). For a long time, such findings were assumed to reflect biologically based personality "defects" within women: excessive feelings of guilt, undue submissiveness, extreme passivity, and so on. These defects were, in turn, thought to lead to a greater need for the forgiveness, comfort, and direction that religion can provide.

But it is a non sequitur to assume that because pervasive sex differences exist, the differences are biological. Parents and society in general tend to respond to little boys very differently than to little girls (Maccoby & Jacklin, 1974). This difference in social response could easily lead to dramatic differences in personality. Consistent with this possibility, in the relatively few studies where attempts have been made to control for socially based differences between the sexes, many of the personality differences that had been assumed to be biologically based have disappeared. The only personality difference that has been clearly traced to a biological base is level of aggressive activity; males tend to display more aggressive behavior than females (Gray, 1971; Maccoby & Jacklin, 1974). It is not clear how this difference, by itself, could account for the observed sex differences in religion.

Due in part to these problems with the biological explanations, sex differences in religion have more recently been explained in terms of social influence. Two different but not contradictory explanations have been proposed. One focuses on personality differences that could arise from sex differences in socialization. If little girls are responded to differently and provided with different role models than little boys, it is reasonable to expect them to grow up having different personality characteristics. Specifically, because of the great emphasis on little girls behaving properly, women may develop the higher degree of guilt, submissiveness, anxiety, and so on, noted above. These personality characteristics could lead to a greater concern about personal worth and purpose. And, consistent with our definition of religion—what the individual does to deal with existential concerns (see Chapter 1)—these concerns could lead to more interest and involvement in religion.

There is some empirical evidence in line with this explanation, although it is by no means conclusive. Barry, Bacon, and Child (1957) report that across 110 cultures little girls are almost always trained more for nurturance, obedience, and responsibility, whereas little boys are almost always trained more for self-reliance and independence (see also D'Andrade, 1967). The former set of characteristics might easily evoke greater concern about personal worth and the meaning of life than the latter. Thompson (1991) found that within *each* sex, feminine gender orientation—that is, reporting oneself as being more nurturant, expressive, dependent, and relational—was associated with higher religiousness among undergraduates; this association was, if anything, stronger among men than among women. Moreover, these sex role differences appear to be reflected in the child's conception of God. Cox (1967) and Wright and Cox (1967) found that girls were more likely to depict God as loving, comforting, and forgiving, whereas boys tended to view God as a supreme power, forceful planner, and controller. It seems, then, that women may be socialized to have those personality characteristics that would lead them not only to raise existential questions, but also to view God as able to meet their existential needs. These socialized personality characteristics could account for the relatively greater involvement of women in religion.

A second social influence explanation proposes an even more direct link between socially created sex roles and religion. At least in Western society, the script for the role of woman seems to include the expectation of more involvement in religion than does the script for the role of man. If this is true, then it may be possible to account for the greater involvement of women in religion without having to assume that certain personality traits, more characteristic of women, lead to an increased interest in religion. It may be that women are simply under more social pressure to display interest and involvement in religion, and so they do. This last explanation is certainly the most parsimonious for the observed relationship between sex and religion.

If it is true that the observed sex differences in religion are a result of social influence rather than biological differences, then recent pressures toward sexual equality, including challenges to traditional male and female roles, should lead to a diminution of these differences. At least within certain segments of modern society, new roles and scripts are being written for women, ones that do not appear to include "be religious" as a necessary component. Within these segments of society, we would expect replications of the studies that have found sex differences in religion to reveal decreases in the observed differences. In fact, if the relationship between sex and religion were *not* affected by these cultural changes, it would lend support to the possibility that the sex differences in religion might be biological after all.

Race. In the United States, race is also a powerful predictor of religious experience. If you are black as opposed to white you are more likely (1) to attend religious services (McConahay, 1970; Sasaki, 1979); (2) to hold traditional religious beliefs (Glenn, 1964); (3) to feel strongly about your religious beliefs (Alston, 1973; Sasaki, 1979); (4) to report having had religious experiences (Back & Bourque, 1970; Sasaki, 1979); and (5) to consider religion to be important in your life—both when you were growing up (McConahay, 1970) and as an adult (Cameron, 1969). Gallup and Castelli (1989) conclude: "American blacks are, by some measures, the most religious people in the world" (p. 122).

When we try to account for these racial differences, one historical fact stands out: In America, religious institutions have occupied a more central position in the black community than in the white community. During slavery, the only regular community meetings blacks were permitted were religious. As a result, the black church came to serve more social functions than the white church. In many black communities, the church still serves roles that in white communities are handled by social and civic clubs, political caucuses, entertainment and cultural centers, day-care centers, even the PTA.

This historical fact suggests that racial differences in religion, like sex differences, are due to the influence of social norms and customs. Because of the wider range of social functions associated with religious institutions, religion is more central in the role definition of members of the black community. Holding firm religious beliefs and having, or at least reporting, religious experiences receive stronger social support in black than in white communities.[2]

Socioeconomic status. Socioeconomic status (SES) is also a predictor of religion, although it seems to affect how, rather than whether, a person is

2. A different explanation for racial differences in religion is frequently invoked by sociologists. This explanation recognizes the differences in social roles for blacks and whites, but it is still not a social influence explanation. Instead, it contends that the experience of blacks as an oppressed minority in American society has intensified their need for religion by making more salient for them existential questions about the meaning of life, about how one should live one's life, about good and evil in society, and about how one should relate to others (cf., Back & Bourque, 1970; Davis, 1948; Glock, 1964).

Proponents of this *oppression-intensification explanation* often note that two rather distinct forms of religious response have developed within black religion. One is otherworldly; it assumes that life on earth is necessarily full of pain, indignity, and injustice; happiness is to be expected only in the life to come. This response leads to acceptance of the present social order and to an emphasis on, as Malcolm X (1964) characterized it, "pie in the sky and heaven in the hereafter." The second response is more this-worldly; it also recognizes that life is full of suffering but does not accept this as the necessary order of things. Instead, it includes active criticism and pressure for social change, seeking to bring more happiness into life on earth. Martin Luther King's dream of a free society and Malcolm X's vision of universal brotherhood are both examples of this kind of religious response. Far from leading to acceptance of the social order,

religious. Members of the middle class are more likely than members of the lower class to be church members and to attend church (Burchinal, 1959; Hollingshead, 1949; Lenski, 1953) but less likely to report having religious or mystical experiences (Back & Bourque, 1970). Moreover, lower SES is associated with more traditional and more fundamental religion, at least among Protestants (deJong & Ford, 1965; Demerath, 1965; Johnson, 1962; Gallup Report, 1986). It is also associated with involvement in sect-type religious organizations—those in which the follower is expected to give his or her all, often including renunciation of friends, family, and possessions (Hine, 1969; Schwartz, 1970; Wilson, 1970)—rather than involvement in more formal churches (Dynes, 1955; Sasaki, 1979). The relationship between lower SES and involvement in sect, as opposed to church, religion is reflected in the relationship between SES and the Protestant denominations. In the United States, Presbyterians and Episcopalians tend to be above average in SES; Methodists and Lutherans about average; and Baptists and members of Protestant fundamentalist sects below average (Laumann, 1969; Lazerwitz, 1964; Warren, 1970; Wilson, 1978).

To explain SES differences in how one is religious, some researchers (e.g., Goode, 1966) have suggested that religion has become secularized in the middle class, that only the less institutionalized religion of the lower class maintains the authenticity of intense personal involvement. But instead of assuming that one social class is more religious than another, the differences

---

this response can serve as a catalyst for social change. Although these two responses are radically different, Alland (1962; see also Cameron, 1971) suggested that both grow from the same motivational roots, intensification of religious questions for those oppressed by social injustice.

Consistent with the possibility of these two distinct responses to oppression, Gary Marx (1967) found that during the 1960s blacks with an otherworldly religious commitment tended to be less militant in their opposition to racial injustice and more accepting of the social status quo than blacks with a temporal or this-worldly religious commitment. Marx's results have been interpreted as support for the oppression-intensification explanation.

But one must be careful when interpreting the pattern of causation in Marx's results. The oppression-intensification explanation assumes that the two approaches to religion studied by Marx are both responses to the experience of oppression and, in turn, causes of the differences in militancy. It is possible, however, that these approaches to religion and militancy are both components of more general sets of social attitudes, one set conservative, the other liberal.

Some evidence that seems to support this possibility has been provided by Eckhardt (1970). Eckhardt carefully replicated Marx's study, except that he studied the attitudes of white students at nine Midwestern colleges. His results closely paralleled those obtained by Marx; white students with an otherworldly religious commitment tended to be less concerned about racial injustice and more accepting of the status quo than those with a this-worldly religious commitment. It seems unlikely that these white college students had experienced the oppression assumed to underlie racial differences in religion. More likely, some were relatively conservative, identifying with traditional, otherworldly views of religion and the social status quo; others were relatively liberal, identifying with temporal religion and social activism. This interpretation suggests that adopting liberal or conservative social roles and norms may be more important than the experience of oppression in producing Marx's (1967) results.

In sum, we would not question that many blacks in the United States have experienced oppression; moreover, it seems likely that for some this experience has intensified religious questions. But we believe that social influence resulting from the unique role of the church in the black community provides a more parsimonious explanation for the pervasive racial differences in religion than does oppression-intensification.

in types of religious affiliation seem more appropriately attributed to strong norm and reference group pressure to maintain a religious affiliation that is consistent with one's social and economic level (Hoge & Carroll, 1978). This pressure is obvious when an individual is coolly received while visiting a church that does not match his or her SES. It is also obvious when an individual, through education or wealth, is promoted to a new social class; if Protestant, he or she will likely feel pressure to change denominational affiliation. As Gibson Winter (1962) put it, "The Church is now a reflection of the economic ladder. Ascent on this ladder is validated by escalation to congregations of higher social and economic rank. For every rung on the ladder there is an appropriate congregation, with ushers of slightly more refined dress, and somewhat more cultivated ladies' affairs" (p. 77).

If you are a Protestant church member, you may object to this picture of economic segregation, noting: "From richest to poorest, everyone is welcome at my church." You may even add, "People of different social status just will not come." And you are probably right; they won't. But why? Once again, social influence suggests an answer: Subtle social pressures are operating to make sure that people get involved in the form of religion that society deems appropriate for a person of a given social class. Demerath (1965) has suggested that middle-class social roles tend to be characterized by a verbal, cognitive, reflective, organized approach to life, whereas lower-class social roles are characterized by a more physical, emotional, actional, spontaneous approach. Adoption of these role characteristics can have subtle but dramatic effects on the social environments, including religious environments, in which a person will feel at home. If a person's religion is to feel "right," it must be compatible with his or her general approach to life.

If, for example, a man has learned at work that the most effective way to deal with problems that arise is by applying more force and breaking the logjam (as is often the case when working on construction or maintenance jobs), he is not likely to respond to a careful, reflective approach when dealing with religious concerns. He will look for decisive, forceful, clear solutions to religious problems as well. As a result, the child of the lower class will find middle-class religion too dry, too dull, too uninvolving. In contrast, the child of the middle class will probably not feel comfortable in a lower-class religious service; the service will seem too emotional, too spontaneous, too disorganized. Without being ostracized or criticized for being out of place socially, each has been socialized to feel pressure from within to stay in those religious settings that feel "right."

Educational level. Educational level and SES are highly correlated. Therefore, one would expect patterns between educational level and religion to parallel those between SES and religion. They do. Increased education correlates positively with church membership and attendance (Burchinal, 1959; Cantril, 1943; Gallup Report, 1986) and negatively with holding traditional or fundamentalist religious beliefs (Feldman, 1969; Ferman, 1960; Ford, 1960) and reporting having religious or mystical experiences (Back &

Bourque, 1970). These effects of educational level are amenable to the same kinds of social influence explanations used to account for SES differences.

There is, however, a specific effect of education that deserves more detailed consideration; this is the effect of attending college or university. Research indicates that college students are considerably less likely to endorse orthodox religious beliefs than are people who have not gone to college (Feldman, 1969; Ford, 1960). It is tempting to view these findings as evidence that higher education teaches people to think critically and not simply to accept socially prescribed religious pronouncements. But this optimistic explanation is not fully adequate because studies that measure students' attitudes after they have graduated and entered adult society reveal that their religious beliefs and attitudes tend to become more orthodox and conservative (e.g., Feldman & Newcomb, 1969). Apparently, for many people college brings about only a temporary decline in religious orthodoxy.

This pattern suggests that the effect of college may be largely due to shifts in reference groups. Leaving home and going to college, the student weakens ties with hometown reference groups and comes under the influence of new ones, most notably other students and the faculty (Ozorak, 1989; Woodroof, 1986). Academic reference groups typically prescribe a more liberal, skeptical attitude toward religion (Havens, 1963). There is even evidence of differences among academic disciplines in the degree of religious skepticism. At secular colleges and universities, psychologists tend to be the least religious, sociologists next, followed by other social scientists, and finally, by faculty members in the natural sciences and humanities (Hoge & Keeter, 1976; Lehman, 1974; Lehman & Shriver, 1968). Thus, college students, especially in the social and behavioral sciences, are likely to face considerable social pressure toward greater religious skepticism.

There are, of course, exceptions. The student may attend a conservative religious college or join a conservative campus religious group, in which case he or she will likely face reference-group pressure to maintain or intensify earlier religious beliefs (see Christensen & Cannon, 1978; Hammersla, Andrews-Qualls, & Frease, 1986; Hammond & Hunter, 1984; Hunsberger, 1978).

The social pressure that students can feel is dramatically reflected in the comments of students at Bennington College, a small, very liberal, women's college in Vermont. In the mid-1930s the entire student body of Bennington participated in what has become a classic study of the liberalizing influence of college. Here are some students' observations about their shift toward less orthodox beliefs:

> All my life I've resented the protection of governesses and parents. At college I got away from that, or rather, I guess I should say, I changed it to wanting the intellectual approval of teachers and more advanced students. Then I found that you can't be reactionary and be intellectually respectable. (Newcomb, 1943, p. 134)

> Becoming radical meant thinking for myself, and, figuratively, thumbing my nose at my family. It also meant intellectual identification with the faculty and students that I most wanted to be like. (p. 131)

Even the students who resisted the influence of the college environment felt its pressure:

> Family against faculty has been my struggle here. . . . Every time I've tried to rebel against my family I've found out how terribly wrong I am, and I've very naturally kept to my parents' attitudes. (p. 124)
>
> I wanted to disagree with all the noisy liberals, but I was afraid that I couldn't. So I built up a wall inside me against what they said. I found I couldn't compete, so I decided to stick to my father's ideas. For at least two years I've been insulated against all college influences. (p. 119)

Such insulation was relatively rare. Far more often the students at Bennington, like students elsewhere, developed beliefs and attitudes that corresponded closely to those of their campus reference groups.

When students graduate and return to the nonacademic community, they leave the student role and academic reference group behind. They face new roles, new norms, and a new set of reference groups. Beliefs that were considered courageous and open-minded in college may, in the eyes of the new reference groups, be considered reckless and naive. If so, there is once again social pressure to change one's beliefs, this time toward greater orthodoxy and conservatism, and, according to the empirical evidence (Feldman & Newcomb, 1969), such a change is likely.

It is possible, then, that rather than leading to a permanent change toward more independent, critical thought, college leads to little more than compliance with a new set of norms under the social pressure of new reference groups. When a person leaves these pressures behind and moves into a new social environment, he or she encounters new social pressures and, consistent with what a social influence explanation has led us to expect, the person's beliefs are likely to change accordingly.

Town size. Does it seem farfetched to claim that a person's religious involvement can be predicted from the size of the town where he or she lives? There is evidence that it can. Ogburn and Tibbits (1933) and Lenski (1953) both reported a higher percentage of church attendance in smaller communities. There is also evidence of greater orthodoxy and conservatism of religious belief, as well as more mystical experiences, among those living in small towns and rural areas than among those living in larger cities (Back & Bourque, 1970; Glock & Stark, 1966; Light, 1970; Marty, Rosenberg, & Greeley, 1968; Nelsen, Yorkley, & Madron, 1971).

Social influence may help explain these differences. A person is more likely to know and be known by neighbors in smaller towns. As a result, neighbors form a more important reference group. The small-town dweller cares more what his neighbors think about what he does and believes; as the saying goes, "Everybody's business is everybody's business in a small town."

This greater social cohesion is likely to lead to greater compliance with established norms, including norms concerning religious beliefs and practices.

Parents' religion. The most powerful social background predictor of a person's religious involvement appears to be the religious involvement of his or her parents (Hoge & Petrillo, 1978a). In an early study, Newcomb and Svehla (1937) measured the attitudes of 548 sets of parents and children toward the church. The children's ages ranged from 14 to 38; most were living at home. Correlating attitudes of fathers and sons, fathers and daughters, mothers and sons, and mothers and daughters, Newcomb and Svehla consistently found strong positive correlations, ranging from .58 to .69. Although there is some evidence that these correlations would have been lower if more children had been living away from home (Hirschberg & Gilliland, 1942), Stark (1963) found that even among young adults living away from home, a high percentage reported the same religious affiliation as their parents (for Catholics, 85 percent, Protestants, 71 percent, and Jews, 65 percent). Recent surveys suggest that, at least for the major Christian denominations, the majority of adults still affiliate with their parents' denomination (Spilka, Hood, & Gorsuch, 1985). Percentages are quite consistent with the earlier findings, with an average of 63 percent for Protestant denominations and 85 percent for Catholics. The influence of parents' religion has been found to be stronger the more important religion is for the parents (Hunsberger, 1976; Hunsberger & Brown, 1984; Strole, Langner, Michael, Opler, & Rennie, 1962); when both parents share the same religious beliefs (Lenski, 1953; Putney & Middleton, 1961); and the more the child likes, identifies with, and has a close relationship with the parent (Erickson, 1964; Hoge & Petrillo, 1978a; Ozorak, 1989; Weigert & Thomas, 1972).

The strong positive correlation with parents' religion is easily explained in terms of social influence. Parents are a major source of social rewards and punishments; they are also a major reference group. Therefore, the child experiences strong social pressure to conform to their wishes with regard to religion. Further, this influence is stronger when the parents believe religion to be important and when the parent-child relationship is optimal for reference-group effects, that is, when the child likes, identifies with, and has a close relationship with the parent (Bandura & Walters, 1963). It is weaker when the child leaves home and is not only out from under direct parental influence but also confronted with potentially conflicting pressure from other reference groups.

Using Social Influence To Predict Personal Religion

In light of this brief review of the evidence for social background as a predictor of personal religion, our rather detailed predictions for the three newborns, Sally, Gloria, and Tony, do not seem so extreme. It can be seen that every major prediction was based on empirical evidence that can be explained in terms of social influence. Think back over the three personal histories.

Sally Morrison's parents were both skeptical of religion and only peripherally involved in the local Episcopal church. Consistent with the evidence suggesting the importance of parental influence on religion, we predicted that Sally, too, would adopt a skeptical attitude. Given her SES, it seemed quite likely that she would attend college, and that she would identify strongly with the academic norms for skepticism and independence of thought. Because her parents supported these values as well, she would not experience conflict between family and college reference groups; rather, college would reinforce and intensify her skepticism. Whether Sally will become especially interested in existentialism as we predicted rather than, for example, nihilism, we cannot say with confidence. But given the general normative agreement between her reference groups at home and college, it is likely that she will adopt some form of skeptical, cynical attitude toward institutional religion. After college, Sally can be expected to move into upper-middle-class adult American society. There she will be bombarded with information about an endless series of self-improvement and personal growth techniques—from aerobics to psychotherapy to meditation and visits to Zen retreats. Her friends will be sampling and talking about such techniques, and it seems quite likely that Sally will too.

Gloria Jackson's social background is quite different. As a lower-middle-class black female born in a small town in North Carolina, she may well live her entire life in that town under the influence of her family, especially her mother, and her friends. The norms and expectations of these reference groups do not include pressure on Gloria to get the education necessary to break out of the pattern of living in a small town and working at the mill; they do include pressure to get "that old-time religion." Assuming that she stays near home, she is very likely to become involved in the same Pentecostal church as her mother and to have religious experiences much like her mother's. If, through education or marriage, Gloria enters the middle class, we would need to change our predictions. Consistent with the evidence for SES differences in religion, we would then expect her to leave the Pentecostal church and tent revivals and join a more sedate Baptist or perhaps Methodist church. We would also expect her intensely emotional religious experiences to end.

As a male, Tony should be less interested in religion than his sisters, although we noted that sex differences are less pronounced for Catholics than Protestants. We also noted that the child of two Catholic parents is very likely to remain Catholic. Balancing these conflicting pressures, we predicted Tony's continued membership in and affection for the Church, but without intense emotion or heavy personal investment. We allowed ourselves a bit of license in predicting Tony's adolescent experiences of the presence of the Blessed Virgin. Although such experiences are clearly valued within some segments of the Catholic tradition and so Tony may experience some normative pressure to have them, we do not have clear enough evidence about the frequency of their occurrence for us to know how likely it is that he will. We can be far more confident, however, about his continued membership in and affection for the Catholic Church.

Our predictions about Sally, Gloria, and Tony, although generally based on solid empirical and theoretical foundations, are only hypothetical. You may, quite rightly, feel that we have risked little by making predictions about hypothetical people; their actual personal histories will not come back to haunt us. If a social influence interpretation is to have any force, it must be able to account for the religion of actual people as well. Therefore, to test the validity of the social influence interpretation, we would suggest that you try it out by conducting an analysis of the actual personal history that you know best, your own. Relying on the general model of social influence through roles, norms, and reference groups, and on the evidence presented for the effects of sex, race, SES, educational level, town size, and parents' religion, see how well you can account for your own religious stance—your membership, if any, in religious organizations, your religious beliefs or disbeliefs, even the frequency and nature of your religious experiences. If you think carefully about the important dimensions of your social background and are honest with yourself, we think that you will be surprised at how much of what had seemed to be an intensely personal religious stance appears to be a product of social influence. As we said at the beginning of this chapter, it is not particularly flattering to think that our beliefs or doubts that appear to be freely chosen are a product of social influence—but a strong case can be made that they are.

THE SOCIETAL FUNCTION OF PERSONAL RELIGION

Once one accepts that the personally real experiences of one's religious life are largely a product of social influence, it is natural to ask why society should want at least some of its members to be religious. Two major contributors to modern thought, Karl Marx and Sigmund Freud, join together to present the same simple answer: control.[3]

Marx's view of religion is nicely encapsulated in his famous dictum, "Religion is the opium of the masses." He believed that the wealthy, controlling classes relied on religion to keep the poor, oppressed proletariat in their place. "Religion is the sigh of the oppressed creature, the heart of a heartless world, and the soul of soulless conditions" (Marx, 1964, p. 43). Marx believed that as long as their sighs were channeled into religion, the oppressed would accept their lot. Religion drugged the restless spirit of the

[3] Of course, this is not the only answer that has been proposed. Sociologist Emile Durkheim (1915), for example, suggested that societies develop religions as a symbolic expression of the ideals and values implicit in the social structure. In Durkhein's view, religion does not control individuals so much as it frees them to attain the uniquely human level of thought that he called "collective consciousness."

impoverished by teaching the virtues of poverty and submission to authority and, at the same time, by promising riches in the life to come. Because of this oppressive character, religion was a key link in the chains that Marx called the workers of the world to unite and cast off.

Freud presented his view of the social function of religion in two books, *The Future of an Illusion* (1964, first published in 1927) and *Civilization and Its Discontents* (1961, first published in 1930). Like Marx, Freud recognized the role that religion could play in political oppression, but his view was considerably broader. Freud believed that religion was an illusion, a myth, that society had developed to keep the aggressive, destructive side of human nature in check.

The horror of World War I had a great impact on Freud. It led him to reflect more and more on what he believed to be humanity's destructive instincts and on the role of civilization in keeping these instincts from destroying the human race. He concluded that each individual wants to gratify his or her instincts but at the same time recognizes the consequences of permitting others to do the same. Civilization arbitrates this conflict through religion, its master illusion. The religious illusion reassures us and leads us to hope for a more satisfying life in the future, while at the same time enjoining against immediate gratification. By thus taming the "asocial instincts," Freud felt that religion had "performed great services for human civilization" (1964, p. 60).

But Freud did not stop here. He went on to suggest that while performing this service religion had enslaved humanity, and so ultimately failed at its task.

> It [religion] has ruled human society for many thousands of years and has had time to show what it can achieve. If it had succeeded in making the majority of mankind happy, in comforting them, in reconciling them to life and in making them into vehicles of civilization, no one would dream of attempting to alter the existing conditions. But what do we see instead? We see that an appallingly large number of people are dissatisfied with civilization and unhappy in it, and feel it as a yoke which must be shaken off; and that these people either do everything in their power to change that civilization, or else go so far in their hostility to it that they will have nothing to do with civilization or with a restriction of instinct. (*The Future of an Illusion,* 1964, pp. 60–61)

As an alternative to religion, Freud proposed an irreligious "education to reality," in which we humans forthrightly and rationally face the dilemma posed by our aggressive instincts and admit our helplessness and insignificance in the machinery of the universe. Freud recognized that this proposal did not mean eliminating illusion, only substituting a different illusion for religion. But he felt that the irreligious illusion was superior for two reasons: It did not require punishment or persecution of those who did not adhere to it, and it was amenable to correction. Freud believed that only such an illusion could save the human race. It could save people because

> by withdrawing their expectations from the other world and concentrating all their liberated energies into their life on earth, they will probably succeed in achieving a state of things in which life will become tolerable for everyone and civilization no longer oppressive to anyone. Then, with one of our fellow-unbelievers, they will be able to say without regret:
>
> Den Himmel überlassen wir
> Den Engeln und den Spatzen
> [We leave Heaven to the angels
> and the sparrows—Heine].
>
> (*The Future of an Illusion,* 1964, p. 82)

The view that religion serves the social function of controlling individual aggressive, selfish impulses is by no means dead in psychology. In his 1975 presidential address to the American Psychological Association, Donald Campbell presented an updated version of it. Campbell's position differed from Freud's in two important respects. First, Campbell was able to build on far more scientific evidence, not only from anthropology, sociology, and psychology, but also from the relatively new discipline of sociobiology (Wilson, 1975). Second, whereas Freud felt that the religious illusion needed to be replaced, Campbell suggested that religion was necessary and constructive in human society.

Based on a review of the biological and sociobiological evidence, Campbell accepted the "thesis of biological selfishness," that our genetic heritage leads humans to have a "social personality of self-serving opportunism" (Campbell, 1975, p. 1111). Campbell then turned to social evolution to account for the goodness that exists in human life: "Social evolution has had to counter individual selfish tendencies which biological evolution has continued to select" (1975, p. 1115).

According to Campbell, religion is one of the major components of social evolution. Religious preaching, indoctrination, and moralizing serve to shift the direction of individual behavior away from personal, selfish goals and toward the more socially oriented ends that are necessary to perpetuate society. Campbell even suggested that to counteract the innate selfishness of human nature, religion's preaching of concern for others must be extreme.

The controlling function of religion is apparent in the views of Marx, Freud, and Campbell. For all three, religion is a social creation; it is passed on from generation to generation by social influence. It serves to restrain some (Marx) or all (Freud and Campbell) people from acting on selfish, aggressive impulses.

To say that religion is a social creation suggests, as Freud made clear, that religion is an illusion; that what may appear to be an intensely personal response to the Divine is actually a product of civilization's attempt to keep human destructiveness and selfishness in check. Such a view suggests that the ancients got it backward: We are not God's creation; He is ours.

PUTTING SOCIAL INFLUENCE IN PERSPECTIVE

A social influence analysis seems to provide clear, simple answers to two basic questions: Where does personal religion come from? Any why? The answers: It comes from society through the pressure of social roles, norms, and reference groups. It functions to keep individuals from acting only to meet their personal wants and needs. Although these answers are appealing in their clarity and simplicity, it is time for us to admit that they are inadequate. Each seems to contain a kernel of truth but is by no means the whole story.

The problem with these answers is primarily logical and linguistic, not empirical, and so we must turn to philosophy for some help. Implicit in our entire discussion of social influence has been the assumption that religious beliefs and experience are a result either of social pressure, as the case for social influence suggests,or of personal choice. But this either-or assumption is probably wrong.

The error becomes clearer when this assumption is recognized to be a special case of an old dilemma: Is our behavior a result of our personal free will or is it determined by environmental influences? Linguistic philosopher Gilbert Ryle (1949) argued that this dilemma rests on a logical confusion between different levels of conceptual analysis. To say that an individual's behavior is either free or else determined is, Ryle suggests, like saying of a young woman traveling in India that "she came home either in a flood of tears or else a sedan chair" (1949, p. 22). One can readily recognize the logical absurdity of setting up an either-or dichotomy between the young woman's emotional state and her mode of transportation. Each is an entirely appropriate answer to the question of how she came home, and to accept the truth of one in no way rules out the truth of the other. Ryle argued that just such a logical and linguistic absurdity is involved in asking whether our behavior is freely chosen or environmentally determined. The terms "freely chosen" and "environmentally determined" are from different linguistic systems, and to conclude that behavior is environmentally determined need not rule out the possibility that it is freely chosen as well.

When applied to the issue of the origin of personal religion, Ryle's argument suggests that to decide that our religion is a product of social influence does not mean that it cannot also be a product of individual choice. The two possibilities are not mutually exclusive. Instead, the question of the origin of personal religion can and should be answered at both the level of social influence and the level of individual, or intrapsychic, processes.

Perhaps the easiest way to appreciate this philosophical argument is to remember that the press of our environment, and especially social influence, contributes to who we are as individuals. It is not simply that we are individuals complying with social pressures; social influence contributes to making us who we are. It affects the way we see the world, the way we think, what we want, and what we choose to do. Over time, we not only comply with but also internalize beliefs and values from those people we admire and respect (Kelman, 1961). To focus on social influence or personal freedom is not to focus on competing alternatives but on different points in a continuous process of individual development. We shall consider this point in more detail in the next chapter.

The philosophical point that a social influence analysis does not replace but stands alongside an intrapsychic analysis has been reflected in psychology as *interactionism* (Endler & Magnusson, 1976; Pervin & Lewis, 1978). Rather than viewing human experience as a function of either social influence or individual initiative, interactionism sees experience as a product of the interaction between human potential and the social situation. Such a view has had a long history in psychology (see, for example, Lewin, 1935; Murray, 1938).

Albert Bandura (1978; see also Overton & Reese, 1973) has taken interactionism a step further by suggesting a three-way "reciprocal determinism" among (1) processes within the individual, (2) the individual's physical and social environment, and (3) his or her behavior. Each of these components is assumed to influence and to be influenced by the other two. On the one hand, an individual's social environment helps determine his or her internal processes and behavior. On the other hand, thoughts and feelings within the individual and the individual's behavior both help determine the social environments, including the roles, norms, and reference groups, that the individual encounters. To illustrate, we have commented on the powerful way that the social environment of total-commitment religious groups can shape the beliefs and behavior of group members. But most of us have not come under this influence because, due in part to other social pressures on us, we have chosen to avoid these social environments. As Bandura concludes, "Because people's conceptions, their behavior, and their environments are reciprocal determinants of each other, individuals are neither powerless objects controlled by environmental forces nor entirely free agents who can do whatever they choose" (1978, pp. 356–357).

The interactionist view, and especially Bandura's three-way reciprocal determinism, underscores the philosophical point that to answer the question of the source of personal religion exclusively in terms of social influence is too simple; we must consider the influence of processes within the individual as well. And just as answering the question of the *origin* of personal religion exclusively in terms of social influence is too simple, so answering the question of the *function* of religion exclusively in terms of social control of individuals' selfish, aggressive impulses is too simple. For, once again, this answer is limited to the societal level. Religion serves important functions at the personal level as well; most notably, it helps the individual deal with existential questions. This function must also be considered if we are to understand the nature of individual religion.

Social influence provides, then, important but only partial answers to the questions of the origin and function of religion. These answers can and should be supplemented by answers based on an intrapsychic analysis. To provide such an analysis, we must turn inward to consider how religion emerges from and contributes to the personality structure of the developing individual. This journey inward lies before us in the next chapter.

SUMMARY AND CONCLUSION

What leads a person to be religious? In spite of the popular view that our religion, or lack of it, is a freely chosen and very personal matter, much social-psychological theory and research points to a very different answer: Our religious beliefs and experiences are determined by our social environment.

A fundamental principle of social psychology is that each of us is continually under the pressure of social influence. Not only when we are in the presence of others, but even in our most private moments, we are subject to subtle social pressures through the combined impact of social roles, norms, and reference groups. As William Shakespeare put it, "All the world's a stage, and all the men and women merely players. . . ." In this social drama, our particular social background determines the audiences to which each of us plays (our reference groups) and provides us with scripts (norms) that specify how we should act in the parts that we have been assigned (roles). The combined pressure of these social roles, norms, and reference groups determines how we think and act, including how we think and act concerning religion.

Consistent with this social influence analysis, empirical evidence suggests that a number of social background variables—sex, race, socioeconomic status, educational level, town size, and parents' religion—have a significant influence on our religious experience. This evidence has often been interpreted as proving that our personal religious stance is determined by social influence rather than by free choice. Each of us, it is said, is free to choose only that religious stance that our particular place in society dictates.

Why should society pressure its members to be religious? Both Karl Marx and Sigmund Freud answer by arguing that society pressures some, if not all, of its members to be religious to keep them from upsetting the social order by acting in their own self-interest. Both Marx and Freud also argue that by serving this function, religion has become an agent of social oppression. If we are to be free as individuals, then we must cast religion aside.

Although there seems to be much truth in the view that individual religion is determined by social influence, we believe that it is only a partial answer. Philosophers concerned with the nature and function of language have pointed out that there is a logical and linguistic error in assuming that an individual's beliefs and experiences are either a product of personal choice or else of social influence. The concepts of free choice and social influence are from different linguistic systems that operate at different levels of analysis; to affirm the importance of one does not rule out the possibility that the other is important as well. Instead of assuming that evidence for social influence demonstrates the lack of importance of intrapsychic processes, a more defensible view is that social influence and these intrapsychic processes are both important in shaping an individual's experience. Such an interactionist view has recently received renewed emphasis in psychology. According to this view, we should not look to *either* the social environment *or* the depths of the individual psyche to uncover the source of religion; we should look to *both.*

Thus, even though social influence and social background are clearly powerful and important determinants of religion, they are not the whole story. To provide an adequate answer to the question of where religion comes from, we must also consider psychological processes within the individual. Let us turn, then, to an analysis of the way processes within the developing individual affect his or her religion.

3

Individual Development and Religion

In the previous chapter we considered social influence as an answer to the question of how an individual acquires religion. Yet we found that answer incomplete; we found we also need to look at processes within the individual.

When we look within, one fact immediately stands out. People are not just passive receptacles of culture; they are not glasses into which society's beliefs and values are poured. Instead, they are active, living organisms that are born, develop toward maturity, and die. Our physical, intellectual, and psychosocial development creates possibilities for religion, but it also sets limits. In the present chapter we shall explore some of these possibilities and limits, beginning with the possibility that religion is innate.

IS RELIGION INNATE?

At the opposite extreme from a social influence analysis is the view that the need for religion—if not the specific content of a person's religion—is innate, that it is genetically determined. Such a view was quite popular among anthropologists, sociologists, and social psychologists around 1900, when new cross-cultural research revealed the near universal existence of religion in human societies, no matter how remote or how diverse. This discovery, coupled with the enormous popularity of Darwin's (1859) theory of natural selection, led to talk of a genetic basis for religion (Coe, 1900; Hall, 1882; McDougall, 1908), even of a religious instinct (Jastrow, 1902).

Instinct theories lost favor, however, once psychologists like Knight Dunlap (1919, 1946) and Edward Toman (1923) pointed out that, in the absence of any knowledge of the underlying neurophysiology, these theories lack explanatory power. They involve circular reasoning: Why is religion so prevalent in diverse societies? Because of the religious instinct. How do we know there is a religious instinct? Because religion is so prevalent in diverse societies.

The demise of instinct explanations notwithstanding, belief that religion is at least in part a response to an innate need remains both popular and plausible. Gordon Allport (1950), who rejected the notion of a specific religious instinct or an innate religious sentiment, still considered religion a product of basic human desires, such as our needs for security, provision, and companionship. Viktor Frankl (1962) wrote of a universal search for meaning. And in Chapter 1, we noted M. Brewster Smith's (1978) claim that human self-consciousness inevitably leads to reflection on existential questions of the sort that are the basis for religion.

Yet clearly, even if we have a universal, inborn capacity to raise the existential questions that evoke religion, the range of responses to these questions is enormous. Responses of different individuals differ, running the gamut from (1) a firm conviction that "God's in his heaven, All's right with the world," to (2) an equally firm conviction that there is no God and no meaning or purpose beyond the everyday, to (3) a question-deflecting shrug and return to matters at hand. Responses of a given individual also differ as he or she matures physically, intellectually, and psychosocially. The young child's capacity and inclination to address existential questions differ dramatically from those of the adolescent, which in turn differ dramatically from those of this same person at age 65. How are we to understand these differences?

SOCIAL LEARNING OF RELIGION

Social learning theory (Bandura, 1977) suggests that the individual gets his or her religion through a gradual process of social learning. By modeling the behavior of others, especially our parents, and by social reinforcement—receiving praise or an encouraging smile when right but punishment or a discouraging frown when wrong—we learn over time which questions to ask and which answers to give. Social learning theory is quite compatible with the social influence analysis presented in the previous chapter. Indeed, it may be considered a nuts-and-bolts description of how the social influence machine works.

Social learning theory deviates from the simplest form of social influence analysis, however, in that social learning theory emphasizes the active role of the learner. The learner is not simply a passive recipient of information and values but one who actively seeks to know and to understand, learning by observing other people's behavior and its consequences, as well as by observing the consequences of his or her own behavior. Herbert Kelman (1958) highlighted this active role of the learner by pointing out three different ways a person can appropriate new attitudes: compliance, identification, and internalization. Although Kelman was interested specifically in the learning of attitudes, these concepts are worth exploring because they are relevant to the appropriation of a wide range of new beliefs and behaviors, including religious ones.

Compliance

Through modeling and reinforcement a person can learn to express certain beliefs and behaviors, valuing them only as a means of receiving reward or avoiding punishment. In this case, the person shows compliance. Examples of compliance in the religious domain abound: A child, following the lead of his parents, may recite a prayer before each meal or may sing a religious song yet not even understand what the prayer or song means. (Think, for example, of the famous Christmas carol about "Round John Virgin.") A man who has no faith in any church or temple may attend services and even affirm belief to please his wife. A teenage girl may express far more cynicism than she actually feels in order to fit in with and be accepted by her sophisticated and skeptical friends.

Compliance is a means to the end of gaining reinforcement. As a result, if a belief or behavior appropriated in this way is not reinforced, it will disappear. A child who prays daily for the reconciliation of his divorced parents, but to no avail, is likely to quit praying.

Compliance may seem quite simple and straightforward, but at times it can have surprising effects. What is learned may not be what was intended. A parent who preaches one thing yet practices another is apt to find that his or her child learns exactly that—to preach one thing and practice another. After all, preaching without practicing is what is being modeled. A preschooler who makes noise during a church service and is expelled to the play nursery has, most likely, not learned to be quiet in church. Quite the opposite, he has learned to make noise because, if he does, he gets to go play. Noise, not silence, is being reinforced.

Although compliance may be the basis for much that we do and say, religious and otherwise, few people would consider beliefs and behavior based on compliance all there is to religion. Religion is a matter of the heart, not merely of outward compliance. Identification, Kelman's second mode of appropriation, takes us closer to the heart.

Identification

When we comply, we do not really value what we do; it is only a means to an end, a way of gaining reinforcement. When we identify with another person, however, we value being like that person. No longer is what we do only a means to get rewards; now we want to look like, act like, think like—indeed, be like—the person with whom we identify. The other's behavior is not simply a source of information about what is possible and permissible, as in modeling; instead, the other's behavior is imitated precisely because it *is* the other's behavior. We do more than comply with what the other wants; we conform to the image of the other.

Anyone who has had a younger brother or sister, or who has seen the clothes and gestures of fans leaving a rock concert, knows the power of identification. It can be a powerful force in our religious life as well. It can lead us to try our utmost to follow in the footsteps of an esteemed religious leader—the Buddha, Jesus, Muhammad. It can also lead us to talk and even to think about religion like our parents or like an admired minister, priest, rabbi, teacher, or friend. Of course, there can be conflicts. In the words of one fourth-grade girl: "I'm not sure there *is* a God! *Is* there a God? My dad says no, and my mom says maybe!" (Coles, 1990, p. 113).

Unlike compliance, identification can lead us to persist in a belief or behavior when it is not reinforced—it may even be severely punished—as long as we are convinced that doing so is what the person with whom we identify would do. A number of early Christian martyrs identified so strongly that they chose the horror of death by crucifixion in order to follow in the footsteps of their Savior.

Internalization

If identification involves *conforming* oneself to think and act like an admired person, then internalization involves *transforming* oneself, incorporating a new way of thinking and acting into one's personality. The new way of thinking and acting is valued not as a means to gain reinforcements nor as a means to be like one's idol; it is valued as an end in itself and can exist independent of reinforcement or what one thinks admired others would say or do. Only when dealing with religious beliefs and behaviors that have been internalized would most people feel that we are dealing with the heart of an individual's religion.

Internalization is not always a conscious process. It can occur at the level of unconscious habit or classical conditioning, as when we learn to value certain words or songs because of positive associations. People often internalize a preference for one or another style of religious worship this way; in the words of the old dictum, "Give us a child until age 7, and he is ours for life." Internalization can, however, also be the product of deep, conscious thought, as when people think their way to a personally meaningful stance on such issues as the purpose of their life, the existence of God, life after death, or any of a range of social and moral issues.

Consistent with our suggestion in the previous chapter that personal freedom and determinism are not really opposites, internalized beliefs are at once the most freely chosen and the most determined. They are no longer ideas or standards outside us that pressure us to do this or that; they are inside, so we feel no coercion or constraint from them. But, at the same time, internalized beliefs cannot easily be laid aside, any more than an arm or a leg can easily be laid aside. They have become part of who we are. Martin Luther expressed this character of internalized beliefs poignantly when he was called to account for his radical ideas that sparked the Reformation: "Here stand I. I can do no other. God help me."

Social learning theory, when elaborated using Kelman's (1958) distinctions among compliance, identification, and internalization, provides a useful general picture of how our thoughts, actions, and even basic personality can change over time. From shortly after birth to the last days before death, social learning takes place. But this theory, in spite of its enormous range of applicability, does not provide a sufficient picture of human development. It fails to consider the physical changes that take place as we grow, as well as the psychological consequences of these changes. These are serious omissions because ours is not simply the active, learning mind that social learning theory rightly recognizes; ours is also an *embodied* mind.

As our body grows and develops, we experience new possibilities and new problems. Four aspects of physical development seem especially crucial for personal religion: (1) Our brain develops rapidly throughout childhood and so does our capacity to think, requiring us to think again. (2) At birth, our limbs and muscles lack the size, strength, and coordination to permit active exploration of the environment. Soon, however, crawling is followed by toddling and then by dashing excitedly from place to place. The experiences that exploration of the environment provides—experiences today vastly extended by electronic and print media—are a major source of knowledge and a continual challenge to what we know. (3) Our sexual development brings new possibilities and problems, dramatically changing who we are, especially at puberty, through adolescence, and beyond. (4) Before we have lived many years, our bodies begin to sing a new refrain. All is not growth and development of new strengths, abilities, and skills. There is also physical decline, loss of capacity, and, ultimately, death. As the decades of life go by, this refrain—first heard as a whisper—becomes louder and louder. Each of these physical changes has important implications for the life of the individual, including the religious life. Developmental psychologists have highlighted several key implications of these changes.

COGNITIVE DEVELOPMENT AND RELIGIOUS THINKING

First and most obviously, these physical changes affect our cognitive development. This is as true for religion as for other areas of life. It is not simply that the young child has not yet been reinforced for asking existential questions about death or the meaning of life. The young child lacks the cognitive capability to ask these questions.

Social learning theory focuses on how the individual acquires new ideas and behaviors, new cognitive content. But cognitive development involves more than change in what the person knows, thinks, and believes. At an even more fundamental level, cognitive development involves change in *how* the person knows, thinks, and believes. These changes in cognitive structure produce new assumptions about the nature of reality and new ways of thinking about experience. The consequences of these structural changes can be dramatic. No one has made this point more forcefully than Swiss developmental psychologist Jean Piaget.

Piaget's Analysis of Cognitive Development

Piaget (1926, 1953) revolutionized our thinking about thinking by employing a wonderfully simple research strategy. He carefully observed his own and other children as they grew up. He asked himself why they found certain games, such as peekaboo, so much fun at certain ages but not at others. He asked his children at different ages questions about the world and their experience of it (e.g., See the moon? How is it that when we drive to grandmother's you see the moon there too?), and he compared their responses at different ages. He gave children logical problems to solve (e.g., he poured water from a tall, thin glass into a short, wide glass and asked: Is the water now more, less, or the same?), and he recorded not only their answers but also the reasoning they used to reach their answers.

Reflecting his biological background, Piaget assumed that the child's most fundamental task is to adapt to its physical and social environment. Further, he assumed that adaptation is achieved through a mix of *assimilation* (fitting new experience into existing cognitive structures, as when we store the memories of a friend's home after a first visit) and *accommodation* (changing existing cognitive structures to fit new experience, as when we learn that, in spite of appearance, it is the earth that moves rather than the sun). Accommodation is promoted by (1) neurophysiological and linguistic development and (2) the increasing diversity of experience. Piaget's observations led him to conclude that, as a result of accommodation, the child develops four distinct ways of thinking. These four ways of thinking emerge in an orderly, invariant sequence of stages.

1. Sensorimotor stage. Spanning the period from birth to 2 years of age, the sensorimotor stage is characterized by expression of internal needs—crying when hungry, wet, or tired—and by gradually increasing attention to and cognitive representation of the world outside oneself. Initially, the distinction between oneself and the world outside does not exist; all that exists is immediate experience. Soon, however, the child learns that external events have a predictable pattern, which he or she can sometimes affect. The child begins to use trial and error to explore the physical properties and the uses of objects.

Still, lacking language, the infant has a markedly limited ability to keep track of and organize information about the environment. A 6-month-old may delight in banging his rattle on the shelf of a high chair, but if the rattle falls to the floor, he does not look for it. He turns his attention to some object he can see. For the child at this stage, it is "out of sight, out of mind."

As awareness of the outside world grows, cause-and-effect relations among events become clearer. By 18 months, the child can learn to anticipate the effect of pulling the string on an action toy and realizes that inverting the wastebasket produces a glorious pile on the floor. Exploration becomes increasingly systematic through the second year of life, and, toward the end of the sensorimotor stage, the beginnings of symbolic thought are evident.

2. Preoperational stage. The preoperational stage extends from about 2 to 7 years of age and is characterized by fantasy. The child acquires language. Thinking now includes the use of symbols but is still egocentric, magical, and largely limited to what is immediately perceived; distant goals and long-term consequences are difficult to grasp. Logical relations are not yet a concern. The preoperational child is not troubled if there is an inconsistency between two pieces of information, or by the impossibility of a circumstance imagined. A 5-year-old may suddenly declare that his favorite toy, an anatomically correct male doll, is now a girl. His fantasy play is unconstrained by the logic that constrains an older child.

3. Concrete-operational stage. The concrete-operational stage extends roughly from 7 to 11 years of age. Important changes in perception of the environment occur when the child's thinking develops to include the principle of conservation—the awareness that essential properties of objects remain the same despite changes in appearance or arrangement. When seeing the water poured from a tall, thin glass to a short, wide glass, the child at the concrete-operational stage answers correctly that the amount remains the same. The child at the earlier preoperational stage does not.

At the stage of concrete operations, the child can recognize logical inconsistencies if they are represented in a concrete, tangible way. The child now actively tries to understand events, including those related to human existence. It is not uncommon for children at the concrete-operational stage to ask questions about the origins of life and death and to begin to think about religious issues. But the reflection is concrete rather than abstract; questions such as "What does God look like?" and "Do they have ice cream in heaven?" are typical.

4. Formal-operational stage. The formal-operational stage begins at about 11 years of age. At this stage the individual becomes capable of abstract reasoning and using formal logic. Symbolic language, analogy, and metaphor can be understood as such. A more systematic approach is now used when exploring a problem: Thinking broadens to encompass what is possible, as well as what is present, and the individual can employ systematic hypothesis testing to sort out correct interpretations from false ones. Points of view other than one's own can be recognized, even on abstract issues such as the existence of God, the purpose of life, and life after death.

Implications of Cognitive Development for Religion

Piaget did not dwell on the implications for religion of his four-stage model of cognitive development, but the model suggests two important limitations. First, if Piaget's analysis is correct, then the young child lacks the way of thinking necessary to understand or ask the existential questions that we have suggested are the basis of religion. To confront the reality of your own death as an existential question or to question the meaning of your life requires formal-operational thought. You must not only have a sense of self as a person distinct from other people and things, but you must also be able to imagine a world in which the person who you are has no part, at least not in your present form, and to ask about meaning and purpose beyond concrete day-to-day activity. According to Piaget, the cognitive structures necessary for such thought do not exist until about age 11.

Second, to the extent that religious language is abstract and symbolic, analogic and metaphorical, alluding to a transcendent reality beyond concrete, everyday experience, the young child cannot adequately understand it. To understand this kind of language requires, once again, formal operations. Gordon Allport (1950, p. 30) illustrated the problem dramatically with the example of a young boy who one day announced that God is a weathercock. When asked how this could be, the boy explained that he had been told that God was "high" and "bright," and the weathercock on a neighborhood barn was the highest and brightest object he knew, so it must be God. In a similar way, many children are led by talk of God's eternity and omniscience into thinking of God as a bearded, grandfatherly figure who watches us from the clouds.

These two limitations led religious educator Ronald Goldman to an unsettling conclusion in his book *Religious Thinking from Childhood to Adolescence* (1964; see also Lawrence, 1965): Teaching young children about religion is potentially dangerous. Think what will happen when young children encounter abstract, symbolic religious language designed to express perspectives on existential questions that these children cannot yet understand or ask. They will make sense of this language using either the magical (preoperational) or literal (concrete-operational) thinking characteristic of their current stage of cognitive development. The understanding that results will be a misunderstanding of the true meaning and purpose of the religious concepts.

Empirical evidence that young children understand religious concepts magically or literally. Goldman (1964) provided some empirical support for his concern through a study of British children's responses to questions about Bible stories. He found that up to age 13 (mental age 12.5), about 80 percent of the children interviewed gave magical or literal interpretations of most Bible stories. To illustrate, when asked about the statement in the story of Moses and the burning bush (Exod. 3:1–4:17) that the ground on which Moses stood was holy, a young child explained: "It was where God was standing." And when that explanation was followed by the question, "How did that make it holy?" the child replied, "Because the holy would go down through God's feet into the ground and make it holy" (Goldman, 1964, p. 56).

A more recent study by David Heller (1986, 1987) has provided further support for Goldman's concern. Heller interviewed children ranging from 4 to 12 years of age about their conception of God, and he invited them to write letters to God, producing amusing but telling concrete-operational gems like the letter of 9-year-old Craig: "Dear, Dear, Dear God, I see you in my dreams all the time. I know it is you because you have a crown on and you are always fishing." And 7-year-old Ralph: "Dear God, I love to eat. Thanks for all the food. Pizza was the best idea you had."

Consistent with Piaget's claim of emerging capacity for abstract, symbolic thought as children reach formal operations, Goldman (1964) found that when children 13 years of age and older explained the story of Moses and the burning bush, they focused more on the awe-inspiring nature of God. In the words of one 13-year-old, "God was a much greater person than himself [Moses]. There was something over-awing about it. . . . God was so great and Moses was like a worm in importance" (p. 120). Letters by Heller's (1987) older subjects also showed movement toward formal-operational thinking, including consideration of multiple perspectives and logical possibilities. For example, 11-year-old Jose wrote: "Dear God, I was watching TV when the *Challenger* shuttle exploded. That was a sad thing. Was there anything that you could have done? Were you mad because they came too close to your territory? We're sorry." And 10-year-old Ian raised probing questions: "Dear God, I have doubts about you sometimes. Sometimes I really believe. . . . But my question is . . . why don't you stop all the bad in the world. Like war. Like diseases. Like famine. Like drugs. . . . I'll try to believe more." Robert Coles reported similar multifaceted probing in *The Spiritual Life of Children* (1990); for example, a 12-year-old girl from a Boston suburb told him: "I wonder about God, who He is, and whether He's just someone who got made up a long time ago by people—and if He's real, what He thinks we should be like" (p. xvii).

Consequences as the young child matures. Goldman's concern extended beyond the possibility that young children will misunderstand religious concepts by making sense of them using preformal cognitive structures. He was also concerned that once children make sense of religion in magical or literal terms, it will be more difficult for them in later years to appreciate the abstract, symbolic nature of religious language and concepts. Having made sense of concepts like *God* and *holy* magically or literally, children may class religion with fairy tales, Santa Claus, and the Easter bunny. As the child grows older and leaves the world of make-believe behind, he or she is faced with three options: (1) Change the understanding of religion to allow for its abstract, symbolic, existential nature; (2) adhere to a magical or literal understanding of religion and accept this understanding as true; or (3) adhere to a magical, literal understanding and reject it as childish.

Without encouragement and careful tutelage, Option 1 seems unlikely. If parents, teachers, and peers provide clear models and social reinforcement for adherence to literal religious beliefs, Option 2 seems likely. In the absence of extensive social support, however, Option 3 seems most likely. As Goldman (1964) put it:

> Literalism seems to continue far too long for the healthy religious development of young people. [As their thinking becomes more abstract,] they may equate religious belief to uncritical childish acceptance and the only valid alternative is to jettison the whole structure as rationally untenable. (p.115)

To the degree that this scenario is correct, the individual is cut off from the abstract, symbolic potential of the one language system and set of concepts specifically designed to provide some perspective on existential questions at the very point in life—early adolescence—that these questions begin to arise. Goldman concluded that "the Bible is not a children's book" and that "the teaching of large areas of it may do more damage than good to a child's religious understanding" (1965, p. 7).

Empirical evidence supporting Goldman's analysis. Several studies have provided support for Goldman's analysis. Hoge and Petrillo (1978b) found a general tendency among tenth-graders (approximately 16 years old) for those who scored higher on a measure of abstract religious thinking to score lower on a measure of traditional religious beliefs, especially when factors such as amount of religious education and knowledge of the Bible were controlled. Moreover, except for those tenth-graders who were Catholics attending private and religious schools, there was a positive correlation between abstractness of religious thinking and answering yes to the question: "Has there ever been a period in your life when you reacted either partially or wholly against the beliefs taught you?"

Apparently, most of the tenth-graders were pursuing Option 3 above, adherence to a literal interpretation of religion and, as their religious thinking became more abstract, rejecting these literal beliefs. Under the influence of their more intellectually open—presumably formal-operational—religious education, however, the private-school Catholics were more likely to pursue Option 1; they changed their understanding of religion to allow for nonliteral, symbolic interpretations, which they could then affirm. In contrast, Southern Baptist tenth-graders showed signs of pursuing Option

2, adherence to a literal interpretation of religion and acceptance of this literal understanding as true; they scored lower compared with the other students on abstractness of religious thinking and higher on religious belief. Surprisingly, Hoge and Petrillo (1978b) interpreted these results as contradicting Goldman; we believe they are precisely what Goldman would have predicted.

In a study of United Methodist youth in Oregon, Abraham (1981) compared the effects of a religious education curriculum explicitly designed to induce cognitive conflict, and thereby stimulate formal-operational religious thinking, with the effects of a more traditional religious education curriculum. Abraham found that among sixth-graders (approximately 12 years old) those who received the conflict-based curriculum showed reduced concrete and increased abstract religious thought relative to those who received the more traditional curriculum. There were, however, no differences in the effects of the two curricula among fifth-graders, presumably because fifth-graders had not yet developed the general formal-operational skills necessary to benefit from the conflict-based curriculum. Especially telling, sixth-graders taught using the traditional curriculum showed *more* concrete and *less* abstract religious thought than did the fifth-graders taught using either curriculum.

Apparently, as Goldman feared, these traditionally taught sixth-graders were stagnating in a literal, concrete understanding of religion. Such stagnation may, in turn, set the stage for later rejection of religion, as is commonly reported by college students. In surveys spanning three decades, the number of college students who report having reacted either partially or wholly against the religious beliefs they were taught as children is consistently around 70 percent (Hoge & Petrillo, 1978b). Clearly, the structural changes in how we think that occur as we mature have the potential to create not only important possibilities but also important problems for our experience of religion.

MORAL DEVELOPMENT

To the degree that religion reflects response to existential questions about our relations with others, moral thinking is an integral part of religion. And, just as religious thinking develops and changes as we mature physically and intellectually, so does moral thinking. Extending Piaget's analysis of general cognitive development, Lawrence Kohlberg attempted to trace the development of moral thinking.

Kohlberg's Analysis of Moral Development

Kohlberg (1969, 1976) claimed to find six stages of moral thinking, arranged in three levels of two stages each. We all begin at Stage 1, claimed Kohlberg, and many of us progress through Stage 2 only as far as Stage 3 or, more likely, Stage 4 in our lifetime. Stage 5 is unusual; Stage 6, extremely rare. Adopting Piaget's understanding of what a stage is, Kohlberg claimed that each of his stages involves a qualitatively distinct way of thinking about moral issues, that the six stages are universal, and that they are hierarchically arranged, with movement from one stage to the next occurring in an invariant sequence.

To get a general sense of Kohlberg's levels and stages of moral thinking, consider a dilemma similar to one you may have faced: Imagine that your good friend Bob asks your opinion of a painting he has done. You know that Bob wants to be a good painter and thinks he is, but you also know that you think the painting is pretty awful and you have heard several people who are very knowledgeable about art say that Bob has no real talent. What should you do? Should you report your honest judgment, leaving Bob hurt, discouraged, and quite possibly very mad at you? Should you lie to protect Bob's feelings, allowing him to think he has talent even if he does not? What is the morally right thing to do, and why? Kohlberg claimed that, if you are like most people, you will answer these questions differently as your moral thinking develops.

Preconventional level (Stages 1 and 2). Young children, who operate at the level of preconventional morality, make moral judgments solely on the basis of consequences for themselves. Whatever brings them pleasure is right; whatever brings them pain is wrong. Of course, adults also at times display preconventional morality. If you decide to tell Bob you like his painting because you do not want to face his anger or risk losing him as a friend, then your moral reasoning is preconventional. If you decide to tell him the truth because you are afraid that you might be laughed at by the experts if you say the painting is good, then, once again, your reasoning is preconventional. In Kohlberg's analysis, as in Piaget's, it is not what decision you reach but the factors you consider in reaching the decision that determine your level of moral thinking. At the preconventional level, producing the best outcome for you is the only factor considered in deciding what is morally right.

Conventional level (Stages 3 and 4). At the conventional level, expectations of others or society, not what is best for you personally, determine what is morally right. People reasoning at this level uphold the rules, expectations, and conventions of society just because they are society's rules, expectations, and conventions. Law and order reign. It is at this level that people are most likely to base their moral decisions on religious precepts or commandments. You may, for example, reason that you cannot tell Bob the truth because you have been taught that good friends never do anything to hurt each other, or you may reason that you must tell Bob the truth because it is a sin to tell a lie.

Postconventional (principled) morality (Stages 5 and 6). At the postconventional level, personally derived moral principles that transcend specific social rules or laws, including religious rules or laws, determine what is morally right. No longer does the individual perceive a single moral reality; instead, multiple possibilities are seen among which he or she must choose. A person operating at this level, which Kohlberg claimed many of us never reach, sees social rules and institutions as created to serve rather than to determine morality. There is recognition of the underlying principles—such as justice, equality, and the rights of the individual—that social rules and institutions were created to uphold, and moral judgments are made on the basis of these principles. There is also recognition that social rules and institutions sometimes fail to serve these principles and that, when this occurs, the morally right action is to disobey the rules or laws.

You may, for example, decide to tell Bob the truth not to avoid telling a lie but because you know that you would want him to tell you the truth, however painful, if the roles were reversed. Or you may decide not to tell him, because you know he is feeling particularly insecure right now, and the greatest good for all concerned would be served by withholding the truth.

Measuring a Person's Level of Moral Thinking

As we have described each level in Kohlberg's model, you may have said to yourself, "Oh yes, I sometimes think that way." So what is your level of moral thinking? Kohlberg attempted to identify individuals' level of moral thought by using an extensive standardized interview in which a series of moral dilemmas was presented. For each dilemma, respondents were asked to make a judgment about the right thing to do and to explain in detail why this judgment was reached. A coding system was then used to rate the typical level of moral thought displayed by a given individual when responding to the dilemmas.

Kohlberg's procedure for assessing individuals' level of moral thought was quite complicated and time-consuming. James Rest (1979, 1983), a former student and colleague of Kohlberg, developed a less time-consuming paper-and-pencil measure, the Defining Issues Test (DIT). The DIT presents six moral dilemmas, each followed by twelve statements expressing considerations reflecting different levels of moral thought. For example, one dilemma on the DIT is Kohlberg's classic, "Heinz and the Drug":

> In Europe, a woman was near death from a special kind of cancer. There was one drug that the doctors thought might save her. It was a form of radium that a druggist in the same town had recently discovered. The drug was expensive to make, but the druggist was charging ten times what the drug cost him to make. He paid $200 for the radium and charged $2,000 for a small dose of the drug. The sick woman's husband, Heinz, went to everyone he knew to borrow the money, but he could only get together about $1,000, which is half of what it cost. He told the druggist that his wife was dying, and asked him to sell it cheaper or let him pay later. But the druggist said, "No, I discovered the drug and I'm going to make money from it." So Heinz got desperate and began to think about breaking into the man's store to steal the drug for his wife. (Rest, 1979, p. 8)

On the DIT, respondents are first asked to decide whether Heinz should steal the drug. Next, they read the twelve statements expressing possible considerations, such as: "Whether or not the community's laws are going to be upheld." "Would stealing in such a case bring about more total good for the whole society or not?" Respondents rate how important each of the twelve considerations was in making their decision about the dilemma; then they rank-order the four considerations that were most important.

To score the DIT, these rankings are summed for each stage across dilemmas. Rest (1983) recommended using the scores for Postconventional Stages 5 and 6 combined, which he called the DIT Principled score, to measure level of moral thought. Of the two illustrative considerations quoted above, the first is not principled; it is Conventional. The second is principled; it is Postconventional. The DIT Principled score, or P-score, has become the most popular method for assessing moral thinking.

As would be expected, P-scores on the DIT tend to increase with age. Retesting the same adolescents at two-year intervals over four years, Rest (1979) found that their mean P-score increased from 33 percent in 1972 to 40 percent in 1974 to 44 percent in 1976; this increase was highly reliable ($p < .0001$). Analysis of individual cases showed that 66 percent of the individuals increased their score, whereas only 7 percent went down. Still, this 7 percent, although small, is a potential embarrassment, either for the assumption that Kohlberg's levels and stages form an invariant, hierarchical sequence or for the reliability of the DIT.

Criticisms of Kohlberg's Analysis

Kohlberg's stage model of moral thinking has generated much interest but also much criticism. Some have criticized the empirical status of the model: Are the three levels and six stages really qualitatively distinct ways of thinking about moral issues, or only quantitatively different? Are these ways of thinking hierarchically ordered, as Kohlberg claimed? Is the sequence really universal and invariant? To the extent that qualitative differences and sequencing are observed, are these features simply a product of the stages of cognitive development described by Piaget, coupled with social learning principles? (For discussion of these and related empirical criticisms, see Haan, Weiss, & Johnson, 1982; Kurtines, 1986; Kurtines & Greif, 1974.)

Others have criticized the conceptual status of Kohlberg's model: Is it not really a prescription of what, in Kohlberg's view, moral development ought to be instead of a description of what moral development actually is? Is the sequence described not a reflection of Western thought (especially Western moral philosophy) and so of limited relevance when describing moral development in other cultures? Is Kohlberg's claim that abstract principles like justice are at the pinnacle of morality sex biased? That is, is there another way of approaching moral dilemmas, thinking in terms of concrete relationships and the feelings and welfare of the people involved, that many people—especially many women—employ and that is at least as developmentally advanced as thinking in terms of abstract universal principles? (For discussion of this last possibility, see Bussey & Maughan, 1982; Gilligan, 1982.)

Level of Moral Thinking and Traditional Religious Beliefs

Keeping these criticisms in mind, it is still worth considering the implications of Kohlberg's analysis for religion. Recall Goldman's concerns about the consequences of Piaget's analysis for religious thinking, that the young child's inevitably concrete, literal interpretation can inhibit later appreciation and use of the abstract, symbolic nature of religious concepts. Given that Kohlberg's analysis of moral development is based on Piaget's analysis of cognitive development, one might suspect a parallel process in moral thought. Specifically, one might suspect that adherence to a concrete, literal interpretation of religion can also inhibit development beyond the level of conventional, rule-based, law-and-order morality to the level of postconventional, principled morality. The limited evidence available suggests that such a link may indeed exist.

For example, Haan, Smith, and Block (1968), in a study of college students and Peace Corps volunteers, found that individuals whose level of moral thinking was Conventional based on Kohlberg's interview assessment were likely to hold traditional religious beliefs; those whose level of moral thinking was Postconventional were likely to describe themselves as agnostic, atheist, or nonreligious. Ernsberger and Manaster (1981) found that members of churches adhering to a more literal, traditional interpretation of religious concepts and teachings (Conservative Baptists and Missouri Synod Lutherans) showed a far lower percentage of principled moral thought (P-score) on Rest's DIT (*M*s = 30.1 and 34.9 percent, respectively) than did members of churches encouraging more abstract, symbolic interpretation (United Methodists and Unitarian Universalists—*M*s = 46.6 and 52.6 percent, respectively). Moreover, lay leaders in the Baptist and Lutheran churches had significantly lower P-scores than the membership at large, whereas lay leaders in the Methodist and Unitarian churches had significantly higher P-scores than the membership at large, highlighting the different directions in which the members of the different churches were being socialized.

In an unpublished dissertation done under Rest's direction, Lawrence (1978, reported in Rest, 1979) studied a group of radical fundamentalist seminarians who closely adhered to a literal interpretation of the Bible and its teachings. He found that these seminarians had an extraordinarily high Conventional (Stage 4) score on the DIT and an extraordinarily low Principled score: 22 percent. This P-score was considerably lower than that of the Baptists and Lutherans in the Ernsberger and Manaster study; it was also considerably lower than the mean P-score for a group of ninth-graders (approximately 15 years of age): 31 percent.

In sum, there is evidence that level of cognitive development influences religious thinking, which in turn influences how one understands religious concepts. There is also evidence that this influence has implications not only for how one responds to religion in later life but also for how one thinks about moral issues. Adopting a concrete, literal interpretation of religion may inhibit movement beyond a conventional, rule-based morality to use of postconventional, abstract principles when deciding what is morally right. In light of this evidence, one may well ask how much of the shouting at one another by opponents on issues such as abortion, affirmative action, and welfare is a result of conflicting values, and how much is a result of conflict between Conventional and Postconventional (or Preconventional?) levels of moral reasoning. This is an important, as yet unanswered, question.

PSYCHOSOCIAL DEVELOPMENT

Physical changes across the life span affect more than our way of thinking. They also shape the personal and interpersonal issues that are important to us. The newborn has, for example, no concern about getting into trouble with its parents. But as the brain develops, as arms and legs grow longer and stronger, and as coordination improves, getting into trouble can be a major concern. Later, the onset of puberty raises a whole host of new issues concerning individuality, sexuality, intimacy, responsibility, and parenthood. Even later, awareness of physical decline and impending death raises yet another set of issues: reconciling oneself to unrealized goals, turning over the reins to others, deciding whether one's life has been worthwhile.

Beginning with Freud (1917), many psychologists and psychiatrists have explored the implications of these issues for personal development. One of the most comprehensive and insightful analyses has been provided by psychoanalyst Erik Erikson.

Erikson's Analysis of Psychosocial Development

Based on his clinical practice and cross-cultural studies, Erikson (1950, 1959) identified eight basic psychosocial conflicts that he believed we each confront in life. He also identified eight basic stages of life. Although all eight conflicts are to some degree present throughout the life span, Erikson suggested that a different conflict comes to the fore at each of the eight stages. The way we resolve the focal conflict at one stage influences how we deal with this and other conflicts at later stages. Positive resolution of the focal conflict at one stage puts us on solid footing to face future conflicts; negative resolution causes difficulty later on.

Erikson's eight basic psychosocial conflicts, and the stages of life at which each is focal, are presented in Table 3.1. The off-diagonal boxes that are empty in the table contain the seven nondominant conflicts for each stage. Thus, for example, the first column contains the issue of Basic Trust versus Mistrust as it appears at each of the eight stages of life, taking on a

Table 3.1 Summary of Erikson's model of psychosocial development

	Eight basic psychosocial conflicts							
Stage of life	1	2	3	4	5	6	7	8
VIII. Maturity (about 60+ years old)								Ego integrity versus despair
VII. Adulthood (about 35–60 years old)							Generativity versus stagnation	
VI. Young Adulthood (about 20–35 years old)						Intimacy versus isolation		
V. Puberty and adolescence (about 12–19 years old)					Identity versus role confusion			
IV. Latency (about 6–11 years old)				Industry versus inferiority				
III. Locomotor-genital (about 4–5 years old)			Initiative versus guilt					
II. Muscular-anal (about 2–3 years old)		Autonomy versus shame, doubt						
I. Oral-sensory (about 1 year old)	Basic trust versus mistrust							

Source: Adapted from Erikson (1950, 1959).

different shading in light of the different focal conflict at each stage. As can be seen from the labels in Table 3.1, Erikson explicitly linked his first four stages to Freud's stages of psychosexual development: oral, anal, genital, and latency. A brief description of the eight conflicts as they appear when focal will give the flavor of Erikson's analysis.

1. Basic trust versus mistrust. The infant is dependent on those around it to meet its needs for food, warmth, stimulation, and security. Its central concern is whether this new world into which it has been thrust can be trusted. If needs are reliably met, a deep-seated sense of trust will develop and undergird all of life; if needs are not reliably met, mistrust of the world and other people will develop. Erikson saw this as the basic conflict faced by the child during the first year, during what Freud (1935) called the oral stage of psychosexual development, when nursing and sensory stimulation—especially tactile stimulation—dominate. "The infant's first social achievement, then, is his willingness to let the mother out of sight without undue anxiety or rage, because she has become an inner certainty as well as an outer predictability" (Erikson, 1950, p. 247). In reaching a successful resolution of this conflict, the key is not the quantity but the quality of care, reflected in sensitive response to the infant's needs and a firm sense of personal trustworthiness.

2. Autonomy versus shame and doubt. As the child begins to gain control of its own body, to "hold on" and "let go" at will, a new conflict arises: Will the child develop a sense of comfortable control of these abilities, or will mistakes lead to shame and doubt about one's capacity to do things right? The answer depends on the degree of trust that has been and continues to develop and on the firm reassurance that the child receives. The key area of muscular control for the child at this period is toilet training, which is why Freud called this the anal stage of psychosexual development.

3. Initiative versus guilt. The growing child not only learns to control bodily functions, it also learns to move about and explore its world with increasing ease. By age 3 or 4, the child can undertake activities, planning and attacking a task, getting into things. To approach these opportunities positively, the child must develop a sense of initiative, a confidence that getting into things brings good outcomes. The child must also develop a sense of timing, knowing when to move forward and when to hold back. "The danger at this stage is a sense of guilt over the goals contemplated and the acts initiated in one's exuberant enjoyment of new locomotor and mental power" (Erikson, 1950, p. 255). Rivalry with older siblings can become a major issue, as can rivalry with one parent for the affection of the other. Freud called this the genital or phallic stage of psychosexual development, the time of Oedipus and Electra conflicts.

4. Industry versus inferiority. When the child begins school and social interactions broaden beyond the family, new challenges await. Exuberance and fantasy must be tempered to the demands of the outside world for performance to standard. The key challenge is to develop industry—a sense of joy in making things, in using tools, in working beside and with others, and in doing a job well. The danger is a sense of inadequacy of performance and inferiority relative to peers. Freud called this the latency stage of psychosexual development; in other areas of life, however, it is a period of intense activity.

5. Identity versus role confusion. Puberty and adolescence bring on Erikson's most famous conflict, the identity crisis. Sexual maturity and the resulting pleasure in sexual intimacy and romance, fascination with the differences among friends and acquaintances, concern over how one is viewed by others, the increasing range of social roles one is called on to play, issues of career choice, and the recognition of the different people one might be, all combine to force the question: Who *am* I? The challenge at this stage is to arrive at a personally satisfying, coherent, and consistent answer to this question, a positive identity that others as well as oneself can count on. The danger is to arrive at a series of incoherent, different answers for different people and different circumstances—role confusion.

6. Intimacy versus isolation. Erikson (1950) presented the conflict of intimacy versus isolation, central for young adults, in these well-chosen words:

> The strength acquired at any stage is tested by the necessity to transcend it in such a way that the individual can take chances in the next stage with what was most vulnerably precious in the previous one. Thus, the young adult, emerging from the search for and the insistence on identity, is eager and willing to fuse his identity with that of others. He is ready for intimacy, that is, the capacity to commit himself to concrete affiliations and partnerships and to develop the ethical strength to abide by such commitments, even though they may call for significant sacrifices and compromises. . . . The avoidance of such experiences because of a fear of ego loss may lead to a deep sense of isolation and consequent self-absorption. (pp.263–264)

7. Generativity versus stagnation. Up to young adulthood, the physical changes underlying the stages of psychosocial development have been those of growth and expansion—increased cognitive, motor, and sexual capability. These physical changes, combined with ever-increasing interaction with the social environment, have, ideally, produced a person who embodies Freud's deceptively profound prescription for living: "*Lieben und arbeiten*" (to love and to work). As one reaches adulthood, however, the whisper of physical decline and personal limitation becomes more and more audible. Physically, one can no longer do or look as one did. Personally and professionally, it becomes increasingly clear that some goals will forever remain out of reach. Socially and culturally, the times they are a-changin'. A new generation, young and eager to deal with this brave new world, is fast rising.

The opportunity at this stage is generativity, gaining satisfaction in helping this new generation—one's children, students, younger friends, and colleagues—to face the new world and assume responsibility, enabling them to love and to work. The danger is stagnation, becoming self-preoccupied, self-indulgent, defensive, and self-protective, seeing the new generation as a threat and trying to maintain dominance, becoming one's own coddled child.

8. Ego integrity versus despair. Especially (but by no means exclusively) toward the end of life, one asks oneself: Is it all worth it? When the fruits of the preceding seven stages have been positive, one's answer is likely to be ego integrity, which Erikson (1950) described as "the acceptance of one's one and only life cycle as something that had to be and that, by necessity, permitted of no substitutions" (p. 268). With this final consolidation, letting go of one's active life—even impending death—can be faced with tranquility. The negative answer to this question is despair, feeling that one's life as lived is not acceptable and time is too short to make a new start, producing bitterness, anger, and a fear of death. To emphasize the cross-generational implications of his analysis, Erikson (1950) bent his linear sequence of psychosocial stages into a circle. One generation's sense of integrity becomes the foundation for a new generation's basic trust: "Healthy children will not fear life if their elders have integrity enough not to fear death" (p. 269).

Erikson's model of psychosocial development depicting these eight basic conflicts is, in many ways, a model of religious development. After all, the questions that underlie each of the conflicts from adolescence on—Who am I? How do I relate to others? Does my life have meaning? How do I deal with my impending death?—are precisely the kind of existential questions that, as we suggested in Chapter 1, are the basis of one's religion. Indeed, Erikson himself displayed the usefulness of his analysis for understanding religious life with insightful psychobiographies of Martin Luther (*Young Man Luther,* 1958) and Mahatma Gandhi (*Gandhi's Truth,* 1969). These psychobiographies explore the religious implications of the eight basic conflicts, especially identity and integrity. Theologian James Fowler has, however, sought to make the religious implications of Erikson's analysis even more explicit by using it, along with Piaget's and Kohlberg's stage models, as the basis for a stage model of faith development.

Fowler's Analysis of Faith Development

Fowler (1981) does not consider faith to be the same as believing that an idea is true; nor is faith necessarily religious in a traditional sense, although it often is. Instead, faith "is our way of finding coherence in and giving meaning to the multiple forces and relations that make up our lives. Faith is a person's way of seeing him- or herself in relation to others against a background of shared meaning and purpose" (Fowler, 1981, p. 4). Under the influence of Erikson's writings, Fowler became convinced that it was possible to provide an ordering of predictable stages of growth in faith, with emergent strengths and potential dangers at each stage; this he attempted to do by describing seven stagelike, developmentally related styles of faith.

Although Erikson's writings provide the deep structure for Fowler's description, Kohlberg's model of moral reasoning provided the surface structure, serving as a template for what a developmental stage analysis should look like. Fowler claimed that his faith stages, like Kohlberg's moral stages, form an invariant sequence, with each new stage integrating and carrying forward the operations of the previous stage. A person may only progress through three or four faith stages in a lifetime, but the stages are, Fowler claimed, always experienced in the same order, and none can be left out.

Fowler's sequence begins with a prestage called Undifferentiated Faith that is characteristic of the first two years of life. His description of this prestage closely parallels Erikson's description of the conflict between Basic Trust versus Mistrust. Six stages follow.

1. Intuitive-projective faith. From approximately 3 to 7 years of age, Piaget's preoperational stage, the child's faith is in a fantasy-filled, imitative phase heavily influenced by examples, actions, and stories of the visible faith of key adults. The first awareness of self, as well as the first awareness of death and sex and the strong taboos surrounding each, occurs during this stage. The emergent strength of this stage is intuitive understanding through imagination; the danger is that the imagination will be overpowered with visions of destruction, taboos, and severe moral demands.

2. Mythic-literal faith. The second stage of faith occurs at Piaget's stage of concrete operations (ages 7–11). The child now appropriates the stories, beliefs, and practices that symbolize belonging to his or her community of faith. Earlier episodic perception of experience gives way to logical construction employing sequence and order to provide meaning. There is an increased ability to take the perspective of others. Narrative stories, drama, and myth become important means of understanding experience. Interpretation is, however, concrete and literal rather than abstract and symbolic.

3. Synthetic-conventional faith. Around adolescence, with the emergence of formal operations and the identity crisis, the individual is likely to begin to display a third style of faith. Life is now much more diverse, and faith must interpret this diversity. The individual begins to define an identity, to establish the meaning of various narratives for self and others, and to synthesize an individual story of life, particularly in relation to others. To provide stability, deeply held beliefs and values may be sought, often by identifying with and internalizing the views of important authority figures or peer role models. These beliefs and values take the form of an "ideology," an uncritically embraced worldview that the individual is unaware is only one possibility among many.

4. Individuative-reflective faith. During young adulthood, the individual assumes responsibility for his or her own commitments, life-style, beliefs, and attitudes; the self becomes more integrated, less a composite of roles and meanings for others. As a result, a new style of faith may emerge, Fowler claimed, one that explicitly involves a system of meaning that is "demythologized," with a recognition of the relativity of one's inherited worldview and rejection of literal interpretation of faith stories and myths. The emergent strength of this style of faith is its capacity for critical reflection on oneself and on one's worldview; the danger is an overreliance on critical, analytic thought.

5. Conjunctive faith. Sometime during the midlife period, conjunctive faith may emerge. This style of faith is sensitive to the pattern of interrelatedness in things; there is a "second naiveté," an opening to the voices of one's "deeper self," including the myths and ideals one has inherited from one's social class, ethnic background, and religious group. Connections that transcend differences are sought. Symbols are appreciated as a source of nonlogical insight, as are paradox and contradiction. Effort is made to accept and unify apparent opposites, often with irony. The dangers of this stage are paralyzing passivity, complacency, and cynical withdrawal.

6. Universalizing faith. Just as Kohlberg claimed that his highest stage of moral reasoning is rarely reached, Fowler claimed that his highest stage of faith is rarely reached. Those exceptional individuals who attain universalizing faith (including, Fowler believed, Gandhi, Martin Luther King, Dag Hammarskjöld, Abraham Heschel, Thomas Merton, and Mother Teresa) have a sense of an ultimate environment that is inclusive of all being. "They have become incarnators and actualizers of the spirit of an inclusive and fulfilled human community. They are 'contagious' in the sense that they create zones of liberation from the social, political, economic, and ideological shackles" (Fowler, 1981, pp. 199–200). Because of their universal, affirming, transcendent view, these individuals are often seen as subversive by social institutions, including religious institutions. Yet, sitting at the eye of the storm, they display a self-transcending simplicity and tranquility.

Reading these descriptions of Fowler's six faith stages, you may have an even stronger sense than with Kohlberg's model that, rather than a description of what is, the ordering is a prescription of what Fowler thinks should be. Fowler (1981) would only partially disagree. He has admitted a normative ordering of the stages; from his perspective as a liberal Christian theologian, Stage 6 is the ideal, and the closer to Stage 6 the better. He recognizes that religious individuals with different perspectives might well propose a different prescriptive ordering of the stages. Fowler (1981) wishes, however, to claim a special status for his ordering. He claims that his model is not just a prescription for what should be; it is also an accurate description of what is. What is Fowler's basis for this bold descriptive claim?

Fowler and his associates conducted interviews, averaging over two hours in length, with more than three hundred people from 4 to 80 years old. These people were asked to share their life histories with regard to universal life issues (dilemmas of existence) through a brief life review, followed by discussion of life-shaping experiences (e.g., significant people, moments of joy), present values and commitments (e.g., purpose in life, important symbols and rituals), and religion (e.g., feelings associated with deity, areas of growth and change). Interview responses were transcribed and subjected to content analysis by trained scorers, using a procedure modeled on Kohlberg's procedure for assessing level of moral thinking. The scorers assigned a stage score to each interview transcript for each of seven aspects thought to be a part of faith development: (1) form of logic, (2) perspective taking, (3) form of moral judgment, (4) bounds of social awareness, (5) locus of authority, (6) form of world coherence, and (7) symbolic function. The first and third of these aspects were explicitly based on the ideas of Piaget and Kohlberg, respectively, and the rest were heavily influenced by these ideas, especially when identifying Faith Stages 1 through 4. After stage scores were assigned to each aspect, these scores were averaged to provide a stage assignment for the respondent.

Fowler (1981) did not report which of the seven aspects proved most diagnostic, accounting for most of the variance, but he did report that the stage assignment ratings on the aspects could be made with good reliability. Apparently, however, many respondents did not have the same stage score on different aspects (which they should if the assessment was reliable and the stages involve a coherent combination of aspects); the averages tended to form a continuum of scores rather than to cluster around the integers. Fowler dealt with this problem by classifying the faith of some respondents as "in transition"; for example, individuals with a mean from 3.4 to 3.6 were classified as Stage 3–4 transitional.

Looking at the stage assignment for respondents of different ages, 88.0 percent of the 4- to 6-year-olds were assigned to Stage 1; 72.4 percent of the 7- to 12-year-olds were assigned to Stage 2; 50.0 percent of the 13- to 20-year-olds were assigned to Stage 3, with another 28.6 percent assigned to Stage 3–4 transitional; 40.0 percent of the 21- to 30-year-olds were assigned to Stage 4, with another 33.3 percent assigned to Stage 3–4 transitional; 37.5 percent of the 31- to 40-year-olds were assigned to Stage 3, with the rest spread fairly evenly from Stage 3–4 transitional to Stage 5; 56.2 percent of the 41- to 50-year-olds were assigned to Stage 5, with another 21.9 percent assigned to Stage 4–5 transitional; 35.3 percent of the 51- to 60-year-olds were assigned to Stage 3, with another 29.4 percent assigned to Stage 4 and 23.5 percent assigned to Stage 5; 27.4 percent of those over 60 were assigned to Stage 4, with another 24.2 percent assigned to Stage 3 and 16.1 percent assigned to Stage 5.

Up to about age 20, then, there is a clear tendency for stage score to increase with age; from about age 20 on, however, it is difficult to see any clear pattern to the stage scores. Roughly equal numbers of respondents are at Stages 3 and 4, with a somewhat smaller percentage at Stage 5. The one notable exception is for respondents in their 40s; the majority of these were assigned to Stage 5.

What do these results tell us about the accuracy of Fowler's model as a description of people's faith development? Fowler (1981) cautiously interpreted the results as supporting his claim of an invariant sequence of his six stages. Yet even his cautious claim of support seems unjustified. These results could as easily reflect a situation in which there is a developmental sequence that moves from Stage 1 to Stage 2 and then to one of the higher stages, probably due to cognitive maturation as described by Piaget (which is heavily represented in the scoring of Stages 1 through 3). Rather than Stages 3, 4, and 5 being hierarchically ordered, one following the other, these three forms of faith may lie alongside one another, much like the three options noted earlier in Goldman's analysis. Consistent with this possibility, Green and Hoffman (1989) found Stage 4 and 5 responses were as common as Stage 3 responses among college students. Finally, about the existence of Stage 6, Fowler's research can say nothing because only one of the more than three hundred people interviewed was classified as Stage 6.

Overall, then, the results suggest that for adults it may be more appropriate to speak of styles of faith, as Fowler sometimes has, not stages (see also Barnes, Doyle, & Johnson, 1989). One style involves orthodox adherence to traditional religious beliefs; a second involves critical analysis and believing for oneself; and a third involves a symbolic and paradoxical interpretation of religious concepts. Some researchers report that the last two styles often appear together (Green & Hoffman, 1989).

Ultimately, the cross-sectional interviews that Fowler conducted cannot provide the information necessary to assess his claim of a stage sequence. Longitudinal research is needed, in which changes in style of faith are measured within individuals over time. In 1981 Fowler reported that longitudinal follow-up interviews with some of his initial respondents were under way, but as far as we know there is still no published report of these interviews. Until supportive longitudinal data are available, it seems premature to accept Fowler's prescriptive ordering of these different styles of faith as a valid description of the way faith develops in individuals' lives.

Attachment to Parents and to God

Erikson (1950) believed that basic trust, the "willingness to let the mother out of sight without undue anxiety or rage," was the touchstone for later religious commitment because "all religions have in common the periodical childlike surrender to a Provider or providers who dispense earthly fortune as well as spiritual health" (p. 250). Lee Kirkpatrick and Phillip Shaver (1990) recently reported an interesting preliminary study, based on Mary Ainsworth's (Ainsworth, Blehar, Waters, & Wall, 1978) extensions of John Bowlby's (1969) theory of infant attachment, that examined the association between adults' reported style of attachment to their mothers during childhood and (1) their current religious beliefs and activity, (2) their sense of having a close, personal relationship with God, and (3) their likelihood of having a sudden conversion experience. Kirkpatrick and Shaver did not make the connection, but we would suggest that their study can be viewed as an exploration and extension of Erikson's ideas concerning the religious significance of basic trust.

Borrowing Ainsworth's concepts, Kirkpatrick and Shaver had their research participants (213 adult respondents to a newspaper survey) classify their pre-adolescent relationship with their mothers as secure, avoidant, or anxious/ambivalent based on the following descriptions (without the labels). The percentage of participants checking each alternative is in parentheses.

> *Secure:* She was generally warm and responsive; she was good at knowing when to be supportive and when to let me operate on my own; our relationship was almost always comfortable, and I have no major reservations or complaints about it. (50.7 percent).
>
> *Avoidant:* She was fairly cold, distant, and rejecting, and not very responsive; I often felt that her concerns were elsewhere; I frequently had the feeling that she would just as soon not have had me. (8.1 percent)
>
> *Anxious/Ambivalent:* She was noticeably inconsistent in her reactions to me, sometimes warm and sometimes not; she had her own needs and agendas which sometimes got in the way of her receptiveness and responsiveness to my needs; she definitely loved me but didn't always show it in the best way. (41.2 percent) (Kirkpatrick & Shaver, 1990, p. 323).

The secure attachment style as described here seems closely akin to Erikson's basic trust; the avoidant style seems akin to mistrust; the anxious/ambivalent style seems to lie between these extremes.

To the extent that these parallels are valid, we can use the Kirkpatrick and Shaver data to test Erikson's claim that basic trust is the touchstone for later religious commitment. The answer provided by their data is, as it turns out, a bit of a surprise; it is certainly not what Erikson's analysis would lead us to expect.

Kirkpatrick and Shaver found that associations between attachment style and religion were qualified by participants' perceptions of their mother's religiousness. Among participants who saw their mothers as highly religious, there was no apparent association between childhood attachment style and current religious beliefs or relationship with God; reports of belief and relationship with God were fairly high for all three attachment-style groups. Among participants who saw their mothers as not very religious, there was evidence of a compensation effect. Those who reported an avoidant attachment style, reflecting mistrust, were more likely to report belief in a loving, personal God, to report having a personal relationship with God, and to report frequent attendance at religious services than were those who reported a secure attachment style, reflecting basic trust. Responses of those who reported an anxious/ambivalent attachment style tended to fall in between, although they were usually closer to the reponses of the secure group.

It appeared, then, that the religion of individuals with a secure attachment style was heavily influenced by the religion of their mothers. If their mother was highly religious, so were they; if she was not, neither were they. This pattern suggests the effects of modeling, identification, and other forms of social learning. In contrast, individuals with an avoidant style were likely to report being highly religious regardless of their mother's religion. Interestingly, they were also more likely to report having had a sudden religious conversion than were individuals in either of the other two attachment-style groups.

Kirkpatrick and Shaver (1990) concluded that their results "suggest that God and religion may function in a compensatory role for people with a history of avoidant attachment; that is, God may serve as a substitute attachment figure" (p. 315). Their results also suggest that, contrary to Erikson's assumption that basic maternal trust provides a necessary foundation for later religious commitment, insecure mistrust in childhood may be at least as powerful an impetus to seek the divine.

Our confidence in these suggestions is tempered by remembering that in their study Kirkpatrick and Shaver employed retrospective self-reports by self-selected participants. Such self-reports are notoriously subject to bias, so this research should be regarded as only preliminary. Still, the results of this study make clear that even an analysis as broad, complex, and subtle as Erikson's may, in important respects, be too simple. Empirical observations like those of Kirkpatrick and Shaver are badly needed to check, correct, and refine our broad, theoretical understanding of the effects of individual development on personal religion. Indeed, study of developmental influences may well be the one area in the social psychology of religion where our need for more and better empirical observation exceeds our need for more and better theoretical analysis.

SUMMARY AND CONCLUSION

In the previous chapter we considered the possibilities for and limitations to our religious experience resulting from our place in society. In this chapter we considered the possibilities and limitations resulting from our physical, intellectual, and psychosocial development.

Set against the general backdrop of social learning based on modeling and reinforcement, we suggested that specific cognitive and psychosocial changes are sparked by specific physical changes. Four physical changes seem particularly important for the cognitive and psychosocial changes related to religion: (1) continuing development of our brain throughout childhood, (2) growth and coordination of our limbs and muscles, permitting active exploration of the environment and performance of complex motor tasks, (3) sexual development at puberty, and (4) loss of physical capacity with age, leading ultimately to death.

As Jean Piaget made clear, the first two of these changes have dramatic effects on our cognitive development during childhood. Not only do we learn many new things, but we also learn new ways of thinking. Based on Piaget's analysis, Ronald Goldman issued warnings about the possibilities and limitations for personal religion. Only with the emergence of formal-operational thinking, roughly around 11 years of age, is it possible for the child to understand and ask the existential questions that we have suggested are the source of one's religion. So, to the extent that religious concepts, teachings, and writings address these questions, the young child is severely limited in his or her ability to understand and appreciate religious thought and language. The young child who succeeds in making sense of religious concepts using magical or literal preformal modes of thought will of necessity misunderstand them. As a result, this child may later be cut off from meaningful, formal-operational use of these concepts when addressing existential questions. Lawrence Kohlberg's analysis of moral development, heavily dependent on Piaget's analysis of cognitive development, suggested that adoption of literal religious beliefs may also limit the individual's ability to move beyond conventional to postconventional or principled moral reasoning.

In his wide-ranging analysis of psychosocial development from birth to death, Erik Erikson considered the impact of all four of the physical changes we noted. Examining the effects of these physical changes on the way the individual relates to self and important others, Erikson produced a rich analysis of eight psychosocial conflicts to be addressed throughout life. Especially from the identity crisis of adolescence on, these conflicts are closely linked to existential questions: Who am I? What is the purpose of my life? How do I relate to others? How do I deal with death? So, in Erikson's analysis, individual development not only permits religion; the interpersonal conflicts that psychosocial development provokes actively encourage it. Indeed, recent research on attachment styles raises the possibility that this encouragement may be even more pervasive than Erikson thought; deficiencies in early psychosocial development may lead to a compensatory need for religion later on.

As Chapter 2 and this chapter make clear, the external social environment and internal developmental processes provide the context for one's religious experience, setting limits but also permitting—even provoking—existential questions. Yet there is more to religion than context; people often consider the heart and soul of their religion to be one or more life-transforming experiences in response to these existential questions. The context of an experience is not the same as the experience itself, any more than the setting that holds the jewel is the jewel. How are we to understand these life-transforming religious experiences psychologically? In the next chapter, as we shift our focus from the sources of individual religion to its nature, we must try.

II

Nature of Individual Religion

4

Religious Experience and Personal Transformation

When we turn to religious experience, we are immediately confronted with overwhelming diversity; personal religious experience comes in many forms. For people with what Edwin Starbuck (1899) called once-born religion, it takes the form of an unspectacular but pervasive illumination of everything that happens in day-to-day life. For those with twice-born religion, it involves dramatic, personally overwhelming events that shine forth from everyday life as beacons in the night. Clearly, whatever we say about religious experience will have its exceptions. Yet something must be said.

In our analysis we shall follow the advice of the foremost student of religious experience, William James (1902). He suggested that the best approach is to focus on the most dramatic and intense experiences because in them one finds most clearly displayed the psychological process also present in less dramatic experiences. Therefore, let us begin our analysis with a brief look at ten dramatic religious experiences. Then we shall try to uncover the psychological process that underlies them.

TEN DRAMATIC RELIGIOUS EXPERIENCES

1. Siddhartha, of the family of Gautama, was born a prince of the Sakya clan in India in the first half of the sixth century BC. He grew up surrounded by luxury and sensuous enjoyment, carefully protected by his father from the sorrows and frustrations of life. Somehow, when in his mid-twenties, he became aware of the sad truths of disease, old age, and death. This knowledge provoked Siddhartha to anxious and puzzled reflection, and finally to determined action. At the age of 29 he left his father's palace, his beautiful wife, and newborn son, and he set out to find a meaningful way to live in this world of suffering, sorrow, and death. For seven years he sought enlightenment. He consulted hermit sages, but did not find the answer. He tried ascetic self-denial, but found that prolonged fasting and other punishment of the body brought only exhaustion and impotence of mind. Finally, his quest reached its culmination in a long period of meditation under a spreading Bo tree, not far from the present city of Gaya in northern India. When he arose, he knew that he had found enlightenment; it lay in recognition and acceptance of the essential unity and harmony of all life.

Siddhartha's insight has provided direction to millions since. For through it, he had become the Buddha.

2. Moses was unhappily living a life of ease, tending his father-in-law's flocks, while his kinsmen remained slaves in Egypt. Suddenly, he was directed by a voice from a burning bush that he was to be the "servant of the Lord" who would free his people. From this experience, a man who had earlier fled from Egypt to save his own skin drew the strength to go back and confront the Pharoah (Exod. 3:1–4:17).

3. In the New Testament we are presented with the following account of the conversion of Saul of Tarsus.

> Meanwhile Saul, still breathing threats and murder against the disciples of the Lord, went to the high priest and asked him for letters to the synagogues at Damascus, so that if he found any who belonged to the Way, men or women, he might bring them bound to Jerusalem. Now as he was going along and approaching Damascus, suddenly a light from heaven flashed around him. He fell to the ground and heard a voice saying to him, "Saul, Saul, why do you persecute me?" He asked, "Who are you, Lord?" The reply came, "I am Jesus, whom you are persecuting. But get up and enter the city, and you will be told what you are to do." The men who were travelling with him stood speechless because they heard the voice but saw no one. Saul got up from the ground, and though his eyes were open, he could see nothing; so they led him by the hand and brought him into Damascus. For three days he was without sight, and neither ate nor drank. (Acts 9:1–9 NRSV)

4. Saint Augustine (354–430) experienced a dramatic conversion when he was 32 years old. While living the life of a carefree bachelor, he became tormented by doubts.

> Troubled in mind and countenance, I turned to Alypius. "What ails us?" I exclaimed. "What is it? what heardest thou? The unlearned start up and take heaven by force, and we with our learning, and without heart, lo, where we wallow in flesh and blood! Are we ashamed to follow, because others are gone before, and not ashamed not even to follow?" Some such words I uttered, [but] . . . my forehead, cheeks, eyes, color, tone of voice, spake my mind more than the words I uttered. (*Confessions,* 1843, VIII, 19)

Augustine then retreated in anguish to a small garden, threw himself down under a fig tree, and cried to God for an end to his uncleanness.

> So was I speaking and weeping in the most bitter contrition of my heart, when, lo! I heard from a neighboring house a voice, as of a boy or girl, I know not, chanting, and oft repeating, "Take up and read; take up and read." Instantly, my countenance altered, I began to think most intently whether children were wont in any kind of play to sing such words: nor could I remember ever to have heard the like. So checking the torrent of my tears, I arose; interpreting it to be no other than a command from God to open the book, and read the first chapter I should find. . . . I seized, opened, and in silence read that section on which my eyes first fell; "Not in rioting and drunkenness, not in chambering and wantonness, not in strife and envying; but put ye on the Lord Jesus Christ, and make not provision for the flesh, in concupiscence." No further would I read; nor needed I: for instantly at the end of this sentence, by a light as it were of serenity infused into my heart, all the darkness of doubt vanished away. (*Confessions,* 1843, VIII, 28).

From this experience Augustine went on to become bishop of Hippo and one of the foremost Christian theologians.

5. Saint Teresa of Avila (1515–1582) reports a similar conversion experience, prompted by reading the preceding account by Augustine of his own conversion.

> At that time, they gave me [Augustine's] *Confessions.* It seems as if the Lord ordained it, for I did not try to get it for myself and had never seen a copy.
>
> Oh, God help me, how all the hard resistance of my soul to all the help God gave me shocks me now! . . . When I got as far as his conversion and read how he heard that voice in the garden, it was just as if the Lord gave it to me, too, to judge from the grief that filled my heart. For a long time I was wholly undone by my weeping, and with Augustine's very same love and anguish within my own self, too. . . .
>
> Oh, God help us, what a soul suffers when it loses the freedom to rule itself that it would have! I wonder that I could have lived so long in such torment! God be praised who gave me life so that I could rise up from such a mortal death! (Santa Teresa de Jesus, 1554/1962, quoted by Lincoln, 1984, p. 40)

6. Henry David Thoreau (1817–1862) describes a less traditional religious experience that occurred during his chosen solitude at Walden Pond.

> Once, a few weeks after I came to the woods, for an hour I doubted whether the near neighborhood of man was not essential to the serene and healthy life. To be alone was somewhat unpleasant. But, in the midst of a gentle rain, while these thoughts prevailed, I was suddenly sensible of such sweet and beneficent society in nature, in the very pattering of the drops, and in every sight and sound around my house, an infinite and unaccountable friendliness all at once, like an atmosphere, sustaining me, as made the fancied advantages of human neighborhood insignificant, and I have never thought of them since. Every little pine-needle expanded and swelled with sympathy and befriended me. I was so distinctly made aware of the presence of something kindred to me, that I thought no place could ever be strange to me again. (Thoreau, 1854, p. 116).

7. The revivalism of the late nineteenth century produced many accounts of dramatic religious experiences. Here is a woman's report that William James (1902) selected from Edwin Starbuck's manuscript collection.

> I was taken to a camp-meeting, mother and religious friends seeking and praying for my conversion. My emotional nature was stirred to its depths; confessions of depravity and pleading with God for salvation from sin made me oblivious of all surroundings. I pled for mercy, and had a vivid realization of forgiveness and renewal of my nature. When rising from my knees I exclaimed, "Old things have passed away, all things have become new." It was like entering another world, a new state of existence. Natural objects were glorified, my spiritual vision was so clarified that I saw beauty in every material object in the universe, the woods were vocal with heavenly music; my soul exulted in the love of God, and I wanted everybody to share in my joy. (James, 1902, p. 200)

Reading these accounts, you may wonder why such experiences do not occur today. The answer is, they do.

8. A 28-year-old student told us of a mountaintop experience that marked a turning point in his life. He was born into a wealthy family, but on his 16th birthday his parents divorced. Shortly afterward, he began to drink heavily and use a variety of drugs, narrowly escaping being expelled from high school. After graduation, he joined the air force. Yet, his drug use did not stop; it intensified, as did a general sense of depression and personal worthlessness. In a desperate attempt to fight the depression, he threw himself into his job, often working over one hundred hours a week. Although these work binges produced considerable success and recognition, they invariably ended in exhaustion, drink, drugs, and more depression. Finally, while stationed in Berlin, he sought a ten-day leave to rest and recover, for he feared that he was near physical and emotional collapse. He went to a retreat in the Alps.

There, he walked out one morning and sat quietly on a mountainside, trying to get some perspective on things. He felt lost and desperately in need of something to take control of his life. Suddenly, he knew that he had found it. Heretofore only a ritual Catholic, he felt an unexpected assurance that God existed and, more importantly, that God was in control of, cared about, and accepted him. And if God cared about and accepted him, he could care about and accept himself.

A cloud had been rising from the valley toward him when he sat down. As it approached, the feeling of being lost intensified. Then the cloud engulfed him in a fog. It was in the midst of this fog that he felt assurance that God was in control of his life. As the cloud passed, he found that "there was a whole new me inside." This change was underscored by a changed perception of his physical surroundings; there was now a warm, luminous glow to everything. The green valley, the white clouds, the trees, and grass were all bathed in an almost iridescent light.

Although it was several years before his religious transformation was complete, the young man is convinced that this experience saved his life. The sense of contact with God that began there has stayed with him since; indeed, he now considers his mountaintop experience to be rather bland compared with the experience that he has each day of the presence of God.

9. While in prison for armed robbery, and having narrowly escaped death, Malcolm Little first encountered Black Muslim teachings. As he described it, "I had sunk to the very bottom of the American white man's society when—in prison—I found Allah and the religion of Islam and it completely transformed my life. . . ." (Malcolm X, 1964, p. 150). To reflect the change from seeing himself as a worthless victim of white oppression to a black man and a follower of Allah, Malcom Little changed his name to Malcolm X. He also became a black Muslim minister.

But this experience was not the end of Malcolm X's religious transformation. When he visited Mecca a few years later, he gained new insights that led him to attempt to transcend the sectarian character of the Black Muslim movement by affirming the worth and dignity of all people, regardless of race. He wrote to his friends back in the United States:

> You may be shocked by these words coming from me. But on this pilgrimage, what I have seen, and experienced, has forced me to *re-arrange* much of my thought-patterns previously held, and to *toss aside* some of my previous conclusions. . . .
>
> During the past eleven days here in the Muslim world, I have eaten from the same plate, drunk from the same glass, and slept in the same bed (or on the same rug)—while praying to the *same* God—with fellow Muslims, whose eyes were the bluest of blue, whose hair was the blondest of blond, and whose skin was the whitest of white. And in the *words* and in the *actions* and in the *deeds* of the "white" Muslims, I felt the same sincerity that I felt among the black African Muslims of Nigeria, Sudan, and Ghana.
>
> We were *truly* all the same (brothers)—because their belief in one God had removed the "white" from their *minds,* the "white" from their *behavior,* and the "white" from their *attitude.*

> I could see from this, that perhaps if white Americans could accept the Oneness of God, then perhaps, too, they could accept *in reality* the Oneness of Man—and cease to measure, and hinder, and harm others in terms of their "differences" in color. (1964, pp. 340–341, italics in original)

Nor was this insight without personal consequences. On his return to the United States, Malcolm X affirmed:

> Since I learned the *truth* in Mecca, my dearest friends have come to include *all* kinds—some Christians, Jews, Buddhists, Hindus, agnostics, and even atheists! I have friends who are called capitalists, Socialists, and Communists! Some of my friends are moderates, conservatives, extremists—some are even Uncle Toms! My friends today are black, brown, red, yellow, and *white*! (1964, p. 375, italics in original)

Shortly after making this statement Malcolm X was assassinated, allegedly by Black Muslim opponents of his new vision of universal brotherhood.

10. Finally, consider the experience of a psychologist who in his late thirties had taken the psychedelic drug LSD. Looking back on his experience, the psychologist sets the stage:

> All of my life I have been trying to cut loose from something at the bottom of myself that prevented me from going where I wanted to go and also from knowing what I wanted to know. What I wanted to know was, essentially, God. But before I could get to know God I had to cut loose from most of what bound me to the Devil. I am sorry that what I have learned cannot be put into terms that would seem to me more scientific. I continue to have some resistance to understanding myself in these terms of God and Devil, Heaven and Hell, although I believe that these terms are the only ones really acceptable to me and effective as instruments of change. (Masters & Houston, 1966, p. 292)

What follows is a transcript of the experience expressed in dialogue between the psychologist (S) and a therapist who served as his guide (G) during the drug session. The psychologist had been looking at a little porcelain mermaid for a long time.

> G: You have mentioned many times your "evil roots," those roots going down to the place you feel that you came from. Do you still feel those roots now?
>
> S: My roots extended down to that other place. I have had to cut myself away from my roots one by one. I have a sense now of having cut through so many of these roots that there may not be too many of them left.
>
> G: Good, then maybe now you can pull free. Try pulling free. *Pull free now!*
>
> S: (Waves his feet in the air, makes jerking motions with his feet and legs, etc.) I feel like I really am free! But it was so easy! I broke them off where they came into the soles of my feet. They were dry as dust and just crumbled when I started to pull away from them. Like dried old umbilicals, attached to the bottoms of my feet, and I've broken them all off. Why didn't I know before that they were ready to crumble? How long could they have been like

that? Why, now I am free! (S is smiling, very excited, and looking extremely pleased and happy.)
G: And this hold that you say the Devil has had on you? What about that?
S: Satan has no more power to control me! I still have habit to fear, but the organic link is gone! What I just kicked loose was the whole serpent identification and the dead crumbling umiblical cord that still was tying me down to Hell. I seem to have shattered every physical connection with the place below. Look! (S gets up and stamps his feet against the ground.) I am crumbling the last remnants of the connection under my feet. I shake off the last of the dust and I step free of it all. My perception with regard to matter was what triggered everything off—seeing in the face of the little mermaid that it could be shaped in so many ways according to the way I looked at it. Intellectually, of course, I was aware of this before. But now I really knew it to be so and it seemed that from there I could go on to other real knowledge. (Masters & Houston, 1966, p. 295)

Shortly thereafter, the effects of the drug were gone "about as abruptly as lights go off when someone flips the switch" (p. 296). Reflecting on this experience later, S said that he felt that "a destructive response to the world has been replaced by a response that is essentially creative" (p. 298).

More examples of contemporary religious experiences could be added, for there is little doubt that such experiences remain central to the religious life of many individuals (Wills, 1978). Indeed, a Gallup Poll conducted in 1986 revealed that among Americans 18 and over, more than 50 million (33 percent of the adult population) report having had one or more "born-again" experiences (Gallup Reports, 1987).

TOWARD A PSYCHOLOGICAL UNDERSTANDING OF RELIGIOUS EXPERIENCES: A CREATIVITY ANALOGY

Clearly, religious experience knows no bounds of creed, color, or nationality. Even within our small sample we find four major religions represented—Buddhism, Judaism, Christianity, and Islam; there are also several experiences that involve personal, idiosyncratic beliefs not easily related to any institutional religion. Yet in spite of their obvious variety, the experiences in our sample do seem to have at least one common characteristic. Each involves dramatic change, both in the way the person sees the world and in the person's behavior; each is reality-transforming. How are we to account for such dramatic change?

In the preceding two chapters we explored the social and developmental context of religion. But these factors cannot explain what happens to the individual in a religious experience or how the experience can have such dramatic effects on his or her life. The time has come for us, with some trepidation, to try to understand the psychology of the experience itself. Our trepidation is magnified by our knowledge that even William James did not attempt this task. He limited himself to collecting diverse examples of religious experience, trying to detect common characteristics of such experiences, and classifying the experiences as to type. He did not offer any systematic explanation of the underlying psychological process. But psychology has come a long way since 1901 when James delivered the lectures that provided the basis for his *Varieties of Religious Experience,* and we believe that it is now possible to present a tentative psychological understanding of what happens during religious experiences, or at least during a substantial number of them.

This understanding is built on the assumption that the psychological process involved in religious experiences also appears in other profound, reality-transforming experiences. If this assumption is valid, then we may get some help in our attempt to understand religious experience by borrowing clues from psychological analyses of another kind of reality-transforming experience. The experience of this kind that has been most carefully studied by psychologists is the creative experience, especially as it occurs in art and science. Therefore, in our attempt to understand religious experience we shall use an analogic approach, employing insights gained from psychological analyses of creativity.

Like any analogy, this one has its limits. Our claim is not that creativity and religious experience are the same. Creativity typically involves questioning some established view of the physical or social world; it concerns external reality. Religion is more personal. As the definition proposed in Chapter 1 suggests, it involves questions close to the core of the individual's personality, life-and-death issues concerning the nature and meaning of existence itself. This difference between creativity and religious experience, although important, is primarily a difference in content and personal centrality, not process. To the extent that the psychological process involved is the same, the understanding that psychologists have developed of the reality transformation that occurs in creativity may help us understand religious experience. This is the assumption on which we shall build our analysis.

Psychological Process involved in Creativity

To make our analysis of the process involved in religious experience as clear as possible, we shall present it in nine explicit propositions. Employing our analogy, the first six propositions concern the psychological dynamics of creativity. In combination, they provide an overview of one currently popular psychological interpretation of the creative process. We shall then build on this understanding of creativity in our analysis of religious experience. Needless to say, our analysis is only suggestive. Many extremely complex issues are raised; few are dealt with in detail. We hope, however, that a brief, nontechnical presentation will most clearly reveal the basic assumptions and steps in the argument.

1. Our reality is constructed. This first proposition is a philosophical one, and philosopher Alfred North Whitehead stated it forcefully:

> Nature gets credit which in truth should be reserved for ourselves, the rose for its scent, the nightingale for his song, and the sun for its radiance. The poets are entirely mistaken. They should address their lyrics to themselves and should turn them into odes of self-congratulations on the excellence of the human mind. Nature is a dull affair, soundless, scentless, colorless, merely the hurrying of material, endlessly, meaninglessly. (Ornstein, 1972, p. 45)

Although we tend to think of reality as something "out there" and quite independent of ourselves, this conviction is based entirely on our experience, experience that without the imposition of meaning on it by our minds would be, as William James said, a "blooming, buzzing confusion." To say this does not, of course, mean that we can make of our experience what we will; should you have any doubt, try walking through a wall. But the meaning that we attach to our experience is what gives it the structure and stability of "reality." And this meaning is very much a human creation.

The point that reality is constructed often seems unimportant, because at the level of simple, direct experience we have few difficulties agreeing what reality is. The heat of fire and the chill of ice are as real for you as they are for us. But the importance of this point becomes apparent when one considers more complex experiences, for then there is far less consensus as to what constitutes reality. It is not uncommon to be engaged in an intense discussion until an "Oh, is *that* what you mean by. . . ." reveals that the participants actually live in different worlds.

Among philosophers, phenomenologists like Husserl (1960) and Merleau-Ponty (1962, 1963) are well known for their emphasis on the constructed nature of reality. Among psychologists, the Gestalt school has most clearly made this point. *Gestalt* is a German word meaning form, and the major point of this school is that we form our experience into meaningful objects and relations. Gestalt psychology was born, in part, out of Max Wertheimer's reflection in 1912 on the newly developed movies. Although a movie is a sequence of separate still shots projected onto the screen, we see motion. This fascinated Wertheimer. He reasoned that if we can so easily construct a moving reality from the experience of a series of still shots, then our power to create reality must be great indeed. He spent much of his life providing evidence of how true this is.

What determines the reality we construct? In making sense of any given experience, context is extremely important. Consider an example presented by Robert Ornstein in *The Psychology of Consciousness* (1972). First, look at the sequences of numbers and letters in Figure 4.1. Now look at Figure 4.2. In Figure 4.1 you probably had no difficulty reading the number *13* in the sequence of numbers and the letter *B* in the sequence of letters, even though the physical stimuli were identical. Because of the different context, you constructed two different realities out of exactly the same sensory input.

Figure 4.1 Numbers and Letters . . .

2. The reality we construct is based on our cognitive structures. This second point builds on Piaget's analysis of the different ways children think at different stages of development. Recall from Chapter 3 that, according to Piaget, these different ways of thinking are a product of the child at each stage having different cognitive structures. Now we need to say a little more about these structures. Cognitive structures are conceptual dimensions on which we scale our experience; they allow us to compare one experience with another. This ability to classify and differentiate experiences enables us to construct a reality.

To illustrate, we construe objects along the dimensions of color, size, weight, function, and so on. We employ even more cognitive structures in our perceptions of other people—intelligence, attractiveness, age, sex, size, friendliness, sincerity—the list could go on and on (see Kelly, 1955; Jones, 1990). Our cognitive structures are, in the words of existential phenomenologist Maurice Merleau-Ponty, "the framework on which reality is woven" (see also Markus & Zajonc, 1985).

The effect of cognitive structures on the construction of reality is nicely demonstrated in a classic study by Hastorf and Cantril (1954). One cognition that most of us hold is the belief that we and others like us are fair. But this cognition, within the heads of members of two different groups that are in conflict, can produce quite different realities. Hastorf and Cantril dem-

Figure 4.2 . . . From Identical Stimuli. *Source:* Adapted from *The Psychology of Consciousness,* Copyright © 1972 by Robert E. Ornstein. Reprinted by permission of Harcourt Brace Jovanovich, Inc.

onstrated this dramatically by showing films of a bitterly contested and violent football game between Princeton and Dartmouth to members of each student body. The game involved a number of serious injuries, the most notable being an injury that forced Princeton's star quarterback to leave the game. Most Princeton students were convinced that the Dartmouth players purposely ganged up and were trying to injure the Princeton quarterback. Most Dartmouth students, on the other hand, felt that the game, although rough, was fairly played.

3. Our cognitive structures are hierarchically arranged. Not only do we construe our experience along dimensions, the dimensions themselves are organized under more or less complex cognitive principles. This proposition has been central to many of the models of human thought or information processing based on a computer analogy (see, for example, Miller, Galanter, & Pribram, 1960; Newell, Shaw, & Simon, 1958; Schank & Abelson, 1977).

Building on such models, as well as on Piaget's earlier work, Schroder, Driver, and Streufert (1967) offer a schematic representation of hierarchical cognitive structures that has been related to creativity (Karlins, 1966). In their scheme, Schroder, Driver, and Streufert use horizontal lines to depict conceptual dimensions and circles to depict organizing principles. Diagonal lines indicate paths of interrelationship. Figure 4.3 depicts a relatively simple and a relatively complex cognitive organization using the Schroder, Driver, and Streufert scheme. In the simple organization, only a few dimensions are related, and by only simple organizing pr inciples, called perspectives. In the complex organization, however, numerous dimensions are related by different perspectives and, further, the perspectives are themselves related by higher-level rules and principles.

According to Schroder, Driver, and Streufert, a person's cognitive orga-

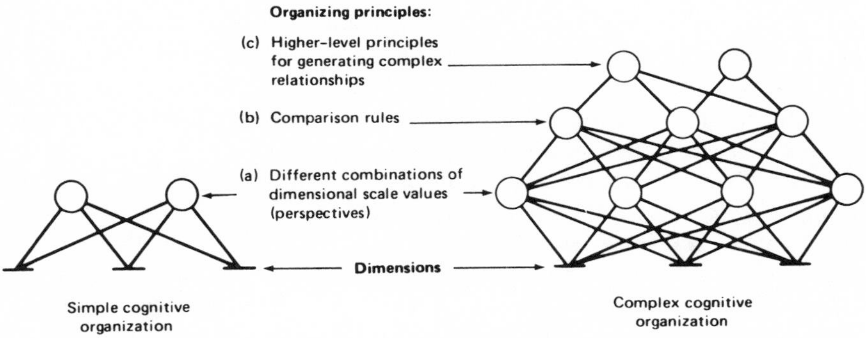

Figure 4.3 Simple and Complex Cognitive Organization. *Source:* Adapted from *Human Information Processing* by H. M. Schroder, M. J. Driver, and S. Streufert. Copyright © 1967 by Holt, Rinehart and Winston, Inc. Reprinted by permission of Holt, Rinehart and Winston, Inc.

nization can vary both in degree of differentiation and degree of integration. *Differentiation* here means the number of distinct levels of stimuli that can be recognized along a given dimension. *Integration* here means the degree of relatedness, both between the organizing principles and the dimensions and between different levels of organizing principles.

To put some flesh on the bones of the Schroder, Driver, and Streufert scheme, think of the way two different people might perceive a particular individual. A person with a simple cognitive organization may have an organizing principle that positively relates the dimensions of attractiveness and intelligence (e.g., the more attractive the individual, the more intelligent) and a different organizing principle that negatively relates the dimensions of friendliness and wealth (e.g., the friendlier, the less wealthy). A person with a complex organization may have a much more sophisticated view. He or she may have principles that suggest that intelligence and attractiveness are positively related up to the point of moderately high intelligence, but that above this point the relation is negative. Or a global dimension like friendliness may be broken into a number of more specific dimensions, such as longtime devotion, business friends, friendship based on ingratiation, and so on.

To say that our cognitive structures are hierarchically arranged means that relatively specific dimensions are grouped under more general organizing principles, which are grouped under even more abstract and general organizing principles. Information processing or problem solving tends to occur at the most specific, concrete level possible, for it would be unnecessarily time-consuming and effortful to do otherwise. A problem like "what is 4 × 282?" is not likely to be referred to the highly abstract principles of general number theory or even to principles of base-ten number systems; instead, it is dealt with in terms of relatively simple rules for multiplication and the recall of memorized multiplication tables.

When we are presented with a problem that requires organizing principles at a higher level of conceptual complexity than we have developed, it will appear to be insoluble. Indeed, it *is* insoluble within the existing cognitive structures. Herman Melville's short novel *Billy Budd* (1948) presents a tragic example of such a situation. Billy is a paragon of innocence and virtue. But when a malicious and conniving junior officer brings false charges against him, Billy loses control and strikes the man. The blow proves fatal. Captain Vere and his comrades are then faced with a dilemma: They feel compelled to uphold the dictates of martial law, which they consider necessary on a naval vessel at sea in time of war. At the same time, they strongly believe that intention and mitigating circumstances should be taken into account in judging Billy's action. Unfortunately for Billy, the captain and his associates are unable to see this dilemma from the perspective of any higher-order organizing principle. Instead, bound by their way of thinking about the problem, they are forced to choose. They decide that they must uphold martial law, and so Billy, after uttering his final virtuous line, "God bless Captain Vere," is put to death.

4. Creativity involves an improvement in one's cognitive organization. When some problem is insoluble within the existing cognitive structures, a new organization is needed. Gestalt psychologist Max Wertheimer defines creative thinking as "the process of destroying one Gestalt in favor of a better one." That is, one cognitive organization is lost and is replaced by another. This is not a logical transformation; as Piaget pointed out, logic operates within the context of a given cognitive organization. Instead, in creative thought the cognitive structures themselves, the very framework within which reflected, rational, logical thought is possible, are changed.

To provide a relatively trivial, noncreative example, Gestalt psychologists have long pointed to the nonlogical shift of meaning involved in the figure-ground reversal. What do you see in Figure 4.4? A vase . . . or two faces? As you stare at the figure, it will shift abruptly and without apparent effort from one figure to the other. What had been the background becomes the figure and vice versa. A new world or reality is created. Because these two realities require mutually exclusive organizations, you cannot see both figures at once. At any given time, you must live with one reality or the other.

Figure 4.4 A Figure-Ground Reversal.

Wertheimer's definition of creativity requires that a *better* Gestalt emerge; the new organization must be an improvement on the old. Beyond the level of simple perceptual arrays, however, Gestalt psychologists have not been very explicit about the underlying characteristics that make one Gestalt or cognitive organization better than another. Fortunately, Schroder, Driver, and Streufert's hierarchical scheme of cognitive structures enables us to state more explicitly what a better organization would be; it would be one that, through greater differentiation and integration, makes it possible to think what was previously unthinkable. Employing this conception of better organization, *creative thought* may be defined as *the process whereby one's cognitive structures are changed toward greater flexibility and adaptability through greater differentiation and integration.* With the emergence through creativity of new organizing principles, new realities are born that allow the individual to think constructively about previously insoluble problems; a greater range of experiences can be handled effectively.

This conception of creativity suggests that any adaptive increase in complexity of the cognitive structures or any emergence of a new level of organization is a product of creative thought. Creativity is not reserved for the artistic or scientific elite, although they may be especially creative in certain areas. Instead, as each of us has developed personally and intellectually, we have had many creative experiences through which our cognitive structures have evolved to their present level of complexity.

But, you may wonder, what provokes a creative shift toward greater differentiation and integration within the cognitive organization? In simple perceptual processes like the figure-ground reversal, retinal fatigue can produce a shift. More generally, changes in cognitive structure appear to result when one's current reality ceases to function effectively. If, for example, one believes that performing certain incantations will produce rain, but the drought persists, then it is time to think again. Under such circumstances, as Piaget (1953) suggested, pressure arises to accommodate our cognitive structures to our experience. It is not, of course, a question of finding the "right" or "true" structures, for rightness and truth can be defined only *within* a set of cognitive structures. It is instead a question of finding a functionally better reality, one that enables the individual to expect and to respond more effectively to experiences of the sort that actually occur.

When one thinks of possible changes in the cognitive organization, it is clear that there are a number of different types. Some changes are not creative, at least not by the definition stated above; others are. Let us look first at some noncreative changes.

Noncreative changes. Acquisition of new knowledge is an extremely important process, but it is not, in itself, creative. Instead of a change in the cognitive structures, it involves a change within them. One or more new bits of information are stored using the existing structure. For example, you may learn the current population of New York City, or that the chemical composition of water is H_2O, or that there is a movie in town that you want to see. Each bit of information adds new content, but it does not change the cognitive structures themselves. Using Piaget's terms, such knowledge involves assimilation rather than accommodation.

A second type of noncreative change is *change toward a simpler organization.* Such changes can be produced by ego-defensive suppression or repression of some aspect of experience; as such, they are common in psychopathology. For example, if you believe that you are extremely competent in mathematics but you are getting failing grades in a math course, you may resolve this tension by adding cognitive elements to the effect that the instructor is out to get you and has been reading your mind so as to include problems on the exams that he knows you cannot solve. Or you may resolve the tension by refusing to think about the implications of your grades for your assumed ability. By keeping these two cognitions separate you can avoid dealing with the cognitive dissonance (Festinger, 1957) implied by your assumption of high ability and your knowledge of your exam performance. Neither of these solutions to your dilemma can be considered creative because each restricts rather than expands the areas of experience that your cognitively constructed reality allows you to confront effectively.

A third type of noncreative change is what Berger and Luckmann (1966) have called *alternation.* Alternation involves a shift from one cognitive organization to another, but at the same level of complexity. Although a new reality is constructed, it is one that is functionally no better than the original. The figure-ground reversal is an example of alternation. Another example would be an abrupt shift from unquestioning allegiance to a radical left-wing political group to unquestioning allegiance to a reactionary right-wing group. Even though such a change involves a dramatic shift in one's reality, if it does not involve any increase in the differentiation or integration of the cognitive structures, then it does not allow one to deal any more effectively with the complexities and nuances of political experience.

Creative changes. Creative change in the cognitive structures involves a shift toward greater differentiation and integration, that is, an increase in the number of organizing principles, the level of organization, or the interaction and interpenetration of existing principles. In a creative change, the old reality is not denied but is transcended; it is seen for what it is, one way of looking at the world that has only a limited range of application. Here are some examples of creative changes.

First, mind-teasers usually require some form of creative restructuring for solution. Look at Figure 4.5. Can you connect all the dots with four straight lines without raising your pen from the page? Try it before reading on. As long as you see the dots as forming a square and work within the boundaries of the square, you cannot succeed. If, however, you extend your lines beyond the boundaries of the implicit square, a solution is possible. As in this one, mind-teasers typically take advantage of dominant cognitive organizations, binding us by our own intelligence. When a solution occurs, it usually comes with an abrupt "Aha!" because once we are able to see the

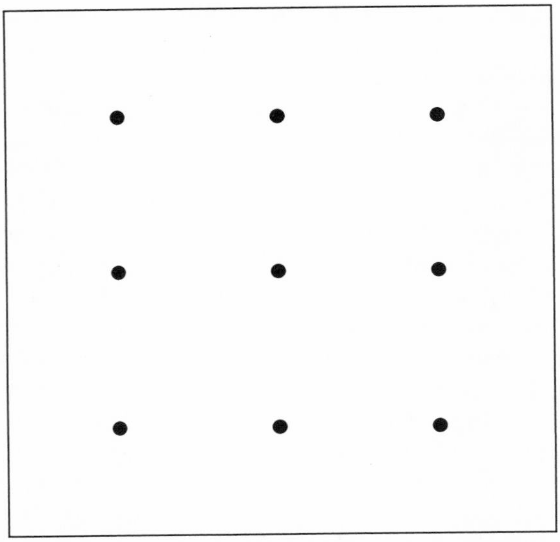

Figure 4.5 A Mind-Teaser: Connect All the Dots with Four Straight Lines Without Raising Your Pen.

problem correctly a solution is straightforward. But to see it correctly, we must be able to break set and recognize that the compelling organizing principle is only one way of viewing the problem, that it is only one reality among many.

Mind-teasers are relatively trivial examples of creativity; but a similar cognitive process may be found in far more profound examples. Consider the following four cases of creativity in science and mathematics.

1. The story of Archimedes's (ca. 287–212 BC) discovery of the principle of specific gravity is well known. His ruler, Hiero, had been presented with a new crown, claimed by the maker to be solid gold. Archimedes was given the task of determining whether the claim was true, or whether Hiero had been cheated by a crown adulterated with silver. Archimedes's life rested on his success. He could not melt down the crown to determine its composition, because if it were solid gold he would be killed for destroying a priceless treasure. On the other hand, if he said it was gold and it was found not to be, he would be killed for letting his ruler be cheated.

Archimedes knew that silver and gold were different in weight, but in order to test the composition of the crown by weight he would have to know its exact volume. And to determine the exact volume of a crown by measuring the thickness of the metal at each point along its face would be an endless task. While puzzling over this problem, Archimedes went to the baths.

Suddenly, as he stepped into the water, he had it! He noticed the familiar phenomenon that as he entered the pool the water level on the side rose slightly. He could determine the volume of the crown by the amount of water it displaced. Ecstatic, he ran through the streets, nude it is said, shouting, "Eureka!" ("I have found it!").

2. Charles Darwin (1809–1882) has gathered data on various species over many years; then one day the idea came that provided the basis for his theory of evolution, the idea of natural selection. As Darwin records in his autobiography: "I can remember the very spot on the road, whilst in my carriage, when to my joy the solution occurred to me" (1958, pp. 120–121).

3. The chemist Kekulé (1829–1896) presents a fascinating account of his discovery of the benzene ring. He had been working on the problem of the molecular structure of these hydrocarbons for days, without success. Then, one afternoon,

> I turned my chair to the fire and dozed. . . . Again the atoms were gambolling before my eyes. This time the smaller groups kept modestly in the background. My mental eye, rendered more acute by repeated visions of this kind, could now distinguish larger structures, of manifold conformation; long rows, sometimes more closely fitted together; all twining and twisting in snakelike motion. But look! What was that? One of the snakes had seized hold of its own tail, and the form whirled mockingly before my eyes. As if by a flash of lightning I awoke. . . . (Findlay, 1948, p. 36)

The insight for which Kekulé had been searching was that the structure of these carbon compounds was not a chain but, like the snake biting its own tail, a closed ring. This insight led to what has been called "'the most brilliant piece of prediction in the whole range or organic chemistry' and . . . one of the cornerstones of modern science" (Koestler, 1964).

4. The French mathematician Poincaré (1854–1912) described his discovery of Fuchsian equations as follows:

> For fifteen days I strove to prove that there could not be any functions like those I have since called Fuchsian functions. I was then very ignorant; every day I seated myself at my work table, stayed an hour or two, tried a great number of combinations and reached no results. One evening, contrary to my custom, I drank black coffee and could not sleep. Ideas rose in crowds; I felt them collide until pairs interlocked, so to speak, making a stable combination. By the next morning I had established the existence of a class of Fuchsian functions, those which come from the hypergeometric series; I had only to write out the results, which took but a few hours. . . .
>
> Just at this time I left Caen, where I was then living, to go on a geologic excursion under the auspices of the school of mines. The changes of travel made me forget my mathematical work. Having reached Coutances, we entered an omnibus to go some place or other. At the moment when I put my foot on the step the idea came to me, without anything in my former thoughts seeming to have paved the way for it, that the transformations I had used to define the Fuchsian functions were identical with those of non-

Euclidian geometry. I did not verify the idea; I should not have had time, as, upon taking my seat in the omnibus, I went on with a conversation already commenced, but I felt a perfect certainty. On my return to Caen, for conscience's sake I verified the result at my leisure. (Poincaré, 1913)

It is hoped that these four examples from science and mathematics will suffice to give a flavor of the creative process. In each, insight came when a new cognitive organization allowed the person to see elements of the problem in a new relationship.

Art and literature, too, provide numerous examples of the process of creative cognitive restructuring. The history of art is a history of seeing in a new way; think of the shift from medieval to Renaissance art or from classical to modern art. Similarly, the novelist and playwright use stories to provide a new conceptual framework for examining personal and social issues, offering new ways to think about the human experience. Based on his extensive study of many forms of creativity, Brewster Gheslin (1952) concluded:

The creative process is the process of change, of development, of evolution, in the organization of subjective life. . . . Although a problem which stubbornly resists solution by traditional means may perhaps be insoluble, the probability is rather that those means are themselves inadequate: the concepts, attitudes, and procedures employed are probably at fault and in need of being transcended in a fresh approach. (p. 12)

5. There appear to be identifiable stages in the creative process. A number of individuals, including Poincaré and Gheslin, have suggested that there are identifiable stages in the creative process. Best known is the sequence suggested by Graham Wallas (1926); he identified four stages: preparation, incubation, illumination, and verification.

Preparation. Creative thought begins with a period of baffled struggle in which the individual attempts to solve the problem in terms of his or her existing cognitive structures. If this effort produces a satisfactory solution, then there is no need for creativity. But what if it does not? Typically, even though the existing structures do not permit a solution, the thinker keeps trying to make them work; they are pushed to the limits. He or she begins to feel trapped within the current organization with no way out; the problem becomes an obsession. Most students of creativity are convinced that this preparatory period of beating one's head against the problem within the existing cognitive structures is a necessary precondition to the emergence of a creative solution.

Incubation. The second stage in the creative process occurs when, exhausted, one finally gives up the attempt to solve the problem. As physicist Peter Carruthers put it, "You have to stuff yourself—gorge yourself on a problem—and then go and leave it." (*New York Times Magazine,* May 6, 1984). In giving up, one relaxes active use of the existing cognitive structures. This relaxation appears necessary if one is to think about the problem in a new way, if a more adaptive organization is to evolve. Reflecting the importance of this incubation stage, some scholars speak of the three Bs of creativity—the bed, the bus, and the bath. As the foregoing examples illustrate, these seem to be places where creative insights often occur. Presumably, this is because they are places in which one is not actively pursuing the problem.

Illumination. Once one has given up the attempt to solve the problem, the stage is set for a new, more appropriate cognitive organization to emerge. The new organization permits insight; the elements of the problem can be seen in a new way, a way that allows solution. Often, as in the case of Kekulé's carbon chains that turned to snakes, the insight first appears in the form of a visual image. Albert Einstein emphasized the importance of imagery in his thinking: "The words or the language, as they are written or spoken, do not seem to play any role in my mechanism of thought. The psychical entities which seem to serve as elements in thought are certain signs and more or less clear images which can be 'voluntarily' reproduced and combined. . . . The above mentioned elements are, in my case, of visual and some of muscular type" (1945).

Wallas speaks of illumination as the emergence of the "happy idea," which provides release of the tension that has been building through the preparation and incubation stages. Psychoanalytic writers suggest that this illumination occurs at the level of the unconscious or nonconscious mind. In terms of our cognitive-structure analysis, we might say that it does not occur in one's thoughts but in what one uses to think, the cognitive structures themselves. Perhaps this is the reason that the creative process is not directly accessible to conscious thought and so is perceived to be illogical, mysterious, or unconscious.

Unfortunately, preparation and incubation do not always lead to illumination. Sometimes, the result is only frustration and disappointment. Set against this background, the joy of the happy idea can be exquisite indeed.

Verification. Once a happy idea occurs, one must elaborate it and test it against experience to find out if it works. One can have "aha" or insight experiences that involve looking at a problem in a new way but prove to be no more effective in dealing with the problem than was the old way. It is worth noting, however, that most of us seem to have a hit rate far better than chance; the solutions that emerge from cognitive restructuring tend to be adaptive. Of course, it may be that this impression is due to selective reporting: we are not likely to proclaim abroad an insight that failed.

6. The creative sequence outlined may have a physiological base. Recent theory and research on hemisphere specificity in the brain may have uncovered a neurophysiological base for these four stages of the creative process. The two cerebral hemispheres, left and right, are the parts of the brain responsible for abstract thought. But it has been found that these hemispheres typically have different predominant functions: The left hemisphere specializes in logic, language, and linear thought; the right hemisphere, in perceptual organization, spatial relations, and insight. This hemisphere specificity seems quite common among right-handed individuals, who constitute about 90 percent of the population. Among left-handers, some show the same pattern; others show more balanced functioning, and some even show a reversal (Springer & Deutsch, 1989).

The claim of hemisphere specificity is not a new one. As early as 1864, neurologist Hughlings Jackson noted that tumors in the left hemisphere affected language, whereas tumors in the right hemisphere affected spatial relations. He also found similar effects among patients suffering from brain lesions or from war injuries to the head.

The most dramatic demonstrations of hemisphere specificity come however, from the split-brain research of Nobel laureate Roger Sperry (1964, 1982) and his associates Michael Gazzaniga (1967) and neurosurgeon Joseph Bogen. In extreme cases of epilepsy, to prevent death from increasingly severe seizures, physicians sometimes resort to a drastic but highly effective surgical procedure. They sever the corpus callosum, the nerve bundle that connects the two hemispheres of the brain. After this operation, patients have two independently functioning cerebral hemispheres that cannot communicate directly with one another. Sperry, Gazzaniga, and Bogen have conducted research on these split-brain patients.

Surprisingly, the effects of this operation are not apparent in day-to-day activities. Testing of the patients under carefully controlled laboratory conditions, however, reveals dramatic effects. For example, a pencil placed in a patient's right hand when the hand is out of the patient's view behind a screen is easily identified and described. But when the pencil is similarly placed in the left hand, the patient is unable to say what it is. The explanation for this apparent discrepancy is that information from the right hand goes to the left hemisphere of the brain, the seat of language, whereas information from the left hand goes to the right hemisphere, which lacks language. Hence, on this task the left hand seems stupid by comparison with the right.

But change the task, and performance is dramatically altered. If one places an object in the right hand when it is out of view, and subsequently asks the patient to use this hand to select the object from a group, the right hand cannot do so. Perform the same task using the left hand, and the patient easily succeeds. Presumably, the left hand succeeds because it is linked to the right hemisphere, which specializes in perceptual and spatial relations.

Sperry has made films of patients' responses in laboratory situations. It is dramatic indeed to watch a sequence in which a middle-aged woman is presented in the course of a series of slides with a picture of a pinup nude on the left side of her visual field. Since this information goes to her right hemisphere, she is not able to say what she has seen. When asked, she reports what the left hemisphere saw, "Nothing." But at the same time, she squirms in her seat, smiles, and looks uncomfortable and confused. Finally, she remarks, "Oh, that funny machine."

Research with nonpatients suggests the same hemisphere specificity found with split-brain patients. At least among right-handers, the left hemisphere appears to be linguistic and oriented toward logical, linear thought; the right hemisphere is oriented toward spatial relations and perceptual organization (see Filbey & Gazziniga, 1969; Galin & Ornstein 1972; Kinsbourne & Cook, 1971; Springer & Deutsch, 1989).

Applying the theory and research on hemisphere specificity to creativity, it has been suggested that formation and maintenance of the cognitive structures is a right-hemisphere function, whereas information processing within the structures is a left-hemisphere function (see Ornstein, 1972). During the preparation stage of the creative process, the individual attempts to deal with the problem in terms of the logical, linear thought of the dominant left hemisphere. During the incubation stage, active processing by the left hemisphere is relaxed, permitting the less dominant, perceptually oriented right hemisphere to go to work reorganizing the cognitive structures. This reorganization leads to the new insight or illumination. Verification involves a return to left-hemisphere dominance; the individual logically tests the functional value of the new insight.

Although suggestive, it must be emphasized that the application of research on hemisphere specificity to creativity is, at present, highly speculative. It is too soon to tell whether the hemispheres of the brain perform different functions at different stages of the creative process in the manner suggested. All we can say is that the possibility merits further exploration. Fortunately, such exploration is under way at a number of research centers.

Psychological Process Involved in Religious Experience

The next three propositions build on the preceding six to provide the framework for an understanding of what happens psychologically during a religious experience.

7. A stage sequence similar to the one outlined for creatively solving intellectual problems can occur in dealing with personal problems. One of the major contributions of researchers attempting to understand creativity from a pscyhoanalytic viewpoint (e.g., Kubie, Kris, Schafer, Rugg) is their suggestion that the process of dealing with problems by a restructuring of constructed reality applies equally well to personal as to intellectual problems. Building on the psychoanalytic work, it is possible to present a stage sequence for dealing with personal problems that closely parallels Wallas's sequence.

The process begins with the individual experiencing some *personal conflict or crisis,* like the eight psychosocial conflicts identified by Erik Erikson

(1950) that were presented in Table 3.1. Karen Horney (1951) suggested that personal conflicts or crises may be characterized as resulting from a discrepancy between our real and ideal self. One way to view this discrepancy is as a difference between the view of ourself within our constructed reality (our ideal self) and the view of ourself that we get from our experience (our real self); there is conflict between who we think we should be and who we know we are. Paralleling the incubation stage, if the conflict is not resolved within our current cognitive structures, it may lead to a state of *confusion and exhaustion.* We begin to lose faith in ourselves; our personal identity begins to crumble. At the extreme, such an experience may be described as a mental breakdown.

But as psychoanalytic writers have noted, this disintegration can have a positive function; the most dramatic personality growth often takes place during such periods of personal crisis and ego disintegration (see Boisen, 1936; Dabrowski, 1964). Paralleling the illumination stage of the creative process, after having given up on ourselves, we may catch a glimpse of a *new self-image,* a new way of seeing ourselves in our world, a way that provides a foundation for building a new reality that is more in tune with our experience. Such a new self-image is personally creative. Of course, a new self may emerge that is not creative, that reflects nothing more than an attempt to assimilate experience into the constructed reality. This happens in cases of pathological fantasy and psychosis.

A pathological flight into fantasy may remove some of the pain of the discrepancy between what a person is and what that person feels he or she ought to be, but at a tremendous price; the person's self-image must become increasingly divorced from his or her experience and so the person becomes increasingly unable to function effectively. This danger points to a final stage in the process of personal creativity, a stage paralleling the verification stage in Wallas's sequence. The new self-image must be expressed and tested in one's life; if the restructuring is creative, the new self-image should lead to *improved personal and social functioning.* It should permit the person to interact positively with a wider range of experiences and social situations.

8. A similar stage sequence may be found in many religious experiences. William James suggests that there is a certain "uniform deliverance" that characterizes all religious experience. "It consists of two parts:—(1) an uneasiness and (2) its solution. The uneasiness, reduced to its simplest terms, is a sense that there is *something wrong about us* as we naturally stand. The solution is a sense that *we are saved from the wrongness* by making proper connection with higher powers" (1902, p. 383, italics in the original). Following the lead of Becker (1973), Bertocci (1958), Clark (1958), Kierkegaard (1844/1957, 1849/1954), Loder (1966, 1981), May (1975), and Rugg (1963), we would suggest that this sequence of uneasiness and solution in religious experience may proceed through four stages analogous to those involved in the creative process.

Existential crisis. Often, religious experience is rooted in a personal existential crisis. Recall from Chapter 1 that existential questions are not abstract, philosophical questions; they are intensely personal: What is the meaning of my life? How shall I relate to others? How do I deal with the fact that I am going to die? An existential crisis involves a discrepancy between what is and what one feels ought to be with regard to one or more of these questions. The individual may try to overcome this discrepancy by discovering a solution using his or her present cognitive structures. If the individual succeeds, or if more pressing, immediate problems intervene, the existential question will be set aside, at least for the time being. If, however, the individual fails, an existential crisis ensues.

The great novelist Leo Tolstoy (1828–1910) described his own existential crisis in telling words:

> I felt that something had broken within me on which my life had always rested, that I had nothing left to hold on to, and that morally my life had stopped. An invincible force impelled me to get rid of my existence, in one way or another. It cannot be said exactly that I *wished* to kill myself, for the force which drew me away from life was fuller, more powerful, more general than any mere desire. It was a force like my old aspiration to live, only it impelled me in the opposite direction. It was an aspiration of my whole being to get out of life. . . .
>
> It could give no reasonable meaning to any actions of my life. And I was surprised that I had not understood this from the very beginning. My state of mind was as if some wicked and stupid jest was being played upon me by someone. One can live only so long as one is intoxicated, drunk with life; but when one grows sober one cannot fail to see that it is all a stupid cheat. What is truest about it is that there is nothing even funny or silly in it; it is cruel and stupid, purely and simply. . . .
>
> What will be the outcome of what I do today? Of what I shall do tomorrow? What will be the outcome of my life? Why should I live? Why should I do anything? Is there in life any purpose which the inevitable death which awaits me does not undo and destroy? (*My Confessions,* 1904, pp. 20–22)

For some—soldiers awaiting battle, travelers in a storm, the seriously ill or bereaved—existential crises may be precipitated by immediate circumstances. But for many, they come when the individual should be happiest, when in Abraham Maslow's (1954) terms, all deficiency needs are met. Crisis may come, in the words of Harold Kushner's popular title, *When All You've Ever Wanted Isn't Enough* (1986). Perhaps existential questions arise at such times because other problems and shortcomings can no longer be blamed for our dissatisfaction and unhappiness. Tolstoy, for example, confronted his crisis "at a time when so far as all my outer circumstances went, I ought to have been completely happy"; he had attained wealth, fame, a blissful family life, and was in good health. Siddhartha was living in the lap of luxury when he began his anxious and puzzled reflection on the miseries of disease, old age, and death. Augustine was a well-educated young man with bright prospects and engaged in a social whirl when he made his anguished cry,

"What ails us? What is it? What heardest thou?" As William James comments, "How irrelevantly remote seem all our usual refined optimisms and intellectual and moral consolations in the presence of a need of help like this: Here is the real core of the religious problem: Help! help!" (1902, p. 137).[1]

Self-surrender. Trying and failing to regain existential meaning within one's existing reality, one is driven to a point of despair and hopelessness. Analogous to the giving up that occurs in Wallas's incubation stage, religious writers speak of self-surrender at this point. Often, as in several of the experiences described at the beginning of this chapter, there is a loss of consciousness or at least loss of direct contact with day-to-day reality. The grip of one's old way of thinking about the crisis loosens.

New Vision. Into this "dark night of the soul" may blaze the light of new vision. This new vision is analogous to Wallas's illumination. It transcends the old ways of thinking based on the old cognitive structures (e.g., one's desire to live versus the inevitability of one's own death) and permits a new way of looking at the elements of the crisis (e.g., one has already died to the old life and is living an eternal life); new truth is revealed. Perhaps because it involves cognitive transcendence, the new vision often seems to come from a transcendent realm outside oneself. The vision and one's place within it feel "bestowed."

Few accounts can rival scientist Blaise Pascal's (1623–1662) description of such a religious vision. Sitting alone in his room one November night in 1654, reading the seventeenth chapter of Saint John's Gospel, Pascal was suddenly consumed by:

FIRE

God of Abraham, God of Isaac, God of Jacob, not of the
philosophers and savants
Certitude, Certitude. Feeling. Joy. Peace.
God of Jesus Christ.
My God and Thy God
"Thy God shall be my God"
Forgetfulness of the world and of everything except God
He is to be found only in the ways taught in the Gospel

1. It should be noted that some religious experiences do not appear to be precipitated by an existential crisis. For example, a Princeton undergraduate told us of an experience that occurred one evening after he returned to his room from the library. His roommates were not in, so he just sat for a bit in the dark. Suddenly, all became light around him, and he was flooded with a tremendous sense of peace, exultation, and in his words, "at-easement with the world." The experience lasted about ten minutes, leaving him emotionally exhausted, confused, and concerned about his sanity. In reporting the experience, this young man insisted that he had had no serious problems or concerns at the time and had no idea why or how this "white light" experience occurred. Assuming that he was right in his insistence, the experience does not appear to have been precipitated by an existential crisis, at least not a conscious one. If it was not, we must conclude that it lies outside the scope of our present analysis.

Grandeur of the human soul
Righteous Father, the world has not known Thee, but I have
Known Thee
Joy, joy, joy, tears of joy. . . .

(Pascal, 1670/1889, p. 2)

Less dramatic but thoroughly enchanting is the description of newness of the transformed reality in one of the examples presented at the beginning of this chapter: "I pled for mercy, and had a vivid realization of forgiveness and renewal of my nature. When rising from my knees I exclaimed, 'Old things have passed away, all things have become new,' It was like entering another world, a new stage of existence. Natural objects were glorified, my spiritual vision was so clarified that I saw beauty in every natural object in the universe, the woods were vocal with heavenly music. . . ." Or, in the words of a farmer whose religious experience also was recounted by William James (1902), "My horses and hogs and even everybody seemed changed" (p. 200).

With the new vision comes rescue from the grips of the precipitating existential crisis. Consider three typical reports from Rodney Stark's (1965) survey of Protestant and Catholic church members in the San Francisco Bay area:

> When I got saved . . . the burden of guilt and sin was lifted, the peace of God flooded my soul.
>
> Christ came into my heart and took the load of sin and guilt away.
>
> One night I awoke gasping for breath—I thought I was dying and felt like I was—Just about to give up—I saw a vision of Jesus at the foot of my bed—the complete figure—He stretched out His hand and said, "No—not yet—Be not afraid." At that moment I felt a *peace* and *joy* come over me—such as I have never experienced in my life. (italics in original)

Of course, the new vision need not conform to traditional religious faiths. One may come to see, like Thomas Hudson in Ernest Hemingway's *Islands in the Stream* (1970), that "there aren't any answers. . . . There aren't any answers at all" (p. 319). One may even adopt the view that there is no ultimate meaning in life and no God, that the only meaning is to be found in being able to live without meaning. Such was the vision of Albert Camus's Stranger: "For the first time, the first, I laid my heart open to the benign indifference of the universe" (1946, p. 154).

New Life. If the new vision, whatever its form, is to be effective in dealing with the existential questions that precipitated the crisis, the individual must live the vision. A new life must follow. Analogous to Wallas's verification stage, a dramatic shift in reality should work to produce a dramatic shift in behavior as well. In theological terms, revelation should lead to sanctification.

As part of the new life, religious individuals often speak of a new "state of assurance." James (1902) describes this state of assurance as including (1) a loss of worry, especially loss of those concerns that produced the religious crisis; (2) a new sense of truth in which mysteries of life become lucid; and (3) a sense of newness to the objects in one's environment. In addition, James suggests that the new life involves "a new zest which adds itself like a gift to life, and takes the form either of lyrical enchantment or of appeal to earnestness and heroism. . . . An assurance of safety and a temper of peace, and, in relation to others, a preponderance of loving affections" (1902, p. 367). Summing up these characteristics, the new vision allows the religious individual to return to the world of the everyday with new assurance and a new perspective; these, in turn, enable him or her to deal more positively and effectively with a wider range of experiences and people. The person is, to some degree, re-created more whole than before.

Summarizing this four-stage model, we may say that *religious experience involves cognitive restructuring in an attempt to deal with one or more existential questions.* Consistent with our proposed analogy, the cognitive process involved seems quite similar to that involved in creativity, although the problems at issue are existential, not intellectual. In the words of Joel Allison (1968), "As in creativity . . . , the religious conversion experience may tap more primitive or unconscious modes of thought, affect, and action in order to acheive a new and more advanced level of personality integration and organization." Jerome Frank (1977; see also Jaynes, 1977; Ornstein, 1972) even suggests the possibility that religious experience may have the same neurophysiological base as creativity, a temporary shift from left to right-hemisphere dominance: "Some researchers believe that the transcendental experience is mediated primarily by the right hemisphere, the one concerned with patterns and emotions, in contrast to the analytic and verbal left hemisphere. This would account for the ineffability of the experience" (Frank, 1977, p. 559).

As a preliminary test of the usefulness of our four-stage model, turn back to the ten descriptions of religious experience with which we began this chapter. We think that you will find it relatively easy to interpret each using the model. In each, the individual is overwhelmed by an existential crisis. Then, in a moment of exhaustion and self-surrender, a new vision emerges, a vision that enables the individual to see the existential question(s) that precipitated the crisis in a new way. This new vision, in turn, provides the basis for a richer, fuller, more positive life. Thus, at the heart of each of these dramatic, emotional, life-changing experiences seems to lie some cognitive restructuring that enables the individual to deal more effectively with one or more existential questions.

Sometimes cognition and emotion—thought and feeling—are juxtaposed in psychology. Therefore, we wish to emphasize that by suggesting that religious experience involves cognitive restructuring in an attempt to deal with existential questions, we do not mean to imply that emotions are not involved. Obviously they are. As our ten examples illustrate, an existential crisis is often accompanied by intense feelings of fear, anxiety, and yearning. It is a time of "wailing and gnashing of teeth." When the crises reaches the point of despair and hopelessness, there is likely to be a complex mix of terror, depression, and resignation; often, the person collapses in exhaustion. New vision brings a dramatic emotional shift; from the depths of despair one soars to the heights of triumph, exultation, and bliss. Once again, there may be tears, but now they are tears of joy. The new life, as it unfolds, is apt to be accompanied by less intense but more enduring emotions; feelings of satisfaction, serenity, and assurance seem to dominate.

Some scholars have attempted to understand religious experience by focusing on these emotional aspects (see Otto, 1923; Pruyser, 1968). We have based our understanding instead on the cognitive process, because we believe that it, and not the emotion, reveals the basic nature of the experience—transformation in the cognitive structures for dealing with existential questions. The major importance of the emotion is, we believe, to provide motivation for the transformation process (Ullman, 1982, 1989). Still, it should be recognized that the cognitions in question, because they lie close to the core of the individual's reality structure, are not cold, calculated facts. Instead, they are what Robert Abelson (1963) called "hot cognitions"; they are invested with great personal meaning and so are accompanied by strong emotions.

9. Religious experiences may be noncreative as well as creative. Just as cognitive restructuring in response to intellectual problems may not be creative, so also restructuring in response to an existential crisis may not be creative. One of the advantages of relating the cognitive process involved in religious experience to a hierarchical model of cognitive organization is that it underscores this point. A given religious experience may allow the individual to deal more positively and effectively with a wider range of experiences and people, and so be creative. Alternatively, it may restrict one's ability to deal positively with one's environment (1) by encouraging a flight from everyday life into an otherworldly fantasy, (2) by engendering emotional dependence through attachment to or infatuation with a religious leader or group (Jacobs, 1987; Ullman, 1982, 1989), or (3) by imposing rigid and arbitrary conceptualizations on one's experience in the form of dogmatic beliefs and rules for conduct. None of these alternative visions would be creative. As Walter Houston Clark (1958) has suggested, "Religion's influence is paradoxical, for often its role, wrongly directed, may be the exact reverse of creative. Its coercive hand may lie dead and stultifying on many a creative spirit" (p. 415).

Our creativity analogy suggests that not all religious experiences are stultifying; in some cases the new Gestalt is indeed a better one, one that allows the individual to deal more positively and effectively with a wider range of experiences and people. Our analysis also suggests that even among positive religious experiences an important distinction can be made. One may have a reality-transforming religious experience that invites further transformation or one that forecloses it. In the former case, the new reality is recognized as a tentative and transient construction, one that will probably undergo future change. In the latter case, the new reality is perceived as *true* reality. It is assumed that one has been given an insight into the mysteries of life that cannot be improved upon, an insight that has definitively answered one or more existential questions. Although such insight may have dramatically positive effects in infusing life with meaning and direction, it would seem to discourage further religious insight. The rest of one's life becomes a postscript to the insight already attained. Both of these types of religious experience involve new vision and so are creative, but the former opens the door to further religious growth; the latter closes the door.

As this distinction illustrates, understanding religious experience in terms of cognitive restructuring permits a more fine-grained analysis of the types and effects of religious experience than is usually achieved. One is able to get beyond the undifferentiated, global question of whether religious experience is personally destructive (Salzman, 1953) or constructive (Christensen, 1963; Fingarette, 1958) to consider the ways that different types of religious experiences are more or less constructive. Further, more or less constructive experiences are not differentiated in terms of what the individual comes to believe but in terms of the nature of the cognitive restructuring that underlies the experience.

How does one determine the nature of the cognitive restructuring? As William James (1902) paraphrased, "By their fruits you shall know them." That is, we can evaluate the constructiveness of a given religious experience by looking at its effects on the individual's subsequent behavior. Does it provide the individual a greater sense of direction and well-being? Does it allow the individual to deal more positively and effectively with his or her physical and social environment? Is there consistency between the values espoused and actions taken; does the individual practice what he or she preaches?

Of course, to evaluate religious experience in terms of these behavioral consequences is to use a psychological and not a theological criterion. Theologically, one may feel that there are right and wrong answers to existential questions. If so, holding the right beliefs may be considered constructive, even if those beliefs have a negative effect on the person's behavior. Such a criterion may make sense theologically (though even its theological validity may be questioned); it does not make sense psychologically. Following James, we believe that the psychological criterion for evaluation must be the way a given experience fits into and affects the indivdual's ongoing life. Evaluation of religious experience using this criterion will be our concern in Part III of this book.

EMPIRICAL STATUS OF THE PROPOSED ANALYSIS OF RELIGIOUS EXPERIENCE

Before moving on, however, we need to consider the empirical status of our analysis of religious experience. For, although one can never empirically prove the truth of an analogy, empirical evidence is still very relevant. Our four-stage model suggests a number of empirical relationships, and only to the degree that these relationships exist can we have confidence in the model.

Association of New Religious Vision with Existential Crisis

If the creativity analogy is valid, new religious vision should follow an existential crisis. Empirical evidence is generally consistent with this expectation, although the evidence is far from conclusive. Seggar and Kunz (1972) interviewed seventy-seven recent converts to Mormonism in urban Kentucky. Among other questions, each convert was asked to indicate whether he or she had considered one or more existential issues (from a list proposed by Glock & Stark, 1965, pp. 246–250) during the previous five years. All of the converts reported that they had (see also Ullman, 1989).

Unfortunately, there was no comparison to nonconverts in this study. If it were found that nonconverts also reported consideration of these issues, then the implied link between consideration of existential issues and conversion would be less clear. Nor was there any attempt to consider the psychological process involved in the experience of the converts. A person who, for example, "converted" because the Mormon church was closest to his newly bought home was not differentiated from a person who converted as a result of a dramatic, life-changing experience.

Heirich (1977) improved on the Seggar and Kunz design. He interviewed 310 Catholics in the Ann Arbor, Michigan, area. Of these, 152 were members of a "Spirit-baptized" Pentecostal group, and 158 were university students not involved in the Pentecostal group. Heirich found that 83 percent of the Pentecostals reported having experienced some form of personal stress prior to conversion to Pentecostalism; but he also found that 67 percent of the non-Pentecostal students reported experiencing personal stress during the same period. Heirich interpreted his results as suggesting little relationship between prior personal stress and intense religious experience.

On closer examination, however, the meaning of Heirich's results is also unclear. First, as Heirich admitted, his concept of personal stress was probably too broad. In addition, to including existential crises, it included problems with members of one's family, with sex, and any other problem for which the individual sought counseling. It is possible that the Pentecostals experienced more existential crises, whereas the university students experienced other forms of stress. Second, there was again no consideration of the psychological process involved in the religious experience of different individuals, whether in the Pentecostal or non-Pentecostal group. If we are to identify experiences in which a creative religious vision was born, whether of Pentecostals or non-Pentecostals, we need to know more about the experience itself. Similar interpretative problems exist with Marc Galanter's

(1989) evidence that individuals join the Unification Church (Moonies) to gain relief from psychological distress.

Brown, Spilka, and Cassidy (1978) reported a study that explored the relationship between existential crisis and religious experience in a little more depth. They administered an extensive questionnaire to 192 Christians (96 men, 96 women) who reported having had one or more mystical experiences. The questionnaire included twenty-five true-false items concerning the respondent's life before the mystical experience(s), divided into a number of subscales. One of the subscales reflected a sense of existential crisis: *self-dissatisfaction* (sample items on this subscale were: "I liked myself"—false; "I was frequently depressed"—true). The questionnaire also included forty-five items concerning the experience itself, again broken into a number of subscales. Three of these seem to reflect characteristics of personal transformation that we have associated with new religious vision: *unity-completeness* ("Unity with the outside world"—true; "Unity with an inner world within myself"—true); *enlightenment and new knowledge* ("Gain of insightful new knowledge or intuitive illumination"—true); and *sensory stimulation* ("I heard voices which were not from anyone present"—true; "An actual vision of a recognizable religious figure"—true).

Correlations revealed statistically reliable ($p < .05$) relationships between self-dissatisfaction and each of the signs of new religious vision: unity-completeness ($r = .22$), enlightenment and new knowledge ($r = .18$), and sensory stimulation ($r = .31$). These correlations suggest that personal dissatisfaction, which would seem to reflect a sense of existential crisis, is associated with signs of creative illumination in religious experience. But it should be noted, as Brown, Spilka, and Cassidy (1978) were careful to point out, that these correlations are not especially large and, moreover, they are based on respondents' memory of what their life was like before the experience and of what happened during the experience. Snow and Machalek (1983) have emphasized that such memories are refracted through the prism of one's beliefs about the effects of the experience. Thus, although suggestive, these results are by no means conclusive.

Association of New Religious Vision with Potential for Incubation and Illumination

Five studies suggest an association between reality-transforming religious experience and three personality characteristics that have been associated with the incubation and illumination stages of the creative process: constructive use of nonlogical thinking, openness to experience, and hypnotic susceptibility.

Constructive use of primitive, nonlogical thinking. Allison (1968) administered Rorschach inkblot tests to twenty seminary students classed into three groups depending on the nature of their religious experience. Seven of the students reported intense, dramatic, life-changing conversion experiences; seven reported mild conversion experiences that led to only minor, often temporary, change; and six reported no experiences of religious insight. Although the samples were small, Allison found a significant difference in the way the three groups responded to the inkblots. Those having conversion experiences, and especially those having intense, life-changing experiences, gave significantly more responses that appeared to reflect what in psychoanalytic terms is called primitive, nonlogical thinking. Such responses included the use of symbols, imagery, and integration of logically unrelated conceptual categories (e.g., the description of an inkblot as "a lion's egg" because it was the shape of an egg and the color of a lion). More important, in the responses of those who had intense, life-changing conversion experiences, this primitive "regression" appeared to be adaptive because these indiviudals also scored significantly higher on a measure of meaningful integration of primitive, nonlogical thinking.

According to Allison (1968), his findings indicate that stronger, more intense conversion experiences of sudden and dramatic type

> are associated with greater amounts of primitive, nonlogical thought . . . and, particularly significant, that they are also associated with better integration of such ideation. Thus, persons with more intense experiences appear to demonstrate a more pronounced capacity for regressive experiences of an adaptive nature. (p. 458)

Within the psychoanalytic tradition, creativity has often been associated with such "regression in the service of the ego" (see Kris, 1952; Kubie, 1958; Pine & Holt, 1960; Schafer, 1960).

Openness to experience. Creativity has also been associated with "openness to experience"—readiness to allow one's experience to influence one's cognitive structures (cf. Piaget's concept of accommodation). Two studies suggest that openness to experience may be associated with life-changing religious experience as well. Hood (1975) constructed a scale to identify individuals who have had intense mystical experiences involving a sense of ineffability and loss of self into unity with a larger reality. He administered this questionnaire and Taft's (1969) Ego Permissiveness scale to a sample of eighty-three undergraduates in Chattanooga, Tennessee. The Ego Permissiveness scale is designed to measure openness to experience (defined as the ability to use preconscious and unconscious potentialities in the service of the ego). Hood found a highly significant correlation ($r = .75, p < .001$) between scores on the Mysticism and Ego Permissiveness scales, suggesting that individuals who have intense, life-changing mystical experiences are more open to nonlogical aspects of experience.

But as Hood noted, the meaning of this correlation is clouded by the overlap in content between the two scales. Among the five subscales of the Ego Permissiveness scale are ones measuring "peak experiences" and "belief in the supernatural." Items on these subscales are very similar to items on the Mysticism scale. Unfortunately, Hood did not report correlations between his Mysticism scale and each different subscale of the Ego Permissiveness scale. Had he, it would be possible to assess whether the overall correlation reflected anything more than item overlap.

Hoffeldt and Batson (1971) administered Byrne's (1961) Repression-Sensitization scale to twenty individuals, ten who reported having at last one dramatic religious experience involving a vision and ten with similar religious affiliation who reported no such experience. Higher scores on the Repression-Sensitization scale are thought to reflect greater sensitivity and openness to unusual, reality-threatening aspects of experience. Even with these small samples, those reporting religious experiences involving visions scored significantly higher ($p < .005$) on the Repression-Sensitization scale than those not reporting such experiences; indeed, there was no overlap in the distribution of scores for the two groups.

Although these results are consistent with the suggestion that dramtic, life-changing religious experiences are associated with openness to experience, they are still not conclusive. Individuals reporting experiences involving visions probably differ from individuals not reporting such experiences on a number of dimensions, and one or more of the other differences could account for the observed differences in scores on the Repression-Sensitization scale. As we have noted before, the causal pattern underlying a correlation is often unclear.

Hypnotic susceptibility. Hypnotic susceptibility has been found to relate to creativity (Bowers & Bowers, 1972), and in two studies it has been found to relate to life-changing religious experience as well. Gibbons and de Jarnette (1972) gave a questionnaire measure of hypnotic susceptibility (Shor & Orne, 1962) to 185 West Georgia College undergraduates volunteering for hypnosis research. Comparing ten of the high-susceptibility students with thirteen low-susceptibility students (it is not clear from the research report how the students who were compared were selected), all of the high-susceptibility group reported having religious conversion experiences characterized by loss of personal control and dramatic affective, perceptual, cognitive, and behavioral effects. In contrast, only eight of the low-susceptibility group reported conversion experiences, and their reports generally lacked these characteristics.

To illustrate the difference in the reports of the two groups, typical of the high-susceptibility group were the following: "I began to feel a warm tingling glow inside of me. The next thing I knew, I was down in front of the altar, and I was crying." "Everything seemed so different and unreal. . . . It was like I'd been hit by a bolt of lightning." Typical of the low-susceptibility group was a student who reported, "No, I never felt too much emotion about it, but one day I just went forward and accepted the Lord" (Gibbons & de Jarnette, 1972, pp. 154–155). The difference in frequency of reporting conversion experiences between the high- and low-susceptibility groups was of marginal statistical significance ($p < .08$).

Hood (1973) measured hypnotic susceptibility of eighty-one fundamentalist Protestant undergraduates using the same questionnaire used by Gibbons and de Jarnette. He also administered a scale designed to detect dramatic, life-changing religious experiences similar to those presented at the beginning of this chapter. Hood found that the likelihood of having such experiences correlated positively ($r = .36, p < .01$) with greater hypnotic susceptibility. Once again, although not conclusive, the results of these studies are consistent with the view that new religious vision is associated with variables that are also associated with the incubation and illumination stages of the creative process.

Association of New Religious Vision with New Life

In addition to assessing the association of characteristics of religious vision with an antecedent existential crisis, Brown, Spilka, and Cassidy (1978) assessed the association of these characteristics with a subsequent life change. Most relevant for the assumption that new religious vision leads to a new life was the subscale *positive and fundamental change* (sample items on this scale were: "Others have remarked about a positive change in me"—true: "The experience has resolved personal problems in my life"—true). The three characteristics of religious vision that we identified earlier—unity-completeness, enlightenment and new knowledge, and sensory stimulation—all correlated significantly ($p < .05$) with reports of more positive and fundamental change (rs = .30, 32, and .18, respectively). Of course, the problem with this study noted previously applies to these findings as well; the results are based entirely on respondents' self-reports of characteristics of the experience and of their subsequent life. So these results are only suggestive.

Also relying on self-reports, Paloutzian (1981) found that college students who identified themselves as having had a conversion experience scored higher on the Purpose-in-Life test, which asks respondents to rate items such as "I see a reason for why I exist" (Crumbaugh & Maholick, 1969), than did students who did not report having had a conversion experience. Again, these results are suggestive but only suggestive.

Association of Signs of Creative Religious Experience with Cognitive Complexity in the Religious Domain

Batson (1971) reasoned that if the psychological processes involved in religious experience and creativity are similar, individuals whose prior religious experience reflected elements of the stage sequence of creative thought (preparation, incubation, illumination, verification) should have a more complex cognitive organization for dealing with existential issues. To test this reasoning, he developed a measure of complexity of cognitive organization in the religious domain. This measure involved having research participants write brief paragraphs in response to sentence stems designed to evoke thought about existential conflicts ("When someone challenges my religious beliefs . . ."; "When I have to make an ethical decision . . ."). The paragraphs were then scored for cognitive complexity by assessing the presence of alternative ways of viewing the conflict, integrations of these alternatives, and recognition of the relativity of these integrations. The scoring system was modeled after the one developed by Schroder and his associates (Phares & Schroder, 1969; Schroder, Driver, & Streufert, 1967) to evaluate complexity in paragraph completions concerning conflicts in social interaction.

To assess the degree to which religious experience follows the stage sequence of creativity, seventy-six students at Princeton Theological Seminary were asked to write autobiographical statements about their religious experience. Each autobiography was then coded by two independent judges for the degree to which it reflected five characteristics of the creative process. The first three were characteristics of the preparation stage—(1) willingness to admit, tolerate, and even actively seek conflict on existential issues; (2) ability to reflect critically and constructively on one's own earlier religious experiences; and (3) perception of one's religious development as fluid and open to further change rather than fixed and permanent. The last two were characteristics of the verification stage—(4) effect of religious experiences on other areas of the individual's life, including behavior; and (5) increasing interaction with new areas of one's personal and social environment rather than insulation and withdrawal.

Results revealed that for each of these characteristics of the creative process, seminarians whose autobiographies reflected more of the characteristic also displayed significantly more cognitive complexity in their paragraphs written in response to the stems evoking thought about existential conflicts (all $ps < .001$).

These results are quite consistent with our creativity analogy. For, if it is through cognitive restructuring that greater structural complexity emerges, then cognitive complexity should reflect the degree of cognitive restructuring that has occurred. But these results still cannot be considered proof of our analysis of religious experience in terms of creative reality transformation. It is possible that the causal sequence was actually the reverse of that implied. That is, greater complexity may have led some seminarians to report their prior religious development in a way that sounded more creative, instead of their more creative prior development leading to greater complexity in religious thought. As with the other research considered in this section, the evidence is supportive but by no means conclusive.

SUMMARY AND CONCLUSION

To understand dramatic, life-changing religious experiences, we made use of psychological analyses of another type of reality-transforming experience, creativity. It was suggested that in creativity the cognitive structures that the individual uses to think about the world are changed. This cognitive restructuring leads to the creation of a new reality for the individual. Typically, this process of reality transformation involves four stages: *preparation*—unsuccessful attempts to solve the problem by using the old cognitive structures; *incubation*—giving up the attempt to solve the problem; *illumination*—emergence of a new cognitive organization that enables the individual suddenly to see the components of the problem in a new way, permitting solution; and *verification*—testing the functional value of the new solution.

Generalizing from this understanding, we suggested that a similar sequence occurs in many religious experiences, although the problems addressed are not intellectual but personally significant existential questions. The religious experience stage sequence includes *existential crisis, self-surrender, new vision,* and *new life.* Moreover, just as it is possible to identify more or less creative changes in the cognitive structures in response to intellectual problems, it seems possible to identify more or less creative changes in the cognitive structures in response to existential problems. Relatively uncreative religious experiences involve rigid adherence to a specific solution that emphasizes only one aspect of the problem while ignoring others (e.g., solving the problem of death by believing that one is going to live forever because one has mouthed certain phrases); in contrast, relatively creative experiences involve a higher-level integration that takes account of various aspects of the problem and resists simplified, absolutistic solutions. The psychological consequences of these different types of experiences will be explored in some detail in Chapters 6 through 10.

Finally, we considered empirical research bearing on the appropriateness of using a creativity analogy to understand the psychological processes underlying religious experience. Although most of the research suffers from one or more methodological weaknesses, results were supportive. Factors that the creativity analogy suggested should precede and follow a creative religious experience generally did seem to. Moreover, several variables that relate to creativity—constructive use of nonlogical thinking, openness to experience, and hypnotic susceptibility—also relate to life-changing religious experience. The research to date by no means proves the validity of our understanding (indeed, it is not clear that empirical research ever could), but it is encouraging.

We have proposed a model of what happens psychologically during dramatic, reality-transforming religious experiences. But even for the individual who has one or more of these experiences, they are usually not an everyday occurrence. Trips to the mountaintop are rare. In the next chapter we shall look at a number of techniques that have been employed to facilitate such trips. The techniques run the gamut from evangelical preaching to psychedelic drugs.

5

Facilitators of Religious Experience

At the first sign of an existential crisis, most of us quickly mobilize our defenses. We increase the tempo of our life, throw ourselves into our work, seek new friends, or try to "get away from away it all" through travel, relaxation, and retreat. We do whatever we can to escape those whispering doubts:

> What will be the outcome of what I do today? Of what I shall do tomorrow? What will be the outcome of all my life? Why should I live? Why should I do anything? Is there in life any purpose which the inevitable death which awaits me does not undo and destroy? (Tolstoy, 1904, p. 21).

Our reluctance to face existential questions is easy to understand; they can quickly bring us, like Tolstoy, to the brink of total despair over the "meaningless absurdity of life." Our present reality may no longer make sense, but there is no guarantee that a new, more meaningful one lies ahead. What confronts us instead is the vast abyss of meaningless and the terrifying possibility of plunging into deep depression, if not psychosis. And even if we hold out hope of emerging safe on the other side, who will be there to greet us? Will our family and friends? Perhaps there will be no room for them in the "new heaven and new earth." Naturally, we shrink back from the abyss in fear.

Recognizing the ambivalence between our desire for a new reality and our terror of losing the old, most religious traditions seek to smooth the path to religious insight. They do this by providing a facilitative physical and social environment in the form of worship services, rites and rituals, holy writings, preaching, and teaching. Some traditions encourage meditation and fasting, and some even use alcohol or psychedelic drugs.

In this chapter we shall consider how four of these facilitative techniques—psychedelic drugs, meditation, religious language, and music—may stimulate religious experience of the sort discussed in Chapter 4. Consistent with the interactionist perspective proposed at the end of Chapter 2, our goal will be to understand as precisely as possible how each potential facilitator contributes to an environment that affects the intrapsychic process of creative religious transformation. Although we shall limit our discussion to drugs, meditation, language, and music, we believe that our strategy of considering the way that potential facilitators affect one or more stages of the creative process provides a theoretical framework for understanding the psychological significance of facilitative techniques in general; our discussion of these four is intended to be illustrative.

We shall begin by considering psychedelic drugs, for two reasons. First, these drugs have powerful and dramatic effects. So, once again adopting William James's (1902) principle that extreme cases reveal more clearly the psychological processes also present in other cases, we may hope to learn from looking at drug experiences how other less extreme facilitative techniques might affect religious transformation. Second, there is more and better empirical research on the effects of psychedelic drugs than any other technique. This may seem surprising because research on these drugs has been legally restricted since 1966, but it is true. Although research on the religious impact of psychedelic drugs is neither plentiful nor conclusive, it is more plentiful and conclusive than research on the effects of more commonly employed facilitative techniques, such as meditation, religious language, or music.

PSYCHEDELIC DRUGS

You may think that accounts of religious experience under the influence of psychedelic drugs were part of a fad that burst on the scene in the 1960s and quickly fizzled. Not so; psychedelic drugs like peyote cactus, psilocybin mushrooms, and marijuana have been used to stimulate religious experience since the dawn of history (Wasson, 1968). Of course, you may well ask whether drug experiences are truly religious or only cheap imitations. To help you decide, try the following exercise devised by philosopher Huston Smith (1964). See if you can correctly identify which of the following experiences was drug-induced and which was the experience of a famous religious mystic.

> Suddenly I burst into a vast, new, indescribably wonderful universe. Although I am writing this over a year later, the thrill of the surprise and amazement, the awesomeness of the revelation, the engulfment in an overwhelming feeling-wave of gratitude and blessed wonderment, are as fresh, and the memory of the experience is as vivid, as if it had happened five minutes ago. And yet to concoct anything by way of description that would even hint at the magnitude, the sense of ultimate reality . . . this seems such an impossible task. The knowledge which has infused and affected every aspect of my life came instantaneously and with such complete force of certainty that it was impossible, then or since, to doubt its validity.

> All at once, without warning of any kind, I found myself wrapped in a flame-colored cloud. For an instant I thought of fire . . . the next, I knew that the fire was within myself. Directly afterward there came upon me a sense of exultation, of immense joyousness accompanied or immediately followed by an intellectual illumination impossible to describe. Among other things, I did not merely come to believe, but I saw that the universe is not composed of dead matter, but is, on the contrary, a living Presence; I became conscious in myself of eternal life . . . I saw that all men are immortal; that the cosmic order is such that without any preadventure all things work together for the good of each and all; that the foundation principle of the world . . . is what we call love, and that the happiness of each and all is in the long run absolutely certain. (Smith, 1964, p. 522)

Among Smith's sample of sixty-nine Princeton University students, only one-third were able correctly to identify the first as the drug-induced experience.

But even if psychedelic drugs can produce experiences that are hard to distinguish from profound religious experiences, does the similarity go beyond surface appearance? Many scholars, even many who were initially skeptical, believe that it does. Here, for example, is the testimony of former Episcopal priest Allan Watts:

> When I was first invited to test the mystical qualities of LSD-25 by Dr. Keith Ditman of the Neuropsychiatric Clinic at UCLA Medical School, I was unwilling to believe that any mere chemical could induce a genuine mystical experience. At most, it might bring about a state of spiritual insight analogous to swimming with water wings. Indeed, my first experiment with LSD-25 was not mystical. It was an intensely interesting aesthetic and intellectual experience that challenged my powers of analysis and careful description to the utmost.
>
> Some months later, in 1959, I tried LSD-25 again with Drs. Sterling Bunnell and Michael Agron, who were then associated with the Langley-Porter Clinic, in San Francisco. In the course of two experiments I was amazed and somewhat embarrassed to find myself going through states of consciousness

> that corresponded precisely with every description of major mystical experiences that I had ever read. Furthermore, they exceeded both in depth and in a peculiar quality of unexpectedness the three "natural and spontaneous" experiences of this kind that had happened to me in previous years.
>
> Through subsequent experimentation with LSD-25 and the other chemicals . . . , I found I could move with ease into the state of "cosmic consciousness," and in due course became less and less dependent on the chemicals themselves for "tuning in" to this particular wavelength of experience. Of the five psychedelics tried, I found that LSD-25 and cannabis [marijuana] suited my purposes best. Of these two, the latter—cannabis—which I had to use abroad in countries where it is not outlawed, proved to be the better. It does not induce bizarre alterations of sensory perception, and medical studies indicate that it may not, save in great excess, have the dangerous side effects of LSD. (Watts, 1968, pp. 75–76)

Walter Houston Clark, a well-known scholar in the field of psychology of religion, also attests to the religious significance of psychedelic drugs.

> Most of what I have learned about religion at first hand I have learned from my encounter with the psychedelics. I speak advisedly, deliberately and thoughtfully. As a scholar, I have learned at least as much, though not more, from my six "trips" as I have from all the plodding study in my field of the psychology of religion. . . .
>
> "Except a man be born again he cannot see the kindgom of God," said Jesus to the bewildered Nicodemus. This is exactly what some favored spirits have reported through the drugs. They have found their lives by losing them. It is for these reasons that neither scholarship nor religious study, neither the university nor the church, nor the scientist, nor the artist, the educator, the prophet, nor the mystic can neglect informing himself of the opportunities for personal growth available through chemical ecstasy. (1969, pp. 155–156)

LSD and marijuana were not available to William James, but other psychedelic drugs were. And he too was impressed with their religious significance. Based in part on his own experience with nitrous oxide, James concluded that these drugs provided a window on new forms of consciousness: "Normal waking consciousness, rational consciousness as we call it, is but one special type of consciousness, whilst all about it, parted from it by the filmiest of screens, there lie potential forms of consciousness entirely different" (1902, p. 298). James believed that drugs can reveal these other forms of consciousness, and because they can, they have important, if somewhat mercurial and mysterious, implications for religious experience.

> Nitrous oxide and ether, especially nitrous oxide, when sufficiently diluted with air, stimulate the mystical consciousness in an extraordinary degree. Depth beyond depth of truth seems revealed to the inhaler. This truth fades out, however, or escapes, at the moment of coming to; and if any words remain over in which it seemed to clothe itself, they prove to be the veriest nonsense. Nevertheless, the sense of a profound meaning having been there persists; and I know more than one person who is persuaded that in the nitrous oxide trance we have a genuine metaphysical revelation. . . .

> Looking back on my own experiences, they all converge towards a kind of insight to which I cannot help ascribing some metaphysical significance. The keynote of it is invariably a reconciliation. It is as if the opposites of the world, whose contradictoriness and conflict make all our difficulties and troubles, were melted into unity. Not only do they, as contrasted species, belong to one and the same genus, but *one of the species,* the nobler and better one, *is itself the genus, and so soaks up and absorbs its opposite into itself.* This is a dark saying, I know, when thus expressed in terms of common logic, but I cannot wholly escape from its authority (James, 1902, p. 298, italics in original)

Not all scholars have been impressed with the religious implications of psychedelic drugs. Perhaps the best-known critic was Oxford professor R. C. Zaehner (1957), an expert on mysticism. He tried psychedelic drugs (mescaline) and came away convinced that the drug experience was but a pale shadow of true religious experience.

Given the controversy surrounding discussion of the religious potential of psychedelic drugs, it seems clear that we need to resist rushing either to jump on the bandwagon or to cast the first stone. Instead, we need to weigh the empirical evidence, both pro and con, with care. Relying on the analogy developed in Chapter 4 between creativity and religious experience, we shall first consider how psychedelics might facilitate creative religious experience. Then we shall turn to the empirical evidence to find out whether they do.

Some Speculation on How Drugs Might Facilitate Religious Experience

To begin our analysis, let us ask how the physiological and psychological effects of psychedelic drugs might be expected to relate to the stages of the creative process outlined in Chapter 4. In *The Doors of Perception* (1954), Aldous Huxley suggested three consequences of psychedelic drugs, each of which might facilitate creativity.

1. Ability to remember and to "think straight" is little if at all impaired.

2. Visual impressions are greatly intensified. "The eye recovers some of the perceptual innocence of childhood, when the sensum was not immediately and automatically subordinated to the concept" (p. 25).

3. The will suffers a profound change for the worse. The individual has no reason to do anything and finds most causes for which he might ordinarily act and suffer, profoundly uninteresting.

To this list we may add two more consequences noted by Harman and Fadiman (1970):

4. Increased access to memories, including preconscious and unconscious material.

5. More fluent free association, imagery, fantasy, and symbolic thought. Increased ability to play spontaneously with hypotheses, metaphors, paradoxes, transformations, and relationships.

Finally, in a summary statement of his research into the effect on creativity of one psychedelic drug, psilocybin, Frank Barron (1963) comments: "What psilocybin does is dissolve many definitions and melt many boundaries. . . ."

These observations suggest that psychedelic drugs have implications for two stages of the creative process: incubation and illumination. Under the influence of the drug, the grip of the present reality is loosened; the power of social norms, values, and habitual ways of thinking is weakened. This first change would seem to encourage incubation, the stage in which one gives up the attempt to solve the problem using the old cognitive structures. This change may even reflect a temporary weakening of left-hemisphere dominance in the brain (see Ornstein, 1972).

At the same time, psychedelic drugs intensify mental associations, imagery, and symbolic thought; the mind is alive with new combinations of sensations, ideas, and memories. This second change would seem to encourage illumination, the stage in which a solution emerges from a new cognitive organization, because within these new combinations is the potential for seeing oneself and one's world differently. This change may reflect a stimulation of right-hemisphere activity.[1]

1. The empirical evidence on psychedelics and creativity is generally consistent with these suggestions. Perhaps the most readily available source of evidence is the report of drug use by the creative vanguard of society—by writers, artists, and musicians. The list of creative people who have used drugs includes such well-known names as Samuel Taylor Coleridge, Aldous Huxley, Arthur Rimbaud, and the Beatles. Of course, even though it is known that these and many other creative people have used drugs, it is not necessarily true that they were more creative as a result. It may even be that they were creative in spite of the drugs.

Somewhat clearer evidence comes from a systematic survey by Stanley Krippner (1967). Krippner interviewed ninety-one artists who were reputed to have had one or more psychedelic experiences. His subjects included an award-winning film maker, a Guggenheim Fellow in poetry, and a recipient of Ford, Fulbright, and Rockefeller Study grants in painting. A heavy majority (91 percent) found their drug experiences pleasant and 81 percent considered themselves to be "psychedelic artists"; that is, they believed that psychedelic drugs contributed significantly and positively to their work.

Krippner's evidence has two major weaknesses. First, at best it reveals a correlation between psychedelic drug use and creativity; it does not demonstrate a causal link. Second and of even greater concern, his evidence is entirely dependent on self-reports.

Two studies using more objective measures provide clearer, if more complex, evidence. In the first, McGlothlin, Cohen, & McGlothlin (1967) examined the effects of LSD on creativity in seventy-two graduate students. Each student participated in three drug sessions, with two weeks between sessions. The students were divided into three groups. Those in the experimental group received a large dose of LSD (200 micrograms—about twice the normal clinical dosage) per session. Those in a second group received 25 micrograms of LSD per session, not enough to produce psychedelic effects. The third group received 20 milligrams of an amphetamine per session. The last two groups were control groups; they were not expected to show enhanced creativity as a result of their drug experience. The experimental group was. To assess changes in creativity, a number of paper-and-pencil tests designed to measure divergent think-

Building on these suggestions and on the analogy between creativity and religious experience developed in Chapter 4, we would speculate that psychedelic drugs can facilitate the self-surrender (incubation) and new vision (illumination) stages of creative religious experience. We would also speculate that drugs cannot produce such an experience if there has been no prior preparation; they can facilitate religious transformation only if the individual has already reached the point of existential crisis. How do these speculations stack up against the empirical evidence?

Empirical Evidence that Psychedelic Drugs Facilitate Religious Experience

Evidence from self-reports. It is not difficult to collect dramatic self-reports that psychedelics evoke religious experience. We presented several at the beginning of this chapter, and it is easy to add to the collection. In 1964 Timothy Leary reported research in which he and his associates gave psychedelics (typically LSD or psilocybin) to over one thousand persons, including sixty-nine religious professionals. He found that more than 75

---

ing were administered approximately one week before the first drug session and two weeks and six months after the final session.

Many students in the experimental group reported at the six-month follow-up that the drug experience had increased their creativity. But test results for students in this group showed no increase; in fact, there were no clear changes in test scores for members of any of the three groups. As a further check for possible effects, McGlothlin et al. looked at the test scores for only those students in the experimental group who reported enhanced creativity, but again no increase was found. Thus, despite these students' subjective impressions, the objective tests provided no evidence that the drug experience had made them more creative.

There is however, some reason to doubt the appropriateness of the creativity tests used in this study. Frank Barron (1969) states the problem succinctly:

> The tests are certainly very useful . . .; however, they are not the instruments of choice for observing creative problem solving in which a high-level integral act of intellect is called for. Moreover, they put a premium upon speed of response and leave no room for the incubation process or for the sort of mental state we call reverie (musing, meditation, contemplation, "brown study"). In fact, they call for precisely the sorts of behavior that we would not expect a psychedelic drug to affect to any great extent. (p. 156)

Because of this measurement problem, Barron questions the significance of the McGlothlin et al. finding that the drug experience did not enhance creativity. We are inclined to agree with Barron, especially in light of the results of a second study.

Harman and Fadiman (1970) had twenty-seven professional men (engineers, mathematicians, architects, management personnel, etc.) work on job-related problems under the influence of a psychedelic drug, mescaline (200 milligrams). Nineteen of the men had had no previous experience with psychedelics. The problems that each man worked on were ones that he brought with him to the session, problems that he was currently trying to solve in his work.

As in the McGlothlin et al. study, the drug experience produced self-reports of enhanced creativity; the men reported reduced inhibition, increased capacity to restructure problems in a larger context, enhanced fluency and flexibility of ideation, heightened capacity for visual imagery and fantasy, association of dissimilar ideas, heightened motivation to obtain closure, and easier visualization of the completed solution. But unlike the previous study, in this study the drug experience appeared to produce objectively measureable consequences as well. While under the influence of the drug, the twenty-seven men attempted to solve forty-four problems.

percent of these religious professionals described "intense mystico-religious responses, and considerably more than half claim[ed] that they had the deepest spiritual experience of their life" (p. 325). Of course, one might speculate that these religious leaders reported religious experiences simply because they were used to thinking in religious terms; that is, they had a religous *set*.

In addition to set, a religious *setting* might also be expected to affect self-reports. Two studies summarized by Masters and Houston (1966) demonstrate a setting effect. Savage, Harman, Fadiman, and Savage (1963) administered LSD to ninety-six people in a supportive setting that included a number of religious stimuli. Of these people, 85 percent reported that the experience was the greatest thing that ever happened to them; 83 percent called it a religious experience; and 90 percent reported greater awareness of God, a Higher Power, or Ultimate Reality. In contrast, Ditman, Hayman, and Whittlesay (1962) administered LSD to seventy-four people in a supportive setting without religious stimuli. Of these people, a much smaller percentage said that the experience was the greatest ever (49 percent), religious (32 percent), and produced greater awareness of God, a Higher Power, or Ultimate Reality (40 percent). Still, even in this second study, the

---

They were able to solve or make substantial progress on thirty-nine. Moreover, the solutions were typically judged by people knowledgeable in the area to be highly creative and satisfactory by practical standards. The usefulness and validity of the solutions are reflected in the following statement written by one of the men several months after the session.

> In the area of ionospheric source location and layer tilt analysis, I was able in the weeks following the session to build on the ideas generated to the extent of working out the mathematics of the schemes proposed, and of making them more definite. The steps made in the session were the correct ones to start with . . . the ideas considered and developed in the session appear as important steps, and the period of the session as the single most productive period of work on this problem I have had in the several months either preceding or following the session. (Harman & Fadiman, 1970, pp. 253–254)

Harman and Fadiman report that this statement was typical of the follow-up statements they received.

Although at first glance the results of this study and of the McGlothlin et al. study would seem to conflict, a closer look suggests that they do not. Indeed, a careful look at the differences between the two studies proves most instructive. It suggests both the potential and the limitations of psychedelics in enhancing creativity. First, in the McGlothlin et al. study, creativity was not assessed during the drug experience, only before and after it; in the Harman and Fadiman study participants sought to solve problems while under the influence of the drug. The different results suggest that drugs can enhance creativity only while they are in effect; they cannot produce more creative persons. Second, the measure of creativity differed in the two studies. McGlothlin et al. used a paper-and-pencil measure of divergent thinking; Harman and Fadiman used more complex real-world problems. Again the different results suggest that drugs do not enhance all forms of thinking, only the cognitive reorganization that we have associated with the creative process. Third, McGlothlin et al.'s students had not been working on the test problems over a period of time, whereas Harman and Fadiman's subjects were professionals who had already been working on the problems that they brought to the session, often for several weeks or months. In terms of the stage model of creativity presented in Chapter 4, Harman and Fadiman's subjects had gone through the preparation stage of unsuccessfully beating their heads against the problem; McGlothlin et al.'s subjects had not. Overall, these results seem quite consistent with the suggestion that psychedelics affect the second and the third stages of the creative process, incubation and illumination.

percentage of people reporting a profound religious experience is far from small.

The tendency to report religious significance in drug experiences even in the absence of a clear religious set or setting is further reflected in a study by Janiger and McGlothlin (also reported in Masters & Houston, 1966). They adminsitered LSD to 194 people. On a self-report questionnaire completed ten months after the session, 24 percent considered the experience religious; 35 percent reported an increased interest in morals and ethics; and 48 percent an increased interest in the meaning of life. Seventy-five percent thought that LSD should be used to help people become aware of themselves; 58 percent to gain meaning in life; and 42 percent to get people to understand each other.

Clearly, a substantial proportion of those who have taken psychedelic drugs report religious experiences. The presence of a religious set or setting may increase the frequency, but the reports do not seem to be attributable to set or setting factors alone. Still, these self-reports must be regarded with caution. Although self-reports are an important source of information about the subjective meaning of drug experiences, they cannot be taken at face value. Self-reports are very subject to self-deception. And with drugs, self-deception can be a major problem. This point deserves some elaboration.

Danger of self-deception in psychedelic self-reports. Psychedelic experiences are typically very different from anything the person has experienced before. In trying to make sense of this new and ambiguous experience, there is a strong tendency to create a meaningful theme around which one's perceptions are assimilated, with consequent leveling and sharpening of details (see Asch, 1952). As a result, the drug experience is likely to be perceived in line with expectations. If one has heard that a particular drug will induce creativity or religious insight, the drug experience is more likely to be perceived in this light. Yet the meaning that one subjectively assigns can differ radically from what others observe. An example illustrates this point.

Carlos Castaneda was a graduate student in anthropology at UCLA when he placed himself under the tutelage of an old Yaqui Indian, don Juan. In his popular book *The Teachings of Don Juan: A Yaqui Way of Knowledge* (1968), Castaneda described the experience of taking the psychedelic drug peyote for the first time. The incident occurred one night at a secluded cabin; don Juan and five other Indians were present. Only Carlos ingested the drug. Here is his self-report of some of what he experienced.

> I saw the juncture of the porch floor and the wall. I turned my head slowly to the right, following the wall, and saw don Juan sitting against it. I shifted my head to the left in order to focus on the water. [A saucepan of water had been brought because Carlos was thirsty.] I found the bottom of the pan; I raised my head slightly and saw a medium-sized black dog approaching. I saw him coming toward the water. The dog began to drink. I raised my hand to push him away from the water; I focused my pinpoint vision on the dog to

> carry on the movement, and suddenly I saw him become transparent. The water was a shiny, viscous liquid. I saw it going down the dog's throat into his body. I saw it floating evenly through his entire length and then shooting out through each one of the hairs. I saw the iridescent fluid traveling along the length of each individual hair and then projecting out of the hairs to form a long, white, silky mane. . . .
>
> I turned around to look for don Juan, but I could not distinguish anything or anyone. All I was capable of seeing was the dog becoming iridescent; an intense light radiated from his body. I saw again the water flowing through him, kindling him like a bonfire. I got to the water, sank my face in the pan, and drank with him. My hands were in front of me on the ground and, as I drank, I saw the fluid running through my veins setting up hues of red and yellow and green. I drank more and more. I drank until I was all afire; I was all aglow. I drank until the fluid went out of my body through each pore, and projected out like fibers of silk, and I too acquired a long, lustrous, iridescent mane. I looked at the dog and his mane was like mine. A supreme happiness filled my body, and we ran together toward a sort of yellow warmth that came from some indefinite place. And there we played. We played and wrestled until I knew his wishes and he knew mine. We took turns manipulating each other in the fashion of a puppet show. I could make him move his legs by twisting my toes, and every time he nodded his head I felt an irresistible impulse to jump. But his most impish act was to make me scratch my head with my foot while I sat; he did it by flapping his ears from side to side. This action was to me utterly, unbearably funny. Such a touch of grace and irony; such mastery, I thought. The euphoria that possessed me was indescribable. I laughed until it was almost impossible to breathe. (pp. 24–25)

This was Carlos's self-report. But as a budding social scientist he went back the next day to check his subjective impression by asking the others who were present what they saw. He found that their report differed dramatically from his. John, the owner of the cabin, provided the following account of the events described above:

> Don Juan brought you more water. You sat quietly in front of the pan. Then you jumped up and took off all of your clothes. You were kneeling in front of the water, drinking in big gulps. Then you just sat there and stared into space. We thought you were going to be there forever. Nearly everybody was asleep, including don Juan, when suddenly you jumped up again, howling, and took after the dog. The dog got scared and howled too, and ran to the back of the house. Then everybody woke up. . . .
>
> The dog was running ahead of you barking and howling. I think you must have gone twenty times around the house, running in circles, barking like a dog. I was afraid people were going to be curious. There are no neighbors close, but your howling was so loud it could have been heard for miles. (p. 28)

After a little encouragement, John shed additional light on the running and playing with the dog:

> You don't think the dog was running because he was afraid of you, do you? The dog was running because you were pissing on him. . . . My dog got even though; he pissed on you too! (p. 29)

Clearly, there was a radical difference between the subjective experience ("I drank until the fluid went out of my body through each pore"; "We ran together toward a sort of yellow warmth") and what happened objectively. Clearly too, although it is important to gather self-reports about psychedelic experiences, it is necessary to gather more objective evidence as well. Therefore, let us turn to three research programs that have provided more objective evidence that psychedelics can facilitate religious experience, at least for some people.

LSD and mystical states: Masters and Houston. Masters and Houston (1966) reported an extensive research project in which they administered LSD to 206 people in a variety of settings. Although 96 percent reported some form of religious imagery, most of the imagery was experienced without accompanying religious emotion. This led Masters and Houston to conclude that the imagery did not establish or portend the presence of religious or mystical states of consciousness. Building on the classic views of Carl Jung (1964) and W. T. Stace (1960), Masters and Houston defined religious or mystical states in terms of three criteria: encounter with some Other; transformation of self; and progression through sensory, recollective, analytic, and symbolic levels to an integral level of thought. They believed that of their 206 people, only 6 experienced a religious or mystical state by this definition. All 6 of these had previously actively sought mystical experience through meditation or spiritual discipline, or had for many years been interested in integral states of consciousness. Moreover, according to Masters and Houston, all 6 were of superior intelligence, at least 40 years old, and had well-adjusted, creative personalities. This description suggests that these 6 may have been unique in that before the drug session they had completed the necessary preparation for a creative religious experience.

Psychedelic therapy for the terminally ill: The Spring Grove project. Starting in 1963, a group of psychiatrists, psychologists, and social workers at the Research Unit of Spring Grove State Hospital (now the Maryland Psychiatric Research Center) began studying LSD-assisted psychotherapy with alcoholic and neurotic patients. They found this form of therapy especially effective in treating depression and anxiety. In 1965 a member of the research team, Gloria, developed breast cancer, and the staff decided to try to extend the LSD therapy to deal with the depression and anxiety associated with her terminal illness. Knowing that she was soon to die precipitated an existential crisis for Gloria; she was in great distress and despair. It was hoped that LSD therapy would relieve her distress.

After a week of preparatory discussion, Gloria was given 200 micrograms of LSD under the guidance of Dr. Sidney Wolf. Here is part of her retrospective report of the drug experience:

> Mainly I remember two experiences. I was alone in a timeless world with no boundaries. There was no atmosphere; there was no color, no imagery, but there may have been light. Suddenly I recognized that I was a moment in

> time, created by those before me and in turn the creator of others. This was my moment, and my major function had been completed. By being born, I had given meaning to my parents' existence.
>
> Again in the void, alone without the time-space boundaries. Life reduced itself over and over again to the least common denominator. I cannot remember the logic of the experience, but I became poignantly aware that the core of life is love. At this moment I felt that I was reaching out to the world—to all people—but especially to those closest to me. I wept long for the wasted years, the search for identity in false places, the neglected opportunities, the emotional energy lost in basically meaningless pursuits. (Grof & Halifax, 1977, p. 23)

Gloria's insights put her life in a broader, timeless perspective and identified the core of life as love, but they were not linked to any religious tradition. Still, by our definition of religion—whatever one does to deal with existential questions (Chapter 1)—these insights would seem to be profoundly religious. And by Gloria's report they had a profoundly positive effect on the rest of her life.

> All noticed a change in me. I was radiant, and I seemed at peace, they said. I felt that way too. What has changed for me? I am living now, and being. I can take it as it comes. Some of my physical symptoms are gone. The excessive fatigue, some of the pains. I still get irritated occasionally and yell. I am still me, but more at peace. My family senses this and we are closer. (Grof & Halifax, 1977, pp. 23–24)

Five weeks after the drug experience, Gloria quietly died.

Encouraged by Gloria's experience, the Spring Grove staff decided to explore further the potential of psychedelic therapy for those facing death. This exploration took the form of a pilot study under the direction of Walter Pahnke. Pahnke and others (Pahnke, Kurland, Unger, Savage, Wolf, & Goodman, 1970) administered LSD (usually 200 micrograms) to five more terminal cancer patients. Treatment consisted of from one to four drug sessions. Although this therapy program was not explicitly concerned with religious experience, and measures of religion were not taken, it seems safe to assume that these patients, like Gloria, were deeply involved in an existential crisis; they too were face-to-face with their own death.

Two measures were taken to assess each patient's improvement. First, the amount of pain killing narcotics required was recorded before and after treatment. Second, ratings of change in the patient's depression, sense of isolation, anxiety, fear of death, and preoccupation with pain and physical suffering were made by the attending physicians, nurses, family, and therapist. Ratings from all these people were averaged to form a global index of psychological improvement.

All five patients were taking narcotics before the LSD therapy; four showed dramatic reductions in the amount of medication needed. And for all five, ratings on the global index indicated improvement; for three, the improvement was at or above a moderate level. The sicker and more nearly terminal patients showed the least benefit, but even they experienced less worry about the future and increased enjoyment of their remaining time.

Grof and Halifax (1977) summarized results of LSD therapy for thirty-one terminal cancer patients in the Spring Grove project (presumably including the six just mentioned). They reported that of the thirty-one, nine showed "dramatic improvement" (an increase of four or more points on the thirteen-point global index); thirteen showed "moderate improvement" (an increase of two to four points); and nine were "essentially unchanged" (an increase of less than two points).

Grof and Halifax (1977) also briefly described a study of DPT therapy that involved forty-five terminal cancer patients. DPT is a psychedelic drug having shorter-term effects than LSD. In addition to measures of therapeutic effects, a measure was taken of the degree to which each patient's drug experience could be classified as mystical (defined in terms of unity, transcendence of time and space, objectivity and reality, feelings of sacredness, deeply felt positive mood, and ineffability). Therapeutic results were reported to be better for those patients whose drug experience was classified as mystical.

Summarizing the overall implications of the Spring Grove project, Grof and Halifax conclude:

> The changes that occur in cancer patients following psychedelic therapy are extremely varied, complex, and multidimensional. Some of them are of a familiar nature, such as alleviation of depression, tension, anxiety, sleep disturbance, and psychological withdrawal. Others involve phenomena that are quite new in Western psychiatry and psychology; especially specific changes in basic life philosophy, spiritual orientation, and the hierarchy of values. (1977, p. 36)

For many of these terminally ill cancer patients, the drugs seem to have facilitated significant, creative religious experiences.

The Miracle at Marsh Chapel experiment: Pahnke. The best-known study of the relationship between psychedelic drugs and religious experience is sometimes called the Miracle at Marsh Chapel experiment. It was conducted by Walter Pahnke (1964) as his Ph.D. dissertation research at Harvard. Pahnke set out to test the hypothesis that a psychedelic drug, psilocybin, can facilitate religious or mystical experience. He defined mystical experience in terms of W. T. Stace's (1960) seven categories: unity, transcendence of time and space, deeply felt positive mood, a sense of sacredness, personally authoritative insight, paradoxicality, and alleged ineffability. To Stace's categories, Pahnke added two of his own: an experience of limited duration and a persistent positive change in attitude and behavior.

Twenty Protestant first-year theology students participated in Pahnke's experiment. All were screened in advance for potential psychological or physical problems, and none had any preivous experience with psychedelic drugs. During the experiment, half of the students were given 30 milligrams of psilocybin, a moderately large dosage. The others were given 200 milligrams of nicotinic acid, enough nicotine to produce a tingling sensation but, of course, no psychedelic effects. A double-blind procedure was used; neither the experimental guides nor the students were told who received which substance until after the experiment was over.

The drugs were administered on Good Friday evening. After allowing time for the drugs to take effect, the twenty students were escorted to a private chapel, where they listened over loudspeakers to a two-and-one-half hour religious service that was in progress in another part of the building. The service included organ music, four solos, readings, prayers, and personal meditation. This environment was chosen as one "most conducive to a mystical experience" (Pahnke, 1966, p. 301).

A number of measures were taken in an effort to determine the nature of the students' experiences. First, immediately after the service, tape recordings were made of individual reactions to the session, as well as of a group discussion. Second, each student wrote an account of his experience as soon as was convenient. Third, within a week, all students completed a 147-item questionnaire about the experience; the questionnaire was designed to detect each of the nine categories of mysticism. Fourth, an extensive tape-recorded interview followed the questionnaire. Finally, six months after the Good Friday service, the students were interviewed again and were given a follow-up questionnaire designed to assess positive and negative attitudinal and behavioral changes resulting from the experience.

Based on the questionnaire responses and independent judges' ratings of the tape recordings, each student was classified as either having or not having experienced each of the categories of mysticism. The percentage of those students receiving psilocybin and those students receiving nicotine who were so classed are presented in Table 5.1. As can be seen from the table, more students receiving psilocybin were classified as having experienced each category of mysticism. Nine of the ten who received psilocybin

Table 5.1 Percentage of experiences classed as mystical of students receiving psilocybin versus nicotine

Mystical category	Students receiving psilocybin (percent)	Students receiving nicotine (percent)	$p<$
Unity	62	7	.001
Transcendence	84	6	.001
Positive mood	57	23	.02
Sacredness	53	28	.02
Personally authoritative insight	63	18	.02
Paradoxicality	61	13	.001
Alleged ineffability	66	18	.001
Limited duration	79	8	.001
Persistent positive change	51	8	.001

Source: Adapted from Pahnke (1966).

were classed as showing unmistakable evidence of at least one of the criteria of mystical consciousness. The tenth reported later that he "wished to demonstrate that no religious experience could result from ingesting drugs" and that he had purposely made no religious preparation for the session. Only one of the ten who received nicotine was classed as having a clear mystical experience, and it was judged to be of mild intensity.

Based on these results Pahnke concluded that "those subjects who received psilocybin experienced phenomena which were indistinguishable from, if not identical with . . . the categories defined by our typology of mysticism" (Pahnke, 1964). "The experience . . . motivated them to appreciate more deeply the meaning of their lives, to gain more depth and authenticity in ordinary living, and to rethink their philosophies of life and values. . . . The results of our experiment would indicate that psilocybin (and LSD and mescaline, by analogy) are important tools for the study of the mystical state of consciousness" (Pahnke, 1966, pp. 307–308).

We consider this to be an important and suggestive experiment, but we do not believe the results are as conclusive as Pahnke claimed. Our reservations are based on two concerns. First, although many measures were taken, the only dimension on which these measures varied was the presence or absence of mysticism. As a result, the students and judges may have been forced to describe the psychedelic experience as mystical. Think how this might happen. It is clear that psychedelic drugs produce extremely unusual and intense experiences; production of such experiences is the defining feature of these drugs. So, if a person were presented with only two categories, mystical and ordinary, he or she would probably place a psychedelic experience in the mystical category, if only to reflect its unusualness and intensity. Had nonmystical but still "wholly other," "far out" categories been available, they might have been used instead of the mystical ones to describe the experience.

Our second concern is whether the students and guides in this experiment were really unaware who received psilocybin and who received nicotine. They may have been unaware at first, but after the drugs began to take effect, it seems doubtful that they remained unaware long. And if they became aware, they may have either intentionally or unintentionally influenced the results of the study in order to support their own or the experimenter's hypothesis that psychedelics can enhance mystical consciousness.

Timothy Leary was a guide in this experiment, and his description of an episode that occurred shortly after the students took the drugs suggests that everyone soon knew who had which drug.

> I looked up and saw that two students had flushed faces. They were squirming with pleased expressions. One of them winked at the other. He rose and said he was going to the toilet. The other red-faced student joined him. As guide, I trailed along. Inside the john they were exulting like happy conspirators. We must have got the mushroom. Yeah, I can feel it. We're the lucky ones. I smiled and kidded them about playing the placebo game. While we

stood there the door banged open. A third student from our group walked in. He looked neither left nor right. No greetings. His eyes were glowing and he was smiling. He walked to the window and stood for a long time looking out. Jesus, he cried, God is everywhere. Oh the Glory of it!. Then he walked out without a word. No social games for him. The two red-faced students looked solemn. Hopes dashed. (1968, p. 311)

Leary continues:

> It's a ridiculous ritual to run a double blind study using psychedelic drugs. After thirty minutes everyone knows what has happened, who has taken the sacrament. . . .
>
> It was easy to tell who had taken the psychedelics. Ten students sat attentively like good worshipers. Facing the altar. Silent. The others were less conventional. Some lay on the benches—one lay on the floor. Some wandered around the chapel murmuring in prayer and wonderment. One chanted a hymn. One wandered to the altar and held his hands aloft. One sat at the organ bench and played weird, exciting chords. (p. 311)

In light of these two weaknesses of this study, it is important to know that Pahnke's six-month follow-up provided some evidence that the experiences classified as mystical were indeed mystical. Even after six months there were differences in the way students in the two groups described the effects of the Good Friday experience. Here are some statements from those who had received psilocybin:

> Very strong benefit: a profound recognition of the "mystical" in the full religious life—but this attitude seen not as an escape from the world, rather giving me a greater sense of concern for the here and now.
>
> Very strong benefit: a startling sensitivity to others—especially those with "problems."
>
> Very strong benefit: a sense of "call"—insofar as this means that the Word must be proclaimed to the "world"—not so much verbally as "existentially," and that somehow I must respond to this challenge, as it has appeared to me.
>
> I have made reference to the joy I experienced when I came back to life since the Good Friday afternoon experience. At times I have felt a joy at being alive and having real existence, but I do not believe I have ever experienced it previous to Good Friday to the degree I did then or to the degree I have since, even though I intellectually knew of it. (Pahnke, 1964)

Those who received nicotine did not make similar statements at the follow-up. Still, although the statements quoted here have the ring of authenticity, they are only self-reports.

Implications

What, then, does our review of the available research suggest about the effect of psychedelic drugs on religious experience? Although the research is not conclusive, we believe that it *suggests* psychedelic drugs can and do facilitate religious experience. Moreover, it suggests they facilitate religious experience in the way we proposed, by disrupting the individual's current way of thinking about one or more existential concerns (the self-surrender stage of creative religious experience) and by stimulating the imaginal process, making cognitive reorganization more likely (the new vision stage). Aldous Huxley put it well in the concluding lines of *The Doors of Perception* (1954):

> The man who comes back through the Door in the Wall will never be quite the same as the man who went out. He will be wiser but less cocksure, happier but less self-satisfied, humbler in acknowledging his ignorance yet better equipped to understand the relationship of words to things, of systematic reasoning to the unfathomable Mystery which it tries, forever vainly, to comprehend. (p. 79)

Or as William James (1902) said, "It is as if the opposites of the world, whose contradictoriness and conflict make all our difficulties and troubles, were melted into unity" (p. 298).

If this analysis is correct, two implications follow. First, drugs can *facilitate* but cannot *produce* religious experience. They can facilitate it if they are used in the context of an ongoing intrapsychic process that includes not only self-surrender (incubation) and new vision (illumination) but also a preceding struggle with one or more existential questions (preparation) and a subsequent new life (verification). If the individual is not already wrestling with existential concerns, psychedelics are not likely to evoke a religious transformation. This point is underscored by the findings of Masters and Houston, of the Spring Grove project, and of Pahnke; in each study religious insight seemed limited to those actively addressing existential questions (preparation). At the same time, if the experience is to be more than psychic "fireworks," there must be positive consequences for one's everyday life (verification). Joseph Havens (1964) makes this point:

> In overturning one's narrow self-limited world and opening him to the possibility of non-ego-centered seeing, they [psychedelic experiences] light the path ahead. In short, they consolidate the past, and envisage the future. . . . How may one determine the trustworthiness of the wisdom and insight which seem to flow from them? It is my view that they cannot be trusted without check and confirmation of some kind. Experience can deceive, just as can the senses and the demonstrations of logic. "Discerning the spirits" has ever been a problem to religious people. It seems clear that any new knowledge acquired under the psychedelic drugs must be subjected to the tests of *reason* and of *subsequent experience* (one writer calls the latter "existential validation"). Do the insights lead toward the deepening of human relations, toward perceiving the world more accurately, toward freedom from ego-centeredness? (p. 220, italics in original)

This first implication leads us to a second; the religious import of psychedelic drugs does not lie in the drugs themselves but in using the drugs as tools in a larger quest for insight. To suggest that drugs should be used as a means to another end and not as an end in themselves may seem dreadfully

Western, even middle class. But it is not. Drugs have long been used in this pragmatic way in non-Western cultures, as is made clear by Carlos Castaneda's Yaqui Indian teacher, don Juan. Don Juan spoke of psychedelic drugs as "allies"; they and the "nonordinary reality" that they could evoke were of value only as part of a larger growth process. Castaneda summarized don Juan's view:

> Don Juan explained time and time again that the encompassing concern of his knowledge was the pursuit of practical results, and that such a pursuit was pertinent in ordinary as well as in nonordinary reality. He maintained that in his knowledge there were the means of putting nonordinary reality into service, in the same way as ordinary reality. According to that assertion, the states induced by the allies were elicited with the deliberate intention of being used. (1968, p. 158)

This approach to the psychedelic experience is a far cry from getting high to see what happens or because it is fun or feels good. These latter approaches are more uniquely Western and middle class. Don Juan instead taught a carefully disciplined use of drugs as vehicles to carry the individual to ever higher levels of insight into the mysteries of life. And the empirical research seems quite consistent with his teaching. Only when so used would we expect psychedelic drugs to have the potential to facilitate religious experience.

MEDITATION

If psychedelic drugs were the spiritual fad of the 1960s, then meditation was the fad of the 1970s. One of the many people who turned from drugs to meditation was Richard Alpert, Timothy Leary's associate in the research at Harvard on spiritual effects of psilocybin and LSD. Alpert's experience with meditation was so profound that it led him to change his name. As Ram Dass, he describes some of what occurred after he went to India in 1967:

> In India I met Neemkaroli Baba, who was far more than I could have hoped for. He lived in the state called sahaj samadhi, in which altered states of consciousness were an integral part of his life. In his presence one had the feeling of boundless space and timelessness, as well as vast love and compassion. Maharaji, as we called him, once ingested a huge dose of psychedelics and, to my complete surprise, nothing happened. If his awareness was not limited to any place, then there was nowhere to go, for he was already here, in all its possibilities. . . .
>
> In the presence of Maharaji I experienced my heart opening and felt previously unexperienced waves of ever more consuming love. Perhaps this was the way—drowning in love. But my mind would not be quiet. The social scientist—that skeptic—was not to be drowned without a struggle. Using all the tools, including my sensual desire and intellect, as well as guilt and sense of responsibility, my ego structure fought back. For example, in the temples in which Maharaji stayed, there were statues of Hanuman, a monkey-God who had all power due to his total devotion to God. Hanuman is deeply loved and

> honored by Maharaji's devotees. I sat before an eight-foot cement statue of a monkey, painted red, and I sang to him and meditated upon him. Every now and then a voice would observe, "Ah, sitting worshipping a cement monkey idol. You've really gone over the edge." This was the inner battle. . . .
>
> My Buddhist friends said that the problem was a matter of discipline of mind and, upon questioning, Maharaji affirmed that if you brought your mind to one-pointedness you would know God. Perhaps that was what I had to do. . . . In 1971 I began serious meditation practice in Bodh Gaya, where Buddha had been enlightened. In a series of ten day courses I, along with about 100 Westerners, was gently guided into Theravadan Buddhist meditation techniques—the ultimate in simplicity of practice. . . . Finally, I, a Western psychologist, was truly humbled intellectually. For I saw what *psyche logos* was really about. Here . . . [was a] method for extricating your awareness from the tyranny of your own mind. (From Goleman, 1977, pp. xiii–xv)

When one begins to explore the literature on meditation, two features stand out. First, there are the frequent claims of dramatic effects—physiological, psychological, and spiritual. The statement above by Ram Dass (who has since returned to calling himself Alpert) is one example. Others include stories of yogis who remain immobile for days, who can walk on hot coals, and who even stop breathing but do not die.

Second, there is a seemingly infinite variety of meditative traditions and practices. Probably the most diverse tradition is the Hindu. It encompasses the range of yoga practices: (1) controlling bodily states such as breathing; (2) attending to a visual image or mandala (e.g., a circle); (3) repeating a mantram, a significant word or phrase such as the name of a deity (e.g., the Hare Krishna chant); or (4) repeating a simple bodily movement, called a mundra. Transcendental Meditation (TM) is a Westernized form of yoga meditation; in TM the meditator silently repeats a personal mantram twice a day for fifteen to thirty minutes.

The Theraveda Buddhist tradition, the one followed by Alpert, is less varied; in this tradition the meditator almost always focuses his or her attention on some object. But the object of meditation can be almost anything; it can be a colored wheel, a decaying corpse, or a very abstract concept such as infinite space, infinite consciousness, fire, or water—even one's own mental process of attending. In the Zen Buddhist tradition the meditator may count breaths without any attempt to control breathing, may try to "solve" a logically unsolvable puzzle or Koan (e.g., "What is the sound of one hand clapping?" or "What is the size of the real you?") or may just sit and attend to, but not be distracted by, each new thought or experience.

In the Islamic Sufi tradition the dervish meditates while engaging in a whirling dance and chant. Christian meditation typically involves long vigils, asceticism, contemplation of the cross, or repetition of simple prayers.

Although it is easy to be overwhelmed by all this variety, these different forms of meditation actually share much common ground. This becomes apparent when we separate the belief systems of the various traditions from the practice of meditation itself. The belief systems differ greatly and, as a result, the religious experience of a Buddhist monk who finally reaches the dissolution of self into the infinite sea of nothingness (nirvana) is very different from the religious experience of the Christian ascetic who finally meets the eternal, omnipotent God face-to-face. But the role of meditation in facilitating these experiences seems much the same; it stops the flow of thought and brings the mind to one-pointedness. We shall have more to say about the combined impact of meditation and the belief system of a religious tradition after we consider the facilitative effect of religious language. For now, we shall focus on how meditation as a technique, independent of any particular religious tradition, might facilitate religious experience.

Some Speculations on How Meditation Might Facilitate Religious Experience

In suggesting that the myriad meditative practices have essentially the same impact on religious experience, we are following the lead of four experts on the psychology of meditation: Daniel Goleman (1977), Claudio Naranjo (1971), Robert Ornstein (1971), and Arthur Deikman (1966). Not only do each of these experts emphasize that the impact of various meditative practices is essentially the same; they agree on what the impact is: By disciplined focus of attention on some object, idea, or activity, the meditator is able to break down his or her present reality. Approaching one-pointedness of thought, the current cognitive organization begins to disintegrate, and the meditator is able to see anew.

Daniel Goleman, speaking of the mindfulness *(satipatthana)* that takes one beyond the levels of concentration with which most forms of meditation begin, says it this way:

> Mindfulness entails breaking through stereotyped perception. Our natural tendency is to become habituated to the world around us, no longer to notice the familiar. We also substitute abstract names or preconceptions for the raw evidence of our senses. In mindfulness, the meditator methodically faces the bare facts of his experience, seeing each event as though occurring for the first time. . . .
>
> Mindfulness will break through the illusions of continuity and reasonableness that sustain our mental life. In mindfulness, the meditator begins to witness the random units of mind stuff from which his reality is built. . . .
>
> The goal of all meditation paths, whatever their ideology, source, or methods, is to transform the meditator's consciousness. In the process, the meditator dies to his past self and is reborn to a new level of experience. (1977, pp. 21, 24, 116)

Naranjo says it likes this:

> While practice in most activities implies the development of habits and the establishment of conditioning, the practice of meditation can be better

> understood as quite the opposite: a persistent effort to detect and become free from all conditioning, compulsive functioning of mind and body, habitual emotional responses. . . .
>
> It may be readily seen, in fact, that the concentrative effort involved in meditation upon a *single* object is of an eliminative nature. . . . The practice in "letting go" that this meditation entails, in the sense of "surrendering to" or "allowing" cannot be completely divorced from a letting go in another sense . . .: letting go of habits, preconceptions, and expectations; letting go of control and of the filtering mechanisms of ego. (1971, pp. 9, 75)

Ornstein says:

> An aim of meditation, and more generally of the disciplines involving meditation, is the removal of "blindness," or the illusion, and an "awakening" of "fresh" perception. Enlightenment or illumination are words often used for progress in these disciplines, for a breakthrough in the level of awareness—flooding a dark spot with light. The Indian tradition speaks of opening the third eye, seeing more, and from a new vantage point. *Satori,* the desired state in Zen, is considered an "awakening." The Sufis speak of growing a new organ of perception. . . . The practice of meditation, then, can be considered as an attempt to turn off conceptual activity temporarily, to shut off all input processing for a period of time, to get away for a while from the external environment. . . .
>
> We can consider the process of meditation as similar to that of taking a vacation—leaving the situation, "turning off" our routine way of dealing with the external world for a period, later returning to find it "fresh," "new," "different," our awareness "deautomatized." (1971, pp. 192–194)

Finally, based on his own research and the research of others, Deikman suggests:

> Since, in the meditative experience, the object world as a perceptual experience is broken down or de-differentiated, the cognitive organization based on that world is disrupted in a parallel fashion. . . . Meditation . . . is potentially a very powerful technique for undoing of the normal cognitive and perceptual modes. Such an undoing might be expected to result in a mobility of "reality quality." . . . (1966, pp. 110–111)

Relating this expert testimony to the stage model of religious experience developed in Chapter 4, we would suggest that meditation practices affect one and only one stage of the process of creative transformation: self-surrender (incubation). The various practices seem directed toward one common goal, bringing to a halt the meditator's processing of information through the channels dictated by the current cognitive structures. When active processing through the current structures ceases, the current reality disintegrates; it then becomes possible for a new reality, a new vision, to emerge. Meditation does not offer a new vision, but it weakens the hold of the old one and so makes a new vision possible. As Naranjo (1971) says, its role is eliminative, not constructive.

EMPIRICAL EVIDENCE THAT MEDITATION FACILITATES RELIGIOUS EXPERIENCE

Although there is some evidence that meditation can facilitate religious experience (Hood, Morris, & Watson, 1990; van der Lans, 1987), there is no unequivocal evidence that it does so by affecting only the self-surrender (incubation) stage. There are, however, three lines of research consistent with this view.

Transcendental Meditation and self-actualization. First, there is research suggesting that meditation can lead to increased self-acceptance and to the sense of personal fulfillment, spontaneity, and integrity described by Abraham Maslow (1954) as "self-actualization." The evidence comes from research by William Seeman and his associates.

In a first study, Seeman, Nidich, and Banta (1972) twice administered Shostrom's (1964) Personal Orientation Inventory (POI)—a psychological test designed to measure twelve dimensions of Maslow's concept of self-actualization—to thirty-five undergraduates (eighteen men, seventeen women) at the University of Cincinnati. The first administration was two days before fifteen of the undergraduates (eight men, seven women) began to practice Transcendental Meditation; the second administration was two months later. Change scores were created for the twelve subscales of the POI by subtracting each individual's score for each subscale at the first administration from his or her score at the second. The investigators found no statistically reliable differences between the two groups at the time of the first administration, but they found significant differences in the change scores. Relative to the nonmeditators, the meditators showed changes in the direction of increased self-actualization on six of the twelve subscales. There were nonsignificant trends toward increased self-actualization among meditators on five of the other six subscales.

In a replication study, Nidich, Seeman, and Dreskin (1973) administered the POI twice to eighteen more undergraduates. The first administration was again two days before nine of them began a program of TM; the second administration was ten weeks later. This time, change scores revealed significant increases in the direction of self-actualization for meditators relative to nonmeditators on ten of the twelve subscales of the POI; the other two subscales showed nonsignificant trends in the same direction.

Seeman and his associates interpreted the results of these two studies as evidence that TM increases self-actualization. If this interpretation is correct, and if, as Maslow claimed, greater self-actualization reflects a more creative approach to the broad, existential issues of life, then these results would seem to provide evidence that this form of meditation can facilitate creative religious experience.

But, even though the results of these two studies are consistent with such a view, they are far from conclusive. First, the link between responses to the forced-choice items on Shostrom's Personal Orientation Inventory and the concept of self-actualization as developed by Maslow remains tenuous. Second, the changes toward higher scores among the meditators may not reflect profound personal change so much as a desire to advertise the benefits of meditation by *reporting* more self-actualization. This possibility is all the more likely because apparently research participants were neither randomly selected nor randomly assigned to the meditation and nonmeditation groups; the meditators assigned themselves by choosing to participate in a program of training in TM. Finally, even if it is true that TM can move one toward a more self-actualized, creative response to questions of existence, it is not clear from Seeman's research that this movement is a result of the effect of meditation on the self-surrender (incubation) stage per se. Fortunately, there is a second line of research that provides some evidence concerning the specific effects of meditation on incubation.

Meditation and brain waves. A number of studies have examined the effects of meditation on the meditator's brain waves, or electroencephalographic (EEG) patterns. Before describing the results of some of these studies, we should say a bit about the nature and possible significance of these brain waves. An EEG pattern is a record of the slight electrical potentials that continually cross the surface of the brain. These potentials can be recorded by electrodes attached to the scalp, and the recordings amplified and transformed into an ink tracing on a continuously moving strip of paper. The tracing provides the EEG pattern; it reveals the frequency and amplitude of the electrical potentials over time.

Four basic EEG patterns have been identified, each associated with a different type of mental experience. They are called Beta, Alpha, Theta, and Delta. *Beta* is a high-frequency, low-amplitude pattern that occurs when the person is actively thinking about some problem or is processing information from the environment. *Alpha* is a lower-frequency, higher-amplitude pattern that occurs during relaxed awareness, for example, when a person is sitting quietly with closed eyes. *Theta* is an even slower pattern that occurs during the hypnagogic (falling asleep) and hypnopompic (waking up) states, that is, when a person is drowsy but still has some awareness of his or her environment. Finally, *Delta* is a very slow pattern that occurs during deep sleep.

The high-amplitude Alpha waves that occur during relaxed awareness and the Theta waves that occur in the hypnagogic and hypnopompic states are believed by many scholars to be the EEG patterns associated with the incubation stage of the creative process (see, for example, Ornstein, 1972; Rapaport, 1951; Rugg, 1963; and Singer, 1974). Thus, if our suggestion is correct that meditation facilitates the self-surrender (incubation) stage, we would expect meditators to produce high-amplitude Alpha and Theta waves.

In perhaps the best-known study in this area, Kasamatsu and Hirai (1966) measured the EEG patterns of Zen masters during meditation, comparing them with the pattern of individuals practicing Zen meditation for the first time. Those with no prior experience produced a predominance of Beta waves throughout the meditation period, mixed with short periods of Alpha when their eyes were closed. The Zen masters showed a very different set of patterns. Before meditation they produced predominantly Beta, indicating normal, active thought. But when they started meditating, Alpha waves of moderate amplitude (40–50 microvolts) and frequency (11–12 per second) appeared. The Alpha became more stable and persistent as the meditation continued, and the waves increased in amplitude and decreased in frequency. Finally, high-amplitude (70–100 microvolts), low-frequency (6–7 per second) Theta waves began to appear among some of the masters rated by other Zen masters as highly proficient in meditation.

Kasamatsu and Hirai noted that the high-amplitude, low-frequency Alpha and Theta waves of the Zen masters were quite similar to the patterns observed in individuals in the drowsy, hypnagogic state. But the Zen masters produced high-amplitude Alpha with their eyes open which is quite unusual. Moreover, they did not seem drowsy, and they did not pass into sleep but remained responsive to environmental stimuli.

In related studies, Anand, Chhina, and Singh (1961) measured the EEG patterns of four yogi meditators both before and during Raj Yoga meditation. They found that these yogis showed prominent Alpha activity even *before* starting to meditate. During meditation, the Alpha activity increased, as did the amplitude of the Alpha waves. William Johnston (1974, p. 37) reported that experienced Christian meditators (men and women) also produced high-amplitude Alpha during meditation. Robert Wallace (1970) found that fifteen college students who had practiced Transcendental Meditation from six months to three years showed increased regularity and amplitude of Alpha waves as they went from sitting quietly with their eyes open, to sitting with eyes closed, to meditating. Wallace reported that Theta waves appeared for a few of these TM meditators. Finally, Fenwick (1969) observed Londoners who practiced a meditation technique similar to TM. He, too, noted an initial increase in Alpha waves and, as meditation progressed, occasional bursts of Theta waves.

These five studies suggest that very different meditation techniques have similar effects on brain waves. The effects include high-amplitude Alpha, followed by Theta waves among some experienced meditators. Because these are the EEG patterns that have most frequently been associated with the incubation stage of the creative process, the results of these five studies are entirely consistent with our suggestion that meditation facilitates religious experience by encouraging self-surrender (incubation). There is also some very tentative evidence that meditation may produce "a weakening of left hemisphere cognitive structures" (Fenwick, 1987, p. 117), which we noted in Chapter 4 may be associated with the incubation stage of the creative process.

Once again, however, a note of caution is in order. Although observation of these specific brain-wave patterns during meditation is certainly intriguing, it remains unclear exactly what these, or any, brain waves mean.

These EEG patterns may reflect a special and potentially creative state of consciousness, or they may reflect nothing more than the neurophysiological correlates of other physiological changes resulting from meditation, such as slower breathing, reduced oxygen consumption, and slower heart rate. To our knowledge, high-amplitude Alpha and Theta waves have never been clearly and uniquely linked to either creativity or religious experience. That is, no one has measured EEG in people while they try to solve a problem or conflict, finally give up, and then experience insight. Nor has anyone measured EEG in people while they try to deal creatively with one or more of the questions of existence. At present, EEG evidence for a link between meditation and self-surrender (incubation) is only suggestive.

Transcendental Meditation and field-independent perception. Given the lack of any real understanding of the relationship between brain waves and perceptual and cognitive processes, it is important to know that there is one published study that suggests that meditation affects perception. Kenneth Pelletier (1974) measured the effects of Transcendental Meditation on perception, using five indices of perceptual style. Two of the indices seem particularly relevant to our concerns, the embedded-figures test and the rod-and-frame test. On the former, an individual is presented with a complex pattern of lines and asked to trace the outline of a simple figure (e.g., a star) that is embedded within it. On the latter, he or she is presented with a blank visual field, except for a rod mounted within a rectangular frame. The frame is tilted either to the right or left, and the task is to rotate the rod until it is straight up and down. To the extent that a person relies on the sides of the frame to provide a reality orientation, he or she will not succeed. The person must resist the preconception that the frame is hanging straight. Thus, both of these tasks require the ability to perceive objects as they are, without having that perception distorted by either environmental cues or habitual modes of seeing. This ability is called *field independence.*

Participants in Pelletier's study were twenty men and twenty women volunteers selected from a group attending an introductory lecture on TM (average age, 24.7 years). Equal numbers of each sex were randomly assigned to meditating and nonmeditating groups. Individuals in the meditating group were permitted to begin practicing TM, whereas those in the nonmeditating group were instructed to sit quietly for twenty minutes each morning. After three months, the indices of perceptual style were administered to all participants.

Results revealed that the meditators showed more accuracy than the nonmeditators on both the embedded-figures test ($F = 48.76$, $p < .001$) and the rod-and-frame test ($F = 35.91$, $p < .001$). Moreover, these differences were not due to initial differences between the groups because half of the members of each group had been tested before the three-month meditation period, and at that point the groups did not differ. Apparently, TM enabled members of the meditation group to see things more for what they are, independent of personal preconceptions and distracting environmental cues.

Once again, these results are quite consistent with the suggestion that meditation facilitates the self-surrender (incubation) stage of religious experience. Moreover, this experiment permits a clearer inference that meditation produced the effects because participants were randomly assigned to the meditating and nonmeditating groups. At the same time, it must be admitted that the link is indirect between displaying field independence on the embedded-figures and rod-and-frame tests and the ability creatively to surrender one's existing mode of seeing oneself and one's world.

Implications

Overall, our speculation that meditative practices encourage self-surrender (incubation) by bringing to a halt use of the current cognitive organization seems quite consistent with the existing research. There is evidence that meditation may lead to increased self-actualization, that it may lead to more field-independent perceptions, and that it produces the high-amplitude Alpha and Theta waves thought to be associated with the incubation stage of the creative process. But as with psychedelic drugs, the available evidence is not yet conclusive. It only serves to demonstrate the plausibility of the proposed relationship.

RELIGIOUS LANGUAGE

Language, written or spoken, is the technique that we most frequently use to influence the experience of others. We write books, papers, and letters to provide new information and to suggest new ways of looking at what is already known. We speak, both publicly and privately, to the same end.

The importance of language as a facilitator of new experience would seem to be as true for religion as for any other area of life. Every major religion has its sacred writings—its Torah, Bible, Vedas, Bhagavad-Gita, Koran, or I Ching. Each also has a wealth of literature interpreting and explaining the holy texts. Many of the major religions can trace their origins to a great teacher and preacher: After the Buddha attained Enlightenment he did not go his own way but devoted his life to preaching the Way to others; Jesus raised his call to humility, love, and service in the Sermon on the Mount; Mohammed began proclaiming his message of strict monotheism and human brotherhood after the angel Gabriel appeared in a vision before him, saying, "Read thou, in the name of the Lord."

Nor is the oral tradition in religion a thing of the ancient past. Jonathan Edwards sparked a major religious revival in eighteenth-century America with his sermons, in which he graphically described our souls "dangling over the pits of Hell by a strand no stronger than the web of a spider." Martin Luther King, Jr., crystallized the hopes of the civil rights movement in the

1960s with his resonant proclamations, "I have a dream!" and "I have seen the Promised Land." Television evangelists weekly call millions to give their lives (and their money) to God. Children are taught the stories, both historical and apocryphal, of their religious tradition in Sunday schools, Hebrew schools, and catechetical classes. Language is so central to most religious traditions that religion is often accused of being little more than words, endless preaching and teaching with very little practice.

Thinking historically, it is hard to deny that religious language is capable of facilitating religious experience. Writing, teaching, and preaching have been central to the spread of all major religious movements. But it is also hard to deny that for many people, religious language is a stumbling block that inhibits religious insight. For some, like Friedrich Nietzsche (1844–1900), it is impossible to confront questions of existence seriously until all talk of God has been cast aside; for these people, "God is dead." For others, religious language becomes a password, unlocking all the puzzles of life. It provides such clear, final answers to questions of existence that it inhibits any deeper insight into these questions.

In an attempt to account for both these facilitating and inhibiting effects, we shall consider how religious language relates to the religious experience of both the speaker (writer) and listener (reader). Our analysis will be entirely speculative, because we know of no empirical research that directly addresses the question of the impact of religious language on religious experience. (Staples & Mauss, 1987, get close, however.) We hope that our speculations will encourage empirical research in the future.

Some Speculations on How Language Might Facilitate Religious Experience

Expression of religious experience in synthetic symbols. Imagine that you have experienced a nonlogical creative reality transformation of the sort that we have suggested characterizes religious experience. How will you think and talk about this experience? Ordinary discursive, referential language seems to miss the mark. You cannot point to something in your reality and say, "I experienced that." What you experienced was instead a change in your reality itself, a change in the cognitive structures that you use to make sense of your perceptions and actions. Ordinary language also falls short in a second respect; it fails to reflect the emotional intensity and personal profundity of the experience. Among those who have been "saved," one often hears phrases like, "I can't begin to describe it. It was wonderful. It totally changed my life." Given the inadequacy of ordinary language, you may be reduced to silence and awe by your reality-transforming experience.

But so significant an experience begs for expression. And if you are like most people, it is likely that you will speak, though in a special way. You will use statements that are literally nonsense but communicate your meaning better than any ordinary, logical statement. If you look back over the statements in Chapter 4 and this chapter that people used to describe their religious experiences, you will see that the language is at heart metaphorical and symbolic: "What ails us?" "Fire!" "My roots are free!" "Every little pine-needle expanded and swelled with sympathy and befriended me." "All at once without warning of any kind, I found myself wrapped in a flame-colored cloud." "I experienced my heart opening and felt previously unexperienced waves of ever more consuming love." The symbols used to describe religious experiences often involve logical contradictions "dazzling obscurity," "whispering silence," "teeming desert," "soundless sound," "the voice of silence" (James, 1902, p. 322).

What is the psychological significance of these nonlogical symbols? Psycholinguistics is a rapidly developing area of psychological research, but until recently it has had relatively little to say about symbolic language of this kind. Its focus has instead been on ordinary language, the assumption apparently being that we need to understand ordinary discursive, referential language before trying to understand symbolic language (Pollio, Smith, & Pollio, 1990). Recently, however, several psycholinguists have begun to consider the function of metaphorical, figurative language.

George Miller (1979) has suggested that images and metaphors serve to evoke an understanding that cannot be objectively or logically true but can only be true given the state of mind of the speaker. Consider the statement "Man is a wolf." This metaphor forces us to attend to the speaker's perception of reality and, therefore, to his or her experience. It is an attempt to present a way of looking at one aspect of experience.

Lakoff and Johnson (1980) illustrate the reality-forming power of metaphor with the example of a student from Iran who heard his American friends talk about "the solution of my problems." Rather than thinking of solving a puzzle, the student interpreted this common phrase as a chemical metaphor; he saw "a large volume of liquid, bubbling and smoking, containing all of your problems, either dissolved or in the form of precipitates" (p. 143). Using the chemical metaphor, problems are no longer seen as amenable to a permanent resolution; they are always present in some more or less troubling form. The chemical metaphor produces a new reality.

Howard Pollio and his associates have examined the use of figurative language in poetry, jokes, politics, psychotherapy, and education (Pollio, Barlow, Fine, & Pollio, 1977). Reflecting on the discussion of figurative language by Gestalt psychologists (e.g., Kurt Koffka) and in the psychoanalytic tradition (e.g., William Gordon, Arthur Koestler, and J. J. Leedy), as well as the treatments of metaphorical language within mainstream psycholinguistics (e.g., Katz and Fodor, Johnson), Pollio et al. emphasize the close link between figurative language and creative problem solving. "In situations ranging from a psychotherapist's couch to an industrial consultant's laboratory, figurative language has been shown to promote innovative problem setting and problem solving" (1977, p. 30).

Applying these observations to religious language, we would suggest that much religious language is metaphorical and symbolic for a specific reason.

It is an attempt on the part of the speaker (writer) to talk about an experience that is literally incomprehensible, the nonlogical, creative transformation of his or her existential reality. Because the experience of reality transformation transcends our shared, ordinary reality, it cannot be talked about or represented directly. Instead, a nonlogical juxtaposition of ordinary terms is used to allude to the transcendant nature of the experience. Carl Jung said it with characteristic murkiness: "Nonambiguity and noncontradiction are one-sided and thus unsuited to express the incomprehensible" (1953, p. 15).

More specifically, we would suggest that these religious symbols contain in kernelized form an expression of both the existential question that provoked the religious experience and the new vision that allows the experiencer to see this question in a new way. Because they kernelize a way of making sense of seemingly conflicting concerns, we shall call such symbols *synthetic.*

Not all religious language is of this type, but synthetic symbols seem to lie at the heart of religious language. For example, one finds a synthetic symbol in the Psalmist's famous expression of assurance that threats to life and limb need not lead to existential terror. We may be helpless sheep, but we are under the care of a loving shepherd:

> The Lord is my shepherd, I shall not want.
> He makes me lie down in green pastures;
> He leads me beside still waters; he restores my soul.
> He leads me in right paths for his name's sake.
>
> Even though I walk through the darkest valley, I fear no evil;
> For you are with me; your rod and your staff—they comfort me.
> (Psalm 23:1–4 NRSV)

One also finds a synthetic symbol in the Christian images of rebirth and resurrection; these images transform the terror of death by putting it in the past tense. If one has already died to one's old life and is born again into a new, eternal life, then physical death becomes a relatively minor event, a going home. Jesus' use of this rebirth image confused the literal-minded Nicodemus, who asked, "How can anyone be born after having grown old? Can one enter a second time into the mother's womb and be born?" (John 3:4 NRSV). But we have no difficulty recognizing that Jesus was speaking figuratively of a transformation of heart and mind, not of the physical body.

The image of kinship provides powerful synthetic symbols in many religious traditions (Batson, 1983). Seeing others as "the Children of God" or "Brothers and Sisters in Christ" suggests an answer to the existential question of how we should relate to one another; we should relate like family. In the words of the motto of Boys' Town, the internationally known orphanage in Nebraska: "He ain't heavy; he's my brother."

All major world religions seem to have developed one or more *supreme synthetic symbols;* these symbols kernelize a new vision that deals with a range of existential questions simultaneously. For Christians, the symbol of the cross deals simultaneously with the questions of meaning in life, impending personal death, and relations to others; meaning is to be found in dying to self to be free to live for others. For Jews, the symbol of the Chosen People deals simultaneously with these same concerns; meaning is to be found in serving the nation Israel, both now and in the future through one's descendants. For the Buddhist, symbols like a drop of water falling into the sea serve a supreme synthetic function; meaning is to be found in the dissolution of self into the eternal oneness of all. We suspect that these supreme synthetic symbols have assumed a role of centrality in their respective traditions because they contain in capsule form the basic existential questions and new visions experienced by followers of these traditions, allowing the faithful to think and talk about the reality transformation they have experienced.

These suggestions are, of course, quite speculative. Because they are, it is somewhat reassuring to know that we are not alone in our view of the origin and function of religious symbols. After an extensive study of religious language, Thomas Fawcett (1970) came to a very similar view. He suggested that religious symbols emerge from the speaker's experience of reality transformation, and the symbols contain an expression of both the descent into the depths of existential crisis and the subsequent ascent to a new perspective on the crisis-provoking question. Thus, he too saw religious symbols as synthetic. Fawcett considered his descent-ascent model an oversimplification; still he argued:

> Its fundamental veracity is perhaps indicated by certain recurring features of religious experience and their symbols. Symbolic language is dualistic throughout and consists largely of contrasts between two realms: light and darkness, death and life, high and low. . . . In the characterization of existential estrangement [i.e., descent] we can recognize a return to the primeval symbol of the deep ocean, the threatening chaos, the unfathomable absurdity. . . . In the creative integration of the second phase [i.e., ascent] there appear the symbols of the victor. . . . The boundless desert becomes the infinity of the divine presence as life once more flows through to dispel death-producing anxiety. (1970, pp. 172–173)

Synthetic symbols as facilitators of religious experience. Up to this point, we have been considering the origin of synthetic religious symbols. We have suggested that they arise out of the attempt of one or more individuals to express an experience of religious reality transformation. The symbols are synthetic in that they contain the crisis-provoking questions viewed in a new way that allows them to be dealt with positively. Now we must extend our analysis to include the use of religious language to facilitate a parallel experience in the life of others.

Once again, psycholinguistic research can only offer suggestive guidelines. Lakoff and Johnson (1980) have provided a general analysis of the power of metaphors to give new understanding to experience. More specifically, in the area of social policy, Donald Schön has spoken of what he calls *generative* metaphors, metaphors that account "for our perspectives on the world: how we think about things, make sense of reality, and set the problems we later try to solve" (1979, p. 254). He suggests that these metaphors have the potential to guide a cognitive restructuring that enables us to see social problems in a new way. Pollio et al. (1977) suggest that metaphoric language may have a parallel function in psychotherapy.

Thomas Fawcett (1970) develops a similar, although somewhat more detailed, analysis of the function of religious symbols. He suggests that because religious symbols arise from an attempt to express the descent-ascent dialectic of a reality-transforming experience, they can evoke a parallel experience in others: "Symbolic discourse is rooted in human experience as subject and results in deep psychological change. Symbols speak to the ontological anxiety of man, his concern to understand the roots of his own existence" (1970, p. 34). Fawcett contends that religious symbols can do this only if "they produce specific reactions in us . . . at the personal level of emotion and imagination . . . ," if "something new appears to be given in the experience they create" (1970, p. 174). Donald Capps (1988) makes a similar claim: "Religious symbols, such as the symbol of Christ, have the power to initiate the transformation of the self" (p. 62). Of course, religious symbols need not be linguistic; they may take the form of icons, statues, paintings, even buildings. Regardless of the form, the facilitative function seems the same.

To illustrate, as we read Psalm 23, we are reminded of the frailty of our existence; we are defenseless sheep in "the darkest valley." But we are also presented with a new vision—we are not lost sheep because "The Lord is my shepherd." We are under the care of a concerned and competent guardian.

Building on these clues, we can speculate about how religious language might facilitate religious experience. If synthetic religious symbols contain in kernel form the existential questions and way of seeing life anew, then religious language is capable of facilitating three stages of religious transformation. It can heighten existential crisis (preparation), suggest a new vision (illumination), and, embedded within a larger interpretative language system such as a theology, provide guidance in how this vision is to be put into practice in a new life (verification). The only stage of the transformation process that religious language does not facilitate is self-surrender (incubation); it does not because the active information processing necessary to understand language is incompatible with the letting go of the self-surrender stage. Perhaps this is why it often seems necessary for the individual who has been carried to the point of crisis by a synthetic symbol temporarily to turn away from the symbol before grasping the positive, synthetic element that permits new vision. Recall the example of religious experience in response to evangelical preaching presented in Chapter 4; the distraught woman lost consciousness only to regain it in the peaceful bliss of a new vision.

Implications

We are suggesting, then, that religious language, and specifically synthetic symbolic religious language, has the power to facilitate religious experience in others because it arises from an attempt to express the speaker's (writer's) religious experience. As a result, it can evoke an understanding of both the existential question and new vision on which the initial experience was based. It can intensify the existential crisis, suggest a new vision, and provide guidance for a new life.

Limits to the Facilitative Power of Religious Language

If our speculations are correct about the way that religious language can facilitate religious experience, then there would seem to be two important limits on the power of such language.

The speaker's (writer's) questions are not the listener's (reader's) questions. First, consider what would happen if the existential question addressed by a synthetic symbol was not a concern for a particular listener (reader). Presumably, the symbol would then be unable to facilitate a reality-transforming experience. For this listener, the symbol would lack creative power; it would be dead.

Of course, existential questions such as finding meaning in life and reconciling oneself to one's own death are widely shared, across cultures and across centuries. It is, we suspect, for this reason that religious language translates across time and place far better than other forms of language. "The Lord is my shepherd . . .," still lives for us, although written thousands of years ago in a very different culture. In contrast, the scientific, economic, and technical language of that age does not live; it is only of historical interest. This generality of existential questions may account for the apparent universality of what Carl Jung calls *archetypal symbols* and what structuralists, like Claude Lévi-Strauss, call *universal myths*.

We may share basic existential questions with people of other ages and other cultures, but even if we share a question, we may not share the conceptual system in which the new vision is framed. For example, we may not conceive of the issue of our own death in terms either of reincarnation or of heaven and hell. If we do not, symbols cast in these terms will not live for us unless we can translate the underlying concepts into our own terms. The religious symbols that are most long-lived seem to be those cast in terms of enduring elements of human experience—family relationships (God as father) and elements of the physical and social environment (the bread of life). Symbols tied to a particular metaphysical worldview die more quickly.

The language is taken literally, not symbolically. There is a second limit on the facilitative power of religious language. Synthetic symbolic religious language has creative potential only to the degree that it is recognized to be symbolic, not literal, language. If it is treated as literal, then the symbols themselves become the focus of attention, and the reality-transforming experience that they were originally coined to express tends to be ignored. Instead of facilitating a process of descent into self-examination and surrender followed by an ascent into a transformed reality, the symbols become logical answers to the questions of existence. When this happens, the questions are trivialized. Treated as logical answers to life's questions, religious symbols do not stimulate the process of religious reality transformation; they stifle it by rendering it unnecessary. As discussed in Chapter 3, interpreting synthetic symbols literally is a particular problem for young children. This is because the existential questions that are addressed in synthetic symbolic religious language presuppose the abstract, hypothetical thinking that Piaget (1926) called formal operations.

Of course, literal interpretations of religious symbols and stories are not limited to children. Protestant fundamentalism is founded on the principle of the literal truth of the Bible. It is ironic that fundamentalism is also deeply concerned that individuals personally experience religious transformation. If the power of religious language to facilitate the transforming process rests on an appreciation of the nonliteral, symbolic nature of this language, then the literalism of the fundamentalist would seem to inhibit religious transformation. We shall have far more to say in the next few chapters about the nature and function of devout religious belief of the sort typical of fundamentalism.

MUSIC

Across centuries and across continents, music has been included in religious services and ceremonies. Why? Could it be that music facilitates religious experience? We cannot say with any confidence; indeed, to say anything about music we must speculate even more wildly than we have about religious language. Yet we believe that something should be said. So, if speculation is a scientific sin, we shall sin boldly.

We would suggest that music can facilitate each of the four stages of religious transformation: existential crisis (preparation), self-surrender (incubation), new vision (illumination), and new life (verification). Music's facilitative power stems from its ability to elicit emotion. As noted in Chapter 4, religious transformation in response to existential questions involves cognitive restructuring. But emotions are also involved in this restructuring because the cognitions are "hot": Existential crises—whether concerning the meaning and purpose of one's life, or the inevitability of one's death, or how one should relate to others—are likely to be accompanied by intense feelings of fear, anxiety, and yearning. When the crisis reaches the point of hopeless self-surrender, one may experience despair and resignation, but also relaxation and relief. New vision is accompanied by, in Pascal's fiery words, "Joy, joy, joy, tears of joy"; the crisis-provoking elements are seen in a new way, transforming terror and despair into triumph and bliss. Finally, the resulting new life is accompanied by feelings of confidence, serenity, and "peace, perfect peace."

Leonard Meyer, in his now-classic *Emotion and Meaning in Music* (1956), suggested that the major psychological significance of music is its ability to create, express, and solidify emotion (see also, Radocy & Boyle, 1988). The poets have said much the same. For example, John Dryden (1631–1700) asks, "What passion cannot Music raise and quell?" And Wallace Stevens (1879–1955) suggests in "Peter Quince at the Clavier":

> Just as my fingers on these keys
> Make music, so the selfsame sounds
> On my spirit make a music, too.
>
> Music is feeling, then, not sound.

Building on these suggestions, we would propose that to the extent a piece of music evokes or intensifies the emotions associated with a given stage of religious transformation, the music has the potential to facilitate this stage. Let us try to be a little more specific.

Existential crisis (preparation). Music that evokes a sense of discord and tension, a feeling that, as Shakespeare said, "time is out of joint," which much contemporary music—both classical and rock—does, can heighten a sense of existential crisis. Confronted with feelings of discontent or even torment, the hearer is impelled to search for a new harmony. For example, the deep, rumbling of anticipation and yearning in the first measures of Richard Strauss's *Also sprach Zarathustra,* the theme song for the movie *2001: A Space Odyssey,* would seem to facilitate preparation. The controlled straining, the low tones of the timpani, suggest that the old order is about to break; something new is needed.

Yet, as with other facilitators we have considered, music in and of itself is not likely to provoke an existential crisis. If one has not already begun to hear, like Tolstoy, the whispering doubts from within, then such music is likely to fall on deaf ears, to strike no resonant chord. But if the doubts have been heard, even if now repressed, then such music can add a torrent of emotional force to the urgency of finding a way out of the dark night of the soul.

Self-surrender (incubation). Other forms of music, especially soft, slow-paced rhythmic music such as a simple chant, can help the individual let go, facilitating the self-surrender stage of religious experience. Such music, as William Congreve (1670–1729) said, "has charms to sooth the savage breast." It can encourage the individual to lay aside active, reasoned mental effort and let the mind idle and play, providing the context for insight, for seeing oneself and one's life in a new way. Thus, the singing of a mantra during meditation or of Gregorian-style chants in a worship service may facilitate religious experience. Once again, however, this facilitating effect is possible only if one has prepared the way by actively confronting the existential crisis. Without this preparation, soothing music is likely to provide nothing more than a pleasant interlude.

New vision (illumination). Especially in classical music, themes are often woven into a fabric in which the emotions of crisis are integrated in a new way that evokes feelings of joy, comfort, and renewal—feelings that reflect a new vision. For example, Chopin's funeral march, the well-known first line of which children sing the words " Come to the morgue, it's the only place to be," begins as a dirge of mourning, loss, and sorrow. By the end, however, the dirge has been transformed into a march of triumph and affirmation. It is hard to hear this piece in its entirety without having a sense of death-transcending vision of the sort expressed by the words of Saint Paul: "O death, where is thy sting? O grave, where is thy victory?" (I Cor. 15:55). Similarly, the strains of Samuel Barber's "Adagio for Strings," which captures wrenching sadness and places it in the context of peace and reconciliation, was used on TV newscasts in the 1960s to accompany the nightly reports of the horrors of the war in Vietnam.

Think too of the spirituals sung by slaves in the early days of the United States. The words and music of these songs evoke a remarkable, redeeming perspective on a life of pain, suffering, and injustice. Pain and hardship are not denied but put in a new, affirmative light. Think of "Jacob's Ladder," "Go Down, Moses," "Down by the River Side," and "Were You There?" And think of the call to new vision and the feeling of resolve and reassurance provided by "Amazing Grace," "The Battle Hymn of the Republic," "We Shall Overcome," and "We Are the World."

At a more personal level, but reflecting much the same process, cellist Yo-Yo Ma (1990) reported playing a particular Bach sarabande when, on concert tour, he became lonely for the company of his family. He found that this particular piece evoked a new perspective on his loneliness, a sense of "wanting what you cannot have and being comforted nevertheless."

New life (verification). The role of music in facilitating the new life stage of religious experience lies less in the specific emotions evoked and more in the link to others that music can provide. In much the same way that religious language can offer an interpretative context for new vision, music can too. As one Christian worshiper told us, "When I sing the *Te Deum* [a canticle of the ancient Christian Church] I feel that I'm united with all the people in the faith who went before me—that I am part of a deep spiritual tradition, and that these earlier believers are somehow watching me and encouraging me."

Perhaps this is why Reformation leader Martin Luther declared, "Music is an endowment and a gift of God. . . . I place music next to theology and give it the highest praise" (Plass, 1959, p. 979). Indeed, because music speaks the universal language of emotion, one may wonder whether Luther did not get the priority wrong. Music may have broader applicability than theology.

Once again, we must emphasize the speculative nature of our suggestions here. Anecdotes and examples are all we have offered in support of our claim that music can facilitate religious experience by evoking relevant emotions. We have no solid empirical evidence to support or contradict this claim; indeed, we know of no published research whatsoever on the ability of music to facilitate religious experience. It is our hope that calling attention to the potential facilitative effects of music may prompt badly overdue research on the topic.

COMBINING FACILITATORS

We have considered four possible facilitators of religious experience—psychedelic drugs, meditation, religious language, and music. We suggested that although none has the power to *produce* religious experience, each has the power to *facilitate* it. Moreover, we suggested that each works in its own unique way: Drugs affect both the self-surrender and new vision stages; meditation only the self-surrender stage; religious language the existential crisis, new vision, and new life stages; and various forms of music affect all four stages. Note that if these suggestions are correct, then to facilitate all four stages using drugs, meditation, and religious language, two or more techniques must be combined. To combine drugs with meditation would be largely redundant, and it would still leave two stages uncovered. So we would not expect such a combination to occur. But to combine either drugs or meditation with religious language would cover all four stages. Therefore, we would expect such combinations to occur and to prove effective. We would expect various forms of music, which affect emotional rather than cognitive processes, to be combined with any and all of the other facilitators.

There is some observational evidence that these expectations are justified. Drugs were effectively combined with religious language and music in Pahnke's Miracle at Marsh Chapel experiment and with language in Carlos Castaneda's spiritual pilgrimage under the tutelage of don Juan. A drug-language-music combination exists in the native American church, where peyote is used in conjunction with Christian teachings and rhythmic music, and among the Rastafarians of Jamaica. As we have already noted, meditation—with or without accompanying music—is combined with religious language in a number of traditions.

When facilitators are combined, we begin to see the unique characteristics associated with the religious experience of different religious traditions. This uniqueness is most clearly revealed in the studies of the brain-wave patterns of Zen and Yogi meditators. Earlier we noted that both Zen and Yogi meditators show high-amplitude Alpha waves during meditation. But it has also been found that there is a dramatic difference in the experiences of meditators from these two traditions. This difference is revealed in their reactions to environmental stimulation. Typically, when a person in an Alpha state is presented with a stimulus (e.g., a loud click), the EEG pattern shifts temporarily to Beta and then returns to Alpha. This shift is called *alpha blocking.* If the stimulus is presented in a regular pattern (e.g., the clicking of a metronome), then alpha blocking soon begins to diminish and finally disappears. Kasamatsu and Hirai (1966) reported that Zen meditators showed clear alpha blocking to a click, but surprisingly, this response did not diminish over time. In contrast, Anand, Chhina, and Singh (1961) reported that Yogi meditators showed no alpha blocking at all, even to extreme stimuli such as strong light, a loud, banging noise, being touched by a hot glass tube, or having their hand thrust into ice water.

These differences in EEG response to environmental stimuli on the part of Zen and Yogi meditators would seem entirely consistent with the different teachings of these two religious traditions. Zen teaches attention to and appreciation of each new sensory experience for what it is. In the words of one Zen verse:

> Blue mountains are of themselves blue mountains;
> White clouds are of themselves white clouds.

And another:

> If you understand, things are just as they are;
> If you do not understand, things are just as they are.
>
> (From Watts, 1972)

Finally,

> If your mind is empty, it is always ready for anything;
> It is open to everything.
> In the beginner's mind there are many possibilities;
> In the expert's mind there are few.
>
> (From Ram Dass, 1978, p. 11)

In contrast, the Raj Yoga tradition teaches one-pointed concentration that takes the person away from the world of sensory experience toward the union of experiencer and object. It teaches that only by calming one's thoughts and stilling one's mind can this union be found. In this stillness the meditator comes to know himself as he really is, to know God, and to know the unity of self with God. The meditator moves toward a point where

> He does not dwell on the past, takes no thought for the future, and looks with indifference on the present. He surveys everything in the world with an eye of equality; he is no longer touched by the infinite variety of phenomena; he no longer reacts to pleasure and pain. (Goleman, 1977, pp. 78–79)

Zen teachings focus on opening one's mind to see anew, so each click is taken as a new event. Yoga teachings take one away from sensory experience; stimulation is disregarded.

Generalizing from these observations, we would hypothesize that characteristic differences in religious experience across traditions are at least in part a product of the way each tradition has developed its unique combination of facilitative techniques in order to touch all four stages of the process of creative religious experience, while at the same time minimizing redundancy. Although this hypothesis grows out of the preceding observations and is quite consistent with them, it clearly goes beyond the existing data and should be regarded with caution (see Fenwick, 1987). It remains to be tested in future research.

SUMMARY AND CONCLUSION

When we look at religious institutions in society, we are struck by the variety of teachings and the different forms of worship services, rituals, and personal devotions. In this chapter we have tried to understand the psychological significance of these socially shared teachings and practices by considering how they might affect the stages of religious experience outlined in Chapter 4. In doing so, we continue to build on the principle of interaction between environmental forces and intrapsychic processes proposed at the end of Chapter 2.

We examined four facilitative techniques—psychedelic drugs, meditation, religious language, and music—and speculated that although none of these techniques can *produce* religious experience, each has the potential to *facilitate* one or more stages of religious transformation. Psychedelic drugs can facilitate the self-surrender (incubation) and new vision (illumination) stages; meditation the self-surrender stage; religious language the existential crisis (preparation), new vision, and new life (verification) stages; and music in its various forms can facilitate all four stages. We presented some empirical evidence that, although certainly not conclusive, is consistent with our speculations about the facilitative effects of psychedelic drugs and meditation. We presented no empirical evidence that religious language and music affect religious experience in the way suggested because we know of none. For these facilitators, we had to be content with a set of speculations that might guide future research.

We also suggested a general hypothesis about the combination of facilitative techniques within religious traditions: A tradition will tend to develop a pattern of facilitators that encourages each of the four stages of the process of creative religious experience and at the same time minimizes redundancy. Most frequently, some form of meditation, contemplation, or personal prayer will be combined with public or private reflection on the synthetic symbols of the tradition. Alternatively, drugs could be substituted for meditation. But drugs will not be combined only with meditation; that would leave the existential crisis and new life stages untouched. Because music facilitates emotional rather than cognitive processes, it may be combined with any of the other facilitators without redundancy.

Finally, as we noted in discussing both drugs and religious language, there is a danger inherent in the use of any facilitator. The danger is that one will become focused on the facilitator rather than the personal transformation being facilitated. One may, for example, come to believe that the psychedelic or meditative state is itself the goal of one's religious quest, or that knowing and saying certain creeds and religious stories, or singing certain songs and hymns, provides the answer to one or more existential questions. Such a belief might enable a person to feel some security in the face of existential doubt, but it would undercut the power of the facilitator to promote personal transformation and insight. The experience would be religious, but it would not be creative.

This last observation returns us to our conclusion at the end of Chapter 4, that there may be different ways of being religious, some of which are more creative than others. In the next chapter we shall explore this important possibility in more detail.

6

Dimensions of Individual Religion

"Are you religious?" You have probably been asked this question at one time or another. And it probably evoked some uncertainty and discomfort about how to answer because it can be doubled-barreled, much like the question "Are you an intellectual?" The problem is that there are different ways of being religious, and although you might be pleased and even honored to be considered religious in some ways, you would be ashamed and upset to be considered religious in others. For example, you might be pleased to be considered religious like the compassionate Good Samaritan but upset to be thought to be like the priest and Levite in the parable, recognized religious leaders who callously passed by on the other side.

TRUE VERSUS FALSE RELIGION

From the Perspective of Religious Traditions

In most religious traditions the major reason for identifying different ways of being religious is to distinguish between true and false religion. In the

Judeo-Christian tradition, for example, the prophets of the Old Testament sought to turn the people of Israel away from superficial religious practices and toward sincere devotion to the law of God. As James Dittes (1969) has observed, "The prophets distinguished between solemn assemblies and righteousness (Amos 5:21–24), between sacrifices and steadfast love, between burnt offerings and knowledge of God (Hosea 6:6)" (p. 618). Jesus also devoted much of his energy to railing against the falseness of the institutional religion of his day:

> The scribes and the Pharisees sit in Moses's seat; therefore, do whatever they teach you and follow it; but do not do as they do, for they do not practice what they teach. They tie up heavy burdens, hard to bear, and lay them on the shoulders of others; but they themselves are unwilling to lift a finger to move them. They do all their deeds to be seen by others. . . . But woe to you, scribes and Pharisees, hypocrites! For you lock people out of the kingdom of heaven. For you do not go in yourselves, and when others are going in, you stop them. . . . Woe to you, scribes and Pharisees, hypocrites! For you are like whitewashed tombs, which on the outside look beautiful, but inside they are full of the bones of the dead and of all kinds of filth. So you also on the outside look righteous to others, but inside you are full of hypocrisy and lawlessness. (Matt. 23:2–5, 13, 27–28 NRSV)

You would hardly want to say that you were religious, if being religious meant being like these scribes and Pharisees!

The distinction between true and false religion can also be found in more recent Christian theology. Danish existentialist Søren Kierkegaard (1813–1855) differentiated "official Christianity" from "the radical Christian." And in the twentieth century there has been an emphasis on "religionless Christianity"; Dietrich Bonhoeffer asked, "If religion is no more than the garment of Christianity . . . then what is a religionless Christianity?" (1953, p. 163), and Karl Barth (1956) spoke of "the revelation of God as the abolition of religion." Building on such ideas, it has become common in many Christian churches to make a distinction between "having faith" and "being religious" or between being a "true Christian" and only a "Sunday Christian."

Given this long-standing concern to distinguish between true and false religion, you are well advised to hesitate before saying that you are or are not religious. And there is a further reason for hesitation. As we noted in Chapter 1, a person who has no interest in formalized, institutional religion may have an intense interest in religious questions. How is this person to answer? He or she may reject not only the superficial commitment of the Sunday Christian but also the total devotion of the true Christian. And yet, this individual may be seriously attempting to deal with existential questions. Is he or she religious? Some would say yes, more truly religious than a person with strong, clear beliefs. Our answer depends on what we consider true religion to be.

No doubt, personal and institutional biases strongly influence our views of what true religion is. If, for example, you have found some particular form of religion to be personally meaningful and satisfying, this form is likely to be labeled true religion, not only for yourself but also for others. Moreover, our biases are usually not limited to *what* a person believes; they extend to *how* the person believes as well, that is, to how dominant religious beliefs are in the person's life. If religion is a central, integrating value for you, you are likely to believe that it should be central and integrating for any truly religious individual, whether Christian, Jew, Buddhist, or Moslem. On the other hand, if you consider religion to be but one concern among many, all of which should be carefully orchestrated and harmonized, you are likely to view the totally committed individual as a fanatic who has lost perspective on what religion should be.

From the Perspective of Social-Psychological Research

Because personal and institutional biases often underlie the distinctions between true and false religion, the social psychologist is well advised to regard them with caution. At the same time, even though the value-laden labels "true" and "false" should be regarded skeptically, the psychologist should not overlook the possibility that the concern to distinguish true from false religion may reveal an aspect of personal religion that is real and important. It seems quite possible that there are different ways of being religious and that distinguishing among them may be of great importance in any attempt to understand the impact of religion on people's lives. For example, it may be that those who are devout in their adherence to religious beliefs are likely to show more love and concern for others in need, whereas those who are religious only in the nominal sense of being members of a local church and occasionally attending services are not likely to show increased concern. Testing hypotheses like this one will be our major concern in Part III of this book.

But before testing any hypotheses about the consequences of different ways of being religious, it is necessary to have a clear conception of these different ways. It is also necessary to have a means of detecting the different ways in human life. Arriving at a clear conception and means of detecting ways of being religious is the task before us in the present chapter.

The argument that we shall present in this chapter is somewhat controversial. We shall not simply adopt the most popular conception of different ways of being religious; we shall modify it with some ideas of our own. To make our reasons for doing this as clear as possible, we shall go into a bit more detail than in other chapters. In addition to looking closely at the popular conceptions of ways of being religious, we shall look closely at the techniques that have been developed to detect or measure these ways because, from a research standpoint, the conceptions cannot be understood independently of the techniques used to measure them. Then we shall relate the different ways to the model of religious experience discussed in Chapter 4, suggesting that different ways of being religious may be associated with different types of cognitive restructuring in response to existential questions.

TWO WAYS OF BEING RELIGIOUS: EXTRINSIC VERSUS INTRINSIC

Among psychologists, Gordon Allport's distinction between extrinsic and intrinsic religion is the most popular conception of ways of being religious. According to Allport, this distinction "helps us to separate churchgoers whose communal type of membership supports and serves other, nonreligious ends, from those for whom religion is an end in itself—a final, not instrumental, good" (1966, p. 454).

> While there are several varieties of extrinsic religious orientation, we may say they all point to a type of religion that is strictly utilitarian: useful for the self in granting safety, social standing, solace, and endorsement for one's chosen way of life. . . . By contrast, the intrinsic form of the religious sentiment regards faith as a supreme value in its own right. . . . A religious sentiment of this sort floods the whole life with motivation and meaning. Religion is no longer limited to single segments of self-interest. (Allport, 1966, p. 455)

The businessman we met in Chapter 1 who went to church only because it was "good for business" would typify an extrinsic orientation; he was using his religion as a means of self-serving ends.[1] The young student we met in Chapter 4 who found meaning and purpose on a mountainside in the Alps would typify an intrinsic orientation; his religion was an active, directing force, not just a tool used to reach self-serving ends.

As may be apparent, the extrinsic versus intrinsic distinction parallels the theological distinction between false and true religion, between the Sunday Christian and the true Christian. This parallel gives the distinction considerable intuitive appeal. But, in spite of this appeal and its popularity, we believe that the extrinsic-intrinsic distinction provides an inadequate conception of ways of being religious and that it should be modified. In order to explain why we think this, we need to look at the distinction more closely. First, let us trace its development.

Development of the Extrinsic Versus Intrinsic Distinction

As early as 1945, social psychologists began speaking of two different ways of being religious, one in which religion was used to justify self-centered

1 You may recall that in Chapter 1 we said that this businessman was not religious by our definition of religion. He still is not. More generally, Allport's extrinsic orientation is not religious by our definition because, although the extrinsically religious individual may display beliefs and behavior that we associate with religion, these beliefs and behavior are used for ends other than to deal with existential questions. In spite of this, we shall follow the convention established by Allport and speak of the extrinsic orientation as a way of being religious. But from our perspective, this orientation might be more appropriately called an *appearance* of being religious rather than a way.

ends, another in which religious commitments were carefully thought out and taken seriously as a major goal in life (see Allport & Kramer, 1946; Frenkel-Brunswik & Sanford, 1945). This distinction was maintained and amplified in the mammoth report on research into *The Authoritarian Personality*, published in 1950.

Neutralized religion versus taking religion seriously: The authoritarian personality research. The authoritarian personality research, a six-year project begun in 1944, had as a goal the identification of personality characteristics of individuals to whom Nazism might appeal. Interviews were conducted with hundreds of individuals, and questionnaires were developed to measure two major personality dimensions, authoritarianism and ethnocentrism. *Authoritarianism* was defined by (1) a high regard for and tendency to acquiesce to authority, (2) adherence to conventional, middle-class values, (3) rigidity in thinking, and (4) need for clear structure. *Ethnocentrism* was a closely related concept defined by (1) in-group loyalty and (2) distrust and dislike for members of out-groups.

Questions about religion were included in both the interviews and questionnaires designed to measure authoritarianism and ethnocentrism. Theodore Adorno found in his analysis of the interview data that those who scored high on authoritarianism and ethnocentrism reported a high incidence of "neutralized" religion. Adorno described neutralized religion as an emasculation of the more profound claims of religion while preserving the doctrinal shell in a rather rigid and haphazard way. Individuals displaying this type of religion appeared to subordinate religion to self-centered aims, "to make use of religious ideas in order to gain some immediate practical advantage or to aid in the manipulation of other people" (Adorno et al., 1950, p. 733).

Adorno also found that neutralized religion frequently correlated negatively with a second way of being religious. This second way involved a "personally experienced belief" that led the believer to "take religion seriously in a more internalized sense" (Adorno et al., 1950, p. 731).

Similarly, in analyzing responses to one open-ended questionnaire item—"How important in your opinion are religion and the church?"—Nevitt Sanford found that some people distinguished between the church and "real" religion. He found that anti-Semitism—negative attitudes toward Jews—tended to correlate positively with the amount of importance attached to the church but not with importance attached to "real" religion.

Immature versus mature religion: Allport's early formulation. Also in 1950, Gordon Allport published his first major statement of a similar distinction; he differentiated immature and mature religion. In his earlier work on personality, Allport (1937) had suggested three attributes of a mature personality: (1) interest in ideals and values beyond immediate physical needs (what he called psychogenic values); (2) the ability to objectify oneself, including an ability to see oneself from others' point of view and to laugh at oneself; and (3) the possession of some unifying philosophy of life, although it need not be religious in character, articulated in words, or entirely complete. Given this conception of maturity, Allport believed that religion might either enhance or inhibit it.

> Most of the criticism of religion is directed to its immature forms. When immature it has not evolved beyond the level of impulsive self-gratification. Instead of dealing with psychogenic values it serves either a wish-fulfilling or soporific function for the self-centered interests. When immature it does not entail self-objectification, but remains unreflective, failing to provide a context of meaning in which the individual can locate himself, and with perspective judge the quality of his conduct. Finally, the immature sentiment is not really unifying in its effect upon the personality. Excluding, as it does, whole regions of experience, it is spasmodic, segmented, and even when fanatic in intensity, it is but partially integrative of the personality. . . .
>
> While we guard against overestimating the consistency and completeness of the mature religious sentiment, we may nonetheless list the attributes that mark if off from the immature sentiment. By comparison, the mature sentiment is (1) well differentiated; (2) dynamic in character in spite of its derivative nature; (3) productive of a consistent morality; (4) comprehensive; (5) integral; and (6) fundamentally heuristic. It will be seen that these criteria are nothing else than special applications in the religious sphere of the tests for maturity of personality: a widened range of interests, insight into oneself, and the development of an adequately embracing philosophy of life. (Allport, 1950, pp. 54, 57)

Mature religion is, then, characterized by complex, critical reflection on religious issues; it "is the outgrowth of many successive discriminations and continuous reorganization" (Allport, 1950, p. 59). At the same time that it provides direction to life as a "master-motive," it is flexible and responsive to new information, neither fanatic nor compulsive. It deals openly and honestly with "matters central to all existence," including the difficult questions of ethical responsibility and evil. It produces the ability to "act wholeheartedly even without absolute certainty. It can be sure without being cocksure" (Allport, 1950, p. 72).

In light of our analysis of religious experience in Chapter 4, Allport's conception of mature religion seems most interesting. Although it predates cognitive structure models of personality change (e.g., Harvey, Hunt, & Schroeder, 1961; Rokeach, 1960), it provides a clear description of an orientation toward religion that is the product of a highly complex cognitive organization for dealing with existential questions, an organization that has emerged from repeated creative changes in response to existential conflicts.

Unfortunately, in 1950 Allport offered no empirical means for identifying immature and mature religion. And without this, one is forced to rely on personal judgments, which are very subject to bias. Well aware of this problem, Allport and his students turned their attention to the development of an objective questionnaire that could identify and distinguish the two ways of being religious. This effort produced the currently popular extrinsic versus intrinsic distinction.

Extrinsic versus intrinsic religion: Allport's later formulation. In the process of developing an empirical measure of immature and mature religion, Allport's conception of these two ways of being religious changed. First, by the late 1950s he had dropped the heavily value-laden labels "immature" and "mature" and spoke instead of extrinsic and intrinsic religion (Allport, 1959). Second, the definitions of these new concepts were, perhaps necessarily, narrower than the definitions of immature and mature religion.

In his classic 1967 paper written with Michael Ross, Allport suggested that "the extrinsically motivated individual *uses* his religion, whereas the intrinsically motivated *lives* his" (Allport & Ross, 1967, p. 434). Allport and Ross expanded on this distinction as follows:

> *Extrinstic orientation.* Persons with this orientation are disposed to use religion for their own ends. The term is borrowed from axiology, to designate an interest that is held because it serves other, more ultimate interests. Extrinsic values are always instrumental and utilitarian. Persons with this orientation may find religion useful in a variety of ways—to provide security and solace, sociability and distraction, status and self-justification. The embraced creed is lightly held or else selectively shaped to fit more primary needs. In theological terms the extrinsic type turns to God, but without turning away from self.
>
> *Intrinsic orientation.* Persons with this orientation find their master motive in religion. Other needs, strong as they may be, are regarded as of less ultimate significance, and they are, so far as possible, brought into harmony with the religious beliefs and prescriptions. Having embraced a creed the individual endeavors to internalize it and follow it fully. It is in this sense that he *lives* his religion. (Allport & Ross, 1967, p. 434)

These definitions maintain much of the flavor of Allport's earlier distinction between immature and mature religion, with one important difference. Compared with the concept of mature religion, there seems to be less emphasis in the notion of intrinsic religion on flexibility, skepticism, and resistance to absolutistic thinking, and more on religion as a master motive that is internalized and followed fully. This shift in emphasis is even more apparent when one looks at the questionnaire that Allport and Ross used to measure extrinsic and intrinsic religion.

The Religious Orientation Scale: An Empirical Measure of Extrinsic versus Intrinsic Religion

The scale. The questionnaire Allport and Ross used to measure extrinsic and intrinsic religion is called the Religious Orientation scale. Actually, the Religious Orientation scale consists of two scales, one designed to measure extrinsic religion and one to measure intrinsic religion. The items on each of these scales are presented in Table 6.1. Read the items over carefully to form your own impression of what each scale is measuring.

What does it measure? Now that you have had a chance to form your own impression, we can tell you that we doubt the Religious Orientation scale

Table 6.1 Items on the Extrinsic and Intrinsic scales of the Religious Orientation scale used by Allport and Ross (1967)

Extrinsic scale

1. Although I believe in my religion, I feel there are many more important things in my life.
2. It doesn't matter so much what I believe so long as I lead a moral life.
3. The primary purpose of prayer is to gain relief and protection.
4. The church is most important as a place to formulate good social relationships.
5. What religion offers me most is comfort when sorrows and misfortune strike.
6. I pray chiefly because I have been taught to pray.
7. Although I am a religious person I refuse to let religious considerations influence my everyday affairs.
8. A primary reason for my interest in religion is that my church is a congenial social activity.
9. Occasionally I find it necessary to compromise my religious beliefs in order to protect my social and economic well-being.
10. One reason for my being a church member is that such membership helps to establish a person in the community.
11. The purpose of prayer is to secure a happy and peaceful life.

Intrinsic scale

1. It is important for me to spend periods of time in private religious thought and meditation.
2. If not prevented by unavoidable circumstances, I attend church.
3. I try hard to carry my religion over into all my other dealings in life.
4. The prayers I say when I am alone carry as much meaning and personal emotion as those said by me during services.
5. Quite often I have been keenly aware of the presence of God or the Divine Being.
6. I read literature about my faith (or church).
7. If I were to join a church group I would prefer to join a Bible study group rather than a social fellowship.
8. My religious beliefs are what really lie behind my whole approach to life.
9. Religion is especially important to me because it answers many questions about the meaning of life.

Note: For several items the wording has been changed slightly to permit responses on a nine-point scale from strongly disagree (1) to strongly agree (9). Allport and Ross limited responses to two categories, disagree or agree, or to a forced-choice between two alternatives, e.g., Bible study or social fellowship.

measures what it is supposed to. Consider the items in relation to Allport's concepts of extrinsic and intrinsic religion and his earlier concepts of immature and mature religion. The items used to measure the extrinsic orientation to religion seem fairly consistent with the concepts of extrinsic and immature religion; they suggest an approach in which the individual uses religion in a self-centered way to serve a range of other needs. But the relation of a number of items on the Intrinsic scale to the concept of intrinsic religion—and especially to the concept of mature religion—seems less clear. Consider such items as: "I try hard to carry my religion over into all my other dealings in life"; "Religion is especially important to me because it answers many questions about the meaning of life"; "If not prevented by unavoidable circumstances, I attend church." Although it is possible that these statements would be strongly endorsed by a person whose religion was "mature" by Allport's 1950 definition, it is also possible that they would receive strong endorsement from a person who tended to identify with and accept religious dogma, authority figures, or institutions in a rigid, uncritical, and dependent fashion.

This possibility leads us to suggest that, as measured by the Religious Orientation scale, intrinsic religion may have at least as much in common with Erik Hoffer's (1951) concept of the "true believer" as with Allport's concept of mature religion. Hoffer defined the *true believer* as a person

> of fanatical faith who is ready to sacrifice his life for a holy cause. . . . The fanatic is convinced that the cause he holds on to is monolithic and eternal—a rock of ages. Still, his sense of security is derived from his passionate attachment and not from the excellence of his cause. The fanatic is not really a stickler to principle. He embraces a cause not primarily because of its justness and holiness but because of his desperate need for something to hold on to. (pp. x, 80)

Such a true believer is far removed from, even antithetical to, Allport's views of intrinsic and mature religion. Yet when we read through the Religious Orientation scale and try to imagine the responses of a religious true beilever, we find that such an individual would probably score very high on the Intrinsic scale.

There is considerable empirical evidence that lends support to this suggestion. It has been found that intrinsic items like those quoted above correlate positively with a tendency to see the world in terms of absolute, rigid categories (King & Hunt, 1975). There is also evidence that the Intrinsic scale as a whole correlates negatively with a measure of open-mindedness in pursuing religious questions, positively with at least some aspects of authoritarianism, and positively with a measure of agreement with the teachings of one's church (Kahoe, 1974, 1977; Kahoe & Meadow, 1977). Finally, it has been found by Gorsuch & McFarland (1972) that scores on a revised version of the Intrinsic scale (Hoge, 1972) correlate positively with responses to three items concerning orthodox religious involvement: (1) frequency of attendance at worship service ($r = .61$); (2) personal importance of religion ($r = .84$); and (3) belief that Jesus is the Christ, the Son of the Living God ($r = .69$). These correlations underscore the close relationship between intrinsic religion and orthodox religious involvement; indeed, they suggest that one can get a good measure of what the Intrinsic scale measures simply by asking individuals how involved they are in religion and how strongly they hold orthodox beliefs.

Taken as a whole, these findings seem difficult to reconcile with Allport's concept of the intrinsic orientation; they seem even more difficult to reconcile with his earlier concept of mature religion. They lead us to conclude that in most samples the Intrinsic scale probably measures something other than what Allport intended; it probably measures intense, perhaps even rigid, devotion to orthodox religious beliefs and practices—or, using the terminology of Kirkpatrick and Hood (1990), it probably measures "religious commitment."

The Religious Orientation scale has produced results other than those Allport intended in another way as well. Allport viewed the extrinsic and intrinsic orientations as distinct religious "types" or, at times, as opposite ends of a single continuum. Viewed in this way, if a person's religious orientation is intrinsic, it cannot be extrinsic; the two are mutually exclusive. But Allport and Ross (1967) found that those who scored high on the Extrinsic scale did not necessarily score low on the Intrinsic scale; the correlation between the scales was close to zero. Other studies using the Religious Orientation scale have typically found the same (see the review by Hunt & King, 1971), except within religiously conservative samples where moderate negative correlations appear (Donahue, 1985). These findings suggest that the Intrinsic and Extrinsic scales do not measure two distinct types of religious orientation, such that a person is one or the other; they instead measure two independent continuous dimensions. A given individual may be more or less concerned to maintain a devout adherence to his or her religion (measured by the Intrinsic scale) and at the same time may be more or less willing to admit the personal and social gains derived therefrom (measured by the Extrinsic scale).[2]

AN ALTERNATIVE CONCEPTION OF TWO WAYS OF BEING RELIGIOUS: CONSENSUAL VERSUS COMMITTED

If the extrinsic versus intrinsic distinction as measured by the Extrinsic and Intrinsic scales is inadequate, what other conceptions of ways of being religious have been proposed? The second most popular conception is the distinction between consensual and committed religion employed by Bernard Spilka and his associates. Allen and Spilka (1967) defined *committed religion*

2. The Intrinsic scale has also been criticized because individuals' responses to the different items on the scale do not always correlate highly with one another (Hunt & King, 1971). This criticism appears to have been adequately answered by Dean Hoge (1972). Hoge developed a revised version of the Intrinsic scale that has satisfactory inter-item correlations and, moreover, correlates well ($r = .59$) with judgments by ministers about whether respondents' orientation toward religion is extrinsic or intrinsic.

Hoge's scale does not, however, answer the more basic criticism, that the Intrinsic scale actually measures intense devotion to orthodox religion. On the contrary, his scale provides additional evidence for this suggestion. First, scores on his scale correlate very highly with scores on Allport and Ross's Intrinsic scale ($r = .86$), indicating that the two measure the same underlying dimension. Second, a look at the items on Hoge's scale suggests even more strongly that this underlying dimension is devout orthodoxy. Not only does Hoge's scale employ several of the Allport and Ross "true believer" items (e.g., "I try hard to carry my religion over into all my other dealings in life"; "My religious beliefs are what really lie behind my whole approach to life"), but the items added to stabilize the scale are also ones likely to receive endorsement from a rigid, true believer: "One should seek God's guidance when making every important decision"; "My faith sometimes restricts my actions"; "Nothing is as important to me as serving God as best I know how." Thus, by providing a more internally consistent set of items, Hoge has revealed even more clearly that the Intrinsic scale measures devout—perhaps rigid—orthodoxy more than it measures the mature, flexible approach to religion that Allport set out to measure.

as a discerning, highly differentiated, candid, open, self-critical, abstract, and relational approach to religious questions. Moreover, for the committed individual, religion is a central value. They defined *consensual religion* as the opposite of each of these characteristics. To measure these two ways of being religious, Allen and Spilka used a complex multidimensional coding of interview responses.

Although Allen and Spilka did not explicitly make the comparison, one cannot help being struck by the similarity between their description of the characteristics of committed and consensual religion and Allport's (1950) earlier description of the characteristics of mature and immature religion. Indeed, with their multidimensional coding technique, Allen and Spilka may well have empirically identified Allport's concepts better than did Allport himself. Perhaps it is for this reason that James Dittes, in his major review of research in psychology of religion in 1969, indicated a preference for Spilka's consensual-committed distinction over Allport's extrinsic-intrinsic distinction.

But multidimensional coding of interview responses is difficult and cumbersome, so during the 1970s Spilka attempted to develop a more easily administered questionnaire measure of the consensual-committed distinction. In doing so, his distinction suffered a fate similar to Allport's. Much of the emphasis in the initial concept of committed religion on complexity, flexibility, and self-criticism was lost; more emphasis was placed on religion as a central value.

As a result, although Allen and Spilka (1967) found little relationship between their classification into consensual versus committed and a measure of Allport's extrinsic versus intrinsic distinction, studies during the 1970s found positive correlations between the questionnaire measures of consensual and committed religion on the one hand and extrinsic and intrinsic religion on the other. For example, in one study with a diverse sample of respondents, Spilka, Stout, Minton, and Sizemore (1977) reported positive correlations of .45 between their Consensual scale and the Allport and Ross Extrinsic scale and of .64 between their Committed scale and the Allport and Ross Intrinsic scale (see also Spilka, Read, Allen, & Dailey, 1968). When one looks more closely at the Committed scale, this high positive correlation with the Intrinsic scale is not surprising; seven of the nine items on Allport and Ross's Intrinsic scale are included in the fifteen items on Spilka's Committed scale.

Comparing the consensual-committed distinction as measured by questionnaire with the extrinsic-intrinsic distinction, Spilka concluded in 1977: "Recent work (Spilka & Minton, 1975; Spilka & Mullin, 1977) strongly implies that these forms of personal religion really represent different facets of the same phenomenon, and it is not inappropriate to refer to Intrinsic-Committed and Extrinsic-Consensual orientations" (Spilka, Stout, Minton, & Sizemore, 1977, p. 170). We would agree that as measured by questionnaire, the consensual-committed distinction is essentially the same as the extrinsic-intrinsic distinction. But because of the problems with the Intrinsic scale noted above, we find this development regrettable. The Committed scale, like the Intrinsic scale, seems to be primarily a measure of intense devotion to orthodox religious beliefs.

A THREE-DIMENSIONAL ANALYSIS OF INDIVIDUAL RELIGION: AS MEANS, END, AND QUEST

In translating Allport's concept of mature religion into the empirically identifiable concepts of intrinsic or committed religion, some aspects of the initial concept were lost. Allport and Ross's Intrinsic scale and Spilka's Committed scale are primarily measures of single-minded commitment to religion and reliance on religion as a central, master motive in life. Single-mindedness and centrality were part of Allport's conception of mature religion, but they were not all. Mature religion also included a critical, open-ended approach to existential questions.

To be more specific, Allport's concept of mature religion included three characteristics that seem to be missing from the questionnaire measures of intrinsic or committed religion. First, Allport suggested that the mature religious sentiment is integrative in the sense of encouraging the individual to face complex problems like ethical responsibility and evil without reducing their complexity. Second, mature religion involves a readiness to doubt and be self-critical: "The mature religious sentiment is ordinarily fashioned in the workshop of doubt" (Allport, 1950, p. 73). In this regard, it seems reminiscent of the approach to religion proposed by the poet Tennyson: "There lives more faith in honest doubt, believe me, than in half your creeds." Third, there is an emphasis on incompleteness and tentativeness; the mature religious sentiment involves a continual search for more light on religious questions. As Walter Huston Clark (1958) said when summarizing Allport's concept of mature religion, "Maturity requires an admixture of humility and makes it possible for the true believer to absorb new points of view into his truth system and so to make his religious progress a genuine quest" (p. 247).

A Third Dimension: Religion as Quest

These characteristics of complexity, doubt, and tentativeness suggest a way of being religious that is very different from either the extrinsic or the intrinsic (at least as the latter is measured by the Intrinsic or Committed scale); they suggest an approach that involves honestly facing existential questions in all their complexity, while at the same time resisting clear-cut, pat answers. An individual who approaches religion in this way recognizes that he or she does not know, and probably never will know, the final truth about such matters. Still, the questions are deemed important, and however tentative and subject to change, answers are sought. There may or may not be a clear belief in a transcendent reality, but there is a transcendent, religious aspect to the individual's life. We shall call this open-ended, questioning approach *religion as quest*.

A number of writers, both theologians and psychologists, have suggested the importance of a quest dimension to religion. Perhaps the clearest theological statement comes from H. Richard Niebuhr. In *The Responsible Self* (1963) Niebuhr presented a picture of a religious individual who participates in an open-ended dialogue with his or her physical and social environment; existential questions are confronted, but definitive answers are not obtained or even expected (see also Batson, Beker, & Clark, 1973; Bonhoeffer, 1953; Gandhi, 1948; Rubenstein, 1965; Tillich, 1951, for similar views).

On the psychological side, Erich Fromm (1950) made a distinction between "authoritarian" and "humanistic" religion. Fromm suggested that often religion is borrowed from other people or social institutions. He believed that religion acquired in this way imposes tyrannical control over the native impulses of the individual; it is authoritarian. But sometimes religion is a product of creative forces within the individual; this kind of religion Fromm called humanistic. It involves the individual hammering out his or her own stance on religious questions, refusing to be dominated by the views advocated by the religious institutions of society. In a similar vein, Peter Bertocci (1958) spoke of "religion as creative insecurity," suggesting that "to flee from insecurity is to miss the whole point of being human, the whole point of religion" (p. ix).

From these authors and others (for example, Barron, 1968; Bergson, 1935; Maslow, 1964; Rugg, 1963) a picture begins to emerge of a dimension of personal religion that is quite different from either the extrinsic or the intrinsic dimension. To highlight the difference, compare the extrinsic religion of the businessman who attends church solely because "it's good for business" and the intrinsic religion of the affirmation "I *know* God exists; I talk to Him every day" with the quest approach to religion displayed by Siddhartha, Malcolm X, and Mahatma Gandhi.

Siddhartha searched for seven years before attaining the enlightenment that made him the Buddha. And even then he had not found the answer; he had found a path, a direction to go. Malcolm X was continually seeking a broader and deeper religious perspective. This search first led him to reject the Christianity of his childhood, a Christianity that he found personally dehumanizing and racially oppressive, to turn to Black Muslim teachings. But he did not uncritically embrace these teachings as the final, absolute answer. Rather, his trip to Mecca led him to reject as well the reverse racism that he saw in the Black Muslim movement and to turn to a new understanding of Islamic faith in terms of universal love and brotherhood.

Gandhi clearly displayed a quest orientation in his "experiments with Truth." In his own words,

> What I want to achieve—what I have been striving and pining to achieve these thirty years—is self-realization, to see God face to face. . . . I live and move and have my being in pursuit of this goal. All that I do by way of speaking and writing, and all my ventures in the political field, are directed to this same end. . . .

> I worship God as Truth only. I have not yet found Him, but I am seeking after Him. I am prepared to sacrifice the things dearest to me in pursuit of this quest. Even if the sacrifice demanded my very life, I hope I may be prepared to give it. But as long as I have not realized this Absolute Truth, so long must I hold by the relative truth as I have conceived it. That relative truth must, meanwhile, be my beacon, my shield and buckler. . . . The instruments for the quest of truth are as simple as they are difficult. They may appear quite impossible to an arrogant person, and quite possible to an innocent child. The seeker after truth should be humbler than the dust. The world crushes the dust under its feet, but the seeker after truth should be so humble himself that even the dust could crush him. Only then, and not till then, will he have a glimpse of truth. . . .
>
> I hope and pray that no one will regard [my] advice . . . as authoritative. [My] experiments . . . should be regarded as illustrations, in the light of which every one may carry on his own experiments according to his own inclinations and capacity. (Gandhi, 1948, pp. 4–7)

Although many writers have pointed to the existence of a quest dimension of personal religion, and although we can identify people whose religious experience seems to exemplify this quest, none of the writers have provided an efficient empirical method for measuring the quest dimension. Therefore, we have undertaken the task of developing questionnaire scales to measure it, as well as to measure two other dimensions—a *means* dimension, in which religion is a means to other self-serving ends, and an *end* dimension, in which religion is an ultimate end in itself. The means and end dimensions are based on our understanding of Allport's extrinsic-intrinsic distinction.[3]

To make our technique for measuring the means, end, and quest dimensions as clear as possible, we shall present it in some detail. Development and revision of this technique have been in progress since 1969. Because the presentation here includes the latest revisions, it differs somewhat from earlier presentations (e.g., Batson, 1971, 1976; Batson & Ventis, 1982).

Measuring the Means, End, and Quest Dimensions

In developing empirical measures of the means, end, and quest dimensions, we decided that we needed not only to add a measure of religion as a quest, but also to pin down more explicitly our assumptions about the means (extrinsic) and end (intrinsic) dimensions. In order to accomplish these aims, we developed four new questionnaire scales; three were combined into a Religious Life Inventory; the fourth was an Orthodoxy scale. We also employed the Extrinsic and Intrinsic scales developed by Allport and Ross. Thus, to measure the three dimensions, we used six different scales: the Extrinsic and Intrinsic scales and our four new scales.

3. An alternative approach would have been to develop a questionnaire that combined elements from Allport's intrinsic, end dimension and the quest dimension, creating a single scale to measure Allport's original concept of religious maturity. For an example of this alternative approach, see Dudley and Cruise (1990).

Four new religious orientation scales. The first new scale is called the External scale; it was designed to measure a component of the extrinsic, means dimension—the degree to which an individual's external social environment has influenced his or her personal religion. We assumed that religion that was a response to social influence would reflect an extrinsic, means orientation because it would presumably be motivated by a desire to gain the self-serving, extrinsic end of social approval. Accordingly, this scale included six items that assess the importance of authority figures and social institutions in shaping one's religious experience. In fact, our assumption that this scale would be associated with an extrinsic, means orientation has proved wrong. In most samples, higher scores on this scale are associated with higher scores on the Intrinsic rather than the Extrinsic scale, suggesting the importance of social influence in the development of strong, intrinsic devotion to religion as the master motive in life. The six items on the External scale are presented in the first section of Table 6.2.

The second new scale is called the Internal scale; it was designed to measure a component of the intrinsic, end dimension—the degree to which an individual's religion is a result of internal needs for certainty, strength, and direction. Building on Hoffer's (1951) understanding of the motives of the true believer, we assumed that these needs would reflect an intrinsic, end orientation because this orientation seems to be based on a need to find firm, clear answers to existential questions. Subsequent research has supported this assumption. The nine items on the Internal scale are presented in the second section of Table 6.2.

Perhaps the most important new scale is the Quest scale; it was designed to measure the basic component of the quest dimension—the degree to which an individual's religion involves an open-ended, responsive dialogue with existential questions raised by the contradictions and tragedies of life. The twelve items on this scale are presented in the third section of Table 6.2. These items were designed to address the three aspects of Allport's concept of mature religion that we found to be missing from the Intrinsic and Committed scales: readiness to face existential questions without reducing their complexity (Items 4, 8, 9, and 11); self-criticism and perception of religious doubts as positive (Items 3, 5, 7, and 12); and openness to change (Items 1, 2, 6, and 10).

The fourth new scale is called the Orthodoxy scale. It was patterned after an orthodoxy scale developed by Glock and Stark (1966) and was designed to measure belief in traditional religious doctrines. We assumed that such beliefs were an important component of the intrinsic, end dimension. Once again, subsequent research has supported this assumption. The twelve items on the Orthodoxy scale are presented in Table 6.3.

Traditional religious doctrines must, of course, be viewed from the perspective of some specific religious tradition. We chose to base our Orthodoxy scale on the Christian tradition because of its relative predominance in Western society. More precisely, the belief statements on the Orthodoxy scale come from American Protestantism. Although research suggests that

Table 6.2 Items on the External, Internal, and Quest scales of the Religious Life Inventory

External scale

1. The church has been very important for my religious development. (1)[a]
2. My minister (or youth director, camp counselor, etc.) has had a profound influence on my personal religious development. (7)
3. A major factor in my religious development has been the importance of religion for my parents. (15)
4. My religion serves to satisfy needs for fellowship and security. (21)
5. Certain people have served as "models" for my religious development. (26)
6. (−) Outside forces (other persons, church, etc.) have been relatively unimportant in my religious development. (34)[b]

Internal scale

1. My religious development is a natural response to our innate need for devotion to God. (4)
2. God's will should shape my life. (9)
3. It is necessary for me to have a religious belief. (12)
4. When it comes to religious questions, I feel driven to know the truth. (13)
5. (−) Religion is something I have never felt personally compelled to consider. (18)
6. (−) Whether I turn out to be religious or not doesn't make much difference to me. (24)
7. I have found it essential to have faith. (28)
8. I find it impossible to conceive of myself not being religious. (31)
9. (−) For me, religion has not been a "must." (35)

Quest scale

1. As I grow and change, I expect my religion also to grow and change. (3)
2. I am constantly questioning my religious beliefs. (5)
3. It might be said that I value my religious doubts and uncertainties. (6)
4. I was not very interested in religion until I began to ask questions about the meaning and purpose of my life. (8)
5. For me, doubting is an important part of what it means to be religious. (11)
6. (−) I do not expect my religious convictions to change in the next few years. (16)
7. (−) I find religious doubts upsetting. (17)
8. I have been driven to ask religious questions out of a growing awareness of the tensions in my world and in my relation to my world. (20)
9. My life experiences have led me to rethink my religious convictions. (25)
10. There are many religious issues on which my views are still changing. (27)
11. God wasn't very important for me until I began to ask questions about the meaning of my own life. (30)
12. Questions are far more central to my religious experience than are answers. (33)

Unscored buffer items

1. Wordly events cannot affect the eternal truths of my religion. (2)
2. On religious issues, I find the opinions of others irrelevant. (10)
3. I find my everyday experiences severely test my religious convictions. (14)
4. My religious development has emerged out of my growing sense of personal identity. (22)
5. My religion is a personal matter, independent of the influence of organized religion. (23)
6. It is important for me to learn about religion from those who know more about it than I do. (29)
7. The "me" of a few years back would be surprised at my present religious stance. (32)

[a]The number in parentheses indicates where the item appears among the thirty-five items on the Religious Life Inventory. All items are responded to on a nine-point scale from strongly disagree (1) to strongly agree (9).

[b]A minus sign preceding an item indicates that it is reversed in scoring (i.e., the number circled is subtracted from 10).

Table 6.3 Items on the Doctrinal Orthodoxy scale

1. I believe in the existence of a just and merciful personal God.
2. I believe God created the universe.
3. I believe God has a plan for the universe.
4. I believe Jesus Christ is the Divine Son of God.
5. I believe Jesus Christ was resurrected (raised from the dead).
6. I believe Jesus Christ is the Messiah promised in the Old Testament.
7. I believe one must accept Jesus Christ as Lord and Savior to be saved from sin.
8. I believe in the "second coming" (that Jesus Christ will one day return to judge and rule the world).
9. I believe in "original sin" (we are all born sinners).
10. I believe in life after death.
11. I believe there is a transcendent realm (an "other" world, not just this world in which we live).
12. I believe the Bible is the unique authority for God's will.

Note: All items are responded to on a nine-point scale from strongly disagree (1) to strongly agree (9).

the scale is appropriate for use with Catholics as well, at least American Catholics, it is clearly inappropriate for use with people whose religious tradition is not Christian. As would be expected, highly orthodox Jews, Moslems, and Buddhists score quite low. This restriction to a specific religious tradition seems unavoidable when one is measuring adherence to institutional beliefs, but it clearly limits the range of applicability of the measure and, as a result, the generality of the conclusions that can be drawn.

Combining these four scales with Allport and Ross's Extrinsic and Intrinsic scales, we expected to be able to measure each of the proposed three dimensions of being religious: as a means to some other end, as an end in itself, and as a quest. We expected Allport and Ross's Extrinsic scale to measure religion as a means. We expected Allport and Ross's Intrinsic scale and our External, Internal, and Orthodoxy scales to be highly correlated and to measure religion as an end. This expectation was based, first, on the finding that the External scale was associated with an intrinsic, end orientation rather than the extrinsic, means orientation, and second, on our belief that Allport and Ross's Intrinsic scale, contrary to their intent, measured devout allegiance to institutional religious orthodoxy. Finally, we expected our Quest scale to stand alone as a measure of religion as a quest.

Intercorrelation of the six religious orientation scales. Since 1969, various versions of these scales have been administered to numerous samples of undergraduates with at least a moderate interest in religion, as well as to several samples of seminary students and adult church members. Batson and Ventis (1982) presented mean scores (and standard deviations) on each of the scales for 258 undergraduates and for 67 seminarians, using an earlier six-item version of the Quest scale. They also presented correlations among the six scales for these undergraduates and seminarians. We shall present similar descriptive statistics for 424 undergraduates, using the latest

Table 6.4 Means and standard deviations on six religious orientation scales for 424 undergraduates interested in religion

Scales	Mean[a]	Standard deviation[a]
Extrinsic	4.54	1.04
Intrinsic	5.26	1.45
External	5.80	1.59
Internal	6.44	1.35
Quest	4.99	1.17
Orthodoxy	7.37	1.43

[a]All means and standard deviations are on nine-point response scales (1 = strongly disagree; 9 = strongly agree), having been adjusted for the number of items on each scale.

twelve-item version of the Quest scale presented in Table 6.2. Mean scores on each scale for the 424 undergraduates are presented in Table 6.4; so are the standard deviations. The correlations among the six scales for these undergraduates are presented in Table 6.5, including internal-consistency reliability coefficients (Cronbach's alpha) on the diagonal.

The correlations in Table 6.5 reveal that the six scales relate to one another very much as expected. Allport and Ross's Intrinsic scale correlates positively with our External, Internal, and Orthodoxy scales, providing additional support for our suggestion that, contrary to Allport's intent, the Intrinsic scale measures devout—perhaps even rigid—adherence to orthodox beliefs. Neither the Extrinsic nor the Quest scale correlates highly with any of the other scales. This is as expected because the Extrinsic scale is the only one measuring the extrinsic, means dimension, and the Quest scale is the only one designed to measure the quest dimension.

Combining the six scales through principal-components analysis to measure the means, end, and quest dimensions. In order to use these six scales to measure the three dimensions of individual religion—as a means, end, and quest—we employed principal-components analysis. Principal-components analysis is a form of factor analysis, a complex statistical technique

Table 6.5 Correlations among six religious orientation scales for 424 undergraduates interested in religion

Scales	Extrinsic	Intrinsic	External	Internal	Quest	Orthodoxy
Extrinsic	.72[a]	−.05	.03	−.12	.16	−.04
Intrinsic		.83	.59	.73	−.05	.55
External			.79	.62	−.17	.49
Internal				.84	−.22	.68
Quest					.78	−.25
Orthodoxy						.91

[a]Entries on the diagonal are internal-consistency reliability coefficients (Cronbach's alpha).

well beyond the scope of this book. Still, the basic function of principal-components analysis is easy to understand. Through comparison and contrast of different individuals' responses to the six scales, it is possible to detect the conceptual dimensions that underlie these responses, as well as how each of the scales relates to each of these underlying dimensions. The underlying dimensions are called *components,* and the relationship of a scale to a given component is called its *loading* on that component.

When responses to the six religious orientation scales were component analyzed, they produced three independent components, one corresponding to the means dimension, one to the end dimension, and one to the quest dimension. Accordingly, we named the components Religion as Means, Religion as End, and Religion as Quest. The loadings of each of the six scales on each component are presented in Table 6.6.

As can be seen in Table 6.6, the contribution of each of the scales to each component is very much as expected. The Religion-as-Means component is defined primarily by the Allport and Ross Extrinsic scale; the Religion-as-End component is defined primarily by four scales—Allport and Ross's Intrinsic scale and our External, Internal, and Orthodoxy scales; finally, the Religion-as-Quest component is defined primarily by our Quest scale.

Once one has determined the relationship between the scales and the underlying components, it is possible to compute scores for each individual on each of the three components. This is done by multiplying each individual's score on each scale (standardized) by a component-score coefficient and then summing these products. The three scores resulting from this computation reflect an individual's score relative to other individuals on each of the three components. These component scores, then, provide an empirical measure of the degree to which an individual orients toward religion in each of the three ways—as a means, end, and quest. And this was our goal. The component-score coefficients for the Means, End, and Quest components for the 424 undergraduates are presented in Table 6.7.

Table 6.6 Component loadings of six religious orientation scales for 424 undergraduates interested in religion

	Components		
Scales	Religion as Means	Religion as End	Religion as Quest
Extrinsic	.991*	−.023	.084
Intrinsic	−.068	.876*	.118
External	.106	.797*	−.086
Internal	−.115	.895*	−.120
Quest	.087	−.109	.975*
Orthodoxy	.003	.777*	−.253

Note: Principal-components analysis with a varimax rotation.
*Indicates highest component loading for each scale.

Table 6.7 Component-score coefficients for 424 undergraduates interested in religion

Scales	Components: Religion as Means	Religion as End	Religion as Quest
Extrinsic	.99	.02	−.07
Intrinsic	−.07	.34	.24
External	.13	.29	.00
Internal	−.08	.32	.01
Quest	−.06	.09	.96
Orthodoxy	.05	.26	−.16

Two characteristics of our three-dimensional measure of ways of being religious. Two characteristics of our approach to measuring these three ways of being religious should be emphasized. First, even though most researchers would agree that a person's orientation to religion need not be of one or another single type, the existing literature on different ways of being religious suggests that it is difficult to resist typological thinking. Researchers have often typed individuals as extrinsic *or* intrinsic (or, if they score high on both scales, as "indiscriminately proreligious" or, if they score low on both, as "indiscriminately antireligious"—see Allport & Ross, 1967), consensual *or* committed, end *or* quest. This practice of typing persists even though there is much evidence suggesting that it is inappropriate, at least when using the currently available questionnaire measures of religious orientation (see Hunt & King, 1971, for a review). In spite of attempts to justify typing (e.g., Donahue, 1985; Hood, 1978), we know of no clear evidence that the responses of people typed in one way or another cannot be explained by where these individuals score on one or another of the continuous dimensions. Fortunately, there are some recent signs that the practice of typing may be losing favor (Gorsuch, 1988; Kirkpatrick & Hood, 1990).

In our approach, we have avoided typing. We have not classified religious individuals as being of a means type, end type, or quest type. Instead, we have measured the degree to which each individual's religion can be characterized in *each* of these ways. Each individual receives a score on each component, and each component is a continuous dimension. We believe that this shift from talking about types to talking about continuous dimensions is an important advantage of our approach.

Second, the three dimensions in our model are independent of one another. Consistent with standard practice, our principal-components analysis was carried out in such a way that each of the components is uncorrelated with the other two (in factor-analysis terms, an orthogonal rotation was employed). This means that, for example, if you score high on the Quest component you need not score low on either the Means or the End component. Indeed, how you score on one component says precisely nothing about how you will score on the other two. The three are independent dimensions. You might score high on all three components, low on all three (if you are relatively nonreligious), or high on one or two and low on another.

These two points are important to keep in mind when considering the research reported in Part III of this book concerning the behavioral consequences of each of these ways of being religious. In Part III we shall *not* be considering how, for example, a quest-type person responds as opposed to an end-type person. We shall not, because we have not classified people into religious types. We shall instead consider how each of the three independent, continuous dimensions of personal religion relates to behavior.

A simplified procedure for obtaining scores on the means, end, and quest dimensions. We must admit that our technique for deriving scores on the means, end, and quest dimensions through the use of principal-components analysis is complex and cumbersome. Some of the complexity is necessary because the six religious orientation scales do not relate to one another in a simple fashion. Still, you may be disappointed not to be able to determine your own score on each of the three dimensions.

If so, then you may be interested to learn that some researchers have employed a simpler strategy for obtaining scores on the means, end, and quest dimensions. The three religious orientation scales that are conceptually most relevant to the three dimensions—the Extrinsic, Intrinsic, and Quest scales—are almost always highly associated with the Means, End, and Quest components, respectively (see the component loadings in Table 6.6), and only slightly correlated with one another. So scores on these three scales provide reasonably good approximations of scores on the three independent dimensions. In most cases, this simpler measurement strategy has produced results that closely parallel results based on component analysis.

We would encourage you to take a few minutes now to compute your own scores on the means, ends, and quest dimensions using this simplified procedure (the necessary steps are described in Table 6.8). Computing your own score on each dimension is probably the best way to gain an understanding of our three-dimensional model. In addition, when in Part III we consider the psychological consequences of these three dimensions, the discussion will have more personal relevance if you have some idea of your own score on each dimension. Of course, you should not take your scores too seriously because you are aware of the intent of the scales. Also, we have arranged the items in Tables 6.1 and 6.2 by scale, whereas normally they are intermixed.

Initial Discriminant Validity of Our Measure of the Means, End, and Quest Dimensions

To provide an initial check whether our three-dimensional analysis including religion as quest actually measured the open-ended search dimension in Allport's concept of mature religion in addition to the devout belief (end)

Table 6.8 Steps in a simplified procedure for obtaining scores on the means, end, and quest dimensions by computing scores on the Extrinsic, Intrinsic, and Quest scales

1. Each individual to be tested should consent to having his or her religious orientation measured.
2. After consent is obtained, have each individual respond to each item on each of the three key religious orientation scales—Extrinsic, Intrinsic, and Quest—using a nine-point response scale ranging from strongly disagree (1) to strongly agree (9). Each individual should be encouraged to give the response that best reflects his or her own true opinion. There are, of course, no right or wrong answers; some people will agree and some disagree with each item.
3. To determine an individual's score on the Extrinsic, Intrinsic, and Quest scales, first reverse the individual's score on each item on the Quest scale preceded by a minus sign in Table 6.2. This is done by subtracting the marked response from 10. Each item now has a corrected response.
4. For each scale, add up the individual's corrected responses to all the items on the scale and divide the sum by the number of items on the scale to get an average response (AR). You will now have three scores, one for each scale.
5. These scores can be compared to the means for each scale in Table 6.4 to see if the individual's score is below or above the average on that scale.
6. For a more precise assessment, you can compute the individual's standard score (SS) on each scale. This is done by subtracting the mean (M) for each scale from the individual's average response (AR) obtained in Step 4 for that scale, then dividing the remainder by the standard deviation (SD) for that scale. Thus, SS = (AR − M)/SD. The means and standard deviations for each scale are reported in Table 6.4. (If you are computing scores for a sample of thirty or more individuals, scores can be standardized using means and standard deviations computed from that sample.) An individual's standard score on the Extrinsic, Intrinsic, and Quest scale will, in most cases, closely approximate that individual's score on the Means, End, and Quest dimensions. These standard scores for the entire sample will have a mean of 0.0 and a standard deviation of 1.0. And, for a given dimension, scores below −1.0 (one standard deviation below the mean) are below the 16th percentile; scores below −2.0 are below the 3rd percentile. Scores above 1.0 are above the 84th percentile; scores above 2.0 are above the 97th percentile.

dimension tapped by the Intrinsic scale, we administered the six scales to individuals whom we thought should score especially high or low on the end and quest dimensions. This way, we could find out whether these individuals did. The individuals selected for initial comparison were fifteen Princeton University undergraduates who were members of one of two campus organizations. Eight were members of a nondenominational evangelical Christian group; for them, Christ was the answer. We expected that these individuals would score especially high on the end dimension and relatively low on the quest dimension. The other seven were members of a social service organization; they were involved in dealing with personal and social crises through work in local mental hospitals, hot-line organizations, or Big Brother programs. We expected that these individuals would score especially high on the quest dimension.

Even though these samples were quite small, making it more difficult to obtain statistically reliable differences, the predicted pattern of results was found. Relative to a comparison sample of thirty-one Princeton undergraduates from Christian backgrounds not involved in either of these groups, the evangelicals scored significantly ($p < .05$) higher on the End component (and also, as it turned out, on the Means component) and significantly ($p <$ .05) lower on the Quest component. The social service group scored significantly ($p < .05$) higher than the comparison sample on the Quest component. These results indicated that the End and Quest components could discriminate in a predictable fashion between individuals that one would expect to be especially high or low on these two dimensions of personal religion (see Batson, 1976, for a more detailed discussion of this validation study). Still, questions about the validity of the Quest scale have persisted.

More Questions about the Validity of the Quest Scale

Perhaps because the concept of religion as quest challenges an exclusively positive view of Allport's highly popular concept of intrinsic religion, a number of questions have been raised in recent years about the validity of the Quest scale. Critics have asked: Is not the Quest scale really a measure of agnosticism, of anti-orthodoxy, or sophomoric religious doubt, or of religious conflict? Indeed, is it a measure of anything religious at all?

Before adopting the Quest scale as the key measure of a third dimension of individual religion that is independent of the means (extrinsic) and end (intrinsic) dimensions, it is important to address these questions about the scale's validity. We need to know whether the Quest scale measures something other than is measured by the Extrinsic and Intrinsic scales, and if so, what.

Virtually every one of the over fifty studies conducted to date using the Quest scale has found low correlations between it and the Extrinsic and the Intrinsic scales. Correlations with the Extrinsic scale are typically in the .00 to .25 range; correlations with the Intrinsic scale are typically in the −.10 to .10 range. Moreover, virtually every one of the approximately thirty studies that has included a principal-components analysis of the six religious orientation scales has found that these three scales load clearly and distinctly on three separate, independent components: Means (Extrinsic), End (Intrinsic), and Quest. Therefore, there seems little question that the Quest scale is measuring something different from the Extrinsic and Intrinsic scales. Questions remain, however, about what the something different measured by the Quest scale really is.

Does the Quest Scale measure anything religious? In 1985 Michael Donahue expressed concern that the Quest scale might not measure a religious dimension at all, let alone the intended religious dimension. In Donahue's words, "Means, end, and quest are certainly three separate, orthogonal, replicable dimensions, but they may not all be dimensions of religiousness" (1985, p. 413). He suggested that "until some group of individuals reasonably identifiable as religious can be demonstrated to have higher *Q* [Quest] scores than another group, it seems invalid to call this a measure of religiousness" (1985, p. 413).

Comparing seminarians to undergraduates. We can only assume that when making this statement, Donahue was unconvinced by the initial validity study already described and had overlooked the scores on the Quest scale reported by Batson and Ventis (1982, p. 155) not only for undergraduates with at least a moderate interest in religion but also for seminarians. Assuming that the seminarians, who were Princeton Theological Seminary students training for the Presbyterian ministry, are "reasonably identifiable as religious," then their significantly higher mean on the Quest scale (6.67) relative to the undergraduates (5.15; $p < .001$) would seem to meet Donahue's criterion for concluding that the Quest scale is a valid measure of something religious.

Comparing members of a charismatic Bible study to members of a traditional Bible study. Further evidence that the Quest scale measures something religious comes from a validation study by Ferriani and Batson (1990). They compared scores on the six religious orientation scales of two quite different interdenominational Bible study groups. One was a traditional group (9 men, 17 women; 25 Protestant, 1 Catholic); the other was a nontraditional, charismatic group (17 men, 15 women; 28 Protestant, 4 Catholic). The nontraditional group placed emphasis on religion as a shared search; some members spoke in tongues, and some prayed with hands raised.

Members of both groups reported a very high interest in religion; means were 7.96 and 8.06 for the traditional and nontraditional groups, respectively, on a 1 *(not at all)* to 9 *(extremely)* response scale. Both groups also reported very frequent participation in religious activities; means were 5.35 and 5.43 for the traditional and nontraditional groups, respectively, on a 1 *(never)* to 6 *(more than once a day)* response scale.

The two groups differed significantly on only one of the six religious orientation scales. As would be expected if the Quest scale measured a dimension of religiousness concerned with an open-ended search without exclusive reliance on traditional answers, the mean score on the Quest scale was higher for the members of the nontraditional, charismatic Bible study group (5.45) than for members of the traditional Bible study group (4.46; $p < .001$).

In light of the undergraduate versus seminarian comparison and the traditional versus charismatic Bible study comparison, it seems clear that certain groups of individuals reasonably identifiable as religious can be demonstrated to have higher Quest scores than another group. So, following Donahue's (1985) logic, it seems appropriate to accept the Quest scale as a measure of a third dimension of personal religion, independent of the means (extrinsic) and end (intrinsic) dimensions. Is, however, this third dimension the one intended? Several alternatives have been suggested.

Does the Quest scale measure agnosticism or sophomoric doubt? Allowing that the Quest scale might measure something religious, but doubting that it measured what was intended, Donahue (1985) suggested a second possibility: The Quest scale "might best be characterized as an agnosticism scale" (p. 413). Donahue admitted that "persons with mature and differentiated religious orientations might agree with [Quest] items," but, he argued, "so might iconoclasts who sophomorically and reflexively respond 'why' to every answer given" (p. 413). Donahue suggested that the Quest scale may simply be picking up agnosticism or sophomoric doubt, especially since so many of the studies employing the Quest scale have used college freshmen and sophomores as participants.

One can certainly imagine agnostics who would score high on the Quest scale. Apparently, however, there are many orthodox believers who do too. Correlations between scores on this scale and scores on the Orthodoxy scale are typically in the .00 to −.20 range. If the Quest scale is actually measuring agnosticism with regard to orthodox beliefs, this correlation should be strongly negative. So, if the Quest scale is measuring agnosticism, it is doing a very bad job.

One can also imagine sophomoric doubters who would score high on the Quest scale. Apparently, however, there are many who are not sophomores who do too. If, as Donahue (1985) suggested, the Quest scale is actually measuring sophomoric doubt, then we would expect scores on the scale to drop as the sophomores "wise up" and mature. We would not, for example, expect the Princeton Theological Seminary students, who were not only older but who presumably also took their religion rather seriously, to score significantly higher than freshmen and sophomore undergraduates on the Quest scale, but—as already noted—they did.

Nor would we expect studies of adult church members to produce means on the Quest scale quite similar to those of undergraduates, but they typically have. Batson and Ventis (1982) reported a mean Quest score of 5.15 for undergraduates. Similarly, Acklin (1984) reported a mean of 5.00 for 120 adults ranging from 15 to over 60 years old; Finney and Malony (1985) reported a mean of 5.20 for 50 Presbyterian adult church members; Walters (1980) reported a mean of 5.12 for 223 volunteer teachers of religion in the archdiocese of Detroit (96 percent were laity). Sampling age cohorts from teens to over 60, both Acklin (1984) and McFarland (1990b) found that adults had scores as high as undergraduates' scores on the Quest scale at least up to age 50, and McFarland found scores that were slightly higher for respondents in their 60s. Thus, we find little evidence of the decline in Quest scores after age 20 that Donahue's (1985) sophomoric-doubt interpretation of the Quest scale would lead us to expect. If the Quest scale is measuring only sophomoric doubt, then we have some very old sophomores—including some over 60 years of age. The Quest scores of post-college samples leave the sophomoric-doubt explanation of what the Quest scale measures very much in doubt.

Does the Quest scale measure religious conflict? Taking a different tack, Spilka, Kojetin, and McIntosh (1985) suggested that what is being measured by the Quest scale "may be religious conflict with anxiety" (p. 440). Kojetin, McIntosh, Bridges, and Spilka (1987) claimed some empirical support for this possibility. They administered religious orientation measures and Funk's (1955) religious conflict scale to three different samples: undergraduates (104), Methodist seminary students (49), and United Church of Christ adults (85). In each sample, scores on the Quest scale correlated positively ($p < .01$) with scores on the religious conflict scale.

More recently, however, Kojetin (1988) has made a distinction between "religious doubt or confusion and an active questioning or seeking" (p. 3). On the basis of factor analyses of six Quest scale items and a number of Funk's religious conflict scale items, Kojetin presented two small scales: a six-item Doubt and Confusion scale and a five-item Active Questioning scale. Interestingly, the Doubt and Confusion scale, which was described as having the flavor of troubling or upsetting doubt, contained *no* items from the Quest scale; all were from the religious conflict scale. The Active Questioning scale contained three of the six Quest items.

It seems, then, that as Kojetin and his colleagues have pursued the possibility that the Quest scale is measuring only religious conflict, they have produced a negative answer. Although individuals scoring higher on the Quest scale are likely to experience—or at least to report experiencing—more religious conflict, this conflict is not what the Quest scale is measuring; the Quest items load on a different factor. Just as children's ages and their heights are correlated but not the same thing, so, it seems, the Quest scale and religious conflict are correlated but not the same thing. Rather than measuring conflict per se, the Quest scale seems to be measuring a more active search in which doubts are viewed as positive and not simply as a threat. To find that the Quest scale is associated with, but not the same as, religious conflict is entirely consistent with the conception of the quest dimension presented earlier in this chapter.

Does the Quest scale measure what was intended? Having reviewed the major claims suggesting that the Quest scale is measuring something other than was intended, the evidence seems surprisingly supportive of the possibility that this scale is actually measuring something close to what it was designed to measure. Seminarians and members of a nontraditional, charismatic Bible study score high on the Quest scale relative to undergraduates and other adults. Quest scale scores have at most a weak negative correlation with measures of intensity of orthodox belief (see Table 6.5). Until at least about age 50, adults do not score noticeably lower on the Quest scale than do undergraduates. Quest scores correlate with religious conflict scores, but they seem to reflect conflict that is part of active seeking, not just troubled doubt and confusion. Thus, not only do we have evidence that this scale is measuring a third dimension of personal religion independent of the means (extrinsic) and end (intrinsic) dimensions, but we also have evidence that this dimension incorporates aspects of the three basic components of the quest orientation: (1) readiness to face existential questions without reducing their complexity, (2) self-criticism and perception of religious doubts as positive, and (3) openness to change. (For a more detailed discussion of validity and reliability of the Quest scale, see Batson & Schoenrade, 1991a, b.)

RELATIONSHIP OF THE THREE DIMENSIONS TO RELIGIOUS EXPERIENCE

Having presented our three-dimensional conception of ways of being religious, and having presented evidence for the validity of the Quest scale used to measure the new dimension, we can now consider how these three ways of being religious might relate to the analysis of religious experience presented in Chapter 4. If, as was suggested in Chapter 4, a person's present religious orientation emerges from a process of cognitive restructuring in response to existential questions, then it seems reasonable that different kinds of restructuring would lie behind development along the means, end, and quest dimensions. Speculate with us about the relationships of these three religious dimensions to religious experience.

Some Speculations

First, development along the means (extrinsic) dimension should involve little change in an individual's religious cognitive structures because such development does not require that existential questions be seriously confronted at all. The appearance of religion is important, but only as a means to other ends. Therefore, creative religious experience should not be a prerequisite for relatively high scores on this dimension.

In contrast, development along either the end or quest dimensions should involve religious cognitive restructuring. The structural change for the two dimensions should, however, be very different. Development along the end (intrinsic) dimension seems likely to reflect a dramatic change in the person's reality, the emergence of a new vision. But this new vision may not involve an increase in the complexity and flexibility of the person's religious cognitive structures. To the extent that the end dimension reflects devout "true belief," the new vision is likely to be one that provides clear, final answers, and may even be adhered to in a rigid, absolutistic fashion. The person is likely to believe that he or she now knows the Truth about religion, the Truth that sets one free. There is no need to consider new information or points of view. Restructuring of this kind is only partly creative; it may enable the individual to deal positively with existential questions, but it may also inhibit further development in the way he or she deals with these questions. It may reflect religious growth but restrict the chance for future religious growth.

Development along the quest dimension should also reflect creative cognitive restructuring in the religious domain, but restructuring that is less complete and more open to future change. The new vision is likely to be seen only "through a glass darkly"; there should be less sense of having had *an* experience because tension and a push toward further insight remain. As a result, the new vision should be expansive rather than restricting; it should allow the individual to see existential questions from a variety of perspectives. There should be an interest in and openness to new information and points of view. As Allport suggested when describing the mature religious individual, the open-ended search that characterizes the quest orientation should be "the outgrowth of many successive discriminations and continuous reorganization" (1950, p. 59).

In considering development along each of the three dimensions, it is important to remember that the dimensions are independent and unrelated. Development involves movement in a three-dimensional space, and development along one dimension may or may not be accompanied by development along another dimension. It is, for example, possible for a person to develop along the end (intrinsic) dimension through a dramatic religious experience that floods his or her life with meaning and provides a master motive in life. At the same time, this experience may be viewed critically and seen as only a partial grasp on the Truth—one important step in an ongoing quest. In this case, there would be simultaneous positive movement on both the end and quest dimensions. Alternatively, it is possible for such an experience to be viewed as The Answer, embraced with certainty and foreclosing further inquiry. In this case, there would be positive movement on the end dimension and negative movement on the quest dimension.

Do Means, End, and Quest Religion Form a Developmental Sequence?

Our analysis here is quite different from several recent stage models that have proposed a developmental ordering of the three ways of being religious—means, end, and quest. These models, which are based on treating the three ways of being religious as types rather than independent dimensions, attempt to specify which type is least and which is most mature. For example, Kahoe and Meadow (1981) proposed a means (extrinsic) followed by end (intrinsic) followed by quest developmental sequence. Hood (1985) proposed a means (extrinsic) followed by quest followed by end (intrinsic) sequence, although he noted that Clark (1958) put end (intrinsic) first, followed by means (extrinsic). Soon, we suspect, researchers will have proposed all six of the logical permutations for arranging these three ways of being religious.

We remain skeptical about all attempts to specify a developmental sequence of these three ways of being religious, because we remain skeptical about the practice of typing on which these attempts rest. Moreover, although it may turn out that over the life span there is a typical pattern of movement through the three-dimensional space of ways of being religious, we know of no good evidence that this is true. To provide good evidence of a typical pattern, it is necessary to conduct longitudinal studies in which the same individuals' scores on all three religious orientation dimensions are measured at a number of points in time. To our knowledge, no such studies have been done.

Hypotheses Based on Our Speculations

In light of our speculations about the way religious experience might relate to development along each of the three dimensions, we wish to propose two hypotheses. First, we hypothesize that higher scores on the intrinsic, end dimension will correlate positively with the presence of one or more dramatic and personally definitive religious experiences in a person's life, whereas higher scores on the means and quest dimensions will not. The means dimension might even correlate negatively with such experience. Second, we hypothesize that higher scores on the quest dimension will correlate positively with the presence of relatively complex cognitive structures for dealing with existential questions, whereas higher scores on the means and end dimensions will not. The end dimension might even correlate negatively with complexity in dealing with existential questions because, to the degree that this dimension reflects ready, absolute answers to such questions, higher scores may undercut even the complexity that existed before one "saw the light."

Empirical Evidence

Is there any empirical evidence to support these two hypotheses? Unfortunately, there is little evidence that is even relevant. We know of only three lines of research, one relevant to the first hypothesis and two to the second.

Intrinsic religion and religious experience: Hood. Concerning the first hypothesis, Ralph Hood (1970, 1972; Hood, Morris, & Watson, 1990) has presented data suggesting that individuals who report having had more religious experiences similar to those presented at the beginning of Chapter 4 are more likely to be classified as intrinsic rather than extrinsic using the Allport and Ross scales ($p < .001$). (Hood did not include any measure of the quest dimension in his research.) This finding is quite consistent with our first hypothesis. It should, however, be noted that Hood's results were based on typing of individuals as either intrinsic or extrinsic (or both or neither); therefore, individuals classified as reflecting one orientation not only scored high (above the fiftieth percentile) on that orientation but also scored low (below the fiftieth percentile) on the other. Hood did not report how the Intrinsic and Extrinsic scales themselves related to frequency of religious experience. This omission is regrettable because Hood found little correlation between the Intrinsic and Extrinsic scales, suggesting that they were measuring two independent dimensions and so should have been considered separately.

Response to crisis in belief: Barron. Turning to our second hypothesis, Frank Barron (1968) reported an interesting study of how people respond to an existential crisis, or, as he called it, a "crisis in belief":

> The crisis in belief is often a time of categorical repudiation or total acceptance, of radical change or of rigid stasis. It is no exaggeration to say that it is a time of the greatest psychological danger, in which the integrity of the self is challenged, and in which old selves die and new selves are born. (p. 148)

Barron conducted intensive interviews twenty-five years after their graduation with fifty alumnae of a college for women. The women selected for interviews had each undergone a period of serious religious doubt and skepticism—a crisis in belief—while in college. Barron did not administer any of the scales for measuring dimensions of individual religion that we have described. Based on his interviews he did, however, make a distinction between three different ways of dealing with the crisis in belief. One response was to reject religion and embrace atheism or agnosticism. A second was to return to traditional religious beliefs. The third response Barron called "believing for oneself"; it involved developing one's own religious beilefs and values through a process of thoughtful, critical reflection. The second response seems to reflect Allport's intrinsic and our end orientation; the third seems to reflect our quest orientation.

Of those employing either the first or second solution to their crisis of belief, Barron observed:

> Speaking as a psychologist, what I find primarily . . . in both these ways of resolving the crisis in belief (i.e, in the atheistic resolution and in the repudiation of a transitory atheism in favor of a return to religion) is an acceptance of emotional polarities as being genuine oppositions which necessitate a choice between them. . . . Essentially what I think we have observed in these crises is not resolution at all, in the sense of establishment of a higher-level integration, but rather perpetuation of the conflict through acceptance of polarities as real, and deferment of the decision to a later point in life. (1968, p. 159)

In contrast, Barron observed that the group that dealt with the crisis by "believing for oneself" seemed to display more ego strength, a personality characteristic he had previously found to be a predictor of creative thinking in response to both intellectual and personal problems. Barron summarized the personality characteristics of members of this group as follows:

> It is noteworthy that in some ways the subjects who hold to a personally evolved religious belief are similar to the group of atheists and agnostics, while in other ways they are distinctly different. The ways in which they are similar are in their relatively high valuation of the thinking processes and of intellectual achievement, and in the absence of ethnocentrism or authoritar-

> ianism in their make-up; the ways in which they are different are in their robust psychological health, their genuine independence, originality, and growth-orientation, and in their relatively high degree of desire for positions of community leadership and status, as contrasted with the degree of social isolation and preference for going-it-alone which marked the radically skeptical group. (1968, p. 168)

Barron's conclusions would appear to be entirely consistent with our suggestion that the more critical, open-ended quest orientation correlates positively with the presence of relatively complex cognitive structures for dealing with religious questions, whereas the end (intrinsic) orientation does not. (Barron did not have a category reflecting a means or extrinsic orientation.) One must be cautious, however, about placing much weight on Barron's conclusions because they are based on highly subjective interviews. Further, the link between his categories of ways of dealing with crises of belief and our end and quest orientations is only inferred; it has not been demonstrated empirically.

Cognitive complexity in the religious domain: Batson and Raynor-Prince. The study with the most direct relevance to our second hypothesis is one by Batson and Raynor-Prince (1983). They administered the six religious orientation scales in Tables 6.1, 6.2, and 6.3 to thirty-five undergraduates interested in religion, providing a direct measure of the means, end, and quest dimensions (they used an earlier six-item version of the Quest scale). To measure complexity of the cognitive structures for dealing with existential questions, they used a technique similar to that developed by Batson (1971) and described in Chapter 4: The undergraduates wrote paragraphs in response to four sentence stems that presented them with existential conflicts ("When I am trying to decide whether to do something that may be morally wrong . . ."; "When I consider my own death . . ."; "When questions about the purpose of my life arise . . ."; "When someone challenges my beliefs about God . . .").

Each paragraph was scored for cognitive complexity independently by two judges, employing the scoring system for paragraph completions developed by Schroder and his associates (Phares & Schroder, 1969). Then an overall complexity score was obtained by summing the scores for each of the four paragraphs. Higher complexity scores reflected greater differentiation and integration based on six criteria: (1) tolerance of ambiguity and conflict; (2) openness to alternative points of view and to new information; (3) ability to incorporate apparently disparate views within a larger synthetic view; (4) avoidance of compartmentalized, rigid thought; (5) recognition of the fallibility of one's own understanding; and (6) appreciation of the diverse functions served by different points of view. It was not *what* the person believed but the underlying cognitive complexity implied by the response that was scored. To give you some understanding of this scoring procedure, examples of relatively low- and high-complexity responses to two of the sentence stems are presented in Table 6.9.

Table 6.9 Examples of paragraph completion responses indicating low and high complexity in dealing with existential questions

When trying to decide whether to do something that may be morally wrong . . .

. . . it usually bothers me to even think of the bad consequences, but I still go on with it. (Low complexity)

. . . I turn to the Lord for help. Usually if there's a possibility it may be morally wrong I try not to do it. I ask the Lord to give me strength to overcome temptations to do things that I feel are unpleasing in His righteous and just sight. (Low complexity)

. . . I may encounter certain conflicts. It is hard to decide about certain things—if they are worth the danger, if they may be morally wrong. Such as stealing to save a person's life—it could be a tough question. (High complexity)

. . . I give it quite a bit of thought. How I feel about it, how I might feel afterwards, what my true feelings are. Does it hurt anyone else? Can I accept the consequences? Basically, I think about it inside and out. (High complexity)

When I consider my own death . . .

. . . I have no fear. I know some day I will die. And when I do, I know I will have eternity. (Low complexity)

. . . I know there is nothing I can do about it when the time comes. (Low complexity)

. . . I am scared and curious at the same time. It is something to fear, but on the other hand, it is as natural as birth. I feel my fear is only because I'm young and not ready to die, but someday I will accept it and be willing to die. (High complexity)

. . . I am not too concerned. Death is inevitable and natural. It may hold a few surprises but I like surprises. It should be fun to find out, but I'm in no rush. (High complexity)

Source: Adapted from Batson and Raynor-Prince (1983).

Based on our hypothesis about the relationship between the three dimensions of personal religion and the complexity of one's cognitive structures for dealing with existential questions, we would expect that scores on the quest dimension should correlate positively with higher complexity, whereas scores on the other two dimensions should not. Scores on the end dimension might even correlate negatively with complexity.

Column 1 of Table 6.10 presents the correlations between the measures of religious orientation—the six scales and the Means, End, and Quest components—and complexity in dealing with the existential conflicts. As expected, the Quest component correlated significantly in a positive direction ($p < .01$); the End component correlated marginally significantly in a negative direction ($p < .06$); and there was no clear relationship for the Means component. The six religious orientation scales related in a similar way to complexity in dealing with the existential conflicts; there was a positive correlation with the Quest scale and a negative correlation with two scales that load highly on the End component, the Intrinsic and Orthodoxy scales.

For two reasons, it does not seem possible to dismiss these results as being a product of general differences in cognitive complexity. First, the same pattern of effects remained when differences in complexity in dealing with interpersonal conflicts were removed through the use of partial correlations (see Column 2 of Table 6.10). Second, Spilka, Kojetin, and McIntosh (1985) and Watson, Morris, and Hood (1988, 1989a) have presented

Table 6.10 Correlations of six religious orientation scales and the means, end, and quest dimensions with cognitive complexity in dealing with existential questions

Measures of religious orientation	Religious cognitive complexity	Religious cognitive complexity independent of general interpersonal cognitive complexity
Religious orientation scales		
Extrinsic	−.07	.04
Intrinsic	−.25	−.30*
External	−.11	−.11
Internal	−.08	−.13
Quest	.37*	.30*
Orthodoxy	−.41**	−.37*
Religious orientation dimensions		
Religion as means	−.13	−.01
Religion as end	−.27	−.28
Religion as quest	.46**	.37*

Source: Adapted from Batson and Raynor-Prince (1983).
Note: Correlations in first column are partial correlations adjusting for sex differences; correlations in second column are partial correlations adjusting for sex differences and general interpersonal cognitive complexity.
$*p < .05$; $**p < .01$, one-tailed.

evidence that the Quest scale is not positively associated with cognitive complexity outside the religious domain.

In sum, the results of this study seem entirely consistent with our second hypothesis, that the quest dimension relates to higher complexity of thought about existential questions, whereas the means (extrinsic) and end (intrinsic) dimensions do not. If anything, the end dimension seems to be associated with reduced complexity in one's thinking about existential questions.

Implications. In Chapter 4 we presented some evidence that higher complexity in dealing with existential questions is the product of religious experiences that involve creative cognitive restructuring, that is, experiences that include elements reflecting stages of the creative process. Now we find that cognitive complexity in dealing with existential questions correlates positively with higher scores on the quest dimension. These relationships suggest that higher scores on the quest dimension reflect a religious development that includes more experiences involving creative cognitive restructuring. In contrast, higher scores on the intrinsic, end dimension may reflect less creative religious development. There is evidence that the end (intrinsic) dimension is associated with dramatic religious experiences that involve cognitive restructuring. But this restructuring is not associated with the increased cognitive complexity that is a hallmark of the creative process. If anything, it seems to be associated with greater reliance on absolutistic answers.

Having noted these possible relationships between the relative creativity of a person's religious experience and development along the various dimensions of personal religion, three points must be emphasized. First and most obviously, more empirical evidence is needed. Second, the inferences drawn from the available evidence are only suggestive. The inference in the previous paragraph concerning the quest dimension was of the following type: A relates to B and B relates to C; therefore, A relates to C. Although such an inference *may* be correct, it is not necessarily so. Therefore, our suggestion that higher scores on the quest dimension reflect more creative religious development, whereas higher scores on the other two dimensions do not, is quite tentative. Rather than a firm conclusion, it is a possibility to be pursued in further research.

Third, even if it turns out that higher scores on the quest dimension relate to more creative religious experience, whereas higher scores on the intrinsic, end dimension relate to less, these relationships should not be considered a basis for acceptance of the quest dimension as a "good" or "true" way to be religious or for indictment of the end (intrinsic) dimension as a "bad" or "false" way to be religious. One must consider not only the origin of these religious dimensions but also their consequences. Even if, for example, those scoring higher on the end dimension display more rigid dependence on orthodox religious answers and less open, critical reflection on existential questions, it is possible that these characteristics are necessary prices one must pay to obtain certain other personal and social benefits that this way of being religious provides. Such a possibility should, of course, be considered empirically, not simply speculated on from our armchairs. Empirical assessment of the personal and social consequences of all three dimensions of personal religion discussed in this chapter—means, end, and quest—is the task that lies before us in Part III of this book.

SUMMARY AND CONCLUSION

Are you religious? Answering is difficult because we have suggested that there are at least three distinct ways of being religious—as a means, an end, and a quest. You may be very religious in one or another of these ways but not at all religious in some other.

Our three-dimensional analysis of ways of being religious was proposed to correct an omission in the currently popular two-dimensional analyses of Allport (extrinsic versus intrinsic) and Spilka (consensual versus committed). A re-examination of Allport's earlier and more comprehensive discussion of immature and mature religion revealed that embedded within the concept of mature religion were two distinct and apparently independent dimensions of personal religion—the *end (intrinsic, committed) dimension,* which concerns degree of devout commitment to traditional religious beliefs and practices, and the *quest dimension,* which concerns degree of open-ended, critical struggle with existential questions. Further, we found that Allport's concept of immature religion was not the polar opposite of either end or quest religion but a third distinct and independent dimension—the *means (extrinsic, consensual) dimension,* which concerns the degree to which one uses religion as a means to other, self-serving ends. Finally, we emphasized that rather than thinking of these ways of being religious as distinct types, it is more appropriate to think of them as three independent continuous dimensions, each uncorrelated with the other two. Together, they provide a three-dimensional framework on which the fabric of religious life is woven. As you religious? A separate and potentially different answer can be given for each of these three dimensions of personal religion.

Turning to the kind of religious experience that lies behind development along each of these three dimensions, we hypothesized, first, that higher scores on the end dimension will be associated with dramatic experiences that involve clear-cut transformations of one's religious reality as one attempts to deal with existential questions, whereas higher scores on the means and quest dimensions will not. These transformations are not, however, likely to increase—they may even reduce—the complexity of the cognitive structures for dealing with existential questions; they may reflect absolutistic and uncritical reliance on traditional, orthodox doctrines and practice. We hypothesized, second, that higher scores on the quest dimension are a result of more creative transformations in one's religious reality, transformations that increase the complexity of the cognitive structures, lead to skepticism of absolute answers, and encourage critical and flexible thinking about existential questions. Although the empirical evidence relevant to these hypotheses is very meager, the evidence that exists supports each.

Many psychologists of religion, following Allport, have assumed that the end (intrinsic) orientation defines "true" religion, at least from a psychological perspective. Our analysis suggests that such a conclusion is premature. Indeed, our analysis may seem to suggest a very different conclusion, that the quest orientation defines true religion. But to draw any conclusion about a true or even better way of being religious would be to misunderstand our analysis. Far from allowing us to identify true religion, our analysis suggests renewed caution about making any evaluative comparisons among the different ways of being religious.

Remember: The different ways that we have identified are independent dimensions, not types. It makes no more sense to ask whether one dimension is best in this three-dimensional space than it does to ask whether depth is best in the three-dimensional space of height, width, and depth. The dimensions are independent, unrelated, and not interchangeable. One can ask which dimension correlates more strongly with some other variable (such as devoutness of belief, cognitive complexity, self-esteem, racial prejudice, or helping behavior), just as one can ask which physical dimension correlates more strongly with some other variable (such as visibility). Whether, however, one considers a stronger correlation good, bad, or indifferent depends entirely on whether one considers the other variable good, bad, or indifferent.

We do well also to remember that both the end and quest dimensions reflect some characteritics of Allport's (1950) concept of mature religion, but neither includes all. Even if intrinsic, end religion restricts one's ability to deal creatively with existential questions, it may still provide other benefits, both to the believer and to society. Indeed, it may provide more benefits than does quest religion. The openness, flexibility, and skepticism that appear to characterize the quest dimension may carry with them a lack of personal direction and peace of mind.

Before we draw any conclusions about which dimensions of individual religion, if any, we wish to promote and develop, we must look at the role of each in the life of the individual. We must judge their psychological value, as William James (1902) said, "by their fruits." This is our task in the next four chapters.

III

Consequences of Individual Religion

7

Personal Freedom or Bondage?

Talk to anyone who is devoutly religious, especially someone who has recently become so, about the effects of religion on his or her life. You will likely get an enthusiastic account of new freedoms obtained: freedom from a sense of worthlessness, from guilt, meaninglessness, and fear. This liberation is well typified by Pilgrim in John Bunyan's *Pilgrim's Progress* (1678) when, as he at last approaches the Celestial City, the great burden that he has been carrying suddenly rolls from his back. He is free at last. A similar refrain is echoed by the deeply religious in every age, even those bound by the chains of slavery, "Free at last! Free at last! Thank God Almighty, I'm free at last!"

IS RELIGION FREEING OR ENSLAVING?

Religion as Freeing

The freedoms obtained by the religious convert can be impressive, as the following testimonials reveal.

Freedom from fear of death. In a highly publicized interview with *Playboy* magazine (November 1976) during his first presidential campaign, Jimmy Carter revealed a freedom from fear of death.

> Playboy: . . . You don't fear death. Why not?
> Carter: It's part of my religious belief. I just look at death as not a threat. It's inevitable, and I have an assurance of eternal life. There is no feeling on my part that I *have* to be President, or that I *have* to live, or that I'm immune to danger. It's just that the termination of my physical life is relatively insignificant in my concept of over-all existence. I don't say that in a mysterious way; I recognize the possibility of assassination. But I guess everybody recognizes the possibility of other forms of death—automobile accidents, airplane accidents, cancer. I just don't worry. (p. 84)

During the Persian Gulf Crisis, Saddam Hussein sent a chill through the world with his reminder that the devout Muslim feels much the same; to die fighting the "Great Satan of the West" is not to be feared; it is a high honor.

Freedom from fear in life. The brilliant novelist and poet Emily Brontë (1818–1848) could face not only death but also her hard life on the Yorkshire moors with a freedom from fear.

> No coward soul is mine.
> No trembler in the world's storm-troubled sphere:
> I see Heaven's glories shine,
> And faith shines equal, arming me from fear. (1941)

Freedom from temptation. William James (1902) presents many dramatic examples of the way religion can free one from the vices of the day. To provide just one, hear the testimony of a young man who could not control his drinking. After his religious conversion he was able to say, "From that hour drink has had no terrors for me: I never touch it, never want it" (James, 1902, p. 213). Anyone who has faced alcoholism, either in his or her own life or in the life of a friend or relative, will be impressed by such a dramatic and effective cure. And to those of us who have been unable to stop ourselves from smoking, this same young man was able to add, "The same thing occurred with my pipe, . . . the desire for it went at once and has never returned. So with every known sin, the deliverance in each case being permanent and complete. I have had no temptations since conversion" (p. 213).

Similarly, literally millions of members of Alcoholics Anonymous (AA) have testified to the power of religion in their efforts to fight the temptation to drink. The first three of AA's Twelve Steps are:

1. We admitted we were powerless over alcohol—that our lives had become unmanageable.

2. Came to believe that a Power greater than ourselves could restore us to sanity.

> 3. Made a Decision to turn our will and our lives over to the care of God, *as we understood Him.* (Alcoholics Anonymous, 1976, italics in original)

Freedom from concern over possessions. Many testify to a freedom from concern for worldly goods and money. For example, the effect of religious conversion on John Cennick, Methodism's first lay preacher, has been described as follows:

> [He] at once left off song-singing, card-playing, and attending theatres. Sometimes he wished to go to a popish monastery, to spend his life in devout retirement. At other times he longed to live in a cave, sleeping on fallen leaves, and feeding on forest fruits. He fasted long and often, and prayed nine times a day. . . . Fancying dry bread too great an indulgence for so great a sinner as himself, he began to feed on potatoes, acorns, crabs, and grass; and often wished that he could live on roots and herbs. (Tyerman, quoted in James, 1902, p. 238)

Freedom from social conventions. George Fox (1624–1691), the founder of Quakerism, was freed from the need to observe many petty social conventions:

> When the Lord sent me into the world, he forbade me to put off my hat to any, high or low; and I was required to "thee" and "thou" all men and women, without any respect to rich or poor, great or small. And as I traveled up and down, I was not to bid people Good-morning, or Good-evening, neither might I bow or scrape with my leg to anyone. . . . Oh! the blows, punchings, beatings, and imprisonments that we underwent for not putting off our hats to men! Some had their hats violently plucked off and thrown away, so that they quite lost them. . . . And though it was but a small thing in the eye of man, yet a wonderful confusion it brought among all professors and priests; but, blessed be the Lord, many came to see the vanity of that custom of putting off hats to men, and felt the weight of Truth's testimony against it. (Fox, 1952)

In recent years members of several religious groups have asserted, at times in court, that their beliefs exempt them from the dictates of social institutions. They claim freedom from reciting any pledge or oath of loyalty, reading certain classics of literature as part of school assignments, serving in the military, even paying taxes.

Freedom from sexual desire. William James (1902) reports Colonel Gardiner's testimony of dramatic liberation from sexual desire:

> I was effectually cured of all inclination to that sin I was so strongly addicted to that I thought nothing but shooting me through the head could have cured me of it; and all desire and inclination to it was removed, as entirely as if I had been a sucking child; nor did the temptation return to this day. (p. 214)

Even more impressive is the freedom from sexual desire obtained by Saint Louis of Gonzaga. His biographer recounts that at the age of ten

> the inspiration came to him to consecrate to the Mother of God his own virginity—that being to her the most agreeable of possible presents. Without delay, then, and with all the fervor there was in him, joyous of heart, and burning with love, he made his vow of perpetual chastity. Mary accepted the offering of his innocent heart, and obtained for him from God, as a recompense, the extraordinary grace of never feeling during his entire life the slightest touch of temptation against the virtue of purity. . . . He, who by an extraordinary protection of God's grace was never tempted, measured all his steps as if he were threatened on every side by particular dangers. Thenceforward he never raised his eyes, either when walking in the streets, or when in society. Not only did he avoid all business with females even more scrupulously than before, but he renounced all conversation and every kind of social recreation with them. . . . If by chance his mother sent one of her maids of honor to him with a message, he never allowed her to come in, but listened to her through the barely opened door, and dismissed her immediately. He did not like to be alone with his own mother, whether at table or in conversation; and when the rest of the company withdrew, he sought also a pretext for retiring. . . . Several great ladies, relatives of his, he avoided learning to know even by sight; and he made a sort of treaty with his father, engaging promptly and readily to accede to all his wishes, if he might only be excused from all visits to ladies. (Meschler, 1891, pp. 40, 71)

Religion as Enslaving

As you read through this series of testimonies, you may have experienced a growing sense of uneasiness. Especially in several of the later examples, one gets a picture of a very strange sort of freedom. The believer seems to be freed not from bondage but *for* bondage. The "blessed freedom" of Saint Louis of Gonzaga would appear to be extremely confining. Can one who never raised his eyes, either when walking in the streets or when in society, who renounced all conversation and every kind of social recreation with women, and who could not be alone even with his own mother, be considered in any sense free? Indeed, how free was George Fox, whom the Lord forbade to put off his hat and who felt required to say Thee and Thou? How free is a person who cannot read literary classics? How free was John Cennick, who considered dry bread too great an indulgence and began to feed on potatoes, acorns, crabs, and grass? Such "freedoms" seem extremely confining, an endless set of enslaving restrictions.

Many people see religion, especially devout religion, in just this way; it is not freeing but confining, an endless string of don'ts and can'ts. The religious person can't drink, can't smoke, can't play around, can't engage in premarital sex, and in some circles can't even go to the movies or dance. As was stated in a letter to the editor of *Time* magazine, "Most . . . unchurched people feel that organized religion is a form of mental enslavement. I believe that what we really yearn for is freedom from religion" (December, 1977).

Such concerns have even led to the formation of groups such as Fundamentalists Anonymous, designed to free people from one form of devout religion. As described by founder and former fundamentalist Richard Yao,

> In Fundamentalists Anonymous we are talking of what we call the "fundamentalist mindset"—a mindset that tends to be authoritarian, intolerant, and compulsive about control; an absolute all-or-nothing, either-or, us-against-them, I've-got-the-truth-and-you-don't mindset. (Quoted in Buie, 1987)

In 1987 Yao claimed that forty thousand people had already sought help from the organization, which was only founded in 1985, seeking to break free of their "addiction" to devout religion.

Devout Religion as Freedom with Bondage

We find, then, two very different views. The devout claim that their religion is liberating; others see it as enslaving. How are we to resolve this apparent contradiction? Is one view right and the other wrong? We think not. Instead, each view seems to tell the truth about religion—as some people experience it. As we noted in Chapter 6, people experience religion along different dimensions. For the person who relates to religion primarily as an extrinsic means to other self-centered ends, religion is likely to appear restricting. It presents a series of obligations one must fulfill in order to qualify for desired selfish ends. To illustrate, if one says Hail Marys to escape the consequences of sin, it is not surprising that this penance is perceived as a somewhat tedious burden. In line with this reasoning, there is preliminary empirical evidence that the extrinsic dimension is associated with a concept of God as "wrathful," "vindictive," and "impersonal" (Spilka & Mullin, 1977).

For the person who relates to religion primarily as an intrinsic end in itself, however, activities like saying Hail Marys are likely to be perceived quite differently, and so is the deity. Such activities may be seen as freely chosen opportunities to serve and adore a loving, merciful Father. It is at least conceivable that Saint Louis of Gonzaga, George Fox, and John Cennick, all of whom appear to be highly intrinsic in their approach to religion, felt no bondage or burden. What may appear as a restriction to the outside observer may in fact be freely chosen as a road to spiritual blessing. In the words of psychologist L. B. Brown (1964), the intrinsic believer carries his beliefs "into his every day dealings with others, gaining freedom by serving them" (p. 94). Saint Augustine put the matter even more clearly in his famous dictum, "Love God and do as you please." The person who loves God as an ultimate value may freely and willingly choose to restrict him- or herself in various ways; it becomes a source of pleasure.

Still, as psychologists we cannot simply take at face value the devout, intrinsic believer's claim that such restrictions are liberating rather than enslaving. Although they may not be experienced as confining by the believer, they may be confining nonetheless.

Of course, a believer may ask what right we have to say he is not free, when he says that he is. An analogy may help. Think about a person who is schizophrenic; he has, it may be said, freely chosen the idiosyncratic reality that he creates. He may even find some comfort, solace, and happiness within it. Still, a therapist may have good reason to believe that this reality is actually a prison, locking the person in and preventing effective coping with life. If so, the therapist does not hesitate to question the schizophrenic's reality. It may be necessary for us to do the same with the reality of the devout, intrinsic religious believer. Although this reality may provide comfort, solace, and happiness, it may also lock the believer in and prevent effective living. To decide whether it does, we must assess the effects of this reality on the individual's life; we must consider not only whether it is *experienced* as liberating or enslaving but also whether it *functions* to liberate or enslave.

Let us state our view forthrightly at the outset. We believe that devout, intrinsic religion is simultaneously liberating *and* enslaving. Devout beliefs may free the believer from many of the burdens of life, but in so doing, they enslave. The believer becomes less capable of free, critical reflection on the beliefs or of rethinking them, even if they are shown to be unequivocally wrong. In this way devout, intrinsic religion seems to offer freedom *with* bondage, bondage to the religious beliefs themselves.

William James suggests a similar view when he quotes a medical man: "The only radical remedy I know for dipsomania [alcoholism] is religiomania" (James, 1902, p. 213n). In more modern terms we might say that devout religion is like methadone, an addictive drug used to replace heroin; religion is an addiction that can free the believer from other addictions. Or we might say that devout religion is like a crutch. It enables the crippled soul to rise, but having risen, the soul cannot let go of the crutch and can go only where it permits.

These statements are very strong, but we have not made them lightly. We believe that there is a sound theoretical and empirical basis for the view that devout, intrinsic religious belief produces freedom with bondage. Given the obvious importance of this issue, we shall consider the theory and research in some detail.

EVIDENCE THAT DEVOUT BELIEF PRODUCES FREEDOM WITH BONDAGE

Our view involves two basic assertions: (1) devout beliefs free the believer from existential concerns; (2) at the same time, they bind the believer to themselves, preventing free critical reflection on their truth or value. First, let us consider evidence that devout beliefs are freeing.

Evidence That Devout Beliefs Provide Freedom from Existential Concerns

The testimonies at the beginning of this chapter provide anecdotal evidence that devout, intrinsic religious beliefs provide meaningful answers to existential questions. There is empirical evidence as well. The contribution of devout religion to a sense of existential meaning is reflected in a series of studies using Crumbaugh's (1968) Purpose-in-Life (PIL) test, a questionnaire designed to measure existential meaning and purpose. Unusually high PIL scores have been reported for a group of Dominican trainees (Crumbaugh, Raphael, & Shrader, 1970), leading Protestant parishioners (Crumbaugh, 1968), and those who believe that they have been "saved" (Soderstrom & Wright, 1977) or are "basic Biblical Christians" (Paloutzian, 1976). In four different studies (Bolt, 1975; Crandall & Rasmussen, 1975; Paloutzian, Jackson, & Crandall, 1978; and Soderstrom & Wright, 1977), PIL scores have been found to correlate positively with scores on Allport and Ross's (1967) Intrinsic scale, the most popular measure of devout, intrinsic religion (see Chapter 6). These studies suggest that devout, intrinsic believers do indeed experience more meaning in life than do nonbelievers.

The power of intrinsic religion to free the believer from existential concern is also indicated by a number of studies on death anxiety. Magni (1971) administered questionnaires designed to assess (1) attitudes toward death; (2) fear of death; and (3) death anxiety, to fifty-three student nurses in Uppsala, Sweden. He also administered Feagin's (1964) version of the Allport Extrinsic and Intrinsic scales. Magni found that higher scores on the Extrinsic scale were associated with less favorable attitudes toward death, more fear of death, and more death anxiety (all ps $< .05$). In contrast, higher scores on the Intrinsic scale were associated with more favorable attitudes, less fear, and less anxiety, although the last two relationships were not statistically significant.

Kahoe and Dunn (1975) administered a fear of death scale and Allport and Ross's Extrinsic and Intrinsic scales to seventy people attending church one Sunday morning in a small Kentucky town. They found a weak, nonsignificant positive correlation between fear of death and scores on the Extrinsic scale, but a significant ($p < .05$) negative correlation between fear of death and scores on the Intrinsic scale. Using undergraduates, Morris (1980) found the same pattern—the Extrinsic scale correlated positively and the Intrinsic scale negatively with fear of death. Spilka, Stout, Minton, and Sizemore (1977) administered the Extrinsic and Intrinsic scales to a sample of 167 adults involved in religion; they found that scores on the Extrinsic scale correlated negatively with a positive perspective on death, whereas scores on the Intrinsic scale correlated positively. Hood and Morris (1983) administered the Extrinsic and Intrinsic scales to both college students and to people older than 65. For both groups, the Intrinsic scale correlated negatively with fear of death ($p < .05$); correlations for the Extrinsic scale were positive but not reliable. Much the same results have been found by Kraft, Litwin, and Barber (1987), Levick and Delaney (1987), and Springer (1987). These eight studies provide consistent evidence that more intrinsically religious individuals report less concern about death, but the studies provide no clear evidence that their religious beliefs are the cause of the reduced concern. The causal relation could be the reverse as well. Perhaps, as suggested by Cook and Wimberley (1983) after their retrospective study on religious belief and parents' reactions to the death of a child, "Religious commitment is both cause and consequence of adjustment to the death" (p. 222). Or perhaps both the beliefs and reduced concern are the product of some third factor.

Clearer evidence that religious beliefs cause reduced fear of death comes from a study by Osarchuk and Tatz (1973). These researchers first measured the strength of belief in an afterlife for each of more than three hundred male and female college students (aged 18 to 22); they then selected thirty students with very high belief and thirty with very low belief and had them participate in an experiment. In the experiment, equal numbers of students from the high and low belief groups were exposed to three experimental treatments—death threat, shock threat, and no threat. Those in the death-threat condition heard a taped communication giving exaggerated estimates of the probability of an early death due to accident or disease for individuals aged 18 to 22; at the same time, students in this condition watched a series of forty-two death-related slides, including scenes of auto wrecks, realistically feigned murder and suicide victims, and corpses in a funeral home. Students in the shock-threat condition were informed that they would soon be receiving a series of potentially painful electric shocks; students in the no-threat condition were asked to perform a bland, unarousing task (trying to flip a ball into a cup, to which the ball was attached by a string). After these experiences, the students' belief in an afterlife was measured again.

Osarchuk and Tatz reasoned that if belief in an afterlife serves to allay fear of death, then those individuals initially high in belief in an afterlife who were exposed to the death-threat experience would become even higher in their belief. Such an increase should not occur, however, for those initially low in belief, nor should it occur for either high or low believers not exposed to the death threat, that is, those in the shock-threat or no-threat conditions. The results followed precisely this pattern, leading Osarchuk and Tatz to conclude that strong belief in an afterlife does indeed function to enable the believer to deal with fear of death.

Osarchuk and Tatz's conclusion received further support in a study by Schoenrade (1989). In this study participants' belief in an afterlife was first assessed. Then, at an experimental session several weeks later, participants completed a questionnaire concerning their views of death. Just prior to completing the questionnaire, some participants listened to an audiotape that led them to imagine their own death (death-threat condition); others completed the questinonaire without imagining their own death (no death-threat condition). Among participants who had initially expressed a strong belief in an afterlife, those in the death-threat condition reported perceiving both more positive and more negative aspects of death compared with those in the no death-threat condition. Among participants who had initially expressed weak belief in an afterlife, death-threat led to a nonsignificant shift toward perceiving death as less positive.

It seems reasonable to assume that those students in these two studies who were initially high in belief in an afterlife were highly intrinsic in their orientation to religion. And if this assumption is true, then these studies provide evidence that devout, intrinsic religion functions to protect the believer from concern about death. But is this assumption true? As a check, Batson, Duncan, Levy, Major, and Miller (1980) administered the belief in afterlife scale used by Osarchuk and Tatz, as well as Allport and Ross's (1967) Extrinsic and Intrinsic scales, to seventy-two undergraduates. As expected, the Intrinsic scale showed a strong positive correlation with belief in afterlife scores ($r = .72, p < .001$); the Extrinsic scale correlated negatively ($r = -.32, p < .01$). These results suggest that the assumption is correct; those high in belief in an afterlife are highly intrinsic in their approach to religion.

Even clearer evidence that devout, intrinsic religion functions to protect the believer from concern about death was reported by Batson, Burris, Wagoner, and Wolgast (1991). They conducted a conceptual replication of the Osarchuk and Tatz study described above except, instead of measuring the effects of a death threat on belief in an afterlife, they measured the effect on the three dimensions of personal religion discussed in Chapter 6—as an extrinsic means, an intrinsic end, and a quest. They found that among individuals with a confident belief in an afterlife, exposure to a death threat increased scores on the intrinsic, end dimension ($p < .05$); it did not increase scores on either of the other two dimensions. These results indicate that devout, intrinsic religion functions to buffer anxiety over death—as long as one has a confident belief in an afterlife.

When these results are combined with results of the eight correlational studies and results of the experiments reported by Osarchuk and Tatz (1973) and Schoenrade (1989), we have quite strong support for our first assertion, that devout, intrinsic religion can provide freedom from at least one major existential concern, fear of death. In addition, the results of these studies indicate that neither extrinsic nor quest religion is associated with such freedom; if anything, extrinsic religion is associated with an increase in existential anxiety.

The evidence that devout religious belief can provide freedom from fear of death is quite consistent with Freud's analysis of the function of religion in *The Future of an Illusion* and *Civilization and Its Discontents,* which was discussed in Chapter 2. It is also consistent with Ernest Becker's analysis in *The Denial of Death* (1973) and with the recent analysis based on Becker's work by Sheldon Solomon, Jeff Greenberg, and Tom Pyszczynski (1991), which they call terror-management theory. Like Freud and Becker, Solomon et al. suggest that both culture (including religious institutions) and personality (including self-concept, self-esteem, and deeply held beliefs) are the result of our attempt to deal with the existential anxiety that awareness of mortality brings.

We would, however, suggest a more general conclusion. Fear of one's own mortality is not the only source of existential anxiety. As Freud (1961) noted, our physical and social environment can be full of upsetting, potentially frightening events that are not directly life-threatening. These events confront us with a whole host of troubling questions: How do we explain our inability to succeed when we think we should? Or our bad luck in having a dead battery on the morning of an all-important interview? Or a tragic accident that takes the life of an innocent child?

Religion can provide anxiety-reducing explanations for such seemingly inexplicable events. Devout, intrinsic believers are likely to attribute them to "God's will," to "God's judgment," or even to "God's blessing" (Gorsuch & Smith, 1983; Pargament & Hahn, 1986; Spilka & Schmidt, 1983; Spilka, Shaver, & Kirkpatrick, 1985), making these events easier to bear. Consistent with this suggestion, Park, Cohen, and Herb (1990) recently presented evidence that, at least among Protestant undergraduates, intrinsic religion helps buffer the depressing effects of uncontrollable life stresses "by providing a framework of meaning, helping individuals make sense of negative experiences" (p. 572; also see Pargament, Ensing, Falgout, Olsen, Reilly, Van Haitsma, & Warren, 1990).

To the degree that devout beliefs provide something of value by freeing the believer from existential concerns, the believer has something valuable to lose. This leads to our second assertion, that devout, intrinsic beliefs are binding, rendering the believer incapable of free, open reflection on their truth.

Evidence That Devout Beliefs Are Psychologically Binding

Theoretical basis. The theoretical basis for the contention that deeply held beliefs are psychologically binding lies in the need for cognitive consistency. Since the mid-1950s social psychologists have recognized that we humans have a need to maintain some consistency in our cognitively constructed reality. If the reality is to function, the various cognitive elements that make it up must fit together into a coherent whole; they must make sense in relation to one another. The most dramatic and influential statement of this principle of cognitive consistency was made by Leon Festinger (1957), who contrasted cognitive consonance with *cognitive dissonance.*

According to Festinger, two cognitive elements are in a dissonant relation if "the obverse of one element would follow from the other" (1957, p. 13). That is, dissonance results when a person simultaneously accepts as true two cognitions that are inconsistent with one another. Festinger suggested that cognitive dissonance is an unpleasant, aversive state that the person tries to escape. The person can escape dissonance either by changing one of the cognitions or by adding new cognitions consonant (i.e., in agreement) with whichever of the cognitions is most resistant to change. Adding new consonant cognitions cannot eliminate dissonance entirely, but it can swamp the dissonant elements and thereby diminish their effect.

Festinger made it clear that his theory of cognitive dissonance deals with *psychological* rather than logical inconsistency. Logical inconsistency between important cognitions is likely to produce dissonance, but cognitions that are not logically inconsistent can also be dissonant. For example, there is no logical inconsistency between the two cognitions "I believe that research has demonstrated that smoking causes cancer" and "I smoke." But there is considerable psychological inconsistency, as long as I also believe that I am not the sort of person who would intentionally do something to give myself cancer.

Festinger's theory of cognitive dissonance suggests important psychological consequences of holding devout religious beliefs. The individual who approaches religion as an intrinsic end in itself places central importance and value on his or her religious beliefs; they are the pivotal truth around which reality and life revolve. Imagine what would happen if such an individual were presented with clear, irrefutable evidence that these religious beliefs were wrong, that the Truth was false. Would he or she reassess the beliefs and, reluctantly perhaps, bring them in line with the new information? The theory of cognitive dissonance suggests not. In Festinger's words,

> Man's resourcefulness goes beyond simply protecting a belief. Suppose an individual believes something with his whole heart; suppose further that he has a commitment to this belief, that he has taken irrevocable actions because of it; finally, suppose that he is presented with evidence, unequivocal and undeniable evidence, that his belief is wrong: what will happen? The individual will frequently emerge, not only unshaken, but even more convinced of the truth of his beliefs than ever before. Indeed, he may even show a new fervor about convincing and converting other people to his view. (Festinger, Riecken, & Schachter, 1956, p. 3)

Festinger and his associates were quite clear about the conditions under which such a process would occur.

> 1. There must be a firm conviction.
>
> 2. There must be public commitment to this conviction.
>
> 3. The conviction must be amenable to unequivocal disconfirmation.
>
> 4. Such unequivocal disconfirmation must occur.
>
> 5. Social support must be available to the believer subsequent to the disconfirmation. (Festinger et al., 1956, p. 216)

Under these circumstances Festinger predicted that the devout believer would not loosen his grip on the belief but would be driven, in an attempt to reduce dissonance, to hold the belief even more firmly.

Festinger's prediction of intensification of belief in the face of unequivocal disconfirmation is based on the assumption that devout religious beliefs are highly resistant to change. What makes them so resistant? Three characteristics seem especially important. First, devout, intrinsic religious beliefs provide important personal benefits to the believer. These benefits take two forms. As we have noted, religious beliefs provide meaningful answers to a range of existential concerns. In so doing, they also provide a sense of personal significance. Personal esteem is enhanced by believing that one has some special insight into the mysteries of life, that one knows the Truth. A person is not likely to let go of an esteem-enhancing belief easily.

Second, deeply held religious beliefs are resistant to change because they almost always involve public commitment. Typically, the devout believer has acted on his or her beliefs in a number of ways: attending worship services, engaging in personal devotions, reading religious literature, perhaps even trying to convert other people. Friends and acquaintances, both inside and outside the family of faith, know where the devout believer stands. Such public commitment makes it difficult subsequently to deny that one took the beliefs seriously. To change them, the believer would have to admit being wrong.

Third, the devout believer typically does not pursue his or her faith in isolation. The believer is involved in a community of individuals who hold the same beliefs. When the beliefs are challenged, the community serves as an important source of social support. Even if the believer has doubts, he or she has only to look to the community to be reminded that others still believe. Ironically, other community members may be having the same doubts, but a process called *pluralistic ignorance* may keep their doubts from being recognized. Here is how.

Picture the situation in which a group of devout believers is confronted with belief-disconfirming information. Each believer may experience doubt. But, unsure what to do, each masks this doubt while looking to other members of the group to see how they are responding. Meanwhile, the other group members are doing the same. To each believer, the other group members appear calm and unruffled by the new information. So each concludes that the disconfirming information must not be as devastating as he or she thought. Through this process of pluralistic ignorance, believers in a group are more resistant to disconfirming information than believers who are alone.[1]

1. The importance of group support in increasing resistance to information that challenges one's beliefs was nicely illustrated in an experiment by Harold Kelley (1955). Catholic high school students' opinions about censorship, parental control, traditional religious practices, and church loyalty were challenged by having them complete an opinion questionnaire on which responses were already marked. These responses were said to indicate the average opinion of a large number of other high school students. Moreover, the responses were always fairly divergent from responses most acceptable to Catholics. Before being given the questionnaire, some students were given a short reading that highlighted the activities of the Catholic Church; this reading was intended to make their group identity as Catholics more salient. Other students were given a reading that had nothing to do with church or religion. The students reminded of

These three characteristics—personal benefits derived from the beliefs, public commitment to the beliefs, and social support from the community of believers—make deeply held religious beliefs highly resistant to change. Of course, irrefutable disconfirming information is also highly resistant to change. Given the unacceptability of surrendering either cognition, Festinger's theory predicts that the dissonance produced by disconfirming information will be reduced by adding new cognitions consonant with the set of cognitions that is most resistant to change. For the highly devout, intrinsic believer the set most resistant to change is likely to be the religious beliefs. And if it is, presenting this believer with information that irrefutably disconfirms the beliefs should lead, not to rejection or even weakening of the beliefs, but to bolstering them with additional consonant cognitions. As Festinger says, the believer should come away "even more convinced of the truth of his beliefs than ever before."

Empirical evidence. Festinger's theory of cognitive dissonance provides a theoretical basis for our contention that deeply held religious beliefs can be binding because it suggests that once a person holds such beliefs, clear evidence that they are wrong only ties the person more tightly to them. But the basis for this contention is not only theoretical; there is empirical evidence as well, evidence from historical examples, field studies, and quasi-experimental studies.

Historical examples. First, let us consider two historical examples of belief intensification in the face of disconfirming information. These examples were cited by Festinger et al. (1956). One concerns the development of Montanism, a second-century Christian sect.

> Montanus, who appeared in the second half of the second century, does not appear as an innovator in matters of belief. His one personal contribution to the life of the time was the fixed conviction that the second coming of Our Lord was at hand. The event was to take place at Pepuza—near the modern Angora—and thither all true followers of Our Lord should make their way. His authority for the statement was an alleged private inspiration, and the new prophet's personality and eloquence won him a host of disciples, who flocked in such numbers to the appointed spot that a new town sprang up to house them. *Nor did the delay of the second advent put an end to the movement. On the contrary, it gave it new life and form* as a kind of Christianity of the elite, whom no other authority guided in their new life but the Holy Spirit working directly upon them. . . . (Hughes, 1954, p. 10, italics added)

---

their religious group identity as Catholics were less likely to shift their opinions toward the responses marked on their questionnaire. Presumably, reminding them that there were others who held the same opinions as they did enabled them to resist the peer pressure to modify their beliefs. Jean-Pierre Deconchy (1980) has also reported research indicating that threatening the beliefs of orthodox believers leads them to rely even more heavily on their religious reference group for social support.

The second historical example concerns the Millerite movement in the mid-nineteenth century. William Miller was a New England farmer with a belief in the literal fulfillment of biblical prophecy. In 1818 he concluded from his study of the scriptures that the end of the world would come about 1843. As the time for the End approached, public interest in Miller's predictions grew, and by 1840 the Millerites had become a recognizable religious movement. The beginning of 1843 ushered in considerable interest in the specific date of the Advent. Up to that point Miller had simply said that the Second Coming would be "about the year 1843." On January 1, 1843, however, Miller published a synopsis of his beliefs, in which he stated his expectations about the date as follows:

> I believe the time can be known by all who desire to understand and to be ready for His coming. And I am fully convinced that sometime between March 21st, 1843, and March 21st, 1844, according to the Jewish mode of computation of time, Christ will come, and bring all His Saints with Him; and that then He will reward every man as his work shall be. (Miller, 1843, p. 147)

Although Miller had resisted setting a specific day, a number of his followers expected the End to come on April 23, 1843. When this day came and went, these followers reacted as follows:

> At first there was evidence of surprise and disappointment among the Millerites, but it quickly gave way to renewed confidence. "After all," they reminded one another, "there is a whole year in which to look for the Coming;—we looked for it too soon, that was all."—and the singing and exhorting took on a new fervor. (Sears, 1924, p. 119)

Next, a number of Millerites placed their hopes on December 31, 1843. When this day came and went, Miller issued a statement:

> Brethren, the Roman [year] 1843 is past [the Jewish sacred year would end in the spring of 1844] and our hopes are not realized. Shall we give up the ship? No, no. . . . We do not yet believe our reckoning has run out. It takes all of 457 and 1843 to make 2300, and must of course run as far into '44 as it began in the year 457 before Christ. (Quoted in Nichol, 1944, p. 160n)

Again, fervor increased; Millerite conferences in New York and Philadelphia were crowded, and in Washington there had to be a last-minute change to a larger hall.

But March 21, 1844, the last day in the year specified by Miller, also came and went with no sign of the Second Coming. What happened? The reaction of non-Millerites was strong and unequivocal. They made jokes and taunted and jeered Miller and his followers: "What—not gone up yet?—We thought you'd gone up! Aren't you going up soon?—Wife didn't go up and leave you behind to burn, did she?" (Sears, 1924, p. 144). Among the Millerites there was strong and severe disappointment, but this was of brief duration. Soon the energy and enthusiam were greater than ever before. During the summer of 1844 the faithful expended more and more energy to convert people to their beliefs. A number were so convinced that the End was imminent that they did not plant crops; some even sold their possessions.

Toward the end of the summer, many of the faithful were accepting October 22, 1844, as the date for the Second Coming. When this day passed without event, the Millerite movement finally began to wither and die. But it had taken a series of disconfirmations over a period of eighteen months to shake the beliefs of the faithful. The early disconfirmations seemed to lead, as dissonance theory would predict, to an intensification of belief.

Field Studies. Historical examples are suggestive, but there is always the danger of biased selection, that only examples clearly consistent with the theory in question are chosen. As a social scientist, Festinger naturally wished to study the process of belief intensification at first hand. And while working out the basic ideas of his theory of cognitive dissonance, he unexpectedly got the chance. A newspaper in a nearby city carried a back-page story with the headline: PROPHECY FROM PLANET. CLARION CALL TO CITY: FLEE THAT FLOOD. IT'LL SWAMP US ON DEC. 21, OUTER SPACE TELLS SUBURBANITE. The accompanying story explained:

> Lake City will be destroyed by a flood from Great Lake just before dawn, Dec. 21, according to a suburban housewife. Mrs. Marian Keech, of 847 West School Street, says the prophecy is not her own. It is the purport of many messages she has received by automatic writing, she says. . . . The messages, according to Mrs. Keech, are sent to her by superior beings from a planet called "Clarion." These beings have been visiting earth, she says, in what we call flying saucers. During their visits, she says, they have observed fault lines in the earth's crust that foretoken the deluge. Mrs. Keech reports she was told the flood will spread to form an inland sea stretching from the Arctic Circle to the Gulf of Mexico. At the same time, she says, a cataclysm will submerge the West Coast from Seattle, Washington, to Chile in South America. (Quoted in Festinger et al., 1956, pp. 30–31, with names changed)

This seemed to be just the sort of situation that Festinger was looking for; here was public commitment to the occurrence of specific events on a particular date. Assuming that the flood did not take place, Mrs. Keech would be faced with unequivocal disconfirmation of her beliefs. Festinger and two of his associates, Henry Riecken and Stanley Schachter, went to see Mrs. Keech. They found her cordial but not at all interested in trying to persuade them to adopt her beliefs. Indeed, she had not been the one to release the story to the press; that was done by a friend and fellow believer, Dr. Armstrong.

Festinger and his associates learned that in addition to Mrs. Keech and Dr. Armstrong, there were a number of other people interested in Mrs. Keech's messages from outer space; these people belonged to a group called the Seekers. Actually, there were two small groups, one in Lake City led by Mrs. Keech, and one in Collegeville, a nearby university town, led by Dr. Armstrong (again, all names are fictitious). Dr. Armstrong worked at the University health center, and most of the members of the Collegeville group were university students. Based on Mrs. Keech's messages, the Seekers not only believed that the great flood was coming on December 21; they also believed that the faithful would be spared, rescued by a flying saucer at midnight on December 20. Festinger and his associates quickly joined the Seekers so as to be present on the night of December 20 to witness firsthand the group's response to unequivocal disconfirmation of their publicly stated beliefs.

As you might imagine, field research of this kind presents some practical difficulties. The social psychologists wished to keep accurate, verbatim records of what groups members said and did, but they did not wish to "blow their cover." Further, although they wanted to be accepted as members of the group, they did not want to influence the beliefs of other group members. In order to get as accurate a record as possible, they frequently resorted to hiding in the bathroom or on the porch, where they frantically scribbled notes. The effort to avoid too direct participation reached a droll climax when one of the social psychologists was asked to act as a medium and receive messages from outer space. He kept a long silence. Finally, Mrs. Keech said with some irritation, "What do you see?" "Nothing," he replied. "That's not nothing," he was told, "that's the Void" (Festinger et al., 1956, p. 243).

When December 20 arrived, many of the Seekers from Collegeville were home on Christmas vacation, but ten of those who lived in Lake City assembled at Mrs. Keech's house and prepared to be picked up by the flying saucers. They readied themselves by rehearsing passwords and removing metal from their clothing. (Mrs. Keech had been informed that metallic objects would be dangerous on the saucer.) When midnight was close, the group went into the backyard to wait, but it was a bitterly cold night, so they soon returned inside. As the clock hand approached twelve, the ten believers sat in strained expectation of a knock at the door. The clock ticked past the hour, and for a few minutes there was discussion of who had the right time and whose watch was fast. Soon, however, it became clear that midnight had passed without the prophesied arrival of the saucer.

At first, the believers seemed stunned; their faces were frozen and expressionless. Gradually and painfully, despair and disappointment engulfed them. They re-examined the messages that Mrs. Keech had received, searching for some explanation. Near 4:00 A.M. Mrs. Keech began to cry, saying bitterly that she knew that some of the group were beginning to doubt her. But at 4:45 she summoned the group together and, with radiant face, read a new message that she had received:

> For this day it is established that there is but one God of Earth, and He is in thy midst, and from His hand thou hast written these words. And mighty is the word of God—and by His word have ye been saved—for from the mouth of death have ye been delivered and at no time has there been such a force loosed upon the Earth. (Quoted in Festinger et al., 1956, p. 169)

The message went on in this King James–style English to explain that the flood had been averted because of the impressive faith of the small group of believers; they had saved the country from disaster.

This explanation was received by the group with great enthusiasm. Soon the believers began to take turns telephoning newspapers and wire services to publicize their explanation of the failure of the prophecy. Although they had avoided publicity and proselytizing previously, they now turned to their task with vigor. In Mrs. Keech's words, "Now it is important."

The role of social support in the process of belief intensification was made clear by the reactions of the Seekers who were not present that night. All of them responded to the disconfirmation either by relinquishing their beliefs or by having greatly diminished faith in Mrs. Keech's prophecies.

The reaction of the Seekers who were present seems to provide dramatic support for Festinger's predictions. Still, two observations should be made. First, it is not really true that the Seekers emerged from the disconfirmation experience even more convinced of the truth of their beliefs than before, at least not all of their beliefs. For example, they did not maintain their belief in the flood. Instead, what occurred was a reinterpretation that allowed them to maintain their basic beliefs in communication with powerful extraterrestrial beings, while at the same time taking account of the disconfirmation. Of course, you might feel that Mrs. Keech and her followers would have been well advised to drop their beliefs entirely, as did most of the Seekers who were not present that night. We would agree. But it is important to note that Mrs. Keech and her followers did not resort to total irrationality, maintaining that the flood had occurred; instead, they resorted to rationalization.

Second, results of this study cannot really be considered an independent test of predictions from dissonance theory because the experience of the Seekers contributed to development of the theory. This study was conducted while the theory was being formulated, and several of the specific predictions that seem so dramatically supported were actually derived from reflection on what happened to Mrs. Keech and her followers. This has not proved to be a serious problem, however, because the essential pattern of results found by Festinger, Riecken, and Schachter has also been found in several subsequent studies.

In a second field study, Hardyck and Braden (1962) observed members of a Pentecostal sect after one of the group's leaders prophesied that there would be a major nuclear attack in six months. Upon receiving this message, more than a hundred members of the group promptly packed up their belongings and moved to a remote area in the southwestern United States, where they constructed an elaborate bomb shelter. When the date of the nuclear attack drew nigh, approximately 135 believers entered the shelter. Of these, 103 remained in the shelter for forty-two days, until it was clear that the attack was not coming.

As with the Seekers, when these faithful emerged from the shelter they had developed a reinterpretation that allowed them to maintain and even intensify their faith while at the same time rationalizing the unequivocal disconfirmation. They claimed, first, that there had never been a clear, unequivocal message of impending attack; second, that God had used them to warn an unvigilant world; and third, that God was testing their faith. They concluded that they had passed the test and were now especially worthy in the eyes of God. Interestingly, they continued to believe that a nuclear attack would be forthcoming, yet this did not prompt them to return to their shelter.

Once again, as predicted by dissonance theory, disconfirmation led to a rationalizing reinterpretation and, if anything, a strengthening of belief. But in one respect the group studied by Hardyck and Braden did not conform to Festinger's predictions. There was no increase in proselytizing after the disconfirmation. Hardyck and Braden suggest that this may have been due to the separatism of the group, which produced extremely high within-group cohesion and support, and to the lack of harassment from the surrounding community. Apparently, this group was able to reduce all dissonance without resorting to proselytizing.

Quasi-Experimental Studies. These historical examples and field studies deal with religious movements that appealed to only a small fraction of the population. You may be hesitant to generalize from the behavior of such individuals to the devout, intrinsically religious as a whole. Further, although field studies allow an investigator to examine the effects of belief disconfirmation firsthand, the investigator's observations may still be subject to bias. In each of the studies described, the investigators had clear expectations of what would happen. It is difficult to be sure that these expectations did not lead to some selective perception. Fortunately, several quasi-experimental studies have been conducted, which are less subject to these criticisms. The results again provide evidence for rationalization in the face of belief disconfirmation.

In one, Norman Feather (1964) examined the tendency of highly devout individuals to judge the truth or falsity of arguments about religion on the basis of whether the conclusions were consistent with their beliefs rather than on the logical merits of the argument. He had 131 religious and 34 nonreligious Australian university students judge the logical validity of forty syllogisms. Twelve of the syllogisms were proreligious in their conclusion and twelve antireligious; the remaining sixteen were not about religion at all. Further, half of the syllogisms in each category were logically valid, and half were invalid. Examples of syllogisms of each type are presented in Table 7.1. For each of the syllogisms the students were instructed: "You may or may not agree with the premises. What is important is to determine whether the argument is logically sound or logically unsound."

Feather expected that religious students would be more likely to make proreligious than antireligious errors; that is, they would be more likely to judge valid antireligious syllogisms to be unsound and invalid proreligious syllogisms to be sound (proreligious errors) than to judge valid proreligious syllogisms to be unsound and invalid antireligious syllogisms to be sound (antireligious errors). His results strongly supported this expectation ($p <$

Table 7.1 Examples of syllogisms used by Feather (1964) to test logical distortion of belief-relevant arguments by highly religious individuals

Proreligious syllogisms	
Valid	People who are without religion are spiritually devoid and need the Christian teachings to show them the true way of life. Atheists and agnostics are people without religion and devoid of spiritual life. Therefore, atheists and agnostics need Christian teachings to show them the true way of life.
Invalid	A charitable and tolerant attitude toward mankind helps to bring people together in love and harmony. Christianity always helps to bring people together in love and harmony. Therefore, a consequence of Christianity is a charitable and tolerant attitude toward mankind.
Antireligious syllogisms	
Valid	The reality of any phenomenon is established by scientific investigation and treatment. The existence of God is not established by scientific investigation and treatment. Therefore, the existence of God is not real.
Invalid	If thorough scientific investigation cannot prove that the Christian religion is superstition then belief in Christian miracles is justified. But thorough scientific investigation is able to prove that the Christian religion is superstition, so it follows that belief in Christian miracles is not justified.
Neutral syllogisms	
Valid	All members of the finance committee are members of the executive committee. No members of the library committee are members of the executive committee. Therefore, no members of the library committee are members of the finance committee.
Invalid	Some artists are unconventional and all portrait painters are known to be artists. It follows, therefore, that some portrait painters are unconventional.

Source: Adapted from Feather (1964).

.001); moreover, the tendency to make proreligious errors was especially strong among the most devout religious students. These students were almost twice as likely to make proreligious as antireligious errors.

Feather did not find the reverse effect among nonreligious students. They tended to make the same number of proreligious and antireligious errors. Given the population from which the students came, however, Feather did not think that the members of his nonreligious group were intensely opposed to religion. He suggested that a group of "devout" atheists would likely make a predominance of antireligious errors.

Feather's study provides clear evidence that the highly religious are likely to judge the truth or falsity of an argument about religion, at least in part, on whether the conclusion of the argument is consistent with their beliefs. One interpretation of this finding is that the need for cognitive consistency undermines these individuals' ability to judge a logical argument on its logical merits. But there is another possible interpretation. The errors observed by Feather among the highly religious may have been honest ones. The content of the valid antireligious syllogisms may have been quite unfamiliar to them; if so, these syllogisms could have been harder for them to understand. Difficulty in understanding could have led to more errors, just as it might if the syllogisms concerned some highly technical subject.

A second quasi-experimental study provides clearer evidence of belief intensification in the face of disconfirming evidence. In this study, Batson (1975) examined the reactions to belief disconfirming information of fifty female high school students who were members of a mainstream Protestant denomination. The study took place during weekend retreats held by several Presbyterian churches in New Jersey. On each retreat, the research was conducted with the cooperation of the youth minister in charge, who served as the leader of the research session.

As participants came into a large room for the session, they were asked to seat themselves in one of two locations depending on how they would answer the question "Do you believe Jesus is the Son of God?" This separation into believing and nonbelieving groups served two purposes. First, it forced each individual to make a visible, public commitment to her belief or nonbelief, one of the requirements for belief intensification specified by Festinger. Second, it provided at least some sense of group identity with others holding similar beliefs, fulfilling the requirement of having group support. After all participants had assigned themselves to one of the two groups, the leader introduced the research, emphasizing its potentially unsettling nature. Participants were told that if they became uneasy or afraid, they should feel free to excuse themselves. He then told them what their task would be.

Their task was to complete a questionnaire "devised to be given to small groups in several areas of the Unites States. Its purpose is to measure the effect of certain information on parts of the American public to determine whether the information should be circulated generally." The questionnaire consisted of three parts. The first part contained thirty items designed to measure intensity of orthodox Christian belief. The items focused on two specific beliefs, belief that Jesus was divine and that the Bible was the infallible Word of God. Typical items included: "Jesus actually performed miracles." "The Bible contains many errors" (reversed). "The Bible is the Word of God." "Jesus was only human" (reversed). Participants were asked to indicate agreement or disagreement with each statement using a five-point scale ranging from strongly disagree (1) to strongly agree (5). An approximate balance was maintained between positive and negative wordings to control for response bias.

After everyone had completed Part One of the questionnaire, they were instructed to turn to Part Two, in which they read the following article, "written anonymously and denied publication in the *New York Times* at the request of the World Council of Churches because of the obvious crushing effect that it would have on the entire Christian world":

> —Geneva, Switzerland. It was learned today here in Geneva from a top source in the World Council of Churches offices that scholars in Jordan have

> conclusively proved that the major writings in what is today called the New Testament are fraudulent.
>
> According to the information gained from the unnamed source within the headquarters of the World Council of Churches, Professor R. R. Lowry (author of *The Zarondike Fragments and the Dead Sea Scrolls*), assisted by other scholars, has been carefully analyzing a collection of papyrus scrolls discovered in a cave in the Jordanian desert near where the famous Dead Sea Scrolls were found. Contained within this collection of scrolls, Lowry and his associates have found letters, apparently written between the composers of various New Testament books, bluntly stating: "Since our great teacher Jesus of Nazareth was killed by the Romans, I am sure we were justified in stealing away his body and claiming that he rose from the dead. For, although his death clearly proves he was not the Son of God as we had hoped, if we did not claim that he was, both his great teaching and our lives as his disciples would be wasted!"
>
> Though Lowry initially suspected the authenticity of these scrolls, he was later quoted as saying, "Through radiocarbon dating and careful study of the Aramaic dialect used in writing these letters, I have found it impossible to deny that the manuscripts are authentic. You can't image what a struggle this has been; I find no alternative but to renounce my former belief that Jesus Christ was the Son of God. I can no longer be a Christian."
>
> When Dr. Ernest Carson Baker, the general secretary of the World Council of Churches, was confronted with Lowry's statement by this reporter, he at first denied that it was true. After a few minutes of questioning, however, he broke down and admitted, "This thing has got us so upset we're just not sure what to do. We just can't let this story get out!" Apparently the only avenue open to the Church in the twentieth century is the same avenue that it took in the first century—conceal the facts and proclaim Jesus as the divine Son of God, even though it knows such a claim is a lie.

This article was designed to present information that, if believed, would clearly disconfirm both belief in Jesus as divine and in the infallibility of the Bible.

After reading the article, participants were instructed to complete Part Three of the questionnaire. Part Three served two purposes. First, it contained twenty more items concerning belief in Jesus' divinity and the infallibility of the Bible. These items, drawn from the same pool as the thirty items in Part One of the questionnaire, were included to measure intensity of belief after reading the article. Twelve other items in Part Three served a second purpose; they were designed to assess participants' reactions to the article. These items ranged from "Lowry's discovery truly proves that Jesus was not the Son of God" to "The article was probably written by a communist." Such items were included for two reasons: First, they were consistent with the stated purpose of the research project, to determine public reaction to the article on a small scale before deciding about its wider dissemination. Second, they allowed assessment of participants' acceptance of the veracity of the article. According to dissonance theory, one would expect reactions to be quite different for believers who thought the article was true as opposed to those who thought it was untrue. Disagreement with one item, "The article is untrue," was the criterion for concluding that an individual accepted the article as true.

After all participants had completed Part Three, the leader encouraged them to express reactions to the questionnaire. Then he assured everyone that the article in Part Two was totally untrue, and he outlined reasons for the administration of the questionnaire and for the deception involved in the research. In his explanation he included a brief description of the field study by Festinger, Riecken, and Schachter (1956). He then went on to suggest possible implications of participants' reactions for understanding the way religious beliefs function, and a lively discussion of the nature of religious beliefs and reactions to belief-disconfirming evidence followed. Care was taken to encourage anyone disturbed by the research to discuss it personally with the leader. This precaution proved unnecessary, however, for participants expressed considerable interest in the research and enthusiasm in discussing its implications. All seemed to understand the reason for the deception involved, and none appeared upset by it.

Assuming that disconfirming information leads to belief intensification in the way that dissonance theory predicts, what results should we see in this study? Any change in belief should depend on the participant's initial belief and her acceptance of the truth of the article in Part Two. Taking these two variables into account, the participants were divided into three groups. First, there were eight nonbelievers, individuals who answered no to the initial question of whether Jesus was the Son of God. We would not expect the article in Part Two to arouse any dissonance for them because it was not inconsistent with their initial beliefs. Second, there were thirty-one believers who said that they did not accept the veracity of the article. We would not expect them to experience dissonance either because, although the article contained information inconsistent with their initial belief, they did not accept the information as true. There were, however, eleven believers who said that they did accept the article as true. These eleven should have experienced dissonance between their publicly stated belief in the divinity of Jesus and the information in the article revealing that this belief was based on a hoax. If clear disconfirmation leads to belief intensification, we would expect these eleven participants to express stronger religious belief after reading the article than they did before. We would not expect to see an increase for either of the other two groups.

Mean religious belief scores on Part One and Part Three of the questionnaire for members of each of the three groups are presented in Table 7.2. The *t*-scores and *p*-values presented in the last two columns of the table reveal the statistical significance of changes in stated belief from Part One to Part Three. Both the nonbelievers and the believers who said that they doubted the disconfirming information indicated less belief after having read the article in Part Two; this difference was statistically significant for the nonbelievers ($p < .01$). Results were quite different for the believers who said that they accepted the article as true. As dissonance theory pre-

Table 7.2. Differences between the pretest and posttest scores of religious belief for believers and nonbelievers

Groups	Mean pretest scores	Mean posttest scores	t	p
Nonbelievers ($n = 8$)	3.37	2.91	−3.70	<.01
Believers doubting the belief-disconfirming information ($n = 31$)	3.97	3.90	−1.17	ns
Believers accepting the belief-disconfirming information ($n = 11$)	4.07	4.30	3.61	<.005

Source: Adapted from Batson (1975).

dicted, these individuals appeared to become stronger in their beliefs. Although members of this group had indicated strong religious belief on Part One of the questionnaire (mean response approximately 4.0 on a five-point scale), they indicated even stronger belief after reading the belief-disconfirming article ($p < .005$).

How did the believers who indicated that they accepted the veracity of the article and yet became stronger in their statement of belief justify this apparent discrepancy? Data were not available to answer this question. Indeed, it seems quite possible that most of the individuals did not have time to work out the discrepancy before they were informed that the article was, in fact, false. Recall that it took Mrs. Keech over four hours to develop a plausible and effective rationalization, and the dissonance of participants in this study was relieved much sooner than that—when they were informed that the article was untrue.

Results paralleling those of this quasi-experimental study have been found in a clever series of quasi-experiments by Jean-Pierre Deconchy (1980). Deconchy found that when Catholic clergy were confronted with evidence challenging the security of their orthodox beliefs (either by pointing out logical contradictions in the Bible or by leading them to believe their peers in the clergy held more liberal beliefs) they intensified their strict allegiance to these beliefs as the basis of church membership.

In the quasi-experimental studies described so far, exposure to belief-disconfirming information was unavoidable. But, if given a choice, the devout believer might be expected to avoid encountering such information and the dissonance that would result (Festinger, 1957). Schoenrade (1987) found evidence consistent with this reasoning in a study in which participants were asked to choose one of two essays to read. The title and written comments (ostensibly from other students who had read the essay) revealed that one essay was clearly supportive of belief in afterlife; the other was clearly opposed. As dissonance theory would predict, the stronger a participant's belief in afterlife the more likely the participant was not to choose the antibelief essay ($p < .05$), which could threaten this belief.

Recently, McFarland and Warren (1992) conducted a similar study with a sample of adult fundamentalist Christians living in small towns and rural areas in south-central Kentucky and north-central Tennessee. Ostensibly as part of a project to select articles for a new periodical, *Christian Reflection*, participants were asked to rate how much they would or would not like to read each of twenty-four articles. Titles and abstracts revealed that six of the articles support fundamentalist beliefs and six opposed these beliefs; the remaining twelve were on nonreligious topics of current interest. For example, the abstract for a belief-supporting article, "The Prophetic Vision," said that the article documented the accuracy of Old Testament prophecies of Jesus, whereas the abstract for a belief-challenging article, "The Illusion of Prophecy," said the article argued that "there are no true prophecies of Jesus in the Old Testament." Overall, these fundamentalist Christians preferred the belief-supporting articles. Moreover, higher scores on Allport's Intrinsic scale were positively correlated with desire to read the belief-supporting articles but not the belief-challenging ones.

To summarize the empirical evidence, the historical examples, field studies, and quasi-experimental studies all point to the same conclusion: a deeply held religious belief can, indeed, be binding. Faced with belief-disconfirming information, the devout believer is not free to critically re-examine and perhaps reject the belief. Instead, he or she is likely to be driven to even stronger belief.

One need not assume, of course, that the devout, intrinisic believer perceives his or her beliefs to be binding. On the contrary, the beliefs are likely to be seen as the freely chosen foundation on which the individual's entire reality is built. Mrs. Keech would doubtless say that she had freely chosen her beliefs, and in a sense she had. She would probably also say that she was in no way bound by them, that they were instead a source of liberating strength. But a more objective view suggests that her beliefs had her trapped and were pushing her farther and farther into a personally constricting, delusional reality. And does not a more objective view suggest a similar conclusion about the restricting effects of any deeply held religious beliefs? Do not such beliefs chain the devout, intrinsic believer to one view of reality, prohibiting adaptive change in response to new information?

IMPLICATIONS OF THE EVIDENCE: AN EXPLANATION FOR THE ORIGIN OF CHRISTIANITY?

In reading the evidence for intensification of belief in the face of disconfirmation, you may have wondered why such an analysis could not be applied to the origin of major world religions. Consider, for example, Christianity. Records indicate that in his brief ministry Jesus attracted a large number of enthusiastic and hopeful followers; they looked to him as their savior. Then he was seized by the Roman soldiers and put to death. Would this not create considerable cognitive dissonance, especially for his closest followers and disciples, those who had given up all to follow him? And if it created dissonance, would these followers not be motivated to develop some face-saving reinterpretation in which their belief in Jesus as savior would be intensified and their proselytizing efforts would increase? And could this not account for the fact that after a period of initial confusion and disappointment, Jesus' death was no longer a stumbling block for his followers but the pillar of their faith, the culminating event in which he atoned for the sins of the world and conquered the power of death through resurrection?

Festinger et al. (1956) noted the possibility of a dissonance interpretation of the origin of Christianity, but they were careful to emphasize its speculative nature and to caution against quick and uncritical adoption of such a view. Wernik (1975), however, argued that dissonance principles not only can but *do* account for the rise of Christianity. Employing Robert Abelson's (1959) analysis of four strategies available to reduce inconsistency between existing beliefs and disconfirming information—denial, bolstering, differentiation, and transcendence—Wernik builds a case that these strategies underlie the development of a number of key beliefs among the early Christians. Beliefs that Wernik claims are a product of dissonance reduction include the following: (1) Jesus was not only a great teacher but the Messiah predicted by the prophets; (2) Jesus had an extraordinary and prodigious birth and childhood; (3) Jesus was endorsed as savior by God, holy men (e.g., John the Baptist), and himself; (4) Jesus' death was transitory and for a purpose, and (5) Jesus knew about, predicted, and chose his own death. Wernik contends that these and similar beliefs served to rationalize the dashed hopes of Jesus' followers and that out of this intensification and rationalization, Christianity was born.

What is one to make of Wernik's argument? Certainly, many of the events surrounding the death of Jesus and the emergence of early Christianity can be fitted into a dissonance analysis. Yet we would echo the caution of Festinger et al. (1956); it is important to resist an overly quick and facile interpretation. Because events can be fitted into a dissonance framework does not, by itself, prove that this is the correct or even the best interpretation of them. Still, Wernik's (1975) analysis provides much food for thought, and just as it should not be prematurely adopted, it should not be prematurely rejected.

DEVELOPMENT OF ENSLAVING BELIEFS: SOME FACTORS IN THE BELIEF ESCALATION PROCESS

In our discussion so far we have been looking at the effect of disconfirming information on devout religious belief once the beliefs are well formed. But we also need to consider how beliefs that are so deeply held that they lead one to distort and deny disconfirming information can develop in the first place. We would suggest that the same forces that lead to intensification can, when they operate over a longer period of time, account for the emergence of deeply held, devout beliefs. The need for cognitive consistency, although a seemingly benign principle, creates pressure toward escalation and intensification of *any* publicly stated belief, even if the belief is initially stated tentatively and with considerable reservation. Like the swirling waters of a whirlpool, this need subtly but powerfully draws the believer, little by little, into deeper and deeper commitment. How does it do this? Through the combined effect of the same three factors that we previously suggested make devout religious beliefs particularly resistant to change—esteem enhancement, public commitment, and social support.

Esteem Enhancement

The new believer is usually told that he or she is now one of a select group of individuals who have "seen the light." This enhances his or her self-esteem. And enhanced self-esteem can make the believer more likely to reject the arguments of anyone who questions the new belief.

Indirect evidence for this reasoning has been provided by David Glass (1964), who found that individuals who have had their self-esteem enhanced are especially likely to resort to derogation of others to reduce dissonance. Glass led individuals to believe that they had delivered shocks to an innocent victim. Participants were then given an opportunity to state their impression of the victim. Based on dissonance theory, Glass reasoned that individuals with enhanced self-esteem, those who saw themselves as good, noble people, would have more dissonance to reduce as a result of delivering shocks to the innocent victim. Although they could reduce the dissonance by re-evaluating themselves, deciding that they were not as good and noble as they had thought, Glass expected that they would instead derogate the victim. By seeing the victim as a relatively worthless individual, they could rationalize their delivery of the shocks without losing their high opinion of themselves. This is exactly what happened. Compared with low-self-esteem individuals, high-self-esteem individuals derogated the victim more.

We would suggest that a parallel process can occur as a result of the esteem enhancement derived from religious commitment. Imagine a believer motivated to retain the esteem that comes from being a person with special insight into the mysteries of life. What will be his response when people present arguments and evidence that contradict his beliefs? He knows who is right and who is wrong: he is right, and they are wrong. After all, they do not have his special insight. In this way, the esteem-enhancing nature of the beliefs may lead the believer toward relatively greater reliance on his own perceptions and derogation of the perceptions of anyone who challenges the beliefs.

Public Commitment

Charles Kiesler has studied the escalating consequences of public behavioral commitment. Based on studies of social and political beliefs, both in the laboratory and the field, Kiesler (1971) reports what he calls a *boomerang effect:* If individuals are publicly committed to action consistent with their belief, then hearing arguments that challenge the belief can intensify it. This boomerang effect is another example of belief intensification in the face of opposition. It is important to note, however, that the beliefs Kiesler studied were not nearly as personally important as are deeply held religious beliefs. Further, participants in Kiesler's research were not presented with unequivocal disconfirmation, only with forcefully stated counterarguments.

To find tnat opposition as well as unequivocal disconfirmation can produce belief intensification carries important implications for the emergence of devout religious beliefs, because most religious beliefs, such as a belief in God, are not stated in such a way that they can be unequivocally disconfirmed. Instead, they are subject to, and are frequently subjected to, challenges of varying intensity.

Kiesler's analysis carries another important implication concerning the consequences of public commitment over time. Imagine that an individual publicly states a tentative and moderately held belief. Imagine further that he is met with counterarguments from friends and acquaintances. What will happen? Although he may simply drop his belief, the evidence for the boomerang effect, as well as our previous argument for esteem enhancement, suggests that he will probably state his belief a bit more strongly in both word and deed. What happens then? Kiesler suggests that this public commitment to a more extreme belief has two consequences. First, it makes the believer more accepting of even more extreme related beliefs; beliefs that he initially might have considered outlandish and fanatical are now not that far removed from what he himself has proclaimed. Second, it makes him even more likely to be confronted with opposition. The more extreme his own belief, the more likely it is to meet with disagreement from others. This opposition should drive him even further toward extreme statements and acts (again, the boomerang effect), making him susceptible to influence by even more extreme related beliefs and to new, even more intense opposition. Step-by-step, public behavioral commitment to the belief, and the belief itself, both move toward extremity.

Michael Pallak and his associates have presented research that lends empirical support to several of the steps in this process of escalation due to public commitment. Sullivan and Pallak (1976; see also Pallak & Sullivan, 1979) found that once an individual had publicly stated a belief, he or she was more likely to agree to take other actions consistent with that belief. Pallak, Mueller, Dollar, and Pallak (1972) found that public, behavioral commitment to a relatively moderate stance on an issue made the person more susceptible to an extremist appeal. And Halverson and Pallak (1978) found that taking public action consistent with one's beliefs led to changes in one's cognitive structure toward greater "ego-involvement" in the belief. Ego-involvment is important, because previous research by Sherif and her associates has indicated that ego-involvement is associated with greater likelihood of taking subsequent action in line with one's belief (Sherif, Kelley, Rodgers, Sarup, & Tittler, 1973) and being more accepting of extreme statements of the belief (Sherif, Sherif, & Nubergall, 1965).

In combination, these findings seem to provide rather clear documentation of the process of belief-behavior escalation. Taking public action consistent with a belief, even a moderate and tenatively held belief, leads to greater ego-involvement in the belief, greater susceptibility to extreme statements of the belief, and greater resistance to opposition to the belief. These consequences, in turn, increase the likelihood of taking further public action and the likelihood of more opposition. Round by round, the individual is moved toward increasing ego-involvement with an increasingly extreme belief.

Religious groups seem well aware of this process of belief-behavior escalation. Typically, the new convert is asked to make some public, behavioral commitment of a relatively minor sort, to "come forward" or at least to "tell someone else." Over time, the behavioral demands are increased as the belief intensifies. Getting a believer to distribute information door-to-door, to sell flowers, or to preach on the street corner not only leads to the possibility of new converts and to increased revenues for a religious movement. It also intensifies the devotion and commitment of the believer.

Social Support

As the belief escalates and becomes more extreme, so does the believer's dependence for social support on others who share the belief. He or she is likely to become more isolated and cut off from former friends and family who do not share the belief, and this weakening of former ties is likely to be matched by an increasing dependence on the new reference group, the community of faith (Galanter, 1989; Staples & Mauss, 1987). Empirical evidence of increased dependency on those who share one's view of reality comes from an experiment by Darley, Moriarty, Darley, and Berscheid (1974).

These researchers used a research technique developed by Solomon Asch (1956) to study conformity. Groups of individuals were presented with a series of judgments on which there were clearly correct answers. Each group contained only one naive research participant; all other members were confederates of the experimenter. The naive participant always made his judgments near the end of the group, and unknown to him, the situation was set up to study the effect of the confederates' judgments on his judgments. Asch had found in such a situation that if the confederates all made a clearly incorrect choice, many participants are unable to resist this group pressure; they too make the incorrect choice. Asch also found that if just one of the confederates gives the correct response, the pressure to conform is broken; participants almost invariably make the correct response also.

Darley et al. took the analysis of the pressure to conform one step further. As a first phase of their experiment they subjected participants to a situation similar to the one used by Asch in which one of the confederates deviated from the others, always making correct responses. As Asch had found, participants easily resisted the majority pressure and made correct responses. But Darley et al. added a second phase to their experiment. The participants were placed in a second judgment situation in which some were paired with the confederate who had previously deviated from the majority, always making correct responses, whereas others were paired with a different confederate. In the new situation the confederate made some responses that were clearly incorrect. What effect did these errors have on the judgments of research participants? Participants who were paired with the confederate who had previously been their ally in truth were far more likely to conform to his incorrect responses in this new situation. Thus, although having an ally allowed the participants to be independent and resist the pressure to conform in the larger group situation, the subsequent session revealed that they had become increasingly dependent on the opinions of the ally.

It seems likely that a similar process can occur for the member of a religious community. Knowing that there are others who think as you do may enable you to resist outside opposition, but at the same time, it may make you less able to resist opinions endorsed by the group or its leader (Galanter, 1989; Hammond & Hunter, 1984; Jacobs, 1984). Moreover, research by Dittes and Kelley (1956) suggests that pressure to conform to group opinion may be especially strong for those who (1) highly value membership in the group and (2) feel only moderately accepted as opposed to totally accepted by the group. These characteristics would seem to describe the new group member, who is acutely aware of his or her dependence on the group and also of having only marginal status within the group. Thus, there would seem to be especially strong pressures on the "novitiate" to conform to group opinion, stronger pressure than might be felt by a well-accepted long-term group member. Of course, by the time one becomes a long-term group member one has burnt many bridges to other social support systems, and even if one feels free to deviate from group opinion and still remain accepted by the group, one is not likely to do so.

In combination, the effects of esteem enhancement, public commitment, and social support seem likely to lead to a gradual escalation in the intensity of even moderate and tentative beliefs. (The importance of all three factors being present is suggested by Long & Hadden, 1983.) This escalation can produce deeply held, devout beliefs capable of maintaining their hold on the believer even in the face of unequivocal disconfirmation. Perhaps the clearest example of this escalation process is to be found in religious cults.

BELIEF ESCALATION IN ACTION: RELIGIOUS CULTS

One of the questions that we have most frequently encountered from students and friends concerning the endless procession of new total-commitment religious groups—often called *cults*—goes something like this: "How can they believe *that* . . . and with such *zeal?*" The foregoing analysis of the processes that operate to increase the extremity of and behavioral commitment to a religious belief would seem to go a long way toward answering this question. It suggests that the answer need not lie in some personality defect or pathological need on the part of the person joining a cult, nor need it lie in the use of physical coercion (Richardson, 1980; Snow & Machalek, 1982). Instead, two perfectly normal needs, when operating in a particular social environment, appear quite capable of accounting for the emergence of intense allegiance to virtually any set of beliefs. The needs are (1) the need to make sense of one's life by dealing with various existential questions and (2) the need to maintain an internally consistent cognitive organization. The particular social enviroment is one of opposition from those outside the community of believers and support from those within. Given these environmental conditions, all that seems required for zealous allegiance is that the beliefs be capable of providing a sense of meaning in life and a sense of personal worth. Then the need for consistency takes hold. Supported by the forces of esteem enhancement, public commitment, and social support, it can propel the individual into escalating involvement with increasingly extreme beliefs.

How far can this escalation process go? Far, very far. We believe that it led to the following interchange among those who, step-by-step, had given up their time, money, possessions, and even their homeland, to live for their religious beliefs in the jungle of Guyana:

> Rev. Jim Jones: To me death is not a fearful thing. It's living that's cursed. It's not worth living like this.
> Cultist Christine Miller: I think that there were too few who left for 1,200 people to give their lives for those people that left.
> Jones: Do you know how many left?
> Miller: Oh, 20-odd. That's small compared to what's here.
> Jones: 20-odd. But what's gonna happen when they don't leave? When they get on the plane and the plane goes down? That plane'll come out of the air. There's no way you fly a plane without a pilot. You think Russia's gonna want us with all this stigma? We had some value, but now we don't have any value. [Jones, who called his political philosophy "socialistic Communism," had talked of moving the community to Russia.]
> Miller: Well, I don't see it like that. I mean, I feel like that as long as there's life there's hope.
> Jones: Well, everybody dies. I haven't seen anybody yet didn't die. And I'd like to choose my own kind of death for a change. I'm tired of being tormented to hell. Tired of it. [Applause.]
> Miller: But I look at all the babies and I think they deserve to live.
> Jones: But don't they deserve much more? They deserve peace.
> Miller: I think we all have a right to our own destiny as individuals. And I have a right to choose mine, and everybody else has a right to choose theirs.
> Jones: The best testimony we can make is to leave this goddam world. [After applause, more argument breaks out in the crowd. Jones' voice, remarkably controlled, begins to rise.] Everybody hold it! Hold it! Hold it! Lay down your

burdens. Down by the riverside. Shall we lay them down here by the side of Guyana? When they start parachuting out of the air, they'll shoot some of our innocent babies. Can you let them take your child?

Voices: No! No! No!

Man: I'm ready to go. If you tell us we have to give our lives now, we're ready: all the rest of the sisters and brothers are with me.

Jones: I've tried to keep this thing from happening. But I now see it's the will of sovereign Being that we lay down our lives in protest against what's been done. If they come after our children, and we give them our children, then our children will suffer forever. [Cultists returning from the airstrip tell Jones that Congressman Ryan, who had been visiting the community on a fact-finding trip, has been killed.]

Jones: Please get us some medication. It's simple, there's no convulsions with it. Just, please get it. Before it's too late. The G.D.F. [Guyanese army] will be here. Get movin', get movin'. Don't be afraid to die. Are you going to separate yourself from whoever shot the Congressman? I don't know who shot him.

Voices: No! No! No!

Jones: How many are dead? [One of the airstrip party reports that others were killed.] Aw, God, Almighty God. It's too late. They're all laying out there dead. Please, can we hasten our medication?

Woman: OK. There's nothing to worry about. Everybody keep calm and try to keep your children calm. Let the little children in and reassure them. [The children are given the poison first.] They're not crying from pain; it's just a little bitter-tasting.

Jones: It's hard only at first. Living is much, much more difficult. Rising in the morning and not knowing what the night's bringing.

Woman: This is nothing to cry about. This is something we could all rejoice about. I'm looking at so many people crying. I wish you would not cry. [Applause.]

Jones: Please, for God's sake, let's get on with it. We've lived as no other people lived and loved. We've had as much of this world as you're gonna get. Let's just be done with it. I want to see you go. They can take me and do what they want, whatever they want to do. I don't want to see you go through this hell no more. No more.

Man: The way the children are laying there now, I'd rather see them lay like that than to see them have to die like the Jews did, which was pitiful. Like Dad [the cultists called Jones "Dad"] said, when they come in, they're going to massacre our children. And the ones that they take capture, they're gonna just let them grow up and be dummies. And not grow up to be a person like the one and only Jim Jones. [Applause.]

Jones: Let's get gone. Let's get gone. We tried to find a new beginning. But it's too late. I don't know who killed the Congressman. But as far as I'm concerned I killed him. He had no business coming, I told him not to come.

Lay down your life with dignity. Don't lay down with tears and agony. It's just stepping over into another plane. [Crying and screaming in the background.] Stop this hysterics. This is not the way for people who are socialistic Communists to die. Children, it's just something to put you to rest. Oh, God. [Continued crying.]

Mother, mother, please. Don't do this. Lay down your life with your

> child. Free at last. Keep your emotions down. Children, it will not hurt. If you be quiet. [Music in background. Children still crying.] I don't care how many screams you hear; death is a million times preferable to spend more days in this life. If you knew what was ahead of you, you'd be glad to be stepping over tonight.
>
> I call on you to quit exciting your children. Stop this nonsense. Hurry, my children, hurry. Quickly. Quickly. Quickly. No more pain. No more pain. All they do is take a drink to go to sleep. That's what death is, sleep. Have trust. You have to step across. This world was not our home. (Transcript of tape found in a recorder in Jonestown, Guyana; reproduced in *Time* magazine, March 26, 1979, pp. 17–19)

After all his "children" were "free at last." Jim Jones died too, presumably by his own hand. In all, 913 people died in Jonestown on that afternoon in November 1978. The very beliefs that freed them from worldly cares to live "as no other people lived and loved" compelled them to "die with dignity."

Bondage to these beliefs and to Jones's authority did not come quickly. Had Jones proposed such a course of action in the early days of the cult back in California, it would probably have been rejected. We would suggest that the bondage was reached by a long, slow process of escalating intensification of belief and behavior built on enhanced self-esteem, public commitment, and intense social support. By small steps, these devout believers reached the point of no return.

SUMMARY AND CONCLUSION

Is religion a source of personal freedom or bondage? We believe that an answer depends on how one approaches religion. To the extent that people use their religion as an extrinsic means to self-serving ends, religion is likely to be perceived as an oppressive set of prescribed beliefs and behaviors. It is restricting, a drag. But to the extent that religion is an intrinsic end in itself, it is likely to be perceived as an important source of personal freedom. It is a joy; it provides freedom from existential doubt and fear (e.g., fear of death), as well as from a variety of self-destructive behaviors (e.g., excessive drinking and lust). But the freedom obtained by devout, intrinsic belief is obtained at a price; it is freedom with bondage, bondage to the belief system itself.

Because the beliefs meet important personal needs, they are highly valued by the believer. As a result, they are highly resistant to change. The devout believer can quickly reach the point where he or she will react to well-founded counterarguments against the beliefs not by critically re-examining the beliefs but by endorsing them even more strongly. This reaction is dramatically displayed in belief intensification in the face of disconfirming information.

To understand this belief-intensification process, we turned to Festinger's theory of cognitive dissonance. Dissonance theory predicts that intensification will occur when (1) the discomfirmed belief is deeply held; (2) the believer has made public his or her commitment to the belief; and (3) he or she is in contact with other believers who can provide social support. Evidence from history, field observation, and quasi-experimental studies provides support for this prediction.

But why should clear disconfirmation under these conditions lead the believer to cling even more firmly to his or her belief? Dissonance theory suggests that the reason lies in the need to maintain a consistent, meaningful cognitive organization. In an attempt to maintain consistency, the believer is motivated to reduce the dissonance between the belief and the disconfirming information. And in this attempt, he or she is in a bind. On the one hand, the disconfirming information cannot be denied; on the other, the believer does not want to let go of a personally meaningful, liberating belief. As a result, rather than changing the belief, he or she attempts to drown out the dissonance in a chorus of cognitions consonant with the belief, including both reinterpretations to explain the disconfirmation in a manner consistent with the belief and more intense statements of the belief itself.

It has been suggested that such a process of intensification in the face of disconfirmation can account for the origin of major world religions such as Christianity. Whether this is so remains unclear. It is clear, however, that many religious communities create a psychological environment that encourages a step-by-step escalation toward increasing dependence on the community's beliefs, making intensification the most likely response to challenge. Important features of this environment include (1) providing the individual with a sense of special identity and esteem; (2) encouraging him or her to act publicly on the belief; and (3) providing a cohesive system of social support. We believe that the fruits of a belief nurtured in such an environment were dramatically, if tragically, displayed at Jonestown, Guyana. But we also believe that a similar escalation process is operating in a less spectacular, and less destructive, way in the lives of the devout followers of any set of religious beliefs, including major world religions.

"You will know the truth, and the truth will make you free" (John 8:32 NRSV). There seems to be psychological truth in this statement because there is much evidence that the truth found through devout religious belief provides important personal freedoms. But there is also much evidence that this freedom comes at the price of uncritical allegiance to the beliefs themselves. The very truth that makes you free, because it makes you free, can enslave. We began this chapter with the joyous cry of the faithful, "Free at last." We ended with this same cry, made by Jim Jones as he admonished mothers to "lay down your life with your child." Devout religious beliefs can bind one so tightly that one is "freely" compelled to die for them.

Are the personal freedoms obtained through devout religious belief worth the price? At one level this is a question that each individual must answer for him- or herself. But as psychologists, we would like to know more about the consequences of a devout intrinsic belief before coming to any conclusion. We need to know more about what such beliefs do for the individual, both in terms of personal adjustment, satisfaction, and happiness, and in terms of ability to respond positively and openly to a wider range of people and situations. It is possible that the personal and social benefits obtained from devout belief more than justify the cost of uncritical bondage. In the next three chapters we shall consider this possibility. Chapter 8 concerns the effect of devout religious belief on personal adjustment and mental health; Chapters 9 and 10, the effect on response to others, especially the outcast, downtrodden, and the needy.

A POSTSCRIPT: FREEDOM OR BONDAGE AND THE QUEST DIMENSION

In Chapter 6 we suggested that the popular distinction between two dimensions of individual religion, as an extrinsic means to self-serving ends and as an intrinsic end in itself, needed to be amended to include a third dimension, as an open-ended quest. In this chapter we have had much to say about the freedom and bondage that result from an intrinsic, end orientation to religion. But we have said almost nothing about the quest orientation. This omission was forced on us, because there is almost no theory or research that has any clear bearing on the question of whether a quest orientation to religion is personally liberating or enslaving. This paucity of evidence makes us hesitant even to comment on the question, but we feel that something should be said. Here are some thoughts and a summary of the limited empirical evidence.

First, some thoughts. We would suggest that the quest dimension will be associated with less bondage than the intrinsic, end dimension but that it will also be associated with less freedom. Recall the dual emphasis within the quest dimension on skepticism toward traditional religious answers and critical reflection on religious questions. This emphasis suggests that the person who orients toward religion as a quest has neither the positive, affirmative answers nor the social support of a community of believers to entrap him or her into an escalating intensification of belief. Therefore, the quest dimension should not be associated with the bondage that is associated with the intrinsic, end dimension. At the same time, the lack of positive, affirmative answers makes it likely that the quest dimension will not produce the freedom associated with devout, intrinsic belief. A quest orientation does not provide the assurance of special insight into the mysteries of life and, as a result, is not likely to produce either the liberation from existential fear and doubt or the dramatic behavioral changes that the devout, intrinsic believer enjoys.

Although attempts to collect data to test this reasoning are few, results so far seem quite supportive. In one study, Batson (1980) constructed three brief scales designed to assess the degree to which individuals perceived their religion as (1) restricting their behavior; (2) freeing them from existential doubts and fears; and (3) binding them to unquestioning allegiance. Items on these Restriction, Freedom, and Bondage scales are presented in

Table 7.3. Batson administered these scales and the six scales used to measure the means, end, and quest dimensions (see Chapter 6) to eighty undergraduates (forty men, forty women) with at least a moderate interest in religion. Based on the reasoning in the preceding paragraph, he predicted that those scoring higher on the End component and related scales (Intrinsic, External, Internal, and Orthodoxy) would be less likely to perceive their religion as restricting, would be more likely to perceive it as freeing, and would be more willing to be bound by it. In contrast, those scoring higher on the Quest component and scale would not perceive their religion as either restricting or liberating, and would be less willing to be bound by it. Finally, those scoring higher on the Means component and related Extrinsic scale would perceive their religion as more restricting and as neither more freeing nor more binding.

The correlations found between the various measures of religious orientation and the Restriction, Freedom, and Bondage scales are reproduced in Table 7.4. As can be seen, they are quite consistent with the predictions. The End component and related scales were negatively correlated with the Restriction scale and positively correlated with the Freedom and Bondage scales. The Quest component and scale correlated significantly only with the

Table 7.3. Items on Batson's (1980) Religious Restriction, Freedom, and Bondage scales

Restriction scale

1. To me, religion comes across as an endless string of rules and prohibitions.
2. If I really lived the way my religious beliefs say I should, I would have to give up a lot that is important to me.
3. (−) I do not find that my religious beliefs have forced me to give up anything really important.
4. I often experience conflict between what my religious beliefs say I should do and what I want to do.
5. Religion often seems like a "drag" to me.

Freedom scale

1. My religious beliefs provide me with meaning and purpose for my life.
2. My religion frees me from doubts and uncertainties about myself.
3. Because of my religious beliefs I do not worry about money and success the way many other people do.
4. My religious beliefs give me strength to resist the temptation to do wrong.
5. Because of my religious beliefs I do not fear death.

Bondage scale

1. (−) I want to avoid becoming too strongly committed to any one set of religious beliefs.
2. It is not, nor should it be, within my power to change my religious beliefs.
3. I would rather risk being accused of being a fanatic than to be wishy-washy in my religious beliefs.
4. I do not think anything could make me change my present religious beliefs.
5. I would feel totally lost without my present religious beliefs.
6. (−) I think it is important not to get locked into any one set of religious beliefs.

Note: Items preceded by a minus sign are reversed in scoring.

Table 7.4 Correlations between measures of religious orientation and the Religious Restriction, Freedom, and Bondage scales ($N = 80$)

Measures of religious orientation	Restriction scale	Freedom scale	Bondage scale
Religious orientation scales			
Extrinsic	30**	−.02	−.07
Intrinsic	−.17	.65***	.48***
External	−.10	.44***	.47***
Internal	−.37***	.61***	.58***
Quest	.21	.05	−.28*
Orthodoxy	−.23*	.47***	.47***
Religion orientation components			
Religion as Means	.26*	.00	.04
Religion as End	−.28*	.66***	.63***
Religion as Quest	.18	.05	−.30**

Source: Adapted from Batson (1980).
*$p < .05$; ** $p < .01$; *** $P < .001$, two-tailed.

Bondage scale, and these correlations were negative. Finally, the Means component and related Extrinsic scale correlated significantly only with the Restriction scale, and these correlations were positive.

To summarize the implications of these correlations, they suggest, first of all, that the extrinsic, means dimension is associated with a view of religion as personally restricting rather than liberating. Second, the intrinsic, end dimension is associated with a view of religion as personally freeing and not restricting. At the same time, this dimension is associated with a readiness to bind oneself to one's religion. And finally, the quest dimension is associated with neither a clear view of religion as restricting nor freeing, only with a reduced readiness to bind oneself to one's present religious beliefs. This rather complex pattern of relationships is entirely consistent with our suggestion that a quest orientation is at once less binding and less freeing than an intrinsic, end orientation.

A second study (Batson et al., 1980) also provided some data consistent with this suggestion. In this study, thirty-six male and thirty-six female undergraduates who had previously completed the six scales used to measure the means, end, and quest dimensions were given a chance to indicate their desire to listen to a number of short audiotapes concerning religion. One of the tapes was described as "a forceful argument that your religious beliefs, or lack of beliefs, are determined by your social environment." It was noted that this tape was very controversial and had "led a number of students to reject their beliefs about religion." As expected, higher scores on the End component and related scales correlated negatively with expressed preference for hearing this belief-challenging tape, presumably because higher scorers felt more dependent on their beliefs and feared having them challenged. But higher scores on the Quest component and scale correlated positively with preference for hearing this tape. Correlations for the Means component and related Extrinsic scale were not reliably different from zero.

Results of the recent study by McFarland and Warren (1992), in which devoutly religious individuals were asked to indicate how much they wished to read belief-supporting and belief-challenging articles, paralleled and extended results of the previous study. Whereas both the Intrinsic and Quest scales were significantly ($p < .05$) positively correlated with desire to read the belief-supporting articles, only the Quest scale was significantly positively correlated with desire to read the belief-challenging articles. The extrinsic scale was significantly negatively correlated with desire to read the belief-supporting articles.

The results of these three studies, although far from conclusive, are quite consistent with the suggestion that a quest orientation to religion is less enslaving but also less freeing than an intrinsic, end orientation. Assuming that future research also supports this suggestion, should we conclude that the quest dimension is more psychologically adaptive than the intrinsic, end dimension because it does not involve enslavement to one's religious beliefs? No. Instead, we should recognize that the quest dimension confronts us with the flip side of the question raised earlier concerning the psychological consequences of the intrinsic, end dimension. It leads us to ask: Is the benefit of avoiding allegiance to a set of beliefs worth the cost of not being freed from existential fear and doubt? As with the earlier question of whether the freedom from fear and doubt obtained by intrinsic belief is worth the cost of enslaving allegiance, we must withhold an answer to this question until we have had a chance in Chapters 8, 9, and 10, to look at the personal and social benefits associated with the quest dimension.

8

Mental Health or Sickness?

Consider the case of a popular, slightly spoiled young man from an upper-middle-class family. In adolescence the young man becomes well known in his community for his fashionable, flashy clothes and his enthusiasm for partying with his friends. But as he grows a little older, he comes under the influence of religion. He gives up partying because he takes his religious beliefs very seriously. Indeed, he takes them so seriously that he becomes intensely dissatisfied with the materialism around him and starts giving away his possessions. He even gives a religious group a large sum of his father's money. His father tries to deal with these disturbing developments by confining the boy to the house, hoping to bring him to his senses. When this fails, the angry and exasperated father subjects his son to severe physical punishment, again without effect.

Finally, the father brings his son into court to recover the money. When the young man is ordered to return his father's money, he does so. But in protest he also gives back everything else that his parents have given him, including the clothes he is wearing. He then walks out of the court and through the streets, naked. Later, the young man becomes part of a religious sect whose members support themselves by begging, and he never returns to life in normal society.

Would you say that for this young man religion encouraged mental health or sickness? You may find it hard to say. An answer would, perhaps, be easier if you were told that the religion by which he was influenced was the Hare Krishnas or the Unification Church of the Reverend Sun Myung Moon. But this would not be true. The religion was Catholicism, and the young man was a well-known Catholic saint. The description is of the early life of Saint Francis of Assisi (1182–1226).

The case of Saint Francis suggests how difficult it can be to determine whether religion is a force for mental health or for sickness. Saint Francis acted in ways that may seem to suggest mental illness, and yet he has been called one of the most psychologically whole, healthy people who ever lived (see Sabatier, 1904). Clearly, the relationship between religion and mental health can be both complex and confusing. And, unfortunately, when we turn to the experts for some clarity, they only magnify the confusion.

EXPERTS' VIEWS OF THE RELATIONSHIP BETWEEN RELIGION AND MENTAL HEALTH

James's Dualistic View: Sick-Souled Versus Healthy-Minded Religion

William James found it necessary to distinguish between two different forms of religion and two related personality types when describing the relationship between religion and mental health. He suggested that one form of religion is closely tied to psychopathology; this form he called the twice-born religion of sick-souled individuals.

> The securest way to the rapturous sorts of happiness of which the twice-born make report has as an historic matter of fact been through a more radical pessimism than anything that we have yet considered. . . . For this extremity of pessimism to be reached, something more is needed than observation of life and reflection upon death. The individual must in his own person become the prey of a pathological melancholy. . . . Such sensitiveness and susceptibility to mental pain is a rare occurrence where the nervous constitution is entirely normal; one seldom finds it in a healthy subject even where he is the victim of the most atrocious cruelties of outward fortune. So we note here the neurotic constitution . . . destined to play a part in much that follows. (1902, p. 124)

James saw religion as an important, possibly essential, source of health in the lives of at least some sick-souled individuals. He saw such effects in the life of Tolstoy, among others.

But James also recognized that a quite different relationship between religion and mental health could exist. For those whom he called healthy-minded, religion was associated with a marked absence of signs of pathological melancholy. Consider, for example, the statement of a healthy-minded Unitarian preacher.

> I observe, with profound regret, the religious struggles which come into many biographies, as if almost essential to the formation of the hero. I ought to speak of these, to say that any man has an advantage, not to be estimated, who is born, as I was, into a family where the religion is simple and rational; who is trained in the theory of such a religion, so that he never knows, for an hour, what these religious or irreligious struggles are. . . . I can remember perfectly that when I was coming to manhood, the half-philosophical novels of the time had a deal to say about the young men and maidens who were facing the "problem of life." I had no idea whatever what the problem of life was. To live with all my might seemed to me easy; to learn where there was so much to learn seemed pleasant and almost of course; to lend a hand, if one had a chance, natural; and if one did this, why, he enjoyed life because he could not help it, and without proving to himself that he ought to enjoy it. (Starbuck, 1899, pp. 305–306)

Psychotherapeutic Views: Looking below the Surface

Freud. This Unitarian preacher's relaxed and natural expression of religion certainly appears psychologically healthy. But in the realm of mental health and illness it is easy to be deceived by appearance. Sigmund Freud made this point forcefully with his careful analysis of pathological symptoms and dreams. And Freud did not hesitate to suggest that mankind was being deceived by religion. For him, religion was not only associated with mental illness, it *was* mental illness; he called it a "universal obsessional neurosis of humanity":

> Like the obsessional neurosis of children, it [religion] arose out of the Oedipus complex, out of the relation to the father. . . . If, on the one hand, religion brings with it obsessional restrictions, exactly as an individual obsessional neurosis does, on the other hand it comprises a system of wishful illusions together with a disavowal of reality, such as we find in an isolated form nowhere else but in . . . a state of blissful hallucinatory confusion. . . .
>
> It has been repeatedly pointed out (by myself and in particular by Theodor Reik) in how great detail the analogy between religion and obsessional neurosis can be followed out, and how many of the peculiarities and vicissitudes in the formation of religion can be understood in that light. And it tallies well with this that devout believers are safeguarded in a high degree against the risk of certain neurotic illnesses; their acceptance of the universal neurosis spares them the task of constructing a personal one. (1964, pp. 71–72)

Only through the therapeutic experience of "education to reality" (see Chapter 2) did Freud hold out hope that mankind could be cured from this religious neurosis. For him the answer was clear: Religion was associated with mental illness, not mental health.

Jung. For Freud's most famous student, colleague, and eventual rival, Carl Jung, the answer was quite different. Jung considered religion necessary for mental health. Jung was a minister's son, and he found that among his thousands of patients in the second half of life, that is, over the age of thirty-five, "there has not been one whose problem in the last resort was not that of finding a religious outlook on life" (1933, p. 229).

> Man positively needs general ideas and convictions that will give a meaning to his life and enable him to find a place for himself in the universe. He can stand the most incredible hardships when he is convinced that they make sense; he is crushed when, on top of all his misfortunes, he has to admit that he is taking part in a "tale told by an idiot." It is the role of religion to give a meaning to the life of man. (Jung, 1964, p. 89)

Allport. Gordon Allport, like Jung, considered religion to be a potentially important contributor to mental health. Noting the shift in our society away from seeking help for personal problems through religion and toward seeking help through psychotherapy, Allport observed:

> The single fact that weighs against this wholly secular solution is the ever insistent truth that what a man believes to a large extent determines his mental and physical health. What he believes about his business, his associates, his wife, his immediate future, is important; even more so, what he believes about life in general, its purpose and design. Religious belief, simply because it deals with fundamentals, often turns out to be the most important belief of all. (1950, p. 79)

Even though Allport believed that religion had often failed to actualize its insights, he contended that religion "is superior to psychotherapy in the allowance it makes for the affiliative need in human nature" (1950, p. 82). Religion focuses on the important human need for love and relationship to a degree that psychotherapy does not.

Boisen. Anton Boisen was a minister and therapist who had himself experienced schizophrenic madness, which he described as "of the most profound and unmistakable variety" (1960, p. 9). Like Freud, Boisen recognized a link between religion and mental illness. But he considered the link to be far more positive than did Freud. Boisen believed that psychosis is a potentially health-giving, essentially religious experience because psychosis often involves an attempt to deal with one or more ultimate, existential concerns (Boisen, 1936). Although a psychotic break could destroy the person, it could also provide the context for the person to reconstruct his or her reality in a positive, healing way. Boisen was convinced that his own psychosis served this therapeutic, religious function: "It was necessary for me to pass through the purgatorial fires of horrifying psychosis before I could set foot in my promised land of creative activity" (1960, p. 208).

Bergin; Ellis. The debate among psychotherapists about the association between personal religion and mental health has not subsided in recent years. Allen Bergin (1980a; 1991) lamented the lack of attention paid by psychologists to the potential therapeutic value of religion, and strongly affirmed his own positive view: "I believe that religion can be powerfully benevolent" (1980b, p. 643). In response, Albert Ellis (1980) hypothesized:

> Devout, orthodox, or dogmatic religion (or what might be called religiosity) is significantly correlated with emotional disturbance. People largely disturb themselves by believing strongly in absolutistic shoulds, oughts, and musts. . . . The devoutly religious person tends to be inflexibly closed, intolerant, and unchanging. Religiosity, therefore, is in many respects equivalent to irrational thinking and emotional disturbance. (p. 637)

Clearly, the views of psychotherapists on the relationship between religion and mental health cover a very wide spectrum. They run the gamut from the contention of Freud and Ellis that religion is a form of mental illness, through the contention of Boisen that mental illness is potentially religious, to the contentions of Jung, Allport, and Bergin that religion, conceived broadly, either can or must be a powerful contributor to mental health. Nor does the matter become clearer when we turn to the views of more empirically oriented psychologists. Three major reviews of the empirical evidence appeared around 1970, but they too covered a wide spectrum.

Empirically Based Views: Looking at the Data

Becker. Russell Becker concluded from his review of studies examining the relationship between religion and mental health that the relationship is positive: "The absence of mental illness and neurotic symptoms does have certain favorable correlations with religious identity and activity" (1971, p. 415). But Becker qualified this conclusion by noting that "the attempt to find detailed points of relationship between positive psychological traits and religion has produced very few clues" (1971, p. 415).

Dittes. At the other end of the empirical spectrum is James Dittes. By no means an opponent of religion, Dittes felt compelled to organize his review of the empirical evidence "around the general supposition that religion is associated with deficiencies of personality, with a 'weak ego' or 'constricted ego'" (1969, p. 636). He felt it was necessary to adopt this supposition because:

> The psychological research reflects an overwhelming consensus that religion (at least as measured in the research, usually institutional affiliation or adherence to conservative traditional doctrines) is associated with awareness of personal inadequacies, either generally or in response to particular crisis or threat situations; with objective evidence of inadequacy, such as low intelligence; with a strong responsiveness to the suggestions of other persons or other external influences; and with an array of what may be called desperate and generally unadaptive defensive maneuvers. (Dittes, 1969, p. 636)

Sanua. Finally, Victor Sanua (1969) took a far less controversial stance after his review of the available empirical research; he declined to draw any clear conclusion:

> What may be said at this point is that a substantial number of additional empirical findings would be necessary before any valid conclusions could be drawn as to the relationship between religiousness and mental health. (p. 120; similarly, see Lea, 1982)

Who is right about the relationship between religion and mental health? Apparently not everyone can be because regardless whether we turn to therapists or researchers, we are offered a range of views, and at least some of the views are diametrically opposed. Instead of relying on the opinions of the experts, it seems that we must turn to the evidence and try to sort it out for ourselves. This is not an easy task, for the evidence forms a large and tangled mass. If we are to have any success making sense of it we need to have a clear idea of what we are about. Most important, we need a clear idea of what we mean by mental health.

SEVEN DIFFERENT CONCEPTIONS OF MENTAL HEALTH

Defining mental health is not easy. Think back to the case of Saint Francis of Assisi. He, like Thoreau, marched to the sound of a different drummer. But was his noncomformity a sign of mental illness or of unusual mental health? An answer will vary depending on our conception of mental health. If, for example, we conceive of mental health in terms of social adjustment and the absence of bizarre behavior, we might pronounce Saint Francis sick. If, instead, we conceive of mental health in terms of the ability to reach a higher level of self-expression that transcends social convention, we would probably consider him very healthy. Recognizing this variety of conceptions adds considerably to the complexity and confusion surrounding interpretations of the relationship between religion and mental health. It also suggests an explanation for all the disagreement. If different psychologists mean different things when they refer to mental health, then it is not surprising that they do not agree on the relationship between religion and mental health.

Different psychologists, working within different traditions and settings, do indeed appear to mean different things by mental health. Based on our review of well over one hundred articles examining the relationship between religion and mental health, we have been able to identify seven distinct conceptions.

1. Absence of Mental Illness

The most straightforward conception of mental health is simply the absence of mental illness; this is the legal definition. If you show none of the identifiable symptoms of psychopathology listed in the Diagnostic and Statistical Manual of the American Psychiatric Association (DSM III-R), then you are mentally healthy or "normal." You may be filled with tension, anxiety, and guilt, but you are healthy, at least in court. This first conception and the next two define mental health negatively; rather than specifying what it is, they specify what it is not.

2. Appropriate Social Behavior

Viewing mental health as appropriate social behavior is popular among some psychologists, especially behavior therapists and social learning theorists (e.g., Bandura, 1969). The popularity of this view is understandable. First, a person is not likely to become a candidate for psychotherapy unless he or she is displaying some inappropriate behavior. Second, using such a conception, mental health and illness are relatively easy to detect.

But this conception also has limitations. Most obviously, it provides a culturally relative and, within a given culture, a conservative definition of mental health. Behavior that is considered appropriate in one society may be inappropriate in another. To present an extreme example, in Nazi Germany it was considered inappropriate *not* to assist in the extermination of Jews, so according to an appropriateness definition, refusal to assist was a sign of potential mental illness; assistance was a sign of mental health. Of course, from the perspective of our society it was the mild-mannered, cooperative Eichmann who was sick.

3. Freedom from Worry and Guilt

Psychoanalysts typically conceive of mental health as freedom from psychological conflict, anxiety, and guilt. As noted in Chapter 3, Freud specified the ability "to love and to work" as the hallmark of mental health, and he devoted most of his energy to unearthing factors that inhibit this ability. For it to flower, the choking weeds of guilt and anxiety must be removed. The emphasis within psychoanalysis on this conception of mental health seems to be, at least in part, a product of the types of clients that psychoanalysts have typically treated—middle- and upper-class neurotics tortured by self-doubt and a lack of sense of purpose.

One of the clearest and most insightful statements of this conception of mental health comes from Karen Horney (1951). She suggested that neurotic conflicts usually arise from the adoption by an individual of an idealized view of what he or she should be (the ideal self), a view that makes what the individual knows that he or she is (the real self) seem horribly inadequate. The result is self-hate, self-effacement, and other forms of reality distortion. Therapy involves freeing the client from the grip of this unrealistic ideal self, allowing acceptance of the real self and freedom from neurotic anxiety, worry, and guilt.

In recent years, psychologists have tended to focus on positive personality characteristics as well as on the absence of negatives when defining mental health. The next four conceptions are a product of this focus on the positive.

4. Personal Competence and Control

Emphasis on a sense of personal competence as an aspect of mental health grew out of a revolution in psychological theories of motivation. Both psychoanalytic and behaviorist theories assume that tension reduction lies at the heart of all human motivation. If the individual is not uncomfortable in some way, he or she will not be motivated. In the 1950s, this assumption was exploded by research on curiosity and puzzle solving; it was found that well-fed, contented animals will work at puzzles for long hours without any extrinsic reward, and they will expend considerable energy just to have a look at a different environment.

Reflecting on the implications of such research, Robert White (1959) postulated a need for competence; he suggested that organisms need to have a sense that they can deal effectively with their environment, that they are in control. A number of other psychologists have also emphasized the importance of a sense of competence or control for mental health: Alfred Adler (1956) spoke of the will to power; both Julian Rotter (1954) and Richard deCharms (1968) made a distinction between having an internal (personal) as opposed to external (environmental) locus of control, and Frank Barron (1953) developed a measure of ego strength, a sense of inner control that seems important in determining positive responses to psychotherapy. Conversely, Martin Seligman (1975) has suggested that a sense of helplessness or lack of personal control is an important component of psychological depression.

5. Self-Acceptance or Self-Actualization

Carl Rogers (1951) suggested that self-acceptance is a crucial component of mental health. Like Karen Horney, Rogers believed that at the heart of most neuroses lies a discrepancy between the person's view of who he or she is and who he or she should be. Health is found in being able to accept oneself as one is.

Abraham Maslow (1954) went beyond the concept of self-acceptance to speak of self-actualization, the ability freely to express one's true nature.

> All trees need sunlight and all human beings need love, and yet, once satiated with these elementary necessities, each tree and each human being proceeds to develop in his own style, uniquely, using these universal necessities to his own private purposes. In a word, development then proceeds from within rather than from without, and paradoxically the highest motive is to be unmotivated, i.e., to behave purely expressively. Or, to say it in another way, self-actualization is growth motivated rather than deficiency motivated. (Maslow, 1954, p. 183)

Maslow believed that self-actualization defined the apex of psychological health. He also believed that only a small percentage of the population is truly self-actualized; the rest of us approach this zenith in differing degrees.

As Maslow spoke of it, self-actualization was an enticing yet rather vague and mysterious concept. Everett Shostrom (1964) sought to remove some of the mystery by providing a paper-and-pencil measure of self-actualization, the Personal Orientation Inventory. This instrument has been used with some success to identify individuals who fit Maslow's conception of self-actualization. Often, however, the POI is administered to samples of undergraduates or young adults. It is less clear that it can or should be expected to detect differences in self-actualization in these relatively homogenous groups.

6. Personality Unification and Organization

Gordon Allport conceived of the healthy, mature personality in terms of a unified and hierarchically organized personality structure. In his classic work on personality in 1937, Allport defined personality as "the dynamic organization within the individual of those psychophysical systems that determine his unique adjustments to his environment" (p. 48). Within the healthy, mature individual, these systems are organized hierarchically; there is a central one, and others are arranged in subordination to it. Allport felt that

> a mature personality always has some unifying philosophy of life, although not necessarily religious in type, nor articulated in words, nor entirely complete. But without the direction and coherence supplied by some dominant integrative pattern any life seems fragmented and aimless. (1950, p. 53)

Allport believed that religion and psychotherapy were aligned in their concern for personality unification:

> Religion and therapy are alike in their insistence upon the need for greater unification and order in personality. Both recognize that the healthy mind requires an hierarchical organization of sentiments, ordinarily with one master-sentiment holding the dominant position. . . . In principle, the religious interest, being most comprehensive, is best able to serve as an integrative agent. (1950, pp. 79, 92)

7. Open-Mindedness and Flexibility

Social psychologists such as Adorno et al. (1950) and Rokeach (1960) and rational-emotive psychotherapists such as Ellis (1980) have stressed the importance for mental health of being able to adapt to new information and to new experiences. The individual who responds openly and flexibly is considered more psychologically healthy than the individual who is closed-minded and rigid. The closed-minded individual blocks out new information, refusing to adjust his or her view of reality in its light. Over time, such closed-mindedness can leave the individual living in a reality of illusion that is quite divorced from his or her experience.

Harvey, Hunt, and Schroder (1961) offered a detailed analysis of the psychological importance of open-mindedness and flexibility. They identified four discriminable personality systems, progressing from extremely concrete and rigid to highly abstract and flexible. And they suggested that increases in openness and flexibility are a result of increases in differentiation and integration (i.e., complexity) of the individual's cognitive structures. Thus, their emphasis on open-mindedness and flexibility as components of mental health involves an emphasis on personal creativity of the sort discussed in Chapter 4.

EMPIRICAL EVIDENCE OF A RELATIONSHIP BETWEEN MENTAL HEALTH AND AMOUNT OF RELIGIOUS INVOLVEMENT

With these seven different conceptions of mental health before us, we can turn to the task of trying to sort out the empirical evidence concerning the relationship between mental health and religion. In the vast majority of studies, the question asked has been: Is being more religious associated with greater mental health or with greater sickness? Although this question may seem quite straightforward, it actually contains two restricting assumptions. First, religion has been considered quantitatively; at issue is the *amount* of religious involvement. Amount of involvement has, in turn, been measured empirically in a number of different ways: (1) having versus not having some religious affiliation; (2) frequency of attendance at religious services; (3) amount of reported interest in religion; (4) stength of religious attitudes; (5) strength of religious values; and (6) strength of orthodox religious beliefs. In many studies a number of possible correlates of mental health are measured, not just religion. And when, as is often true, the relationship to religion is not a focal concern of the study, the measures of religious involvement can be rather crude. To provide just one example, in the research reported by von Hentig (1948) involvement was measured by whether a criminal did or did not report having some church affiliation at the time that he was booked.

Second, the question asked is one of association between religion and mental health, not causation. As a result, the findings can provide only a partial answer to our question of whether religion leads to mental health or sickness. If religion causes health, there should be a positive correlation between measures of religion and mental health. Therefore, if we do *not* find such a correlation, we have evidence that religion does not cause health. Yet even if we do find such a correlation, this does not provide clear evidence that religion causes health; it only provides evidence consistent with this possiblity. Such a correlation is also consistent with other possiblities—that mental health leads to more religious involvement or that some other variable or variables (e.g., stable family structure, intelligence, sociability) causes both. (See Appendix for further discussion of the problems involved in using correlation data to assess the validity of causal hypotheses.)

The Empirical Evidence

What, then, does the available research tell us about the correlation between amount of religious involvement and mental health? We have collected 115 findings based on ninety-one different studies that provide empirical evidence relevant to this question. To discuss each of these ninety-one studies in any detail would not be feasible, nor would it be very helpful; the general contours of the forest would almost certainly be obscured by the overwhelming number of individual trees. We have, therefore, summarized the findings of these studies in tabular form. We have also developed a "line score" table that presents the number of times that one or another relationship between mental health and amount of religious involvement has been found. The findings, grouped by conception of mental health, are summarized in Table 8.1, and the line score is presented in Table 8.2.[1]

Although we encourage you to look over the summaries in Table 8.1 to get a flavor of the type of research that has been done, we shall move directly to the line score in Table 8.2. When we look at the line score for the relationship between amount of religious involvement and mental health, several points stand out. First, if we ignore differences among the seven different conceptions of mental health and just look at the totals across the bottom of the table, the relationship between religious involvement and mental health seems weak, but, if anything, it appears to be *negative* rather than positive. Forty-seven findings are of a negative relationship; thirty-seven are of a positive relationship; and thirty-one show no clear relationship. It must be emphasized, however, that many of the statistically significant relationships—especially the positive ones—are very weak. Correlations are rarely above .20, which means that the association with the measure of religion is accounting for less than 5 percent of the variance in the measure of mental health. Still, looking at the empirical evidence in this global way, it appears that religion is, if anything, associated with mental illness more than with mental health.

If we take a closer look, we find that we must qualify this sweeping conclusion. We find that the evidence suggests a negative relationship between amount of religious involvement and three of our seven conceptions of mental health: personal competence and control, self-acceptance or self-actualization, and open-mindedness and flexibility. The evidence also sug-

1. Although the list of studies in Table 8.1 is long, it is by no means exhaustive. To the best of our knowledge, however, it includes all major studies and is an accurate reflection of the existing empirical evidence as a whole. In compiling these tables, we were greatly helped by the reviews of research on religion and mental health provided by Argyle and Beit-Hallahmi (1975), Dittes (1969), Sanua (1969), and Spilka and Werme (1971). The uneven quality of research methods in these studies makes a formal meta-analysis inappropriate. See Cooper & Lemke, 1991, and other articles in the special issue of *Personality and Social Psychology Bulletin,* 1991, *17*(3), "Meta-Analysis in Personality and Social Psychology."

Table 8.1 Summary of research examining the relationship between mental health and amount of religious involvement

Authors	Sample population	Measure of religion	Measure of mental health	Findings
1. Using absence of illness as the criterion of mental health				
Schofield and Balian (1959)	Matched groups of 178 schizophrenics and 150 nonschizophrenics	Church attendance in childhood	Schizophrenic diagnosis	Nonsignificant tendency for schizophrenics to have attended less ($p < .10$)
Roe (1956)	Seminary students and students of other professions	Seminary student status	Neuroticism	Seminary students more neurotic than students of other professions
Gurin, Veroff, and Feld (1960)	Survey of 2460 U.S. adults	Frequency of church attendance	Self-report of mental health adjustment (including job and marital happiness)	Positive relationship
Brown (1962)	203 Australian university students	Intensity of religious belief	Neuroticism	No significant correlation ($r = -.07$)
Srole et al. (1962)	Adults in midtown Manhattan, New York	Self-report of importance of religion	Self-report of psychiatric impairment	Less pathology among more religious, except among upper-class Protestants
Webster (1967)	191 Protestant seminarians	Seminarian status	MMPI	Seminarians poorer in mental health than nonclergy
Mayo, Puryear, and Richek (1969)	166 college students (67 males, 99 females)	Self-report as religious	Absence of depression as measured by the MMPI	For males, being religious was positively associated with absence of depression; no clear relationship for females
Stark (1971)	Survey of 1976 U.S. adults	Church attendance, orthodoxy	Self-report of psychiatric impairment	Both church attendance and orthodoxy were associated with less impairment
Comstock and Partridge (1972)	1963 Washington County census (western Maryland)	Church attendance	Absence of physical disease	Higher church attendance associated with less heart disease, emphysema, cirrhosis, tuberculosis, cancer of the cervix

Table 8.1 Summary of research examining the relationship between mental health and amount of religious involvement (*Continued*)

Authors	Sample population	Measure of religion	Measure of mental health	Findings
Comstock and Partridge (1972)	1963 Washington County census (western Maryland)	Church attendance	Recuced likelihood of suicide	Higher church attendance associated with lower suicide rate (.45 suicides per 1000 for frequent attenders, .95 per 1000 for infrequent attenders)
Hood (1974)	114 undergraduates	Index of intense religious experience	Index of Psychic Inadequacy	Intense religious experience more frequent among those scoring low on psychic inadequacy (i.e., those showing greater adequacy)
Hadaway (1978)	2164 adults in U.S. national survey	Frequency of church attendance, self-reported "religious mindedness"	Self-report of personal well-being or life satisfaction	Both religion measures had low but significant positive correlations with reported well-being (rs = .12 and .17, $p < .001$)
Steinitz (1980)	1493 persons aged 65 or older in U.S. national survey	Frequency of church attendance, strength of religious affiliation, belief, and confidence	Self-report of happiness and satisfaction	No consistent positive relation except for church attendance, for which relation appeared to be effect of physical health permitting attendance
Francis et al. (1981a,b)	1088 15- and 16-year olds in England	Francis's Attitude Towards Religion scale	Junior Eysenck Neuroticism and Extraversion scales	No reliable relationship between religiosity and neuroticism when sex difference was controlled; low but significant negative correlation with extraversion ($r = -.15, p < .001$)
Thoits (1982)	1095 adult men and women in New Haven Connecticut	Frequency of church attendance	Vulnerability to undesirable life events and negative health events	Attendance not associated with vulnerability to undesirable life events but associated with reduced adverse reaction to health events

Stack (1983)	U.S. National Center for Health Statistics (Data on U.S. as a whole from 1954 to 1978)	Frequency of church attendance in U.S. during year	Suicide rate in U.S. during year	Over years, church attendance has decreased and suicide rate has increased (especially among those under age 30)
St. George and McNamara (1984)	3877 white and 449 black adults in U.S. national survey	Frequency of church attendance; strength of religious affiliation	Self-reported happiness and satisfaction	For whites, relation weak; for black, religion positively associated with reported well-being
Petersen and Roy (1985)	318 citizens of Memphis, Tennessee, in telephone interview	Frequency of church attendance, self-reported importance of religion	Self-report of meaning and purpose in life	Both religion measures were positively correlated with reported meaning and purpose ($rs = .19$ and $.25$, $p < .01$)
Levin and Markides (1986)	1125 young, middle-aged, and elderly Mexican-American adults in San Antonio, Texas	Frequency of attendance at religious services; self-rated religiosity	Self-report of health	Frequency of attendance had low positive correlation with self-reported health, but relation disappeared when physical capacity was controlled; no relation for self-rated religiosity
Pollner (1989)	Approximately 2000 adults in U.S. national survey	Self-reported closeness to God and frequency of prayer and church attendance	Self-reported happiness, life excitement, and life satisfaction	Positive correlations between measures of religious involvement and measures of happiness and satisfaction ($ps < .01$)
Pargament et al. (1990)	586 members from 10 midwestern churches	Self-reported frequency of church attendance and prayer	Self-reported general health; perception of having handled a negative life event well	Frequency of attendance and prayer had low positive correlations with perceptions ($.10 < r < .15$); no relation to general health
Ross (1990)	401 adults in Chicago area	Self-reported strength of religious belief	Self-report of fewer symptoms of depression and anxiety in past year	Among believers, strength of belief was positively correlated with reporting fewer symptoms; nonreligious reported fewest symptoms but not significantly fewer than strong believers

Table 8.1 Summary of research examining the relationship between mental health and amount of religious involvement (*Continued*)

Authors	Sample population	Measure of religion	Measure of mental health	Findings
Schwab and Petersen (1990)	115 women and 91 men in Hamburg, Germany	Questionnaire measure of belief in God and of religious commitment	Questionnaire measure of loneliness and neuroticism	Belief unrelated to reported loneliness; commitment was associated with reduced loneliness; correlations of religious measures with neuroticism were generally negative but low
Weiss and Mendoza (1990)	132 men and 94 women members of Hare Krishna movement at 8 sites in U.S.	Degree of involvement or acculturation in Hare Krishna movement	Mental Health Inventory and Comrey Personality scales	For men, greater involvement was associated with higher psychological well-being scores (similar but weaker pattern for women); no other mental health effects, except that more involved members appeared to be more compulsive
Ferraro and Albrecht-Jensen (1991)	2939 adults in U.S. national survey	Self-reported religious practice, conservatism, closeness to God, and belief in life after death	Self-reported health status	Religious practice was positively correlated with health status, religious conservatism was negatively correlated; closeness to God and belief in afterlife not related to health
2. Using appropriate social behavior as the criterion of mental health				
Hartshore and May (1928)	Children in U.S.	Religious training, belief, and participation	Moral behavior	No relationship
Middleton and Fay (1941)	83 delinquent and 102 nondelinquent girls	Attitide toward Sunday service and Bible readings	Absence of delinquent record	Delinquent girls were more favorable toward both Sunday service and Bible reading

Bonger (1943)	Holland, 1910–1915, 1919	Denominational affiliation	Absence of criminal conviction	Nonreligious and Jews underrepresented among criminals; Protestants and Catholics overrepresented
von Hentig (1948)	Criminals and noncriminals in Pennsylvania	Religious affiliation	Absence of criminal sentence	Religious affiliation was positively correlated with being a criminal
Kinsey, Pomeroy, and Martin (1948)	Survey of U.S. male adults	Devoutness (religious activity)	Masturbation, premarital intercourse, marital intercourse, and homosexuality	More devout report less masturbation, premarital intercourse, marital intercourse, and homosexuality
Landis and Landis (1953)	409 U.S. couples	Frequency of church attendance	Self-report of marital happiness	Regular church attenders more frequently reported "very happy" marriages
Strunk (1959)	60 preministerial and 50 business students	Preministerial student	Nonagressive social behavior measured by Bell Adjustment inventory	Preministerial students were more aggressive ($p < .01$)
Middleton and Putney (1962)	U.S. adults	Religious belief	Absence of antisocial behavior	No relationship
Scholl and Beker (1964)	52 delinquent and 28 nondelinquent boys (Protestant)	Religious belief and attitudes	Absence of delinquent record	No clear relationship for either belief or attitudes
Masters and Johnson (1970)	Sex therapy patients	Religious background	Absence of sexual dysfunction	Strict religious unbringing was associated with dysfunction
Kantner and Zelnik (1972)	4240 unmarried women, 15–19 years old	Frequency of church attendance	Self-report of premarital intercourse	Frequent attenders less likely to report having premarital intercourse than nonattenders

Table 8.1 Summary of research examining the relationship between mental health and amount of religious involvement (*Continued*)

Authors	Sample population	Measure of religion	Measure of mental health	Findings
Goldsen et al. (1960)	1600 (approx.) undergraduates at Cornell University	Religiousness scale, measuring belief in God and importance of religion	Self-report of frequency of drinking, cutting classes, and premarital sex	Respondents who were more religious reported less drinking, less cutting of classes, and less acceptance of premarital sex
Gorsuch and Butler (1976)	Review of results of over 15 studies	Various—including church membership and participation, religious upbringing, and self-reported meaningfulness of religion	Illicit drug use	Religion, however defined, was associated with lower probability of illicit drug use
Hadaway, Elifson, and Peterson (1984)	600 white adolescents in Atlanta, Georgia	Self-reported church attendance, importance of religion, and orthodoxy	Self-reported use of alchohol, marijuana, and other illicit drugs	All religious measures were associated with less use of alcohol, marijuana, and other illict drugs ($ps < .01$)
Hoge and de Zulueta (1985)	1729 adults in U.S. national survey	Orthodoxy scale; perception of self as religious	Self-report of honesty on taxes, etc.; alcohol drinking	Weak positive correlations ($rs = .08$ to .24), except no relation to alcohol drinking among Catholics
Woodroof (1985)	447 freshmen at colleges affiliated with the churches of Christ	Frequency of church attendance	Self-reported status as a sexual virgin	Church attendance was positively associated with being a virgin ($p < .0001$)
Dudley, Mutch, and Cruise (1987)	801 Seventh-Day Adventist youth from 71 churches in North America	Frequency of family worship, church attendance, and personal devotions	Self-reported frequency of use of alcohol and tobacco	Religion measures were positively related to less frequent use of alcohol and tobacco

Perkins (1987)	860 undergraduates at liberal arts college in upstate New York	Questionnaire measure of strength of religious commitment	Self-reported alcohol consumption and frequency of intoxication	Strength of religious commitment was negatively associated with reports of frequent consumption (especially among Protestants) and reports of intoxication ($ps < .05$)
Jensen, Newell, and Holman (1990)	423 single undergraduates (191 men, 232 women) in Midwest	Frequency of church attendance	Self-reported frequency of sexual intercourse	No reliable relationship; very frequent attenders and nonattenders scored low, but only if they disapproved of sexual permissiveness
Welch, Tittle, and Petee (1991)	2487 Catholic parishioners in U.S.	Self-reported freuqency of private, family-centered religious activity	Self-report of unwillingness to cheat on taxes, to drink excessively, etc.	Very low but statistically significant ($p < .05$) positive correlation
Beck, Cole, and Hammond (1991)	888 male and 1031 female "teen virgins" in U.S.	Frequency of church attendance	Self-report of not having engaged in premarital intercourse when interviewed 4 years later	Church attendance was positively correlated with remaining a virgin ($p < .01$)
3. Using freedom from worry and guilt as the criterion of mental health				
Funk (1956)	255 college students	Orthodoxy of belief	Taylor Manifest Anxiety scale	No significant relationship
O'Reilly (1957)	Noninstitutionalized Catholic elderly (108 males, 102 females)	Religious activity	Self-report of happiness	Religious activity was positively related to reported happiness
Rokeach (1960)	College students	Believers versus nonbelievers	Self-report of tension, fitful sleep, and anxiety	Believers complained of more tension, fitful sleep, and anxiety ($p < .01$)
Argyle and Delin (1965)	700 British children	Church attendance	Self-report of guilt feelings	Church attendance positively correlated with guilt for Protestant females ($r = .30$, $p < .01$), but not for males

Table 8.1 Summary of research examining the relationship between mental health and amount of religious involvement (*Continued*)

Authors	Sample population	Measure of religion	Measure of mental health	Findings
Peterson (1964)	420 married people	Religious affiliation	Sex guilt	Sex guilt highest among members of conservative denominations, lowest among those with no religious affiliation
Moberg (1965)	Institutionalized elderly	Religious activities	Assessment of personal adjustment	Involvement in religious activities positively correlated with personal adjustment
Moberg and Taves (1965)	1340 men and women over 60 years old (Minnesota)	Church membership and involvement	Self-report of happiness enjoyment, and satisfaction	Among those not fully employed, church leaders and members reported more happiness, enjoyment, and satisfaction. Among those fully employed, there were no differences
Spellman, Baskett, and Byrne (1971)	60 citizens of a small farming community in Texas	Three categories: nonreligious; regular church attenders; those experiencing a sudden conversion	Taylor Manifest Anxiety scale	Sudden converts had higher anxiety scores than nonreligious ($p < .05$); regular attenders and nonreligious did not differ reliably
Hoelter and Epley (1979)	375 undergraduates at a midwestern university	Frequency of church attendance, self-perceived religiosity, orthodoxy	8 multidimensional fear of death subscales	All religion measures correlated negatively with fear of death as unknown; self-perceived religiosity and orthodoxy correlated positively with fear of death due to consequences for others and fear due to self-destruction
Peterson and Roy (1985)	318 citizens of Memphis, Tennessee, in telephone interview	Frequency of church attendance; self-reported importance of religion	Self-reports of worry, discouragement, and unfair treatment	Frequency of church attendance was negatively correlated with reported unfair treatment; otherwise, no reliable relationship

4. Using personal competence and control as the criterion of mental health				
Symington (1935)	300 adults	Conservative versus liberal denominational affiliation	Independence of group pressure	Conservatively religious were more dependent on group opinion
Prothro and Jensen (1950)	Adults in southern U.S.	Religious value score on Allport, Vernon, and Lindzey scale	Self-reliance	Importance of religion was negatively correlated with self-reliance among Protestants
Dreger (1952)	30 most conservative and 30 most liberal from 490 California church members	Degree of religious conservatism	Independence, measured by projective techniques	Conservatively religious were more dependent ($p < .02$)
Lasagna et al. (1954)	27 hospital patients	Church attendance	Response to placebo for pain relief	Church attendance correlated positively with responsiveness to a placebo ($p < .01$)
Clark (1955)	Scholars and scientists in U.S.	Religious affiliation and belief	Appearance in "Who's Who"	Both religious affiliation and belief were negatively correlated with appearance in "Who's Who"
Ranck (1961)	800 male Protestant theological students	Conservative versus liberal religious attitude and belief	Independence and assertiveness	Conservatively religious were both more dependent and more submissive
Stark (1963)	2601 U.S. graduate students	Religious involvement	Self-report of valuing self-expression	Religious involvement was negatively related to valuing self-expression
Dunn (1965)	Religious professionals (Catholic)	Comparison with population norms	Personality assessment, typically using MMPI	Religious professionals were more perfectionistic, insecure, withdrawn, and socially inept
Shrauger and Silverman (1971)	465 college students	Frequency of church attendance	Rotter's Locus of Control scale	Among females, more frequent attenders had more internal sense of control ($p < .001$); no relationship for males

Table 8.1 Summary of research examining the relationship between mental health and amount of religious involvement (*Continued*)

Authors	Sample population	Measure of religion	Measure of mental health	Findings
Hood (1974)	82 undergraduates	Index of intense religious experience	Barron's Ego-Strength scale	Those reporting intense religious experience scored lower on ego-strength, but not significantly so when religious items on the Ego-Strength Scale were removed
Graff and Ladd (1971)	152 male college students	Religious involvement	Self-report of independence and self-acceptance	More religiously involved were more dependent, less inner-directed, and less self-accepting
Pargament, Steele, and Tyler (1978)	133 U.S. adults (Protestant, Catholic, and Jewish)	Frequency of attendance at religious services	Levinson's Control scales: a personal efficacy scale	More frequent attenders had less sense of personal control and chance control, more sense of God's control, and less sense of personal efficacy
Hadaway (1978)	2164 adults in U.S. national survey	Frequency of church attendance; self-reported "religious mindedness"	Self-report of degree of control one has in one's life	Both religious measures had very low but significant positive correlations with reported control (*rs* = .08 and .07, $ps < .001$)
Kaiser (1991)	121 college students	Self-reported interest in religion and participation in religious activities	Self-directing, deferring, and collaborative problem solving	Religious interest and participation were negatively correlated with a self-directing problem-sovling style and positively correlated with a deferring and a collaborative problem-solving style ($p < .001$)
5. Using self-acceptance or self-actualization as the criterion of mental health				
Dreger (1952)	30 most conservative and 30 most liberal from 490 California church members	Degree of religious conservatism	Absence of ego defensiveness as measured by a projective test	Conservatively religious were found to be more defensive ($t = 2.45$, $p < .02$)

Cowen (1954)	81 college students	Strength of belief in God and reliance on church for ethical code	Self-acceptance as measured by high negative self-concept score on Brownfain's Self-Rating Inventory	Belief in God and reliance on church both negatively associated with self-acceptance; association statistically reliable for reliance on church ($p < .05$)
Strunk (1958)	136 U.S. youth (55 males, 81 females)	Self-report of religious involvement	Self-acceptance as measured by Brownfain's Self-Rating Inventory	Religious involvement was positively correlated with self-acceptance ($p < .01$)
Bender (1958)	84 male college graduates while in school and 15 years later	Religious value score on Allport, Vernon, and Lindzey scale	Ego-strength as reflected in diagnostic interview of self-development	Nonsignificant positive correlation when measured as students; significant positive correlation 15 years later ($p < .05$)
Armstrong, Larsen, and Mourer (1962)	121 U.S. adults (Catholic and Protestant)	Conservative versus liberal religious beliefs	Self-acceptance as measured by Osgood's Semantic Differential	No clear difference between conservatives and liberals in discrepancy between ratings of real and ideal self
Fisher (1964)	49 male and 49 female university students	Religious value score on Allport, Vernon, and Lindzey scale; self-rating of religiosity; frequency of church attendance	Absence of acquiescence as measured by Bass's Social Acquiescence scale	All three measures of religious involvement were positively associated with greater social acquiescences for both males and females
Maslow (1964)	U.S. adults Maslow considered self-actualized	Self-report of involvement in conventional religion	Self-actualization and psychological health	Only one person classed as self-actualized reported being religious in a conventional way
Webster (1967)	191 Protestant seminary students compared with nonseminary norms	Seminarian status	Self-actualization as measured by Shostrom's Personal Orientation Inventory	Seminarians scored lower on self-actualization than nonseminarians

Table 8.1 Summary of research examining the relationship between mental health and amount of religious involvement (*Continued*)

Authors	Sample population	Measure of religion	Measure of mental health	Findings
Mayo, Puryear, and Richek (1969)	166 college students (67 males, 99 females)	Self-report as religious	Ego strength as measured by the MMPI	For females, being religious was associated with less ego-strength ($p < .01$); no reliable difference for males
Graff and Ladd (1971)	152 male college students	Religious commitment scale measuring belief, practice, experience, and knowledge	Self-actualization as measured by Shostrom's Personal Orientation Inventory	Religious commitment was negatively correlated with self-actualization; more religious were less self-accepting and spontaneous, more dependent
Lindskoog and Kirk (1975)	45 Protestant seminary students	Church activity, intensity of belief, presence of mystical experience	High, moderate, and low self-actualization as measured by Shostrom's Personal Orientation Inventory	No relationship between any of the measures of religious involvement and self-actualization
Pargament, Steele, and Tyler (1978)	133 U.S. adults (Protestant, Catholic, and Jewish)	Frequency of attendance at religious services	Absence of self-criticism as measured by self-criticism scale	More frequent attenders were more self-critical than less frequent attenders
Hjelle (1975)	63 male freshman at Catholic college in Rochester, New York	Frequency of participation in church activities	Self-actualization as measured by Shostrom's Personal Orientation Inventory	Frequency of participation was negatively correlated with self-actualization
Smith, Weigert, and Thomas (1979)	Middle-class Catholic high school students in 6 cities representing 5 cultures	Self-reported religious belief, practice, and experience	Semantic differential measure of self-esteem	Religion, especially religious practice, was significantly positively correlated with self-esteem in 3 of 5 cultures (i.e., in U.S., Spain, and Germany but not in Puerto Rico or the Yucatan)
Ventis, Batson, and Burke (1982)	16 male and 18 female undergraduates	Self-report of interest in religion	Self-actualization as measured by Shostrom's Personal Orientation Inventory	Interest in religion was negatively correlated with self-actualization for males; no clear relationship for females

Bahr and Martin (1983)	1673 "Middletown" (Muncie, Indiana) high school students	Frequency of church attendance; self-rated evangelicalism	Rosenberg Self-Esteem scale	No reliable relationship
6. Using personality unification and organization as the criterion of mental health				
Carr and Hauser (1976)	219 adults in small industrial town in midwestern U.S.	Self-report of religious activity	Sense of personal integration expressed in absence of alienation from others	No relationship
7. Using open-mindedness and flexibility as the criterion of mental health				
Ranck (1955)	800 male Protestant theological students	Intensity of conservative religious attitudes and belief	Absence of authoritarianism	Conservative religious attitudes and belief were positively correlated with authoritarianism ($r = .53$, $p < .01$)
Appleby (1957)	42 male Jewish college students	Frequency of religious activity	Absence of rigidity	Those reporting either high or no religious participation were more rigid than those reporting moderate amount of participation
Gregory (1957)	596 students and members of church and civic groups	Religious orthodoxy	Absence of authoritarianism as measured by the F-scale	Orthodoxy positively correlated ($r = .53$, $p < .001$) with authoritarianism
Spilka (1958)	U.S. adults	Religious orthodoxy	Absence of rigidity	Orthodoxy was positively correlated with rigidity
Brown (1962)	203 Australian university students	Intensity of religious belief	Absence of authoritarianism as measured by the F-scale	Stronger religious belief was positively correlated with authoritarianism ($r = .41$, $p < .001$)
Photiadis and Johnson (1963)	300 U.S. adults	Religious orthodoxy	Absence of authoritarianism as measured by the F-scale	Orthodoxy was positively correlated with authoritarianism ($p < .01$)

Table 8.1 Summary of research examining the relationship between mental health and amount of religious involvement (*Continued*)

Authors	Sample population	Measure of religion	Measure of mental health	Findings
Stark (1963)	2609 U.S. graduate students	Religous involvement	Self-identification as intellectual; positive attitude toward open-minded scholarship	Religious involvement was negatively related to both intellectual identity and positive attitude toward open-minded scholarship
Feather (1964)	165 male Australian college students	Attitude toward religion (pro versus anti)	Accurately judging the falseness of invalid proreligious syllogisms	Religious students made more proreligious errors; nonreligious students did not make more antireligious errors
Stark (1971)	Survey of 1976 U.S. adults	Church attendance	Absence of authoritarianism as measured by the F-scale	No relationship, although author's mode of organizing data may have restricted variance on orthodoxy
Johnson and Tamney (1984)	284 residents of "Middletown" (Muncie, Indiana)	Endorsing a "Christian Right" orientation defined by seeing U.S. as God's instrument and supporting school prayer	Cultural ethnocentrism and authoritarianism questionnaire items	Christian Right orientation was positively correlated with ethnocentrism ($r = .23$) and authoritarianism ($r = .49$), $ps < .01$
Black (1985)	780 Protestant church members in Australia	Questionnaire measure of theological conservatism, frequency of church attendance and church involvement	Questionnaire measures of authoritarianism and dogmatism	Theological conservatism was positively correlated with authoritarianism ($r = .41$); no clear relation to attendance or involvement
Lupfer, Hopkinson, and Kelley (1988)	165 undergraduate volunteers from psychology classes	Fullerton and Hunsberger's Christian Orthodoxy scale	Authoritarianism measured by the Balanced F-scale	Orthodoxy was positively correlated with authoritarianism ($r = .41, p < .001$)
Eisinga, Felling, and Peters (1990)	1190 adults from national survey in The Netherlands	Christian Belief scale	Authoritarianism measured by the F-scale	Strength of Christian belief was positively correlated with authoritarianism ($r = .35, p < .001$)

Table 8.2 Line score on research examining the relationship between mental health and amount of religious involvement

	Relationship with amount of religious involvement			
Conception of mental health	Positive	None	Negative	Total
Absence of illness	17	12	4	33
Appropriate social behavior	12	4	5	21
Freedom from worry and guilt	4	3	5	12
Personal competence and control	2	2	11	15
Self-acceptance, self-actualization	2	6	11	19
Unification and organization	0	1	0	1
Open-mindedness and flexibility	0	3	11	14
Total	37	31	47	115

gests a qualified negative relationship with another conception, freedom from worry and guilt. Only among the elderly do the more religious report less worry; among other age groups (ranging from children to young adults), they tend, if anything, to report more.

For one of the remaining conceptions, personality unification and organization, there is no clear relationship, perhaps because virtually no relevant data exist. For the other two, absence of symptoms of mental illness and appropriate social behavior, there are qualified positive relationships. Among clergy (and seminarians) the relationship between religious involvement and absence of symptoms appears to be negative; among nonclergy it seems, if anything, positive. Among nonclergy, seventeen findings were of a positive relationship; twelve were of no clear relationship; and only two were of a negative relationship. For appropriate social behavior, there is a consistent, if weak, positive relationship between religious involvement and both reduced premarital sex and reduced use of tobacco, alcohol, and illicit drugs among adolescents. For other social behaviors and other age groups, the relationship is not clear. It tends to be positive when the measure of appropriate social behavior is based on self-report of a behavior one's religious institution proscribes (condemns) more clearly than does the culture at large; otherwise, there tends to be no clear relationship.

Using the Seven Conceptions to Account for the Differences among the Empirical Experts

The more complex array of findings suggests an explanation for the apparently contradictory conclusions drawn by Becker, Dittes, and Sanua concerning the relationship between religion and mental health. It suggests that we may be confronted with a situation like the one described in the parable of the blind men and the elephant. Although our experts contradict one another, each may be telling the truth. Directed by different conceptions of mental health, each may, like the blind men, have grabbed hold of a different part of the available evidence.

Looking back at the research reviews presented by Becker, Dittes, and Sanua, we believe that this is, in fact, what happened. Becker focused on the Midtown Manhattan Study (Srole, Langer, Michael, Opler, & Rennie, 1962), a classic study of mental health in New York City that used absence of symptoms of mental illness as the criterion of mental health. Becker's conclusion that "the absence of mental illness and neurotic symptoms does have certain favorable correlations with religious identity and activity" was based primarily on the results of this study. As Tables 8.1 and 8.2 suggest, for this and other studies focusing on absence of illness, the relationship between mental health and religious involvement tends to be positive.

Becker's qualification of his general conclusion is also instructive. When he notes that "the attempt to find any detailed points of relationship between positive psychological traits and religion has produced very few clues," he is referring to research that employed four other conceptions of mental health. The positive psychological traits to which Becker alludes are freedom from worry and guilt, personal competence and control, self-acceptance or self-actualization, and open-mindedness and flexibility. For each of these conceptions we found that the relationship with religious involvement tends to be negative; the only exception is that among the elderly the more religious report less worry and guilt.

Dittes (1969) focused his analysis of the relationship between amount of religious involvement and mental health on three conceptions of mental health: personal competence and control, self-acceptance or self-actualization, and open-mindedness and flexibility. Given this focus, his conclusion that religious involvement is associated with mental sickness rather than with mental health seems quite correct. Summing across these three conceptions, the line score in Table 8.2 reveals thirty-three findings of a negative relationship, eleven of no relationship, and only four of a positive relationship.

Sanua's (1969) equivocal conclusion "that a substantial number of additional empirical findings would be necessary before any valid conclusions could be drawn" was based on a review that ranged across six of our seven conceptions of mental health; only unification and organization was omitted. Within this broad scope, Sanua focused on four conceptions: absence of illness, freedom from worry and guilt, self-acceptance or self-actualization, and open-mindedness and flexibility. Given this focus, his refusal to draw any conclusion seems entirely justified; our line score suggests a positive relationship for one of these conceptions (absence of illness), a negative relationship for two (self-acceptance or self-actualization and open-mindedness and flexibility), and no clear relationship for one (freedom from worry and guilt—when one includes studies of the elderly, as Sanua did).

In sum, our strategy of identifying different conceptions of mental health and then classifying the research on the relationship between mental health and amount of religious involvement by conception seems to have paid off. It has enabled us to make sense of the apparently contradictory conclusions of Becker, Dittes, and Sanua; each drew the right conclusion given that part of the empirical evidence on which each laid his hands.

In addition to allowing us to sort out this apparent confusion, our more comprehensive review has provided a basis for a broader, more differentiated set of conclusions. Except among clergy, religious involvement is positively correlated with absence of mental illness. But it is negatively correlated with personal competence and control, self-actualization, open-mindedness and flexibility, and freedom from worry and guilt (except among the elderly). The relationship to appropriate social behavior is mixed. Among adolescents, there is consistent evidence of a positive correlation with reduced premarital sex and reduced use of tobacco, alcohol, and illicit drugs, especially on self-report measures. For other age groups, other social behaviors, and other modes of measurement, however, the relationship is not clear. (We will present additional research on two other important social behaviors in Chapters 9 and 10—discrimination against minorities and helping people in need.) There is, as yet, no clear evidence of a relationship between amount of religious involvement and personality unification and organization.

Overall, this pattern of results may seem to contradict the views of Carl Jung, Gordon Allport, and Allen Bergin, who have suggested that religion is an important if not essential contributor to mental health. Indeed, when taken as a whole, the evidence may appear to support the suggestion of Freud and Ellis that religion is itself a form of mental illness. The evidence indicates that amount of religious involvement is associated with an array of deficiencies in personality development (Conceptions 4, 5, and 7). And even the positive associations with absence of symptoms of mental illness (Conception 1) and appropriate social behavior (Conception 2) can be viewed as support for Freud's view. If religion is itself a form of pathology—an illusion designed to keep our libidinal impulses in check—then it could, as Freud suggested, render the need for other pathological symptoms superfluous while at the same time increasing conformity to society's demands for appropriate social behavior.

EMPIRICAL EVIDENCE OF A RELATIONSHIP BETWEEN MENTAL HEALTH AND DIFFERENT DIMENSIONS OF INDIVIDUAL RELIGION

The appearance of support for the view that religion is a form of mental illness may, however, be misleading. Even though we have introduced considerable differentiation into the relationship between religion and mental health by distinguishing among seven different conceptions of mental health, we may not have introduced enough. In addition to recognizing different ways of being healthy, we may also need to take account of different ways of being religious.

In Chapter 6 we proposed a three-dimensional analysis of different ways of being religious—as an extrinsic means to some other end, as an intrinsic end in itself, and as a quest. A little reflection suggests that we probably need to take account of these different dimensions in our assessment of the religion–mental health relationship; each dimension may have its own unique pattern of relationships with the various conceptions of mental health.

Expected Relationships to Mental Health for the Three Dimensions of Individual Religion

The extrinsic, means dimension. Following Allport, we viewed the extrinsic, means dimension as reflecting the extent to which the believer uses religion for self-serving ends; "the extrinsic type turns to God, but without turning away from self" (Allport & Ross, 1967, p. 434). Allport originally labeled this orientation to religion "immature," and noted that

> It serves either a wish-fulfilling or soporific function for the self-centered interests. . . . It does not entail self-objectification, but remains unreflective, failing to provide a context of meaning in which the individual can locate himself, and with perspective judge the quality of his conduct. Finally, the immature sentiment is not really unifying in its effect upon the personality. . . . Even when fanatic in intensity, it is but partially integrative. (1950, p. 54)

Such an approach to religion should have a negative influence on virtually all of our conceptions of mental health. Although it might not increase symptoms of mental illness, the self-centeredness and lack of perspective should lead to less appropriate social behavior, at least in situations where there is no fear of punishment or censure. The knowledge that there is a certain hypocrisy in one's beliefs should not provide freedom from worry and guilt. The lack of a "context of meaning in which the individual can locate himself" should discourage both personal competence and self-acceptance. Because this dimension is "not really unifying" and "but partially integrative," it should produce less unity and organization. And because it is characterized by a closed-minded attention to one's own point of view, it should discourage open-mindedness and flexibility. In sum, although it might not lead to increased symptoms of illness, there is no basis for expecting the extrinsic, means dimension to be associated with increased mental health, regardless of how mental health is conceived.

The intrinsic, end dimension. Allport was convinced that intrinsic religion, in which religious beliefs provide the master motive in life and suffuse it with meaning and direction, was a powerful contributor to mental health. As a result, he would almost certainly have expected the intrinsic, end dimension to relate positively to all seven conceptions of mental health. But we would not. The understanding of this dimension that we developed in Chapter 6 differed from Allport's, and so do our expectations for its contribution to mental health. We suggested that the intrinsic, end dimension, at least as measured by Allport's Intrinsic scale and related instruments, includes many of the characteristics of Erik Hoffer's fanatical, rigid, true believer. And if this is true, then we would not expect the relationship between this dimension and the various conceptions of mental health to be uniformly positive.

To be explicit, we would expect positive relationships with four conceptions of mental health. (1) The more devout, intrinsic believer's conformity to the moral prescriptions of orthodox religion should produce an increase in appropriate social behavior, at least behavior defined as appropriate by the religious tradition. (2) The believer's faith that he or she has answers to life's existential questions should increase freedom from worry and guilt. (3) The believer's conviction that not only is he or she on God's side but also that God is on his or her side should increase the sense of personal competence and control. (4) And finally, a devout, intrinsic belief should provide personality unification and organization; the true believer knows who he or she is and what is important.

In addition to these four positive relationships, we would expect this dimension to relate negatively to one conception of mental health, open-mindedness and flexibility. As we suggested in Chapter 6, to the degree that the intrinsic believer is convinced that he or she already knows the truth about life, there is no need to be open to new ideas and other points of view. On the contrary, as discussed in Chapter 7, the intrinsic believer should actively resist these potential threats to the source of his or her comfort and direction.

Finally, we are unable to make clear predictions for the relationship of the intrinsic, end dimension to two conceptions of mental health: absence of illness and self-acceptance or self-actualization. Although, as Freud suggested, devout belief might render personal neurosis unnecessary, it is itself interpreted as a form of mental illness not only by Freud but also by many other psychopathologists (e.g., Erich Fromm, 1950; Albert Ellis, 1980). This interpretation is also reflected in diagnostic instruments like the Minnesota Multiphasic Personality Inventory (MMPI), which include items that ask about religious belief, prayer, and experiences of the presence of God, and treat affirmative answers as evidence of psychopathology.

Turning to self-acceptance or self-actualization, intrinsic belief might increase self-acceptance if the believer focuses on his or her acceptance by God. But it might also reduce self-acceptance if the believer focuses on the equally orthodox doctrines of original sin and total depravity. Moreover, the intrinsic believer's devout allegiance to orthodox religion would not seem to encourage the free self-expression that characterizes Maslow's self-actualized individual. It might lead to a *belief* that one is self-actualized, that one has discovered and is living out one's true nature, but not to genuine self-actualization.

The quest dimension. In Chapter 6 we introduced a third dimension because we felt that Allport's intrinsic dimension omitted three important aspects of his earlier concept of mature religion: complexity, skepticism of traditional orthodox religious answers, and a sense of incompleteness and tentativenss. Each of these aspects was built into the scale we designed to measure the quest dimension.

For three conceptions of mental health, we would expect a relationship to the quest dimension that is just the opposite of the relationship to the intrinsic, end dimension. Whereas the certainty and direction provided by devout, intrinsic belief may be expected to lead to more freedom from worry and guilt and more unification and organization, the skepticism and tentativeness of the quest dimension should produce less of these two characteristics. At the same time, whereas the intrinsic, end dimension may be associated with less open-mindedness and flexibility, the quest dimension should be associated with more.

For two other conceptions we would also expect differences between the relationship to the end and quest dimensions, although not clear opposites. Whereas we expect the intrinsic, end dimension to relate positively to appropriate social behavior, there seems to be no basis for predicting either a positive or negative relationship between the quest dimension and this conception. And whereas we cannot make a clear prediction for the relationship of the end dimension to self-acceptance or self-actualization, we would expect the quest dimension to relate positively to this conception of mental health.

Concerning the remaining two conceptions, we would predict the same relationship for the end and quest dimensions. As noted above, the intrinsic, end dimension should relate positively to personal competence and control because the devout believer is confident that God is on his or her side. The quest dimension should also relate positively to personal competence and control, but for a very different reason. This dimension should reflect a self-directedness and reliance on one's own ability to think through complex, ultimate questions. Finally, as was true for the end dimension, we have no clear expectation concerning the relationship of the quest dimension to the absence of illness.

Obviously, our expectations for the way the means, end, and quest dimensions relate to different conceptions of mental health are complex. To help you keep these expectations in mind as we proceed to check them against the available empirical evidence, we have summarized them in Table 8.3. Where we expect a positive relationship between a religious dimension and a conception of mental health, a plus sign (+) is entered in the table; where we expect a negative relationship, a minus sign (−); and where we have not been able to predict a clear relationship, a question mark (?). Look over the entries in Table 8.3 to be sure that the predicted patterns make sense to you. Then we can move on to see how well these predictions stand up against the available empirical evidence.

The Empirical Evidence

When in 1982 Batson and Ventis reviewed the available evidence on the relationship of the three religious dimensions to the seven conceptions of

Table 8.3 Summary of expected relationships between the seven conceptions of mental health and the three dimensions of individual religion

	Dimension of individual religion		
Conception of mental health	Extrinsic, means	Intrinsic, end	Quest
Absence of illness	?	?	?
Appropriate social behavior	−	+	?
Freedom from worry and guilt	−	+	−
Personal competence and control	−	+	+
Self-acceptance, self-actualization	−	?	+
Unification and organization	−	+	−
Open-mindedness and flexibility	−	−	+

mental health, they were able to report 36 findings from fifteen different studies. We have uncovered some research that Batson and Ventis (1982) missed, and we have added relevant studies done since; during the past decade, there have been many. Now, instead of 36 findings from fifteen different studies, we are able to report 197 findings from sixty-one different studies.

To organize this huge mass of evidence, we have constructed a separate summary table for each of the three dimensions, as well as a line score table that presents side-by-side the pattern of findings for each dimension. (Once again, the uneven quality of research methods makes formal meta-analysis inappropriate.) Table 8.4 summarizes eighty findings from forty-five different studies of the relationship between the extrinsic, means dimension and one or more of the seven conceptions of mental health; Table 8.5 summarizes ninety-three findings from forty-six different studies of the intrinsic, end dimension; and Table 8.6 summarizes twenty-four findings from fifteen different studies of the quest dimension. Note that many of the studies appear in more than one of these tables.

Table 8.7 presents the line score for all 197 findings. As in Table 8.3, a plus sign in Table 8.7 denotes a positive relationship between a given religious dimension and conception of mental health, a minus sign denotes a negative relationship, and a question mark no clear relationship.

How do the expectations summarized in Table 8.3 fare when compared with the available evidence? The easiest way to answer this question is to check the expected patterns for each dimension presented in Table 8.3 with the line score for that dimension presented in Table 8.7. When we make this comparison, we find that our expectations were generally supported, with a few exceptions.

The extrinsic, means dimension. Following Allport, we had expected the extrinsic, means dimension to be negatively related to all but the first conception of mental health. Results of the research summarized in the line score in Table 8.7 are generally consistent with this expectation. Of the eighty relevant findings, forty-eight indicate a negative relationship between

Table 8.4 Summary of research examining the relationship between mental health and the extrinsic, means dimension

Authors	Sample	Measure of mental health	Findings
1. Using absence of illness as the criterion of mental health			
Lovekin and Malony (1977)	51 persons attending Life in the Spirit seminars (encouraging glossolalia)	Depression as measured by the Multiple Affect Adjective Checklist	No reliable relationship
Watson, Hood, and Morris (1984, Study 1)	85 introductory psychology students	Narcissism as measured by the Narcissistic Personality Inventory	No reliable relationship
Bergin, Masters, and Richards (1987)	32 former Mormon missionaries	Neurosis as measured by Irrational Beliefs Inventory; Beck Depression Inventory	Extrinsic religious orientation not reliably related to either measure
Levick and Delaney (1987)	193 introductory psychology students (63 men, 130 women)	Beck Depression Inventory	Extrinsic religious orientation positively correlated with Beck Depression Inventory ($r = .25, p < .01$)
Watson, Hood, Morris, and Hall (1987)	145 introductory psychology students (64 men, 81 women)	Exploitative narcissism as measured by the Narcissistic Personality Inventory and the Narcissistic Personality Disorder scale	Extrinsic religious orientation had low positive correlations with exploitative narcissism as measured by the NPI ($r = .14$, *ns*) and by the NPDS ($r = .28, p < .01$)
Watson, Hood, Foster, and Morris (1988)	198 undergraduates at a state university; 116 Pentecostal college students	Exploitative narcissism as measured by the Narcissistic Personality Inventory; two depression scales	Extrinsic religious orientation had low positive correlations with exploitative narcissism ($r = .28, p < .001$) and both depression scales ($rs = .17$ and $.16, ps < .01$)
Watson, Morris, and Hood (1988b)	Two studies: Samples were 125 and 211 undergraduates	Neurosis as meausred by Irrational Beliefs Inventory and Neuroticism scale	Extrinsic religious orientation had low but significant positive correlation with irrational beliefs ($r = .15$); no relationship with Neuroticism Scale

Watson, Morris, and Hood (1989b)	Summarizes results from 8 samples, ranging in size from 116 to 212, totalling 1397 undergraduates	Depression as measured by Costello and Comrey Depression scale	Extrinsic religious orientation had low positive correlations with depression (*rs* = .13 to .28, *ps* < .05 in 4 of 8 samples); across all samples, *r* = .18
Watson, Morris, and Hood (1989c)	286 undergraduates in psychology classes (110 men, 176 women)	Exploitative narcissism as measured by the Narcissistic Personality Inventory	Extrinsic religious orientation was positively correlated with exploitative narcissism (*r* = .29, *p* < .001)
Park, Cohen, and Herb (1990)	Two studies: 83 undergraduates each	Beck Depression Inventory (BDI)	In Study 1, extrinsic religious orientation was positively correlated with BDI scores among Catholics (*r* = .26) but negatively correlated among Protestants (*r* = −.43); in Study 2, no reliable relationship among either Catholics or Protestants
Pargament et al. (1990)	586 members from 10 midwestern churches	Self-reported general health; perception of having handled negative life event well	Extrinsic religious orientation had low positive correlation with perception (*r* = .15); no relation to general health
Genia and Shaw (1991)	309 adults or college students attending Protestant, Catholic, or Jewish services in Washington, D.C.	Beck Depression Inventory	Extrinsic religious orientation was positively correlated with scores on the Beck Depression Inventory (*r* = .24, *p* < .001)
2. Using appropriate social behavior as the criterion of mental health			
Rice (1971)	151 male members of religious groups (Massachusetts)	Questionnaire measure of social adjustment	Extrinsic religious orientation was negatively correlated with measure of social adjustment
Kahoe (1974)	518 freshmen at conservative college in the Midwest	Responsiblity scale from the California Psychological Inventory	Extrinsic religious orientation was negatively correlated with Responsibility scale (*r* = −.40)

Table 8.4 Summary of research examining the relationship between mental health and the extrinsic, means dimension (*Continued*)

Authors	Sample	Measure of mental health	Findings
Paloutzian, Jackson, and Crandall (1978)	Two samples: 84 introductory psychology students; 177 adults	Crandall's Social Interest scale	Extrinsic religious orientation was negatively correlated with social interest among adults ($r = -.22$, $p < .01$); no reliable relationship among students
Bergin, Masters, and Richards (1987)	78 BYU juniors and seniors	California Personality Inventory Sociability, Social Presence, Responsibility, Socialization, and Good Impression scales	Extrinsic religious orientation was negatively correlated with each of these scales ($rs = -.21$ to $-.26$, $ps < .05$, for all but Socialization, for which $r = -.08$, *ns*)
Also see Chapters 9 and 10 for summary of research on the relationship between extrinsic religion and prejudice and helping			
3. Using freedom from worry and guilt as the criterion of mental health			
Magni (1971)	53 student nurses in Uppsala, Sweden	Attitudes toward death, fear of death, and death anxiety	Extrinsic religious orientation was positively correlated with unfavorable attitudes toward death, fear of death, and death anxiety
Kahoe and Dunn (1975)	70 U.S. adults attending church in a Kentucky town	Absence of fear of death	Extrinsic religious orientation was nonsignificantly positively correlated with fear of death
Minton and Spilka (1976)	67 religiously active people (aged 17 to 83)	Questionnaire measures of positive and negative pespectives on death	Extrinsic religious orientation was negatively correlated with positive view of death and positively correlated with negative view of death (most $rs = .30$ or higher)
Spilka et al. (1977)	167 religiously involved individuals	Questionnaire measures of positive and negative perspectives on death	Extrinsic religious orientation was positively correlated with negative view of death ($p < .01$) and not reliably related to a positive view
Bolt (1977)	62 undergraduate psychology students at Calvin College	Templer's Death Anxiety scale	Extrinsic religious orientation was positively correlated with death anxiety ($r = .29$, $p < .05$)

Lovekin and Malony (1977)	51 persons attending Life in the Spirit seminars (encouraging glossolalia)	Questionnaire measures of state and trait anxiety and of guilt	Extrinsic religious orientation was not reliably related to state anxiety or guilt, but was positively correlated with trait anxiety ($r = .38, p < .01$)
Patrick (1979)	35 Buddhist, 40 Baptist, and 16 Congregationalist worshipers on Christmas Day in Honolulu	Splika's Death Perspectives scales; Templer's Fear of Death scale	Extrinsic religious orientation had a low, nonsignificant positive correlation with positive death outlook for each group, a significant positive correlation with negative death outlook and fear of death for Baptists and Congregationalists (all $rs > .30$, $ps < .05$) but not for Buddhists
Batson (1980)	80 undergraduates interested in religion	Perception of own religion as freeing self from existential concerns	No reliable relationship
Baker and Gorsuch (1982)	52 campers in religious wilderness camp	IPAT Trait Anxiety scale	Extrinsic religious orientation was positively correlated with anxiety ($r = .35, p < .01$)
Hood and Morris (1983)	Two samples: 105 undergraduates; 39 elderly	Questionnaire measures of death transcendence and death perspectives	Extrinsic religious orientation was not reliably related to use of religion for death transcendence but was positively correlated with negative perspectives on death ($rs = .25$ to $.35$, $ps < .01$)
Watson, Hood, Morris, and Hall (1985, Study 2)	194 introductory psychology students (98 men, 96 women)	McConahay and Hough Guilt scale	No reliable relationship
Schoenrade (1986)	100 introductory psychology students (50 men, 50 women)	Questionnaire measures of positive and negative perspectives on death	Extrinsic religious orientation was positively correlated with negative perspective on death ($r = .31, p < .01$), no reliable relationship with positive perspective on death
Kraft, Litwin, and Barber (1987)	107 introductory psychology students (50 men, 57 women)	Death anxiety as measured by Collett-Lester Fear of Death scale	Extrinsic religious orientation was positively correlated with death anxiety ($r = .42, p < .001$)

Table 8.4 Summary of research examining the relationship between mental health and the extrinsic, means dimension (*Continued*)

Authors	Sample	Measure of mental health	Findings
Kojetin et al. (1987)	Three samples: 104 undergraduates; 49 Methodist seminary students; 85 United Church of Christ adults	Questionnaire measures of anxiety and of religious conflict	Extrinsic religious orientation was positively correlated with anxiety and religious conflict
Bergin, Masters, and Richards (1987)	61 BYU juniors and seniors	Taylor Manifest Anxiety scale	Extrinsic religious orientation was positively correlated with anxiety ($r = .27, p < .05$)
Levick and Delaney (1987)	193 introductory pscyhology students (63 men, 130 women)	Templer Death Anxiety scale	Extrinsic religious orientation had a low but significant positive correlation with death anxiety ($r = .15, p < .05$)
Springer (1987)	118 Catholic, Presbyterian, or Baptist church members in northern U.S.	Hoelter's Fear of Death scale	Extrinsic religious orientation was positively correlated with 7 of 9 fear of death dimensions (all $ps < .05$)
Watson, Morris, and Hood (1987)	162 introductory psychology students (75 men, 87 women)	McConahay and Hough Guilt scale	No reliable relationship reported
Watson, Morris, and Hood (1988a,b,c)	Six samples of undergraduates, ranging in size from 125 to 314	Questionnaire measures of social anxiety (3 studies), anxiety (5 studies), anxious overconcern (1 study)	Extrinsic religious orientation had low but significant positive correlations with anxiety in 4 of 5 studies ($rs = .17$ to $.28$); no evidence of relationship with social anxiety or anxious overconcern
4. Using personal competence and control as the criterion of mental health			
Strickland and Shaffer (1971)	104 adolescent and adult church members from a liberal and a conservative church in the Atlanta area	Internal locus of control as measured by Rotter's Locus of Control scale	Extrinsic religious orientation was negatively correlated with internal locus of control ($r = -.30$)

Rice (1971)	151 male members of religious groups (Massachusetts)	Barron's Ego-Strength scale	Extrinsic religious orientation was negatively correlated with ego-strength, but relationship disappeared when age and religious affiliation were controlled
Kahoe (1974)	518 freshman at conservative college in the Midwest	Internal locus of control as measured by Rotter's Locus of Control scale	Extrinsic religious orientation was negatively correlated with internal locus of control ($r = -.25$)
Lovekin and Malony (1977)	51 persons attending Life in the Spirit seminars (encouraging glossolalia)	Barron's Ego-Strength scale	Extrinsic religious orientation had a nonsignificant negative correlation with ego-strength ($r = -.28$)
Acklin (1984)	120 adults ranging in age from 15 to 70 (60 men, 60 women)	Barron's Ego-Strength scale and Loevinger and Wessler test of ego development	Extrinsic religious orientation was negatively correlated with ego-strength ($r = -.16$, $p < .05$) and ego development ($r = -.32$, $p < .001$)
Bergin, Masters, and Richards (1987)	33 BYU juniors and seniors	Self-control as measured by Rosenbaum's Self-Control Schedule	Extrinsic religious orientation was nonsignificantly negatively correlated with self-control ($r = -.19$)
Bergin, Masters, and Richards (1987)	78 BYU juniors and seniors	Self-Control, Achievement by Independence, and Intellectual Efficiency scales from California Psychological Inventory	Extrinsic religious orientation was nonsignificantly negatively correlated with self-control ($r = -.13$); significantly negatively correlated with achievement by independence ($r = -.23$) and intellectual efficiency ($r = -.38$)
Pargament et al. (1988)	197 Presbyterian and Lutheran church members	Self-directing, deferring, and collaborative problem solving	Partialling correlations with other styles; extrinsic religious orientation was positively correlated with deferring problem-solving style ($r = .32$); not related to other two

Table 8.4 Summary of research examining the relationship between mental health and the extrinsic, means dimension (*Continued*)

Authors	Sample	Measure of mental health	Findings
Watson, Morris, and Hood (1988b, Study 2)	125 introductory psychology students (58 men, 67 women)	Questionnaire measures of locus of control, hopelessness, general self-efficacy, and social self-efficacy	Extrinsic religious orientation had low but significant negative correlations with internal locus ($r = -.19$) and general self-efficacy ($r = -.22$); no reliable relation with hopelessness or social self-efficacy
Watson, Morris, and Hood (1988c, Study 1)	157 introductory psychology students (73 men, 84 women)	Problem-avoidance scale of the Irrational Beliefs Test	No reliable relationship
Park, Cohen, and Herb (1990, Study 2)	83 undergraduates	Mirels's Internal Locus of Control scale	Extrinsic religious orientation was negatively correlated with internal locus of control among Catholics ($r = -.37$); no reliable relationship for Protestants
5. Using self-acceptance or self-actualization as the criterion of mental health			
Ventis, Batson, and Burke (1982)	34 introductory psychology students (16 men, 18 women)	Self-actualization as measured by Shostrom's Personal Orientation Inventory	Extrinsic religious orientation was not clearly related to self-actualization
Watson, Hood, and Morris (1984)	Two studies: Samples were 85 and 317 introductory psychology students	Self-actualization as measured by Inner Support scale of Shostrom's Personal Orientation Inventory	No reliable relationship in either study
Watson, Hood, Morris, and Hall (1985)	Two studies: Samples were 227 and 194 undergraduates	Two self-esteem scales (Rosenberg; Coopersmith) and Shostrom's Self-Acceptance scale	No reliable relationships with Rosenberg Self-Esteem Scale in either study; low but significant negative correlations with Coopersmith scale in each study ($rs = -.19$ and $-.14$); low but significant negative correlation with self-acceptance in Study 1 ($r = .15$), no reliable relationship in Study 2

Bergin, Masters, and Richards (1987)	78 BYU juniors and seniors	Self-acceptance scale of the California Psychological Inventory	No reliable relationship
Watson, Morris, and Hood (1987)	162 introductory psychology students (75 men, 87 women)	Two self-esteem scales (Rosenberg; Coopersmith), two self-acceptance scales (Berger; Phillips), and self-actualization as measured by the Inner Support Scale of Shostrom's Personal Orientation Inventory	No reliable relationship with either self-esteem scale; low but significant negative correlations with both self-acceptance scales ($rs = -.23$ and $-.21$) and with inner support ($r = -.17$, all $ps < .05$)
Watson, Morris, and Hood (1989c)	286 undergraduates in psychology classes (110 men, 176 women)	Self-acceptance as measured by Inner Support scale of Shostrom's Personal Orientation Inventory	Extrinsic religious orientation had a low but significant negative correlation with inner support ($r = -.18$, $p < .01$)
6. Using personality unification and organization as the criterion of mental health			
Crandall and Rasmussen (1975)	71 students from adolescent psychology class (34 men, 37 women)	Crumbaugh and Maholick's Purpose-in-Life Test	No reliable relationship
Soderstrom and Wright (1977)	427 introductory psychology students from 6 religious and 2 state colleges in the Midwest	Crumbaugh and Maholick's Purpose-in-Life Test	No reliable relationship to Spilka et al. measure of consensual (extrinsic) religion
Paloutzian, Jackson, and Crandall (1978)	Two samples: 84 introductory psychology students; 177 adults	Crumbaugh and Maholick's Purpose-in-Life Test	No reliable relationship in either sample
7. Using open-mindedness and flexibility as the criterion of mental health			
Tisdale (1966)	292 entering college freshman	Autonomy as measured by the Edwards Personal Preference Schedule	Extrinsic religious orientation was negatively correlated with autonomy ($r = -.35$, $p < .001$)
Hoge and Carroll (1973)	515 church members from northern U.S.; 343 church members from southern U.S.	Dogmatism as measured by Trodahl and Powell's Short Dogmatism scale	Extrinsic religious orientation was positively correlated with dogmatism in both North and South ($rs = .50$ and $.66$, $ps < .001$)

Table 8.4 Summary of research examining the relationship between mental health and the extrinsic, means dimension (*Continued*)

Authors	Sample	Measure of mental health	Findings
Thompson (1974)	532 Catholic mothers, fathers, and adolescents (195 boys, 337 girls)	Dogmatism as measured by Trodahl and Powell's Short Dogmatism scale	Extrinsic religious orientation was positively correlated with dogmatism among mothers, fathers, and adolescents ($rs = .28$, .38, and .28, all $ps < .001$)
Kahoe (1974)	518 freshmen at conservative college in the Midwest	Absence of authoritarianism as measured by the F-scale, and of dogmatism as measured by Rokeach's Dogmatism scale	Extrinsic religious orientation was positively correlated with authoritarianism ($r = .33$) and dogmatism ($r = .30$)
Kahoe (1975)	236 predominantly Baptist college students	Absence of authoritarianism as measured by the F-scale	Extrinsic religious orientation was positively correlated with authoritarianism across each of four subscales of the F-scale
Paloutzian, Jackson, and Crandall (1978)	Two samples: 84 introductory psychology students; 177 adults	Dogmatism as measured by Troldahl and Powell's Short Dogmatism scale	Extrinsic religious orientation had low, nonsignificant positive correlations with dogmatism for both students and adults ($rs =$ .18 and .08)
Batson and Raynor-Prince (1983)	35 undergraduates interested in religion	Cognitive complexity as measured by Schroder's Paragraph Completion Test	Extrinsic religious orientation was nonsignificantly negatively correlated with cognitive complexity in dealing with interpersonal conflict ($r = -.19$)
Bergin, Masters, and Richards (1987)	78 BYU juniors and seniors	Tolerance and Flexibility scales of the California Psychological Inventory	Extrinsic religious orientation was negatively correlated with tolerance ($r = -.24$); not reliably related to flexibility
Watson, Hood, and Morris (1988)	201 introductory psychology students (94 men, 107 women)	Questionnaire measure of avoidance of existential confrontation outside the religious domain	No reliable relationship

Table 8.5 Summary of research examining the relationship between mental health and the intrinsic, end dimension

Authors	Sample	Measure of mental health	Findings
1. Using absence of illness as the criterion of mental health			
Watson, Hood, and Morris (1984, (Study 1)	85 introductory psychology students	Narcissism as measured by the Narcissistic Personality Inventory	Intrinsic religious orientation was negatively correlated with narcissism ($r = -.40, p < .001$)
Bergin, Masters, and Richards (1987)	32 former Mormon missionaries	Neurosis as measured by Irrational Beliefs Inventory; Beck Depression Inventory	Intrinsic religious orientation not reliably related to either measure
Levick and Delaney (1987)	193 introductory psychology students (63 men, 130 women)	Beck Depression Inventory	Intrinsic religious orientation not reliably correlated with Beck Depression Inventory
Watson, Hood, Morris, and Hall (1987)	145 introductory psychology students (64 men, 81 women)	Exploitative narcissism as measured by the Narcissistic Personality Inventory and the Narcissistic Personality Disorder scale	Intrinsic religious orientation was negatively correlated with exploitative narcissism as measured by the NPI and NPDS (both $rs = -.32, ps < .01$)
Chamberlain and Zika (1988)	172 young mothers in New Zealand	Life satisfaction measured by Andrews and Withey's global scale	Intrinsic religious orientation (inferred from two King and Hunt subscales) had low positive correlation with life satisfaction ($r = .17, p < .05$)
Watson, Hood, Foster, and Morris (1988)	198 undergraduates at a state university; 116 Pentecostal college students	Exploitative narcissism as measured by the Narcissistic Personality Inventory; two depression scales	Intrinsic religious orientation had low negative correlations with exploitative narcissism ($r = -.20, p < .001$) and both depressions scales ($rs = -.19$ and $-.26, ps < .01$)
Watson, Morris, and Hood (1988b)	Two studies: Samples were 125 and 211 undergraduates	Neurosis as measured by Irrational Beliefs Inventory and Neuroticism scale	Intrinsic religious orientation had no reliable relationship with irrational beliefs or with neuroticism

Table 8.5 Summary of research examining the relationship between mental health and the intrinsic, end dimension (*Continued*)

Authors	Sample	Measure of mental health	Findings
Watson, Morris, and Hood (1989b)	Summarizes results from 8 samples, ranging in size from 116 to 212, totalling 1397 undergraduates	Depression as measured by Costello and Comrey Depression scale	Intrinsic religious orientation had low negative correlations with depression ($rs = -.11$ to $-.39$, $ps < .05$ in 6 of 8 samples); across all samples, $r = -.20$)
Watson, Morris, and Hood (1989c)	286 undergraduates in psychology classes (110 men, 176 women)	Exploitative narcissism as measured by the Narcissistic Personality Inventory	Intrinsic religious orientation was negatively correlated with exploitative narcissism ($r = -.23$, $p < .001$)
Park, Cohen, and Herb (1990)	Two studies: 83 undergraduates each	Beck Depression Inventory (BDI)	In Study 1, intrinsic religious orientation was positively correlated with future depression among Catholics ($r = .48$), but no reliable relationship among Protestants; in Study 2, no reliable relationship among either Catholics or Protestants
Pargament et al. (1990)	586 members from 10 midwestern churches	Self-reported general health; perception of having handled a negative life event well	Intrinsic religious orientation had low positive correlation with general health ($r = .11$) and with perception ($r = .19$)
Genia and Shaw (1991)	309 adults or college students attending Protestant, Catholic, or Jewish services in Washington, D.C.	Beck Depression Inventory	Intrinsic religious orientation was negatively correlated with scores on the Beck Depression Inventory ($r = -.20$, $p < .001$)
Kass et al. (1991)	83 adult medical outpatients in hospital-based behavioral medicine program	Self-report of physical health on medical symptom checklist	Intrinsic religious orientation (measured by questionnaire assessing commitment and closeness to God) was negatively correlated with reported frequency of symptoms ($p < .01$) but not related to reduced discomfort or interference from symptoms

2. Using appropriate social behavior as the criterion of mental health			
Rice (1971)	151 male members of religious groups (Massachusetts)	Questionnaire measure of social adjustment	Tendency for intrinsically religious to score lower on social adjustment than nonreligious but to score higher than extrinsically religious
McClain (1977)	145 intrinsically religious and 133 nonreligious students from classes preparatory to helping professions	Absence of stereotyped femininity, restlessness, and egocentric sexuality as measured by diagnostic questionnaires	Intrinsically religious scored higher on stereotyped feminity but lower on restlessness and egocentric sexuality than did nonreligious
Kahoe (1974)	518 freshmen at conservative college in the Midwest	Responsibility scale from the California Psychological Inventory	Intrinsic religious orientation was positively correlated with Responsibility scale ($r = .29$)
Paloutzian, Jackson, and Crandall (1978)	Two samples: 84 introductory psychology students; 117 addults	Crandall's Social Interest scale	Intrinsic religious orientation was positively correlated with social interest among both students and adults (*rs* = .53 and .50, *ps* $< .001$)
Woodroof (1985)	447 freshmen at colleges affiliated with the churches of Christ	Self-reported status as a sexual virgin	Classification as intrinsic rather than extrinsic was positively associated with being a virgin ($p < .0001$)
Bergin, Masters, and Richards (1987)	78 BYU juniors and seniors	California Personality Inventory Sociability, Social Presence, Responsibility, Socialization, and Good Impression scales	Intrinsic religious orientation was positively correlated with each of these scales (*rs* = .24 to .44, *ps* $< .05$, for all but Social Presence, for which $r = .07$, *ns*)
Also see Chapters 9 and 10 for summary of research on the relationship between intrinsic religion and prejudice and helping			
3. Using freedom from worry and guilt as the criterion of mental health			
Magni (1971)	53 student nurses in Uppsala, Sweden	Attitudes toward death, fear of death, and death anxiety	Intrinsic religious orientation was negatively correlated with unfavorable attitudes toward death, fear of death, and death anxiety, but last two relationships were not statistically significant

Table 8.5 Summary of research examining the relationship between mental health and the intrinsic, end dimension (*Continued*)

Authors	Sample	Measure of mental health	Findings
Kahoe and Dunn (1975)	70 U.S. adults attending a church in a Kentucky town	Absence of fear of death	Intrinsic religious orientation was negatively correlated with fear of death
Minton and Spilka (1976)	67 religiously active people (aged 17 to 83)	Questionnaire measures of positive and negative perspectives on death	Intrinsic religious orientation tended to correlate positively with positive views of death and negatively with negative views of death, but no correlations were reliable
Spilka et al. (1977)	167 religiously involved individuals	Questionnaire measures of positive and negative perspectives on death	Intrinsic religious orientation was positively correlated with positive views of death and negatively with negative views (ps range from *ns* to $< .01$)
Bolt (1977)	62 undergraduate psychology students at Calvin College	Templer's Death Anxiety scale	Intrinsic religious orientation had low, nonsignificant negative correlation with death anxiety ($r = -.14$)
Patrick (1979)	35 Buddhist, 40 Baptist, and 16 Congregationalist worshipers on Christmas Day in Honolulu	Splika's Death Perspectives scales; Templer's Fear of Death scale	Intrinsic religious orientation had significant positive correlation with positive death outlook only for Buddhists ($r = .40, p < .05$); had significant negative correlation with negative outlook only for Baptists ($r = -.42, p < .01$); and was not reliably related to fear of death for any group
Sturgeon and Hamley (1979)	144 students at a conservative, church-related college	Questionnaire measures of state, trait, and existential anxiety	Group classifed as intrinsic scored lower than group classified as extrinsic on trait and existential anxiety; no reliable difference on state anxiety
Batson (1980)	80 undergraduates interested in religion	Percpetion of own religion as freeing self from existential concerns	Positive relationship ($r = .66, p < .001$)
Baker and Gorsuch (1982)	52 campers in religious wilderness camp	IPAT Trait Anxiety scale	Intrinsic religious orientation was negatively correlated with anxiety ($r = -.33, p < .05$)

Hood and Morris (1983)	Two samples; 105 undergraduates; 39 elderly	Questionnaire measures of death transcendence and death perspectives	Intrinsic religious orientation was positively correlated with use of religion for death transcendence, positively correlated with positive perspective on death, and negatively correlated with some negative perspectives ($ps < .01$)
Watson, Hood, Morris, and Hall (1985, Study 2)	194 introductory psychology students (98 men, 96 women)	McConahay and Hough Guilt scale	Intrinsic religious orientation was positively correlated with guilt ($r = .29, p < .001$)
Schoenrade (1986)	100 introductory psychology students (50 men, 50 women)	Questionnaire measures of positive and negative perspectives on death	Intrinsic religious orientation was positively correlated with positive perspective on death ($r = .52, p < .01$) and negatively correlated with negative perspective ($r = -.22, p < .05$)
Kraft, Litwin, and Barber (1987)	107 introductory psychology students (50 men, 57 women)	Death anxiety as measured by Collett-Lester Fear of Death scale	Intrinsic religious orientation was negatively correlated with death anxiety ($r = -.30, p < .001$)
Bergin, Masters, and Richards (1987)	61 BYU juniors and seniors	Taylor Manifest Anxiety scale	Intrinsic religious orientation was negatively correlated with anxiety ($r = -.27, p < .05$)
Levick and Delaney (1987)	193 introductory psychology students (63 men, 130 women)	Templer Death Anxiety scale	Intrinsic religious orientation had a low but significant negative correlation with death anxiety ($r = -.18, p < .01$)
Kojetin et al. (1987)	Three samples: 104 undergraduates; 49 Methodist seminary students; 85 United Church of Christ adults	Questionnaire measures of anxiety and of religious conflict	Intrinsic religious orientation was either not related or negatively related to anxiety and religous conflict
Springer (1987)	118 Catholic, Presbyterian, or Baptist church members in northern U.S.	Hoelter's Fear of Death scale	Intrinsic religious orientation was positively correlated with fear of being destroyed ($p < .05$) and negatively with fear of the unknown ($p < .001$)

Table 8.5 Summary of research examining the relationship between mental health and the intrinsic, end dimension (*Continued*)

Authors	Sample	Measure of mental health	Findings
Watson, Morris, and Hood (1987)	162 introductory psychology students (75 men, 87 women)	McConahay and Hough Guilt scale	Intrinsic religious orientation was positively correlated with guilt ($r > .50, p < .001$)
Watson, Morris, and Hood (1988a,b,c)	Six samples of undergraduates, ranging in size from 125 to 314	Questionnaire measure of social anxiety (3 studies), anxiety (5 studies), anxious overconcern (1 study)	Overall, intrinsic religious orientation had no reliable relationship with social anxiety or anxiety; it had a low but significant positive correlation with anxious overconcern ($r = .19, p < .05$)
Schaefer and Gorsuch (1991)	161 students at Christian colleges in southern California	IPAT Trait Anxiety Scale; trait anxiety portion of STAI	Intrinsic religious orientation was negatively correlated with both anxiety measures ($rs = -.35$ and $-.30$, $ps < .01$)
4. Using personal competence and control as the criterion of mental health			
Rice (1971)	151 male members of religious groups (Massachusetts)	Barron's Ego-Strength scale	Intrinsically religious scored lower on ego-strength than did relatively nonreligious, but difference may have been a function of age and denominational differences
Kahoe (1974)	518 freshmen at conservative college in the Midwest	Internal locus of control as measured by Rotter's Locus of Control scale	Intrinsic religious orientation was positively correlated with internal locus of control ($r = .24$)
Kopplin (1976)	1546 undergraduate and graduate students in the Midwest and Southwest	Internal locus of control as measured by Levinson's Control scales	Intrinsic (committed) religious orientation was positively correlated with God control and negatively correlated with internal, other, and chance control; only the God-control correlation was large.
McClain (1977)	145 intrinsically religious and 133 nonreligious students from classes preparatory to helping professions	Self-control, achievement potential, and assertiveness or ascendancy as measured by diagnostic questionniares	Intrinsically religious scored higher than nonreligious on self-control; no differences on achievement potential or assertiveness (ascendancy)

Pargament, Steele, and Tyler (1978)	133 U.S. adults (Protestant, Catholic, and Jewish)	Internal locus of control as measured by Levinson's Control scales	Intrinsic religious orientation was positively correlated with God control and internal control; it was negatively correlated with control by chance
Sturgeon and Hamley (1979)	144 students at a conservative, church-related college	Internal locus of control as measured by Rotter's Locus of Control scale	Group classified as intrinsic scored higher than group classified as extrinsic on internal locus of control
Acklin (1984)	120 adults ranging in age from 15 to 70 (60 men, 60 women)	Barron's Ego-Strength scale and Loevinger and Wessler test of ego development	No reliable relationship with either measure
Bergin, Masters, and Richards (1987)	33 BYU juniors and seniors	Self-control as measured by Rosenbaum's Self-Control Schedule	Intrinsic religious orientation was positively correlated with self-control ($r = .38$, $p < .01$)
Bargin, Masters, and Richards (1987)	78 BYU juniors and seniors	Self-Control, Achievement by Independence, and Intellectual Efficiency scales from California Psychological Inventory	Intrinsic religious orientation was positively correlated with self-control ($r = .32$) and intellectual efficiency ($r = .29$); it was nonsignificantly positively correlated with achievement by independence ($r = .17$)
Pargament et al. (1988)	197 Presbyterian and Lutheran church members	Self-directing, deferring, and collaborative problem solving	Partialling correlations with other styles, intrinsic religious orientation was negatively correlated with a self-directing problem-solving style ($r = -.38$), positively correlated with a collaborative style ($r = .23$), and not related to a deferring style
Jackson and Coursey (1988)	98 black adult members of a Baptist church in Washington, D.C.	Internal locus of control (Rotter scale) and God control; psychosocial competence measured by Behavioral Attributes of Psychosocial Competence scale	Intrinsic religious orientation was positively correlated with God control, with internal locus of control, and with psychosocial competence (ps $< .02$)
Waton, Morris, and Hood (1988b, Study 2)	125 introductory psychology students (58 men, 67 women)	Questionnaire measures of locus of control, hopelessness, general self-efficacy and social self-efficacy	Intrinsic religious orientation had low but significant negative correlation with hopelessness ($r = -.22$) and a low but significant positive correlation with general self-efficacy ($r = .16$); no reliable relation with locus of control or social self-efficacy

Table 8.5 Summary of research examining the relationship between mental health and the intrinsic, end dimension (*Continued*)

Authors	Sample	Measure of mental health	Findings
Watson, Morris, and Hood (1988c, Study 1)	157 introductory psychology students (73 men, 84 women)	Problem-avoidance scale of the Irrational Beliefs Test	Intrinsic religious orientation was negatively correlated with problem avoidance ($r = -.32, p < .001$)
Hathaway and Pargament (1990)	108 Presbyterian and Assembly of God church members	Psychosocial competence as measured by Behavioral Attributes of Psychosocial Competence scale	Intrinsic religious orientation was not reliably related to psychosocial competence, but LISREL analysis indicated a positive relationship mediated by religious coping style
Park, Cohen, and Herb (1990, Study 2)	83 undergraduates	Mirels's Internal Locus of Control scale	No reliable relationship
5. Using self-acceptance or self-actualization as the criterion of mental health			
McClain (1977)	145 intrinsically religious and 133 nonreligious students from classes preparatory to helping professions	Sense of personal and social adequacy as measured by diagnostic questionnaires	Intrinsically religious scored higher than nonreligious on sense of personal and social adequacy
Pargament, Steele, and Tyler (1978)	133 U.S. adults (Protestant, Catholic, and Jewish)	Low scores on a self-criticism scale	No relationship between intrinsic religious orientation and self-criticism score
Ventis, Batson, and Burke (1982)	34 introductory psychology students (16 men, 18 women)	Self-actualization as measured by Shostrom's Personal Orientation Inventory	For males, intrinsic religious orientation was negatively correlated with self-actualization; for females, there was no relationship
Watson, Hood, and Morris (1984)	Two studies; Samples were 85 and 317 introductory psychology students	Self-actualization as measured by Inner Support scale of Shostrom's Personal Orientation Inventory	No reliable relationship in either study

Watson, Hood, Morris and Hall (1985)	Two studies: Samples were 227 and 194 undergraduates	2 self-esteem scales (Rosenberg; Coopersmith) and Shostrom's Self-Acceptance scale	No reliable relationships with either self-esteem scale in either study; low but significant negative correlations with self-acceptance in each study ($rs = -.12$ and $-.25$)
Bergin, Masters, and Richards (1987)	78 BYU juniors and seniors	Self-acceptance scale of the California Psychological Inventory	No reliable relationship
Watson, Morris, and Hood (1987)	162 introductory psychology students (75 men, 87 women)	Two self-esteem scales (Rosenberg; Coopersmith), two self-acceptance scales (Berger; Phillips), and self-actualization as measured by the Inner Support scale of Shostrom's Personal Orientation Inventory	No reliable relationship with either self-esteem or self-acceptance measure; low but significant negative correlation with inner support ($r = -.17$, $p < .05$)
Watson, Morris, and Hood (1989c)	286 undergraduates in psychology classes (110 men, 176 women)	Self-acceptance as measured by Inner Support scale of Shostrom's Personal Orientation Inventory	Intrinsic religious orientation had no reliable relationship with inner support
Hathaway and Pargament (1990)	108 Presbyterian and Assembly of God church members	Self-esteem as measured by Rosenberg's Self-Esteem scale	Intrinsic religious orientation had no reliable relationship to self-esteem
6. Using personality unification and organization as the criterion of mental health			
Crandall and Rasmussen (1975)	71 students from adolescent psychology class (34 men, 37 women)	Crumbaugh and Maholick's Prupose-in-Life Test	Intrinsic religious orientation was positively correlated with purpose in life ($r = .31$, $p < .01$)
Soderstrom and Wright (1977)	427 introductory psychology students from 6 religious and 2 state colleges in the Midwest	Crumbaugh and Maholick's Purpose-in-Life Test	High intrinsics scored higher on purpose in life than low intrinsics ($p < .01$)

Table 8.5 Summary of research examining the relationship between mental health and the intrinsic, end dimension (*Continued*)

Authors	Sample	Measure of mental health	Findings
Paloutzian, Jackson, and Crandall (1978)	Two samples: 84 introductory psychology students; 177 adults	Crumbaugh and Maholick's Purpose-in-Life Test	Intrinsic religious orientation was positively correlated with purpose in life among both students and adults ($rs = .34$ and $.37$, $ps < .01$)
Chamberlain and Zika (1988)	172 young mothers in New Zealand	Crumbaugh and Maholick's Purpose-in-Life Test	Intrinsic religious orientation (inferred from two King and Hunt subscales) was positively correlated with purpose in life ($r = .27$, $p < .01$)
Kass et al. (1991)	83 adult medical outpatients in hospital-based behavioral medicine program	Self-report questionnaire measure of life purpose and satisfaction	Intrinsic religious orientation (measured by questionnaire assessing commitment and closeness to God) was positively correlated with self-reported life purpose ($p < .05$)
7. Using open-mindedness and flexibility as the criterion of mental health			
Hoge and Carroll (1973)	515 church members from northern U.S.; 343 church members from southern U.S.	Dogmatism as measured by Trodahl and Powell's Short Dogmatism scale	Intrinsic religious orientation was positively correlated with dogmatism in both North and South ($rs = .24$ and $.25$, $ps < .001$)
Thompson (1974)	532 Catholic mothers, fathers, and adolescents (195 boys, 337 girls)	Dogmatism as measured by Trodahl and Powell's Short Dogmatism scale	No reliable relationship
Kahoe (1974)	518 freshmen at conservative college in the Midwest	Absence of authoritarianism as measured by the F-scale, and of dogmatism as measured by Rokeach's Dogmatism scale	No relationship was found between intrinsic religious orientation and either authoritarianism or dogmatism; but when response-set bias was controlled in a subsample, a positive correlation with authoritarianism was found

Kahoe (1977)	200 Southern Baptist college students selected so as to control for response-set bias	Absence of authoritarianism as measured by Krug's 6 F-scale factors	Intrinsic religious orientation was positively correlated with conventionalism and superstition factors; no relation for other 4 factors
Paloutzian, Jackson, and Crandall (1978)	Two samples: 84 introductory psychology students; 177 adults	Dogmatism as measured by Troldahl and Powell's Short Dogmatism scale	Intrinsic religious orientation had low positive correlation with dogmatism among both students (r = .14, *ns*) and adults (r = .22, $p < .001$)
Batson and Raynor-Prince (1983)	35 undergraduates interested in religion	Cognitive complexity as measured by Schroder's Paragraph Completion Test	No reliable relationship was found between intrinsic religious orientation and cognitive complexity in dealing with interpersonal conflict
Bergin, Masters, and Richards (1987)	78 BYU juniors and seniors	Tolerance and Flexibility scales of the California Psychological Inventory	Intrinsic religious orientation was positively correlated with tolerance (r = .35); not reliably related to flexibility
Watson, Hood, and Morris (1988)	201 introductory psychology students (94 men, 107 women)	Questionnaire measure of avoidance of existential confrontation outside the religious domain	No reliable relationship

Table 8.6 Summary of research examining the relationship between mental health and the quest dimension

Authors	Sample	Measure of mental health	Findings
1. Using absence of illness as the criterion of mental health			
Levick and Delaney (1987)	193 introductory psychology students (63 men, 130 women)	Beck Depression Inventory	Quest orientation had a low but significant positive correlation with Beck Depression Inventory ($r = .15, p < .05$)
Leak, et al. (1990, Study 1)	133 undergraduates from Jesuit or state university	Questionnaire measure of neuroticism	Quest orientation had low, nonsignificant negative correlation with neuroticism ($r = -.17$)
Pargament et al. (1990)	586 members from 10 midwestern churches	Self-reported health; perception of having handled negative life event well	No reliable relationship
2. Using appropriate social behavior as the criterion of mental health			
See Chapters 9 and 10 for summary of research on the relationship between the quest orientation and prejudice and helping			
3. Using freedom from worry and guilt as the criterion of mental health			
Batson (1980)	80 undergraduates interested in religion	Perception of own religion as freeing self from existential concerns	No reliable relationship
Schoenrade (1986)	100 introductory psychology students (50 men, 50 women)	Questionnaire measures of positive and negative perspectives on death	Quest orientation was negatively correlated with positive view of death ($r = -.18, p < .05$) and positively correlated with negative view of death ($r = .25, p < .01$)
Levick and Delaney (1987)	193 introductory psychology students (63 men, 130 women)	Templer Death anxiety scale	No reliable relationship
Kojetin et al. (1987)	Three samples: 104 undergraduates, 49 Methodist seminary students; 85 United Church of Christ adults	Questionnaire measures of anxiety and of religious conflict	Quest orientation was positively correlated with anxiety and religious conflict ($rs = .18$ to $.53$)

Springer (1987)	188 Catholic, Presbyterian, or Baptist church members in northern U.S.	Hoelter's Fear of Death scale	Quest orientation was positively correlated with 2 of 9 fear of death dimensions: fear of the unknown and fear of premature death ($ps < .05$)
Watson, Morris, and Hood (1987)	162 introductory psychology students (75 men, 87 women)	McConahay and Hough Guilt scale	No reliable relationship reported
Leak et al. (1990, Study 1)	133 undergraduates from Jesuit or state university	Questionnaire measure of social anxiety	Quest orientation had low but significant correlation with social anxiety ($r = -.26$, $p < .05$)
4. Using personal competence and control as the criterion of mental health			
Barron (1968)	50 women in their 40s who experienced a "crisis in belief" while in college	Ratings or intellectual excellence, autonomy, and mastery	"Belief for oneself" was positively associated with intellectual excellence ($r = .39$), autonomy ($r = .38$), and mastery ($r = .35$)
Acklin (1984)	120 adults ranging in age from 15 to 70 (60 men, 60 women)	Barrons' Ego-Strength scale and Loevinger and Wessler test of ego development	No reliable relationship
Pargament et al. (1988)	197 Presbyterian and Lutheran church members	Self-directing, deferring, and collaborative problem solving	Partialling correlations with other styles, quest orientation had low but significant positive correlations with self-directing and collaborative problem-solving styles (both $rs = .17$); no reliable relationship with deferring style
Leak et al. (1990, Study 1)	133 undergraduates from Jesuit or state university	Questionnaire measure of will to achieve	No reliable relationship
5. Using self-acceptance or self-actualization as the criterion of mental health			
Barron (1968)	50 women in their 40s who experienced a "crisis in belief" while in college	Ratings of capacity for further growth, self-insight, and self-awareness	"Belief for oneself" was positively associated with capacity for further growth ($r = .36$), self-insight ($r = .38$), and self-awareness ($r = .35$)
Ventis, Batson, and Burke (1982)	34 introductory psychology students (16 men, 18 women)	Self-actualization as measured by Shostrom's Personal Orientation Inventory	No relationship between measures of the quest orientation and self-actualization for either men or women

Table 8.6 Summary of research examining the relationship between mental health and the quest dimension (*Continued*)

Authors	Sample	Measure of mental health	Findings
Watson, Hood, Morris, and Hall (1985, Study 1)	227 introductory psychology students (97 men, 130 women)	Two self-esteem scales (Rosenberg; Coopersmith) and Shostrom's Self-Acceptance scale	No clear relationship with either self-esteem measure or with the Self-Acceptance scale
Watson, Morris, and Hood (1987)	162 introductory psychology students (75 men, 87 women)	Two self-esteem scales (Rosenberg; Coopersmith), two self-acceptance scales (Berger; Phillips), and self-actualization as measured by Inner Support scale of Shostrom's Personal Orientation Inventory	No reliable relationships
Leak et al. (1990, Study 1)	133 undergraduates from Jesuit or state university	Rosenberg's Self-Esteem scale and self-actualization as measured by revised Personal Orientation Inventory	Quest orientation was positively correlated with self-esteem and self-actualization (rs = .28 and .27, $ps < .01$)
6. Using personality unification and organization as the criterion of mental health			
None			

7. Using open-mindedness and flexibility as the criterion of mental health			
Barron (1968)	50 women in their 40s who experienced a "crisis in belief" while in college	Flexibility as measured by the California Personality Inventory; independence of judgment; rating of lack of authoritarianism	"Belief for oneself" was positively associated with flexibility ($r = .31$) and independence ($r = .42$), and negatively with authoritarianism ($r = -.33$)
Batson and Raynor-Prince (1983)	35 undergraduates interested in religion	Cognitive complexity as measured by Schroder's Paragraph Completion Test	Quest orientation was positively associated with cognitive complexity in dealing with interpersonal conflicts ($r = .34$)
Watson, Hood, and Morris (1988)	201 introductory psychology students (94 men, 107 women)	Questionnaire measure of avoidance of existential confrontation outside the religious domain	No reliable relationship
Leak et al. (1990, Study 1)	133 undergraduates from Jesuit or state university	Questionnaire measures of openness to experience and of rigidity	Quest orientation was positively correlated with openness ($r = .36, p < .01$) and negatively correlated with rigidity ($r = -.21, p < .05$)

Table 8.7 Line score on research examining the relationship between mental health and three different dimensions of individual religion

	Dimension of individual religion								
	Extrinsic, means			Intrinsic, end			Quest		
Conception of mental health	+	?	−	+	?	−	+	?	−
Absence of illness	1	7	11	11	7	1	0	2	1
Appropriate social behavior	0	1	4	5	0	1		No data	
Freedom from worry and guilt	0	7	15	15	5	4	1	4	3
Personal competence and control	0	4	9	11	4	3	2	2	0
Self-acceptance, self-actualization	0	5	3	1	8	3	2	3	0
Unification and organization	0	3	0	5	0	0		No data	
Open-mindedness and flexibility	0	4	6	1	6	2	3	1	0
Total	1	31	48	49	30	14	8	12	4

Note: The three columns under each dimension of individual religion indicate first, the number of reports of a positive relationship with each conception of mental health (+); second, the number of reports of no clear relationship (?); and third, the number of reports of a negative relationship (−).

the extrinsic, means dimension and mental health; thirty-one indicate no clear relationship. In only one case has evidence been found of a positive relationship between the extrinsic, means dimension and mental health; Park, Cohen, and Herb (1990) reported a negative correlation with depression among Protestant undegraduates.

Still, there are differences in the relationship to the different conceptions of mental health that are worth noting. The clearest negative relationships are for appropriate social behavior, freedom from worry and guilt, personal competence and control, and open-mindedness and flexibility. Contrary to our expectations, both for self-acceptance or self-actualization and for unification and organization, there is no clear relationship. The negative relationships under self-acceptance and self-actualization are most often for measures of self-acceptance; no-relationship findings are most common for measures of self-esteem. Moreover, concerning freedom from worry and guilt, a relationship is consistently found with measures of general trait anxiety and with measures of death anxiety, but studies using measures of guilt report no reliable relationship.

Although there are more negative than no-relationship findings for absence of illness, the negative correlations are generally low and not consistent across studies. Positive correlations with measures of depression or narcissism appear in some studies but not in others. And there is the one negative correlation with depression.

In sum, the research provides virtually no evidence that the extrinsic, means dimension of personal religion is positively associated with mental health, and it provides considerable evidence that this dimension is negatively associated with several conceptions of mental health. This is very much as Allport (1950) and we, following him, had predicted. On the other hand, some tempering of the extremity of the predictions seems in order. Evidence does not suggest that the relationship of the extrinsic, means dimension to mental health is as uniformly negative as either Allport's expections or ours in Table 8.3 suggest. For several conceptions of mental health—especially for self-acceptance or self-actualization and for unification and organization—there seems to be no clear relationship.

The intrinsic, end dimension. Allport would have expected a positive relationship between the intrinsic, end dimension and all seven conceptions of mental health. We expected a positive relationship with only four: appropriate social behavior, freedom from worry and guilt, personal competence and control, and unification and organization. We expected a negative relationship with open-mindedness and flexibility.

With several important qualifiers, the results of the research summarized in the line score in Table 8.7 support our expectations. The positive association with appropriate social behavior is most apparent on self-report measures. For freedom from worry and guilt, there is consistent evidence of a negative correlation with measures of general trait anxiety and death anxiety, but the limited evidence that exists indicates a positive correlation with measures of guilt. For personal competence and control, as predicted, the major source of the positive relationship is perception of God control; evidence of a relationship with either perceived internal locus of control or ego-strength is mixed, usually indicating either no clear relationship or a negative relationship.

We were unable to predict a clear relationship between the intrinsic, end dimension and two conceptions of mental health: absence of illness and self-acceptance or self-actualization. The evidence shows no clear relationship for self-acceptance or self-actualization. But it tends toward the positive for absence of illness due to generally negative (but low) correlations with measures of depression and exploitative narcissism and generally positive (but low) correlations with measures of life satisfaction, health, and well-being.

Finally, there is little indication that the relationship to measures of open-mindedness and flexibility is positive, as Allport would have predicted, but there is also little evidence that it is negative, as we predicted. The most common finding is no clear relationship. To anticipate our argument in the next chapter, however, there is some reason to believe that people scoring high on the intrinsic, end dimension are especially concerned to *appear* open-minded, so the relationship may be more negative than the results of these nine studies using paper-and-pencil measures suggest.

Overall, measures of the intrinsic, end dimension relate positively to measures of mental health in forty-nine findings, relate negatively in fourteen findings, and show no clear relationship in thirty findings. So, although the relationship of this dimension to the various conceptions of mental health is generally positive, it is not as uniformly positive as Allport (1950) predicted. On the other hand, there is little evidence of the negative relationship with open-mindedness and flexibility that we predicted.

The quest dimension. We had expected the relationship of the quest dimension to mental health to be very different from the relationship of the intrinsic, end dimension. In general, where one related positively, we either expected that the other would relate negatively or we could not make a clear prediction. The only conception to which we expected both dimensions to relate positively was personal competence and control, and even for this conception we assumed the relationship would be a result of very different factors. We expected the intrinsic, end dimension to be associated with reliance on God, and the quest dimension with self-reliance.

When we look at the evidence summarized in Table 8.7 for the quest dimension, we are first and foremost impressed by how limited it is. Data for this dimension are by far the most sparse, although not nearly as sparse now as at the time of Batson and Ventis's (1982) review. They were able to cite only six findings based on four different studies; we now have twenty-four findings based on fifteen different studies.

In the limited research that exists, the dominant finding is of no clear relationship between the quest dimension and measures of the various conceptions of mental health (twelve of the twenty-four findings). Still, the evidence of positive and negative relationships that exists generally patterns as predicted. Evidence generally supports the predicted positive relationship between the quest dimension and measures of open-mindedness and flexibility. Evidence is less supportive of the predicted positive relationships with personal competence and control and with self-acceptance or self-actualization. Some studies report the predicted positive relationship; others report no clear relationship.

We predicted two negative relations for the quest dimension. The available evidence provides qualified support for our prediction of a negative relationship with measures of freedom from worry and guilt. The evidence includes several positive correlations with measures of anxiety, especially death anxiety, but a negative correlation with social anxiety. The one study measuring guilt revealed no reliable relationship. There is still no evidence concerning the relationship to unification and organization, for which we also predicted a negative relationship.

Having looked at the mass of data on the religion–mental health relationship, we must once again emphasize the methodological limitations of this research. The quantity of research is certainly great, and it is increasing all the time; unfortunately, the quality is neither great nor increasing. Virtually all of the studies are correlational, and the measures of religion and mental health are taken at the same time, preventing clear causal inference. Assessment of mental health is almost always based on self-reports, which may at times be biased by a desire to present oneself in a good light. Samples are, at times, from unusual populations, leaving the generalizability of findings unclear. Although we have suggested the need for more data in several areas, quality is a far more important research virtue than is quantity. Therefore, we do not wish to call for more research on the religion–mental health relationship without calling even more loudly for *better* research.

Which of the Three Dimensions of Individual Religion Is Most Closely Associated with Increased Mental Health?

Stepping back from the mass of data and comparing the different patterns for the three dimensions of individual religion, it seems clear that what dimension one looks at will have a dramatic effect on one's conclusions about the relationship between religion and mental health. The generally negative relationship between amount of religious involvement and mental health noted earlier seems to be a product of the extrinsic, means dimension. Neither the intrinsic, end dimension nor the quest dimension appears to be negatively related to mental health; the relationships for each are, if anything, generally positive.

At the same time, the relationships for the end and quest dimensions are quite different. In general, the findings reveal more positive relationships for the intrinsic, end dimension than for the quest dimension. But the pattern shifts depending on the conception of mental health. The clearest positive relations for the end dimension are for appropriate social behavior, freedom from worry (but not guilt), personal competence and control, and unification and organization. For the quest dimension, there are no data for the first and last of these conceptions (although data presented in the next two chapters suggest a positive relation with at least some manifestations of appropriate social behavior), and for freedom from worry (but not guilt) the relationship is, if anything, negative. For personal competence and control, the relationship of the quest dimension seems somewhat positive, but for different reasons than for the end dimension. For the end dimension this relationship is based more on reliance on God; for the quest dimension it is based more on self-reliance. Positive relations for the quest dimension exist with open-mindedness and flexibility and, possibly, with self-acceptance and self-actualization. The end dimension does not appear to relate positively to either of these conceptions of mental health.

Which of these patterns indicates greater mental health—the pattern of relationships associated with the intrinsic, end dimension or the pattern associated with the quest dimension? An answer will, of course, depend on the conception of mental health one prefers. Freedom from worry and guilt is a favorite conception among psychoanalytically oriented therapists; open-mindedness and flexibility are more highly valued by social psychologists. So we might expect individuals more influenced by the psychoanalytic tradition to consider the former a more important sign of health, and those more influenced by social psychology to consider the latter more important. As a result of these preferences, we might expect those influenced by the psychoanalytic tradition to associate the intrinsic, end dimension more closely with mental health, and those influenced by social psychology to associate the quest dimension more closely with mental health.

We would caution against any clear-cut choice between these alternatives. Even though, given our social-psychological perspective, we may be inclined to say that freedom from worry and guilt is not as important for mental health as open-mindedness, we recognize that such freedom may be extremely important to those individuals, like Tolstoy, who are consumed by fear of death or a sense of meaninglessness and worthlessness. For such individuals, freedom from those whispering doubts, "Why should I live? Why should I do anything? Is there in life any purpose which the inevitable death which awaits me does not undo and destroy?" (Tolstoy, 1904, p. 21), may well be the most important thing in life. But having said this, we should not forget the lesson learned in Chapter 7: If this freedom is attained through devout, intrinsic religious belief, it is apt to be bought at the price of bondage to the belief.

SUMMARY AND CONCLUSION

"Divide and conquer" has been our strategy in attacking the complex and contradictory evidence concerning the relationship of religion to mental health. First, we divided the concept of mental health into seven distinct conceptions. This division proved helpful in understanding the mass of data on the relationship between mental health and amount of religious involvement. We found that the seemingly contradictory conclusions in the research reviews of Becker, Dittes, and Sanua could be accounted for by their different conceptions of mental health. Like the legendary blind men describing the elephant, each of these empirical experts appears to have been right for that part of the evidence that he touched. Becker dealt with absence of symptoms of mental illness, and for this conception the relationship between religion and mental health appears to be as he claimed, positive. Dittes dealt with personal competence and control, self-acceptance or self-actualization, and open-mindedness and flexibility, and for these conceptions the relationship appears to be as he claimed, negative. Sanua dealt with absence of illness, freedom from worry and guilt, self-acceptance or self-actualization, and open-mindedness and flexibility, and across these four conceptions the relationship appears to be as he claimed, unclear.

Second, we divided the broad concept of religious involvement into the three dimensions proposed in Chapter 6—as an extrinsic means to self-serving ends, as an intrinsic end in itself, and as a quest. This division also proved helpful because we found that these three dimensions relate to the various conceptions of mental health in very different ways. The extrinsic, means dimension appears to have a rather pervasive negative relationship to mental health, regardless of how mental health is conceived. Both the intrinsic, end dimension and the quest dimension appear to have positive relationships with at least some conceptions of mental health.

The instrinsic, end dimension is positively associated with reports of (1) greater absence of illness, (2) more appropriate social behavior, (3) greater freedom from worry (but not guilt), (4) greater personal competence and control, and (5) greater unification and organization, but not with (6) greater self-acceptance or self-actualization or (7) greater open-mindedness and flexibility. The quest dimension is positively associated with (1) greater open-mindedness and flexibility and, possibly, with (2) greater personal competence and control and (3) greater self-acceptance, but not with (4) greater absence of illness or (5) greater freedom from worry. These different patterns for the end and quest dimensions are generally consistent with the broad hypotheses proposed in Chapter 7: The intrinsic, end dimension leads to freedom from existential concerns and a sense of competence based on one's connectedness to the Almighty but, at the same time, to an inflexible bondage to one's beliefs. In contrast, the quest dimension leads to neither.

Although the empirical evidence generally supports our expectations concerning the relationship between each of the three dimensions and mental health, it also underscores the need for further research. Even excluding the second conception, appropriate social behavior, on which further data will be presented in Chapters 9 and 10, a look at Table 8.7 reveals that often the evidence for a given relationship is limited to less than a half dozen correlational findings. And for the relationship of the quest dimension to unification and organization, there is no evidence at all. Even greater than the need for more research in this area, however, is the need for better research.

We began this chapter with the case of young Francis of Assisi and the question of whether his religion was a force for mental health or sickness. We found that had we been able to take him to some of the leading psychotherapists in history to ask their opinion, we would probably have gotten conflicting views. Freud and Ellis would almost certainly have diagnosed sickness; Boisen might have said that Francis was sick but on his way to health; Jung, Allport, and Bergin would likely have contended that Francis's religion was an important source of mental health. We, if not Francis, would have been left very confused.

But just as our strategy of divide and conquer enabled us to make sense of the apparent contradictions among the empirical experts, it also enables us to make sense of the apparent contradictions among the therapeutic experts. Our analysis suggests that before answering the question of whether religion is a force for health or sickness in the life of Saint Francis—or anyone else—we must specify the dimension of religion and the conception of mental health that we have in mind. If, for example, we are referring to the extrinsic, means dimension and freedom from worry and neurotic anxiety, as Freud seems to have been, then the available evidence supports Freud's diagnosis; the relationship is negative. If we are referring to the intrinsic, end dimension and this same conception of mental health, as Jung and Allport seem to have been, then the available evidence supports their diagnosis; the relationship is positive.

It may seem that our answer to the question of whether religion is a force for mental health or sickness is equivocal, that we are simply saying, "It depends." Indeed, we are saying that it depends, but we do not think our answer is equivocal. We do not think so because we are also saying on *what* it depends. It depends on the particular dimension of religion and particular conception of mental health in question. Once the dimension and conception are specified, then our analysis permits us tentatively to answer whether the relationship is positive, negative, or unclear. Our answer is complex but not, we think, equivocal. To the contrary, we think it has enabled us to sort out at least some of the confusion and apparent contradiction that has for decades entangled the relationship between religion and mental health.

9

Brothers-and-Sisters or Sheep-and-Goats?

In the previous two chapters we have considered the effects of religion on the inner life of the individual, on existential anxiety and openness to new information (Chapter 7), and on personal adjustment and mental health (Chapter 8). Now it is time to broaden our focus and consider the effects of religion on reactions to and actions toward other people. Our basic question in this chapter shall be: Does personal religion increase universal love and acceptance of others, especially others who are different from ourselves? Does it enable us to see all people, no matter how alien, as our brothers and sisters? In the next chapter we shall ask: Does personal religion increase concern and caring for others in need?

All major religions preach love and acceptance of others—all others. The acceptance is to be unconditional, not qualified by race, creed, sex, or color. As Tolstoy (1902/1987) put it:

> In all faiths man [used generically] is regarded as equally insignificant before the infinite; they therefore all include the concept of equality between men in the eyes of what is called God. . . . The acceptance of equality between all men is a necessary and fundamental characteristic of all religions. (p. 91)

Christianity in particular prides itself on its vision of universal love: "There is no longer Jew or Greek, there is no longer slave or free, there is no longer male and female"—and, we might add, there is no longer black and white—"for all of you are one in Christ Jesus" (Gal. 3:28 NRSV). To the degree that a religion enables its followers to adopt and live such a vision, then it is a very welcome antidote for the hatred, suspicion, stereotyping, and prejudice that poison our world.

One can certainly think of dramatic examples in which this vision seems to have been realized. Think of the many Christians who, at the risk of their own lives and the lives of their children, sheltered Jews from the Nazis during World War II. Why did they do it? In the words of one: "My mother was a model of Christian faith and love of neighbor." And another: "He [my father] taught me to love my neighbor—to consider him my equal whatever his nationality or religion. He taught me especially to be tolerant" (Oliner & Oliner, 1988, pp. 164–165). Think of freedom riders who faced insult, jail, beating, and even death to further racial justice in the southern United States during the early 1960s. Many were clergy, and many others said that religion was an important impetus for their action. Think of Catholic clergy who, at the risk of infection, voluntarily served as guinea pigs to test experimental AIDS vaccines in the late 1980s and early 1990s.

These examples are both heartwarming and encouraging. They suggest that Christianity—and by extension other religions as well—can be a powerful stimulus to loving acceptance of "all God's children." Noted historian Arthur Schlesinger, Jr. (1989) calls us to think again:

> As a historian, I confess to a certain amusement when I hear the Judeo-Christian tradition praised as the source of our concern for human rights. In fact, the great religious ages were notable for their indifference to human rights in the contemporary sense. They were notorious not only for acquiescence in poverty, inequality, exploitation, and oppression but for enthusiastic justifications of slavery, persecution, abandonment of small children, torture, genocide.
>
> Religion enshrined and vindicated hierarchy, authority, and inequality and had no compunction about murdering heretics and blasphemers. Till the end of the 18th century, torture was normal investigative procedure in the Roman Catholic church. . . . In Protestant America in the early 19th century, as Larry Hise points out in his book "Pro-Slavery: A History of the Defense of Slavery in America, 1701–1840," men of the cloth "wrote almost half of all the defenses of slavery published in America"; an appendix lists 275 ministers of the Gospel who piously proclaimed the Christian virtue of a system in which one man owned another as private property to be used as he pleased.
>
> Human rights is not a religious idea. It is a secular idea, the product of the last four centuries of Western history. (p. 26)

Clearly, at the same time that we can think of cases in which religion appears as a driving force for universal love, acceptance, and tolerance, we can also think of cases in which it appears as a force for self-righteousness, pious elitism, and cruel, inhuman behavior toward others from different countries, cultures, races, and religions. All too often, it seems, religion functions not as a prophetic voice, calling the faithful to shed their intolerance and bigotry, but as a mighty fortress of ingroup superiority, justifying rejection, oppression, and even destruction of those who are different.

There appears to be a tragic, unintended corollary to knowing that one is among God's elect. If some are the "elect," "sheep," "chosen people," "family of God," then others are the "damned," "goats," "outcasts," "infidels." Far from encouraging universal love and acceptance, such labels are likely to encourage rejection and intolerance. As Robert Brannon (1970) has noted, "Some critics of religion have gone so far as to charge that racial and ethnic intolerance is a natural extension of religious precepts" (p. 42). When one thinks back over the role of religion in Western civilization, as Schlesinger calls us to do, this charge does not seem nearly as extreme as Brannon implies. Examples in which religious institutions and doctrines have encouraged racial and ethnic intolerance come to mind at least as easily as examples in which religion has encouraged acceptance.

Thinking of extreme examples like these certainly sharpens the question of whether personal religion is a force that encourages love, acceptance, and tolerance, or encourages intolerance, prejudice, and bigotry. Yet when addressing so emotionally charged and value-laden a question, extreme examples produce little clarity. If we are to arrive at a meaningful understanding of the role of religion in discouraging or encouraging intolerance, prejudice, and bigotry, then we believe we must depart from William James's maxim of looking at extreme examples and look instead at the social attitudes and behavior of more typical religious individuals. And when we do, we cannot rely on anecdotes; we need objective, empirical evidence.

As it turns out, there is much empirical research concerning the effect of religion on intolerance, prejudice, and bigotry, more than on any other topic in psychology of religion except mental health. When evaluating the research on the religion-prejudice relationship, it is important to keep three points in mind. First, a variety of different measures of intolerance, prejudice, and bigotry have been used. These measures include ethnocentrism (the tendency to be suspicious and rejecting of members of outgroups), racism, anti-Semitism, and what might be called "other prejudice" (i.e., prejudice against any of a number of other ethnic or national groups, such as Chicanos, Puerto Ricans, and Orientals). Second, the research tends to focus on the relationship between religion and prejudice among white, middle-class Christians in the United States. This is both because of the accessibility of such individuals (most of the researchers have worked in the United States) and because prejudice within this group has been a major social problem over the past five decades. Third, the research is correlational. It does not actually assess the influence of religion on prejudice, only the relationship between the two. Any relationship found could result from the influence of prejudice on religion instead of the influence of religion on prejudice, or it could result from the influence of some third variable on each.

Reviewing the research on the relationship between religion and prejudice, we have come across more than eighty different findings based on over sixty different studies. Paralleling our presentation in Chapter 8, we shall not attempt to consider each of these studies in detail. Instead, we shall summarize the findings in tabular form, including line score tables that report the number of findings suggesting one or another relationship.[1]

PREJUDICE AND AMOUNT OF RELIGIOUS INVOLVEMENT

When persons are more religious are they less prejudiced, more prejudiced, or is there no difference? Based on the existing research, an answer is all too clear. In spite of what the religions preach about universal brotherhood, the more religious an individual is, the *more* prejudiced he or she is likely to be. In early studies, for example, Allport and Kramer (1946) found that Protestant and Catholic students were more likely than those with no religious affiliation to be prejudiced against blacks. They also found that strong religious influence in the home correlated positively with racial prejudice. Rosenblith (1949) found a similar trend. In the authoritarian personality research, Adorno and his associates (1950) reported that both authoritarianism and ethnocentrism were higher among church attenders than among nonattenders. Kirkpatrick (1949) found that religious people had more punitive attitudes than nonreligious people toward criminals, delinquents, prostitutes, drug addicts, and those in need of psychiatric treatment. Stouffer (1955) demonstrated that among a representative sample of American church members, those who had attended church within the past month were more intolerant of nonconformists, socialists, and Communists than those who had not attended.

Rather than continue this litany, we refer you to Table 9.1, which summarizes forty-seven different findings relevant to the relationship between one or more of three indices of amount of religious involvement (church membership or attendance, positive attitudes toward religion, and orthodoxy or conservatism of religious beliefs) and one of four types of intolerance or prejudice (ethnocentrism, racial prejudice, anti-Semitism, and other prejudice). These findings were obtained across thirty-eight different studies conducted from 1940 to 1990. Table 9.2 presents a line score of these findings.

1. In the development of our summary tables we owe a large debt to Richard Gorsuch and Daniel Aleshire. In 1974, they published an extensive review of research on the religion-prejudice relationship, including several summary tables. We have relied heavily on their review in constructing our tables.

Table 9.1 Summary of research examining the relationship between prejudice and amount of religious involvement

Study	Sample population	Location	Prejudice measure	Relationship reported	Comments
1. Studies using church membership and/or attendance as measure of amount of religious involvement					
a. Using ethnocentrism as measure of prejudice					
Sanford and Levinson (1948)	1282 white, middle-class adults	California	California Ethnocentrism Scale	Positive	No significance tests reported
Rokeach (1960)	278 college students	Michigan, New York	Ethnocentrism scale	Positive	$p < .05$
Friedrichs (1960)	280 male college students	New York	Revised Ethnocentrism scale	Positive	$r = .24, p < .01$
Eisinga, Felling, and Peters (1990)	1190 adults in a national survey	The Netherlands	Agreement with negative stereotypes of ethnic outgroups	Positive	$p < .001$
b. Using racism as measure of prejudice					
Merton (1940)	522 college students	5 universities	MacCrone's Negro Prejudice scale	Positive	$p < .05$ in both North and South
Turbeville and Hyde (1946)	212 college students	Louisiana	Attitudes toward Negroes	Positive	No significance tests reported
Allport and Kramer (1946)	437 college students	Northeastern U.S.	Attitudes toward minorities	Positive	$p < .05$; but students who said religion was positive influence on racial attitudes were in less prejudiced half of sample

Table 9.1 Summary of research examining the relationship between prejudice and amount of religious involvement (*Continued*)

Study	Sample population	Location	Prejudice measure	Relationship reported	Comments
Rosenblith (1949)	861 college students	South Dakota	Attitudes toward Negroes and Indians	Positive for Catholics, no relationship for Protestants	$p < .05$ for Catholics; students who said religion was positive influence on attitudes toward minorities were in less prejudiced half of sample
Rosenblith (1957)	239 college women (1952); 256 college students (1954)	Boston area	Attitudes toward Negroes	Positive in 1952 sample; negative in 1954 sample	No significance tests reported
Pettigrew (1959)	78 small-town community residents	Southern U.S.	Anti-Negro scale	Positive	$p < .02$
Pettigrew (1959)	110 small-town community residents	Northern U.S.	Anti-Negro scale	No relationship	Nonsignificant negative correlation
Hadden (1963)	261 college students	Wisconsin	Racial segregation	Positive	$r = .17, p = .05$
c. Using anti-Semitism as measure of prejudice					
Levinson and Sanford (1944)	77 college males	California	Anti-Semitism scale	Positive	$p < .01$
Rosenblith (1949)	861 college students	South Dakota	Anti-Semitism scale	Positive	$p < .05$
Pettigrew (1959)	78 small-town community residents	Southern U.S.	Anti-Semitism scale	Nonsignificant positive relationship	$p < .18$
Pettigrew (1959)	110 small-town community residents	Northern U.S.	Anti-Semitism scale	No relationship	Nonsignificant negative correlation

Blum and Mann (1960)	125 college students	New York	Anti-Semitism scale	Positive	$p < .05$
d. Using other measures of prejudice					
Kirkpatrick (1949)	297 college students; 468 nonstudent adults	Minnesota	Attitudes toward criminals, delinquents, prostitutes, drug addicts, and mental patients	Positive	$p < .05$, comparing conservative versus liberal religious affiliation
Stouffer (1955)	4933 adults	U.S.; national cross-section probability sample	Intolerance of noncomformists (socialists, atheists, Communists)	Positive	$p < .01$
2. Studies using strength of religious attitudes as measure of amount of religious involvement					
a. Using ethnocentrism as measure of prejudice					
Friedrichs (1960)	280 male college students	New York	Revised Ethnocentrism scale	Positive	$r = .32, p < .01$
Siegman (1962)	43 male college students	University of North Carolina	Ethnocentrism scale	Positive	$r = .34, p < .05$
Bagley (1970)	200 adults	Holland	Attitudes toward nonwhite immigrants	Positive	No significance tests reported
Nias (1972)	441 11- and 12-year-olds	England	Ethnocentrism factor	Negative	$r = -.36$ for males; $r = -.19$ for females
Eisinga, Felling, and Peters (1990)	1190 adults in a national survey	The Netherlands	Agreement with negative stereotypes of ethnic outgroups	Positive	$r = .25, p < .001$
b. Using racism as measure of prejudice					
Sanai (1952)	250 college students	London	Racial prejudice	Positive	No significance tests reported

Table 9.1 Summary of research examining the relationship between prejudice and amount of religious involvement (*Continued*)

Study	Sample population	Location	Prejudice measure	Relationship reported	Comments
Kelly, Ferson, and Holtzman (1958)	547 undergraduates	Texas	Desegregation scale	Positive	$r = .17, p < .05$
Goldsen et al. (1960)	2161 Protestants and Catholics	U.S., nationwide; 11 universities	Attitudes toward blacks	Positive	No significance tests reported
c. Using anti-Semitism as measure of prejudice					
Evans (1952)	169 students	Michigan	Anti-Semitism scale	No relationship	$r = -.14$
d. Using other measures of prejudice					
Comrey and Newmeyer (1965)	212 adults	Los Angeles	Opposition to social change and racial tolerance	Positive	$r = .31; p < .05$
3. Studies using orthodoxy or conservatism as measure of amount of religious involvement					
a. Using ethnocentrism as measure of prejudice					
Gregory (1957)	596 students and members of church and civic groups	California	Ethnocentrism scale	Positive	$r = .37, p < .05$
Keedy (1958)	138 college students	Southern U.S.	Ethnocentrism scale	Positive	$r = .35, p < .05$
b. Using racism as measure of prejudice					
O'Reilly and O'Reilly (1954)	212 Catholic students	Southern U.S.	Anti-Negro scale	Positive with orthodoxy	$p < .001$
Garrison (1961)	81 college women	Georgia	Racial prejudice	Positive with fundamentalism	$r = .53, p < .05$
Salisbury (1962)	340 students	Southern U.S.	Attitudes toward segregation	Positive	$p < .001$

Salisbury (1962)	180 students	Northeastern U.S.	Attitudes toward segregation	No relationship	Nonsignificant positive correlation
Maranell (1967)	182 college students	Southern U.S.	Anti-Negro scale	Positive with fundamentalism	$p < .05$
Maranell (1967)	177 college students	Midwestern U.S.	Anti-Negro scale	No clear relationship	
c. Using anti-Semitism as measure of prejudice					
O'Reilly and O'Reilly (1954)	212 Catholic students	Southern U.S.	Anti-Semitism scale	Positive with orthodoxy	$p < .01$
Maranell (1967)	182 college students	Southern U.S.	Author-devised Anti-Semitism scale	Positive with fundamentalism	$p < .05$
Maranell (1967)	177 college students	Midwestern U.S.	Author-devised Anti-Semitism scale	No clear relationship	
Selznick and Steinberg (1969)	1093 white adults	U.S., nationwide	Anti-Semitism scale	Positive with conservatism of belief	$p < .05$
Kersten (1970)	886 Lutheran laymen	Detroit	Anti-Semitism scale	Positive with conservatism of belief	$p < .01$
d. Using other measures of prejudice					
Photiadis and Biggar (1962)	300 church members	South Dakota	Bogardus Social Distance scale	No clear relationship	
Whitam (1962)	101 adults	Indiana	Westie Social Distance scale	Positive with fundamentalism	$p < .05$
Strommen (1967)	2609 Lutheran youth	U.S., nationwide	Generalized prejudice scale	Negative with orthodoxy	$r = -.42, p < .01$
Gorsuch and McFarland (1972)	84 introductory psychology students	Nashville, Tenn.	General prejudice scale	Positive with fundamentalism	$r = .32, p < .05$
Johnson (1987)	371 adults in phone survey	"Middletown" (Muncie, Indiana)	Intolerance of person with AIDS at school and work	Positive with fundamentalism	$p < .01$

Source: Table based in part on Gorsuch and Aleshire (1974).

Table 9.2 Line score on research examining the relationship between prejudice and amount of religious involvement

	Index of religious involvement											
	Membership or attendance			Religious attitudes			Orthodoxy or conservatism			Total		
Index of prejudice	+	?	−	+	?	−	+	?	−	+	?	−
Ethnocentrism	4	0	0	4	0	1	2	0	0	10	0	1
Racism	6	2	0	3	0	0	4	2	0	13	4	0
Anti-Semitism	4	1	0	0	1	0	4	1	0	8	3	0
Other measures	2	0	0	1	0	0	3	1	1	6	1	1
Total	16	3	0	8	1	1	13	4	1	37	8	2

Note: Column entries in the table indicate, first, the number of reports of a positive relationship between prejudice and amount of religious involvement (+); second, the number of reports of no relationship (?); and third, the number of reports of a negative relationship (−).

As was true for the studies on religion and mental health reviewed in Chapter 8, the uneven quality of research methods in the studies summarized in Table 9.1 precludes a formal meta-analysis, but one is not necessary to determine the direction of the relationship. All it takes is a brief look at Table 9.2 to see that the score is very lopsided. Overall, thirty-seven of the forty-seven findings show a positive relationship between amount of religious involvement and amount of prejudice. Eight findings show no clear relationship; most of these were conducted in the northern United States. Only two findings indicate a negative relationship; one of these tested preadolescents, and the other tested preadolescents and adolescents. Comparing either the columns or the rows in Table 9.2, one can see that the pattern of results is highly consistent regardless of how religion or prejudice is measured. The pattern is also highly consistent over the years.

If one were to compute the probability of obtaining evidence this strong for a positive relationship between being more religious and being more prejudiced when such a relationship really did not exist, it would not be noticeably different from your chances of winning the New York State lottery—provided that you never entered! The relationship can be taken as a fact. We seem to be presented with a clear, if unsettling, conclusion: At least among white, middle-class Christians in the United States, *religion is not associated with increased love and acceptance but with increased intolerance, prejudice, and bigotry.*

PREJUDICE AND DIFFERENT WAYS OF BEING RELIGIOUS: THE EXTRINSIC-INTRINSIC DISTINCTION

You can well imagine the consternation among religious leaders as the evidence for a positive correlation between religion and prejudice began to pile up. Actually, the consternation was short-lived because several social psychologists pointed out a basic flaw in these studies, the inappropriateness of lumping together all white, middle-class people who identified themselves as Christians. Indeed, the early findings of a positive correlation between religion and prejudice were an important impetus for Gordon Allport and others to argue that it is not enough to measure whether or even to what degree a person is involved in religion; it is also necessary to measure how the person is religious.

In Chapter 6 we considered Allport's (1950) early distinction between immature and mature religion and his later distinction between extrinsic and intrinsic religion. We also noted the distinction made by Adorno et al. (1950) between neutralized religion and taking religion seriously and Spilka's distinction between consensual and committed religion (Allen & Spilka, 1967). Each of these conceptions suggests two different ways of being religious, one in which religion is used as an extrinsic means to reach self-serving ends, another in which religion is taken seriously as an intrinsic end in itself. Allport, Adorno, and Spilka each insist that some such distinction is essential to understand the relationship between religion and prejudice; they claim that although extrinsic, means religion may encourage prejudice, intrinsic, end religion does not. In Allport's (1966) words: "Both prejudice and religion are subjective formulations within the personal life. One of these formulations (the extrinsic) is entirely compatible with prejudice; the other (the intrinsic) rules out enmity, contempt, and bigotry" (p. 456).

Are Allport, Adorno, and Spilka right? To find out, it is necessary, first, to have some way of identifying extrinsic versus intrinsic religion. As we noted in Chapter 6, the most popular strategy has been to type individuals as extrinsic or intrinsic based on scores on the Allport and Ross (1967) Religious Orientation scale (or on some similar instrument). But another strategy has also been used. Gorsuch and McFarland (1972) noted that a fairly reliable index of the distinction between extrinsic and intrinsic religion can be obtained simply by asking people about the frequency of their involvement in religious activities. Individuals who are more religious in either an extrinsic or intrinsic way should, by definition, be more involved in religious activities than nonreligious individuals. But the extrinsically religious should limit their involvement to a moderate level because for them religion is subsumed under other, more important values and goals. The intrinsically religious, on the other hand, should be highly involved in religious activities because for them religion is the master motive in life. Consistent with this reasoning, among religious individuals more involvement is highly positively correlated with scores on Allport's Intrinsic scale but not with scores on his Extrinsic scale (Donahue, 1985; Gorsuch & McFarland, 1972).

This reasoning and evidence suggest a relatively simple, if somewhat crude, index of whether an individual is extrinsically or intrinsically religious—whether the individual is moderately or highly involved in religious activities. Accordingly, a number of researchers have compared three levels of involvement in religious activities: no or low involvement (e.g., less than four times a year), moderate involvement (e.g., less than weekly), and high involvement (e.g., at least weekly). These three levels have been assumed to identify the nonreligious, extrinsically religious, and intrinsically religious, respectively.

Equipped with these two ways of identifying extrinsic versus intrinsic religion, we can turn to the empirical research on the association between these different ways of being religious and prejudice. Table 9.3 summarizes forty-one findings obtained across thirty-two different studies conducted between 1949 and 1990. The first part of the table reports fourteen findings from twelve studies that used some form of questionnaire or interview data to classify religious individuals as extrinsic or intrinsic. The second part reports twenty-seven findings from twenty-three studies in which religious orientation was assessed by amount of religious activity broken either into low (L), moderate (M), and high (H), or into moderate (M) and high (H). A line score of findings is presented in Table 9.4.

Once again, the pattern of results across the studies is extremely clear, even clearer than it was for the relationship between amount of religious involvement and prejudice. As predicted by Allport and others, the way one is religious seems to make a great difference; individuals classified as intrinsically religious are consistently found to be less prejudiced than those classified as extrinsically religious. In all fourteen findings in the first three columns of Table 9.4, those classified as intrinsic scored lower on prejudice, however measured, than those classified as extrinsic. In twenty-five of the twenty-seven findings in the next three columns, those highly involved in religious activities scored lower on prejudice, however measured, than those only moderately involved.

Treating the extrinsic versus intrinsic distinction and the moderate versus high distinction as two different ways to compare the extrinsic and intrinsic orientations, we find that people classified as intrinsic scored lower on prejudice than people classified as extrinsic in thirty-nine of forty-one comparisons based on the results of thirty-two different studies. Moreover, one of the two studies that found no difference assessed attitudes toward political issues concerning minority rights, not prejudice (Rokeach, 1969b). The other assessed racial attitudes of white Catholics in the Florida panhandle who had recently migrated from northern United States and were members of an integrated church (Liu, 1961). Self-selection as a member of an integrated church in the Deep South could easily account for the lack of difference in this study. Overall, it is difficult to conceive of obtaining stronger evidence that the way one is religious affects the religion-prejudice relationship.

It seems clear that the earlier conclusion about a positive relationship between religious involvement and prejudice needs to be revised. Apparently, in studies measuring amount of involvement, the relatively low prejudice of the intrinsically religious minority was masked by the high prejudice of the extrinsically religious majority. When these different ways of being religious are taken into account, the more appropriate conclusion seems to be: *Although the extrinsically religious are high in intolerance and prejudice, the intrinsically religious are relatively low.*

Table 9.3 Summary of research examining the relationship between prejudice and extrinsic versus intrinsic religion

Study	Sample population	Location	Prejudice measure	Relationship reported	Comments
1. Studies using extrinsic (E) versus intrinsic (I) orientation (or related measure) to measure quality of religious involvement					
a. Using athnocentrism as measure of prejudice					
Adorno et al. (1950)	268 men, women, and students	U.S., West Coast	Ethnocentrism scale	E > I	No significance tests reported; using serious versus neutralized religion classification
b. Using racism as measure of prejudice					
Feagin (1964)	286 Southern Baptist church members	Texas and Oklahoma	Anti-Negro scale	E > I	$p < .001$
Allen and Spilka (1967)	497 college students	Colorado	Intolerance for national, ethnic or racial groups	E > I	$p < .01$; using committed versus consensual classification
Allport and Ross (1967)	309 church members	U.S., North and South	Anti-Negro scale	E > I	$p < .01$
Brannon (1970)	81 church members	Atlanta	Leaving integrating church	E > I	$p < .05$
Gray and Revelle (1974)	125 college students	Pennsylvania	10 scales measuring racial attitudes	E > I	Extrinsic religion correlated with prejudice, $p < .05$; intrinsic not correlated
Johnson (1977)	1040 heads of households	North Central Illinois	Racial Intolerance; Social Distance	E > I	$p < .001$; intrinsic measured by religious importance scale
c. Using anti-Semitism as measure of prejudice					
Frenkel-Brunswik and Sanford (1945)	76 female students	California	Anti-Semitism scale	E > I	No significance tests reported; deep versus utilitarian religion classification

Table 9.3 Summary of research examining the relationship between prejudice and extrinsic versus intrinsic religion (*Continued*)

Study	Sample population	Location	Prejudice measure	Relationship reported	Comments
Wilson (1960)	207 adults and college students	Boston	Anti-Semitism scale	E > I	$p < .001$; extrinsic religion correlated .66 with prejudice
Allport and Ross (1967)	309 church members	U.S., North and South	Anti-Jewish scale	E > I	$p < .05$
d. Using other measures of prejudice					
Allport (1954)	77 church members	Northeastern U.S.	General prejudice measure	E > I	No significance tests reported; institutional versus devout religion classification
Photiadis and Biggar (1962)	300 church members	South Dakota	Bogardus Social Distance scale	E > I	$p < .01$
Allport and Ross (1967)	309 church members	U.S., North and South	Anti-Other scale; indirect prejudice measures	E > I	$p < .05$
Tate and Miller (1971)	97 United Methodist adults	U.S., nationwide	Rating value of equality	E > I	Difference not statistically reliable
2. Studies using differentiated assessment of amount of religious activity (L = low—usually less than 4 times a year; M = moderate—usually less than weekly; H = high—usually at least weekly) to measure quality of religious involvement					
a. Using ethnocentrism as measure of prejudice					
Sanford (1950)	123 college females	California	Ethnocentrism scale	M > H > L	No significance tests reported
Shinert and Ford (1958)	327 Catholic students	Unspecified	Ethnocentrism scale	M > H	$p < .01$
Eisinga, Felling, and Peters (1990)	1190 adults in a national survey	The Netherlands	Agreement with negative stereotypes of ethnic outgroups	M > H > L	Only extremes differed reliably by a Scheffé test ($p < .05$)

b. Using racism as measure of prejudice					
Kelley, Ferson, and Holtzman (1958)	547 college students	Texas	Attitudes toward desegregation	M > H, L	$p < .05$
Friedrichs (1959)	112 residents of white, upper-middle-class suburb	New Jersey	Attitudes toward residential and school desegregation	M > L > H	No significance tests reported
Young, Benson, and Holtzman (1960)	497 college students	Texas	Attitudes toward desegregation	M > H, L	$p < .05$
Liu (1961)	196 white Catholics from integrated church	Florida	Racial Attitude scale	No significant relationship	
Lenski (1963)	481 adults	Detroit	Pro or con school integration	M > H	$p < .05$
Ragan (1963)	266 white Methodist church members	Los Angeles	Attitude toward Negro residential proximity	M > H	$p < .05$
Williams (1964)	950 white non-Jewish adults	Ohio, Georgia, and California	Attitudes toward Negroes	M > L > H	True of data as whole, but for Georgia group, M > L, H
Allport and Ross (1967)	309 church members	U.S., North and South	Anti-Negro scale	M > H, L	No significance test reported
Young, Clore, and Holtzman (1968)	578 college students	Texas	Attitudes toward desegregation	M > H > L	$p < .01$
Rokeach (1969b)	1400 adults in nationwide probability sample	U.S.	14 items measuring attitudes toward minority rights	M, H > L	This pattern was observed for all items; it was statistically reliable for 8

Table 9.3 Summary of research examining the relationship between prejudice and extrinsic versus intrinsic religion (*Continued*)

Study	Sample population	Location	Prejudice measure	Relationship reported	Comments
Hoge and Carroll (1973)	858 United Methodist and Presbyterian church members	Philadelphia (N = 515); Atlanta (N = 343)	Antiblack scale	M > H, L	$p < .05$
Johnson (1977)	1040 heads of households	North Central Illinois	Racial Intolerance scale; Social Distance	M > H	$p < .05$ for racial intolerance; nonsignificant trend for social distance
c. Using anti-Semitism as measure of prejudice					
Parry (1949)	612 community residents	Denver	Franzen Anti-Semitism Scale	M > H	$p < .03$
Sanford (1950)	123 college females	California	Anti-Semitism scale	M > H > L	$p < .05$
Williams (1964)	337 white non-Jewish adults	Georgia	Attitudes toward Jews	M > H > L	No significance test reported
Allport and Ross (1967)	309 church members	U.S., North and South	Anti-Jewish scale	M > H, L	No significance test reported
Kersten (1970)	886 Lutheran laymen	Detroit	Anti-Semitism scale	L, M > H	$p < .05$
Hoge and Carroll (1973)	858 United Methodist and Presbyterian church members	Philadelphia (N = 515); Atlanta (N = 343)	Anti-Semitism scale	M > H, L	$p < .05$

d. Using other measures of prejudice					
Rosenblum (1958)	54 Presbyterian, 64 Episocopalian and 54 Jewish middle-class adults	California	Prejudice scale	L, M > H	$p < .01$
Photiadis and Biggar (1962)	300 church members	South Dakota	Bogardus Social Distance scale	M > H	$p < .01$
Struening (1963)	911 university faculty and staff	Midwest	Prejudice scale	M > L, H	$p < .01$
Bagley (1970)	1400 adults	England and Wales	Attitudes toward immigrants, ethnic groups	M, L > H	$p < .01$
Campbell (1971)	2945 white adults	15 U.S. cities	General prejudice items	M > H, L	No significance tests reported
King and Hunt (1972)	1356 church members	Dallas area	Generalized prejudice	M > H	$r = .14$, $p < .05$. Measure of church attendance compiled from 7 attitude items

Source: Table based in part on Gorsuch and Aleshire (1974).

Table 9.4 Line score on research examining the relationship between prejudice and extrinsic versus intrinsic religion

	Index of religious orientation								
	Extrinsic vs. intrinsic			Moderate vs. high					
Index of prejudice	E < I	E = I	E > I	M < H	M = H	M > H	Total		
Ethnocentrism	0	0	1	0	0	3	0	0	4
Racism	0	0	6	0	2	10	0	2	16
Anti-Semitism	0	0	3	0	0	6	0	0	9
Other measures	0	0	4	0	0	6	0	0	10
Total	0	0	14	0	2	25	0	2	39

Note: Column entries in the table indicate, first, the number of reports that E < I (extrinsic less prejudiced than intrinsic) or M < H (moderate attenders less prejudiced than high attenders); second, the number of reports of no difference; and third, the number of reports that E > I or M > H.

This revised conclusion has been and continues to be widely accepted and popular among psychologists of religion. We have already heard Allport's (1966) claim that extrinsic religion "is entirely compatible with prejudice," whereas intrinsic religion "rules out enmity, contempt, and bigotry" (p. 456). Similarly, Gorsuch and Aleshire (1974), after an extensive review of research up to the early 1970s concerning the relationship between religion and prejudice, concluded:

> The extrinsically-oriented person, i.e., one who supports religion for what he can get from it, tends to be prejudiced. On the other hand, a person who is intrinsically committed to his religious position, i.e., supports religion for the sake of religion itself, . . . tends to be less prejudiced. (p. 284)

In recent years, Donahue (1985), Spilka, Hood, and Gorsuch (1985), and Gorsuch (1988) have continued to affirm this highly popular revised conclusion. For example, Gorsuch (1988) succinctly states: "Those with an intrinsic orientation towards religion are relatively unprejudiced, whereas those with an extrinsic view are relatively prejudiced" (p. 212).

The question of the relationship between religion and prejudice seems to be neatly answered. Although being more religious correlates with being more intolerant and prejudiced, this is true only among those who have emasculated the more profound claims of their religion and are using it as an extrinsic means to self-serving ends. Those who take their religion seriously, dealing with it as an intrinsic end in itself, are not more intolerant. Even though there is no clear evidence that the intrinsically religious are less prejudiced than individuals not involved in religion at all—in the first part of Table 9.3, correlations of the Intrinsic scale with the prejudice measures are often close to zero; in the second part, high attenders are rarely less prejudiced than low—there is at least no clear evidence that they are more so. And they certainly appear less prejudiced than the large segment of the population that is involved in religion in a nominal, extrinsic way. Intrinsic religion may not actually be the depressant of intolerance, prejudice, and bigotry that Allport (1966) claimed, but at least it does not seem to be the stimulant that extrinsic religion is.

DOUBTS

Perhaps because this revised conclusion regarding the religion-prejudice relationship has been far more satisfying to researchers interested in religion than was the original conclusion, it has seldom been questioned. We believe, however, that it should be. We have doubts both about the adequacy of the assessment of prejudice in the research summarized in Table 9.3 and about the adequacy of the assessment of extrinsic and intrinsic religion. Let us explain.

The Problem of Self-Presentation When Using Overt, Questionnaire Measures of Prejudice

Concerning the assessment of prejudice, we worry about self-presentation (Jones & Pittman, 1982). Presenting oneself as prejudiced or as a bigot is something that most people in the mainstream of contemporary society wish to avoid. There are side eddies of society where prejudice against certain groups is still overtly encouraged (e.g., against Jews among members of the American Nazi Party or against blacks among members of the Ku Klux Klan), but these are increasingly rare. To the extent that a person wishes to be seen as unprejudiced, we might expect this wish to affect his or her responses to interview questions or questionnaire items concerning prejudice. Consistent with this expectation, a number of social-psychological studies have provided evidence that individuals in contemporary American society show a strong tendency to adjust their responses when answering questions about prejudice; they attempt to appear less prejudiced than they actually are (Gaertner & Dovidio, 1986; Karlins, Coffman, & Walters, 1969; Sigall & Page, 1971; Silverman, 1974).

Evidence of this desire to present oneself as relatively free of prejudice raises serious doubts about the validity of the assessment of prejudice in the studies summarized in Table 9.3. In all but one of the studies summarized (the one exception is a study by Brannon, which we shall consider in more detail shortly), prejudice was measured by questionnaire, and the prejudice questionnaires tend to be quite transparent. Although none directly asks, "Are you a racist bigot?", many come close.

Transparency of prejudice questionnaires. To illustrate our concern, let us ask you to read the three hypothetical situations in Table 9.5 and imagine your responses to the questions posed. These situations and questions are from the prejudice questionnaires used in the classic study of religious orientation and prejudice by Allport and Ross (1967) and were described by them as "subtly worded." In spite of this description, we suspect that you had no difficulty identifying the low-prejudice responses. Similarly, we sus-

Table 9.5 Sample items from the Harding and Schuman Prejudice scale used by Allport and Ross (1967) as a subtle measure of prejudice

1. A Negro girl who had just got a job in San Francisco was looking for a place to live in an all-white neighborhood. She went to see several people who had advertised rooms for rent, but all of them suggested she find a room in a Negro neighborhood instead. They were always pleasant to her, but said that renting to her would make it hard for them to rent their other rooms. Finally she found a landlady in the white neighborhood, Mrs. Williamson, who agreed to take her.

a. If you had been Mrs. Williamson, would you have rented to the Negro girl?	YES	yes	?	no	NO
b. Should the other landladies in the neighborhood have been willing to rent to the Negro girl?	YES	yes	?	no	NO
c. Is it unfair to the white roomers to let a Negro move in?	YES	yes	?	no	NO

2. In a large Western city there has been for many years an informal group called the Businessmen's Luncheon Club. None of the members is Jewish. Recently one of the members proposed they add to the group a Jew who was head buyer for one of the larger clothing stores. A majority of the members voted against this. The president of the club said: "I think Mr. Rothman is a fine person, but I don't think we should add him to the Luncheon Club. This has always been a small, closely knit private group; and if we took in Mr. Rothman we would soon need to admit every Jewish business man in town who wanted to join."

a. If you had been a member of the club, would you have objected to the president's statement?	YES	yes	?	no	NO
b. If the club does admit Jewish members, should it be a little more careful in picking them than in picking non-Jews?	YES	yes	?	no	NO
c. Should business and professional clubs admit members without paying attention to whether the new members are Jewish?	YES	yes	?	no	NO

3. Mr. Ramirez, a Puerto Rican, was looking for an apartment in a New York City suburb. He went into a real estate office which had a list of apartments in the window, and asked about one of the places that was listed. The clerk told him that this apartment was in a private house in a white neighborhood, and the owner would not rent to Puerto Ricans. Also, the white neighbors would probably reject Puerto Ricans and make life unhappy for them. However, he suggested other apartments elsewhere at about the same rent which he thought would be just as satisfactory.

a. Should the owner of the house be willing to rent to Puerto Ricans, regardless of what the neighbors think?	YES	yes	?	no	NO
b. Should there be a law requiring landlords always to rent to the first one applying?	YES	yes	?	no	NO
c. Is it better to keep people such as Puerto Ricans in one section of a city, to avoid tensions and trouble?	YES	yes	?	no	NO

pect that research respondents—well aware of issues of prejudice and discrimination that have been so prominent over the past several decades—could easily detect the purpose of such questions and, if they wished to present themselves as free from prejudice, mark low-prejudice responses.

There have been attempts in recent years to overcome this self-presentation problem by developing more subtle "modern" or "symbolic" racism scales. Unfortunately, what is being measured by these scales still seems readily apparent, as indicated by the fact that scores on these scales are highly correlated with scores on earlier, blatant racism scales. A typical item from the Modern Racism scale (McConahay, 1986), for example, asks respondents to indicate agreement or disagreement with the following statement: "Blacks are getting too demanding in their push for equal rights." We suspect modern respondents would have little difficulty detecting what is being measured by such an item and in knowing whether agreement or disagreement would make them look prejudiced. (See Crosby, Bromley, & Saxe, 1980, and Gaertner & Dovidio, 1986, for further discussion of self-presentation problems with questionnaire measures of prejudice.)

Self-presentation and intrinsic religion. Adding to our concerns about the effects of self-presentation on the evidence summarized in Tables 9.3 and 9.4, there are several reasons to believe that individuals classified as intrinsically religious are likely to be more concerned to present themselves as tolerant and unprejudiced than are individuals classified as extrinsic. Let us mention just two of these reasons.

First, in the United States strong agreement with items assessing intrinsic religion (e.g., "I try hard to carry my religion over into all my other dealings in life") may itself be motivated at least in part by a desire to present oneself in a positive light. This is because both personal religion and living one's beliefs are positively valued in American society. It is less clear that strong agreement with items assessing extrinsic religion (e.g., "Although I believe in my religion, I feel there are many more important things in my life") places the respondent in a favorable light. Thus, high scores on the Intrinsic scale may reflect, at least in part, desire for positive self-presentation, whereas high scores on the Extrinsic scale probably do not.

Once again, there is evidence consistent with this suggestion. Several studies have found that individuals who report being highly devout and committed to their religion present themselves especially positively when asked about their behavior in other areas of life (Crandall & Gozali, 1969; Francis, Pearson, & Kay, 1983; McConahay, 1986). More directly relevant, Batson, Naifeh, and Pate (1978) found a moderate positive correlation between scores on the Intrinsic scale and the Marlowe-Crowne Social Desirability scale ($r = .36, p < .01$). To give you an idea of the kind of item on the Social Desirability scale, the first four are reproduced below. Responses are true or false. Except for reversed items, true responses are taken to reflect a concern to present oneself in a positive, socially desirable light because it is assumed that no one could be as conscientious and thoughtful as the items imply.

1. Before voting I thoroughly investigate the qualifications of all candidates.
2. I never hesitate to go out of my way to help someone in trouble.
3. (reversed) It is sometimes hard for me to go on with my work if I am not encouraged.
4. I have never intensely disliked anyone.

Subsequent research (e.g., Watson, Morris, Foster, & Hood, 1986) has also typically found a positive correlation between the Intrinsic scale and the Marlowe-Crowne Social Desirability scale, although of a lower magnitude than the correlation found by Batson et al. (1978). Based on the research to date, the true correlation between these two scales seems to be around .20. In contrast, correlations of the Extrinsic scale with the Marlowe-Crowne Social Desirability scale are typically either close to zero or low negative.[2]

Second, as already noted, all major religions in our society condemn prejudice and bigotry. Given that their religious community provides an especially important reference group for the devout, intrinsically religious (Brown, 1987; also see Chapter 7), individuals so classified should be especially motivated to live up to the community's standards by presenting themselves as free from prejudice and bigotry. One way to do so would be to circle the easily discernible "right" responses on a prejudice questionnaire.

An alternative explanation. If self-presentation concerns lead individuals classified as intrinsically religious to present themselves as free from prejudice to a greater extent than individuals classified as extrinsic, then the result would be precisely the pattern found in Tables 9.3 and 9.4, *even if*

2. Interpretation of the correlation between the Intrinsic and Social Desirability scales has been the subject of some controversy. Watson et al. (1986) suggested that the Marlowe-Crowne Social Desirability scale (SDS) is not an appropriate measure of social desirability to use with intrinsically religious individuals because "over half of the SDS items have content relevant to religion and religious belief" (p. 228), which "could put the intrinsic . . . subject at a selective disadvantage" (p. 227).

Leak and Fish (1989) have challenged this suggestion on both logical and empirical grounds. Empirically, Leak and Fish found statistically significant ($p < .05$) positive correlations between the Intrinsic scale and both subscales of the Paulhus (1984) Balanced Inventory of Desirable Responding (BIDR), an instrument proposed as an improvement on the Marlowe-Crowne and incorporating separate subscales to assess concern for public and private self-presentation. Correlations were .23 for the public Impression Management subscale; .27 for the private Self-Deception subscale; and .30 for the total BIDR. Additionally, Leak and Fish found near-zero correlations between the Intrinsic scale and subject-rated religious relevance of the items of both BIDR subscales, using a rating procedure modeled after that of Watson et al. (1986). Overall, the research to date seems generally consistent with the suggestion that individuals scoring higher on measures of intrinsic religion are more concerned to present themselves in a positive light, especially but not exclusively on issues related to their religious beliefs.

there were no difference between the groups in prejudice. The former would appear less prejudiced than the latter. Yet the personal transformation that Allport (1966) and others have claimed is associated with intrinsic religion—and that forms the basis for the highly popular revised conclusion concerning the religion-prejudice relationship—would have reached only to the hand that marks the questionnaire, not to the heart.[3]

The Problem of Typing Rather than Using a Multidimensional Assessment of Personal Religion

Concerning the assessment of personal religion, the comparisons in Tables 9.3 and 9.4 are based on Allport's original bipolar conception of extrinsic and intrinsic religion. As you may recall from Chapter 6, Allport originally assumed that these two ways of being religious were mutually exclusive types. To make an extrinsic versus intrinsic comparison, he and other researchers have classified as extrinsic those individuals who scored above the median of the sample on the Extrinsic scale and below the median on the Intrinsic scale. Conversely, they have classified as intrinsic those individuals who scored below the median on the Extrinsic scale and above the median on the Intrinsic scale. But, as you may also recall, this assumption of mutually exclusive types ran into problems early on, when Allport and Ross (1967) found that the Extrinsic and Intrinsic scales were not measuring opposite ends of the same continuum, as had been assumed, but were measuring two independent dimensions of personal religion.

If scores on the Extrinsic and Intrinsic scales are uncorrelated, as they are in most samples, the extrinsic versus intrinsic classification involves an inappropriate confounding of the two dimensions. Attributes associated

3. When one begins to entertain the possibility that the relationship between intrinsic religion and low prejudice could be an artifact of self-presentation, one discovers that there are a number of pieces of evidence consistent with it. First, in the classic and frequently cited study by Allport and Ross (1967), there were actually wide differences in the relationship between the intrinsic-extrinsic classification and prejudice across the six different church groups studied (Baptists and Catholics from Massachusetts, Lutherans from New York, Methodists from Tennessee, Nazarenes from South Carolina, and Presbyterians from Pennsylvania). Considering only racial prejudice, correlations between prejudice and being classified as intrinsic rather than extrinsic ranged from $-.39$ for the Massachusetts Baptists to $+.24$ for the Tennessee Methodists. That is, for the latter group there was a marginally significant tendency for those classified as intrinsic to score *higher* on the prejudice measure than those classified as extrinsic. A nonsignificant positive correlation (.12) was also found for the Pennsylvania Presbyterians.

This wide variation between regional and denominational groups is hard to explain if one assumes that intrinsic religion leads to reduced prejudice. But it is easy to explain if one assumes that the different church groups had different norms for desirable responses and that members of these groups were conforming to these norms. Expression of devout religion and little prejudice might have been desirable among the Baptist, Catholic, and Nazarene samples; in contrast, those members of the Methodist and Presbyterian samples who were more educated and so more likely to be concerned about displaying nonprejudicial attitudes might also have been concerned to present themselves as not unduly fanatical and pious in their orientation to religion.

Evidence for the effect of religious group norms on the religion-prejudice relationship is even clearer in a study by Strickland and Weddell (1972). They administered Allport and Ross's

with extrinsic religion, such as relatively high prejudice, might be a result either of the people classified as extrinsic scoring relatively high on the Extrinsic scale or of these people scoring relatively low on the Intrinsic scale. Attributes associated with intrinsic religion, such as relatively low prejudice, might be a result either of the people classified as intrinsic scoring relatively high on the Intrinsic scale or of these people scoring relatively low on the Extrinsic scale.

Rather than a bipolar classification into extrinsic versus intrinsic, we recommend measuring different ways of being religious through use of the three-dimensional model presented in Chapter 6. This model includes two independent dimensions, means and end, that correspond conceptually to Allport's (1966) extrinsic and intrinsic orientations (and are measured principally by the Extrinsic and Intrinsic scales); it also includes a third dimension, independent of either of the other two, the quest dimension (measured principally by the Quest scale). This third dimension concerns the degree to which the individual seeks to face religious issues—such as issues of personal mortality or meaning in life—in all their complexity, while at the same time resisting clear-cut, pat answers.

A NEW LOOK AT THE RELIGION-PREJUDICE RELATIONSHIP USING NEW RESEARCH STRATEGIES

These doubts about the revised conclusion concerning the religion-prejudice relationship surfaced in the late 1970s. Since then, several researchers have used one of two different strategies to take a new look at the relationship between prejudice and different ways of being religious. One strategy still involves using questionnaires to assess prejudice, but assessing prejudice that the respondents' religious community does not clearly proscribe or condemn, such as prejudice against nonwhites by Afrikaners in South Africa or prejudice against homosexuals or Communists by members of mainline churches in the United States. The second strategy involves assessing a religiously proscribed prejudice, such as racial prejudice by members

---

Intrinsic and Extrinsic scales and a sixty-item form of the Multifactor Racial Attitude Inventory (Woodmansee & Cook, 1967) to forty-seven Baptists and forty-six Unitarians in suburban Atlanta. For the Baptist sample they found, as Allport and Ross had found, that individuals classified as intrinsic were less prejudiced than either those classified as extrinsic or as indiscriminantly proreligious. But they found that the Unitarians, over 80 percent of whom were classified as extrinsic, were significantly less prejudiced than the Baptists ($p < .005$). Once again, these results are not consistent with the view that intrinsic religion leads to reduced prejudice, but they are entirely consistent with the view that different group norms lead to different patterns of socially desirable responses and respondents present themselves accordingly. Among Unitarians the most socially desirable pattern would likely involve appearing relatively independent of traditional religion and opposing zealous piety or fanaticism; at the same time, it would involve placing high value on liberal social views, including an abhorrence of racial prejudice and discrimination. Among Baptists, on the other hand, the most socially desirable pattern would likely be to place high value on religious devotion and orthodoxy and, by the mid-1960s, to show at least moderate support for racial tolerance as well.

of mainline churches in the United States, but doing so using covert, behavioral measures of prejudice, not questionnaires. Although relatively few studies of each type have been conducted, the results are, once again, remarkably consistent.

Questionnaire Measurement of Prejudices Not Clearly Proscribed

To organize the available evidence on the relationship between the three different religious dimensions and prejudice when the prejudice is not clearly proscribed by the respondents' religious community, we have constructed a separate summary table for each of the three dimensions, as well as a line score table that presents in one place the pattern of findings for each of the three dimensions. Table 9.6 summarizes eight findings from five different studies using a questionnaire to assess the relationship of the extrinsic, means dimension to some nonproscribed prejudice; Table 9.7 summarizes nine findings from six studies of the intrinsic, end dimension; and Table 9.8 summarizes seven findings from five studies of the quest dimension. Note that most studies appear in all three tables; in all, only six different studies are reviewed.

Table 9.9 presents the line score for the twenty-four findings obtained in these six different studies. A plus sign in Table 9.9 denotes a positive relationship between a given dimension of personal religion and some measure of nonproscribed prejudice; a minus sign denotes a negative relationship; and a question mark, no clear relationship. The nonproscribed prejudices assessed include prejudice against Rastafarians by Seventh-Day Adventists in the Virgin Islands (Griffin, Gorsuch, & Davis, 1987); prejudice against homosexuals by university students in the United States (Herek, 1987); prejudice against homosexuals and Communists by undergraduate and adult members of mainline churches in the United States (McFarland, 1989, 1990a); social distance from various ethnic minorities among university students in Venezuela (Ponton & Gorsuch, 1988); and social distance from nonwhites among Afrikaners (Snook & Gorsuch, 1985).

Additional evidence for the effect of group norms on the religion-prejudice relationship is provided by a study done by Friedrichs (1971; see also Johnson, 1977). In his 1959 study of attitudes toward open housing in suburban New Jersey, Friedrichs had found that church members were more prejudiced than nonmembers and that moderate attenders were more prejudiced than either frequent attenders or infrequent attenders. In a follow-up study six years later, however, after vigorous efforts by local clergy and others in the community to counteract prejudice among the churchgoers, he found quite different results. Church members were now less prejudiced than nonmembers, and moderate attenders were less prejudiced than either frequent or infrequent attenders. Friedrichs concluded, "There is not an inevitable correlation between church-going and prejudice: Where tolerant attitudes on specific issues are made clear norms for church-goers, church-goers expressed these norms to interviewers" (1971, p. 154). Of course, we may wonder whether respondents' assurances to an interviewer that they would not object to a black family moving into their neighborhood reflected their true attitude or what they had learned was the right response. It seems likely that the church members, especially moderate attenders, became aware of the "wrongness" of their earlier responses, and in the follow-up study were careful to get the answers right.

Table 9.6 Summary of research examining the relationship between nonproscribed prejudice and the extrinsic, means dimension

Study	Sample population	Location	Prejudice measure	Relationship reported
Griffin, Gorsuch, and Davis (1987)	190 West Indian black attenders of Seventh-Day Adventist church (English speaking)	St. Croix, U.S. Virgin Islands	Ratings of vignettes disallowing basic constitutional and human rights to Rastafarians	Extrinsic scale not related to prejudice against Rastafarians ($r = -.01$)
Herek (1987)	126 white (non-Hispanic) students at four U.S. universities	California; Milwaukee; Boston	Adapted Symbolic Racism scale; Attitudes Toward Lesbians scale; Attitudes Toward Gay Men scale	Extrinsic scale correlated positively with racial prejudice ($r = .24, p < .01$) but not related to prejudice against lesbians ($r = -.06$) or gay men ($r = -.07$)
Ponton and Gorsuch (1988)	275 university students (Spanish speaking)	Caracus, Venezuela	Culturally adapted version of Bogardus Social Distance scale, measuring preferred social distance from 8 ethnic groups (Spaniards, Portuguese, Italians, Americans, Colombians, Peruvians, and Chileans)	Extrinsic scale correlated positively with preferred social distance when correlations with religious affiliation, parents' nationality, and SES were partialed out ($p < .05$)
McFarland (1989)	173 white undergraduates with at least a moderate interest in religion	Western Kentucky University	Scales measuring discriminatory attitudes toward blacks, women, homosexuals, and Communists	Extrinsic scale correlated positively with discriminatory attitudes toward blacks ($p < .02$); not reliably related to discriminatory attitudes toward other 3 groups
McFarland (1990a)	470 active adult Christians (ages from 20s to 60s)	Kentucky and Tennessee	Scales measuring discriminatory attitudes toward blacks, women, homosexuals, and Communists	Extrinsic scale not reliably related to discriminatory attitudes toward any of the 4 groups

Table 9.7 Summary of research examining the relationship between nonproscribed prejudice and the intrinsic, end dimension

Study	Sample population	Location	Prejudice measure	Relationship reported
Snook and Gorsuch (1985)	94 Afrikaner and 135 English high school students	South Africa	Modified version of Spangenberg and Nel Social Distance scale	Batson Internal scale correlated positively with preferred social distance from nonwhites among Afrikaners ($r = .21$, $p < .05$); no relation among English
Griffin, Gorsuch, and Davis (1987)	190 West Indian black attenders of Seventh-Day Adventist Church (English speaking)	St. Croix, U.S. Virgin Islands	Ratings of vignettes disallowing basic constitutional and human rights to Rastafarians	Intrinsic scale correlated positively with prejudice against Rastafarians ($r = .23$, $p < .01$)
Herek (1987)	126 white (non-Hispanic students) at four U.S. universities	California; Milwaukee; Boston	Adapted Symbolic Racism scale; Attitudes Toward Lesbians scale; Attitudes Toward Gay Men scale	Intrinsic scale not related to racial prejudice but was positively correlated with prejudice against lesbians ($r = .24$, $p < .01$) and gay men ($r = .18$, $p < .05$)
Ponton and Gorsuch (1988)	275 university students (Spanish speaking)	Caracas, Venezuela	Culturally adapted version of Bogardus Social Distance scale, measuring preferred social distance from 8 ethnic groups (Spaniards, Portuguese, Italians, Americans, Colombians, Peruvians, and Chileans)	Intrinsic scale correlated negatively with preferred social distance when correlations with religious affiliation, parents' nationality, and SES were partialed out ($p < .01$)
McFarland (1989)	173 white undergraduates with at least a moderate interest in religion	Western Kentucky University	Scales measuring discriminatory attitudes toward blacks, women, homosexuals, and Communists	Intrinsic scale not reliably related to discriminatory attitudes toward blacks and women, but positively correlated with discriminatory attitudes toward homosexuals and Communists ($p < .05$)
McFarland (1990a)	470 active adult Christians (ages from 20s to 60s)	Kentucky and Tennessee	Scales measuring discriminatory attitudes toward blacks, women, homosexuals, and Communists	Intrinsic scale not reliably related to discriminatory attitudes toward blacks and women, but positively correlated with discriminatory attitudes toward homosexuals and Communists ($p < .01$)

Table 9.8 Summary of research examining the relationship between nonproscribed prejudice and the quest dimension

Study	Sample population	Location	Prejudice measure	Relationship reported
Snook and Gorsuch (1985)	94 Afrikaner and 135 English high school students	South Africa	Modified version of Spangenberg and Nel Social Distance scale	Quest scale correlated negatively with preferred social distance from nonwhites for both Afrikaners ($r = -.21, p < .05$) and English ($r = -.17, p < .05$)
Griffin, Gorsuch, and Davis (1987)	190 West Indian black attenders of Seventh-Day Adventist church (English speaking)	St. Croix, U.S. Virgin Islands	Ratings of vignettes disallowing basic constitutional and human rights to Rastafarians	Quest scale not reliably related to prejudice against Rastafarians ($r = -.08$)
Ponton and Gorsuch (1988)	275 university students (Spanish speaking)	Caracas, Venezuela	Culturally adapted version of Bogardus Social Distance scale, measuring preferred social distance from 8 ethnic groups (Spaniards, Portuguese, Italians, Americans, Colombians, Peruvians, and Chileans)	Quest scale not reliably related to preferred social distance
McFarland (1989)	173 white undergraduates with at least a moderate interest in religion	Western Kentucky University	Scales measuring discriminatory attitudes toward blacks, women, homosexuals, and Communists	Quest scale correlated negatively with discriminatory attitudes toward all 4 groups ($p < .05$)
McFarland (1990a)	470 active adult Christians (ages from 20s to 60s)	Kentucky and Tennessee	Scales measuring discriminatory attitudes toward blacks, women, homosexuals, and Communists	Quest scale correlated negatively with discriminatory attitudes toward all 4 groups (ps from $< .10$ to $< .001$)

Table 9.9 Line score summary of research examining the relationships between three dimensions of personal religion and prejudices not clearly proscribed by respondents' religious community (twenty-four findings from six different studies, 1985–1990)

Dimension of personal religion	Nature of association		
	+	?	–
Extrinsic	1	7	0
Intrinsic	8	0	1
Quest	0	2	5

Note: Column entries in the table indicate, first, the number of reports of a positive correlation between measures of each dimension of personal religion and some nonproscribed prejudice; second, the number of reports of no reliable correlation; and third, the number of reports of a negative correlation.

The line score in Table 9.9 is extremely interesting. The patterns of association for the extrinsic, means dimension, and the intrinsic, end dimension exactly reverse the patterns of association for these dimensions summarized in Table 9.4 for proscribed prejudice (e.g., racial prejudice). For nonproscribed prejudice, the extrinsic, means dimension shows no clear relationship to prejudice in seven of eight findings; the intrinsic, end dimension shows a positive relationship to prejudice in eight of nine findings. Only the quest dimension shows evidence of a negative relation to prejudice when the prejudice is not clearly proscribed by the religious community (five of seven findings).

Three comments should be made about the studies summarized in Tables 9.6, 9.7, and 9.8, and the line score in Table 9.9. First, two of the studies reviewed assessed prejudice against women by male and female members of mainline churches in the United States (McFarland, 1989, 1990a). Given that these studies were both conducted in the late 1980s, we have considered this a proscribed prejudice and not included findings for it in these tables. The validity of this assumption is supported by the tendency in these studies for correlations with prejudice against women to pattern much like correlations for prejudice against blacks. If, however, you wish to consider prejudice against women nonproscribed, then add two no-relation findings to the extrinsic, means row in Table 9.9, two no-relation findings to the intrinsic, end row, and two negative-correlation findings to the quest row. These additions do not substantially change the overall pattern.

Second, the one outlier in the extrinsic row, the one outlier in the intrinsic row, and one of the two no-relation findings in the quest row all come from a single study by Ponton and Gorsuch (1988). This study assessed the preferred social distance from various ethnic minorities by Spanish-speaking university students in Caracas, Venezuela. The ethnic minorities were Spaniards, Portuguese, Italians, Americans, Canadians, Colombians, Peruvians, and Chileans. Given that social contact with at least some of these groups might have been positively desired rather than merely tolerated, it seems doubtful that the social distance measure in this study was a valid measure of prejudice. If this study is excluded from Tables 9.6 through 9.9, as it probably should be, then the pattern of correlations becomes even clearer.

Finally, it is worth noting that four of the six studies summarized in the line score in Table 9.9 also included questionnaire measure of a proscribed prejudice—racial prejudice in the United States or among English high school students in South Africa (Herek, 1987; McFarland, 1989, 1990; Snook & Gorsuch, 1985). Correlations of the measures of racial prejudice with the extrinsic, means dimension and the intrinsic, end dimension were much the same as in the earlier studies summarized in Table 9.3 and in the line score in Table 9.4. The extrinsic, means dimension correlated positively with proscribed prejudice against blacks in two of three findings (no relation in the third); the intrinsic, end dimension was not reliably correlated with proscribed prejudice against blacks in four of four findings.

Measures of the quest dimension were not included in any of the studies summarized in Table 9.3, and so we could not include the quest dimension in the line score in Table 9.4. Therefore, it is of particular interest to note that in the studies summarized in Table 9.8, the Quest scale was negatively correlated with proscribed prejudice—racial prejudice in the United States—in three findings. As in all of the questionnaire-based research on the religion-prejudice relationship, these three correlations were not especially large (*r*s ranging from −.10 to −.30), but they were all reliably different from zero.

In sum, although the extrinsic, means dimension is related positively to questionnaire measures of a wide range of proscribed prejudices (see Tables 9.3 and 9.4), it generally relates close to zero to questionnaire measures of nonproscribed prejudice (see Tables 9.6 and 9.9). Why might this be? One possibility is that, whereas higher scores on the intrinsic, end dimension are associated with both knowledge and acceptance of the teachings of one's religious community about right and wrong prejudices, higher scores on the extrinsic, means dimension are associated with knowledge but not acceptance (and possibly rejection) of these teachings.

More importantly, it appears that the association between the intrinsic, end dimension and relatively low prejudice is not a general one; it is limited to prejudices that are clearly proscribed by the respondent's religious community (see Tables 9.3 and 9.4 versus Tables 9.7 and 9.9). Apparently, the intrinsic believer is not generally free from enmity, contempt, and bigotry, as Allport (1966) claimed, but instead is conforming to the "right" tolerances and the "right" prejudices as defined by the formal and informal teachings of his or her religious community.

This suggestion is further supported by the finding in three of the studies summarized in Table 9.7 (Herek, 1987; McFarland, 1989, 1990a) that the positive relation of (1) the intrinsic, end dimension to (2) nonproscribed prejudice may be accounted for by the positive association of both *1* and *2* to devout, orthodox beliefs. To the degree that people value their religion intrinsically, wholeheartedly embracing what is taught, they are more likely to report being tolerant of those their religious community tells them they should tolerate and being intolerant of those the community tells them they should not tolerate. At best, the personal transformation produced by their religion seems circumscribed.

We must, however, question even this circumscribed transformation. The evidence we have reviewed thus far suggests that the extrinsic, means dimension correlates positively with questionnaire measures of a clearly proscribed prejudice, racial prejudice; neither the intrinsic, end dimension nor the quest dimension does. The intrinsic, end dimension shows either no relationship or a weak negative relationship to questionnaire measures of racial prejudice; the quest dimension shows a weak-to-moderate negative relationship. But does the tolerance reported on these racial prejudice questionnaires reflect an internalization of the values of the religious community, or only presentation of oneself as exemplifying these values (Jones & Pittman, 1982)? To answer this question, it is necessary to move beyond overt, questionnaire assessment of racial prejudice to examine the relation of the three religious dimensions to racial prejudice using more covert, behavioral measures. This is the second strategy used to take a new look at the religion-prejudice relationship.

Covert, Behavioral Measurement of Racial Prejudice

Assessing prejudice through the use of behavioral measures is almost always more difficult and more time-consuming than administering a prejudice questionnaire. But behavioral measures can have two important advantages. First, the response required can be made more costly to the respondent; second, the relevance of the response to prejudice can often be masked, making the measurement unobtrusive, or covert.

If, for example, I state on a questionnaire that race would make no difference in my choice of a roommate, I need not fear that the statement will actually affect my roommate assignment. The statement carries no behavioral consequences, and so no cost. But what if I make the same statement on an application form from the housing office? Now it carries behavioral consequences and cost.

Not surprisingly, people's responses differ dramatically in these two situations, as Silverman (1974) cleverly demonstrated. He found that white incoming college freshmen reported little concern about the race of their future roommate on an attitude questionnaire; they seemed quite colorblind. But other incoming freshmen from the same group, responding to the same question on a housing office application, reported a definite preference for a white rather than a black roommate. This experiment is one of those clearly demonstrating the importance of moving beyond exclusive reliance on cost-free questionnaire measures of proscribed prejudice.

In Silverman's (1974) experiment, not only did the application form involve potential cost, but it also provided an unobtrusive measure; respondents thought their housing assignment, not prejudice, was at issue. Costs may at times override the motivation to present oneself in a socially desirable light even on obtrusive behavioral measures, but it is preferable to make the measures unobtrusive, or covert (Crosby et al., 1980). With a little imagination, this can usually be done.

Over the past two decades, development of covert, behavioral measures has been one of the major contributions of social psychology to the study of prejudice (see Gaertner & Dovidio, 1986, for a number of examples). Unfortunately, this strategy has rarely been employed in studies of the religion-prejudice relationship. We know of only three studies that have examined the relationship between one or more of the religious dimensions and prejudice using covert, behavioral measures. All three studies focus on racial prejudice.

When integration comes: Brannon (1970). Robert Brannon (1970) administered the Extrinsic and Intrinsic scales to eighty-one white members of a small Protestant church in the southern United States. The church had recently decided to racially integrate, and, as an index of prejudice, Brannon noted whether each individual remained a member of the now-integrated church, showing racial tolerance, or left to join a new, splinter church that vowed to remain segregated. Brannon reported that those who remained with the old church scored significantly higher on the Intrinsic scale and significantly lower on the Extrinsic scale than did those who left, suggesting that the intrinsic, end dimension was negatively associated and the extrinsic, means dimension positively associated with racial prejudice, assessed behaviorally.

Unfortunately, there was an important confound in this study that clouds interpretation of the results. As previously noted, scores on the Intrinsic scale tend to be associated with greater overall religious activity, including church involvement. It is possible that the more intrinsic members stayed with the old church because of this attachment, not because they were more racially tolerant. To disentangle this confound, one would need to compare Brannon's results with results in a situation in which the old church remained segregated and the new splinter church integrated. As far as we know, this comparison has never been made.

Selecting an interviewer: Batson, Naifeh, and Pate (1978). Adapting Silverman's (1974) strategy for covert, behavioral assessment of prejudice, Batson, Naifeh, and Pate (1978) placed fifty-one white undergraduates with at least a moderate interest in religion in a situation where their expressed readiness to interact with a black individual would have behavioral consequences. This was done by telling the undergraduates that later in the study they would be interviewed in depth about their religious views. The undergraduates were given the opportunity to indicate how much they would like each of the available interviewers to interview them. As a basis for their judgment, they were provided information sheets describing each interviewer. Though differing in particulars, each sheet described a well-rounded college graduate, interested in religion, who had grown up in a middle-class Protestant church (Congregational, Lutheran, Methodist, or Presbyterian). Clipped to each information sheet was a photograph. The photographs revealed that one interviewer was white, the other black.

Interviewers were always the same sex as the undergraduate, were nicely dressed and groomed, and had a friendly smile. In order to equalize information about interviewers other than race, information sheets and photographs were counterbalanced. The photograph of the black interviewer was clipped to one information sheet for some undergraduates; it was clipped to a different sheet for others. In addition, photographs of two different individuals were used in each condition. Some male undergraduates saw one black male; some saw another black male, and so on. This was done to ensure that differences across conditions were not the result of idiosyncratic characteristics of particular individuals.

After reading the information sheets, the undergraduates were asked to rate how much they would like each interviewer to interview them. A difference score was created by subtracting the rating of the black interviewer from the rating of the white. Relative preference for the white over the black interviewer on this difference score reflected a preference to interact with one person rather than another solely on the basis of race, providing an index of racial prejudice.

To permit direct comparison of results using this behavioral measure with results using a questionnaire measure of prejudice, Batson et al. (1978) also administered the racial prejudice questionnaire used by Allport and Ross (1967); a sample item from this questionnaire was presented in Table 9.5 (Item 1). Finally, the three dimensions of individual religion were assessed using the six religious orientation scales familiar to you from Chapter 6.

Results of this study are summarized in Table 9.10. As you can see, cor-

Table 9.10 Association between dimensions of personal religion and overt versus covert measures of racial prejudice

	Measure of racial prejudice	
Dimension of personal religion	Overt (questionnaire)	Covert (interview preference)
Extrinsic, means	.18	.17
Intrinsic, end	−.35*	.26
Quest	−.34*	−.16

Source: Adapted from Batson, Naifeh, and Pate (1978).
*$p < .05$, two-tailed.

relations between the religious dimensions and the questionnaire measure of racial prejudice were much as in previous research. The correlation for the extrinsic, means dimension was low positive ($r = .18$, ns); the correlations for the intrinsic, end dimension and quest dimension were both negative ($rs = -.35$ and $-.34$, $ps < .05$).

For the extrinsic, means dimension and for the quest dimension, the correlations with racial prejudice using the behavioral measure did not differ from those using the questionnaire measure. But for the intrinsic, end dimension, there was a clear difference. Using the behavioral measure, the correlation with racial prejudice became significantly more positive ($r = .26$; $z = 3.21$, $p < .005$).

These results were consistent with the suggestion that the intrinsic, end dimension is associated more with a desire to avoid *appearing* racially prejudiced than with a genuine reduction of prejudice. Using the overt, questionnaire measure, this dimension had a significant negative association with racial prejudice; using the covert, behavioral measure, however, the association was nonsignificantly positive. Only the quest dimension appeared to be associated with a genuine reduction of prejudice; it was negatively associated with both the overt and covert measures of prejudice, although the latter association was weak.

Choosing with whom to sit: Batson, Flink, Schoenrade, Fultz, and Pych (1986). Snyder, Kleck, Strenta, and Mentzer (1979) introduced a new technique known as *attributional ambiguity* for detecting prejudicial attitudes that people wish to conceal. They demonstrated the usefulness of this technique in two studies assessing prejudice against the physically handicapped. In each study, participants chose where they would sit to watch a movie: either with a handicapped person or with a nonhandicapped person. In the low-attributional–ambiguity condition, participants had been told that the same movie was being shown in both locations; in the high-attributional–ambiguity condition, they had been told that the movies were different. Snyder et al. (1979) found, as they had predicted, that people avoided a handicapped person more often if the decision to do so was also a decision between two different movies, allowing the avoidance to masquerade as a movie preference.

Batson, Flink, Schoenrade, Fultz, and Pych (1986) used this attributional-ambiguity technique to assess the religion-prejudice relationship. They had forty-four white undergraduates with at least a moderate interest in religion first complete a battery of questionnaires, including the Extrinsic, Intrinsic, and Quest scales. At a later experimental session, these undergraduates participated individually in what was ostensibly a study of factors that affect liking for movies. As part of this study, they were given a choice of whether to watch a movie being shown in "Theater A" or "Theater B." There was already a person (a confederate the same sex as the subject) sitting in each theater; one person was black, the other white. Choosing to sit in the theater with the white person rather than the black person was the measure of racial prejudice.

Attributional ambiguity for the seating choice was manipulated by varying whether participants had been told that the movies being shown in the two theaters were the same (overt racial prejudice condition) or different (covert racial prejudice condition). Pairing of confederate with movie, of confederate with theater, of movie with theater, and of theater with side of room were all counterbalanced.

Results of this study are summarized in Table 9.11. As you can see, they are generally consistent with the results of the Batson, Naifeh, and Pate (1978) study. For the extrinsic, means dimension, there was no reliable correlation with preference for sitting with the white person in either condition. For the intrinsic, end dimension, the correlation with choosing to sit with the white person was significantly negative in the overt condition ($r = -.52$, $p < .05$) but near zero in the covert condition ($r = -.08$). For the quest dimension, the correlation was near zero in the overt condition ($r = -.10$) and significantly negative in the covert condtiion ($r = -.45$, $p < .05$).

As in the Batson, Naifeh, and Pate (1978) study, then, the intrinsic, end dimension correlated negatively with an overt measure of racial prejudice. But this significant negative correlation disappeared when the measure was covert, when choosing to sit with the white person could masquerade as a movie preference. The pattern of behavior associated with devout, intrinsic religion in these two studies is strikingly reminiscent of what Gaertner and Dovidio (1986) have called "aversive racism"; that is, the pattern suggests a concern on the part of the intrinsically religious not to be seen by others, or by themselves, as prejudiced, although "the underlying negative portions of their attitudes are expressed, but in subtle, rationalizable ways" (Gaertner & Dovidio, 1986, p. 62).

Only the quest dimension had a significant negative correlation with the covert measure of prejudice in this study. To check the pattern of choices underlying this negative correlation, Batson et al. (1986) performed median splits on the Quest scale in each attributional-ambiguity condition. Among

Table 9.11 Association between dimensions of personal religion and overt versus covert measures of racial prejudice

	Measure of racial prejudice	
Dimension of personal religion	Overt (same movie)	Covert (different movie)
Extrinsic, means	−.21	−.01
Intrinsic, end	−.52*	−.08
Quest	−.10	−.45*

Source: Adapted from Batson et al. (1986).
Note: Because of the somewhat atypical component structure found in this study, results are reported for the Extrinsic, Intrinsic, and Quest scales, rather than for the Means, End, and Quest components.
*$p < .05$, two-tailed.

participants scoring above the median, the proportions of participants choosing to sit with the white person were .44 and .46 in the overt and covert prejudice conditions, respectively; among participants scoring below the median, the proportions were .75 and .71. Thus, high scorers on the quest dimension showed no preference for black or white persons in either condition, whereas low scorers showed a preference for sitting with the white person ($z = 2.13, p < .04$; observed proportions tested for difference from .50 across experimental conditions).

Similar median splits on the Intrinsic scale revealed that, among participants scoring above the median, the proportions choosing to sit with the white person were .25 and .54 in the overt and covert prejudice conditions, respectively; among participants scoring below the median, the proportions were .89 and .64. Thus, high-intrinsic participants showed a preference for sitting with the black person in the overt condition, in which choice to sit with the white person might appear prejudicial, but not in the covert condition.

Although this pattern of proportions is quite consistent with the suggestion that high scorers on the Intrinsic scale are concerned not to appear prejudiced, it is also consistent with a quite different explanation, suggested by Richard Gorsuch (personal communication, November 1983). Perhaps high-intrinsic participants in the overt condition chose to sit with the black person out of (1) a heightened sensitivity for his or her feelings and (2) a desire to witness to the experimenter about the value of black people. Because of the attributional ambiguity in the covert condition, high-intrinsic participants in that condition may not have been as concerned about what their seating choice would indicate to others about the value of black people. In that condition these participants could express their own feelings, which were quite without prejudice, leading them to show no clear preference for either black or white persons.

This "affirmative-action" alternative explanation seems to fit nicely the responses of the high-intrinsic participants in the study, but it does not seem to fit the responses of the high-intrinsic participants in the previous study by Batson, Naifeh, and Pate (1978). The procedure of that study should have provided participants an opportunity to witness for affirmative action by indicating a preference for being interviewed by a black person. Yet in that study, higher scorers on the Intrinsic scale were no less likely to show a preference for being interviewed by a white person than were low scorers; indeed, they were slightly *more* likely to do so. Nor does it seem possible to reconcile this affirmative-action explanation with the evidence summarized in Table 9.7, indicating that the intrinsic, end dimension correlates positively with prejudices that are not proscribed by the religious community.

These observations illustrate a general principle about the relationship between empirical data and explanation in science. Ruling out alternative explanations is a major reason for testing the same predictions in different studies using different procedures; all studies in which the predictions have been tested should be considered as a set, not in isolation from one another.

When the affirmative-action explanation is viewed in this context, its truth seems doubtful.

SUMMARY AND CONCLUSION

Does religion promote universal love and acceptance, allowing the faithful to see all others, no matter how alien, as brothers and sisters? Or does it promote intolerance, prejudice, and bigotry? We have traveled a long and winding path in our pursuit of an answer to these questions, but we believe that we have gotten somewhere. First, we found much research suggesting a positive correlation between being religious and being prejudiced. Then we found much research suggesting that this was only true for those persons who use their religion as an extrinsic means to self-serving ends. Among religious individuals, those who orient to religion as an intrinsic end in itself almost invariably score lower on questionnaire measures of proscribed prejudice (e.g., racial prejudice) than do the extrinsically religious, although the intrinsically religious rarely score lower on these measures than nonreligious individuals. In sum, neither of these two religious dimensions appears to promote tolerance and acceptance. But at least the devout, sincere belief of high scorers on the intrinsic, end dimension does not appear to be a stimulant of prejudice.

Although these results have led to a more comforting revised conclusion concerning the relationship between religion and prejudice, we expressed doubts. In virtually every study of the relationship between religion and proscribed prejudice, prejudice has been measured by self-report questionnaires. Measuring prejudice in this way opens the door wide for individuals who wish to present themselves as unprejudiced to do so. And there is reason to suspect that individuals scoring high on measures of intrinsic, end religion might wish to do so.

The few studies to date that have attempted to avoid this self-presentation problem, by either (1) assessing forms of prejudice that are not proscribed by respondents' religious community or (2) using covert, behavioral measures of prejudice, suggest a *revised* revised conclusion: *The extrinsic, means dimension is related to increased prejudice, but only when prejudice is proscribed. The quest dimension is related to decreased prejudice, both proscribed and not. The intrinsic, end dimension is related to the appearance of relatively low proscribed prejudice, but only the appearance. It is related to increased prejudice when the prejudice is not proscribed by the religious community.* This is a far more complex answer than we were seeking when we first asked whether religion discourages or encourages intolerance, prejudice, and bigotry; it is, however, the answer to which we believe the existing evidence points. Of course, future research may cause us to rethink matters yet again.

In the interim, we must take issue with earlier reviews (e.g., Donahue, 1985; Gorsuch, 1988; Gorsuch & Aleshire, 1974) and caution against concluding that intrinsic religion is an antidote for prejudice. We find it remarkable that this conclusion persists in the face of the evidence we have reviewed, yet persist it does. We believe the evidence indicates that the devout, sincere belief of the intrinsically religious changes the manifestation of prejudice, making it more covert. But prejudice remains, appearing in subtle ways reminiscent of the "aversive racism" described by Gaertner and Dovidio (1986).

Our interpretation of the intrinsic religion–prejudice relationship may, however, be too pessimistic. Patricia Devine (1989) has recently proposed a "dissociation model of prejudice" that suggests a more optimistic interpretation of the evidence we have reviewed concerning the relationship of devout, intrinsic religion to racial prejudice. Perhaps, stimulated by their religious beliefs and role models, the intrinsically religious are in the process of being resocialized away from prejudice, but the resocialization or dissociation process is not complete. Like trying to break a bad habit, they slip back into their old ways when their new, unprejudicial thoughts and behaviors are not consciously activated by salient cues (such as being asked to complete a prejudice questionnaire or act in a way that might appear overtly prejudicial). If this interpretation is correct, then increasing the salience of the antiprejudice norm of the religious community—consciousness-raising—may lead to reduced prejudice by the more intrinsically religious even in covert behavior, not just on questionnaires.

Once again, we have doubts. This dissociation analysis rests on the assumption that the norm of the religious community is to eschew prejudice and discrimination, that the religious community teaches—to paraphrase McConahay (1986)—"The truly religious can't be racists and racists can't be truly religious." We wonder whether this is the norm. True, every major religion teaches tolerance, and every major denomination is on record opposing racial prejudice and discrimination. Yet we have doubts about the norm when we see a headline that reads, "Sunday morning at 11 remains most segregated hour of week" (*Atlanta Constitutuion,* August 9, 1987). We suspect that in many cases the intrinsic believer, attending to the practice of the religious community as well as to the preaching, is being resocialized to a very different, more hypocritical norm: "The truly religious can't *look* racist." If so, then perhaps the resocialization process is complete. And even if it is not, increased salience of the norm will not reduce subtle, covert prejudice.

The possibility that the open-ended, quest dimension actually is associated with reduced prejudice seems more promising. This dimension generally correlates negatively with measures of both proscribed and nonproscribed prejudice, especially when prejudice is measured covertly. It remains unclear at this point, however, whether the quest dimension should get causal credit for its association with reduced prejudice or vice versa, or whether high quest scores and reduced prejudice are both expressions of a general personal disposition toward openness and tolerance. Until we have an answer to this question, it seems premature to suggest that the quest dimension is a *source* of increased acceptance and tolerance. It may only be a symptom.

10

Concern for Others or Self-Concern?

Some version of the Golden Rule, "Do unto others as you would have others do unto you," is known in all major religions, East and West. The faithful are admonished to love neighbor as self. And who is your neighbor?

> Jesus replied, "A man was going down from Jerusalem to Jericho, and fell into the hands of robbers, who stripped him, beat him, and went away, leaving him half dead. Now by chance a priest was going down that road; and when he saw him, he passed by on the other side. So likewise a Levite, when he came to the place and saw him, passed by on the other side. But a Samaritan while traveling came near him; and when he saw him, he was moved with pity. He went to him and bandaged his wounds, having poured oil and wine on them. Then he put him on his own animal, brought him to an inn, and took care of him. The next day he took out two denarii, gave them to the innkeeper, and said, 'Take care of him; and when I come back, I will repay

> you whatever more you spend.' Which of these three, do you think, was a neighbor to the man who fell into the hands of the robbers?" (Luke 10:30–36 NRSV)

The answer is obvious.

There are even frequent admonitions to extend the scope of concern for others beyond strangers in need to enemies as well: "Love your enemies, and do good to those who hate you. . . . If you love those who love you, what credit is that to you? For even sinners love those who love them . . ." (Luke 6:27, 32 NRSV). Similarly, the Buddhist is taught in the *Sutta Nipata:*

> Just as with her own life
> a mother shields from hurt
> her own, her only, child—
> let all-embracing thoughts
> for all that lives be thine,
>
> An all-embracing love
> for all the universe
> in all its heights and depths
> and breadth—unstinted love,
> unmarred by hate within,
> not rousing enmity.

The universal compassion advocated in such teachings is often considered to be a defining feature of world religions, in contrast to tribal religions. In the words of Edwin Burtt (1957):

> A conviction of moral obligation toward all men, simply because they are men, is born. The wall that circumscribed sympathetic feeling and kept it within the tribe is broken down, and the sense of community is encouraged to open out beyond that limit; the idea takes root that we are essentially members of a society embracing all human beings on the same terms and in which therefore all men are brothers. This involves a radical and decisive transcendence of customary morality and of the attitudes which pervade it. (p. 108)

Such an impulse toward universal love is clearly manifest in the lives of deeply religious individuals like Albert Schweitzer, Mahatma Gandhi, Martin Luther King, Jr., and Mother Teresa.

William James speaks of the concern for others evoked by religion in three lectures on "Saintliness" in his *Varieties of Religious Experience* (1902). Among the features of saintliness, common across religious traditions, James lists:

> A shifting of the emotional center towards loving and harmonious affections, towards "yes, yes" and away from "no," where the claims of the non-ego are concerned. . . . The shifting of the emotional center brings . . . increase of charity, tenderness for fellow-creatures. (1902, p. 217)
>
> Religious rapture, moral enthusiasm, ontological wonder, cosmic emotion, are all unifying states of mind, in which the sand and grit of the selfhood incline to disappear, and tenderness to rule. . . . Like love or fear, the faith-

> state is a natural psychic complex, and carries charity with it by organic consequence. (1902, p. 221)

To illustrate, James recounts a Buddhist legend:

> Where the future Buddha, incarnated as a hare, jumps into the fire to cook himself for a meal for a beggar—having previously shaken himself three times, so that none of the insects in his fur should perish with him. (1902, p. 224n)

But as is characteristic of James, his view of religious charity is not one-sided. Along with the virtue, he also sees excesses that leave us asking, what really is going on?

> Francis of Assisi kisses his lepers; Margaret Mary Alacoque, Francis Xavier, St. John of God, and others are said to have cleansed the sores and ulcers of their patients with their respective tongues; and the lives of such saints as Elizabeth of Hungary and Madame de Chantal are full of a sort of reveling in hospital purulence, disagreeable to read of, and which makes us admire and shudder at the same time. (1902, p. 225)

These last examples suggest an interesting, if troubling, possibility. Rather than the religious individual being concerned for others in need, these examples suggest that the religious individual may be self-concerned, concerned to show others, self, and God that he or she is the good, kind, caring—even heroic—person that his or her religion celebrates. Religious charity may be motivated more by concern to put a star in one's own crown than by concern to alleviate the suffering of those in need.

Now, you may ask, what difference does it make why the religious help others in need, as long as they do? The answer is that motives differ radically in their consequences. If my motive for helping others is actually to benefit myself by looking good, then my helping may be relatively insensitive to others' actual needs. On some occasions my help may be just what does the most good, but on other occasions I may engage in dramatic acts of self-sacrifice that may appear very helpful but do very little real good. What is the possible benefit for patients with sores to have them cleansed by my tongue rather than by normal washing? And on still other occasions, I may fail to respond to the needy at all because they or their needs do not fit my conception of how one responds in order to show compassion.

This latter possibility is clearly recognized in the parable of the Good Samaritan. At the same time that the parable extolls the compassion of the neighborly Samaritan, encouraging the faithful to go and do likewise, it condemns the piety of the priest and Levite, suggesting that it was their very religiousness that led them to pass by on the other side. The problem is not that the priest and Levite, or the legendary scribes and Pharisees of whom Jesus was so critical, never helped others in need. The problem is that their helping was limited to situations in which it would be recognized and applauded. They were quite ready to help the right person at the right time. But heaven help someone who had the wrong need at the wrong time, like the man who fell into the hands of robbers on the road from Jerusalem to Jericho. One can imagine the unhelpful priest and Levite looking with disdainful pity on this man; clearly, he was not the sort of riffraff with whom upstanding, moral pillars of the religious community like they should get involved. One can also imagine the priest and Levite among those who, when called to account for their actions, would say, "Lord, when was it that we saw you hungry or thirsty or a stranger or naked or sick or in prison, and did not take care of you?" (Matt. 25:44 NRSV). They would willingly have helped the right person, but they never saw that person in need; all they saw were the poor, lonely, downtrodden, and diseased.

Does religion produce increased concern for others in need and a desire to relieve those needs—altruistic motivation (Batson, 1991)—or does it produce increased self-concern and a desire to meet one's own need to appear good, kind, and caring—egoistic motivation? As was true at the beginning of Chapter 9, the extreme examples we have considered help sharpen the question, but they do not provide a clear answer. Once again, we must turn to empirical evidence if we are to learn how being religious relates to response to the needs of others.

RELATIONSHIP OF RELIGION TO CARING ATTITUDES AND BEHAVIOR

When we turn to the empirical evidence concerning the relationship of religion to caring for others in need, we find there is relatively little of it, far less than the evidence we reviewed in Chapters 8 and 9 concerning the effects of religion on mental health and on intolerance, prejudice, and bigotry. There would seem to be two historical reasons for this. First, early psychologists devoted most of their efforts to trying to understand and overcome problems in living—neurosis, psychosis, learning dysfunctions, and antisocial behavior. This focus on problems and on attempts to alleviate them was, perhaps, natural. When something does not work well it attracts our attention; when it works unusually well we are not likely to notice. Only in the last few decades have psychologists paid much attention to more positive aspects of human behavior, such as going out of one's way to help someone in need.

A second reason for the lack of attention to possible prosocial effects of religion is that many early psychologists shared Freud's negative view of religion; they believed that it had a pernicious influence on the human spirit and that this influence should be exposed. Such a belief led them to look for evidence of negative rather than positive effects of religion, and as the research summarized in the previous two chapters reveals, they had little difficulty finding it. Indeed, the negative evidence was so strong that psychologists more sympathetic to religion found themselves preoccupied with rebutting it; the hypothesis that religion increases concern for others was seldom even entertained. But this seems to be changing.

As we noted in Chapter 2, in his presidential address to the American

Psychological Association Donald Campbell (1975) suggested that religion is important to society because it inculcates more stringent moral standards, leading individuals to think not only of their own needs but also of the needs of others. Campbell was not the first president to suggest such a view. In his Farewell Address in 1797 George Washington declared:

> Religion and morality are indispensable supports. . . . These great pillars of human happiness [are the] firmest props of the duties of men and citizens. . . . A volume could not trace all their connections with private and public felicity. . . . And let us with caution indulge the supposition that morality can be maintained without religion.

There are two steps in the argument proposed by Campbell and Washington: (1) Religion inculcates more stringent moral standards; and (2) as a result, it leads people to act with more concern for others. Such an argument is both plausible and popular, but is it sound? To answer this question, we need to examine the empirical evidence for each step. As in the previous two chapters, we shall present the evidence in summary tables.

Moral Standards and Amount of Religious Involvement

The eleven studies summarized in Table 10.1 suggest that the first step is sound; being more religious does seem to lead a person to adhere to more stringent moral standards. Those who are more involved in religion more strongly espouse values that involve curbing personal desire and benefit in order to benefit others and society at large.

We should, however, note two qualifications on this conclusion. First, in several of the studies summarized in Table 10.1, a distinction is made between personal "sins" such as gambling, drinking, and premarital sex, and social "sins" such as stealing, lying, and cheating. The effect of religion on standards concerning personal sins appears to be considerably strongly than its effects on standards concerning social sins. This may be because the behaviors classed as social sins are generally considered more serious and so are more likely to be condemned by everyone.

The second qualification concerns the nature of the moral standards that the more religious adopt. If we look closely at the results summarized in Table 10.1, an interesting pattern emerges. The study by Eisenberg-Berg and Roth (1980) suggests that young children with religious training give more other-oriented and fewer self-centered reasons for helping. The study by Boehm (1962) suggests that children in religious (Catholic) schools are more sophisticated earlier in their thinking about moral issues than are children in state schools. But the study by Haan, Smith, and Block (1968) suggests that religious young adults are more likely to appeal to the conventional standards of society than to internalized moral principles when justifying their moral decisions.

Relating these three findings to Lawrence Kohlberg's stage model of moral development described in Chapter 3, it appears that religion first

Table 10.1 Summary of research examining the relationship between moral standards and amount of religious involvement

Study	Sample population	Location	Measure of religion	Measure of moral standards	Relationship reported
Gorer (1955)	5000 (approx.) adults, nationwide sample	England	Frequency of church attendance and prayer	Judgment of various actions as immoral	Respondents who were more religious judged more actions wrong and judged them more wrong
Boehm (1962)	110 children (aged 6–9) attending Catholic schools; 112 attending state schools	Brooklyn, New York; Natick, Massachusetts	Attendance at Catholic or state school	Test of use of intent rather than result as basis for moral evaluation	More children in Catholic school distinguished between intent and result, and they did so younger
Middleton and Putney (1962)	554 undergraduates in social science classes	Florida State University; San Jose State College	Self-report of belief in God, frequency of church attendance, and importance of religion	Self-report of feeling of violation of own ethical standards if engaged in personal "sins" (e.g., gambling, smoking, drinking, sex) and social "sins" (e.g., stealing, lying, cheating)	For all 3 measures of religion, more religious were much more likely to view personal sins as violation of their standards and were less likely to report engaging in them; no reliable differences for social sins
Klinger, Albaum, and Hetherington (1964)	72 introductory psychology students	University of Wisconsin	Religious versus economic or political as highest value on Allport, Vernon, and Lindzey Survey of Values	Degree of condemnation of hypothetical parent who intentionally did not report some income in order to use the extra money to send child to college	Respondents whose highest value was religious most opposed the parent's behavior, although they were not significantly more opposed than those whose highest value was economic
Wright and Cox (1967)	2276 sixth form (i.e., secondary school students, aged 16–18)	England	Self-report of orthodoxy of belief and frequency of church attendance	Rating of wrongness of various behaviors (e.g., gambling, drunkenness, smoking, lying, stealing, premarital sex)	Respondents who were more religious adopted stricter moral stance on most behaviors, especially on personal as opposed to social "sins"

Berkowitz and Lutterman (1968)	766 adults	Wisconsin	Church membership; contribution to religious organizations	Score on Berkowitz's Social Responsibility scale	Positive correlation for both measures of religious involvement
Haan, Smith and Block (1968)	Over 900 college students and Peace Corps volunteers	San Francisco Bay area	Religious affiliation; frequency of church attendance	Level of moral reasoning using Kohlberg's stages	Protestant and Catholic respondents were more likely to make moral judgments by appeal to social convention; agnostic, atheist, or areligious respondents were more likely to appeal to internalized principles; more frequent church attendance was associated with more reliance on social convention
Eisenberg-Berg and Roth (1980)	34 middle-class preschool children	Arizona	Parental report of amount of religious training	Style of prosocial moral reasoning	Religious training was positively related to more needs-oriented and less hedonistic moral reasoning ($p < .05$)
Morgan (1983)	1467 adults in national survey	U.S.	Frequency of prayer	Self-reported goodness, friendliness, and cooperativeness	Positive association ($p < .01$)
Woodrum (1988)	378 adults	U.S.	Frequency of church attendance and personal religious activity	Index of conservative moral attitudes (anti abortion, pornography, extramarital sex, and homosexuality; pro prayer in school)	Both religion measures were positively correlated with conservative moral attitudes (rs = .45 and .44, $ps < .0001$)
Cochran and Beeghley (1991)	Over 10,000 adults in national surveys	U.S.	Frequency of church attendance; strength of religious identification	Attitudes toward nonmarital sex (i.e., premarital, extramarital, and homosexual relations)	Religious involvement associated with more negative attitudes toward nonmarital, especially premarital, sex; effects strongest for members of conservative Protestant denominations

stimulates and then inhibits moral thinking. Recall that Kohlberg (1976) argued that appealing to conventional social standards (Level 2 morality) is a more sophisticated way of thinking about moral issues than appealing to self-benefits (Level 1) but less sophisticated than appealing to internalized principles (Level 3). The evidence from Table 10.1—especially the three studies just mentioned—suggests that, although religion may inculcate more stringent moral standards and less self-centered thought about moral issues in the child, by the time the child grows up, these standards may inhibit more sophisticated moral thinking. Religion may facilitate moral development up to the point of adherence to conventional moral standards and then retard development beyond that point.

Helping Behavior and Amount of Religious Involvement

Given that religion appears successful in inculcating more stringent moral standards, what about the second step in the argument? Do the faithful actually practice what they preach; do they show more loving concern for those in need?

The fifteen findings from fourteen studies summarized in Table 10.2 provide data relevant to this question. In each study, some measure of religious involvement was associated with some measure of compassionate helping of those in need. Table 10.2 is divided into two sections. In the first are nine findings from eight studies that employed either respondents' self-reports or ratings of the respondent by someone else to provide a measure of helping. In the second section are six studies that employed behavioral measures. We have separated these two types of studies, because we fear that studies of the first type might be contaminated by a desire for positive self-presentation. Paralleling the effect of desire for positive self-presentation on questionnaire reports of low prejudice discussed in Chapter 9, it seems likely that self-presentation could affect self-reports of high helpfulness because helpfulness is a desirable trait in our society. Even ratings of a person's helpfulness made by someone else appear to be subject to contamination by positive presentation; Dennis Krebs (1970) has noted that people who are rated as more likable and sociable tend also to be rated as more helpful, even when they are not. All of the studies in the second section of Table 10.2 used behavioral measures of helping; three involved a direct request for help, whereas three did not. The latter should be less subject to contamination by self-presentation than the former.

When we look at the results of the studies summarized in Table 10.2, we find a dramatic difference between those in the first and second sections. The nine findings from studies that used self-report or rating measures suggest that there is a positive, if rather weak, correlation between involvement in religion and helpfulness. The more religious are seen by both themselves and others as valuing helpfulness more and as being somewhat more helpful. Typical are the Gallup Poll results presented by Langford and Langford (1974): 58.7 percent of 526 respondents who reported having attended

Table 10.2 Summary of research examining the relationship between helping and amount of religious involvement

Study	Sample population	Location	Measure of religion	Measure of helping	Relationship reported
1. Studies using self-report ratings by self, peer, or researcher to measure helping					
Hartshorne and May (1929)	Children	U.S.	Frequency of church attendance	Various tests of service	Very slight tendency for frequent church attenders to score higher on service
Clark and Warner (1955)	72 well-known community members	Village in upper New York state	Church attendance	Average rating of person's kindness and honesty by 14 community members	Positive correlations for both kindness (r = .41) and honesty (r = .64)
Friedrichs (1960)	280 fraternity members	Columbia University, New York	Frequency of church attendance; belief in God	Rating of altruism by self and by others in fraternity; self-report of helpfulness in response to hypothetical need situations	Both church attendance and belief in God showed low positive correlations with self-report of helpfulness, rs = .20 and .24, $p < .01$, but neither were related to either self or other ratings of altruism
Cline and Richards (1965)	155 adults, male and female (72% Mormons)	Salt Lake City, Utah	Belief in God, religious activity, and importance of religion based on "depth" interview; self-report of religious involvement on questionnaire	Rating by "depth" interviewer as showing "love and compassion" for others and "being a Good Samaritan"	For males and females, belief in God was not related to either helpfulness rating; religious activity, importance of religion, and self-reported involvement were all positively related (rs ranging from .21 to .50)
Rokeach (1969a)	Nationwide survey of 1406 adults	U.S.	Religious affiliation; church attendance	Ranking "helpful" as important personal value	No significant relation with religious affiliation, but significant positive relation with church attendance

Table 10.2 Summary of research examining the relationship between helping and amount of religious involvement (*Continued*)

Study	Sample population	Location	Measure of religion	Measure of helping	Relationship reported
Rokeach (1969a)	298 college students	Michigan	Church attendance; importance of religion	Ranking "helpful" as important personal value	Significant positive relation with both church attendance and importance of religion
Gallup Poll (Sept., 1973; see Langford and Langford, 1974)	Nationwide survey of adults	U.S.	Attending church during previous 7 days	Self-report of "taking concrete action on behalf of others"	59% of those who had attended said that they "almost always" did; only 31% of the nonattenders claimed this
Nelson and Dynes (1976)	482 male adults returning a mail questionnaire	Medium-sized city in southwestern U.S.	Self-report of regular prayer, church attendance, and regular involvement in religion	Self-report of helping through social service agencies	Significant but low positive correlations (most *r*s between .10 and .20); when correlations adjusted for helping *through* church as well as for income and age, they drop to close to 0
Zook, Koshmider, and Zehr (1982)	300 undergraduates at Mennonite colleges	Midwestern U.S.	Religiosity scale assessing religious activity and belief	Self-report of helpfulness and attitudes toward helping	More religious reported more helpfulness and more positive attitude toward helping ($p < .001$)
2. Studies using a behavioral measure of helping					
Forbes, TeVault, and Gromoll (1971)	People in church doorway or parking lot after Sunday morning service	Medium-sized city in midwestern U.S.	Type of church: conservative versus liberal Protestant and Catholic	Mailing an addressed, unstamped "lost letter" dropped in church doorway or parking lot	No differences in rate of return (approximately 40% for each location), but more letters dropped outside conservative churches were returned unstamped with postage due

Smith, Wheeler, and Diener (1975)	402 introductory psychology students	University of Washington, Seattle	Self-report on questionnaire as evangelical, other religious, nonreligious, or atheist	Volunteering 5 hours to work with profoundly retarded child	No reliable differences in rates of volunteering for different groups (overall, 16% volunteered)
Annis (1975)	68 introductory psychology students	Western Carolina University	Religious value score on Allport, Vernon, and Lindzey scale	Attempting to help after hearing a ladder fall, possibly injuring a young woman	No reliable difference between helpers and nonhelpers in religious value score
Annis (1976)	71 introductory psychology students	University of Mississippi	Self-report of orthodoxy, frequency of prayer, and frequency of church attendance; religious value score on Allport, Vernon, and Lindzey scale	Attempting to help after hearing a ladder fall, possibly injuring a young woman	No reliable differences in rate of helping as a result of any of the measures of religious involvement (overall, 48% attempted to help)
McKenna (1976)	Adults in clergy and nonclergy homes who answered telephone	Selected urban and rural settings in U.S.	Clergy versus nonclergy home	Calling garage for stranded female motorist who mistakenly called the home with her last dime	No reliable difference in rate of calling the garage from clergy and nonclergy homes; in the rural setting both rates were very high, so differences may have been obscured
Yinon and Sharon (1985)	53 men and 54 women in upper-middle-class apartment complex	Central Israel	Religious versus secular self-identification	Contribution of money to help a needy family	Religious individuals donated more money than secular individuals ($p < .002$), but difference reliable only when request came from a religious individual

church in the previous seven days said that they "almost always" took concrete action on behalf of others in need, whereas only 31.4 percent of 862 nonattenders said that they did. Statistically, this difference is overwhelmingly significant ($p < .0001$). Yet even though these self-reports suggest a strong desire on the part of the more religious to show greater concern and compassion, you may still wonder whether this desire is reflected in their behavior.

Your doubts appear well founded. For, when we turn to the results of the studies in the second section of Table 10.2, those that control for positive self-presentation by using behavioral measures, we find a very different pattern of results. Only one of the five studies in the second section provides evidence that the more religious are more helpful.[1]

The one positive finding comes from a study by Yinon and Sharon (1985). Among residents of an upper-middle-class apartment complex in central Israel, Yinon and Sharon found that those residents who had previously identified themselves as religious donated more money to help a needy family than did those residents who had previously identified themselves as secular. But this difference was statistically reliable only when the person soliciting the contribution wore a yarmulke, indicating that he was religious. In light of this qualification, Yinon and Sharon (1985) conclude that their results suggest "the behavior of the religious subjects was guided by the need for positive self-presentation" (p. 726). If their conclusion is correct, then the evidence in Table 10.2 seems even more consistent. This evidence strongly suggests that the more religious show no more active concern for others in need than do the less religious. The more religious only present themselves as more concerned.

It seems that the argument that religion promotes increased helping of others in need stumbles and falls on the second step. Although the highly religious have more stringent moral standards, they are no more likely than the less religious to help someone in need. The more religious may *see* themselves as more helpful and caring; they may even be seen this way by others. But when it comes to action, there is no evidence that they are—except when presented with a low-cost, direct request for help under conditions designed to heighten concern for positive self-presentation.

In Chapter 9 we found that increased religious involvement was associ-

1. It is, of course, possible that no effects of religion on helping behavior were observed in these studies because the measures of helping were insensitive to differences. If, for example, a study were designed so that helping was extremely dangerous, almost no one would help, and if no one helped there would be no relationship between helping and any other factor, including religion. Conversely, if a study were designed so that helping was extremely easy, almost everyone would help, and once again there would be no relationship between helping and any other factor. Some reassurance that the helping measures used in these studies were sensitive is provided by two facts. First, the overall helping rate tended to be about 50 percent in most of the studies. Second, each of the helping measures has been used in other studies, and each has proved sensitive to differences in the rate of helping between different groups (see Batson & Weeks, 1991, for a review of other studies of helping behavior).

ated with more rather than less prejudice and discrimination; now we find that it is associated with no real increase in helpfulness. Of course, advocates of religion might point out that the evidence concerning the effects of religion on helping is not as discouraging as the evidence concerning the effects on prejudice; at least the evidence on helping does not show that religious involvement makes a person *less* helpful. But to rejoice at this lack of evidence for a clear detrimental effect would seem to be grasping at straws. There is, however, a more sound reason for not being discouraged by the evidence that involvement in religion does not increase helpfulness.

HELPING BEHAVIOR AND DIMENSIONS OF INDIVIDUAL RELIGION

When considering the effect of religion on prejudice in Chapter 9, we found that the initial conclusion of a positive relationship between amount of religious involvement and prejudice had to be revised because it failed to take account of the different dimensions of religion. That experience should make us cautious about hasty conclusions based on evidence that religious involvement is not associated with increased helping. Any conclusions need to take account of the ways the different dimensions might affect helping. Two such conclusions have been proposed.

First, paralleling his revised conclusion about the effects of the different dimensions on prejudice, Gordon Allport was quite clear about how he thought the extrinsic, means dimension and the intrinsic, end dimension would affect helping. Although extrinsic religion might lead a person to be self-centered, only looking out for Number One, intrinsic religion should lead a person to transcend self-centered needs and display true compassion and universal love. In Allport's own words, intrinsic religion "is oriented toward a unification of being, takes seriously the commandment of brotherhood, and strives to transcend all self-centered needs" (1966, p. 455). Second, paralleling our suggestion at the end of the previous chapter of a *revised* revised conclusion concerning the religion-prejudice relationship, Batson (1976) proposed a very different possibility than Allport; he proposed that the quest dimension relates to increased compassion, whereas the intrinsic, end dimension relates only to the desire to *appear* compassionate.

Which, if either, of these views is correct? Does the intrinsic, end dimension breed Good Samaritans, whose "neighbor" is whoever is in need, or does it breed scribes and Pharisees, who help only when they can make a show of their helpfulness to other people, to themselves, or to God? And what about the quest dimension? To sharpen these questions with a fanciful reflection, if someone had been administering questionnaires on the road from Jerusalem to Jericho, who—if anyone—would have scored unusually high on the intrinsic, end dimension? Who would have scored high on the quest dimension? Would it have been the Good Samaritan, or the priest and Levite? To decide, we must again look at the relevant empirical evidence.

Self-Report Evidence

First, let us look at the results of three studies using self-report measures of concern, compassion, and helpfulness. Tate and Miller (1971) administered Rokeach's (1969a) value survey and Allport and Ross's (1967) Extrinsic and Intrinsic scales to 236 United Methodist adults from three different geographical areas. They found that respondents who were classified as intrinsically religious (i.e., who scored above the mean on the Intrinsic scale and below the mean on the Extrinsic scale) considered the values *helpful, loving,* and *responsible* to be of greater personal importance than did respondents who were classified as extrinsically religious (i.e., who scored above the mean on the Extrinsic scale and below the mean on the Intrinsic scale). For the values *helpful* and *loving* the difference in ranking by the two groups was statistically reliable; for *responsible* it was not.

Watson, Hood, Morris, and Hall (1984) administered the Mehrabian and Epstein Empathy scale, a popular self-report questionnaire assessing general emotional sensitivity to and concern for the needs of others, and the Extrinsic and Intrinsic scales to 180 undergraduates. Scores on the Intrinsic scale correlated positively with scores on the empathy scale ($r = .26, p < .01$); scores on the Extrinsic scale correlated negatively ($r = -.22$, $p < .01$). In a second study, Watson, Hood, and Morris (1985) administered Davis's Interpersonal Reactivity Index (IRI), a more recent self-report empathy questionnaire designed as an improvement on the Mehrabian and Epstein scale, to 215 undergraduates. They also administered Maranell's Christian Altruism scale, a self-report questionnaire of the degree to which a person shows unselfish concern for the welfare of others. Finally, they administered all six of the religious orientation scales recommended in Chapter 6 as measures of the means, end, and quest dimensions. Scores on the Intrinsic scale correlated positively with scores on Davis's Empathic Concern scale ($r = .31, p < .001$) and the Christian Altruism scale ($r = .51$, $p < .001$). Scores on the Extrinsic scale correlated negatively with scores on the Empathic Concern scale ($r = -.24$, $p < .001$) and were not reliably related to scores on the Christian Altruism scale. Scores on the Quest scale were not reliably related to scores on either the Empathic Concern or Christian Altruism scales. Correlations for the End, Means, and Quest components were quite similar to the correlations for the Intrinsic, Extrinsic, and Quest scales, respectively.

If scores on these self-report measures of helpful values, empathic concern, and selfless altruism can be taken as valid indices of a person's concern for others in need, then the results of these three studies argue persuasively for Allport's view of the effect on helping others of the different religious dimensions. The more intrinsically religious claim that they place high value on being helpful and loving, that they feel more compassion for others in need, and that they show more selfless concern for the welfare of others; the more extrinsically religious are less likely to make these claims. Individuals scoring relatively high on the quest dimension do not report more (or less) compassion than individuals scoring low.

If, however, scores on these self-report measures indicate how respondents would like to be seen by self and others, rather than how they actually are, then these results do not support Allport's view. Instead, they are entirely consistent with Batson's (1976) suggestion that the intrinsic, end dimension is associated with an increased desire to *appear* compassionate, whereas the quest dimension is not.

By themselves, then, these self-reports are consistent with either of the competing views. Clearly, we need to move beyond self-report measures to consider how the different religious dimensions relate to actual helping behavior. If we find that any of the dimensions relate to helping behavior, then we shall need to take our analysis a step further to consider whether this behavior is motivated by concern for the welfare of the person in need or by the helper's self-concern to appear kind and caring.

Behavioral Evidence

Martin Bolt (1982) reported two studies in which scores on the Allport and Ross (1967) Extrinsic and Intrinsic scales were correlated with the amount of help offered in response to specific requests. Bolt included no measure of the quest dimension in these studies. In Study 1, two different requests for help were made during the course of the semester to 124 students in an introductory psychology class at Calvin College in Michigan. The first request was for volunteers to record the required course readings on audiotape for blind students who might enroll in the course in the future. The second was for volunteers to serve as uncompensated participants in psychology department research during the next semester. Scores on the Intrinsic scale had low but statistically significant positive correlations with volunteering in response to these requests ($rs = .23$ and $.29$, $ps < .01$). Scores on the Extrinsic scale had low but significant negative correlations ($rs = -.24$ and $-.25$, $ps < .01$).

In Study 2, fifty-two introductory psychology students were asked to complete a brief survey to help an upper-level psychology major finish a research project for another course. Once again, scores on the Intrinsic scale correlated positively with agreeing to help ($r = .29$, $p < .05$); scores on the Extrinsic scale correlated negatively ($r = -.30$, $p < .05$).

Results of these two studies indicate that intrinsic religion does indeed correlate positively with actual helping behavior, not just with self-reports. Extrinsic religion, on the other hand, correlates negatively. These findings enable us to ask about motivation: Why do the more intrinsically religious help more? Is it out of increased concern for the welfare of those in need, as the more intrinsically religious claim? Or is it out of increased self-concern to present themselves as kind, caring people?

Helping in Bolt's two studies involved a relatively low-cost response to a direct request from a relatively high-status person. This kind of help certainly could be the result of concern for those in need, but it could also be the result of a desire to gain the pat on the back or warm feeling inside that comes from showing oneself to be a kind, caring person. Allport's view predicts the former; Batson's view predicts the latter. Batson's view predicts that it is the quest dimension, not the intrinsic, end dimension, that is associated with greater concern for others in need. How can we know which, if either, of these two views is right? Obviously, it is not easy, but there is some relevant evidence from a series of six rather complex studies that assess the nature of the motivation to help associated with the different dimensions of individual religion.

NATURE OF THE MOTIVATION TO HELP ASSOCIATED WITH THE DIFFERENT DIMENSIONS OF INDIVIDUAL RELIGION

The first three of these studies assess whether helping associated with the different religious dimensions is a response to the expressed needs of the suffering individual or to a personal need to appear helpful. The last three studies more explicitly explore the degree to which this helping is motivated by concern for the person in need—altruistic motivation—or by self-concern.

Responding to the Victim's Needs or to One's Own Needs?

From Jerusalem to Jericho: Darley and Batson. The first study was conducted by Darley and Batson (1973). In it, sixty-seven Princeton Theological Seminary students completed the six religious orientation scales used to measure the means, end, and quest dimensions. Subsequently, forty of these seminarians participated in an experiment in which they were confronted with a young man in possible need. The need situation was modeled after the one in the parable of the Good Samaritan; the young man was somewhat shabbily dressed and was slumped, coughing and groaning, in a doorway in an alley through which each of the seminarians passed. For each seminarian, both whether he offered the young man help, and, if so, the kind of help he offered was recorded.

Sixteen (40 percent) of the forty seminarians stopped to offer aid. None of the three religious dimensions predicted who would stop. Only a situational factor, the degree to which the seminarians were in a hurry, was a significant predictor.

Among those who did stop, however, the dimensions of religion seemed to have an effect on the *kind* of help offered. A coding of kinds of helping had been developed in advance. But, at the suggestion of the confederate acting the part of the young man in distress, a category had been added. This category included helpers who persisted with efforts to help even after receiving assurances from the young man that he was all right, that he had already taken medication, that he just needed to rest for a few minutes, and, finally, that he wished to be left alone. (The young man had been instructed to provide these assurances because another seminarian was being sent into the alley every fifteen minutes, and the young man needed to return to his position to be ready.)

When helping responses were dichotomized between this added category and all less persistent forms of helping, an interesting pattern emerged. The intrinsic, end dimension correlated positively with this persistent helping ($r = .43, p < .12$), whereas the quest dimension correlated negatively ($r = -.54, p < .05$). The difference between these two correlations was highly significant ($p < .01$).

What did the persistent form of helping mean? Darley and Batson suggested that it seemed to be a response more to the helper's own personal need to be helpful than to the expressed needs of the young man. When the more devout, intrinsically religious seminarians encountered the young man in possible need, it seemed to trigger a preprogrammed response (e.g., taking him for coffee, to the infirmary, or praying for his welfare), and this response was little modified by his statements about his needs. In contrast, the tentative helping associated with higher scores on the quest dimension seemed more attuned to the young man's statement that he was all right and, ultimately, wished to be left alone. It seemed less a response to a personal need to be helpful and more to the expressed needs of the young man.

But, as Darley and Batson were aware, this interpretation of their results was entirely after the fact. Perhaps, as some other researchers have suggested (e.g., Gorsuch, 1988; Watson, Hood, & Morris, 1985), the more persistent help associated with the intrinsic, end dimension reflected more genuine caring and concern, whereas the tentative forms of help associated with the quest dimension reflected relatively weak caring. Perhaps at the first obstacle those scoring relatively high on the quest dimension abandoned their halfhearted efforts to help, whereas those scoring high on the intrinsic, end dimension persevered. Clearly, we need more evidence.

Perception of need in Elmdale: Batson. Batson (1976) reported a small study that provided some additional evidence consistent with Darley and Batson's interpretation of their results. This study included male Princeton University undergraduates involved in two campus organizations with different religious orientations—eight from an evangelical group that scored high on the intrinsic, end dimension and seven from a social service organization that scored high on the quest dimension. As noted in Chapter 6, these samples were used to validate the distinction between the end and quest dimensions.

After the validation study, each of these fifteen undergraduates participated in an experiment designed to assess the degree to which they were willing to accept the expressed need of a person seeking help as the person's true need. In the experiment, each undergraduate was asked to adopt the hypothetical role of a lay referral counselor in a voluntary referral agency in a town called Elmdale. Then each was given background information and heard a tape recording of excerpts from the referral interview for six male clients. In their interviews all six clients said that they felt their social situation was the source of the problem, and they expressed hope that something could be done to change the situation. After hearing each client discuss his problem, the undergraduates were asked to fill out a referral form on which they indicated where they thought the client's problem lay, with the client as a person or with his social situation.

Paralleling Darley and Batson's (1973) results, the quest dimension correlated significantly more positively ($p < .05$) with a situational perception of clients' problems ($r = .36$), the perception that the clients themselves expressed, than did the intrinsic, end dimension ($r = -.19$). In interpreting the results of this study, it should be emphasized that the undergraduates were not called on to provide any actual help. So, although the results were generally consistent with the suggestion of Darley and Batson that the quest dimension is associated with more sensitivity to the expressed needs of persons seeking help, whereas the intrinsic, end dimension is not, the results were far from conclusive.

Help that is or is not wanted: Batson and Gray. Somewhat clearer evidence comes from a quasi-experimental study by Batson and Gray (1981). In this study, sixty female undergraduates at the University of Kansas were confronted with a lonely young woman who said either that she wanted help or that she did not. Batson and Gray reasoned that attempts to help the young woman when she said that she did not want it would indicate helping that was a response to a personal need to be helpful rather than to the young woman's expressed need.

The research was introduced to participants as a study of how one person forms an initial impression of another. Each participant was led to believe that she would be getting acquainted with another female undergraduate, Janet Armstrong, by exchanging three notes. After exchanging the notes, the participant would be asked to report her impression of Janet, whom she would never see. In fact, Janet was a fictitious person and her notes, written in advance, were designed to present her as a person suffering from loneliness.

In her first note, Janet hinted that she had found it difficult to adjust to college life, especially since she was so far from her home in Camden, Ohio. In her second note, Janet confessed that she was extremely lonely; she concluded the note by saying, "I'll bet there are some days when I don't say more than a couple dozen words to anybody. Really, I guess I've shared more with you in these two notes than with anyone else since I've been here."

In her third note, Janet went on to observe that it might help if she knew someone with whom she could get together and talk. In the help-wanted condition she said:

> I've often thought, if I could just look forward to getting together with someone—not for anything special, just coffee or a movie or something. That would sure make things better. Sitting here, I've even wondered if you'd be willing to get together a couple of times over the next few weeks.

In the help-not-wanted condition the note included this same passage, but it was followed immediately by an expression of desire to work through the problem on her own:

> . . . But then I thought that that would be a cop out. I think what I really need is to get my own head straight about being alone in a new place. If I don't deal with this problem on my own now, I'll just have to face it again later.

The note each participant wrote in response to Janet's third note provided the measure of helping. If it included an explicit attempt to get together with Janet (e.g., "As soon as this study is over, why don't you wait for me by the elevator?"), it was considered a helping response. If it did not include any explicit attempt to get together, it was considered not helping.

Data were also collected on participants' self-report ratings of their own helpfulness and concern for others. This was done by having each participant complete a self-perception questionnaire before the get-acquainted conversation began. Consistent with the results of other studies using self-report measures, it was expected that scores on the intrinsic, end dimension would correlate positively with self-reported helpfulness and concern, whereas scores on the quest dimension would not.

The results of this study were quite consistent with Darley and Batson's (1973) suggestion that the helping associated with the intrinsic, end dimension is motivated by a personal need to be helpful, whereas the helping associated with the quest dimension is motivated by a desire to relieve the expressed needs of the other person. First consider the self-reports. Across all participants, scores on the intrinsic, end dimension were positively correlated with self-reports of greater helpfulness ($r = .28, p < .05$) and concern ($r = .35, p < .01$), suggesting a desire to be helpful, or at least to appear helpful. Scores on the quest dimension did not correlate reliably with these self-reports.

Turning to helping behavior, a very different pattern appeared, as can be seen from the summary correlations presented in Table 10.3. Scores on the extrinsic, means dimension were unrelated to helping when Janet wanted help and were negatively related to helping when she did not. Scores on the intrinsic, end dimension were moderately positively related to helping in both experimental conditions. Pooled across conditions, this association was statistically reliable ($r = .27, p < .02$). It seems, then, that this dimension was associated with an inclination to help in response to Janet's appeal, but the association was just as strong when Janet said that she did not want help as when she said that she did. This is the pattern of correlations expected if the motivation for helping was to meet a personal need to be helpful rather than to meet Janet's expressed needs. In contrast, scores on the quest dimension were positively associated with helping when Janet

Table 10.3 Association between dimensions of personal religion and helping when help is wanted or not wanted

Dimension of personal religion	Victim's desire regarding help: Help wanted	Help not wanted	z-score testing difference in correlations in the conditions
Extrinsic, means	−.00	−.38**	1.47
Intrinsic, end	.24	.27	−.08
Quest	.37**	−.32*	2.69***

Source: Adapted from Batson and Gray (1981).
Note: $n = 30$ for each experimental condition.
*$p < .05$, one-tailed; **$p < .025$, one-tailed; ***$p < .01$, one-tailed.

said that she wanted help ($r = .37, p < .05$) but negatively associated when she said that she did not ($r = -.32, p < .09$). The difference between these correlations was highly significant ($p < .01$), suggesting motivation to respond to Janet's expressed needs.[2]

Motivated by Concern for Others or Self-Concern?

Three recent studies have sought to move beyond the issue of response to the victim's expressed needs in order to examine more directly the nature of the motivation to help associated with each of the three dimensions of individual religion. Is the motivation altruistic or egoistic?

Volunteering but not qualifying to help: Batson et al. (Study 1). Two of these studies were reported by Batson, Oleson, Weeks, Healy, Reeves, Jen-

2. Reviewing the evidence from the studies by Darley and Batson (1973), Batson (1976), and Batson and Gray (1981), Gorsuch (1988) has suggested that this evidence should be dismissed:

> Batson heavily weights [the] *lack* of a statistically significant relationship between aggregated religious scores [the religious orientation questionnaires] and a specific behavior. However, given the aggregation principle . . . , we must reconsider those studies. One seldom finds that any aggregated variable relates to an individual behavior, because the level of aggregation is inappropriate. Hence all studies comparing a religiousness scale to an individual behavior must be discounted, and cannot be used to suggest that the intrinsically motivated person says one thing and lives another. (p. 214)

What is one to think of Gorsuch's suggestion? It is true that the association of an aggregated questionnaire measure with an individual behavior—such as helping in a particular situation—is likely to be lower than the association with an aggregate behavior. This is the aggregation principle to which Gorsuch refers. Yet we can only assume that when he invoked this principle as a basis for dismissing studies assessing the relationship between the different dimensions of personal religion and helping behavior, either Gorsuch had not looked carefully at the results of those studies or he confused those studies with the studies examining the relationship

nings, and Brown (1989). In the first, undergraduate participants were provided with an opportunity to help under conditions in which, even if they volunteered to help, they would be allowed to do so only if they met a certain performance standard on a qualifying task.

How might introducing a qualifying task disentangle possible motives for helping? An example illustrates the logic. Imagine a young man who wants to appear helpful by volunteering to serve as a bone-marrow donor but who also wants to avoid the discomfort of this rather painful procedure. He should be relieved and quite content if, after having volunteered, a blood-type mismatch disqualifies him as a possible donor. He has displayed his helpfulness because, after all, "It's the thought that counts." Better yet, he has done so without incurring the cost of helping. If, however, this young man is motivated by concern for the other's welfare, the blood-type mismatch should not cause relief and contentment but disappointment; it prevents him from meeting the other's need.

In the bone-marrow example, qualifying to help is entirely out of the potential helper's control; blood types either match or they do not. But now imagine a slightly different situation in which, rather than potential helpers simply learning that they are or are not eligible, they learn that they must perform a task requiring effort in order to qualify to help. In such a situation, how hard a potential helper tries on the qualifying task should give us a basis for inferring whether he or she is motivated by concern for the other's welfare (which requires qualifying) or by concern to appear kind, caring, and helpful (which does not). This should be true, however, only when the qualifying standard is difficult enough that failure can be attributed to the task and not to lack of effort. When the qualifying standard is easy, a person cannot appear helpful without qualifying.

Building on this logic, if the intrinsic, end dimension is associated with motivation to help based on concern for the other's welfare, as Allport claimed, then when the qualifying standard is easy, there might be no rela-

---

between amount of religious involvement and helping behavior (summarized in the second section of Table 10.2). For, in his criticism and dismissal Gorsuch ignores the fact that in each study assessing the relationship of the religious dimensions to helping (but not in the ones in the second section of Table 10.2) there *are* statistically significant relationships between the measures of one or more of the religious dimensions and the individual behavior in question: the kind of helping, the perception of need, or helping that is desired or undesired. Moreover, Gorsuch ignores the evidence of difference in the direction of the relationships for the different dimensions. In key conditions of each study, the intrinsic, end dimension relates to the individual behavior measured in one direction, whereas the quest dimension relates in the other direction. The aggregation principle to which Gorsuch appeals suggests that the true relationships of the religious dimensions to helping may be stronger than observed, but this principle provides no basis for assuming that the direction of the relationship is the *reverse* of what is observed.

In sum, Gorsuch's observations about aggregation actually suggest that the results of these studies should be given more weight rather than less. Because these studies found statistically significant effects using an individual behavior, they would seem to provide especially strong evidence for the view that the intrinsic, end dimension is associated with helping in order to respond to a personal need to appear helpful, whereas the quest dimension is associated with helping that is responsive to the expressed needs of the suffering individual.

tionship to performance on the qualifying task because even those scoring low on this dimension may expend some effort to look good. But when the standard is difficult, low scorers would no longer need to work hard; they could gracefully take a dive. In contrast, high scorers should work even harder in an effort to reach their ultimate goal of relieving the needy person's distress. This pattern should produce a positive correlation between measures of intrinsic religion and performance on the qualifying task when the qualifying standard is difficult.

If, however, the intrinsic, end dimension is associated with helping motivated by a desire to look good, as Batson claimed, then when the qualifying standard is difficult, there should be a positive correlation of measures of the intrinsic, end dimension with volunteering to help but not with performance on the qualifying task. By volunteering to help and then not trying especially hard to qualify, high scorers on the intrinsic, end dimension would be able to reach the goal of appearing helpful without incurring the cost of actually having to help. Batson's view also suggests that measures of the quest dimension should have a positive correlation with performance on the qualifying task when the standard is difficult.

To test these competing predictions, Batson et al. (1989, Study 1) provided forty-six undergraduates with an opportunity to help under conditions in which, even if they volunteered to help, they would be allowed to do so only if they met a certain performance standard on a qualifying task. Ostensibly, the study concerned evaluation of an innovative helping program designed to assist individuals with high medical expenses. This program involved individuals taking part in walkathons, earning donations from local corporations for those in need. As part of the evaluation, participants read a description of one client of the program, Billy, a 7-year-old with a rare genetic disorder that prevented him from having contact with anyone outside his immediate family. Participants were then given an opportunity to volunteer to take part in a walkathon, earning contributions to help Billy get very expensive medication that would enable him to go back to school and play with his friends.

Before being given the opportunity to volunteer, participants read about the qualifying task, a fitness test used to determine who was eligible to participate in a walkathon. Participants read that only those individuals who passed the qualifying task could take part in a walkathon, even if they volunteered. The qualifying task involved stepping up onto a stone block and off again as many times as was comfortable in thirty seconds. Participants were not told what level of performance was necessary to qualify, but they were told about the difficulty of qualifying. Participants in the easy qualifying-standard condition read that the standard was "moderately stringent," that 60 percent of young adults (including college students) qualify. Participants in the difficult qualifying-standard condition read that the standard was "extremely stringent," that only 15 percent of young adults qualify. It was assumed that participants in the easy-standard condition would have some difficulty justifying to themselves and others a failure to qualify;

Table 10.4 Association between dimensions of personal religion and helping when qualifying is easy or difficult

	Difficulty of qualifying standard	
Dimension of personal religion	Easy (n = 24)	Difficult (n = 22)
Extrinsic, means	−.39*	−.33
Intrinsic, end	−.02	.50**
Quest	−.12	.03

Source: Adapted from Batson et al. (1989, Study 1).
*$p < .05$, one-tailed; **$p < .01$, one-tailed.

those in the difficult-standard condition would not. The difficult-standard condition provided a relatively safe opportunity to volunteer because it was unlikely that one would have to follow through.

Results of this study are summarized in Tables 10.4 and 10.5. Table 10.4 presents correlations of the three religious dimensions with helping in the two experimental conditions; Table 10.5 presents correlations with performance on the qualifying task. As you can see, the extrinsic, means dimension correlated negatively with helping Billy in both easy and difficult qualifying-standard conditions (overall $r = -.37, p < .01$), and in neither experimental condition was this dimension associated with performance on the qualifying task among either helpers or nonhelpers. These associations suggested that the extrinsic, means dimension was associated with decreased motivation to help.

The intrinsic, end dimension was significantly positively correlated with volunteering to help only when participants were informed that the standard was difficult, and so the likelihood of actually having to help was low ($r = .50, p < .01$). Moreover, among the volunteers in the difficult-standard condition, the intrinsic, end dimension did not correlate positively with trying harder on the qualifying task; it correlated nonsignificantly negatively

Table 10.5 Association between dimensions of personal religion and performance on qualifying task for helpers and nonhelpers when standard is easy or difficult

	Difficulty of qualifying standard			
	Easy (n = 24)		Difficult (n = 22)	
Dimension of personal religion	Helpers (n = 13)	Nonhelpers (n = 11)	Helpers (n = 14)	Nonhelpers (n = 8)
Extrinsic, means	−.29	.04	−.03	−.20
Intrinsic, end	−.12	.17	−.24	.69*
Quest	−.28	−.13	.51*	−.18

Source: Adapted from Batson et al. (1989, Study 1).
*$p < .05$, one-tailed.

($r = -.24$). The intrinsic, end dimension correlated positively with trying harder in the difficult-standard condition only among participants who had *not* volunteered to help ($r = .69, p < .05$). This pattern of results suggested that the motivation to help associated with the intrinsic, end dimension was not directed toward meeting Billy's need; it was directed toward meeting a personal need to appear helpful without having to follow through.

The quest dimension was not correlated with helping in either experimental condition, suggesting that this dimension was not associated with either an increase or a decrease in the overall amount of motivation to help. Among those who volunteered to help in the difficult qualifying-standard condition, however, scores on the quest dimension were positively correlated with performance on the qualifying task ($r = .51, p < .05$). This pattern of correlations suggested an association between the quest dimension and the *nature* but not the *amount* of motivation to help. The motivation of high scorers on the quest dimension appeared to be directed more toward the goal of benefiting Billy because, when they thought it would be especially difficult to qualify to help, they worked even harder to do so. They did not seem content to use the difficulty of the standard as an excuse for not having to help.

Using the inaction of others to justify not helping: Batson et al. (Study 2). In their second study, Batson et al. (1989) provided another way for participants to justify not helping and still save face. The purpose of this study was to test a variant on Batson's claim that intrinsic religion is associated with the desire to appear helpful; the variant is that intrinsic religion is associated not with gaining the social and self-rewards of appearing helpful but with avoiding the social and self-punishments of appearing unhelpful. Accordingly, rather than enabling some participants to get the benefits of looking kind and caring without having to incur the cost of actually helping, in this study some participants could avoid the threat of looking bad even if they did not help.

Batson et al. (1989) reasoned that one way to provide justification for not helping was to draw on the power of social norms and reference groups that we discussed in Chapter 2. They did this by presenting individuals confronted with a request for help with information about how previously asked peers had responded to the request. If most peers had helped, then the individuals could anticipate looking bad if they did not help too (high social pressure). If, however, most peers had not helped, then the individuals could also decline without looking bad (low social pressure).

Building on this logic, if the intrinsic, end dimension is associated with motivation to help based on concern for the other's welfare, as Allport claimed, then even though there might be no correlation with helping when social pressure to help is high, there should be a positive correlation between measures of intrinsic, end religion and helping when social pressure is low. When pressure is high, even those scoring low on intrinsic, end religion may help in order to avoid looking bad. But when pressure is low,

low scorers no longer need to help to save face. High scorers should still help because that is the only way for them to reach the goal of relieving the needy person's distress. This pattern of helping should produce a positive correlation between measures of intrinsic, end religion and helping when pressure is low.

If, however, intrinsic, end religion is associated with motivation to avoid looking bad, as the variant on Batson's view claimed, then there should be a positive correlation between measures of this dimension and helping when pressure is high. There should not be a positive correlation when pressure is low.

If the quest dimension is associated with motivation to meet the expressed needs of the victim, as Batson claimed, then even though there might not be a positive correlation when pressure is high, there should be a positive correlation between measures of this dimension and helping when pressure is low.

Batson et al. (1989, Study 2) tested these predictions by giving sixty female undergraduates at the University of Kansas the chance to volunteer time to help Katie Banks, a senior at the university who was struggling to support her younger brother and sister after the tragic death of her parents in an automobile accident. For some of the research participants, social pressure to help was high; for others, it was low. Pressure was manipulated by having participants indicate whether they wished to help on a pledge form that included spaces for the names and responses of eight people. The first seven spaces were already filled, ostensibly by previous participants. In the high-pressure condition, five of the seven previous participants had volunteered to help; in the low-pressure condition, only two of seven had volunteered.

Results of this study are summarized in Table 10.6. As you can see, scores on the extrinsic, means dimension were negatively correlated with helping in the low-pressure condition ($r = -.41, p < .025$), suggesting that the relatively weak motivation to help associated with higher scores on this dimension found in previous studies is directed toward the self-serving goal of avoiding looking bad, in one's own eyes or in the eyes of others.

Table 10.6 Association between dimensions of personal religion and helping when pressure to help is high or low

	Pressure to help	
Dimension of personal religion	High pressure ($n = 24$)	Low pressure ($n = 22$)
Extrinsic, means	.05	−.41**
Intrinsic, end	.00	.10
Quest	.13	.36*

Source: Adapted from Batsom et al. (1989, Study 2).
*$p < .05$, one-tailed; **$p < .025$, one-tailed.

Scores on the intrinsic, end dimension failed to correlate significantly with helping in either condition, providing no clear evidence of either motivation to avoid looking bad or motivation to relieve the needy individual's suffering. The pressure manipulation used in this study was not designed to detect motivation to look good, so, in combination with the results of the preceding study, the results of this study suggested that the motivation to help associated with intrinsic, end religion is most likely directed toward obtaining the self-benefits of looking good.

Only measures of the quest dimension were significantly positively correlated with helping in the low-pressure condition ($r = .36, p < .05$). This correlation is the one we would expect if this dimension of personal religion is associated with motivation to relieve the needy person's suffering, not motivation to help in order to avoid looking bad. Results of this and the preceding study appear to lay to rest the suggestion of Gorsuch (1988) and Watson, Hood, and Morris (1985) that the quest dimension is simply associated with halfhearted helping.

Thoughts associated with helping: Batson and Flory. Batson and Flory (1990) used a very different technique to assess the nature of the motivation to help associated with the different religious dimensions. They used a Stroop task to identify the goal-relevant cognitions associated with this helping.

The Stroop task, named for its inventor (Stroop, 1938), is an ingenious method of assessing what a person is thinking about at a given moment. When we see a printed word, we automatically read it. Even if we are asked to respond to some feature of the word, such as naming the color of ink in which it is printed, the meaning of the word is nevertheless processed. And, if the meaning of the word is related to thoughts that are salient at the time, this relation will interfere with naming the color, so our response time will be slower—or, said another way, our color-naming latency will be greater. For example, our color-naming latency for the word *steak* will be greater when we are hungry than when we are not. Taking advantage of this cognitive interference effect, the Stroop task seeks to determine what is on people's minds by asking them to name as quickly as possible the color of the ink in which a word (or other visual stimulus whose meaning might be associated with their thoughts) appears.

Employing the Stroop procedure, Batson and Flory (1990) had research participants first listen to a brief pilot radio broadcast that presented the need of Katie Banks, the young woman who was attempting to care for her younger brother and sister and prevent them being put up for adoption after the tragic death of her parents in an automobile accident. Next, participants learned that in a few minutes they would have a chance to volunteer time to help Katie. It was suggested that they think about what they wanted to do before deciding. In the interim, they performed a Stroop task.

The Stroop task was presented as a reaction-time measure of the effect of the pilot radio broadcast on thoughts. Participants had previously been told that they would be shown a series of words, some relevant to possible thoughts after hearing the broadcast, others not. Different words would appear in different colors. For each word, participants assigned to the test group would say as quickly as possible whether it was relevant to their thoughts; participants assigned to the control group would say as quickly as possible the color in which the word was printed. It was explained, "Responses of people in the control group will provide a baseline needed to interpret the responses of people in the test group. Therefore it is important that you do your best no matter to which group you have been assigned." All participants were informed that they had (ostensibly randomly) been assigned to the control group; their task would be to name the color (red, blue, green, or brown) in which each word appeared. (Mention of the test group made it plausible not only that the reaction-time measure be taken but also that some of the words be relevant to thoughts evoked by the broadcast.)

Participants were then shown reward-relevant words *(nice, merit, honor, praise),* punishment-relevant words *(duty, guilt, shame, punish),* victim-relevant words *(care, needy, adopt, tragic),* and neutral words *(pair, clean, extra, smooth),* and they named as quickly as possible the color of the ink. (The words were intermixed, and both order and pairing with color were counterbalanced.) After they finished the Stroop task, participants were given a form on which to indicate whether they wished to help Katie and, if so, how much time they wished to volunteer.

Batson and Flory (1990) reasoned that if the motivation to help associated with a given religious dimension is directed toward the self-serving goal of looking good by doing the right thing, then helping by high scorers on this dimension should be positively correlated with increased color-naming latency for reward-relevant words on the Stroop task. If the motivation is directed toward the self-serving goal of avoiding looking bad, then helping by high scorers should be positively correlated with increased color-naming latency for guilt-relevant words. If the motivation is directed toward the goal of reducing the young woman's need, then helping by high scorers should be correlated with increased color-naming latency for victim-relevant words.

Results indicated that the helping of high scorers on the extrinsic, means dimension was not reliably related to color-naming latency for any of the three types of words. (To correct for individual differences in general reaction time, all latencies were adjusted for latency to name the color of the neutral words.)

Helping of high scorers on the intrinsic, end dimension was associated with thoughts of the rewards for looking good ($r = .55, p < .01$); it was also nonsignificantly positively correlated with thoughts about the victim ($r = .36$). This latter correlation was not, however, independent of the correlation with thoughts of looking good ($r_{partial} = -.05$), suggesting that attention to the victim's need was only instrumental to reaching the ultimate goal of gaining the self-rewards for doing a good deed. Controlling for associations with the reward-relevant and victim-relevant words, color-naming latency for the punishment-relevant words was negatively correlated with helping among individuals scoring high on the intrinsic, end dimension ($r_{partial} = -.47, p < .03$). This correlation suggested that thoughts about looking bad were more salient for those high scorers who were *less* likely to help, indicating that these thoughts were not a motivator of helping but were triggered by deciding not to help. None of these associations appeared among individuals scoring low on the intrinsic, end dimension.

Helping by high scorers on the quest dimension was nonsignificantly positively correlated with color-naming latency for the victim-relevant words ($r = .24$), and this correlation appeared to be independent of correlations for the reward-relevant or punishment-relevant words. This correlation suggested that the helping of individuals scoring high on the quest dimension might reflect concern for Katie's welfare, but the evidence was weak. It did not contradict Batson's claim that the quest dimension is associated with helping directed to meeting the expressed needs of the victim, but it did not provide clear support for that claim either.

Implications

Looking back over the results of this series of six studies, what implications can we draw about the nature of the motivation to help associated with the different dimensions of individual religion? Specifically, what implications can we draw about Allport's claim that although extrinsic religion might lead to self-centered concern for Number One, and therefore reduced and self-serving motivation to help others in need, intrinsic religion should lead a person to transcend self-centered needs and display true compassion and universal love? What implications can we draw about Batson's competing claim that the intrinsic, end dimension relates not to genuine concern for the other's welfare but to a self-serving desire to appear concerned, whereas the quest dimension relates to genuine concern?

Prosocial motivation and extrinsic religion. The evidence suggests that the first part of Allport's claim is right. In study after study, extrinsic religion is not associated with an increase in helping; if anything, it is associated with a decrease. Moreover, the results of Study 2 by Batson et al. (1989) suggest that the weak motivation to help associated with this dimension is directed not toward concern for the needy person's welfare but toward the self-serving goal of avoiding looking bad. This dimension correlated with helping only when everyone else was helping.

Prosocial motivation and intrinsic religion. The evidence suggests that the more important and controversial second part of Allport's claim—that intrinsic religion evokes true compassion—is wrong. There is evidence that higher scorers on the intrinsic, end dimension report being more compassionate, caring, and helpful (Tate & Miller, 1971; Watson, Hood, & Morris,

1985; Watson, Hood, Morris, & Hall, 1984); there is also evidence that they help more in response to direct, low-cost requests (Bolt, 1982). But Darley and Batson (1973), Batson (1976), and Batson and Gray (1981) each found that responses associated with the intrinsic, end dimension were relatively insensitive to the expressed needs of suffering individuals. The responses appeared to be directed instead toward meeting the helper's own need to be helpful.

Focusing more directly on underlying motives, the combined results of the two studies by Batson et al. (1989) suggest that, although the intrinsic, end dimension can at times be associated with increased helping, this helping is not motivated by altruistic concern for the other person's welfare but by egoistic concern to look good, presenting oneself as a good, kind, caring person. Adding further support to this suggestion, Batson and Flory (1990) found that the helping of individuals scoring high on the intrinsic, end dimension was positively correlated with the salience of thoughts about the personal rewards of helping, thoughts associated with the words *nice, merit, honor,* and *praise.*

These results are hard to reconcile with Allport's claim about the increased selfless concern for others evoked by intrinsic religion. They are far more consistent with Batson's claim that the intrinsic, end dimension of personal religion is associated with increased self-concern—self-concern to gain the rewards of seeing oneself and being seen as concerned. We are reminded of the concern for appearances for which Jesus castigated the scribes and Pharisees.

Prosocial motivation and quest religion. What about the second part of Batson's claim? Is the quest dimension associated with genuine compassion? The answer to this question is not yet clear. Although there is no clear evidence that this dimension is associated with an increase in the *amount* of motivation to help, there is considerable evidence that this dimension is associated with a change in the *nature* of the motivation to help. But what is the character of this change? Is the motivation altruistic?

Darley and Batson (1973) and Batson and Gray (1981) found that this dimension was associated with helping that appeared more responsive to the expressed needs of the suffering individual; Batson (1976) found that this dimension was associated with adopting the suffering individual's perception of the need. These findings suggest that the quest dimension may be associated with increased concern for others' welfare, as Batson claimed. Also consistent with this view were the results of the two studies reported by Batson et al. (1989). In Study 1, although this dimension was not associated with an increased amount of helping, it was associated with trying harder to qualify to help in the difficult-standard condition. In Study 2, scores on the quest dimension were associated with increased helping in the low-pressure condition.

But there is also some evidence that calls this conclusion into question. First, scores on measures of the quest dimension are not positively correlated with reports of increased feelings of sympathy or compassion for people in need, either as a general disposition (Watson, Hood, & Morris, 1985; Watson, Hood, Morris, & Hall, 1984) or in response to specific needs (Batson, Schoenrade, Bolen, Cross, & Neuringer-Benefiel, 1984). If anything, the quest dimension seems to be associated with reduced feelings of sympathy and compassion. Second, in the Batson and Flory (1990) study the correlation between helping and color-naming latency for the victim-relevant words among individuals scoring high on the quest dimension, although positive, was not statistically reliable.

The weakness of this correlation could easily be due to chance variation, but both it and the apparent lack of relation to reports of sympathy and compassion raise the possibility that the quest dimension is not associated with a shift from self-concern toward an increased altruistic concern for individuals in need but with a shift from self-concern toward some other goal. What other goal? Possibly, the goal of upholding some general moral principle, such as a principle of fairness or justice.

Consistent with this possibility, Cheuvront and Ventis (1982) and Sapp and his colleagues (Sapp & Gladding, 1986; Sapp & Jones, 1986) have repeatedly found positive correlations (typically from .30 to .50) between scores on measures of the quest dimension and principled scores on Rest's Defining Issues Test (DIT), the objective measure of Kohlberg's principled morality discussed in Chapter 3. (Correlations for the extrinsic, means dimension are typically close to zero; those for the intrinsic, end dimension are typically negative—ranging from −.20 to −.40.) If a person comes to adopt a moral principle like justice as a guide for action, as higher scorers on the quest dimension apparently do, then this person may be motivated to rectify any situation that violates this principle. An innocent person in need violates this principle. So, relieving this person's suffering may not be the ultimate goal of helping; it may be only an instrumental means to reach the ultimate goal of upholding the principle. In the helping situations used in the studies we have described, pursuit of the impersonal goal of upholding moral principles would produce the same pattern of results predicted if the quest dimension evoked increased compassion for the person in need—the pattern that has been observed.

Because of this last possibility, it seems premature to conclude that the studies we have reviewed provide clear evidence for the second part of Batson's claim, that the quest dimension is related to genuine compassion for others in need. The studies do suggest that the quest dimension is not associated with motivation to help in order to look good or to avoid looking bad, but future research must determine whether the ultimate goal is to enhance the other person's welfare—altruistic motivation—or to uphold one or more moral principles. It may be that those high in quest religion have taken to heart Immanuel Kant's (1785/1889) admonition that we should love our neighbor as ourselves "not from inclination, but from duty" (sec. 1, par. 12).

To return to our fanciful question about who on the road from Jerusalem to Jericho would have scored high on which dimensions of religion, the popular view in psychology of religion has long been that the Good Samaritan would have scored high on the intrinsic, end dimension. In light of our review of the available evidence, however, we doubt this view. Instead, we suspect that, had someone been nearby handing out questionnaires, the priest and Levite, who for all their appearance of goodness did nothing, would have been the ones to score high on the intrinsic, end dimension. In contrast, the Samaritan might well have scored high on the quest dimension.

A Qualification: Institutional Versus Individual Response to Others' Needs

As we noted in Chapter 6, the intrinsic, end dimension is closely associated with high involvement in institutional religion. Does the research we have reviewed imply, then, that active involvement in institutional religion does not lead to more helping of the poor, sick, and downtrodden? Not at all, for two reasons. First, helping through institutional channels is precisely the sort of high-visibility helping with which the research suggests the intrinsic, end dimension is associated. Second, the research we have reviewed concerns the way a person responds as an individual. Although individual response to others in need is clearly covered by religious teachings like the parable of the Good Samaritan, needs in our society are often dealt with at an institutional rather than individual level. And religious institutions have long been among the most likely to respond, whether with Thanksgiving and Christmas baskets for the poor, visits to the sick and elderly, or financial contributions to one or another defense or relief fund.

Given that religious institutions are an important channel for meeting needs in our society, we seem to be faced with an interesting dilemma. The sensitivity to and apparent concern for the expressed needs of others shown by those scoring higher on the quest dimension seems a desirable form of individual response. But, if anything, those scoring higher on this dimension are less likely to be involved in institutional religion. Thus, they are less likely to participate in this important channel for institutional response to others' needs.

In contrast, the relative insensitivity to the wishes of individuals in apparent need and the concern to appear helpful more than actually to help shown by those scoring higher on the intrinsic, end dimension seem less desirable forms of individual response. But those scoring higher on this dimension are more likely to be involved in religious institutions (Gorsuch & McFarland, 1972) and in helping others through these institutions (Benson, Dehority, Garman, Hanson, Hochschwender, Lebold, Rohr, & Sullivan, 1980; Bolt, Pyne, & Shoemaker, 1984; Nelson & Dynes, 1976). Paralleling the apparent insensitivity of the more intrinsically religious to the expressed wishes of Janet in the Batson and Gray (1981) study, the help that religious institutions provide may not always be sensitive to the wishes of the needy, yet it is doubtful whether those in need, or society at large, would be better off without it.

Still, to recognize that the needy benefit from the institutional response of the intrinsically religious does not resolve the dilemma; this only sharpens it. For we may take our fanciful reflection on the parable of the Good Samaritan a step further and ask: Even if we were to learn that the priest and Levite passed by on the other side because they were taking contributions from the Temple in Jerusalem to an orphanage down the road, would we excuse their insensitivity to the needs of the man who fell among thieves?

SUMMARY AND CONCLUSION

Our examination in this chapter of the effects of religion on concern for others in need has led us to conclusions quite similar to those reached in Chapter 9 concerning the effects of religion on intolerance, prejudice, and bigotry. In that chapter we found, first, that there was much research that suggested a positive correlation between being religious and being prejudiced. But then we found that there was also much research suggesting that this was only true for those persons who use their religion as an extrinsic means to self-serving ends. Those who orient to religion as an intrinsic end in itself almost invariably score lower on measures of prejudice than the extrinsically religious; they do not appear to be more prejudiced than nonreligious individuals.

Although this pattern of results presented a rather comforting view of the relationship between religion and antisocial attitudes and behavior, we found that it could not be accepted. For in virtually every study of the relationship between religion and prejudice, prejudice has been measured by self-report questionnaires. Measuring prejudice in this way opens the door wide for individuals who wish to present themselves as good to adjust their responses so as to appear less prejudiced than they actually are.

When we turned to more recent research designed to control for self-presentation, we found that the negative relationship between scores on the intrinsic, end dimension and prejudice disappeared; indeed, the relationship seemed to be positive for nonproscribed prejudices. These results led us to suggest that there was no clear evidence that those scoring high on the intrinsic, end dimension were less prejudiced than those scoring low on this dimension, or indeed than those scoring high on the extrinsic, means dimension. There was only clear evidence that those scoring high on the intrinsic, end dimension *present* themselves as less prejudiced. Finally, research suggested that those scoring high on the quest dimension were less prejudiced than those scoring low even when self-presentation was controlled.

In the present chapter, we shifted focus to the relationship of religion to compassion and caring for others in need, the sort of caring exemplified by the Good Samaritan. Paralleling findings in the previous chapter, we first found that religious involvement is associated with more stringent moral standards and with seeing oneself and being seen by others as more concerned for the welfare of people in need. But when confronted with someone in need, individuals who are more religious are not any more helpful than those who are less religious, unless self-presentation concerns have been aroused.

When we turned to the relationship between helping and different ways of being religious, we found that the intrinsic, end dimension is associated with saying one is helpful and concerned for others, and it is associated with increased helping in response to direct, low-cost requests. But the helping behavior associated with this dimension often is not responsive to the expressed needs of the person seeking help. We concluded that this help was not motivated by altruistic concern for the needy person's welfare but by self-concern to show oneself to be a good, kind, caring person. The quest dimension, on the other hand, is not associated with reports of helpfulness or with increased amounts of helpfulness, but it is associated with helping that seems responsive to the expressed needs of the person seeking help. Whether this helping is motivated by increased concern for those in need as an end in itself—altruistic motivation—or as a means to uphold general moral principles is not as yet clear.

Combining the results of our inquiries into the role of religion in (1) reducing intolerance, prejudice, and bigotry and (2) increasing concern and compassion for others in need, we believe there is sufficient evidence, and the evidence is sufficiently clear, to warrant some general—if tentative—observations about the social consequences of the different dimensions of individual religion. First, there is no evidence that the extrinsic, means dimension is associated with increased acceptance of and concern for others, especially others who are down-and-out, nor is it likely that anyone would have expected it to be.

Second, there is also no clear evidence that the intrinsic, end dimension is associated with increased acceptance of or concern for others who are down-and-out, even though many people, both religious teachers and psychologists of religion, have claimed that it is. This dimension seems instead to reflect an increased concern for looking good in one's own or society's eyes, for showing the world that one possesses the tolerance, concern, and compassion that one's religion preaches. The underlying motivation, however, seems to be self-concern rather than concern for others. The tolerances proclaimed are limited to those deemed acceptable by the religious community, and at a behavioral level the intrinsic, end dimension is not associated with increased tolerance even of those outgroups deemed acceptable, nor is it associated with increased responsiveness to the needs of others. This discrepancy between appearance and action reminded us of the behavior of the priest and Levite in the parable of the Good Samaritan, or of the scribes and Pharisees against whom Jesus railed.

Third, there is evidence that the quest dimension is associated with increased tolerance and sensitivity to the needs of others. Even though higher scores on the quest dimension are not associated with self-reports of greater helpfulness and concern, they relate both to increased tolerance of oppressed minorities and outgroups and to increased sensitivity to others' needs. Importantly, these relationships are found using behavioral measures. This concern for action rather than appearance reminded us of the behavior of the unpretentious Samaritan.

Faced with this general pattern of results, we believe it is time to suggest a general conclusion concerning the social consequences of the end and quest dimensions: *The quest dimension is related to reduced intolerance and increased sensitivity to the needs of others, whereas the intrinsic, end dimension is related to the appearance of these social benefits.* This conclusion is very much at odds with the currently popular view suggested by Gordon Allport that the devout, intrinsic, end dimension reduces intolerance and increases compassion, allowing the individual to transcend all self-centered needs and live his or her religion. But we found that, when examined carefully and critically, the empirical evidence does not support this popular view. Instead, the evidence supports the conclusion we have stated.

Having stated this conclusion, we immediately need to add an important qualifier. We noted that the relevant research and this conclusion focus on the consequences of the religious dimensions for individual, not institutional, response. Intrinsic, end religion, not quest religion, is associated with more involvement in religious institutions. Therefore, we may expect the more intrinsically religious to contribute more to the help that religious institutions provide to those in need. Although we may question the motivation associated with the intrinsic, end dimension and applaud the motivation associated with the quest dimension, the importance of the response of religious institutions in meeting the needs of the downtrodden in society should not be ignored. And when we allow for institutional response, we find ourselves faced with what would seem to be an irresolvable dilemma between the more laudable action at the individual level associated with the quest dimension and the more laudable action at the institutional level associated with the intrinsic, end dimension.

With this chapter we complete our look at theory and research relevant to understanding the sources, nature, and consequences of individual religion. But our task is not done. Now we need to consider the broader implications of our social-psychological analysis. In the final chapter we shall attempt to do this, addressing a fundamental question: Is religion, or at least some form of religion, on our side as individuals and as a society, or is religion our enemy?

IV

Implications

11

Is Religion on Our Side?

Oxford philosopher Basil Mitchell (1955) tells a parable. The parable is set in a war-torn country occupied by enemy forces. One night a member of the resistance, a partisan, meets a stranger. The Stranger deeply impresses him. In the course of a long conversation the Stranger tells the partisan that he too is on the side of the resistance, indeed that he is the leader of it, and urges the partisan to have faith in him no matter what happens. The partisan, utterly convinced of the Stranger's sincerity and constancy, trusts him. In the ensuing months the partisan does not speak to the Stranger. But sometimes he sees the Stranger helping members of the resistance, and he is grateful and says, "He is on our side." Other times he sees the Stranger in the uniform of the police, handing patriots over to the occupying forces. In spite of this behavior and the grumbling of his friends, the partisan maintains that the Stranger is "on our side." At such times the partisan's friends object, asking, "What would he have to do before you will admit that he is not really on our side, that he is a double agent?" Or they complain, "Well, if that's what you mean by his being on our side, the sooner he goes over to the other side the better!"

A strange parable. Mitchell originally presented it to depict the dilemma faced by the person who believes in a loving, just, and omnipotent God, while living in this world of suffering and tragedy. But the parable seems equally applicable to the dilemma posed by the role of religion in human life. Advocates claim that religion works for the betterment of humanity, providing direction and comfort, encouraging tolerance, love, and compassion. Skeptics ask whether religion is on our side. They remind us that religion often appears in the uniform of the opposition. Rather than our salvation, it seems bent on destroying us; rather than calling out the best in us and enabling us to transcend ourselves, it appeals to our weaknesses, our infantile needs for security, easy answers, and seeing ourselves as better than others.

Religious leaders often suggest that the central question about religion in our time is whether living in today's world we can maintain or rediscover a spiritual dimension in life. We would suggest that many of us face an even more basic question: Do we *want* a spiritual dimension in our lives? An answer rests on knowing whether religion is on our side or is a double agent who masquerades as our ally but is actually our enemy. If religion is a positive force, then we need it because we need all the help we can get. But if it is not, then the sooner we recognize the deceit and cast it aside, the better.

The possibility that religion is a deceptive double agent could not be faced head-on in earlier ages; the presumption was too strong that in one form or another, religion *was* on our side. There were grumblings, of course, and even some small rebellions, but nothing like the wholesale desertions that this century has witnessed.

It has become a cliché to attribute the cultural changes of our age to modern technology. Still, even at the risk of invoking a cliché, we suspect that technology deserves much of the credit—or blame—for loosening the hold of religion, for turning it into an elective rather than a requirement. Technology has made our lives so active, comfortable, and secure that it is possible to glide from day to day and never really confront ultimate, existential questions. One can move from work to cocktails, the news, dinner, a party, bed, breakfast, the news, and back to work, inserting some exercise and some serious recreation on the weekend, and never really face more ultimate questions than whether to risk an affair or whether the children will make it through puberty with their sanity, if not their virginity, intact. Life-and-death issues have receded behind a screen of hospital corridors, white uniforms, impressive chrome machines, and plastic tubes. Or they come to us served up by the media, stirred into a thick soup in which the real tragedy of a plane crash or earthquake and the fictional tragedy of a disaster movie are so mixed up that they begin to taste the same. Each provides some macabre spice to life, but not enough to cause any existential heartburn.

In such an age, it is possible to live free of religion, free of the insulating and stultifying security of knowing that "God is in His heaven and all is right with the world," free to face one another and our lives with, as Jean-Paul Sartre said, the unblinking gaze of "lidless eyes." No longer must we assume that religion is necessary for our survival or our sanity; too many people survive and are sane without it.

But even if religion is not necessary, it may still be worth having. Indeed, some would say it is all the more essential. It may keep us from becoming too anxious on those occasions when existential doubts do creep into our lives, or becoming too consumed with our own enjoyment to think of others, or becoming too one-dimensional to recognize and appreciate the fundamental mystery of existence. It may even totally transform our life, flooding it with meaning and purpose and extending us beyond ourselves. It may. The question is, *does* it?

We believe that our social-psychological analysis has implications for an answer to the question of whether religion is on our side, and we would like to spell out these implications. But before we do, we must mention two qualifiers. First, although we have tried to test our analysis against existing empirical research, and have generally found it supported, the research is often far from conclusive. At many points, more research is needed before firm conclusions can be drawn. In the discussion that follows, we shall present the implications of our analysis as clearly and positively as possible, without constant reminders about the inconclusiveness of the supporting evidence. We wish to emphasize, however, that these are often tentative implications based on only suggestive data.

Second, as Mitchell's parable implies, even if the empirical evidence were more conclusive, it would probably not provide a conclusive answer to the question of whether religion is on our side. For, although research can be quite relevant, an answer will also depend on whether we come to the research with a prior belief in the value of religion. Such a belief (or lack of it) can easily shape our interpretation of the empirical evidence. Those who believe and those who do not have often looked at the same evidence, and both claimed support for their views. Each side ends up muttering about the other, "They're *so* biased; I wonder if *any* data would get through to them!" Such encounters remind us that the facts are neither hard nor cold in the case for religion being on our side. They are easily melted into a predetermined mold by the heat generated by our prior beliefs.

Insofar as possible, we need to avoid this bias. There is nothing wrong with having prior beliefs, even strong ones. Most of the best research in social psychology has been done by people who cared deeply about the ideas they were testing. It is a serious problem, however, when we are not open to having our initial beliefs challenged by the evidence. Then our science becomes a sham. Whatever our initial beliefs, we need to try to look at the evidence as openly and honestly as possible, and at the same time, we need to recognize that these beliefs may still distort our view.

We shall approach the question of whether religion is on our side using

Mitchell's parable as a guide. For, in addition to highlighting the problem of prior beliefs shaping our interpretation of the evidence, this parable enables us to see that the question is actually two-sided. It is in part a question about *religion,* about the true identity of the Stranger, but it is also a question about *us,* about which side is our side. We need to consider each of these components if we are to determine whether religion is on our side.

WHO IS THE RELIGIOUS STRANGER?

Concerning the identity of the religious Stranger, one can ask several questions. Most obviously, is the Stranger really who he claims to be? That is, is religion the powerful, positive force in human life that it and its advocates claim? Our social-psychological analysis offers two types of information relevant to an answer to this question. First, it offers information on where the Stranger comes from, on the social and psychological origins of religion. Knowing where the Stranger comes from may be helpful in establishing his true identity. Second, it offers information on what the Stranger does, on the social and psychological consequences of personal religion. Knowing what the Stranger does may help us establish his true intent.

Where Does the Stranger Come From?

In Chapter 2 we suggested that a persuasive case can be made that our social environment has foisted the religious Stranger on us, that whether and how we are religious is a product of the combined influence of our social norms, roles, and reference groups. It has been proposed that, ultimately, the religious Stranger is our own creation, an illusion invented by society to curb self-gratification and to meet our desperate need for comfort and direction. But we also suggested that this was not the whole story, that it would be a mistake to assume that social influence precluded personal initiative and choice; social influence and intrapsychic processes are not mutually exclusive alternatives.

In Chapter 3 we placed religion in the context of psychosocial development of the individual. Much of what we know about the religious Stranger comes to us through socialization in the form of compliance, identification, and internalization of religious beliefs and practices. In addition, our cognitive development shapes the way we think about religion. As children who are unable to ask the existential questions religion seeks to answer and unable to appreciate the symbolic nature of much of religious language, our first impressions may be overly concrete and simplistic, yet lasting; they may lead to serious misunderstandings later on. Still, as we grow and mature we are faced with a number of psychosocial conflicts that are likely to raise various existential questions. From adolescence on, it is hard to ignore the religious Stranger.

In Chapter 4 we examined the internal dynamics of religious experience. We suggested that religious experience can be viewed as a more or less creative transformation of the individual's existential reality. In more creative religious experiences, the individual comes to see crisis-provoking existential questions (What is the meaning and purpose of my life? How should I relate to others? How do I deal with the fact that I am going to die?) in a new light, a light that enables him or her to transcend the existential crisis by means of a more complex, higher-level cognitive organization. This new reality enables the individual to confront a wider range of people and situations positively. In less creative religious experiences, the reality transformation is much more limited. By appeal to some dogmatic formula as *the* answer to one or more existential questions, less creative religious experiences lead to a reduction rather than an increase in the complexity of the cognitive structures that the individual uses to think about these questions. As a result, this kind of reality transformation may restrict the range of people and situations that the individual can confront positively.

In Chapter 5 we considered four of the techniques that various religious traditions have employed to facilitate religious experience—psychedelic drugs, meditation, religious language, and music. We suggested that if these techniques are relied on to produce religion, then they are likely to inhibit rather than encourage religious experience. But if the techniques are used as facilitators of the stages of creative reality transformation, then they may be powerful contributors to religious experience.

Overall, our analysis in Chapters 2 through 5 suggested that although the social environment has a powerful effect on the individual's religious experience (or lack of experience), an experience that transforms the individual's life is not simply a product of the social environment. It is also a response to pressures from within, to psychosocial conflicts, to a dissatisfaction with one's present way of seeing oneself and one's world, and a sincere desire to have it all make better sense. Religion can provide a new vision that transforms a life racked with doubt, contradiction, and despair into one of purpose, contentment, and joy.

To say that religious experience is a product of one's social environment and one's personal desire for existential meaning calls the origin of the religious Stranger into question. He claims to have been sent by God. But our social-psychological analysis raises the possibility that religious experience is not a response to Divine revelation but a product of our social and personal needs—that, as Freud claimed, it is an illusion created to provide meaning and structure in the face of the uncertainties, tragedies, and absurdities of life. Indeed, if one wishes to extend the scientist's rule of parsimony into the realm of faith, as some psychologists (including Freud) clearly do, one may be inclined to proclaim this possibility the most plausible one. It certainly seems simpler to dismiss religious realities as one more example of our ability to create need-fulfilling illusions than to assume that there are whole levels of reality that transcend our observable, social world. It seems simpler to say that we created God than that God created us.

But as we noted in Chapter 1, parsimony is a problematic principle; the simplest explanation is often not the most elegant. Nor is it necessarily the most true. Attempts to solve metaphysical questions by parsimony are suspect. Faith—religious and otherwise—has never been ruled by parsimony; nor is it clear that it should be.

What Does the Stranger Do?

William James takes our thinking a provocative step further by suggesting that even if the religious Stranger *were* only a figment of our imagination, he could still be on our side. James contends that we must judge the Stranger not by where he came from but by his deeds or "fruits." If we follow James's lead and direct our attention to the effects of religion on human life, two more questions about the identity of the religious Stranger arise. First, is the Stranger a leader, as Mitchell's parable suggests, or just a follower? Second, if a leader, where does he lead?

Leader or follower? When we find religion associated with various attitudes and behaviors, is this because religion *produced* these attitudes and behaviors or simply because it *reflects* them? That is, is religion an active force providing direction to life, or is it just one arena among many in which more basic characteristics of the individual—intelligence, sociability, reflectivity, open-mindedness, need for structure, and so on—are at work? If religion is the former, then it deserves our attention because we would like to understand the forces directing our lives. But if religion is only an arena, then it is not clear that it does deserve our attention. We would probably be wiser to focus on the more basic characteristics that account for the direction of a person's life, not only in the arena of religion but in other arenas as well.

The bulk of the research on consequences of religion is correlational, and as such, it does not allow us to determine whether religion is a leader or a follower. So we must look elsewhere. Perhaps the most relevant evidence is to be found in examples of dramatic religious experience like those presented in Chapter 4. Such examples provide strong anecdotal evidence that religion at least has the potential to lead. Experiences like those of Saint Paul and Malcolm X appear to change the entire direction of a person's life. Of course, as William James's distinction between healthy-minded and sick-souled religion reminds us, other characteristics of the individual's personality seem important in determining whether a given person will have such an experience. The healthy-minded are not likely to have dramatic religious experiences; the sick-souled are.

So is religion a leader or a follower of other aspects of personality? At this point, an answer is not clear. Our best guess, however, is that religion is a leader in many people's lives, but that there is a limit on its ability to lead. We suspect that religion can lead only to the degree that it follows as well. Before religion can direct our life, it must speak to problems that are our problems, and speak to them in a style that is our style. Religion can serve as an active, directing force in our life only to the degree that it is responsive to and congruent with other forces within our personality. It can lead, but only if it also follows.

If this guess is correct, then it may explain some of the ambiguity about the direction of causality in research on the relationship between religion and other aspects of the individual's life. Some causal ambiguity may be unavoidable if religious experience is at once a cause and an effect of other aspects of personality, if religion at once emerges from and contributes to the direction of a person's life.

Where does religion lead us? If the religious Stranger can lead, we must ask about the consequences of his leadership. What are the effects of religion on human life? As James suggests, this is the crucial question for determining whether religion is on our side, whether it is a positive or negative force in human life.

When asked in this general way, the available research provides an unsettlingly clear answer: The religious Stranger does *not* appear to be on our side. Being more religious may be positively associated with fewer symptoms of mental illness and with more appropriate social behavior (i.e., reduced alcohol and drug use, smoking, and premarital sex among adolescents), but it is not associated with more positive forms of mental health or with greater social tolerance and compassionate concern. Quite the contrary, there is strong evidence that being more religious is associated with poorer positive mental health (Chapter 8), with greater intolerance of people who are different from ourselves (Chapter 9), and with no greater concern for those in need (Chapter 10). This evidence seems to suggest that, overall, religion is a negative force in human life, one we would be better off without.

Three Strangers Instead of One

But this answer, alhough clear and empirically well grounded, is misleading. It treats religion as a unitary concept. And, as we found in Chapter 6, there are different dimensions of individual religion. We considered three independent dimensions: religion as an extrinsic means to other ends, as an intrinsic end in itself, and as a quest. Doubtless there are other dimensions as well. But considering just these three, it seems that we must modify Mitchell's parable to include not one religious Stranger but three, each claiming to be on our side, each claiming to be a leader—if not *the* leader—of the resistance, and each accusing the other two of being impostors. To have to deal with three Strangers rather than one certainly complicates matters, but there is ample evidence that this complication is necessary. Rather than asking the general question of whether religion is on our side, we need to ask of each Stranger individually and in turn, is this one on our side?

The extrinsic, means dimension. The extrinsic, means dimension involves the use of religion as a means to attain self-serving ends such as going to church for social reasons or praying for a new car, a good grade, or a needed cure. The evidence in Chapters 7 through 10 suggests that this aspect of religion is not on our side. It is not associated with more meaning in life or less anxiety about death; if anything, it is associated with less meaning and more anxiety. It is also associated with a perception of religion as an oppressive set of restrictions (Chapter 7). This dimension is not associated with increased mental health, regardless of how mental health is conceived (Chapter 8). At the social level, it is associated with more rather than less intolerance and prejudice (Chapter 9) and with no increase in compassion for those in need (Chapter 10). Thus, for this dimension of religion the empirical research provides no evidence of beneficial effects. And since we are judging the religious Strangers by what we know of their fruits, this one should probably be branded an enemy.

If Gordon Allport was right in his belief that the extrinsic, means dimension is by far the predominant aspect of religion, then to find that this dimension is not an agent for good has wide-ranging implications. It suggests that the vast majority of what is considered religion in modern society is not a constructive force in human life, that it is not on our side.[1]

But even if the extrinsic, means dimension is the predominant aspect of religion in modern society, it is certainly not the one that religious teachers, preachers, and writers extoll. To embellish Mitchell's parable a bit, one can imagine these partisans jumping up to say of the extrinsic Stranger, "See, we told you that he was no good. But don't be misled, he is not the true religious Stranger; he is an impostor!" We might then expect them to turn to the devout, intrinsic Stranger and say, "This is the true religious Stranger, and he is on our side." Or some might turn to the quest Stranger and say the same. Are these claims true? Our social-psychological analysis permits us to go beyond impassioned advocacy to consider empirically the behavioral consequences of these two Strangers as well.

The evidence for the effects of these two religious dimensions is far less clear-cut than the evidence for the extrinsic, means dimension. Rather than clearly favoring or condemning either dimension, it suggests a complex set of tradeoffs. For each, there is evidence of some beneficial consequences but also some liabilities. Moreover, where one dimension shows benefits, the other tends to show liabilities, and vice versa.

1. There is as yet no clear way of identifying the relative predominance of the three religious dimensions, so we cannot be certain that Allport is right. But the similarity of the results of studies that assess the effects of religious involvement of any kind and the results of studies that assess the effects of extrinsic religion suggest that he is right, at least in contemporary American society.

Still, we should mention another possible interpretation of the observed relationship between the extrinsic, means dimension and various negative personal and social characteristics. It is possible that this relationship arises because those who score higher on extrinsic religion are more self-critical, or at least present themselves in a more self-critical way. A readiness to be self-critical could lead a person to admit to using his or her religion for self-serving ends and also to admit having anxieties, difficulties in personal adjustment, and even some prejudice and callousness. In combination, these admissions could produce many of the observed relationships.

The intrinsic, end dimension. The intrinsic, end dimension involves sincere, devout commitment to a set of religious beliefs. The beliefs are not to be used in the service of other needs; they are to define the master motive in life. What are the consequences of being more religious in this way? This aspect of religion is associated with freedom from existential concerns such as meaninglessness and anxiety over death, but with this freedom comes bondage to the beliefs; the believer is no longer able to reflect openly and honestly on their truth (Chapter 7). Depending on the conception of mental health employed, intrinsic, end religion can be seen as either enhancing or not enhancing personal adjustment and mental health. It is associated with freedom from worry over existential concerns, and with a sense of control over events in one's life (due at least in part to a belief that God is in control). At the same time, there is no clear evidence that this orientation increases self-acceptance or open-mindedness and flexibility (Chapter 8). At a social level, this dimension is associated with claims of greater tolerance, reduced prejudice, and more responsiveness to the needs of the distressed. But none of these claims seems to be borne out in behavior. Rather than genuine impulses toward increased tolerance, reduced prejudice, and increased concern for others, this dimension seems to be associated with a self-serving concern to *appear* tolerant, unprejudiced, and compassionate (Chapters 9 and 10).

Reflecting on this evidence as a whole, it seems that the firmly held commitment and belief that are the hallmark of the intrinsic, end dimension are both a benefit and a burden. Like a pair of crutches, they provide a sense of security and purpose that the believer can lean on but, at the same time, must clutch tightly. And as long as the believer can appear faithful and committed to the beliefs without acting in accord with them, there seems little impetus to do so. In sum, this dimension appears to be associated with a religion of faith more than works, unless the works are on public display.

Our picture of the nature and consequences of the intrinsic, end dimension is very different from the picture painted by most religious leaders and psychologists of religion; this dimension is usually presented in an unequivocally positive light. But when we try to look at the evidence concerning the behavioral correlates of this dimension as objectively as possible, we find that the evidence is, at best, mixed.

The quest dimension. The quest dimension involves an open-ended readiness to confront ultimate, existential questions, coupled with a skepticism

---

If a more candid, self-critical response style were accounting for the relationships, it would cast a very different light on things. It would suggest that the extrinsic, means Stranger might be on our side after all, at least in one respect, because self-critical candor would seem to be a virtue. Unfortunately, the research to date provides no basis for determining whether higher scores on this dimension reflect more use of one's religion for self-serving ends or just more willingness to acknowledge such use. The recent research using behavioral measures to assess the relationship to helping, however, suggests that this dimension is associated with reduced concern for others in need.

of definitive answers to these questions. This dimension seems to be associated with very different effects on human life than the intrinsic, end dimension. Although empirical evidence for the effects of the quest dimension is still sparse, and most of it comes from our own research, the evidence to date suggests that this dimension does not provide the same sense of freedom from existential concerns that the intrinsic, end dimension does, but neither does it produce the same bondage (Chapter 7). The quest dimension is not positively associated with absence of mental illness or freedom from worry and anxiety, but it is positively associated with several other conceptions of mental health: open-mindedness and flexibility and, perhaps, personal competence and control and self-actualization (Chapter 8). It is at the level of social consequences that the quest dimension looks most beneficial. It has been found to relate both to reduced prejudice (Chapter 9) and to increased responsiveness to the needs of the distressed (Chapter 10). Unlike the intrinsic, end dimension, it does not relate to claims of these virtues; it relates to actual behavior.

Reflecting on this evidence as a whole, the quest dimension appears to be associated with a religion of less faith (unless, following Tennyson, one argues that there is "more faith in honest doubt . . . than in half your creeds") but more works.

Given this complex pattern of evidence, it is not clear what we should say about these last two religious Strangers. Sometimes one seems to be on our side and the other not; at other times it seems to be just the reverse. To try to gain some clarity as to what our verdict should be, let us turn to the other basic question implicit in Mitchell's parable: Which side is *our* side?

WHICH SIDE IS OUR SIDE?

Just as we found that we had to consider the possibility that there is more than one religious Stranger, so we must consider the possibility that there is more than one side that is ours. Indeed, a little reflection reveals that there are actually many sides, and some of us are on one, some on another; it even seems likely that most of us are on different sides at different points in our lives or, at times, on several different sides at once.

At a personal level, our sides are determined by our needs and values, and there are wide individual differences among us in needs and values. For those of us who need security and structure, the intrinsic, end Stranger is far more likely than the quest Stranger to be on our side. For those who value open, honest inquiry, the verdict is likely to be just the opposite.

In addition to asking whether religion helps overcome deficiencies or facilitate growth in the life of the individual, we can ask whether it helps overcome deficiencies or facilitate growth in society at large. Once again, at a societal level there are multiple sides. The intrinsic, end dimension would seem to be on the side of maintaining the traditional institutions and values of society, whereas the quest dimension would seem to be on the side of debunking the established institutions and encouraging social change. Although the quest dimension may be on the side of breaking down barriers between people and increasing concern for others in one-to-one relations, the intrinsic, end dimension seems to be on the side of those social institutions, especially religious ones, that attempt to respond to the needs of the poor and downtrodden. One may argue that these institutions are only treating the symptoms of social injustice while at the same time perpetuating the underlying causes by maintaining the status quo, but symptom relief may be better than no relief at all.

It seems, then, that which religious Stranger is on our side depends on which side we are talking about, both personally and socially. To put these sides in an even broader perspective, we might extend Mitchell's parable once again to include two very different wars. In one, we are fighting to adapt to and deal effectively with our cosmic environment; in the other, we are fighting to adapt to and deal effectively with our temporal environment. The cosmic environment is created by our awareness of ourselves as particles in a drop of time falling into a sea of eternity. The temporal environment is created by our awareness that we live in a world with others here and now.

The intrinsic, end Stranger is more oriented to helping us adapt to the cosmic environment rather than to the temporal. He is not of this world but goes to prepare a place for us. The quest Stranger is more oriented to helping us adapt to the temporal environment than to the cosmic. He is very much of this world, and holds out less hope for a secure place in the world beyond.

Which of these two battlefronts is more important, the cosmic or the temporal, will vary from individual to individual; indeed, it often varies for a given individual at different stages of life. As a result, which religious Stranger is on our side will vary from individual to individual, and quite possibly at different stages of our life.

SUMMARY AND CONCLUSION

Our answer to the question of whether religion is on our side is necessarily multifaceted. Although there is little reason to believe that the extrinsic, means dimension of religion is on our side, both the intrinsic, end dimension and the quest dimension are on the side of at least some of us, some of the time. But neither is an unequivocal ally. This is a much more complex and qualified answer than we were initially seeking when we used Mitchell's parable to pose the question of whether religion is on our side. In order to take account of the complex pattern of relationships between religion and other aspects of human life suggested by our social-psychological analysis, we found it necessary to destroy the simple elegance of Mitchell's parable, adding the possibility of different religious Strangers, different sides, even different wars.

But we do not consider this increased complexity to be a problem. On the contrary, we believe that it is a testimony to the power of an empirically based social-psychological analysis of religion. Our analysis has led us to a far more differentiated view than we initially had of religion and of the roles that religion plays in human life. At the same time, it has not led us into a maze of complexity simply to leave us there, confused. It has also provided at least tentative answers to many of our questions concerning which side which religious Stranger is on. Whether a given religious Stranger is on our side is, ultimately, a question that each of us must answer for ourselves, given who we are and where we are in our personal development. But our social-psychological analysis has contributed to an answer. It has suggested some of the heavens and some of the hells to which different ways of being religious are likely to lead.

APPENDIX

The Scientific Method and Social Psychology of Religion

The Scientific Method

Science is a method of knowing. The goal is to provide an understanding of various aspects of human experience, both aspects within ourselves and aspects within our social and physical environment. Such a goal is not, of course, unique to science. Literature, art, history, and theology all provide understanding of various aspects of human experience. Yet they are not sciences. The unique feature of the scientific method is a combination of skepticism, empiricism, and systematic research.

For the scientist, to have a theory that provides an understanding of some aspect of experience is only the beginning. The theory may be wrong. *Skepticism* leads the scientist to construct a situation in which the theory can show its falseness (Popper, 1959). If the theory is a good one, a fairly explicit statement of the falsifying conditions can be made. Moreover, because the scientist is hoping that his or her theory is right, it is important that the falseness, if it exists, be demonstrated as unequivocally as possible. The scientist must not be able to wriggle off the hook by saying that only he or she can know whether things came out as predicted. The outcome must be specifiable in terms of observable events that are just as available to an opponent of the theory as to a proponent. This requirement of public verifiability leads to *empiricism.*

But even publicly verifiable empirical observation is not enough. It is also essential that the scientist not be able to wriggle off the hook by pointing to some additional factors to explain why things did not come out as the theory predicted. To guard against this, the scientist employs *systematic research.* The method of systematic research that has proved most effective is the *experiment.* This is because a good experiment can produce unequivocal disappointment, or falsification, better than any other research method.

Because experiments play such a central role in science, let us look more closely at what an experiment is. An experiment might be described as a *causal caricature.* A caricature is an artificial, usually simplified, reconstruction of some natural phenomenon; it selectively emphasizes essential components. A caricature is not a mirror of reality; it is an intentional distortion. Yet it may reveal reality better than a mirror, because the essential components stand out.

In an experiment the scientist develops a simplified, artificial model of some natural process. This caricature is created with a specific purpose in mind, testing one or more causal explanations. Virtually all scientific explanations are causal; they have an underlying "if . . . , then . . ." form.[1] An experiment allows the scientist to test for the existence of this causal relationship by varying (manipulating) selected "if" dimensions (independent variables) and observing the effect on selected "then" dimensions (dependent variables). Nonessential factors are excluded by one of two techniques. They may be eliminated through control of the environment (as in a laboratory), or they may be neutralized through random assignment of the entities being studied to independent variable conditions.

The resulting caricature provides a situation where, except for chance variation, the only differences between the entities in different experimental conditions are the differences created by manipulation of the independent variables. Under these circumstances, if one or more independent variables correlate with one or more dependent variables, then one can infer with confidence that the independent variables caused change in the dependent variables, and not vice versa. This clarity of causal inference makes experiments ideal for testing explanatory theories. One knows what caused what, not just what was correlated with what.

The symbiotic relationship between the scientist's theoretical explanation and systematic empirical research should be apparent from this sketch of the logic of experimentation. The theory being tested suggests which variables should be included in the experimental caricature and what the causal relationship between these variables should be. A good experiment, in turn, can give the theory an unequivocal opportunity to show itself wrong, when the predicted causal relationships fail to appear.

Even though experiments are the best systematic research method for falsifying theories, scientists cannot always rely on experiments. In some cases

1. A number of social and behavioral scientists have argued that causal explanations are not appropriate for understanding human behavior. Some, notably systems theorists, argue that we should instead view human behavior as a complex system with multiple causation and feedback loops, in which X affects Y which in turn affects X, and so on. Others argue that we should focus not on past causes but on future-directed intentions in understanding human behavior.

We find much merit in both of these arguments, but not a fundamental challenge to the centrality of causal explanations in science. To talk about multiple causation or feedback loops as do systems theorists is still to use causal explanations, only more complex and sophisticated ones. To talk about intentions still implies that if X intention is present, then Y behavior should be observed. Although an analysis in terms of intentions clearly transcends a simple "billiard ball" notion of causation, it still seems to fit the general form of what is meant by a causal explanation in science.

this is because experiments are not practical. In astronomy and astrophysics, for example, one cannot move the stars and planets around to test one's theories about characteristics of space and mass, the existence of black holes, or the origin of the universe. And yet a rich collection of theories has been developed in astronomy, and many theories have been effectively falsified. This has been done through careful observation and correlation of naturally occurring events.

In other cases experiments are not possible for ethical reasons. Our understanding of the effects of neurophysiological processes in the brain on behavior would doubtless advance far more rapidly if we were to conduct experiments in which people's brains were chemically or surgically changed and the effects on behavior observed. But such an approach is not ethical. Instead, research in this important area relies on studies of infrahuman animals or on studies of those few persons whose brain structure or chemistry is different at birth or has been altered in accidents or by medical treatment.

Using the Scientific Method in Social Psychology of Religion

Given this understanding of the scientific method, let us now turn to the specific issue of the use of this method in social psychology of religion. What are the types of systematic research available to the social psychologist studying religion?

Experimental designs. During the past half century social psychology has grown up as a science. The dominant concern has become the development and testing of explanatory theories; the dominant research method has become experimentation. This does not mean that all or even most research done by social psychologists is experimental; ethical and practical considerations often lead to the use of other research techniques, such as correlational studies or naturalistic observation. Nor does it mean that there are no criticisms of the experimental method; there have been many. These limitations and criticisms should not, however, overshadow the fact that most social psychologists consider experimental designs to be the best technique for testing scientific theories. We certainly do.

In spite of this, we do not believe that one can rely heavily on experiments in building a social psychology of religion. Ethical and practical considerations place severe restrictions on their use. For example, a researcher would likely be hesitant to test a theory about the relationship between certain religious beliefs and certain behaviors by randomly selecting some individuals for exposure to these beliefs while preventing others from exposure. If the researcher considered the beliefs to be of value, it would be unethical not to expose everyone to them; if he or she considered the beliefs to be dangerous, it would be unethical to expose anyone. Although experimentation is the preferred research design when it is ethically and practically feasible, the occasions when one can test a theory about religion by using an experiment are relatively rare. Walter Pahnke's (1964) study concerning the effects of psilocybin on mysticism (see Chapter 5) is one of the few true experiments in psychology of religion. (See Batson, 1977, 1979; Deconchy, 1978, 1985; Gorsuch, 1982; Yeatts & Asher, 1979, for further discussion of the ethical and practical limitations on experimentation in social psychology of religion.)

Correlational designs. Because of the difficulties associated with experiments, many psychologists studying religion have come to rely on correlational designs. Correlational designs have the ethical and practical virtue that they do not require one to manipulate or change anything in people's lives, only to measure what is already there. One may, for example, correlate intensity of religious belief with extent of racial prejudice (see Chapter 9) simply by obtaining a measure of the naturally occurring level of each in a number of people. Correlational studies of this kind are the type of empirical research that has been by far the most popular with psychologists studying religion over the past half century. More than 90 percent of the studies in psychology of religion have been correlational (see Argyle & Beit-Hallahmi, 1975; Batson & Ventis, 1982; Capps, 1976; Spilka, Hood, & Gorsuch, 1985).

But, although correlational studies can be of value, they are fraught with problems. First and foremost, one often faces the problem of not knowing what caused what. Assume one finds that variable X correlates with variable Y. Did X cause Y, Y cause X, or were both the result of some other variable, Z? Sometimes the answer to this question is clear. For example, if we observe a systematic correlation between the tides and the location of the moon, we can assume that the location of the moon caused the tides and not vice versa. Similarly, if some measure correlates with another measure taken at a later time, we can assume that the latter did not cause the former. But very often, especially with human behavior, the causal pattern underlying a correlation is not clear.

There is also the problem that correlational studies in the psychology of religion often rely on questionable measures of conceptual variables. If we wish to study the effects of intensity of religious conviction on some other variable, then we must have a measure of intensity of religious conviction. What measure do we use? The most easily quantifiable measures are either frequency of participation in religious activities (going to church, praying, etc.) or the person's self-report of how religious he or she is. Each of these has been used to measure intensity of religious conviction numerous times. But the relationship between either measure and the conceptual variable, religious conviction, is questionable. The first is problematic because one can engage in religious activities like going to church for a wide variety of reasons, many of which have nothing to do with religion. For example, one may go hoping to meet a boy- or girlfriend. This may be a perfectly reasonable thing to do, but it is hardly an indication of religious conviction.

Self-report measures are a problem as well; they fail to make a distinction among (1) what people *say* they believe, value, and do; (2) what they honestly *believe* they believe, value, and do; and (3) what they *actually* believe, value, and do. In some cases the difference among these three levels of response is minor. For example, in the absence of any strong situational pressure to the contrary, we may assume that questionnaire responses about interest in religion or belief in an afterlife are reasonably accurate reflections of what respondents actually feel or believe at the time.

In other cases, however, there may be a tremendous difference. If, for example, we wish to assess the level of racial prejudice or of helping behavior associated with devout, sincere religious belief (see Chapters 9 and 10), then it is not enough to ask people to indicate their agreement or disagreement with questionnaire items such as "I find racial prejudice and discrimination abhorrent" or "It is extremely important to me to help others less fortunate than myself." There may be wide discrepancies between what people say is true of themselves on such items, what they actually believe is true, and how they behave.

Problems may be especially severe when correlating these self-reports with religion. This is because all major religions make rather clear prescriptions about the right answers to such questions. So there is reason to expect a positive correlation between devotion to religious teachings and more positive responses to these questions. But what does this relationship mean? It may mean nothing more than that the person knows what his or her religion teaches about these issues and can respond accordingly, regardless of whether these teachings have had any effect on the person's private attitudes or, more importantly, on the person's behavior.

For this reason we strongly believe the psychology of religion needs to re-examine its use of self-report questionnaires when measuring value-laden psychological and social correlates of religion. Methods are needed that distinguish among the way people present themselves, the way they honestly believe themselves to be, and the way they actually are. If we want to know about people's intensity of religious conviction or their religious beliefs, then it may be best to follow Gordon Allport's advice: Ask them. But if we want to know how individuals who are more or less religious actually behave in value-laden areas, then asking them is not enough. We need to look and see how these individuals actually *do* behave; we need behavioral measures. Self-report questionnaire measures have value, but they cannot always be taken at face value, as results of the research reviewed in Chapters 9 and 10 make clear.

Finally, there is a third problem with correlational designs. They seem to lead to descriptive rather than explanatory research (Gorsuch, 1984). Since it is difficult to test causal theories of the "if X, then Y" variety using correlational techniques, these techniques discourage the researcher from developing such explanations. Instead of considering what is causing an observed relationship between variables X and Y and then trying to think of a research design that will unequivocally test this causal explanation, it is easier to move on and find out whether X is also related to Z. Far too often, researchers studying religion have taken this easier option. As a result, we have a large number of empirical observations about people's religion, but we have very few scientific theories to help us understand them. The heavy reliance on correlational designs has, we believe, contributed to the persistent theoretical weakness in the psychology of religion, a weakness noted years ago by James Dittes in 1969—"the chief problem appears to be in the realm of theory and in the theoretical relevance of data" (p. 603)—and by Bernard Spilka in 1978—"the great weakness is in theory" (p. 97). This weakness still exists today. There continues to be far more interest in using empirical observations to pile up descriptive facts about how religion relates to this or that other aspect of life—age, sex, anxiety about death, mental health, coping, racial prejudice, and so on—than in developing explanatory theories to account for these facts and using empirical observations to test these theories.

French psychologist of religion Jean-Pierre Deconchy (1980) has suggested an intriguing and provocative reason beyond ease and simplicity for this preference for collecting descriptive facts using correlational designs over developing and testing explanatory theories. Deconchy suggests that descriptive data are preferred because they cannot threaten the personal beliefs and values of religious individuals, whereas explanatory theories can, as we pointed out in Chapter 1.

By criticizing the heavy use of correlational designs, we do not mean to suggest that they have no value. They have. Observation of an empirical relationship (i.e., a correlation) can serve as a stepping-stone to explanation and understanding. And, under certain circumstances, such an observation can even make an important contribution to theory testing. If, for example, some theory predicts "if X, then Y," then the *failure* to find a correlation between X and Y can count against the theory as conclusively as finding through an experiment that manipulating X had no effect on Y.

It is when interpreting correlations that come out as predicted, or that are observed in the absence of any clear theory-based prediction, that problems arise. When this happens, one usually is not sure what caused what. The observed correlation may be because "if X, then Y," but in most cases it may also be the result of a number of other causal patterns. Thus, although correlational designs have value, their value is limited. This limited value should be kept in mind when assessing the scientific import of the many correlational findings reported in this and other books in psychology of religion.

Quasi-experimental designs. If experimentation is generally unavailable for use in studying religion and if correlational designs are of only limited value, what are we to do? Donald Campbell (1963, 1969; Campbell & Stanley, 1966) suggests that when experimentation is impossible, the social psychologist should look to *quasi-experimental designs.* The general feature of these designs is that they involve acquiescence to the ethical and practical constraints of reality, while at the same time coming as close as possible to meeting the criteria for a true experiment. For example, when ethical and practical constraints make random assignment of research participants to independent variable comparison groups impossible, nonrandom comparison groups are sought. When manipulation of independent variables is impossible, the researcher looks for naturally occurring differences instead. Campbell hastens to add that the researcher must be well aware of the potential confounds to causal inference introduced as a result of failure to meet all of the criteria of a true experiment.

Campbell and Stanley (1966) present about a dozen different quasi-experimental designs. For purposes of illustration, let us consider just one, the *time-series design.* In this design, measures on some dependent variable are taken at a number of points in time, both prior to and following some naturally occurring event. By comparing differences on the dependent variable across the time periods that bracket the event with differences across other time periods, it is possible to make fairly confident causal inferences about the effects of the naturally occurring event, far more confident than if one simply correlated attendance at the event with scores on the dependent variable. In the study of religion, a time-series design like this could be used to examine, for example, the effect on beliefs or behavior (dependent variables) of various naturally occurring religious activities such as regular worship, catechetical training, a revival, summer camp experience, or festivals (independent variables).

We believe that quasi-experimental designs like this one can and should be widely used by social psychologists studying religion. Such designs have three attractive features: First, they permit the researcher to capitalize on much of the theory-testing potential of experiments. This should encourage development of explanatory theories and theory-relevant research, which would be a major advance over the descriptive summaries of empirical relationships produced by most correlational studies. Second, because quasi-experimental designs are explicitly contrasted with an experimental ideal, the researcher is continually reminded of their inferential limitations. Finally, since quasi-experimental designs can be applied to naturally occurring differences as well as to manipulated differences, they do not involve as many ethical and practical problems as experiments.

A number of studies using quasi-experimental designs are reported in this book, especially in Chapters 7, 9, and 10. But we must admit that we have reported far fewer quasi-experimental studies than we would like. The problem is that only a limited number exist. We hope that in the near future this will cease to be true. Quasi-experimental designs provide the social psychologist studying religion with a happy compromise between inferentially powerful but often impractical experimental designs and easily done but inferentially weak correlational designs. We hope that quasi-experimental designs will soon become the research method of choice in social pscyhology of religion.

Implications: Two Dangers

Use of the scientific method in the psychology of religion can be distorted in two major ways. First, we can distort the search. Intentionally or unintentionally, we can fail to ask the relevant hard questions, the answers to which might embarrass our present understanding of the way personal religion operates. Second, we can distort the results of the search. Even if we ask the potentially embarrassing questions, we can fail to hear the answers given by empirical research. At the most obvious level, we can selectively perceive and report results, taking seriously only those results that support our preconceptions. We hope this is rarely done; yet it clearly is done—most obviously in articles reviewing research on a given topic. There is another more subtle way that we can fail to hear the answer being given. We can fail to show enough bias when evaluating research findings. No doubt it sounds heretical for us to advocate bias, so let us explain.

Bias means preference or prejudice, and when evaluating research findings, we need to show bias—in favor of quality. Not all research is created equal. Yet there is a tendency in the psychology of religion for reviewers of research simply to count the number of findings that support or contradict a particular hypothesis and to decide truth by majority vote. Indeed, we have succumbed to this practice at points in Chapters 8, 9, and 10. This one-study-one-vote approach may be quite objective, but it may also be quite misleading. Weak studies are much easier to do and are far more prevalent than strong studies. If studies differ in quality, then this difference needs to be reflected in our assessment of what the research is saying.

Obviously, when quality judgments are made, there will be disagreements among different interpreters of the research. Still, these judgments need to be made. Science is not value-free; quite the contrary. It involves adherence to a specific set of values—those that enable us to find our errors. If our social psychology of religion is to be scientifically respectable, then we need a clear bias in favor of research that exemplifies these values.

References (indexed)

Numbers in brackets following each reference indicate pages in this book where the reference is discussed.

Abelson, R. P. (1959). Modes of resolution of belief dilemmas. *Journal of Conflict Resolution, 3,* 343–352. [217]

Abelson, R. P. (1963). Computer simulation of "hot" cognition. In S. S. Tomkins & S. Messick (Eds.), *Computer simulation of personality.* New York: Wiley. [107]

Abraham, K. G. (1981). The influence of cognitive conflict on religious thinking in fifth and sixth grade children. *Journal of Early Adolescence, 1,* 147–154. [62]

Acklin, M. W. (1984). An ego developmental study of religious cognition. Unpublished Ph.D. dissertation, Georgia State University, Atlanta, Georgia. [179, 267, 277, 283]

Adler, A. (1956). *The individual psychology of Alfred Adler.* New York: Basic Books. [237]

Adorno, T. W., Frenkel-Brunswik, E., Levinson, D. J., & Sanford, R. N. (1950). *The authoritarian personality.* New York: Norton. [159, 238, 296, 303, 305]

Ainsworth, M.D.S., Blehar, M. C., Waters, E., & Wall, S. (1978). *Patterns of attachment: A psychological study of the strange situation.* Hillsdale, NJ: Lawrence Erlbaum. [75–76]

Alcoholics Anonymous. (1976). *The big book* (3rd ed.). New York: A.A. World Services. [194–195]

Alland, A., Jr. (1962). Possession in a revivalistic Negro church. *Journal for the Scientific Study of Religion, 1,* 204–213. [39n]

Allen, R. O., & Spilka, B. (1967). Committed and consensual religion: A specification of religion-prejudice relationships. *Journal for the Scientific Study of Religion, 6,* 191–206. [164–165, 303, 305]

Allison, J. (1968). Adaptive regression and intense religious experience. *Journal of Nervous and Mental Disease, 145,* 452–463. [106, 110–111]

Allport, G. W. (1937). *Personality: A psychological interpretation.* New York: Holt. [159–160, 238]

Allport, G. W. (1950). *The individual and his religion.* New York: Macmillan. [11, 53, 59, 159, 160, 163, 165, 166, 182, 190, 233, 238, 258, 286–287, 303]

Allport, G. W. (1954). *The nature of prejudice.* Cambridge, Mass.: Addison-Wesley. [306]

Allport, G. W. (1959). Religion and prejudice. *Crane Review, 2,* 1–10. [161]

Allport, G. W. (1966). Religious context of prejudice. *Journal for the Scientific Study of Religion, 5,* 447–457. [158, 303, 310–311, 315, 316, 343, 358–359]

Allport, G. W. (1968). The historical background of social psychology. In G. Lindzey & E. Aronson (Eds.), *The handbook of social psychology* (Vol. 1, pp. 1–80). Reading, MA: Addison-Wesley. [28]

Allport, G. W., & Kramer, B. M. (1946). Some roots of prejudice. *Journal of Psychology, 22,* 9–30. [159, 296, 297]

Allport, G. W., & Ross, J. M. (1967). Personal religious orientation and prejudice. *Journal of Personality and Social Psychology, 5,* 432–443. [161–162, 164, 164n, 165, 174, 199, 201, 258, 303, 305, 306, 307, 308, 311–313, 315, 315n, 325, 344, 345]

Alston, J. P. (1973). Review of the polls. *Journal for the Scientific Study of Religion, 12,* 109–111. [38]

Anand, B. K., Chhina, G. S., & Singh, B. (1961). Some aspects of electroencephalographic studies in Yogis. *Electroencephalographic Clinical Neurophysiology, 13,* 452–456. [139, 152]

Annis, L. V. (1975). Study of values as a predictor of helping behavior. *Psychological Reports, 37,* 717–718. [341]

Annis, L. V. (1976). Emergency helping and religious behavior. *Psychological Reports, 39,* 151–158. [341]

Appleby, L. (1957). The relationship between rigidity and religious participation. *Journal of Pastoral Care, 11,* 73–83. [253]

Argyle, M., & Beit-Hallahmi, B. (1975). *The social psychology of religion.* Boston: Routledge & Kegan Paul. [33, 35, 240n, 382]

Argyle, M., & Delin, P. (1965). Non-universal laws of socialization. *Human Relations, 18,* 77–86. [247]

Armstrong, R. C., Larsen, G. L., & Mourer, S. A. (1962). Religious attitudes and emotional adjustment. *Journal of Psychological Studies, 13,* 35–47. [251]

Asch, S. E. (1952). *Social psychology.* New York: Prentice-Hall. [124]

Asch, S. E. (1956). Studies of independence and conformity: A minority of one against a unanimous majority. *Psychological Monographs, 70* (Whole No. 416). [28, 220]

St. Augustine. (1843). *The confessions* (E. B. Pusey, trans.). Oxford: J. H. Parker. [83]

Back, C. W., & Bourque, L. B. (1970). Can feelings be enumerated? *Behavioral Science, 15,* 487–496. [38, 38n, 39, 40–41, 42]

Bagley, C. (1970). Relation of religion and racial prejudice in Europe. *Journal for the Scientific Study of Religion, 9,* 219–225. [299, 309]

Bahr, H. M., & Martin, T. K. (1983). "And thy neighbor as thyself": Self-esteem and faith in people as correlates of religiosity and family solidarity among Middletown high school students. *Journal for the Scientific Study of Religion, 22,* 132–144. [253]

Baker, M., & Gorsuch, R. (1982). Trait anxiety and intrinsic-extrinsic religiousness. *Journal for the Scientific Study of Religion, 21,* 119–122. [265, 274]

Bandura, A. (1969). *Principles of behavior modification.* New York: Holt, Rinehart & Winston. [236]

Bandura, A. (1977). *Social-learning theory.* Englewood Cliffs, N.J.: Prentice-Hall. [53–54]

Bandura, A. (1978). The self system in reciprocal determinism. *American Psychologist, 33,* 344–358. [49]

Bandura, A., & Walters, R. (1963). *Social learning and personality development.* New York: Holt, Rinehart & Winston. [43]

Barnes, M., Doyle, D., & Johnson, B. (1989). The formulation of a Fowler scale: An empirical assessment among Catholics. *Review of Religious Research, 30,* 412–420. [75]

Barron, F. (1953). An ego-strength scale which predicts response to psychotherapy. *Journal of Consulting Psychology, 17,* 327–333. [237]

Barron, F. (1963). *Creativity and psychological health.* Princeton: Van Nostrand. [121]

Barron, F. (1968). *Creativity and personal freedom.* Princeton: Van Nostrand. [167, 184–185, 283, 285]

Barron, F. (1969). *Creative person and creative process.* New York: Holt, Rinehart & Winston. [122n]

Barry, H., Bacon, M. D., & Child, I. L. (1957). A cross-cultural study of sex differences in socialization. *Journal of Abnormal and Social Psychology, 55,* 327–332. [37]

Barth, K. (1956). *Church dogmatics* (Vol. 1, Part 2). New York: Scribner's. [156]

Batson, C. D. (1971). Creativity and religious development: Toward a structural-functional psychology of religion. Unpublished Th.D. dissertation, Princeton Theological Seminary. [113–114, 168, 185]

Batson, C. D. (1975). Rational processing or rationalization?: The effect of disconfirming information on a stated religious belief. *Journal of Personality and Social Psychology, 32,* 176–184. [212–215]

Batson, C. D. (1976). Religion as prosocial: Agent or double agent? *Journal for the Scientific Study of Religion, 15,* 29–45. [168, 177, 343, 345, 347–348, 350n, 359]

Batson, C. D. (1977). Experimentation in psychology of religion: An impossible dream. *Journal for the Scientific Study of Religion, 16,* 412–418. [382]

Batson, C. D. (1979). Experimentation in psychology of religion: Living with or in a dream? *Journal for the Scientific Study of Religion, 18,* 90–93. [382]

Batson, C. D. (1980). "And the Truth shall make you free": Religion as personally liberating or enslaving? Unpublished manuscript, University of Kansas. [226–228, 265, 274, 282]

Batson, C. D. (1983). Sociobiology and the role of religion in promoting prosocial behavior: An alternative view. *Journal of Personality and Social Psychology, 45,* 1380–1385. [144]

Batson, C. D. (1991a). *The altruism question: Toward a social-psychological answer.* Hillsdale, NJ: Erlbaum Associates. [334]

Batson, C. D., Beker, J. C., & Clark, W. M. (1973). *Commitment without ideology.* Philadelphia: Pilgrim Press. [167]

Batson, C. D., Burris, C. T., Wagoner, K. C., & Wolgast, B. M. (1991, November). Is intrinsic religion used to meet personal needs? Paper presented at the annual convention of the Society for the Scientific Study of Religion, Pittsburgh, PA. [201]

Batson, C. D., Duncan, B. D., Levy, J., Major, S., & Miller, M. (1980). Effects of religious orientation on response to death anxiety and belief-challenging information. Unpublished manuscript, University of Kansas. [201, 228–229]

Batson, C. D., Flink, C. H., Schoenrade, P. A., Fultz, J., & Pych, V. (1986). Religious orientation and overt versus covert racial prejudice. *Journal of Personality and Social Psychology, 50,* 175–181. [326–329]

Batson, C. D., & Flory, J. D. (1990). Goal-relevant cognitions associated with helping by individuals high on intrinsic, end religion. *Journal for the Scientific Study of Religion, 29,* 346–360. [356–358, 359, 360]

Batson, C. D., & Gray, R. A. (1981). Religious orientation and helping behavior: Responding to one's own or to the victim's needs? *Journal of Personality and Social Psychology, 40,* 511–520. [348–350, 350n, 359, 361]

Batson, C. D., Naifeh, S. J., & Pate, S. (1978). Social desirability, religious orientation, and racial prejudice. *Journal for the Scientific Study of Religion, 17,* 31–41. [313–314, 324–326, 327, 328]

Batson, C. D., Oleson, K. C., Weeks, J. L., Healy, S. P., Reeves, P. J., Jennings, P., & Brown, T. (1989). Religious prosocial motivation: Is it altruistic or egoistic? *Journal of Personality and Social Psychology, 57,* 873–884. [350–356, 358, 359]

Batson, C. D., & Raynor-Prince, L. (1983). Religious orientation and complexity of thought about existential concerns. *Journal for the Scientific Study of Religion, 22,* 38–50. [185–187, 270, 281, 285]

Batson, C. D., & Schoenrade, P. A. (1991a). Measuring religion as quest: 1. Validity concerns. *Journal for the Scientific Study of Religion, 30,* 416–429. [181]

Batson, C. D., & Schoenrade, P. A. (1991b). Measuring religion as quest: 2. Reliability concerns. *Journal for the Scientific Study of Religion, 30,* 430–447. [181]

Batson, C. D., Schoenrade, P. A., Bolen, M. H., Cross, J. H., & Neuringer-Benefiel, H. E. (1984, October). Religious orientation and response to a lady in distress: Egoistic or altruistic? Paper presented at the annual convention of the Society for the Scientific Study of Religion, Chicago. [360]

Batson, C. D., & Ventis, W. L. (1982). *The religious experience: A social-psychological perspective.* New York: Oxford University Press. [vii, 168, 171, 178, 179, 260–261, 288, 382]

Batson, C. D., & Weeks, J. L. (1991). Helping. In R. M. Baron & W. G. Graziano (Eds.), *Social Psychology* (pp. 352–393). New York: Holt, Rinehart, & Winston. [342n]

Beck, S. H., Cole, B. S., & Hammond, J. A. (1991). Religious heritage and premarital sex: Evidence from a national sample of young adults. *Journal for the Scientific Study of Religion, 30,* 173–180. [247]

Becker, E. (1973). *The denial of death.* New York: Free Press. [102, 201]

Becker, R. J. (1971). Religion and psychological health. In M. P. Strommen (Ed.), *Research on religious development: A comprehensive handbook.* New York: Hawthorne. [234, 256]

Bem, D. J. (1970). *Beliefs, attitudes, and human affairs.* Monterey, Calif.: Brooks/Cole. [29]

Bender, I. E. (1958). Changes in religious interest: A retest after fifteen years. *Journal of Abnormal and Social Psychology, 57,* 41–46. [251]

Benson, P. L., Dehority, J., Garman, L., Hanson, E., Hochschwender, M., Lebold, C., Rohr, R., & Sullivan, J. (1980). Intrapersonal correlates of nonspontaneous helping behavior. *Journal of Social Psychology, 110,* 87–95. [361]

Berger, P. L. (1974). Some second thoughts on substantive versus functional definitions of religion. *Journal for the Scientific Study of Religion, 13,* 125–133. [11–12]

Berger, P. L., & Luckmann, T. (1966). *The social construction of reality.* Garden City, N.Y.: Doubleday. [95]

Bergin, A. E. (1980a). Psychotherapy and religious values. *Journal of Consulting and Clinical Psychology, 48,* 95–105. [234]

Bergin, A. E. (1980b). Religious and humanistic values: A reply to Ellis and Walls. *Journal of Consulting and Clinical Psychology, 48,* 642–645. [234]

Bergin, A. E. (1991). Values and religious issues in psychotherapy and mental health. *American Psychologist, 46,* 394–403. [234]

Bergin, A. E., Masters, K. S., & Richards, P. S. (1987). Religiousness and mental health reconsidered: A study of an intrinsically religious sample. *Journal of Counseling Psychology, 34,* 197–204. [262, 264, 266, 267, 269, 270, 271, 273, 275, 277, 279, 281]

Bergson, H. (1935). *The two sources of morality and religion.* Garden City, N.Y.: Doubleday. [167]

Berkowitz, L., & Lutterman, K. G. (1968). The traditional socially responsible personality. *Public Opinion Quarterly, 32,* 169–185. [337]

Bertocci, P. A. (1958). *Religion as creative insecurity.* New York: Association Press. [102, 167]

Bible, new revised standard version. (1989). New York: Oxford University Press. [7, 60, 82, 144, 156, 294, 331–332, 334]

Black, A. W. (1985). The impact of theological orientation and of breadth of perspective on church members' attitudes and behaviors: Roof, Moll, and Kaill revisited. *Journal for the Scientific Study of Religion, 24,* 87–100. [254]

Blum, B. S., & Mann, J. H. (1960). The effect of religious membership on religious prejudice. *Journal of Social Psychology, 52,* 97–101. [299]

Boehm, L. (1962). The development of conscience: A comparison of students in Catholic parochial schools and in public schools. *Child Development, 33,* 591–602. [335, 336]

Boisen, A. T. (1936). *The exploration of the inner world.* New York: Harper. [102, 233]

Boisen, A. T. (1960). *Out of the depths.* New York: Harper. [233]

Bolt, M. (1975). Purpose of life and religious orientation. *Journal of Psychology and Theology, 3,* 116–118. [199]

Bolt, M. (1977). Religious orientation and death fears. *Review of Religious Research, 19,* 73–76. [264, 274]

Bolt, M. (1982, August). Religious orientation, belief in a just world, and prosocial behavior. Paper presented at the annual convention of the American Psychological Association, Washington, D.C. [345–346, 359]

Bolt, M., Pyne, C., & Shoemaker, A. (1984, August). Religious orientation, responsibility denial, and nonspontaneous helping. Paper presented at the annual convention of the American Psychological Association, Toronto. [361]

Bonger, W. A. (1943). *Race and crime.* New York: Columbia University Press. [245]

Bonhoeffer, D. (1953). *Letters and papers from prison.* New York: Macmillan. [156, 167]

Bowers, K. J., & Bowers, P. G. (1972). Hypnosis and creativity: A theoretical and empirical rapprochement. In E. Fromm & R. E. Shor (Eds.), *Hypnosis: Research developments and perspectives.* Chicago: Aldine-Atherton Press. [112]

Bowlby, J. (1969). *Attachment and loss* (Vol. 1), *Attachment.* New York: Basic Books. [75]

Braden, C. S. (1947). Why people are religious—a study of religious motivation. *The Journal of Bible and Religion, 15,* 38–45. [9n]

Brannon, R.C.L. (1970). Gimme that old-time racism. *Psychology Today, 3,* 42–44. [295, 305, 311, 324]

Brontë, E. J. (1941). *The complete poems of Emily Jane Brontë, edited from the manuscripts by C. W. Hatfield.* New York: Columbia University Press. [194]

Brown, G. A., Spilka, B., & Cassidy, S. (1978, October). The structure of mystical experience and pre- and post-experience lifestyle correlates. Paper presented at the annual convention of the Society for the Scientific Study of Religion, Hartford, Conn. [110, 113]

Brown, L. B. (1962). A study of religious belief. *British Journal of Psychology, 53,* 259–272. [241, 253]

Brown, L. B. (1964). Classifications of religious orientation. *Journal for the Scientific Study of Religion, 4,* 91–99. [197]

Brown, L. B. (1987). *The psychology of religious belief.* London: Academic Press. [3, 314]

Brown, L. B., & Pallant, D. J. (1962). Religious belief and social pressure. *Psychological Reports, 10,* 269–270. [31–32]

Buie, J. (1987, November). Fundamentalism likened to addiction. *APA Monitor,* p. 11. [197]

Bunyan, J. (1678). *The pilgrim's progress from this world to that which is to come.* London: Nathanael Ponder. [22, 193]

Burchinal, L. G. (1959). Some social status criteria and church membership and church attendance. *Journal of Social Psychology, 49,* 53–64. [39, 40]

Burtt, E. A. (1957). *Man seeks the divine: A study in the history and comparison of religions.* New York: Harper. [332]

Bussey, K., & Maughan, B. (1982). Gender differences in moral reasoning. *Journal of Personality and Social Psychology, 42,* 701–706. [65–66]

Byrne, D. (1961). The repression-sensitization scale: Rationale, reliability, and validity. *Journal of Personality, 29,* 334–349. [112]

Cameron, P. (1969). Valued aspects of religion to Negroes and Whites. *Proceedings of the 77th Annual Convention of the American Psychological Association, 4,* 741–742. (Summary) [38]

Cameron, P. (1971). Personality differences between typical urban Negroes and whites. *Journal of Negro Education, 40,* 66–75. [39n]

Campbell, A. (1971). *White attitudes toward black people.* Ann Arbor: Institute for Social Research, University of Michigan. [309]

Campbell, D. T. (1963). From description to experimentation: Interpreting trends as quasi-experiments. In C. W. Harris (Ed.), *Problems in measuring change.* Madison: University of Wisconsin Press. [384]

Campbell, D. T. (1969). Reforms as experiments. *American Psychologist, 24,* 409–429. [384]

Campbell, D. T. (1975). On the conflicts between biological and social evolution and between psychology and moral tradition. *American Psychologist, 30,* 1103–1126. [15, 47, 334–335]

Campbell, D. T., & Stanley, J. C. (1966). *Experimental and quasi-experimental designs for research.* Chicago: Rand McNally. [384–385]

Camus, A. (1946). *The stranger.* New York: Knopf. [105]

Cantril, H. (1943). Educational and economic composition of religious groups. *American Journal of Sociology, 48,* 574–579. [40]

Capps, D. (1976, June). Personal communication. [382]

Capps, D. (1988). The psychology of religious experience. In C. H. Lippy & P. W. Williams (Eds.), *Encyclopedia of American religious experience: Studies of traditions and movements* (Vol. 1, pp. 51–70). New York: Scribner's. [146]

Carnap, R. (1938). Logical foundations of the unity of science. *International Encyclopedia of Unified Science, 1,* 42–62. [20]

Carr, L. G., & Hauser, W. J. (1976). Anomie and religiosity: An empirical re-examination. *Journal for the Scientific Study of Religion, 15,* 69–74. [253]

Castaneda, C. (1968). *The teachings of Don Juan: A Yaqui way of knowledge.* Berkeley: University of California Press. [124–126, 133]

Chamberlain, K., & Zika, S. (1988). Religiosity, life meaning, and well-being: Some relationships in a sample of women. *Journal for the Scientific Study of Religion, 27,* 411–420. [271, 280]

Cheuvront, J. B., & Ventis, W. L. (1982). A study of the relationship between religious orientation, fundamentalist beliefs, and cognitive moral judgment. Unpublished manuscript, College of William and Mary. [360]

Child, I. L. (1973). *Humanistic psychology and the research tradition: Their several virtues.* New York: Wiley. [20]

Christensen, C. W. (1963). Religious conversion. *Archives of General Psychiatry, 9,* 207–216. [108]

Christensen, H. T., & Cannon, K. L. (1978). The fundamentalist emphasis at Brigham Young University: 1935–1973. *Journal for the Scientific Study of Religion, 17,* 53–57. [41]

Clark, W. H. (1955). A study of some of the factors leading to achievement and creativity, with special reference to religious skepticism and belief. *Journal of Social Psychology, 51,* 57–70. [249]

Clark, W. H. (1958). *The psychology of religion.* New York: Macmillan. [102, 107, 166, 182]

Clark, W. H. (1969). *Chemical ecstasy: Psychedelic drugs and religion.* New York: Sheed & Ward. [119]

Clark, W. H., & Warner, C. M. (1955). The relation of church attendance to honesty and kindness in a small community. *Religious Education, 50,* 340–342. [339]

Cline, V. B., & Richards, J. M. (1965). A factor-analytic study of religious belief and behavior. *Journal of Personality and Social Psychology, 1,* 569–578. [339]

Cochran, J. K., & Beeghley, L. (1991). The influence of religion on attitudes toward non-marital sexuality: A preliminary assessment of reference group theory. *Journal for the Scientific Study of Religion, 30,* 45–62. [337]

Coe, G. A. (1900). *The spiritual life: Studies in the science of religion.* New York: Eaton & Mains. [53]

Coles, R. (1990). *The spiritual life of children.* Boston: Houghton Mifflin. [7, 55, 60]

Comrey, A. L., & Newmeyer, J. A. (1965). Measurement of radicalism-conservatism. *Journal of Social Psychology, 67,* 357–369. [300]

Comstock, G. W., & Partridge, K. B. (1972). Church attendance and health. *Journal of Chronic Diseases, 25,* 665–672. [241, 242]

Cook, J. A., & Wimberley, D. W. (1983). If I should die before I wake: Religious commitment and adjustment to the death of a child. *Journal for the Scientific Study of Religion, 22,* 222–238. [200]

Cooper, H. M., & Lemke, K. M. (1991). On the role of meta-analysis in personality and social psychology. *Personality and Social Psychology Bulletin, 17,* 245–251. [240n]

Cowen, E. L. (1954). The negative concept as a personality measure. *Journal of Consulting Psychology, 18,* 138–142. [251]

Cox, E. (1967). *Sixth form religion.* London: SCM Press. [37]

Crandall, J. E., & Rasmussen, R. D. (1975). Purpose in life as related to specific values. *Journal of Clinical Psychology, 31,* 483–485. [199, 269, 279]

Crandall, V. C., & Gozali, J. (1969). The social desirability responses of children of four religious-cultural groups. *Child Development, 40,* 751–762. [313]

Crosby, F., Bromley, S., & Saxe, L. (1980). Recent unobtrusive studies of black and white discrimination and prejudice: A literature review. *Psychological Bulletin, 87,* 546–563. [313, 324]

Crowne, D., & Marlowe, D. (1964). *The approval motive.* New York: Wiley. [313–314]

Crumbaugh, J. C. (1968). Cross-validation of purpose-in-life test based on Frankl's concepts. *Journal of Individual Psychology, 24,* 74–81. [199]

Crumbaugh, J. C., & Maholick, L. T. (1969). *The Purpose in Life Test.* Munster, IN: Psychometric Affiliates. [113]

Crumbaugh, J. C., Raphael, M., & Shrader, R. R. (1970). Frankl's will to meaning in a religious order. *Journal of Clinical Psychology, 26,* 206–207. [199]

Dabrowski, K. (1964). *Positive disintegration.* Boston: Little, Brown. [102]

D'Andrade, R. G. (1967). Sex differences and cultural institutions. In E. E. Maccoby (Ed.), *The development of sex differences.* London: Tavistock. [37]

Darley, J. M., & Batson, C. D. (1973). "From Jerusalem to Jericho": A study of situational and dispositional variables in helping behavior. *Journal of Personality and Social Psychology, 27,* 100–108. [346–347, 348, 349, 350n, 359]

Darley, J. M., Moriarty, T., Darley, S., & Berscheid, E. (1974). Increased conformity to a fellow deviant as a function of prior deviation. *Journal of Experimental Social Psychology, 10,* 211–223. [220–221]

Darwin, C. (1859). *On the origin of species.* London: J. Murray. [53]

Darwin, C. (1958). *The autobiography of Charles Darwin, 1809–1882.* New York: Harcourt. [97]

Davis, K. (1948). *Human society.* New York: Macmillan. [38n]

deCharms, R. C. (1968). *Personal causation: The internal affective determinants of behavior.* New York: Academic Press. [237]

Deconchy, J.-P. (1978). L'experimentation en psychologie de la religion: Pourquoi ne pas rever? *Archives de Science Sociales des Religions, 46,* 176–192. [382]

Deconchy, J.-P. (1980). *Orthodoxie religieuse et sciences humaines (Religious orthodoxy, rationality, and scientific knowledge).* The Hague: Mouton. [205n, 215, 384]

Deconchy, J.-P. (1985). Non-experimental and experimental methods in the psychology of religion: A few thoughts on their implications and limits. In L. B. Brown (Ed.), *Advances in the psychology of religion* (pp. 76–112). Oxford: Pergamon Press. [382]

Deikman, A. J. (1966). Implications of experimentally induced contemplative meditation. *Journal of Nervous and Mental Disease, 142,* 101–116. [135, 136]

deJong, G. F., & Ford, T. R. (1965). Religious fundamentalism and denominational preference in the southern Appalachian region. *Journal for the Scientific Study of Religion, 5,* 24–33. [39]

Demerath, N. J. (1965). *Social class in American Protestantism.* Chicago: Rand McNally. [39, 40]

Demerath, N. J., & Levinson, R. M. (1971). Baiting the dissident hook: Some effects of bias on measuring religious belief. *Sociometry, 34,* 346–359. [3]

Devine, P. G. (1989). Automatic and controlled processes in prejudice: The role of stereotypes and personal beliefs. In A. R. Pratkanis, S. J. Breckler, & A. G. Greenwald (Eds.), *Attitude structure and function.* Hillsdale, NJ: Erlbaum. [330]

Diagnostic and statistical manual of mental disorders: III-R. (1980). New York: American Psychiatric Association. [235]

Ditman, K. S., Hayman, M., & Whittlesay, J.R.B. (1962). Nature and frequency of claims following LSD. *Journal of Nervous and Mental Disease, 134,* 336–352. [123–124]

Dittes, J. E. (1969). Psychology of religion. In G. Lindzey & E. Aronson (Eds.), *The handbook of social psychology* (Vol. 5). Reading, Mass.: Addison-Wesley. [156, 165, 234, 240n, 256, 384]

Dittes, J. E., & Kelley, H. H. (1956). Effects of different conditions of acceptance upon conformity to group norms. *Journal of Abnormal and Social Psychology, 53,* 100–107. [221]

Donahue, M. J. (1985). Intrinsic and extrinsic religiousness: Review and meta-analysis. *Journal of Personality and Social Psychology, 48,* 400–419. [164, 174, 177–179, 303, 310, 329]

Dreger, R. M. (1952). Some personality correlates of religious attitudes as determined by projective techniques. *Psychological Monographs, 66* (Whole No. 335). [249, 250]

Dudley, R. L., & Cruise, R. J. (1990). Measuring religious maturity: A proposed scale. *Review of Religious Research, 32,* 97–109. [168n]

Dudley, R. L., Mutch, P. B., & Cruise, R. J. (1987). Religious factors and drug usage among Seventh-Day Adventist youth in North America. *Journal for the Scientific Study of Religion, 26,* 218–233. [246]

Dunlap, K. (1919). Are there any instincts? *Journal of Abnormal Psychology, 14,* 307–311. [53]

Dunlap, K. (1946). *Religion: Its functions in human life; a study of religion from the point of view of psychology.* New York: McGraw-Hill. [53]

Dunn, R. F. (1965). Personality patterns among religious personnel: A review. *Catholic Psychological Record, 3,* 125–137. [249]

Durkheim, E. (1915). *The elementary forms of the religious life.* London: George Allen & Unwin Ltd. [45n]

Dynes, R. R. (1955). Church-sect typology and socio-economic status. *American Sociological Review, 20,* 555–560. [39]

Eckhardt, K. W. (1970). Religiosity and civil rights militancy. *Review of Religious Research, 11,* 197–203. [39n]

Einstein, A. (1945). Letter to Jacques Hadamard. In J. Hadamard (Ed.), *The psychology of invention in the mathematical field.* Princeton: Princeton University Press. [99]

Eisenberg-Berg, N., & Roth, K. (1980). Development of young children's prosocial moral judgment: A longitudinal follow-up. *Developmental Psychology, 16,* 375–376. [335, 337]

Eisinga, R., Felling, A., & Peters, J. (1990). Religious belief, church involvement, and ethnocentrism in the Netherlands. *Journal for the Scientific Study of Religion, 29,* 54–75. [254, 297, 299, 306]

Ellis, A. (1980). Psychotherapy and atheistic values: A response to A. E. Bergin's "Psychotherapy and religious values." *Journal of Consulting and Clinical Psychology, 48,* 635–639. [234, 238, 259]

Endler, N., & Magnusson, D. (Eds.). (1976). *Interactional psychology and personality.* Washington, D.C.: Hemisphere. [49]

Erickson, D. (1964). Religious consequences of public and sectarian schooling. *The School Review, 72,* 22–33. [43]

Erikson, E. (1950). *Childhood and society.* New York: Norton. [67–71, 75, 101–102]

Erikson, E. (1958). *Young man Luther: A study in psychoanalysis and history.* New York: Norton. [71]

Erikson, E. (1959). Identity and the life cycle. *Psychological Issues, 1* (Whole issue). [67–71]

Erikson, E. (1969). *Gandhi's truth: On the origins of militant nonviolence.* New York: Norton. [71]

Ernsberger, D. J., & Manaster, G. L. (1981). Moral development, intrinsic/extrinsic religious orientation, and denominational teaching. *Genetic psychology Monographs, 104,* 23–41. [66]

Evans, R. I. (1952). Personal values as factors in antisemitism. *Journal of Abnormal and Social Psychology, 47,* 749–756. [300]

Fawcett, T. (1970). *The symbolic language of religion.* London: SCM Press. [145, 146]

Feagin, J. R. (1964). Prejudice and religious types: A focused study of Southern fundamentalists. *Journal for the Scientific Study of Religion, 4,* 3–13. [199, 305]

Feather, N. T. (1964). Acceptance and rejection of arguments in relation to attitude strength, critical ability, and intolerance of inconsistency. *Journal of Abnormal and Social Psychology, 69,* 127–136. [210–212, 254]

Feldman, K. A. (1969). Change and stability of religious orientations during college. *Review of Religious Research, 11,* 40–60 and 103–128. [40, 41]

Feldman, K. A., & Newcomb, T. M. (1969). *The impact of college on students.* San Francisco: Jossey-Bass. [41, 42]

Fenwick, P. (1969). Computer analysis of the EEG during mantra meditation. Paper presented at a conference on the effects of meditation, concentration, and attention on the EEG, University of Marseilles. [139]

Fenwick, P. (1987). Meditation and the EEG. In M. A. West (Ed.), *The psychology of meditation* (pp. 104–117). Oxford: Clarendon Press. [139, 153]

Ferman, L. A. (1960). Religious change on a college campus. *Journal of College Student Personnel, 1,* 2–12. [40]

Ferraro, K. F., & Albrecht-Jensen, C. M. (1991). Does religion influence adult health? *Journal for the Scientific Study of Religion, 30,* 193–202. [244]

Ferriani, N. A., & Batson, C. D. (1990). Religious orientation and traditional versus charismatic Bible study: A validation study. Unpublished manuscript, University of Kansas. [178]

Festinger, L. (1954). A theory of social comparison processes. *Human Relations, 7,* 117–140. [30–31]

Festinger, L. (1957). *A theory of cognitive dissonance.* Stanford, Calif.: Stanford University Press. [95, 202–203, 215]

Festinger, L., Riecken, H. W., & Schachter, S. (1956). *When prophecy fails.* Minneapolis: University of Minnesota Press. [203–204, 205, 207–209, 214, 217]

Filbey, R. A., & Gazzaniga, M. (1969). Splitting the normal brain with reaction time. *Psychonomic Science, 17,* 335–336. [101]

Findlay, A. (1948). *A hundred years of chemistry* (2nd ed.). London: Duckworth. [97]

Fingarette, H. (1958). The ego and mystic selflessness. *Psychoanalytic Review, 45,* 5–40. [108]

Finney, J. R., & Malony, H. N. (1985). Means, end, and quest: A research note. *Review of Religious Research, 26,* 408–412. [179]

Fisher, S. (1964). Acquiescence and religiosity. *Psychological Reports, 15,* 784. [251]

Forbes, G. B., TeVault, R. K., & Gromoll, H. F. (1971). Willingness to help strangers as a function of liberal, conservative, or Catholic church membership. A field study with the lost-letter technique. *Psychological Reports, 28,* 947–949. [340]

Ford, T. R. (1960). Status, residence, and fundamentalist religious beliefs in the Southern Appalachians. *Social Forces, 39,* 41–49. [40, 41]

Fowler, J. W. (1981). *Stages of faith: The psychology of human development and the quest for meaning.* San Francisco: Harper & Row. [71–75]

Fox, G. (1952). *Journal* (Rev. ed.). Cambridge: Cambridge University Press. [195]

Francis, L. J., Pearson, P. R., Carter, M., & Kay, W. K. (1981a). The relationship between neuroticism and religiosity among English 15 and 16 year olds. *Journal of Social Psychology, 114,* 99–102. [242]

Francis, L. J., Pearson, P. R., Carter, M., & Kay, W. K. (1981b). Are introverts more religious? *British Journal of Social Psychology, 20,* 101–104. [242]

Francis, L. J., Pearson, P. R., & Kay, W. K. (1983). Are religious children bigger liars? *Psychological Reports, 52,* 551–554. [313]

Frank, J. D. (1977). Nature and functions of belief systems: Humanism and transcendental religion. *American Psychologist, 32,* 555–559. [10, 106]

Frankl, V. (1962). *Man's search for meaning: A introduction to logotherapy.* Boston: Beacon Press. [53]

Frenkel-Brunswik, E., & Sanford, R. N. (1945). Some personality correlates of anti-semitism. *Journal of Psychology, 20,* 271–291. [159, 305]

Freud, S. (1913). *Totem and taboo.* London: Hogarth Press. [34]

Freud, S. (1935). *A general introduction to psycho-analysis.* New York: Liveright. (First published, 1917) [67, 69]

Freud, S. (1961). *Civilization and its discontents.* New York: Norton. (First published, 1930). [46, 201, 202]

Freud, S. (1964). *The future of an illusion.* Garden City, N.Y.: Doubleday. (First published, 1927) [46–47, 201, 232]

Friedrichs, R. W. (1959). Christians and residential exclusion: An empirical study of a Northern dilemma. *Journal of Social Issues, 15,* 14–23. [307, 317n]

Friedrichs, R. W. (1960). Alter versus ego: An exploratory assessment of altruism. *American Sociological Review, 25,* 496–508. [297, 299, 339]

Friedrichs, R. W. (1971). Decline in prejudice among churchgoers following clergy-led open housing campaign. *Journal for the Scientific Study of Religion, 10,* 152–156. [317n]

Fromm, E. (1950). *Psychoanalysis and religion.* New Haven: Yale University Press. [167, 259]

Funk, R. A. (1955). A survey of religious attitudes and manifest anxiety in a college population. Unpublished Ph.D. dissertation, Purdue University. [180]

Funk, R. A. (1956). Religious attitudes and manifest anxiety in a college population. *American Psychologist, 11,* 375. [247]

Gaertner, S. L., & Dovidio, J. F. (1986). The aversive form of racism. In J. F. Dovidio & S. L. Gaertner (Eds.), *Prejudice, discrimination, and racism* (pp. 61–89). New York: Academic Press. [311, 313, 324, 327, 330]

Galanter, M. (1989). *Cults: Faith, healing, and coercion.* New York: Oxford University Press. [109–110, 220, 221]

Galin, D., & Ornstein, R. (1972). Lateral specialization of cognitive mode: An EEG study. *Psychophysiology, 9,* 412–418. [101]

Gallup, G. H., Jr., & Castelli, J. (1989). *The people's religion: American faith in the 90's.* New York: Macmillan. [3, 4, 38]

Gallup Poll International: Index to international public opinion, 1983–1984. (1984). (E. H. Hastings & P. K. Hastings, eds.). Westport, CT: Greenwood Press. [3]

Gallup Report: Political, social, and economic trends, 1986 (Report #253). (1986). Princeton, NJ: Gallup Report. [39, 40]

Gallup Report: Political, social, and economic trends, 1987 (Report #259). (1987). Princeton, NJ: Gallup Report. [33, 87]

Gandhi, M. K. (1948). *Gandhi's autobiography: The story of my experiments with truth* (M. Desai, trans.). Washington, D.C.: Public Affairs Press. [167–168]

Garai, J. E. (1970). Sex differences in mental health. *Genetic Psychology Monographs, 81,* 123–142. [36]

Garai, J. E., & Scheinfeld, A. (1968). Sex differences in mental and behavioral traits. *Genetic Psychology Monographs, 77,* 169–299. [36]

Garrison, K. C. (1961). Worldminded attitudes of college students in a Southern university. *Journal of Social Psychology, 54,* 147–153. [300]

Gazzaniga, M. S. (1967). The split brain in man. *Scientific American, 217,* 24–29. [100]

Genia, V., & Shaw, D. G. (1991). Religion, intrinsic-extrinsic orientation, and depression. *Review of Religious Research, 32,* 274–283. [263, 272]

Gheslin, B. (Ed.). (1952). *The creative process.* New York: New American Library. [98]

Gibbons, D., & de Jarnette, J. (1972). Hypnotic susceptibility and religious experience. *Journal for the Scientific Study of Religion, 11,* 152–156. [112]

Gilligan, C. (1982). *In a different voice: Psychological theory and women's development.* Cambridge, MA: Harvard University Press. [65–66]

Glass, D. (1964). Changes in liking as a means of reducing cognitive discrepancies between self-esteem and aggression. *Journal of Personality, 32,* 531–549. [218]

Glenn, N. D. (1964). Negro religion and Negro status in the United States. In L. Schneider (Ed.), *Religion, culture, and society.* New York: Wiley. [38]

Glock, C. Y. (1964). The role of deprivation in the origin and evolution of religious groups. In R. Lee & M. E. Marty (Eds.), *Religion and social conflict.* New York: Oxford University Press. [38n]

Glock, C. Y., & Stark, R. (1965). *Religion and society in tension.* Chicago: Rand McNally. [109]

Glock, C. Y., & Stark, R. (1966). *Christian beliefs and antisemitism.* New York: Harper & Row. [42, 169]

Godin, A., & Hallez, M. (1964). Parental images and divine paternity. In A. Godin (Ed.), *From religious experience to a religious attitude.* Brussels: Lumen Vitae. [35]

Goethals, G. R., & Darley, J. M. (1977). Social comparison theory: An attributional approach. In J. M. Suls & R. M. Miller (Eds.), *Social comparison processes: Theoretical and empirical perspectives.* Washington, D.C.: Hemisphere. [31]

Goffman, E. (1959). *The presentation of self in everyday life.* Garden City, N.Y.: Doubleday. [28]

Goldman, R. (1964). *Religious thinking from childhood to adolescence.* London: Routledge & Kegan Paul. [59–61]

Goldman, R. (1965). *Readiness for religion: A basis for developmental religious education.* New York: Seabury. [61]

Goldsen, R., Rosenberg, M., Williams, R. M., & Suchman, E. A. (1960). *What college students think.* New York: Van Nostrand. [246, 300]

Goleman, D. (1977). *The varieties of meditative experience.* New York: Dutton. [133–134, 135, 152]

Goode, E. (1966). Social class and church participation. *American Journal of Sociology, 72,* 102–111. [39]

Gorer, G. (1955). *Exploring English character.* London: Cresset. [336]

Gorsuch, R. L. (1982). Practicality and ethics of experimental research when studying religion. *Journal for the Scientific Study of Religion, 21,* 370–372. [382]

Gorsuch, R. L. (1984). Measurement: The boon and bane of investigating religion. *American Psychologist, 39,* 228–236. [383]

Gorsuch, R. L. (1988). Psychology of religion. *Annual Review of Psychology, 39,* 201–221. [174, 310, 329, 347, 350n–351n, 356]

Gorsuch, R. L., & Aleshire, D. (1974). Christian faith and ethnic prejudice: A review and interpretation of research. *Journal for the Scientific Study of Religion, 13,* 281–307. [296n, 309, 310, 329]

Gorsuch, R. L., & Butler, M. C. (1976). Initial drug abuse: A review of predisposing social-psychological factors. *Psychological Bulletin, 83,* 120–137. [246]

Gorsuch, R. L., & McFarland, S. (1972). Single- vs. multiple-item scales for measuring religious values. *Journal for the Scientific Study of Religion, 11,* 53–65. [163, 301, 303, 361]

Gorsuch, R. L., & Smith, C. S. (1983). Attributions of responsibility to God: An interaction of religious beliefs and outcomes. *Journal for the Scientific Study of Religion, 22,* 340–352. [202]

Graff, R. W., & Ladd, C. E. (1971). POI [Personal Orientation Inventory] correlates of a religious commitment inventory. *Journal of Clinical Psychology, 27,* 502–504. [250, 252]

Gray, D. B., & Revelle, W. A. (1974). A multidimensional religious attitude inventory related to multiple measures of race. *Journal of Social Psychology, 92,* 153–154. [305]

Gray, J. A. (1971). Sex differences in emotional behavior in mammals including man: Endocrine bases. *Acta Psychologica, 35,* 29–46. [36]

Green, C. W., & Hoffman, C. L. (1989). Stages of faith and perceptions of similar and dissimilar others. *Review of Religious Research, 30,* 246–254. [75]

Gregory, W. E. (1957). The orthodoxy of the authoritarian personality. *Journal of Social Psychology, 45,* 217–232. [253, 300]

Griffin, G.A.E., Gorsuch, R. L., & Davis, A. (1987). A cross-cultural investigation of religious orientation, social norms, and prejudice. *Journal for the Scientific Study of Religion, 26,* 358–365. [317, 318, 319, 320]

Grof, S., & Halifax, J. (1977). *The human encounter with death.* New York: Dutton. [126–128]

Gurin, G., Veroff, J., & Feld, S. (1960). *Americans view their mental health.* New York: Basic Books. [241]

Haan, N., Smith, B., & Block, J. (1968). Moral reasoning of young adults. *Journal of Personality and Social Psychology, 10,* 183–201. [66, 335, 337]

Haan, N., Weiss, R., & Johnson, V. (1982). The role of logic in moral reasoning and development. *Developmental Psychology, 18,* 245–256. [65]

Hadaway, C. K. (1978). Life satisfaction and religion: A reanalysis. *Social Forces, 57,* 636–643. [242, 250]

Hadaway, C. K., Elifson, K. W., & Petersen, D. M. (1984). Religious involvement and drug use among urban adolescents. *Journal for the Scientific Study of Religion, 23,* 109–128. [246]

Hadden, J. K. (1963). An analysis of some factors associated with religion and political affiliation in a college population. *Journal for the Scientific Study of Religion, 2*, 209–216. [298]

Hall, G. S. (1882). The moral and religious training of children. *The Princeton Review, 9*, 26–48. [53]

Halverson, R. R., & Pallak, M. S. (1978). Commitment, ego-involvement, and resistance to attack. *Journal of Experimental Social Psychology, 14*, 1–12. [219]

Hammersla, J. F., Andrews-Qualls, L. C., & Frease, L. G. (1986). God concepts and religious commitment among Christian university students. *Journal for the Scientific Study of Religion, 25*, 424–435. [41]

Hammond, P. E., & Hunter, J. D. (1984). On maintaining plausibility: The worldview of evangelical college students. *Journal for the Scientific Study of Religion, 23*, 221–238. [41, 221]

Hanford, J. T. (1975). A synoptic approach: Resolving problems in empirical and phenomenological approaches to the psychology of religion. *Journal for the Scientific Study of Religion, 14*, 219–227. [17]

Hanson, N. R. (1958). *Patterns of discovery.* New York: Cambridge University Press. [17]

Hardyck, J. A., & Braden, M. (1962). Prophecy fails again: A report of a failure to replicate. *Journal of Abnormal and Social Psychology, 65*, 136–141. [209–210]

Harman, W. W., & Fadiman, J. (1970). Selective enhancement of specific capacities through psychedelic training. In B. Aaronson & H. Osmond (Eds.), *Psychedelics: The uses and implications of hallucinogenic drugs.* Garden City, N.Y.: Doubleday. [120–121, 122n–123n]

Hartshorne, H., & May, M. A. (1928). *Studies in deceit.* New York: Macmillan. [244]

Hartshorne, H., & May, M. A. (1929). *Studies in service and self-control.* New York: Macmillan. [339]

Harvey, O. J., Hunt, D. E., & Schroder, H. M. (1961). *Conceptual systems and personality organization.* New York: Wiley. [160, 239]

Hastorf, A., & Cantril, H. (1954). They saw a game: A case study. *Journal of Abnormal and Social Psychology, 49*, 129–134. [90–91]

Hathaway, W. L., & Pargament, K. I. (1990). Intrinsic religiousness, religious coping, and psychosocial competence: A covariance structure analysis. *Journal for the Scientific Study of Religion, 29*, 423–441. [278, 279]

Havens, J. (1963). The changing climate of research on the college student and his religion. *Journal for the Scientific Study of Religion, 3*, 52–69. [41]

Havens, J. (1964). A working paper: Memo on the religious implications of consciousness-changing drugs (LSD, mescalin, psilocybin). *Journal for the Scientific Study of Religion, 3*, 216–226. [132]

Heirich, M. (1977). Change of heart: A test of some widely held theories about religious conversion. *American Journal of Sociology, 83*, 653–680. [109]

Heller, D. (1986). *The children's God.* Chicago: University of Chicago Press. [60]

Heller, D. (1987). *Dear God: Children's letters to God.* New York: Doubleday. [60]

Hemingway, E. (1970). *Islands in the stream.* New York: Scribner's. [105]

Herek, G. M. (1987). Religious orientation and prejudice: A comparison of racial and sexual attitudes. *Personality and Social Psychology Bulletin, 13*, 34–44. [317, 318, 319, 322–323]

Hesse, H. (1951). *Siddhartha.* New York: New Directions. [9–10]

Hine, V. H. (1969). Pentecostal glossolalia: Toward a functional interpretation. *Journal for the Scientific Study of Religion, 8*, 211–226. [39]

Hirschberg, G., & Gilliland, A. R. (1942). Parent-child relations in attitudes. *Journal of Abnormal and Social Psychology, 37,* 125–130. [43]

Hjelle, L. A. (1975). Relationship of a measure of self-actualization to religious participation. *Journal of Psychology, 89,* 179–182. [252]

Hoelter, J. W., & Epley, R. J. (1979). Religious correlates of fear of death. *Journal for the Scientific Study of Religion, 18,* 404–411. [248]

Hoffeldt, D., & Batson, C. D. (1971). The psychology of religious visions: A study of those who experience them. Unpublished manuscript, Princeton University. [112]

Hoffer, E. (1951). *The true believer.* New York: Harper. [163, 169]

Hoge, D. R. (1972). A validated intrinsic religious motivation scale. *Journal for the Scientific Study of Religion, 11,* 369–376. [163, 164n]

Hoge, D. R., & Carroll, J. W. (1973). Religiosity and prejudice in Northern and Southern churches. *Journal for the Scientific Study of Religion, 12,* 181–197. [269, 280, 308]

Hoge, D. R., & Carroll, J. W. (1978). Determinants of commitment and participation in suburban Protestant churches. *Journal for the Scientific Study of Religion, 17,* 107–127. [40]

Hoge, D. R., & de Zulueta, E. (1985). Salience as a condition for various social consequences of religious commitment. *Journal for the Scientific Study of Religion, 24,* 21–38. [246]

Hoge, D. R., & Keeter, L. G. (1976). Determinants of college teachers' religious beliefs and participation. *Journal for the Scientific Study of Religion, 15,* 221–235. [41]

Hoge, D. R., & Petrillo, G. H. (1978a). Church participation among high school youth. *Journal for the Scientific Study of Religion, 17,* 359–379. [43]

Hoge, D. R., & Petrillo, G. H. (1978b). Development of religious thinking in adolescence: A test of Goldman's theories. *Journal for the Scientific Study of Religion, 17,* 139–154. [61–62]

Hollingshead, A. B. (1949). *Elmtown's youth.* New York: Wiley. [39]

Hood, R. W., Jr. (1970). Religious orientation and the report of religious experience. *Journal for the Scientific Study of Religion, 9,* 285–291. [183]

Hood, R. W., Jr. (1972). Normative and motivational determinants of reported religious experience in two Baptist samples. *Review of Religious Research, 13,* 192–196. [183]

Hood, R. W., Jr. (1973). Hypnotic susceptibility and reported religious experience. *Psychological Reports, 33,* 549–550. [112–113]

Hood, R. W., Jr. (1974). Psychological strength and the report of intense religious experience. *Journal for the Scientific Study of Religion, 13,* 65–71. [242, 250]

Hood, R. W., Jr. (1975). The construction and preliminary validation of a measure of reported mystical experience. *Journal for the Scientific Study of Religion, 14,* 29–41. [111–112]

Hood, R. W., Jr. (1978). The usefulness of the indiscriminantly pro and anti categories of religious orientation. *Journal for the Scientific Study of Religion, 17,* 419–431. [174]

Hood, R. W., Jr. (1985). The conceptualization of religious purity in Allport's typology. *Journal for the Scientific Study of Religion, 24,* 413–417. [182]

Hood, R. W., Jr., & Morris, R. J. (1983). Toward a theory of death transcendence. *Journal for the Scientific Study of Religion, 22,* 353–365. [199–200, 265, 275]

Hood, R. W., Jr., Morris, R. J., & Watson, P. J. (1990). Quasi-experimental elicitation of the differential report of religious experience among intrinsic and indiscriminately pro-religious types. *Journal for the Scientific Study of Religion, 29,* 164–172. [137, 183]

Horney, K. (1951). *Neurosis and human growth.* New York: Norton. [102, 236]

Hughes, P. (1954). *A popular history of the Catholic Church.* New York: Doubleday. [205]

Hunsberger, B. E. (1976). Background religious denomination, parental emphasis, and the religious orientation of university students. *Journal for the Scientific Study of Religion, 15,* 251–255. [43]

Hunsberger, B. E. (1978). The religiosity of college students: Stability and change over years at university. *Journal for the Scientific Study of Religion, 17,* 159–164. [41]

Hunsberger, B. E., & Brown, L. B. (1984). Religious socialization, apostasy, and the impact of family background. *Journal for the Scientific Study of Religion, 23,* 239–251. [43]

Hunt, R. A., & King, M. B. (1971). The intrinsic-extrinsic concept. *Journal for the Scientific Study of Religion, 10,* 339–356. [164, 164n, 174]

Husserl, E. (1960). *Cartesian meditations: An introduction to phenomenology* (D. Cairns, trans.). The Hague: Martinus Nijhoff. [89]

Huxley, A. (1954). *The doors of perception.* New York: Harper. [120, 132]

ITA. (1970). *Religion in Britain and Northern Ireland,* London: Independent Television Authority. [9n]

Jackson, L. E., & Coursey, R. D. (1988). The relationship of God control and internal locus of control to intrinsic religious motivation, coping, and purpose in life. *Journal for the Scientific Study of Religion, 27,* 399–410. [277]

Jacobs, J. (1984). The economy of love in religious commitment: The deconversion of women from nontraditional religious movements. *Journal for the Scientific Study of Religion, 23,* 155–171. [221]

Jacobs, J. (1987). Deconversion from religious movements: An analysis of charismatic bonding and spiritual commitment. *Journal for the Scientific Study of Religion, 26,* 294–308. [32, 107]

James, W. (1902). *The varieties of religious experience.* New York: Longman. [6, 11, 15, 81, 84, 87–88, 102, 104, 105, 106, 108, 117, 119–120, 132, 143, 190, 194–195, 198, 231–232, 332–333]

Jastrow, M. (1902). *The study of religion.* New York: Scribners. [53]

Jaynes, J. (1977). *The origin of consciousness in the breakdown of the bicameral mind.* Boston: Houghton Mifflin. [106]

Jensen, L., Newell, R. J., & Holman, T. (1990). Sexual behavior, church attendance, and permissive beliefs among unmarried young men and women. *Journal for the Scientific Study of Religion, 29,* 113–117. [247]

Johnson, B. (1962). Ascetic Protestantism and political preference. *Public Opinion Quarterly, 26,* 35–46. [39]

Johnson, D. P. (1977). Religious commitment, social distance, and authoritarianism. *Review of Religious Research, 18,* 99–113. [305, 308, 317n]

Johnson, S. D. (1987). Factors related to intolerance of AIDS victims. *Journal for the Scientific Study of Religion, 26,* 105–110. [301]

Johnson, S. D., & Tamney, J. B. (1984). Support for the Moral Majority: A test of a model. *Journal for the Scientific Study of Religion, 23,* 183–196. [254]

Johnston, W. (1974). *Silent music, the science of meditation.* New York: Harper. [139]

Jones, E. E. (1987). Major developments in social psychology during the past five decades. In G. Lindzey & E. Aronson (Eds.), *Handbook of social psychology* (Vol. 1: *Theory and method:* 3rd ed., pp. 47–107). New York: Random House.[28]

Jones, E. E. (1990). *Interpersonal perception.* New York: W. H. Freeman. [90]

Jones, E. E., & Pittman, T. S. (1982). Toward a general theory of strategic self-presentation. In J. Suls (Ed.), *Psychological perspectives on the self* (pp. 231–262). Hillsdale, NJ: Erlbaum. [311, 323]

Jung, C. G. (1933). *Modern man in search of a soul.* New York: Harcourt. [233]

Jung, C. G. (1953). *The collected works of C. G. Jung* (Vol. 12). Trans. R.F.C. Hull. London: Routledge & Kegan Paul. [144]

Jung, C. G. (Ed.). (1964). *Man and his symbols.* London: Aldus Books. [126, 233]

Kahoe, R. D. (1974). Personality and achievement correlates of intrinsic and extrinsic religious orientations. *Journal of Personality and Social Psychology, 29,* 812–818. [163, 263, 267, 270, 273, 276, 280]

Kahoe, R. D. (1975). Authoritarianism and religion: Relationships of F-scale items to intrinsic and extrinsic religious orientations. *JSAS Catalog of Selected Documents in Psychology, 5,* 284–285. (Manuscript No. 1020) [270]

Kahoe, R. D. (1977). Intrinsic religion and authoritarianism: A differentiated relationship. *Journal for the Scientific Study of Religion, 16,* 179–183. [281]

Kahoe, R. D., & Dunn, R. F. (1975). The fear of death and religious attitudes and behavior. *Journal for the Scientific Study of Religion, 14,* 379–382. [199, 264, 274]

Kahoe, R. D., & Meadow, M. J. (1977, October). Religious orientations dimensions: Individual and institutional interrelations. Paper presented at the annual convention of the Society for the Scientific Study of Religion, Chicago. [163]

Kahoe, R. D., & Meadow, M. J. (1981). A developmental perspective on religious orientation dimensions. *Journal of Religion and Health, 20,* 8–17. [182]

Kaiser, D. L. (1991). Religious problem-solving styles and guilt. *Journal for the Scientific Study of Religion, 30,* 94–98. [250]

Kant, I. (1889). Fundamental principles of the metaphysic of morals. In *Kant's critique of practical reason and other works on the theory of ethics* (4th ed., T. K. Abbott, Trans.). New York: Longmans, Green. (First published, 1785) [360]

Kantner, J. F., & Zelnik, M. (1972). Sexual experience of young unmarried women in the United States. *Family Planning Perspectives, 4,* 9–18. [245]

Karlins, M. (1966). Conceptual complexity and remote association proficiency as creativity variables in a complex problem-solving task. Unpublished Ph.D. dissertation, Princeton University. [91]

Karlins, M., Coffman, T. L., & Walters, G. (1969). On the fading of social stereotypes: Studies in three generations of college students. *Journal of Personality and Social Psychology, 13,* 1–16. [311]

Kasamatsu, A., & Hirai, T. (1966). An electroencephalographic study on the Zen meditation (Zazen). *Folio Psychiatrica and Neurologica Japonica, 20,* 315–336. [138–139, 152]

Kass, J. D., Friedman, R., Leserman, J., Zuttermeister, P. C., & Benson, H. (1991). Health outcomes and a new index of spiritual experience. *Journal for the Scientific Study of Religion, 30,* 203–216. [272, 280]

Keedy, T. C. (1958). Anomie and religious orthodoxy. *Sociology and Social Research, 43,* 34–37. [300]

Kelley, H. H. (1955). Salience of membership and resistance to change of group anchored attitudes. *Human Relations, 8,* 275–290. [204n–205n]

Kelly, G. A. (1955). *The psychology of personal constructs.* New York: Norton. [90]

Kelly, J., Ferson, J., & Holtzman, W. (1958). The measurement of attitudes towards the Negro in the South. *Journal of Social Psychology, 48,* 305–317. [300, 307]

Kelman, H. C. (1958). Compliance, identification, and internalization: Three processes of attitude change. *Journal of Conflict Resolution, 2,* 51–60. [54–56]

Kelman, H. C. (1961). Processes of opinion change. *Public Opinion Quarterly, 25,* 57–78. [48–49]

Kersten, L. K. (1970). *The Lutheran ethic.* Detroit: Wayne State University Press. [301, 308]

Kierkegaard, S. (1954). *The sickness unto death.* New York: Anchor Books. (First published, 1849) [102]

Kierkegaard, S. (1957). *The concept of dread.* Princeton: Princeton University Press. (First published, 1844) [102]

Kiesler, C. A. (1971). *The psychology of commitment: Experiments linking behavior to belief.* New York: Academic. [218–219]

King, M. B. (1991). Is scientific study of religion possible? *Journal for the Scientific Study of Religion, 30,* 108–113. [17]

King, M. B., & Hunt, R. A. (1972). *Measuring religious dimensions.* Dallas: Congregational Involvement Study. [309]

King, M. B., & Hunt, R. A. (1975). Measuring the religious variable: National replication. *Journal for the Scientific Study of Religion, 14,* 13–22. [163]

Kinsbourne, M., & Cook, J. (1971). Generalized and lateralized effect of concurrent verbalization on a unimanual skill. *Quarterly Journal of Experimental Psychology, 23,* 341–345. [101]

Kinsey, A. C., Pomeroy, W. B., & Martin, C. E. (1948). *Sexual behavior in the human male.* London: Saunders. [245]

Kirkpatrick, C. (1949). Religion and humanitarianism: A study of institutional implications. *Psychological Monographs, 63,* No. 304. [296, 299]

Kirkpatrick, L. A., & Hood, R. W., Jr. (1990). Intrinsic-extrinsic religious orientation: The boon or bane of contemporary psychology of religion? *Journal for the Scientific Study of Religion, 29,* 442–462. [163–164, 174]

Kirkpatrick, L. A., & Shaver, P. R. (1990). Attachment theory and religion: Childhood attachments, religious beliefs, and conversion. *Journal for the Scientific Study of Religion, 29,* 315–334. [75–77]

Klinger, E., Albaum, A., & Hetherington, M. (1964). Factors influencing the severity of moral judgments. *Journal of Social Psychology, 63,* 319–326. [336]

Koestler, A. (1964). *The act of creation.* New York: Dell. [97]

Kohlberg, L. (1969). Stage and sequence: The cognitive-developmental approach to socialization. In D. Goslin (Ed.), *Handbook of socialization theory and research* (pp. 347–480). Chicago: Rand McNally. [62–64]

Kohlberg, L. (1976). Moral stages and moralization: The cognitive-developmental approach. In T. Lickona (Ed.), *Moral development and behavior: Theory, research, and social issues.* New York: Holt, Rinehart & Winston. [62–64, 338]

Kojetin, B. A. (1988, October). Separating the seekers from the doubters: Quest, self-consciousness, and religious experience. Paper presented at the annual convention of the Society for the Scientific Study of Religion, Chicago. [180]

Kojetin, B. A., McIntosh, D. N., Bridges, R. A., & Spilka, B. (1987). Quest: Constructive search or religious conflict? *Journal for the Scientific Study of Religion, 26,* 111–115. [180, 266, 275, 282]

Kopplin, D. A. (1976, September). Religious orientations of college students and related personality characteristics. Paper presented at the annual convention of the American Psychological Association, Washington, D.C. [276]

Kraft, W. A., Litwin, W. J., & Barber, S. E. (1987). Religious orientation and assertiveness: Relationship to death anxiety. *Journal of Social Psychology, 127,* 93–95. [200, 265, 275]

Krebs, D. L. (1970). Altruism: An examination of the concept and a review of the literature. *Psychological Bulletin, 73,* 258–302. [338]

Krippner, S. (1967). Creative production and "mind-manifesting" experience: A study of the "psychedelic artist." Paper presented at the annual convention of the American Psychological Association, Washington, D.C. [121n]

Kris, E. (1952). *Psychoanalytic explorations in art.* New York: International Universities Press. [101, 111]

Kubie, L. S. (1958). *Neurotic distortions of the creative process.* Lawrence: University of Kansas Press. [101, 111]

Kuhn, T. S. (1962). *The structure of scientific revolutions.* Chicago: University of Chicago Press. [17, 19]

Kurtines, W. M. (1986). Moral behavior as rule-governed behavior: Person and situation effects on moral decision making. *Journal of Personality and Social Psychology, 50,* 784–791. [65]

Kurtines, W. M., & Greif, E. B. (1974). The development of moral thought: Review and evaluation of Kohlberg's approach. *Psychological Bulletin, 81,* 453–470. [65]

Kushner, H. (1986). *When all you've ever wanted isn't enough.* New York: Summit Books. [103]

La Barre, W. (1962). *They shall take up serpents.* Minneapolis: University of Minnesota Press. [34]

Lakoff, G., & Johnson, M. (1980). *Metaphors we live by.* Chicago: University of Chicago Press. [143, 145]

Landis, J. T., & Landis, M. G. (1953). *Building a successful marriage* (2nd ed.). Englewood Cliffs, N.J.: Prentice-Hall. [245]

Langford, B. J., & Langford, C. C. (1974). Church attendance and self-perceived altruism. *Journal for the Scientific Study of Religion, 13,* 221–222. [338, 340]

Lasagna, L., Mosteller, F., von Felsinger, J. M., & Beecher, H. K. (1954). A study of the placebo response. *American Journal of Medicine, 16,* 770–779. [249]

Laumann, E. O. (1969). The social structure of religious and ethno-religious groups in a metropolitan community. *American Sociological Review, 34,* 182–197. [39]

Lawrence, P. J. (1965). Children's thinking about religion: A study of concrete-operational thinking. *Religious Education, 60,* 111–116. [59]

Lazerwitz, B. (1964). Religion and social structure in the United States. In L. Schneider (Ed.), *Religion, culture, and society.* New York: Wiley. [39]

Lea, G. (1982). Religion, mental health, and clinical issues. *Journal of Religion and Health, 21,* 336–351. [235]

Leak, G. K., & Fish, S. (1989). Religious orientation, impression management, and self-deception: Toward a clarification of the link between religiosity and social desirability. *Journal for the Scientific Study of Religion, 28,* 355–359. [314n]

Leak, G. K., Fish, S., Jugel, L., Loucks, A. A., Wood, P., Wright, K., & Williams. D. E. (1990). A multimethod assessment of the construct validity of the Quest religious orientation scale. Unpublished manuscript, Creighton University. [282, 283, 284, 285]

Leary, T. (1964). The religious experience: Its production and interpretation. *Psychedelic Review, 1,* 324–346. [122–123]

Leary, T. (1968). *High priest.* New York: World. [130–131]

Lehman, E. C. (1974). Academic discipline and religiosity in secular and church-related colleges. *Journal for the Scientific Study of Religion, 13,* 205–220. [41]

Lehman, E. C., & Shriver, D. W. (1968). Academic discipline as predictive of faculty religiosity. *Social Forces, 42,* 171–182. [41]

Lenski, G. E. (1953). Social correlates of religious interest. *American Sociological Review, 18,* 533–544. [39, 42, 43]

Lenski, G. E. (1963). *The religious factor* (Rev. ed.). Garden City, N.Y.: Doubleday. [307]

Leuba, J. H. (1912). *A psychological study of religion.* New York: Macmillan. [6]

Levick, M. A., & Delaney, H. D. (1987, October). Religious orientation and overt versus covert death anxiety. Paper presented at the annual convention of the Society for the Scientific Study of Religion, Louisville, KY. [200, 262, 266, 271, 275, 282]

Levin, J. S., & Markides, K. S. (1986). Religious attendance and subjective health. *Journal for the Scientific Study of Religion, 25,* 31–40. [243]

Levinson, D. J., & Sanford, R. N. (1944). A scale for the measurement of antisemitism. *Journal of Psychology, 17,* 339–370. [298]

Lewin, K. (1935). *A dynamic theory of personality.* New York: McGraw-Hill. [49]

Light, H. K. (1970). Attitudes of rural and urban adolescent girls toward selected concepts. *Family Coordinator, 19,* 225–227. [42]

Lincoln, V. (1984). *Teresa: A woman; a biography of Teresa of Avila.* Albany, NY: SUNY Albany Press. [83]

Lindskoog, D., & Kirk, R. E. (1975). Some life-history and attitudinal correlates of self-actualization among evangelical seminary students. *Journal for the Scientific Study of Religion, 14,* 51–55. [252]

Liu, W. T. (1961). The community reference system, religiosity, and race attitudes. *Social Forces, 39,* 324–328. [304, 307]

Loder, J. E. (1966). *Religious pathology and Christian faith.* Philadelphia: Westminster Press. [102]

Loder, J. E. (1981). *The transforming moment: Understanding convictional experiences.* New York: Harper & Row. [102]

Long, T. E., & Hadden, J. K. (1983). Religious conversion and the concept of socialization: Integrating the brainwashing and drift models. *Journal for the Scientific Study of Religion, 22,* 1–14. [32, 221]

Lovekin, A., & Malony, H. N. (1977). Religious glossolalia: A longitudinal study of personality changes. *Journal for the Scientific Study of Religion, 16,* 383–393. [262, 265, 267]

Luckmann, T. (1967). *The invisible religion.* New York: Macmillan. [7]

Lupfer, M. B., Hopkinson, P. L., & Kelley, P. (1988). An exploration of the attributional styles of Christian fundamentalists and of authoritarians. *Journal for the Scientific Study of Religion, 27,* 389–398. [254]

Ma, Yo-Yo (1990). Interview on *Mister Rogers' Neighborhood.* Pittsburgh, PA: Family Communications. [150]

McClain, E. W. (1977, September). Personality differences between intrinsically religious and nonreligious students: A factor analytic study. Paper presented at the annual convention of the American Psychological Association, San Francisco. [273, 276, 278]

Maccoby, E. E., & Jacklin, C. N. (1974). *The psychology of sex differences.* Stanford, Calif.: Stanford University Press. [36]

McConahay, J. B. (1970). Attitudes of Negroes toward the church following the Los Angeles riot. *Sociological Analysis, 31,* 12–22. [38]

McConahay, J. B. (1986). Modern racism, ambivalence, and the Modern Racism scale. In J. F. Dovidio & S. L. Gaertner (Eds.), *Prejudice, discrimination, and racism* (pp. 91–125). New York: Academic Press. [313, 330]

McDougall, W. (1908). *An introduction to social psychology.* London: Methuen. [53]

McFarland, S. G. (1989). Religious orientations and the targets of discrimination. *Journal for the Scientific Study of Religion, 28,* 324–336. [317, 318, 319, 320, 321, 322–323]

McFarland, S. G. (1990, April). Religiously oriented prejudice in communism and Christianity: The role of Quest. Paper presented at the annual convention of the Southeastern Psychological Association, Atlanta. [317, 318, 319, 320, 321, 322–323]

McFarland, S. G. (1990). Is quest a distinct and important religious orientation?: Quest and discrimination revisited. Unpublished manuscript, Western Kentucky University. [179]

McFarland, S. G., & Warren, J. C., Jr. (1992). Religious orientation and selective exposure among fundamentalist Christians. *Journal for the Scientific Study of Religion, 31,* 163–174. [215–216, 229]

McGlothlin, W. S., Cohen, S., & McGlothlin, M. J. (1967). Long-lasting effects of LSD on normals. *Archives of General Psychiatry, 17,* 521–532. [121n–123n]

Machalek, R., & Martin, M. (1976). "Invisible" religions: Some preliminary evidence. *Journal for the Scientific Study of Religion, 15,* 311–321. [6, 7, 10]

McKenna, R. H. (1976). Good Samaritanism in rural and urban settings: A nonreactive comparison of helping behavior of clergy and control subjects. *Representative Research in Social Psychology, 7,* 58–65. [341]

Magni, K. G. (1971). The fear of death: Studies of its character and concomitants.*Lumen Vitae, 5,* 129–142. [199, 264, 273]

Mandler, J. M., & Mandler, G. (1974). Good guys versus bad guys: The subject-object dichotomy. *Journal of Humanistic Psychology, 14,* 63–78. [20]

Maranell, G. M. (1967). An examination of some religious and political attitude correlates of bigotry. *Social Forces, 45,* 356–363. [301]

Markus, H., & Zajonc, R. B. (1985). The cognitive perspective in social psychology. In G. Lindzey & E. Aronson (Eds.), *Handbook of social psychology.* (Vol. 1: *Theory and Method,* pp. 137–230). New York: Random House. [90]

Marshak, A. (1976). Implications of the paleolithic symbolic evidence for the origin of language. *American Scientist, 64,* 136–145. [9n]

Marty, M. E., Rosenberg, S. E., & Greeley, A. M. (1968). *What do we believe?* New York: Meredith Press. [42]

Marx, G. T. (1967). Religion: Opiate or inspiration of civil rights militancy among Negroes? *American Sociological Review, 32,* 64–72. [39n]

Marx, K. (1964). *Early writings.* New York: McGraw-Hill. [45–46]

Maslow, A. H. (1954). *Motivation and personality.* New York: Harper. [103, 137, 237–238]

Maslow, A. H. (1964). *Religions, values, and peak-experiences.* Columbus: Ohio State University Press. [167, 251]

Masters, R.E.L., & Houston, J. (1966). *The varieties of psychedelic experience.* New York: Holt, Rinehart & Winston. [86–87, 123–124, 126]

Masters, W. H., & Johnson, V. (1970). *Human sexual inadequacy.* Boston: Little, Brown. [245]

May, R. (1975). *The courage to create.* New York: Bantam. [102]

Mayo, C. C., Puryear, H. B., & Richek, H. G. (1969). MMPI correlates of religiousness in late adolescent college students. *Journal of Nervous Disorder and Mental Disease, 149,* 381–385. [241, 252]

Melville, H. (1948). *Billy Budd.* Cambridge, Mass.: Harvard University Press. [92]

Merleau-Ponty, M. (1962). *The phenomenology of perception* (C. Smith, trans.). New York: Humanities Press. [89]

Merleau-Ponty, M. (1963). *The structure of behavior* (A. L. Fisher, trans.). Boston: Beacon Press. [89]

Merton, R. K. (1940). Facts and factitiousness in ethnic opinionnaires. *American Sociological Review, 5,* 13–28. [297]

Meschler, M. (1891). *Leben des hl. Aloysius von Gonzaga, Patrons der christlichen Jugend* [*Life of St. Louis of Gonzaga, patron of Christian youth*]. St. Louis: Herder. [196]

Meyer, L. B. (1956). *Emotion and meaning in music.* Chicago: University of Chicago Press. [149]

Middleton, R., & Putney, S. (1962). Religion, normative standards, and behavior. *Sociometry, 25,* 141–152. [245, 336]

Middleton, W. C., & Fay, P. J. (1941). Attitudes of delinquent and nondelinquent girls toward Sunday observance, the Bible, and war. *Journal of Educational Psychology, 32,* 555–558. [244]

Milgram, S. (1963). Behavioral study of obedience. *Journal of Abnormal and Social Psychology, 67,* 371–378. [28]

Miller, G. A. (1979). Images and models, similes and metaphors. In A. Ortony (Ed.), *Metaphor and thought.* New York: Cambridge University Press. [143]

Miller, G. A., Galanter, E., & Pribram, K. H. (1960). *Plans and the structure of behavior.* New York: Holt, Rinehart & Winston. [91]

Miller, W. (1843, January 25). *Signs of the Times.* Boston. [206]

Minton, B., & Spilka, B. (1976). Perspectives on death in relation to powerlessness and form of personal religion. *Omega, 7,* 261–267. [264, 274]

Mitchell, B. (1955). Untitled contribution to the *University* discussion. In A. Flew & A. MacIntyre (Eds.), *New essays in philosophical theology* (pp. 103–105). New York: Macmillan. [367–368]

Moberg, D. O. (1965). Religiosity and old age. *Gerontologist, 5,* 78–87. [248]

Moberg, D. O., & Taves, M. J. (1965). Church participation and adjustment in old age. In A. M. Rose & W. A. Peterson (Eds.), *Older people and their social world.* Philadelphia: F. A. Davis. [248]

Morgan, S. P. (1983). A research note on religion and morality: Are religious people nice people? *Social Forces, 61,* 683–692. [337]

Morris, R. J. (1980, October). Religious orientation, report of mystical experience, and attitudes toward death. Paper presented at the annual convention of the Society for the Scientific Study of Religion, Cincinnati. [199]

Murray, H. A. (1938). *Explorations in personality.* New York: Oxford University Press. [49]

Naranjo, C. (1971). Meditation: Its spirit and technique. In C. Naranjo & R. E. Ornstein, *On the psychology of meditation.* New York: Viking Press. [135–136]

Nelsen, H. M., Yorkley, R. L., & Madron, T. W. (1971). Rural-urban differences in religiosity. *Rural Sociology, 36,* 389–396. [42]

Nelson, L. D., & Dynes, R. R. (1976). The impact of devotionalism and attendance on ordinary and emergency helping behavior. *Journal for the Scientific Study of Religion, 15,* 47–59. [340, 361]

Newcomb, T. M. (1943). *Personality and social change.* New York: Dryden. [41–42]

Newcomb, T. M., & Svehla, G. (1937). Intra-family relationships in attitude. *Sociometry, 1,* 180–205. [43]

Newell, A., Shaw, J. C., & Simon, H. A. (1958). Elements of a theory of human problem solving. *Psychological Review, 65,* 151–166. [91]

Newman, J. S., & Pargament, K. I. (1990). The role of religion in the problem-solving process. *Review of Religious Research, 31,* 390–404. [9n]

Nias, D.K.B. (1972). The structuring of social attitudes in children. *Child Development, 43,* 211–219. [299]

Nichol, F. D. (1944). *The midnight cry.* Washington, D.C.: Review and Herald Publishing Co. [206]

Nidich, S., Seeman, W., & Dreskin, T. (1973). Influence of Transcendental Meditation: A replication. *Journal of Counseling Psychology, 20,* 565–566. [137–138]

Niebuhr, H. R. (1963). *The responsible self.* New York: Harper. [167]

Nietzsche, F. W. (1964). *The complete works of Friedrich Nietzsche.* New York: Russell & Russell. [142]

Ogburn, W. F., & Tibbits, C. (1933). The family and its functions. Chapter 13 in *Recent social trends.* New York: McGraw-Hill. [42]

Oliner, S. P., & Oliner, P. M. (1988). *The altruistic personality: Rescuers of Jews in Nazi Europe.* New York: The Free Press. [294]

O'Reilly, C. T. (1957). Religious practice and personal adjustment. *Sociology and Social Research, 42,* 119–121. [247]

O'Reilly, C. T., & O'Reilly, E. J. (1954). Religious beliefs of Catholic college students and their attitude toward minorities. *Journal of Abnormal and Social Psychology, 49,* 378–380. [300, 301]

Ornstein, R. E. (1971). The techniques of meditation and their implications for modern psychology. In C. Naranjo & R. E. Ornstein, *On the psychology of meditation.* New York: Viking Press. [135, 136]

Ornstein, R. E. (1972). *The psychology of consciousness.* San Francisco: W. H. Freeman. [88–90, 101, 106, 121, 138]

Osarchuk, M., & Tatz, S. J. (1973). Effect of induced fear of death on belief in afterlife. *Journal of Personality and Social Psychology, 27,* 256–260. [200, 201]

Otto, R. (1923). *The idea of the holy.* New York: Oxford University Press. [6, 107]

Overton, W. F., & Reese, H. W. (1973). Models of development: Methodological implications. In J. R. Nesselroade & H. W. Reese (Eds.), *Life span developmental psychology.* New York: Academic Press. [49]

Ozorak, E. W. (1989). Social and cognitive influences on the development of religious beliefs and commitment in adolescence. *Journal for the Scientific Study of Religion, 28,* 448–463. [41, 43]

Pahnke, W. N. (1964). Drugs and mysticism: An analysis of the relationship between psychedelic drugs and mystical consciousness. Unpublished Ph.D. dissertation, Harvard University. [128–130, 131, 381–382]

Pahnke, W. N. (1966). Drugs and mysticism. *International Journal of Parapsychology, 8,* 295–320. [129–130]

Pahnke, W. N., Kurland, A. A., Unger, S., Savage, C., Wolf, S., & Goodman, L. E. (1970). Psychedelic therapy (utilizing LSD) with cancer patients. *Journal of Psychedelic Drugs, 3,* 63–75. [127–128]

Pallak, M. S., Mueller, M., Dollar, K., & Pallak, J. (1972). Effects of commitment on responsiveness to an extreme consonant communication. *Journal of Personality and Social Psychology, 23,* 429–436. [219]

Pallak, M. S., & Sullivan, J. J. (1979). The effect of commitment, threat, and restoration of freedom on attitude change and action-taking. *Personality and Social Psychology Bulletin, 5,* 307–310. [219]

Paloutzian, R. F. (1976, September). Purpose-in-life and value changes following conversion. Paper presented at the annual convention of the American Psychological Association, Washington, D.C. [199]

Paloutzian, R. F. (1981). Purpose in life and value changes following conversion. *Journal of Personality and Social Psychology, 41,* 1153–1160. [113]

Paloutzian, R. F., Jackson, S. L., & Crandall, J. E. (1978). Conversion experience, belief system, and personal and ethical attitudes. *Journal of Psychology and Theology, 6,* 266–275. [119, 264, 269, 270, 273, 279, 281]

Pargament, K. I., Ensing, D. S., Falgout, K., Olsen, H., Reilly, B., Van Haitsma, K., & Warren, R. (1990). God help me (I): Religious coping efforts as predictors of the outcomes to significant negative life events. *American Journal of Community Psychology, 18,* 793–824. [202, 243, 263, 272, 282]

Pargament, K. I., & Hahn, J. (1986). God and the just world: Causal and coping attributions to God in health situations. *Journal for the Scientific Study of Religion, 25,* 193–207. [202]

Pargament, K. I., Kennell, J., Hathaway, W., Grevengoed, N., Newman, J., & Jones, W. (1988). Religion and the problem-solving process: Three styles of coping. *Journal for the Scientific Study of Religion, 27,* 90–104. [267, 277, 283]

Pargament, K. I., Steele, R. E., & Tyler, F. B. (1978, August). Religious practice, religious motivation, religious identification, and individual psychosocial competence. Paper presented at the annual convention of the American Psychological Association, Toronto. [250, 252, 276, 278]

Park, C., Cohen, L. H., & Herb, L. (1990). Intrinsic religiousness and religious coping as life stress moderators for Catholics versus Protestants. *Journal of Personality and Social Psychology, 59,* 562–574. [202, 263, 268, 272, 278, 286]

Parry, H. J. (1949). Protestants, Catholics, and prejudice. *International Journal of Opinion and Attitude Research, 3,* 205–213. [308]

Pascal, B. (1889). *Thoughts of Blaise Pascal* (C. Kegan Paul, Trans.). London: George Bell & Sons (First published, 1670). [104–105]

Patrick, J. W. (1979). Personal faith and the fear of death among divergent religious populations. *Journal for the Scientific Study of Religion, 18,* 298–305. [265, 274]

Paulhus, D. L. (1984). Two-component models of socially desirable responding. *Journal of Personality and Social Psychology, 46,* 598–609. [314n]

Pelletier, K. R. (1974). Influence of transcendental meditation upon autokinetic perception. *Perceptual and Motor Skills, 39,* 1031–1034. [140–141]

Perkins, H. W. (1987). Parental religion and alcohol use problems as intergenerational predictors of problem drinking among college youth. *Journal for the Scientific Study of Religion, 26,* 340–357. [247]

Pervin, L. A., & Lewis, M. (1978). *Perspectives in interactional psychology.* New York: Plenum. [49]

Petersen, L. R., & Roy, A. (1985). Religiosity, anxiety, and meaning and purpose: Religion's consequences for psychological well-being. *Review of Religious Research, 27,* 49–62. [243, 248]

Peterson, J. A. (1964). *Education for marriage* (2nd ed.). New York: Scribner's. [248]

Pettigrew, T. (1959). Regional differences in anti-Negro prejudice. *Journal of Abnormal and Social Psychology, 59,* 28–36. [298]

Phares, J. O., & Schroder, H. M. (1969). Structural scoring manual for Paragraph Completion Test. Unpublished manuscript, Princeton University. [114, 185]

Photiadis, J. D., & Biggar, J. (1962). Religiosity, education, and ethnic distance. *American Journal of Sociology, 67,* 666–672. [301, 306, 309]

Photiadis, J. D., & Johnson, A. L. (1963). Orthodoxy, church participation, and authoritarianism. *American Journal of Sociology, 69,* 244–248. [253]

Piaget, J. (1926). *The language and thought of the child.* New York: Harcourt. [57–59, 148]

Piaget, J. (1953). *The origins of intelligence in the child.* New York: International Universities Press. [57–59, 94]

Pine, F., & Holt, R. R. (1960). Creativity and primary process: A study of adaptive regression. *Journal of Abnormal and Social Psychology, 61,* 370–379. [111]

Plass, E. M. (1959). *What Luther says: A practical in-home anthology for the active Christian.* St. Louis: Concordia Publishing House. [150]

Poincaré, H. (1913). Mathematical creation. In *The foundations of science* (G. B. Halsted, trans.). New York: Science Press. [97–98]

Polanyi, M. (1958). *Personal knowledge: Towards a post-critical philosophy.* Chicago: University of Chicago Press. [19]

Pollio, H. R., Barlow, J. M., Fine, H. J., & Pollio, M. (1977). *Psychology and the poetics of growth: Figurative language in psychology, psychotherapy, and education.* Hillsdale, N.J.: Erlbaum Associates. [143, 146]

Pollio, H. R., Smith, M. K., & Pollio, M. R. (1990). Figurative language and cognitive psychology. *Language and Cognitive Processes, 5,* 141–167. [143]

Pollner, M. (1989). Divine relations, social relations, and well-being. *Journal of Health and Social Behavior, 30,* 92–104. [243]

Ponton, M. O., & Gorsuch, R. L. (1988). Prejudice and religion revisited: A cross-cultural investigation with a Venezuelan sample. *Journal for the Scientific Study of Religion, 27,* 260–271. [317, 318, 319, 320, 321–322]

Popper, K. R. (1959). *The logic of scientific discovery.* New York: Basic Books. [17, 379]

Prothro, E. T., & Jensen, J. A. (1950). Inter-relations of religious and ethnic attitudes in selected Southern populations. *Journal of Social Psychology, 32,* 45–49. [249]

Pruyser, P. W. (1968). *A dynamic psychology of religion.* New York: Harper & Row. [6, 107]

Putney, S., & Middleton, R. (1961). Rebellion, conformity, and parental religious ideologies. *Sociometry, 24,* 125–135. [43]

Radocy, R. E., & Boyle, D. J. (1988). *Psychological foundations of musical behavior* (2nd ed.). New York: C. C. Thomas. [149]

Ragan, R. L. (1963). Attitudes of white Methodist church members in selected Los Angeles metropolitan area churches toward residential segregation of the Negro. *Dissertation Abstracts, 24,* 2615. [307]

Ram Dass. (1978). *Journey of awakening: A meditator's guidebook.* New York: Bantam. [152]

Ranck, J. G. (1955). Some personality correlates of religious attitude and belief. *Dissertation Abstracts, 15,* 878–879. [253]

Ranck, J. G. (1961). Religious conservatism-liberalism and mental health. *Pastoral Psychology, 12,* 34–40. [249]

Rapaport, D. (1951). *Organization and pathology of thought: Selected sources.* New York: Columbia University Press. [138]

Rest, J. R. (1979). *Development in judging moral issues.* Minneapolis: University of Minnesota Press. [64–65, 66]

Rest, J. R. (1983). Morality. In J. Flavell & E. Markham (Eds.), *Manual of child psychology.* (Vol. 3: *Cognitive development,* P. Mussen, general ed., pp. 556–629). New York: Wiley. [64–65]

Rice, C. A. (1971). The relationship of intrinsic and extrinsic religious orientations to selected criteria of mental health. *Dissertation Abstracts, 32*(4-A), 2194. [263, 266, 273, 276]

Richardson, J. T. (1980). People's Temple and Jonestown: A corrective comparison and critique. *Journal for the Scientific Study of Religion, 19,* 239–255. [222]

Roe, A. (1956). *The psychology of occupations.* New York: Wiley. [241]

Rogers, C. (1951). *Client-centered therapy.* Boston: Houghton Mifflin. [237]

Rokeach, M. (1960). *The open and closed mind.* New York: Basic Books. [160, 238, 247, 297]

Rokeach, M. (1969a). Value systems and religion. *Review of Religious Research, 11,* 2–23. [339, 340, 344]

Rokeach, M. (1969b). Religious values and social compassion. *Review of Religious Research, 11,* 24–38. [304, 307]

Rosenblith, J. A. (1949). A replication of "Some roots of prejudice." *Journal of Abnormal and Social Psychology, 44,* 470–489. [296, 298]

Rosenblith, J. (1957). How much invariance is there in the relations of "prejudice scores" to experimental and attitudinal variables? *Psychological Reports, 3,* 217–241. [298]

Rosenblum, A. L. (1958). Ethnic prejudice as related to social class and religiosity. *Sociology and Social Research, 43,* 272–275. [309]

Ross, C. E. (1990). Religion and psychological distress. *Journal for the Scientific Study of Religion, 29,* 236–245. [243]

Rotter, J. B. (1954). *Social learning and clinical psychology.* Englewood Cliffs, N.J.: Prentice-Hall. [237]

Rubenstein, R. L. (1965). The making of a rabbi. In I. Eisenstein (Ed.), *The varieties of Jewish belief.* New York: Jewish Reconstructionist Press. [167]

Rugg, H. (1963). *Imagination.* New York: Harper. [101, 102, 138, 167]

Rychlak, J. (1977). *The psychology of rigorous humanism.* New York: Wiley. [20]

Ryle, G. (1949). *The concept of mind.* New York: Barnes & Noble. [48]

Sabatier, A. (1904). *Religions of authority and religions of the spirit* (L. S. Houghton, trans.). New York: McClure, Phillips, & Co. [231]

St. George, A., & McNamara, P. H. (1984). Religion, race, and psychological well-being. *Journal for the Scientific Study of Religion, 23,* 351–363. [243]

Salisbury, W. S. (1962). Religiosity, regional sub-culture, and social behavior. *Journal for the Scientific Study of Religion, 2,* 94–101. [300, 301]

Salzman, L. (1953). The psychology of religious and ideological conversion. *Psychiatry, 16,* 177–187. [108]

Sanai, M. (1952). An empirical study of political, religious, and social attitudes. *British Journal of Psychology* (Statistics Section), *5,* 81–92. [299]

Sanford, R. N. (1950). Ethnocentrism in relation to some religious attitudes and practices. In T. W. Adorno et al., *The authoritarian personality.* New York: Norton. [306, 308]

Sanford, R. N., & Levinson, D. J. (1948). Ethnocentrism in relation to some religious attitudes and practices. *American Psychologist, 3,* 350–351. [297]

Sanua, V. D. (1969). Religion, mental health, and personality: A review of empirical studies. *American Journal of Psychiatry, 125,* 1203–1213. [235, 240n, 256]

Sapp, G. L., & Gladding, S. T. (1986, August). Correlates of religious orientation, religiosity, and moral judgment. Paper presented at the annual convention of the American Psychological Association, Washington, D.C. [360]

Sapp, G. L., & Jones, L. (1986). Religious orientation and moral judgment. *Journal for the Scientific Study of Religion, 25,* 208–214. [360]

Sasaki, M. S. (1979). Status inconsistency and religious commitment. In R. Wuthnow (Ed.), *The religious dimension: New directions in quantitative research.* (pp. 135–156). New York: Academic Press. [33, 38, 39]

Savage, C., Harman, W. W., Fadiman, J., & Savage, E. (1963, May). A follow-up note on the psychedelic experience. Paper presented at the annual convention of the American Psychiatric Association, St. Louis. [123]

Schaefer, C. A., & Gorsuch, R. L. (1991). Psychological adjustment and religiousness: The multivariate belief-motivation theory of religiousness. *Journal for the Scientific Study of Religion, 30,* 448–461. [276]

Schafer, R. (1960). Regression in the service of the ego: The relevance of a psychoanalytic concept for personality assessment. In G. Lindzey (Ed.), *Assessment of human motives.* New York: Grove Press. [101, 111]

Schank, R. C., & Abelson, R. P. (1977). *Scripts, plans, goals, and understanding.* Hillsdale, N.J.: Erlbaum Associates. [91]

Schlesinger, A., Jr. (1989, July 23). The opening of the American mind. *New York Times Book Review,* 1, 26–27. [294]

Schoenfeld, E., & Mestrovic, S. G. (1991). With justice and mercy: Instrumental-masculine and expressive-feminine elements in religion. *Journal for the Scientific Study of Religion, 30,* 363–380. [36]

Schoenrade, P. A. (1986). Belief in afterlife as a response to awareness of individual mortality. Unpublished Ph.D. dissertation, University of Kansas. [265, 275, 282]

Schoenrade, P. A. (1987, October). Belief in afterlife, religious orientation, and openness to belief challenge. Paper presented at the annual convention of the Society for the Scientific Study of Religion, Louisville, KY. [215]

Schoenrade, P. A. (1989). When I die . . . : Belief in afterlife as a response to mortality. *Personality and Social Psychology Bulletin, 15,* 91–100. [200–201]

Schofield, W., & Balian, L. A. (1959). A comparative study of the personal histories of schizophrenic and nonpsychiatric patients. *Journal of Abnormal and Social Psychology, 59,* 216–225. [241]

Scholl, M. E., & Beker, J. (1964). A comparison of religious beliefs of delinquent and nondelinquent Protestant adolescent boys. *Religious Education, 59,* 250–253. [245]

Schön, D. A. (1979). Generative metaphor: A perspective on problem-setting in social policy. In A. Ortony (Ed.), *Metaphor and thought.* New York: Cambridge University Press. [145–146]

Schroder, H. M., Driver, M. J., & Streufert, S. (1967). *Human information processing.* New York: Holt, Rinehart & Winston. [91–92, 94, 114]

Schwab, R., & Petersen, K. U. (1990). Religiousness: Its relation to loneliness, neuroticism, and subjective well-being. *Journal for the Scientific Study of Religion, 29,* 335–345. [244]

Schwartz, G. (1970). *Sect ideologies and social status.* Chicago: University of Chicago Press. [39]

Sears, C. E. (1924). *Days of delusion—A strange bit of history.* Boston: Houghton Mifflin. [206]

Seeman, W., Nidich, S., & Banta, T. (1972). Influence of Transcendental Meditation on a measure of self-actualization. *Journal of Counseling Psychology, 19,* 184–187. [137]

Seggar, J., & Kunz, P. (1972). Conversion: Evaluation of a step-like process for problem solving. *Review of Religious Research, 13,* 178–184. [109]

Seligman, M.E.P. (1975). *Helplessness.* San Francisco: W. H. Freeman. [237]

Selznick, G. J., & Steinberg, S. (1969). *The tenacity of prejudice: Antisemitism in contemporary America.* New York: Harper. [301]

Sherif, C. W., Kelley, M., Rodgers, H. L., Sarup, G., & Tittler, B. I. (1973). Personal involvement, social judgment, and action. *Journal of Personality and Social Psychology, 27,* 311–328. [219]

Sherif, C. W., Sherif, M., & Nubergall, R. E. (1965). *Attitude and attitude change.* Philadelphia: Saunders. [219]

Shinert, G., & Ford, E. E. (1958). The relation of ethnocentric attitudes to intensity of religious practice. *Journal of Educational Sociology, 32,* 157–162. [306]

Shor, R., & Orne, E. C. (1962). *The Harvard group scale of hypnotic susceptibility.* Palo Alto, Calif.: Consulting Psychologists Press. [112]

Shostrom, E. L. (1964). A test for the measurement of self-actualization. *Educational and Psychological Measurement, 24,* 207–218. [137, 238]

Shrauger, J. S., & Silverman, R. E. (1971). The relationship of religious background and participation to locus of control. *Journal for the Scientific Study of Religion, 10,* 11–16. [249]

Siegman, A. W. (1962). A cross-cultural investigation of the relationship between religiosity, ethnic prejudice, and authoritarianism. *Psychological Reports, 11,* 419–424. [299]

Sigall, H., & Page, R. (1971). Current stereotypes: A little fading, a little faking. *Journal of Personality and Social Psychology, 18,* 247–255. [311]

Silverman, B. I. (1974). Consequences, racial discrimination, and the principle of belief congruence. *Journal of Personality and Social Psychology, 29,* 497–508. [311, 323–324]

Singer, J. L. (1974). *Imagery and daydream methods in psychotherapy and behavior modification.* New York: Academic Press. [138]

Smith, C. B., Weigert, A. J., & Thomas, D. L. (1979). Self-esteem and religiosity: An analysis of Catholic adolescents from five cultures. *Journal for the Scientific Study of Religion, 18,* 51–60. [252]

Smith, H. (1964). Do drugs have religious import? *Journal of Philosophy, 61,* 517–529. [118]

Smith, M. B. (1978). Perspectives on selfhood. *American Psychologist, 33,* 1053–1063. [8, 53]

Smith, R. E., Wheeler, G., & Diener, E. (1975). Faith without works: Jesus people, resistance to temptation, and altruism. *Journal of Applied Social Psychology, 5,* 320–330. [341]

Snook, S. C., & Gorsuch, R. L. (1985, August). Religion and racial prejudice in South Africa. Paper presented at the 92nd Annual Convention of the American Psychological Association, Los Angeles. [317, 319, 320, 322]

Snow, D. A., & Machalek, R. (1982). On the presumed fragility of unconventional beliefs. *Journal for the Scientific Study of Religion, 21,* 15–26. [222]

Snow, D. A., & Machalek, R. (1983). The convert as a social type. In R. Collins (Ed.), *Sociological theory, 1983* (pp. 259–289). San Francisco: Jossey-Bass. [110]

Snyder, M. L., Kleck, R. E., Strenta, A., & Mentzer, S. J. (1979). Avoidance of the handicapped: An attributional ambiguity analysis. *Journal of Personality and Social Psychology, 37,* 2297–2306. [326]

Soderstrom, D., & Wright, E. W. (1977). Religious orientation and meaning in life. *Journal of Clinical Psychology, 33,* 65–68. [199, 269, 279]

Solomon, S., Greenberg, J., & Pyszczynski, T. (1991). A terror-management theory of social behavior: The psychological functions of self-esteem and cultural worldviews. In M. P. Zanna (Ed.), *Advances in Experimental Social Psychology* (Vol. 24, pp. 93–159). San Diego: Academic Press. [8, 201–202]

Spellman, C. M., Baskett, G. D., & Byrne, D. (1971). Manifest anxiety as a contributing factor in religious conversion. *Journal of Consulting and Clinical Psychology, 36,* 245–247. [248]

Sperry, R. W. (1964). The great cerebral commissure. *Scientific American, 210* (1), 42–52. [100–101]

Sperry, R. W. (1982). Some effects of disconnecting the cerebral hemispheres. *Science, 217,* 1223–1226. [100–101]

Spilka, B. (1958). Some personality correlates of interiorized and institutionalized religious belief. *Psychological Newsletter, 9,* 103–107. [253]

Spilka, B. (1977, August). Theory and empirical research in the psychology of religion: Some fundamental issues. Paper presented at the annual convention of the American Psychological Association, San Francisco. [17]

Spilka, B. (1978). The current state of the psychology of religion. *The Council on the Study of Religion Bulletin, 9,* 96–99. [15–16, 384]

Spilka, B., Hood, R. W., Jr., & Gorsuch, R. L. (1985). *The psychology of religion: An empirical approach.* Englewood Cliffs, NJ: Prentice-Hall. [43, 310, 382]

Spilka, B., Kojetin, B. A., & McIntosh, D. (1985). Forms and measures of personal faith: Questions, correlates, and distinctions. *Journal for the Scientific Study of Religion, 24,* 437–442. [180, 186–187]

Spilka, B., & Minton, B. (1975, October). Defining personal religion: Psychometric, cognitive, and instrumental dimensions. Paper presented at the annual convention of the Society for the Scientific Study of Religion, Milwaukee. [165]

Spilka, B., & Mullin, M. (1977). Personal religion and psychosocial schemata: A research approach to a theological psychology of religion. *Character Potential,* 57–66. [165, 197]

Spilka, B., Read, S., Allen, R. O., & Dailey, K. A. (1968, December). Specificity vs. generality: The criterion problem in religious measurement. Paper presented at the annual convention of the American Association for the Advancement of Science, Dallas. [165]

Spilka, B., & Schmidt, G. (1983). General attribution theory for the psychology of religion: The influence of event-character on attributions to God. *Journal for the Scientific Study of Religion, 22,* 326–339. [202]

Spilka, B., Shaver, P., & Kirkpatrick, L. A. (1985). A general attribution theory for the psychology of religion. *Journal for the Scientific Study of Religion, 24,* 1–20. [202]

Spilka, B., Stout, L., Minton, B., & Sizemore, D. (1977). Death and personal faith: A psychometric investigation. *Journal for the Scientific Study of Religion, 16,* 169–178. [165, 199, 264, 274]

Spilka, B., & Werme, P. H. (1971). Religion and mental disorder: A research perspective. In M. P. Strommen (Ed.), *Research on religious development: A comprehensive handbook.* New York: Hawthorne. [240n]

Springer, J. M. (1987). An investigation of the relationship between ways of being religious and a multidimensional fear of death scale. Unpublished Ph.D. dissertation, Temple University. [200, 266, 275, 283]

Springer, S. P. & Deutsch, G. (1989). *Left brain, right brain* (3rd ed.). New York: W. H. Freeman. [100, 101]

Srole, L., Langner, T., Michael, S. T., Opler, M. K., & Rennie, T.A.C. (1962). *Mental health in the metropolis* (Vol. 1). New York: McGraw-Hill. [43, 241, 256]

Stace, W. T. (1960). *Mysticism and philosophy.* Philadelphia: Lippincott. [126, 128]

Stack, S. (1983). The effect of decline in institutionalized religion on suicide, 1954–1978. *Journal for the Scientific Study of Religion, 22,* 239–252. [243]

Staples, C. L., & Mauss, A. L. (1987). Conversion or commitment?: A reassessment of the Snow and Machalek approach to the study of conversion. *Journal for the Scientific Study of Religion, 26,* 133–147. [142, 220]

Starbuck, E. D. (1899). *The psychology of religion.* New York: Scribner's. [81]

Stark, R. (1963). On the incompatibility of religion and science: A survey of American graduate students. *Journal for the Scientific Study of Religion, 3,* 3–21. [43, 249, 254]

Stark, R. (1965). A taxonomy of religious experience. *Journal for the Scientific Study of Religion, 5,* 97–116. [34, 105]

Stark, R. (1971). Psychopathology and religious commitment. *Review of Religious Research, 12,* 165–176. [241, 254]

Steinitz, L. Y. (1980). Religiosity, well-being, and *weltanschauung* among the elderly. *Journal for the Scientific Study of Religion, 19,* 60–67. [242]

Stouffer, S. A. (1955). *Communism, conformity, and civil liberties.* New York: Doubleday. [296, 299]

Strickland, B. R., & Shaffer, S. (1971). I-E., I-E., & F. *Journal for the Scientific Study of Religion, 10,* 366–369. [266]

Strickland, B. R., & Weddell, S. C. (1972). Religious orientation, racial prejudice, and dogmatism: A study of Baptists and Unitarians. *Journal for the Scientific Study of Religion, 11,* 395–399. [315n–316n]

Strommen, M. P. (1967). Religious education and the problem of prejudice. *Religious Education, 62,* 52–59. [301]

Stroop, J. R. (1938). Factors affecting speed in serial verbal reactions. *Psychological Monographs, 50,* 38–48. [356]

Struening, E. L. (1963). Anti-democratic attitudes in a midwestern university. In H. H. Remmers (Ed.), *Anti-democratic attitudes in American schools.* Evanston, Ill.: Northwestern University Press. [309]

Strunk, O. (1958). Relation between self-reports and adolescent religiosity. *Psychological Reports, 4,* 683–686. [251]

Strunk, O. (1959). Interest and personality patterns of pre-ministerial students. *Psychological Reports, 5,* 740. [245]

Sturgeon, R. S., & Hamley, R. W. (1979). Religiosity and anxiety. *Journal of Social Psychology, 108,* 137–138. [274, 277]

Sullivan, J. J., & Pallak, M. S. (1976). The effect of commitment and reactance on action-taking. *Personality and Social Psychology Bulletin, 2,* 179–182. [219]

Symington, T. A. (1935). *Religious liberals and conservatives.* New York: Columbia University Teachers College, Teachers College Contribution in Education No. 640. [249]

Taft, R. (1969). Peak experiences and ego permissiveness, an exploratory factor study of their dimensions in a normal person. *Acta Psychologica, 29,* 35–64. [111]

Tate, E. D., & Miller, G. R. (1971). Differences in value systems of persons with varying religious orientations. *Journal for the Scientific Study of Religion, 10,* 357–365. [306, 344, 358]

St. Teresa of Avila. (1957). *Life of St. Teresa* (J. M. Cohen, trans.). Baltimore: Penguin. (First published, 1562) [34–35]

Thoits, P. A. (1982). Life stress, social support, and psychological vulnerability: Epidemological considerations. *Journal of Community Psychology, 10,* 341–362. [242]

Thompson, A. D. (1974). Open-mindedness and indiscriminate antireligious orientation. *Journal for the Scientific Study of Religion, 13,* 471–477. [270, 280]

Thompson, E. H. (1991). Beneath the status characteristic: Gender variations in religiousness. *Journal for the Scientific Study of Religion, 30,* 381–394. [37]

Thoreau, H. D. (1854). *Walden: or, life in the woods.* Boston: Ticknor & Fields. [84]

Tillich, P. (1951). *Systematic theology* (Vol. 1). Chicago: University of Chicago Press. [167]

Tisdale, J. R. (1966). Selected correlates of extrinsic religious values. *Review of Religious Research, 7,* 78–84. [269]

Tolman, E. E. (1923). The nature of instinct. *Psychological Bulletin, 20,* 200–216. [53]

Tolstoy, L. N. (1904). *My confessions.* Boston: Dana Estes & Co. [103, 116, 290]

Tolstoy, L. N. (1987). Religion and morality. In *A confession and other religious writings* (J. Kentish, trans.). New York: Penguin. (First published, 1893) [8–9]

Tolstoy, L. N. (1987). What is religion and of what does its essence consist? In *A confession and other religious writings* (J. Kentish, trans.). New York: Penguin. (First published, 1902) [293–294].

Turbeville, G., & Hyde, R. E. (1946). A selected sample of attitudes of Louisiana State University students toward the Negro: A study in public opinion. *Social Forces, 24,* 447–450. [297]

Ullman, C. (1982). Cognitive and emotional antecedents of religious conversion. *Journal of Personality and Social Psychology, 43,* 183–192. [107]

Ullman, C. (1989). *The transformed self: The psychology of religious conversion.* New York: Plenum. [107, 109]

van der Lans, J. (1987). The value of Sundén's role theory demonstrated and tested with respect to religious experiences in meditation. *Journal for the Scientific Study of Religion, 26,* 401–412. [137]

Ventis, W. L., Batson, C. D., & Burke, D. (1982, August). Religious orientation and self-actualization: A psychometric study. Paper presented at the annual convention of the American Psychological Association, Washington, D.C. [252, 268, 278, 283]

Vergote, A., Tamayo, A., Pasquali, L., Bonami, M., Pattyn, A., & Custers, A. (1969). Concept of God and parental images. *Journal for the Scientific Study of Religion, 8,* 79–87. [35]

von Hentig, H. (1948). *The criminal and his victim.* New Haven: Yale University Press. [239, 245]

Wallace, R. K. (1970). Physiological effects of Transcendental Meditation. *Science, 167,* 1751–1754. [139]

Wallas, G. (1926). *The art of thought.* New York: Harcourt. [98–99]

Walters, T. P. (1980). A study of the relationship between religious orientation and cognitive moral maturity in volunteer religion teachers from selected suburban Catholic parishes in the Archdiocese of Detroit. Unpublished Ph.D. dissertation, Wayne State University. [179]

Warren, B. L. (1970). Socio-economic achievement and religion: The American case. *Sociological Inquiry, 40,* 130–155. [39]

Wasson, R. G. (1968). *Soma, divine mushroom of immortality.* New York: Harcourt. [117]

Watson, P. J., Hood, R. W., Jr., Foster, S. G., & Morris, R. J. (1988). Sin, depression, and narcissism. *Review of Religious Research, 29,* 295–305. [262, 271]

Watson, P. J., Hood, R. W., Jr., & Morris, R. J. (1984). Religious orientation, humanistic values, and narcissism. *Review of Religious Research, 25,* 257–264. [262, 268, 271, 278]

Watson, P. J., Hood, R. W., Jr., & Morris, R. J. (1985). Dimensions of religiosity and empathy. *Journal of Psychology and Christianity, 4,* 73–85. [344, 347, 356, 358–359, 360]

Watson, P. J., Hood, R. W., Jr., & Morris, R. J. (1988). Existential confrontation and religiosity. *Counseling and Values, 33,* 47–54. [186–187, 270, 281, 285]

Watson, P. J., Hood, R. W., Jr., Morris, R. J., & Hall, J. R. (1984). Empathy, religious orientation, and social desirability. *Journal of Psychology, 117,* 211–216. [344, 358–359, 360]

Watson, P. J., Hood, R. W., Jr., Morris, R. J., & Hall, J. R. (1985). Religiosity, sin, and self-esteem. *Journal of Psychology and Theology, 13,* 116–128. [265, 268, 275, 278, 284]

Watson, P. J., Hood, R. W., Jr., Morris, R. J., & Hall, J. R. (1987). The relationship between religiosity and narcissism. *Counseling and Values, 31,* 179–184. [262, 271]

Watson, P. J., Morris, R. J., Foster, J. E., & Hood, R. W., Jr. (1986). Religiosity and social desirability. *Journal for the Scientific Study of Religion, 25,* 215–232. [314, 314n]

Watson, P. J., Morris, R. J., & Hood, R. W., Jr. (1987). Antireligious humanistic values, guilt, and self-esteem. *Journal for the Scientific Study of Religion, 26,* 535–546. [266, 269, 275, 279, 283, 284]

Watson, P. J., Morris, R. J., & Hood, R. W., Jr. (1988a). Sin and self-functioning, Part 1: Grace, guilt, and self-consciousness. *Journal of Psychology and Theology, 16,* 254–269. [276]

Watson, P. J., Morris, R. J., & Hood, R. W., Jr. (1988b). Sin and self-functioning, Part 2: Grace, guilt, and psychological adjustment. *Journal of Psychology and Theology, 16,* 270–281. [262, 266, 268, 271, 276, 277]

Watson, P. J., Morris, R. J., & Hood, R. W., Jr. (1988c). Sin and self-functioning, Part 3: The psychology and ideology of irrational beliefs. *Journal of Psychology and Theology, 16,* 348–361. [266, 268, 276, 277]

Watson, P. J., Morris, R. J., & Hood, R. W., Jr. (1989a). Interactional factor correlations with means and end religiousness. *Journal for the Scientific Study of Religion, 28,* 337–347. [186–187]

Watson, P. J., Morris, R. J., & Hood, R. W., Jr. (1989b). Sin and self-functioning, Part 4: Depression, assertiveness, and religious commitments. *Journal of Psychology and Theology, 17,* 44–58. [263, 272]

Watson, P. J., Morris, R. J., & Hood, R. W., Jr. (1989c). Sin and self-functioning, Part 5: Antireligious humanistic values, individualism, and the community. *Journal of Psychology and Theology, 17,* 157–172. [263, 269, 272, 279]

Watts, A. (1968). Psychedelics and religious experience. *California Law Review, 56,* 74–85. [118–119]

Watts, A. (1972). *The art of contemplation.* New York: Pantheon Books. [152]

Webster, A. C. (1967). Patterns and relations of dogmatism, mental health, and psychological health in selected religious groups. *Dissertation Abstracts, 27,* 4142–A. [241, 251]

Weigert, A. J., & Thomas, D. L. (1972). Parental support, control, and adolescent religiosity: An extension of previous research. *Journal for the Scientific Study of Religion, 11,* 389–393. [43]

Weiss, A. S., & Mendoza, R. H. (1990). Effects of acculturation into the Hare Krishna movement on mental health and personality. *Journal for the Scientific Study of Religion, 29,* 173–184. [244]

Welch, M. R., Tittle, C. R., & Petee, T. (1991). Religion and deviance among adult Catholics: A test of the "moral communities" hypothesis. *Journal for the Scientific Study of Religion, 30,* 159–172. [247]

Wernik, U. (1975). Frustrated beliefs and early Christianity: A psychological enquiry into the gospels of the New Testament. *Numen, 22,* 96–130. [217]

Wertheimer, M. (1945). *Productive thinking.* New York: Harper. [93–94]

Whitam, F. L. (1962). Subdimensions of religiosity and race prejudice. *Review of Religious Research, 3,* 166–174. [301]

White, R. W. (1959). Motivation reconsidered: The concept of competence. *Psychological Review, 66,* 297–333. [237]

Williams, R. M. (1964). *Strangers next door.* Englewood Cliffs, N.J.: Prentice-Hall. [307, 308]

Wills, G. (1978). What religious revival? *Psychology Today, 11* (11), 74–81. [87]

Wilson, B. R. (1970). *Religious sects.* London: Weidenfeld & Nicolson. [39]

Wilson, E. O. (1975). *Sociobiology: The new synthesis.* Cambridge, Mass.: Harvard University Press. [47]

Wilson, J. (1978). *Religion in American society: The effective presence.* Englewood Cliffs, N.J.: Prentice-Hall. [39]

Wilson, W. C. (1960). Extrinsic religious values and prejudice. *Journal of Abnormal and Social Psychology, 60,* 286–288. [306]

Winter, G. (1962). *The suburban captivity of the churches.* New York: Macmillan. [40]

Wittgenstein, L. (1958). *The blue and brown books.* New York: Harper & Row. [17–18]

Woodmansee, J. J., & Cook, S. W. (1967). Dimensions of verbal racial attitudes: Their identification and measurement. *Journal of Personality and Social Psychology, 7,* 240–250. [316n]

Woodroof, J. T. (1985). Premarital sexual behavior and religious adolescents. *Journal for the Scientific Study of Religion, 24,* 343–366. [246, 273]

Woodroof, J. T. (1986). Reference groups, religiosity, and premarital sexual behavior. *Journal for the Scientific Study of Religion, 25,* 436–460. [41]

Woodrum, E. (1988). Determinants of moral attitudes. *Journal for the Scientific Study of Religion, 27,* 553–573. [337]

Wright, D. (1971). *The psychology of moral behavior.* Baltimore: Penguin. [36]

Wright, D., & Cox, E. (1967). A study of the relationship between moral judgment and religious belief in a sample of English adolescents. *Journal of Social Psychology, 72,* 135–144. [37, 336]

X, Malcolm. (1964). *The autobiography of Malcolm X,* assisted by Alex Haley. New York: Grove Press. [38n, 85–86]

Yeatts, J. R., & Asher, W. (1979). Can we afford *not* to do true experiments in psychology of religion? A reply to Batson. *Journal for the Scientific Study of Religion, 18,* 86–89. [382]

Yinger, J. M. (1967). Pluralism, religion, and secularism. *Journal for the Scientific Study of Religion, 6,* 17–28. [6]

Yinger, J. M. (1970). *The scientific study of religion.* New York: Macmillan. [6, 7, 10]

Yinger, J. M. (1977). A comparative study of the substructures of religion. *Journal for the Scientific Study of Religion, 16,* 67–86. [9n]

Yinon, Y., & Sharon, I. (1985). Similarity in religiousness of the solicitor, the potential helper, and the recipient as determinants of donating behavior. *Journal of Applied Social Psychology, 15,* 726–734. [341, 342]

Young, R. K., Benson, W. M., & Holtzman, W. H. (1960). Change in attitudes toward the Negro in a Southern university. *Journal of Abnormal and Social Psychology, 60,* 131–133. [307]

Young, R. K., Clore, G., & Holtzman, W. H. (1968). Further change in attitudes toward the Negro in a Southern university. In D. Byrne & M. Hamilton (Eds.), *Personality research: A book of readings.* New York: Wiley. [307]

Zaehner, R. C. (1957). *Mysticism: Sacred and profane.* Oxford: Clarendon Press. [120]

Zook, A., Koshmider, J., Kauffman, D., & Zehr, T. (1982). Religion, altruism, and kinship: A study of sociobiological theory. *Journal of Psychology and Christianity, 1*(3), 23–31. [340]

Subject Index